Freedom of Information
The Law, the Practice and the Ideal

Third Edition

Patrick Birkinshaw LLB
Professor of Public Law, Hull University Law School;
Director, Institute of European Public Law, Hull University;
Barrister

Butterworths
A Member of the LexisNexis Group

United Kingdom	Butterworths, a Division of Reed Elsevier (UK) Ltd, Halsbury House, 35 Chancery Lane, LONDON WC2A 1EL and 4 Hill Street, EDINBURGH EH2 3JZ
Australia	Butterworths, a Division of Reed International Books Australia Pty Ltd, CHATSWOOD, New South Wales
Canada	Butterworths Canada Ltd, MARKHAM, Ontario
Hong Kong	Butterworths Hong Kong, a division of Reed Elsevier (Greater China) Ltd, HONG KONG
India	Butterworths India, NEW DELHI
Ireland	Butterworth (Ireland) Ltd, DUBLIN
Malaysia	Malayan Law Journal Sdn Bhd, KUALA LUMPUR
New Zealand	Butterworths of New Zealand Ltd, WELLINGTON
Singapore	Butterworths Asia, SINGAPORE
South Africa	Butterworths Publishers (Pty) Ltd, DURBAN
USA	Lexis Law Publishing, CHARLOTTESVILLE, Virginia

© Patrick Birkinshaw 2001

A CIP Catalogue record for this book is available from the British Library.

ISBN   0 406 91491 5

Printed and bound in Great Britain by Hobbs the Printers Ltd, Totton, Hampshire

Visit Butterworths LEXIS *direct* at: www.butterworths.com

Preface

The major development since the second edition has been the enactment of the Freedom of Information Act 2000. The Act is unlikely to come into effect in Whitehall until the summer of 2002 at the earliest and, even then, only in relation to publication schemes. Between December 1997 and November 1999, I served as a specialist adviser to the House of Commons Public Administration Committee in its review of the White Paper *Your Right to Know* and the *Draft Freedom of Information Bill and Consultation Paper*. It was an enormously rewarding experience and I am grateful to successive Chairs and members of the Committee and the Committee's clerk for their respect, patience and assistance.

Other developments have included the Data Protection Act 1998, the Regulation of Investigatory Powers Act 2000 and the Human Rights Act, as well as the beginning of freedom of information in devolved government and the Local Government Act 2000. As I write, we still await the final agreed version of the Regulation on Access to Information made under Article 255 EC. The interrelationship between EU provisions and domestic provisions governing access is going to be an important development.

Patrick Birkinshaw
April 2001

Law in Context

Below is a listing of the more recent publications in the Law in Context Series

Editors: William Twining (University College, London) and Christopher McCrudden (Lincoln College, Oxford)

Ashworth: *Sentencing and Criminal Justice*
Bercusson: *European Labour Law*
Birkinshaw: *Freedom of Information: The Law, the Practice and the Ideal*
Cane: *Atiyah's Accidents Compensation and the Law*
Collins: *The Law of Contract*
Scott and Black: *Cranston's Consumers and the Law*
Elworthy and Holder: *Environmental Protection: Text and Materials*
Fortin: *Children's Rights and the Developing Law*
Harlow and Rawlings: *Law and Administration: Text and Materials*
Harris: *An Introduction to Law*
Harvey: *Seeking Asylum in the UK: Problems and Prospects*
Lacey and Wells: *Reconstructing Criminal Law*
Moffat: *Trusts Trusts Law- Text and Materials*
Norrie: *Crime, Reason and History*
Oliver and Drewry: *The Law and Parliament*
Oliver: *Common Values and the Public- Private Divide*
O'Dair: *Legal Ethics Text and Materials*
Palmer and Roberts: *Dispute Processes: ADR and the Primary Forms of Decision Making*
Reed: *Internet Law- Text and Materials*
Turpin: *British Government and the Constitution: Text, Cases and Materials*
Twining: *Globalisation and Legal Theory*
Twining and Miers: *How to Do Things with Rules*
Ward: *Shakespeare and the Legal Imagination*
Zander: *Cases and Materials on the English Legal System*
Zander: *The Law Making Process*

Contents

Birkinshaw *Freedom of Information:*
The Law, the Practice and the Ideal (3rd edn)

ERRATUM

Please note that on page 336, line 14, the words 'It does not involve
additional security measures' should read 'It does involve additional
security measures'.

The author and publishers would like to apologise for this error.

July 2001

Chapter 4   Claims and counterclaims   160

Table of statutes

List of cases

C

D

E

PAGE

T

U

V

W

X

Z

Decisions of the European Court of Justice are listed below numerically. These
decisions are also included in the preceding alphabetical list.

Introduction: setting the agenda

'Freedom of Information' has the ability to generate more controversy and heated debate than virtually any other aspect of contemporary government and administration. Press and media make daily references to Public Interest Immunity Certificates (or 'gagging orders'), the perpetuation of official secrecy despite the 'reform' of section 2 of the Official Secrets Acts (the Shayler and Tomlinson episodes) and the introduction of a Freedom of Information Act (FOIA) which was given Royal Assent in November 2000. Few bills have been subjected to such prolonged criticism from government friend and foe alike. The new Act is examined in ch 6. Stories continue of 'cover-ups', 'half truths' and excessive attention to presentation of policy by government, the confidentiality of state secrets, access to files, and protection of information collected by public or private bodies. 'Freedom of Information' has long been a rallying cry of libertarians, if not quite the contemporary equivalent of 'Wilkes and Liberty' in eighteenth-century London or 'Reform' in nineteenth-century England.

But what does Freedom of Information mean? For most of those who employ the phrase it means having access to files, or to information in any form, in order to know what government is up to. In ch 2, I illustrate what is done in other jurisdictions. In some jurisdictions, it may mean not only allowing access to government documents in whatever form they happen to exist, but also opening up the meetings of governments, their advisory bodies and client groups to public scrutiny. Or it may involve access by individuals to files containing information about themselves - and an assurance that the information is not being used for improper or unauthorised purposes. Though it covers individual access to information, and the protection of information upon individuals from unjustified use, and these points are addressed in chapter seven, the scope of this book is much broader. Much of the information, though by no means all, which this book covers is of little or no *direct* concern to individuals as individuals. But it will all, to a greater or lesser degree, constitute data on which decisions affecting the collective welfare, or someone's perception of that welfare, will be taken or influenced. Chapter 3 outlines how in the British tradition that perception had to be cocooned in secrecy. Unless we are very careful, that tradition may develop in the European Union - a point which is examined in chapter eight.

If individual access to such information is too costly, or too sensitive, or not worth the effort because of public apathy, or because there is little public feedback of views or ideas to inform specialists or decision-makers, is this an argument against freedom of information? Or is it an argument in favour of the provision of essential and unadulterated information to bodies whom we trust, so that they may check the policy-making process, render that process accountable, and report on their findings? One can imagine a departmental claim that a request by me to see all the files on the Millennium Dome project or 'Mad Cow Disease' disaster is unreasonable. But that does not mean that nobody outside the Prime Minister's Office, the connected departments or their coterie of 'private' advisers should have access to such documentation in order to assess the project's viability and feasibility or the latter tragedy's causes and lessons for the avoidance of mistakes in the future.

The Freedom of Information debate for much of the 1980s and 1990s tended less to promote this latter aspect but rather the question of individual entitlement to personal files and punitive governmental reaction to a sensational leak. With the publication of the Nolan Report on *Standards in Public Life*[1], the Scott Report into the collapse of the *Matrix Churchill* trial, the *Bovine Spongiform Encephalopathy* Report, the FOIA 2000 itself, the movement to devolution and the incorporation of the European Convention on Human Rights by the Human Rights Act and so much else,[2] the constitutional or collective dimension to the information debate has been reinvigorated. In *Matrix Churchill,* the then Government's refuge in dicta from almost thirty years ago about the 'inner workings' of government needing protection against 'captious' or 'ill informed' criticisms provoked this response from Sir Richard (now Lord) Scott:

1   Cm 2850 I and II. See also *The Civil Service: Continuity and Change* Cm 2627 and *Taking Forward Continuity and Change* Cm 2748 and the *Government's Response* to Nolan Cm 2931 p 168 et seq infra and further reports from the Committee on Standards in Public Life (see chs 4 and 5 below).

2   *Report of the Inquiry into the Export of Defence Equipment and Dual-Use Goods to Iraq and Related Prosecutions* HC 115 (1995-6) Vols. I–V and Index; see *The Report of the Rt Hon Sir Richard Scott's Inquiry: Government Press Pack* February 1996; and for the BSE report, see: HC 887 Vols I-XVI (1999-2000).

An acceptance from time to time of ill-informed or captious public or political criticism is part of the price that has to be paid for a democratic and open system of government. As to criticism being ill-informed, government should .... make it its business to do what it can to ensure that its critics are not ill-informed. The secrecy with which government chooses to surround its inner workings, with light cast only by designer leaks and investigative journalists is not, in my opinion, a reason for perpetuating the sort of Public Interest Immunity claims that were made in the Matrix Churchill case.

The FOIA of Blair's government has given complete protection to these inner workings in a manner criticised by Scott. For former Foreign Secretary Lord Howe, the laying bare of inner processes touching upon the rites of government would be to expose them before a 'world-wide range of uncomprehending or malicious commentators. This is the point. You cannot choose a well-balanced presentation to an elite Parliamentary audience.'[3] Nor, Blair seems to believe, to the public. In the previous edition of this book, I wrote that it was clear that 'major reform is due in our governmental machinery to re-impose constitutionalism, democracy and openness.' Since then, major constitutional change has taken place with the passage of devolution legislation, the Human Rights Act and FOIA; Scotland has produced its own draft FOI bill which in spite of some crucial differences, is modelled on the Whitehall prototype. I return to these points in chapters 4, 5, 6, 9 and 10.

The collective aspect, as well as the individual one, is a central feature of the information debate; its analysis, at all levels of government, pervades the following pages. It makes little sense to be given access to government information when there is no independent method of checking its accuracy and reliability and no way of ensuring that government has given a full account of what it has been up to, and of knowing what alternatives to preferred options there are.

Government, it might be claimed, is the official regulation of human affairs for the greater good. What of government by unofficial means? What of gagging clauses in contracts of commercial bodies seeking to bind public bodies to secrecy 'shades of the Official Secrets Act' and even attempting to restrain publication of reports by public bodies? Does the duty to inform end when regulation of essential interests or decisions affecting the collective welfare are taken by private bodies? Does the bartering between government and organised interests, in the private sphere, over the delivery of services to the public or for the public escape from scrutiny - scrutiny which is performed by the public or on behalf of the public? Is the market a suitable accountability device in itself? No responsible government has accepted such a stark conclusion, though it has accepted that constitutional controls will be much attenuated where the primary actors are private and not public. What place is there for freedom of information in this way of arranging the public interest? Where does the theme of freedom of information stand in relation to the belief that government is also the organisation of information for the use, effective or otherwise, of power in the public interest? The FOIA 2000 is cast in wider terms than any in existence in its coverage of the private sector where private bodies are performing public business. So much depends upon the minister's power of 'designation' as will be explained in ch 6.

Freedom of information naturally flows into topics such as freedom of speech, censorship, the right to remain silent and not to answer incriminating questions, freedom of assembly, and so on. These themes form part of the information debate, but any allusion to them in greater detail than I have allowed would have altered the nature of the work. They are topics which have attracted a considerable amount of critical attention from informed sources. Freedom of information in a British framework has attracted much polemical and political attention. At the time of the first edition there was little sustained analysis by a lawyer of the subject *de profundis*. And yet, without reliable information, freedom of expression may well be deprived of much of its potency. If we do not know and are ill-informed, what reliance can be placed on what we say? Sir Richard Scott has done us all a service in his painstaking analysis of the concealment, half truths, convenient cover-ups and so on that characterised the 'Arms to Iraq' episode. Lord Philips in his report on the BSE scandal has exposed that desire for closure and secrecy in the culture of our government. That the Government should reveal inconsistencies in approaches to secrecy in different cases is understandable albeit worrying when the development reveals a tendency to greater secrecy. That it should reveal inconsistencies in the *same* case is deplorable.[4] Whether FOI laws, or Access to Information laws as they are more commonly referred to today would have prevented the Matrix Churchill or BSE episodes is besides the point. The point is that the absence of such

---

4   No attempt was made by the Attorney-General on behalf of the Government to protect by Public Interest Immunity certificates the production of the highly sensitive 'Crown Jewels' information in the trial of Clive Ponting in 1985: see p 119 et seq infra. Certificates were sought to protect far less sensitive information in the *Matrix Churchill* trial. However, some of the information in the latter trial concerned secret intelligence which was protected but two secret Intelligence Service officers were allowed to give evidence. The witness statements of one of these were read and approved by the Secretary of State Mr K Clarke and clearly fell within the information which it was claimed by the Attorney-General Ministers had an unqualified *duty* to protect by certificates. HC 115 para G13.13.

laws allows the culture of secrecy – which attends any form of government – to fester unabated, to make the lie all too easy, the cover-up all too convenient. It is hoped that with all its faults, the FOIA will help to make such malpractice more difficult to practise and conceal. What follows can only be an introduction to this vast subject. In ch 1 I examine wider arguments about government and information and various case studies to set the scene.

The Shayler trial

The first edition of this book was written amid a frenzied lather of activity relating to *Spycatcher* and reforms of the Official Secrets Act 1911. The OSA 1989 emerged after the first edition was published. The prosecution of former MI5 official David Shayler for breaches of the OSA 1989, s 1 presented an opportunity to apply the rights and obligations of the European Convention of Human Rights incorporated by the Human Rights Act 1998 into domestic law and to assess the compatibility of the 1989 Act, particularly s 1, with Convention rights. The absolute prohibition contained in section 1, although arguably supported by the House of Lords in *A-G v Blake*[5] would be seen by Shayler's lawyers as a breach of Art 10 ECHR which protects freedom of expression and the right to pass on information (see p 412 et seq below). A total ban on *all* disclosures would, it would be argued, be disproportionate and not necessary in a democratic society in the interests of national security or public safety, for the prevention of disorder or crime or to prevent the disclosure of information received in confidence, to pick on some of the relevant grounds justifying state interference with the rights under Art 10. There is no public interest defence and the onus of proof is reversed and placed on the defendant.

Where the information concerns trivia, or repeats what is already known or reveals serious wrongdoing or waste by the services, it is well to remember that there has been a relaxation of prohibitions on press reports of such revelations, a relaxation well under way before the Convention was incorporated under the Human Rights Act 1998. Shayler not only alleged an attempted assassination of Colonel Gadaffi involving MI6 agents, an attempt which led to other deaths. He also revealed to newspapers the identities of two MI6 agents.[6] Under present practice, the latter would have been regarded by the courts as inexcusable.

---

5 [2000] 4 All ER 385 — 'an absolute rule against disclosure, visible to all, makes good sense' per Lord Nicholls at p 400a. Lord Nicholls was here referring not to s 1, but to Blake's contractual undertaking not to publish.

6 See *R v Central Criminal Court ex p Bright etc* [2001] 2 All ER 244 and see pp 138-139 et seq below.

On the other hand we have to focus on the position of the agent, a *secret* agent, and the fact that the damaging effect of a disclosure, including risk of life or security, may not be known until the damage has been effected. The prosecution of offenders under s 1, as under the 1989 Act generally with one exception, has to be agreed by the Attorney-General. This 'safeguard' begs the question of the appropriateness of the Attorney-General in this role (see p 147) and although a sensible Attorney-General would surely not agree to a prosecution that appeared ridiculous or spiteful the past does not provide much cause for comfort. The reliance upon the Attorney-General's (a member of the government) discretion does not conduce to legal certainty. Furthermore, why may the Director of MI5 or a former Director be allowed to give public lectures and in the latter case be allowed to write memoirs when agents are prohibited from publishing *anything*. The spectre of self-authorisation (p 134) and the role of the Cabinet Secretary begin to loom large. Even if a court declared that s 1 was incompatible with the Convention, the government would not have to act on that declaration by repealing legislation.[7] If the absolute prohibition were deemed compatible with Art 10, then surely an internal safety valve should be introduced for officers who wish to 'whistleblow' in the public interest. The present arrangements are not satisfactory and the Public Interests Disclosure Act 1998 does not apply to such agents (see p 192 et seq). Is this not a job for the Chairman of the Security Commission or the Intelligence Services Commissioner? Both of these figures are senior judges. In May 2001, Moses J ruled s 1 OSA was not incompatible with the Human Rights Act and Article 10.

The audience

The primary audience for this book will be students of constitutional, administrative or public law and students of political science and politics. They are concerned with the relationship between law and politics, between law and political choice, political institutions and administration on behalf of the public interest. What sort of questions one poses about the relationship is often a matter of personal or political preference. The provision of information has always been at the centre of the relationship between government and society; provision of information has always been instrumental in the way governmental institutions have been created or allowed to develop. Such developments have occurred to fulfil public expectations in oversight, accountability, explanation or legitimacy for the exercise of power. I would hope, therefore, that the book would be of interest to a much wider audience of concerned citizens.

7   Sections 4(6) and 10(2) HRA.

The use of the courts by individuals to extract information from political and administrative institutions as part of, or to mount, an attack on the exercise or non-exercise of public power depends upon the law. Much of this law, as we shall see in chapter 9, is created or controlled by judges. It has been characteristic of the 1980s and 1990s that we have seen the emergence of a variety of statutory duties to allow access to information in the possession of public and, in the case of the Data Protection Act 1984 and its successor in 1998, private bodies (see chapter 7). Lawyers and administrators will find increasing demands placed upon their services in the 'Information Society' into which we have moved. This book attempts to examine the public law implications of such a movement. Interest in the subject ought to extend well beyond the field of public law. It must be said that telecommunications and computers have made our world a 'Global Information Society'. Our response has largely been nationally based. The future beckons.

1 Persistent themes and novel problems

The popular phrase 'Information Society' was coined to describe the essence of the advanced computerised world. From financial markets to government, from national security to education, from multinational corporations to small employers, from police to social welfare, medical treatment and social services, we are confronted by information repositories and retrieval systems whose capacity to store and transmit information is staggering. A moment's thought should make us appreciate that we have always been an information society. Anyone who has studied the constitutional history of Britain will appreciate that a major factor in the struggle between Crown and Parliament was the latter's desire to be informed about who counselled and advised the monarch in the formulation of policy. That monumental work in the history of our public administration, the Domesday Book, was basically an information exercise to assess the wealth and stock of the nation. Our process of trial by law constitutes an attempt to exclude unreliable evidence and to establish by rules of evidence a more reliably informed basis of fact on which to establish guilt or innocence. Law-making itself 'confessedly needs to be based on an informed judgment' requiring 'the widest access to information'.[1] The spread of information in the form of fact, opinion or ideas has variously been repressed, exhorted, victimised or applauded to advance the ideologies of those whose moment of power is in the ascendant. In this general sense, we can see previous societies as information societies. What is novel in our society, however, is the heightened awareness of the use, collection, dissemination or withholding of information. Such functions are facilitated by artificial intelligence systems, advanced information technology and the opportunities which

1 R. Berger *Executive Privilege* (1974), p 3

exist to influence public opinion through ever more sophisticated broadcasting, telecommunications and information technology networks. Many recent *causes célèbres* have involved information in the form of the giving or keeping of confidences. Socrates would have been in his element in discussing the case of a civil servant deliberately leaking information to 'advance' the public interest; the nature of informed consent before medical treatment;[2] the extent of the duty to inform parents of advice by doctors to their children;[3] a leak of a difference of opinion between the head of state and the prime minister on government policies;[4] the failure to inform those affected of the extent of nuclear accident and disaster; seeking to prevent disclosure of information that would reveal the Government knew that defendants in a criminal trial were wrongfully indicted;[5] abusive use of information stored in computerised retrieval systems. For a Socrates, the details would be novel; there would, however, be a persistence in the nature of the problems they pose. The 'problems' surround the 'use' and 'abuse' of information. 'Use' and 'abuse' in this context are evaluative terms, and ones which I hope will be clarified in the course of this book. They are also relative terms. We may consider that a government abuses information when, without apparent justification, it refuses individuals access to information in its possession. This would not be the case in a system geared towards traditional representative democracy—where our representatives govern on our behalf and account to a collective assembly. It would certainly not be the case where government is absolutist and is accepted as such by those whom it governs.

A further comparative aspect of the terms 'use' and 'abuse' is present in two other features. One concerns the changing nature of the role of government not simply as an agent protecting and defending the realm from external and internal strife, but as a shaper of people's lives in almost every conceivable way. Government intervenes more and more in our society, whatever its political hue. Different roles require different sorts and amounts of information. The administrative regulatory state is the most acquisitive. In addition, the sophistication of information technology has made the collection, storage and retrieval of information not simply a national and corporate preoccupation, but a global one. The speed and ease with which information may be transferred across national

2 *Sidaway v Board of Governors of the Bethlem Royal Hospital etc* [1985] AC 871.
3 *Gillick v West Norfolk and Wisbech Area Health Authority* [1985] 3 All ER 402, HL, concerning contraception for girls under 16.
4 Resulting from a leak by the Queen's Press Officer: *The Times*, 28 July 1986.
5 See Tomkins (1993) Public Law 650 and *The Constitution after Scott: Government Unwrapped* (1998); these were the events behind the Matrix Churchill inquiry by Sir Richard Scott. See Birkinshaw (1996) JLS 406; *Under the Scott-light* B Thompson and F Ridley (1997) OUP; (1996) Public Law Autumn Issue dedicated to The Scott Report.

boundaries, by governments or private concerns, or matched by computers for different purposes from those for which the information was collected, is seen by many as an abuse in itself. The 'abuse' would be in the creation of information systems which are incapable of effective regulation at a price that treasuries would be prepared to tolerate. Privacy protection has not traditionally been afforded a high priority in the United Kingdom; the developments which I have referred to diminish it even further. We shall have to see what the impact of the Data Protection Act 1998 (DPA) and Human Rights Act 1998 (HRA) will be.

Things must be seen in perspective. The UK Government is a holder of vast amounts of manual (ie documentary) information, much of it on individuals. For instance, in 1987, the then Department of Health and Society Security held 75 million personal social security files; the Immigration Department had 3.75 million personal files, 'many over a foot thick'; there were 8.7 million files on current schoolchildren, 11 million on public sector tenants, 1 million social work records, and in 1995, 180 million personal documents held by insurance companies.[6] But the movement towards a 'paperless environment', as IBM's administration was described during the passage of the Access to Personal Files Act in 1987, is a distinct characteristic of our age. The characteristics of information technology, however, require further elaboration.

Computers and information

Information technology is often described in exceptional and dramatic terms. The following from more than a decade ago and before the emergence of the 'super information highway' or internet and its staggering implications is a vivid example:

> In the last hundred years, we see the rapidly accelerating advent of a technology so powerful, novel, widespread, and influential that we may indeed call it the Second Industrial Revolution. Its basis is electromagnetic, in many interconnected forms: photography, photocopying, cinematography, and holography; telegraphy, telephony, radio communication, radar, sonar, and telemetry; sound and video recording and reproduction; vacuum tubes, transistors, printed circuits, masers, lasers, fiber optics, and (in rapid succession) integrated circuits (IC), large-scale integration (LSI), and very large-

6   HC Debs vol 110, col 1172 (20 Feb 1987). In Standing Committee C for the Access To Personal Files Bill, it was stated that government departments hold 12 million linear feet of records, half the files being on individuals (25 March 1987, col 5); D Bainbridge and G Pearce (1995) New LJ 1656.

scale integration (VLSI) of circuitry on a tiny semiconducting 'chip'; and, finally, the bewildering variety of electronic digital computers. All these devices are intimately interrelated, and any advance in one tends to generate advances in all of them. The progress has been truly amazing. In only about 40 years, electronic communications and news media have become commonplace and indispensable; computers have proliferated, becoming increasingly fast, powerful, small and cheap, so that now there is scarcely a human activity in which they are not to be found, bearing an increasing share of the burden of repetitive information processing, just as the machines of the First Industrial Revolution have taken over the majority of heavy and unpleasant physical labor (we may say, energy processing).

Now, information can not only be stored, retrieved, communicated, and broadcast in enormous quantities and at phenomenal speeds; but it can also be rearranged, selected, marshalled, and transformed.[7]

Since that was written there has been an advance in digital systems sweeping away remaining distinctions between data processing and telephony. We have witnessed a growing convergence of computer and telephone systems and a wholesale shift to computer networking. The obvious progeny has been the internet—a network of computer networks which works like a combined telephone and postal service—and the creation of the World Wide Web. In 1988 there were 1 million users of the internet. By 1996, it had reached 210 million with one billion predicted users by 2010. Governments have increasingly taken steps to prevent the transmission of 'obscene' material via the internet, most conspicuously the US government where the President has signed into law the Communications Decency Act 1996 which the Supreme Court ruled unconstitutional.[8] Policing the net has become a global preoccupation.[9]

Over two decades ago, the Lindop Committee[10] offered a thoughtful and informative account of the problems posed by data accumulation and protection. It noted that the electronic computer was 'only a part of any

7   J Halton 'The Anatomy of Computing', in T Forrester (ed) The *Information Technology* (1985). See *Information Technology Futures* (NEDC, 1987); on the internet and law, see: L Edwards and C Waelde *Law and the Internet* (2nd ed 2000); C Reed *Internet Law: Text and Materials* (2000); M Ibusuki ed *Transnational Cyberspace Law* (2001); Y Akdeniz and C Walker *Internet Law and Society* (2001); M Gould *Foundations of Internet Governance* (2001) forthcoming.

8   *ACLU v Reno* 929 F Supp 824, 117 S Ct 2329 (1997); US Communications Decency Act 1996, 47 USC 230.S

9   See note 7 above.

10 Cmnd 7341 (1978), following *Computers and Privacy*, Cmnd 6353 (1975).

information system' and that the rest of the system will perform 'the functions of collecting and preparing the data for the computer, devising its instructions, and transferring the information produced to those who need it'. All of this would require human control and 'often human intervention' and the creation of 'at least some manual records'.

The report spoke quite correctly of the dangers of abuse of information that would come with centralisation of information on computerised systems. Since 1931, for instance, the Driving and Vehicle Licensing Centre had informed the Inland Revenue of the addresses of individuals. More recent examples include the report that MI5—the security service— had access to data on 20 million people by linking its computer, under Prime Ministerial approval, with a growing network of other government computer data banks.[11] MI5 reportedly kept files on over half a million individuals it had targeted since 1909.[12] Computer network contracts have specified how a free flow of information can pass between the major government departments contrary to existing legislative requirements.[13] An increasing number of statutes has facilitated such transfer.[14] Now computer matching is widespread (see chapter seven). A more authoritative source has warned that police officers should be issued with strict guidelines about the use and misuse of the Police National Computer to which police forces are linked, together with the Scottish Criminal Record Office.[15] The Police Act 1997 established the National Criminal Intelligence Service Authority responsible for disseminating criminal intelligence to police forces and law enforcement agencies. The Act also created the Police Information Technology Organisation advising forces on IT. The Police Complaints Authority had found 529 potential causes of complaint on one subject alone concerning misuse of computerised information held by the police.[16] The Criminal Records Bureau will

11 *New Statesman* 4 March 1982.
12 The Government refused to disclose the number of files held by MI5 because the service was not covered by the Code on Open Government; on the Ombudsman's report see: Case No A11/95, HC 758 (1994-95) and ch 5 below. See the written answer of the Home Secretary: HC Debs 29 July 1998 (WA). The Home Secretary disclosed that a file had been kept on himself and also Peter Mandelson. The Ombudsman cannot investigate complaints against the Security Service but he can have access to the files of the service 'if that seemed necessary as part of an investigation' into an admissible complaint, ibid.
13 *The Guardian*, 7 January 1987.
14 Including the TV Licences Act 1999.
15 HC Debs, 2 July 1985 (Written Answers). In December 1991, the Home Office reported that PNC 2 will allow all police forces to access a data base of 5 million 'criminal names'; 40 million vehicle owners, 135,000 missing persons and 450,000 missing vehicles.
16 HC 307 (1985–6), para 3.14. About 125,000 'transactions' can be performed per day on the PNC 2 each taking 2.5 seconds. See also, National Intelligence Criminal Service *Annual Report* (July 1995) and their ALERT computer system.

commence operations in the summer of 2001and will provide checks on those working with children. The Home Affairs Committee of the House of Commons has expressed concerns over the accuracy of data on the Police National Computer from which checks will be made. Error rates were between 15 and 65 per cent.[17] Closed circuit TV, mobile phones and automatic number plate recognition have all facilitated location of individuals and their movements.

In his research Lindop was not given all the detailed information he wanted from the Metropolitan Police.[18] At the time of his investigation the extensive scope and use of their computer was widely reported, especially by the Special Branch.[19]

The use of such information technology (IT) can have a potent impact on centralising and co-ordinating information, facilitating centripetal administrative tendencies within organisations and between hierarchical levels of bureaucracy, but there are dangers in over-sensationalising. It is naive to believe that government in whatever form will not exploit new technology. The Treasury established a Central Computer and Telecommunications Agency (CCTA) which publishes manuals and booklets on all aspects of government and information technology. The E-Government Group (formerly Central Information Technology Unit now the Office of the e-Envoy (OeE)) has the responsibility for assisting and improving the e- delivery of government services and information. All major departments, agencies and public authorities are linked to the web and are increasingly dependent upon IT and online facilities. The OeE asked all governments departments in 2000 to produce strategy documents setting out how they will attain the government target of 100% capacity for delivery of services electronically by 2005. The Treasury has incorporated this target in Public Service Agreements.[20]

No less a figure than the Comptroller and Auditor-General has voiced his misgivings about the lack of appropriate security for government-held data.[1] This is a responsibility that has passed to MI5, the Security Service. It was previously undertaken by CCTA. Data with a comparatively high security rating will 'generate a considerable volume of traffic'. Security procedures for handling classified information are laid down separately for all departments to follow and implementation of IT security procedures

17 *Criminal Records Bureau* HC 227 (2000-2001).
18 And see *Police Computers and the Metropolitan Police* (GLC 1985); *Techno-Cop: New Police Technologies* (Free Enterprise Books 1985).
19 *The Times*, 14 February and 9 September 1977.
20 HC 94 (2000-2001) and see *Government on the WEB* from the National Audit Office: HC 87 (1999-2000). On PSAs, see ....
1   *Information Technology Security in Government Departments*. National Audit Office, 1 March 1995 and see Management of Information Technology Security in Government Departments, Public Accounts Committee, HC 480 (1990-91).

is the responsibility of individual departments.[2] An increasing interface between government officials and their dependence upon private company experts for the installation, operation and management of computer systems has taken place. The contract to establish and operate the biggest and most advanced computer network in Whitehall was put out to tenders from private organisations.

The importance of governmental control over information technology has been dramatically evidenced by the US Department of Commerce's refusal in the 1980s to grant licences to companies to export computers to British universities unless they signed documents giving the American government control over their use. Ostensibly this is to ensure that the technology and information obtained from such computers were not shared with proscribed communist countries while the USA maintained its technological supremacy in this field. Sir Michael Havers, the former Attorney-General and Lord Chancellor, stated his opinion that such a restriction was unlawful. Other security measures were imposed which many believed posed a serious threat to civil liberties in the USA and UK.[3] CIA involvement in gathering information on companies such as British Nuclear Fuels and Amersham International whetted the appetite of conspiracy theorists but nonetheless brought home the importance attached at the highest levels to information technology.

More beneficial features of the brave new world of the computerisation of governmental administration were highlighted several years ago in the evidence of a permanent secretary before the select committee on the Parliamentary Commissioner for Administration. He described how aspects of the social security administration would be simplified by use of computers which the then DHSS had already introduced.[4] Several years later, both the DSS and Benefits Agency have faced enormous difficulties with inadequate computer systems,[5] a fate shared by the Passport Agency and by the Immigration Service at Croydon. The Inland Revenue's attempts to go online for tax returns has not been a success. The Inland Revenue has computerised their whole network,[6] although originally reluctant to use systems in the private sector, which was contrary to US

2   A Central IT Unit was installed in Whitehall to coordinate government IT operations: *Financial Times,* 8 November 1995.
3   See A.V. Lowe and C. Warbrick (1987) 36 ICLQ 398. The refusal of the Department of Trade and Industry to safeguard British subjects has led to applications for judicial review. On the American literature see: H. Relyea *Silencing Science: National Security Controls and Scientific Communication* (1994).
4   HC 312 (1985–6), p 32. The 'Local office project' will link social security offices into a national network starting in 1988–9, HC Debs, 7 March 1985 (WA). See now HC 382 iii (1994-5) *DSS Information Technology Services Agency.*
5   See HC 433 (1999-2000).
6   Private companies operate government's IT services.

practice because of the perceived risks to breaches of confidentiality.[7] This reluctance has, however, been overtaken by events. The Treasury model of the British economy has been available since Sch 5 of the Industry Act 1975 came into effect. The Economic and Social Research Council in conjunction with the Bank of England and the Treasury announced a programme of study to link micro-economic models of companies and local authorities with the macro-economic model of the Treasury in an effort to achieve better understanding between the Government, industry, unions, local authorities and financial centres. In the early days of the internet, the Treasury introduced a service which allowed access to press releases, ministers' speeches, minutes of the Chancellor's monthly monetary meetings with the Governor of the Bank of England, reports of the Panel of Independent Economic Forecasters, details of the fundamental expenditure review of Treasury running costs as well as the Chancellor's budget speech and budget press release shortly after he has finished speaking. The Foreign and Commonwealth Office was an early pioneer in its use of the internet to publicise information. After a slow start, the position with other departments is much improved. However, the National Audit Office has reported that the more recent development of Government websites has been slow (Government on the Web www.nao.gov.uk). Deloitte and Touche have reported that $4.5 billion is needed for 'the UK to become an e-nation (www.deloitte.co.uk). The White Paper on *Communications* observed that more was spent by citizens in the UK on telecommunications than on beer.[8] By 2008, the Prime Minister wants all public services to be delivered electronically with the whole population able to be on-line by 2005. IT is at the centre of his wish for joined up government in his plans for *Modernising Government.*[9] A Government Information Service has existed on the internet since early 1995 (www.open.gov.uk/). In early 1996, the Government relaxed the copyright laws where statutory provisions allowing access to information were concerned.

The US Office of Management and Budget in 1995 launched an ambitious programme or 'electronic open meeting' entitled 'People and their Governments in the Information Age'. Use of the 'information superhighway' in the USA by government is at its most advanced in terms of interfacing the government with the people and providing public service information to citizens. Numerous details on the US freedom of

7   HC 312 (1985-86), p 18.
8   Cm 5010 (2000) para 1.1.18.
9   Cm. 4310 (1999). In HC 94 (2000-2001), the Select Committee on Public Administration said this target was now hoped for by 2005, see note 20 above. It is estimated that a phone call to a call centre costs £2.50 where access via the WEB is marginal once the site is established. The DSS has 300 million calls pa, ibid para. 14.

information laws may be obtained from the internet and such publications have not been protected by copyright. In the UK, *Hansard* and official Bills were protected by copyright and were only available where high fees were expended. Such services still exist but the former documents, and select committee reports and statutory instruments are available through the internet. The availability is revolutionary. In the USA, right wing politicians see the internet as an opportunity to end big centralised government by restoring power to the people—digital democracy as it is known. In the EC the use of IT until the mid 1990s had not been as advanced as its supporters would have wished, to some extent the result of more tightly controlled telecommunications markets in member states. The Bangemann Report *Europe and the Global Information Society* said very little about public information as a driving force behind the information society concentrating instead on deregulation and liberalisation of the European telecommunications industry. The European Commission Green Paper of 1999 *Public Sector Information in the Information Society[10]* was far more sensitive to the use of government held information to improve the quality of government service, make it easier for individuals and business to relate to government and to generate increased wealth and industrial competition. In 1994, 71% of EC citizens did not feel well informed about European institutions. 61% would like more information and 59% said a European telefax 'hotline' would be a good idea.[11] Here is a job for e-government. The potential benefits and dangers are mind-blowing. The EU Council of Ministers has operated an electronic register of documents held as will be seen in chapter 8.

On police computers in particular, the Lindop Report expressed concern at the secrecy attaching to their operation, the classification of information upon, for example, 'political activists', and their potential abuse. He recommended the creation of a data protection authority which would oversee the operation of data systems and which would liaise with the police in setting appropriate standards, as in the case of Sweden.[12] For 'national security' data the authority should have an officer with a

---

10   COM(1998)585.
11   *Eurobarometer 40* cited in A. Donnelly *Rewiring Democracy* Maclennan Ward Research Ltd (1994).
12   *Lindop*, ch 23. In cases of disagreement about the handling of personal information, a code should be approved by Parliament, he recommended. In Sweden, codes are negotiated between the Authority and the police. The European Court of Human Rights has held that there was no breach of arts 8 or 10 of the Convention on Human Rights when the Swedish Government refused access to a register containing personal information relating to national security: *Leander v Sweden* (1987) 9 EHRR 433. See also *Rotaru v Romania* (2000) 8 BHRC 449 (ECtHR). See I Cameron *National Security and the European Convention on Human Rights* (2000).

security clearance sufficiently high to enable him to operate in effect as a consultant to the Home Office and the security services and to establish with them the appropriate rules and safeguards for their systems. None of these recommendations was accepted. Versions of such a scheme are operational in Sweden and France. We will return to the provisions of the Data Protection Act 1998 in a later chapter. National security information may be given a complete exemption from that Act and is also excluded from FOIA where it is held by security and intelligence agencies. Although the police are covered by FOIA and the DPA, personal documents are given the widest of exemptions (chapters 6 and 7).

At this stage the primary focus will be upon a theoretical analysis of information, its importance in human relationships and its treatment in state/civil society compacts. I wish to advance the argument that citizens have a right to expect more information from their government than is currently the case in the UK notwithstanding initiatives in the 1990s and 2000 which I discuss in detail. Legislation, it will be argued later in the book and depending obviously upon its content, can go some way to redressing the current imbalance. It can help to a certain extent in creating a better informed public and establishing the basis of fuller participation of individuals and groups in the process of rule. But we need to understand why the provision of information is limited. Are there justifications for limiting it? Does current practice represent an implicit theory of state/ individual relationships which the overwhelming majority are happy to accept? If so, are they misguided? Claims and counterclaims about freedom of information are couched in terms of a theory of democracy by their respective proponents, often unwittingly. An attempt must be made to unpack and analyse these claims. Ironically, freedom of information could make us a very undemocratic and very unprincipled, indeed a more callous society.

The importance of information

Our capacity as human beings to acquire, use and store information is essential for our survival. This might appear a tall claim for something which in English law cannot be the object of theft.[13] At a practical level, disasters are avoided, accidents prevented and sustenance provided by

13 *Oxford v Moss* (1978) 68 Cr App Rep 183; *R v Absolon* (1983) Times, 14 September. See now, however, Computer Misuse Act 1990 on computer hacking and *A-G's Ref (No 1 of 1991)* [1992] 3 All ER 897, CA and *R v Bow Street Stipendiary Magistrate, ex p United States Government* [1999] 4 All ER 1, HL. Printing or other infringement is an offence under the Copyright Act 1988 and dealing may involve a conspiracy to defraud and note s 107 of that Act; Cf *Rank Film Distributors Ltd v Video Information Centre* [1982] AC 380 and Criminal Justice etc Act 1994, s 165.

our use of information. Hamlet's tragedy was that he was accurately informed; Othello's that he was not. While information itself is important, our ability to discern the degree of the reliability of the information provided is essential in the exploitation of resources or relationships, or in the exposure of sham. Information acquired through scientific inquiry establishes that it is irrational to believe that consulting the auspices, the stars or the tea leaves is a reliable indication of future events. Information is necessary to make sensible choice or wise judgement. Moral and ethical evaluation depends upon information acquired through our own and our predecessors' experience. Information in the form of facts constitutes the basis of order in our lives, of community, regularity and knowledge. Are 'facts' nothing more than the haphazard ascription of names or categories to phenomena impinging on our consciousness, however? And if there are no facts, is it possible to know anything? In order to think or make decisions we apply categories of thought such as quantity, substance and causality, or '*a priori* intuitions' such as space and time, to myriad phenomena which we encounter. These are categories or intuitions which, according to Kant, inhere in the working of the mind itself. They are the starting-point, he argued, of our organisation of confused data. They are the most basic forms of information. Their existence, Kant reasoned, is a basic fact.

Without the application of these categories and intuitions we would be incapable of achieving judgment or making decisions. We would be incapable of existence beyond that of a vegetable. Such intuitions and categories, Kant believed, are inescapable in the human predicament. But the information to which we apply our faculties of judgement and decision-making is far from immutable. It is subject to change, historical development, inaccuracy, distortion or imprecision, and so on. This is why we normally set a high premium on telling the truth, faithful and accurate recording of events, care in the provision of information; and why we punish cheats and frauds or censure liars, or hold as culpable the negligent transmission of information that causes harm.[14] These examples illustrate the importance of the mutual and implicit acceptance of certain ground rules in the use of information and its employment in human communication. Rather like the categories of thought, they are an inescapable feature of existence, in particular of communication.

These are commonsensical observations. Can they be given a theoretical, explanatory framework? A theory of communication that might assist has its most recent expression in the work of Jürgen Habermas.[15]

---

14 For references negligently compiled see: *Spring v Guardian Assurance plc* [1994] 3 All ER 129, HL.

15 J Habermas *Toward a Rational Society* (1971), esp chapters 5 and 6, and *Communication and the Evolution of Society* (1979). See Prosser 'Towards a Critical Public Law' (1982) 9 JLS 1.

Habermas has sought to establish that the process of communication between human beings, of which information is an essential if not exclusive component, is only possible on the basis that certain ground rules representing an underlying consensus are accepted. These will cover such obvious features as: assertions are made on the basis that they are believed to be true, or that the facts that we allude to in our speech are correct. Rational discourse is premised upon norms such as these. Even if we rejected the norms, we would still have to accept them implicitly to communicate. If I operate on the basis that deception is the fundamental truth of communication, I will set out to deceive. But a corollary of what I accept as a fundamental truth is that others may operate on the same basis. If they are attempting to deceive me, how can I assume that what they are uttering is not in fact the truth?—for they will deceive me by telling the truth, which I will not believe since I will accept it as lies. More importantly, in order to deceive, I must have an idea of the concept of truth. Deception implies truth or the concept of truth. If the consensus of the claims inherent in communicative competence is challenged, then its validity, correctness or acceptability can only be tested by debate and argument.[16]

Habermas argues that through discourse, as he calls it, the only form of pressure that is allowed to operate is the force of the better argument. Discourse is a 'special form of communication', but all communicative action implies that those 'interacting in it are discursively justifying their beliefs and norms through the giving of reasons'. As a practical reality, this is very often not the case; but communication must take place on the basis that the 'conditions constituting communicative competence are true'. If not, communication in any meaningful sense of the word would be impossible. What discourse presupposes, Habermas believes, is 'an ideal speech situation'. In this situation all participants must be given the same opportunity to debate and justify according to reasoned argument without external pressure or domination. All assertions and norms and claims are subject to examination and appraisal in discussion. By this method, norms will only be found to be justified when grounded in 'generalisable interests' and not simply on the power of those asserting the norms. The 'ideal speech situation' is precisely that—an ideal, although it is a fulfilment of the conditions which enable meaningful communication. It is forever frustrated as a matter of practice by 'systematically distorted communication'—by, for instance, manipulation of public opinion, misinformation, a lack of full information on which to exercise a proper freedom of choice, or ideologies legitimating class, economic or political domination. Habermas argues that a fundamental question of practical philosophy today 'has been . . . a question of the

16 'Discursive examination' free from domination, per Prosser. op cit.

procedures and presuppositions under which justifications can have the power to produce consensus'.[17] This will be a point to which I shall return. The attempt to convey correct information is the basis on which communication is premised. We are all regular providers of information, and we know the consequences of providing false information if we are caught out. There is a converse side to the provision of information. This is the control of information: that pursuit of secrecy or confidentiality or that quest for privacy which is essential to our full development as human beings. How can this be reconciled with the 'ideal speech situation' advanced by Habermas?

It can be reconciled by accepting that there are spheres of our personal and public lives that are a legitimate object of secrecy. Without adequate protection for justifiable secrets our integrity can be compromised, our identity shaken, our security shattered. Details of legitimate intimate relationships, medical facts, of prolonged sensitive negotiations, extremely delicate investigations in the public interest, development of strategic or commercial plans, often require secrecy. Likewise the long-term development of products requiring constant experimentation and creative thought or the protection of ideas. Without the guarantee of secrecy, there would be no protection for their development. The law has come to recognise this by the enactment of copyright and patent laws, the burgeoning area of intellectual property law, the law of confidentiality and specific privacy laws such as those that have been enacted in America and parts of the Commonwealth and Europe.[18] Some American states have gone further and made unauthorised appropriation of industrial secrets a crime.

In other respects secrecy is essential for and between participants to make sense of a situation; there would be little point in playing cards or chess if one constantly revealed one's future plans. This illustrates a deeper theme. 'What is at issue', argues Bok, 'is not secrecy alone but rather the control over secrecy and openness.'[19] It is very often a question of the timing of the release of information so as not to prejudice legitimate interests. Financial information or examination papers are obvious examples. But with information comes power, and with the exclusive control and use of information power is augmented. The problem then

17 Habermas *Communication etc*, p 205.
18 As well as actions for wrongful invasion of privacy developed after the seminal article of Warren and Brandeis, 'The Right of Privacy' (1890) 4 HLR 193. See the Younger Report on Privacy, Cmnd 5012 (1972). R Wacks *Personal Information: Privacy and the Law* (1993) and *Privacy and Press Freedom* (1995), P Birks ed *Privacy and Loyalty* (1997), R Singh and J Strachan *The Law of Privacy* (2001), D. Feldman *Civil Liberties and Human Rights* Part 2nd ed (2001). See ch 10 below.
19 S Bok *Secrets* (1984). Bok's work has numerous references to theoretical works on secrecy.

becomes one of establishing when secrecy operates not only to protect or advance the interests of those possessing or sharing secrets, but to subvert the interests of those not privy to such secrets. To a lawyer this is familiar territory: a balancing of interests, protection of proprietorial or quasi-proprietorial rights, reasonable behaviour. But the law can only play a minimal role in opening up closed societies or secret relationships given the strength of the attraction of secrecy and confidentiality in business relationships, professional associations, bureaucracy whether private or public, political groups, government, police and Freemasonry.[20] The problem concerning the exclusive use of information is at its most acute when we have a state or an official institution speaking on behalf of the collective or public interest which accumulates unimaginable amounts of information and which carries out its operations, whether by design, stealth or accident, in secrecy or at best under significant limitations on openness and access.

Information and the state

The position that a ruling body adopts towards the provision of information about its activities to a representative chamber or the civil society at large will inevitably be coloured by considerations about the proper role of government, as well as sheer political expedience.

When government was in the personal household of the monarch, the words of James I of England expressed the 'private nature' and arcane mysteries of state business by warning that 'None shall presume henceforth to meddle with anything concerning our government or deep matters of state'.[1] Francis Bacon was more subtle in his justification of state secrecy and in his presaging of a Leviathan, an almighty state:

> Concerning government, it is a part of knowledge secret and retired in both these respects in which things are deemed secret; for some things are secret because they are hard to know, and some because they are not fit to utter. We see all governments as obscure and invisible.

---

20 See the Home Affairs Committee: HC 192 (1997-98) *Freemasonry in the Police and Judiciary* and Government Reply HC 578 (1997-98). See Home Office Press Release 233/2000 on the consultation by the Home Office with police on registering masonic membership. The police were not registering on a voluntary basis to the same extent that judges and magistrates were.

1 Cited in *Bok*. See also W Eamon *Science and the Secrets of Nature: Books of Secrets in Medieval and Early Modern Culture* (1994). In spite of his belief in state secrecy, Francis Bacon advocated promulgation of scientific knowledge beyond a 'privileged few'.

In Leviathan, the all-powerful state, citizens have no need of governmental information and nor do those who purport to speak on their behalf. Government is absolute. It is absolute because it needs absolute power to defend society. Too much information about state activity will demystify the process of government.

When government is limited, however, in the nature of a trust on behalf of the community, such assumptions of absolutism which inform the relationship between state and society, government and the community, can no longer prevail. The nature of the bond between the state and its citizens, and between citizens *inter se,* is formulated in an implied contract, not an unalterable status. Breach by the government justifies its removal. John Locke saw the supreme power of the state residing in a legislature, and behind the legislature the people. The people governed, but they were not government. Nor were they the legislature, although they were represented in it. In matters of government, claims for information could not be made by the community directly, but via their representatives. Part of Locke's philosophy also justified acquisitive individualism and the rights of citizens to own what 'they have mixed their labour with' deriving from a natural right of property antecedent to the existence of government. When property is extended to information we have the joinder of issue with which we are still engaged—the conflict between a representative democracy and a democratically elected government and its preserve upon information on the people's behalf. The force of the argument posed on behalf of society is political not legal.

The growth of governmental power, quite simply, necessitated greater safeguards against abuse. 'Secrecy, being an instrument of conspiracy', said Bentham, 'ought never to be the system of a regular government.'[2] His appeal is to a political morality which government must adhere to and which, for all Bentham's apprehensions on extending the franchise,[3] is sympathetic to representative democracy, and especially publicity 'in matters of government'. 'Without publicity, no good is permanent; under the auspices of publicity no evil can continue.' Secrecy was the climate in which, at worst, those placed in government would abuse the power which had been given to them. It protected misrule. Publicity, regular elections and a free press were needed to safeguard the electorate from their chosen governors—from the excesses of 'bullies, blackguards and buffoons'. The risk that mistake or perversity in the electors' choice would

2   J Bentham, 'On Publicity', *Works of J Bentham* (1843, ed J Bowring), 2, pp 310–17; see also *The Collected Works of J Bentham: Constitutional Code*, vol 1 (1983), ed F Rosen and JH Burns, esp pp 162–8, 283–93; and F Rosen, *Jeremy Bentham and Representative Democracy* (1983), esp ch VII.

3   Rosen, op cit, notes now the *Code* stipulated that no one could be a member of the legislature who had not been admitted and successfully examined in the system of education prescribed for judges and senior civil servants.

increase as the franchise was extended was the dilemma Bentham found. Much has been made of this dilemma in present-day analysis.[4] But elsewhere Bentham represented that rational impulse which insisted on the goodness of publicity, of knowing. He quoted enthusiastically from Pope's *Essays on Man:* 'What can we reason but from what we know?' It was a theme that was to be developed in the liberal tradition.

With the extension of the franchise, liberal democracy proclaimed its strength as a political system in which individuals were given the greatest opportunity for self-development and self-fulfilment, especially under the influence of John Stuart Mill. The author of *On Liberty* would have approved of the words of Adam Smith who, in postulating the example of the 'ideal observer', said it was one who could infer that a moral principle for human guidance was correct after pursuing a mental procedure that was dependent upon such valuable human characteristics as being 'fully informed, free, imaginative, sympathetic, calm, impartial, fair, willing to universalise, acting on principle, considering the good of everyone alike, and so forth'.[5] The emphasis is upon being fully informed and rational. Within limits, modern pleas for freedom of information would have struck a chord of sympathy in Mill's breast, and later liberal philosophers came to realise more keenly that sharing of information was an essential component of democracy itself. Democracy had to be extended to ensure the greater informed participation of citizens in the process of government. It was a representative participation. The questions would be put by elected representatives, and information would filter through the system to the citizens. In spite of Mill's desire for an informed society in which maximum opportunity was available for self-improvement and the development of individuals, he prevaricated upon the extension of the franchise. Freedom was one thing, irresponsibility another. Other notes of caution must be sounded.

Bentham, however, would have seen it as proper for government to have restricted a free flow of information about its activities. Bentham argued for three exceptions to a prohibition on government secrecy: where publicity would assist an enemy of the state, where it would harm the innocent, or where it would inflict unduly harsh punishment on convicted persons. I cannot envisage arguments which would establish and successfully support the need for no restriction on freedom of information. The difficulty lies in allowing government prerogative alone to call the tune.

Secondly, liberal philosophers of a different school have frequently urged caution in so far as the well-informed individual wishes to use

4   C B Macpherson *The Life and Times of Liberal Democracy* (1977).
5   A Gewirth *Reason and Morality* (1978), p 20. See generally JS Mill *Considerations on Representative Government*.

information, or to keep information secret, not only to advance his own position but to distort equality of opportunity or a like liberty for all. In administering a state, Kant argued, there is a problem in knowing how 'to organise a group of rational beings who together require universal laws for their survival, but of whom each separate individual is secretly inclined to exempt himself from them'. Possibly the most influential of present-day liberal theorists, John Rawls, has argued that a fully informed individual *cannot* make the decision to deduce what principles *ought* to govern the operation of social institutions and government. Rawls argues for a method whereby individuals will achieve a state of 'reflective equilibrium' to establish through consensus the basic principles of justice that will be applied in their relationships as individuals and collectively.[6] He imagines rational men and women coming together in a temporary state of ignorance of their own personal strengths and weaknesses to form a compact in which the 'principles of justice', as he calls them, will be arrived at. The individuals will be rational—they will know how to reason and they will have information allowing them to argue on a general rather than a personal level. They will also be self-interested. They will be equipped to assess what their reaction as rational human beings would be to particular situations and what principles justify their decisions. The principles would allow them to assess moral priorities; they are 'constitutive of justice'.[7] As Rawls sees it, the temporary lack of information by each individual of their personal abilities, strengths and weaknesses is an essential ontological feature of the method of establishing 'principles with independent moral appeal'. If they knew of their strengths and weaknesses, they would load the dice to achieve an outcome that would be in their individual interest and not in the collective interest of all or of the whole in which they have an equal part. Rawls's device is a fiction; it is a method to capture an objective analysis required in moral philosophy. Apart from establishing the principles of justice, Rawls would not argue that a lack of information is a good thing *per se;* the principles of justice would be given full publicity in their existence, interpretation and application so that individuals would not misunderstand how they work.[8] But this does not tell us how much they are entitled to know.

It is one aspiration, that social and ethical relations should not essentially rest on ignorance and misunderstanding of what they are, and quite another that all the beliefs and principles involved in

6   J Rawls *A Theory of Justice* (1971).
7   See R Dworkin *Taking Rights Seriously* (1977), ch 6.
8   Rawls refers to this as 'publicity', op cit, p 133. Bernard Williams calls it 'transparency' in *Ethics and the Limits of Philosophy* (1985). See also AMS Piper 'Utility, Publicity and Manipulation' (1978) Ethics 88, p 189.

them should be explicitly stated. That these are two different things is obvious with personal relations, where to hope that they do not rest on deceit and error is merely decent, but to think that their basis can be made totally explicit is idiocy.[9]

It is ironic that Rawls chose for his tableau individuals in a 'veil of ignorance'. To simplify a Marxist critique of liberal philosophy and practice one need only address a Marxist belief that liberalism as an ideology perpetuates a veil of ignorance in as much as it is a legitimating device for capitalist accumulation and exploitation. The class structure is not seen for what it is: an organised enterprise bent on the exploitation of the economically weak by the economically powerful who manage to cloak the partial nature of the exercise of power with the ideologies of equality and liberty emanating from and supporting the material relations of production. The true nature of liberal society will be concealed by providing no information, disinformation or misinformation. Even in its more humane manifestations, the critique continues, it is elitist. In liberal society, information given by the government only serves to mystify because it is either intentionally false or it is part of a matrix in which systemic distortion is generated.

The last note of caution on democracy and information concerns power groups which are not ostensibly governmental, but which may be private and professional or trade associations and unions, and which are often protected by oaths, duties, or a culture, of confidentiality. There are arguable reasons why confidentiality must be maintained or not maintained in various relationships. These relate to individual respect and integrity. A problem arises when the private body in question exercises considerable influence in public life but insists on confidentiality in its operations to such an extent that it is effectively its own master. A lack of information facilitates a lack of accountability for the exercise of power and influence and the impact these forces have upon the public interest where democratic controls are absent.

Information and communication

It will be recalled that Habermas maintained that an 'ideal speech situation' is one where there is no distortion of discourse by contained inequalities or ideologies concealing inequality and that the 'ideal speech situation' was nothing more than the fulfilment of what is presumed in the effort of communication.[10] At the political level, he continues, legitimacy—

---

9   Williams, op cit, p 102.
10   See L Fuller *The Morality of Law* (1969), pp 185–6 on 'communication'.

justification for the exercise or non-exercise of power on the public behalf—can only properly be achieved under certain conditions. These are satisfied where decision-making processes are organised in such a way that arrangements can be found in which the institutions and political decisions would meet with the unforced consensus, if not approval, of the members of society *if they had been allowed* to participate as free and equal in policy-making.[11] The issue then becomes one of organising decision-making processes that provide information about their operations in as full and timeous a manner as possible as well as establishing the most appropriate procedures, organisations and mechanisms which 'are in each case better suited to bring about procedurally legitimate decisions and institutions'. Attempts to arrange a society democratically can only be perceived as 'a self-controlled learning process'[12] for all its members, not simply governmental or other elites.

One response to Habermas's attempt to extend his theory of communicative competence to political institutions and collective decision-making is to assert that it is all visionary and idealistic, that the world does not and cannot work like that. On the other hand, there is a link with the liberal tradition which has argued for liberalism as *the* system for the encouragement of individual development and achievement for all. Participation in government and publicity about the working of government have been consistent themes in the liberal tradition. Where Habermas differs fundamentally is in insisting upon an assessment and reassessment of the procedures and the information which are available so that legitimation can be achieved only after a participation of all as free and equal or, most importantly, who *would agree as such persons* if they had participated in policy and decision-making, ie if the process were seen to be even-handed and above-board. Habermas here accepts, it seems, certain realities of governmental decision-making. The decisions are made by government or elected chambers or elsewhere, and the 'elsewhere' poses particular problems. We cannot all be there in the chamber, in the cabinet, in the department. But what does go on in those places we would agree to, if not in terms of the substantive outcome, then at least on the basis that decisions were made on a rational assessment of the information which was not perverted by ideology, or distorted by influence and domination which is tangible or subliminal.

But if we are not in the chamber or elsewhere, how do we know the debate was rational? Experience may lead us to believe it is anything but. The point is that the more irrational the process, the more governors will want to conceal, the more they pervert the conditions of legitimacy. It must be accepted, however, that we cannot know everything about a government's operations and decision-making whenever we want. Such

---

11 Habermas *Communication etc*, op cit, p 186.
12 Ibid.

a restriction is consistent with Habermas's theory. The reasons for not imparting information, however, must satisfy the test that would justify an unforced consensus which would constitute a sure basis for legitimation. As long as we accept as inescapable that people exercise power on our behalf, then the exercise of power in whatever form must satisfy those ultimate criteria. Where I find strength in Habermas's analysis, which is lacking in the work of much of liberal theory, is his attempt to establish the ontology, the pure conditions of legitimation for the exercise of power through institutional frameworks whose arrangement is only justified to the extent that it facilitates discussion, information, reasoned decisions and supporting evidence. It is not a liberalism which assumes the inherent inequality of the social condition around which the agenda is set. Nor is the *tabula rasa* of Habermas contingent upon material forces of production distorting the information which shapes its inscriptions, as Marxists believe. Economic inequality is a distorting feature of domination preventing true consensus. It must be seen for what it is, and the interests of the economically weaker must be equally represented, *and represented with equal efficacy, as* other interests. When a government does not wish to publish its cabinet proposals for changes in child benefit[13] or when it makes 19 changes in the formula for calculating the number of unemployed,[14] or provides information on the increase of poverty and its effects in a manner designed to attract as little attention as possible,[15] or in a form which is incomprehensible,[16] or it does not publish figures for deaths from hypothermia among pensioners until after the November 2000 Budget Forecast announced increases for fuel allowance, or where it distorts the truth about the safety of food production[17] or it becomes obsessed by the 'packaging' of its policies, one can see the forces of domination perverting the discussion.

Freedom of information—the good, the bad and the ugly

The 'information society', or its members, are making increasing claims for Freedom of Information and open government (the two are not the same although they are very closely related).[18] Some use 'open

13 The revelations by Frank Field in 1976.

14 HC Debs 25 July 1986.

15 HL Debs, 30 March 1987 – a controversy surrounding the alleged suppression of the Health Education Council's Report *The Health Divide* on poverty and sickness, two hours before it was due to be published.

16 Occupational Morality: The Registrar-General's Decennial Supplement for Great Britain 1979–80/1982–83 Part II. It consists of microfiche tables.

17 See the Bovine Spongiform Encephalopathy Inquiry Report: HC 887 Vols I-IX (1999-00).

18 Freedom of Information may be seen as wider in so far as it covers, potentially, all information in the public and private domain. The phrase 'open government'

government' in a derogatory sense to mean what government promises but never delivers. This is contrasted with Freedom of Information which gives a legal entitlement to official information. In my view this robs open government of a powerful significance which is broader than access to information or documents. Freedom of information does not mean access to brute information alone such as documents or records in whatever form, as we shall see. It leads into open government in so far as it necessitates access to governmental decision-making in a more public and participatory form. The claims for such are couched in terms of a right to know, a democratic right. Such claims are easily made, but more difficult to justify if one has not established what theory of democracy one accepts. Information is inherently a feature of power. So too is its control, use and regulation. Government, to repeat, is the organisation of information for the use, effective or otherwise, of power in the public interest. Take away a government's preserve on information, and its preserve of when and what to release, then take away a fundamental bulwark of its power. This may be desirable or it may not. It is undeniable, however, that its impact is potentially profound. Such developments could establish new centres of power and organisation outside of government, where 'government' would be 'all inside and no outside', to rearrange Woodrow Wilson's snappy phrase. It could facilitate an even more acquisitive and inquisitive and captious society, or an oppressive one. One has only to remember that the president who coined the phrase 'executive privilege' in 1958 to circumscribe Congressional investigations was the same president who refused to hand over executive documents to Senator McCarthy in his witch-hunt of Un-American 'activists'. An investigative press or lightly regulated broadcasting system could do untold damage to individuals in a freedom of information state. Any responsible advocate for open government and freedom of information must accept that there are subjects which we do not all need to know and be informed on and which we cannot insist on knowing as of right. The question then becomes: what kind of information is this and, if I do not know, is someone entitled to know on my behalf and to what extent are they entitled to know?

Information and institutional structure

This leads us to the question of institutional structure. How do we best organise our institutions which are responsible for making decisions

---

refers to the openness of processes, as well as documentation and may concern private institutions in so far as they are used as a surrogate for governmental decision-making.

affecting the public and the public interest? How can they be structured to ensure that the debate is carried on in as informed a manner as possible? What allows unjustifiable domination in present institutions? On what, if any, issues should information be the preserve of the Prime Minister and one or two others? Is it wrong that it is so restricted, and why? When should information be exclusive to the Cabinet? When should it go to an assembly of elected members and how should it go—to the whole chamber or to specific committees? When is there a need for wider public debate at either inquiries or other public meetings, and how well informed will the public be? When is a subject appropriate for a judicial body or tribunal, and how widely should such bodies, especially courts, range in seeking information? Should there be a difference between litigation between private individuals according to law, which is therefore a matter of public interest, and litigation about the public interest itself? When do we need to present information for the assessment of outside experts who will assist either ministers, the elected and representative chambers or the nation at large? The reaction of British governments to such questions as these has been a tinkering at the edges and an insistence on the maintenance of the status quo. This is not simply because of the power of tradition and confidentiality. It is because in the British tradition, unlike the American or Scandinavian traditions which provided the prototype of freedom of information legislation, political power and survival are inextricably bound up with control of information.[19] Any information is used by the Opposition to make political capital out of the Government's position. Hence the increasing concern of successive governments to put 'spin' on the presentation of policy; to put their policies in their best light which is often assisted by the timing of disclosures.[20] However, there is evidence of secrecy in the operation of the Council and Commission of the EC where political power is not so dependent upon the control of information. This point can be more conveniently discussed in a later chapter, but it is interesting to speculate on the implications of the 'hiving off' of departmental responsibilities to 'independent' governmental executive agencies and contracting out where the traditional convention of ministerial responsibility has shown signs of considerable modification if not erasure.

It is now time to move from the general and fairly abstract to the particular and to examine a problematic area which poses significant political, legal and practical difficulties in relation to information control and its regulation and to see how the government has responded to the competing claims of security and accountability.

---

19 KG Robertson *Public Secrets* (1982)
20 See HC 770 (1997-98) and *Government Reply* HC 162 (1998-99) on *Government Information and Communications Service*; see also HC 511 (1999-00).

Information and national security[1]

National security poses the most difficult of practical problems in respect of information. 'Information Warfare' has become an important feature of the agencies who defend national security.[2] It concerns what many regard as *the* quintessential function of the state. National security involves the most developed form of information technology—much of it highly secret and according to renegade security agent David Shayler much of it incompetent, an accusation that was vigorously denied.[3] The area covers the most intrusive of information-gathering exercises conducted on behalf of government agencies. National security is also a virtually unanswerable plea to immunity, preventing access by individuals to information upon those individuals, and confidentiality. As we shall see in ch 9, the courts have long shown themselves sensitive to executive assertions of national security precluding judicial investigation of an individual grievance, although there are indications of increasing unease where the plea is put to a strained use.[4] Many of the most controversial cases concerning information in recent years have related to national security. The peculiar potency of the subject must be fully realised. It is not characteristic of all areas of government activity. However, it will provide an interesting area of human activity in which some of the theoretical points set out above may be tested. This is because the subject poses the most difficult of questions about executive action and its relationship with effective accountability and informed public opinion. The culture of government secrecy which will occupy our attention in later chapters owes much of its inspiration to this responsibility of government.

Is distortion of the truth allowable for the greater public good? Is this an area which is appropriately colonised by the powers of 'democratisation', as Habermas advocated? If so, with what necessary concessions to the claims of responsible and efficient government? Is distortion permissible in the conduct of trials where a relevant defence may not be invoked because of public interest immunity protection for vital information (see chapter 9) or to prevent the identity of witnesses?[5] Does distortion make such trials unfair?

1   I Cameron *National Security and the ECHR* (2000).
2   See Security and Intelligence Committee *Annual Report 2000* Cm 4897 (2000) pp.28-29.
3   Ibid p 18.
4   Cf *R v Secretary of State for the Home Department, ex p Ruddock* [1987] 2 All ER 518; *R v Secretary of State for the Home Department, ex p McQuillan* [1995] 4 All ER 400 and ch 7 note 1, p 290, below depriving judges of 'anxious scrutiny' to review interference with fundamental rights per Sedley J.. See also *R v MOD, ex p Smith* [1995] 4 All ER 427, QB, [1996] 1 All ER 257, CA, and what is rightly ascribed to 'national security'. *Tinnelly & Son Ltd v UK* (1998) 27 EHRR 249, *Svenska Journalistförbundet v EU Council* Case T-174/95 [1998] ECR II-2289, CFI.
5   Sir Richard Scott answered with a categorical 'no' in Matrix Churchill: HC 115

On national security, the UK approach has meant that the assessment of such an important matter and its requirements are for the executive alone.[6] Even the definition relating to security of the state and community against threats to their well-being is hopelessly glib, and has in fact assumed more of an international security dimension[7] as well as counter espionage, counter terrorism and counter subversion dimensions. This latter feature, which is notoriously broad, still survives in the legislation even though the anti-subversive unit of the security service was wound up in 1992.[8] Should national security not involve some objective assessment of well-being on the basis of political and civil rights, open democracy, and participative processes of rule? Surely these are features of a 'secure nation' moving towards a more secure international order?[9] What ought we to know about decisions on national security, the security and intelligence services, their general operations and those of the police in security work or indeed on the extent to which the security service is assuming the role of a police force? What should we know of their techniques for obtaining and dealing with information, and what safeguards exist, and should exist, to prevent abuse?

The answer given by the Freedom of Information Act 2000 to these questions is negative. Security and Intelligence bodies are excluded from the Act and information from such bodies or about such bodies held by public authorities is given a class exemption which is protected by a ministerial certificate. This is subject to a very limited challenge in the Information Tribunal.[10] Where records from the security and intelligence services are placed in the Public Records Office or the Northern Ireland PRO, they lose their absolute exemption after 30 years (see pp .... below). However, most of these records are not placed in the PRO and will retain their absolute exemption.[11]

(1995-6) Vols I-V and Index. On secrecy for witnesses, see: M Gilbert (1990) *Public Law* 207 and *R v HM Coroner Greater Belfast, ex p MOD* [1994] NICA Transcript 2439-2441; and *R v Lord Saville of Newdigate, ex p A* [1999] 4 All ER 860, CA. See Cameron n 19 p 28 and *McCann v UK* (1995) 21 EHRR 97 following the death on the rock shootings involving IRA terrorists. Failure to conduct proper investigations into shooting of terrorists has been ruled a breach of Art 2, ECHR: *Hugh Jordan v UK* ECtHR (4 May 2001, unreported).

6   On the role of the judiciary, see below.

7   Under the Criminal Justice (Terrorism and Conspiracy) Act 1998 hearsay evidence may be given in court by a senior police officer that the defendant is a member of a proscribed organisation; the Act extended the criminal law to cover conspiracies in the UK to commit crimes abroad. See now the Terrorism Act 2000. The Third Pillar of the Treaty on European Union covers Judicial and Police cooperation in Criminal Matters. The EComHR has stated that 'national security' cannot be defined 'exhaustively': *Hewitt and Harman v UK* 12/75/86 and *Esbester v UK* (1993) 18 EHRR CD 72.

8   See R Norton-Taylor in R Blackburn and R Plant eds *Constitutional Reform* (1999).

9   See Cameron note 19 p 28 and Lustgarten and Leigh below.

10 See ch 6 p 308 et seq. Under DPA s 28. See ch 7.

11 FOIA 2000, s 64.

From the many points which arouse interest and controversy on the subject of security, two are particularly pertinent for this study. The first concerns our information, or lack of it, about the security and intelligence services (MI5, MI6 and GCHQ (General Communications HQ) respectively and related bodies) and their activities. The second concerns the methods the services adopt to extract information from individuals or institutions and the use which they make of such information. In so far as security involves the police it will be pertinent to examine developments augmenting police powers while maintaining a suspect's right to silence.

The 'covert' ethos of the security services has undoubtedly helped to present an extraordinary picture of botched amateurism and eccentricity.[12] The whole question of accountability of these services in a democratic state was given dramatic not to say sensational prominence by the events in a Sydney courtroom, and later in English courts, when the British Government sought to restrict publication of the memoirs of the former MI5[13] agent Peter Wright. There were allegations of the infiltration by foreign spies at the highest level in the service, and a catalogue of 'dirty tricks' regularly practised by security officials, which involved their role in the resignation of a prime minister and the undermining of British governments in the past as well as assassination plots on a foreign head of state, President Nasser of Egypt. There was also the question of an eccentric and highly questionable individual being placed in such a sensitive position as Wright had been. Suppressing Wright's memoirs became a worldwide drama. It was an extraordinary episode in which the

12 For a history, see C Andrew *Secret Service: The Making of the British Intelligence Community* (1985). A particularly useful study written by lawyers is L Lustgarten and I Leigh *In From the Cold: National Security and Parliamentary Democracy* (1994) which also contains a very helpful bibliography. If anything it has been more accentuated in the last five years: the Shayler etc episodes do raise serious questions about the quality of people hired by the services.

13 MI5 is the security service. MI6 is the secret intelligence service – on the latter see S Dorril *MI6:Fifty Years of Special Operations* (2000). The Regulation of Investigatory Powers Act 2000 refers to them as 'the intelligence services'. MI5 was established in 1909. The 'arms and legs' are provided by the Special Branch and even the SAS as events in Gibraltar indicated in 1988 when three IRA terrorists were shot by that service. Lord Windlesham and R Rampton QC wrote a report *Report on Death on the Rock* (1989) on the affair. In July 1995, the European Court of Human Rights, overruling the Commission, ruled that the shootings were in breach of art 2 ECHR. MI5 has 'close relations' with chief constables. With the end of the Cold War, the security and intelligence services have been seeking new fields of activity and investigations and organised crime, money laundering and international fraud have been areas where they are reputedly seeking engagement as well as environmental and animal rights groups. The services are co-ordinated through the Joint Intelligence Committee and Intelligence Co-ordinator. In October 1995, the Prime Minister announced new powers for MI5 to engage in policing activities: *The Times* 14 October 1995 and Security Services Act 1996. See below.

public caught a glimpse of the working of British government at the highest level. One of the most dramatic moments was the rare scenario of a Cabinet Secretary upon oath under hostile cross-examination in a court of law both in Australia and in England. Such a picture re-emerged albeit less dramatically in the case of former MI5 officer David Shayler who was charged with offences under the Official Secrets Act 1989 in the Autumn of 2000 after revealing various alleged malpractices about the services. These cases precipitated further calls for reform of the security services in the UK, which have been not only distant but isolated from any form of democratic oversight or accountability commensurate with their power and influence. Until 1989, one statute, Cook has claimed, named the secret service: the Civil List and Secret Service Money Act of 1782, which restricted the issue of public money to the service to £10,000 per annum. When the statute was repealed in 1977 expenditure was estimated at £30 million per annum, and by the year 2001-02 expenditure was forecast at £867.00 million per annum.[14] Unofficial estimates vastly exceed this amount.

The services owe their origin and operations to the murkier side of the Crown prerogative. Nor should we forget that the Crown possesses a prerogative power not to prosecute charges, and to stop criminal proceedings, as was evidenced by the 'shoot to kill' policy practised by the RUC in Northern Ireland which was originally investigated by John Stalker.[15]

In 1984, the former Prime Minister claimed that she had, if anything, been 'too forthcoming' in her disclosure on security matters.[16] Since then, the public has witnessed a growing body of information – including publication of the identities of the Heads of the Services and official publications about them[17] — and speculation about the security services and its operations. Scandals and revelations throughout the late 1970s, 1980s and 1990s coincided with the prolonged dispute surrounding the

14 The Government's budget for the services; and see Cm 4897 (2000) p 20. In 1997, the services were subject to a Treasury driven Comprehensive Spending Review from a zero base. The details were not published. The 1782 Act was repealed by the Statute Law (Repeals) Act 1978, s 1 and Sch 1, Part II. Accounts of expenditure vary widely. Formally speaking, the service was not known by common law and had no executive powers. See now the Security Service Act 1989 and Intelligence Services Act 1994 under which the services may apply for warrants for certain activities p 41 et seq below. The Comptroller and Auditor-General had suggested the suitability of his office to oversee expenditure of the security services; see p 49 *et seq* below on his remit under the Intelligence Services Act 1994.

15 See HC Debs, 25 January 1988. See J Stalker *Stalker* (1988).

16 HC Debs Vol 59, col 187 (1 May 1984).

17 Eg *MI5 The Security Service* Home Office (1998). The former Director of MI5, Stella Rimington gave the Dimbleby Lecture as Director on TV and the present Director Stephen Lander gave a public lecture in March 2001.

introduction of polygraph 'lie detectors' at General Communications Headquarters,[18] the subsequent banning of trade unions at GCHQ, the Peter Wright, David Shayler and Richard Tomlinson affairs among others.

The Security Commission made intermittent appearances to examine breaches of security and advise on security procedures.[19] This body was established in 1964 following the Denning Report on the Profumo scandal.[20] Its chairman was a senior judge and it has seven members. The Prime Minister, traditionally, after consulting the Leader of the Opposition, refers cases to the Commission. In 1982, the Commission, then under Lord Diplock, recommended a relaxation of positive vetting in the civil service,[1] and a relaxation of the rules governing release of classified information especially where it was held back to prevent

---

18   'A branch of the civil service' whose main functions are to ensure the security of the UK military and official communications and to provide signals intelligence for the Government. They are part of the intelligence services.

19   See eg, Cm 4532 (2000).

20   Cmnd 2152. He described its functions as 'the Defence of the Realm, from external and internal dangers arising from attempts at espionage and sabotage' or actions 'subversive of the State'.

1   Cmnd 8540 a Government *Statement on the Recommendations*. A procedure to 'purge' communists and fascists from vital security-sensitive operations was revised in 1957: HC Debs, vol 563, cols 152–6 (WA) (29 January 1957). A procedure involving the 'Three Advisers' advised the secretary of state and heard the civil servant, though s/he was not allowed to cross-examine government witnesses. 'Positive vetting' was introduced to confirm the reliability of a candidate for a post involving access to 'top secret' information in 1952: see HC 242 (1982–3) and the memorandum from the MoD. Vetting policy guidelines were revised in 1990 and 1994 (HC Debs Vol 177 cols 159-161, and HC Debs Vol 251 cols 764-66) and overt reference to communism or fascism have been erased although no one should be employed in work which is vital to the security of the state where they have been engaged in espionage, terrorism, sabotage or actions intended to overthrow or undermine parliamentary democracy by political, industrial or violent means. Where they have connections with such organisations or are susceptible to pressure from such bodies or foreign agents or have defects of character which render the person susceptible to blackmail they are likewise not to be employed. Complaints provisions involve the Tribunal created by RIPA—see the legislation at p 47 *et seq* below and a Security Vetting Appeals Panel was established in 1997, HC cols 243-244 (19 June 1997). There are 'counter terrorist checks', 'security checks' which allow access to secret and sometimes top secret information and is reviewed every ten years. The highest level is 'developed vetting' allowing uncontrolled access to top secret information and which is reviewed after five years and thereafter every seven years. Over 160,000 vetting cases and checks are carried out each year. There are also basic identity checks. A Defence Vetting Agency was established in 1997 to take responsibility for vetting. See *Lustgarten and Leigh* ch 6 and Cameron pp 215 et seq and K McEvoy and C White (1998) Mod LR 341. See further the *Trestrail* case, HC 59 (1982–3) and the *Prime* case, Cmnd 8876. The Government has introduced polygraph (lie-detector) security screening, HC Debs vol 42, cols 431–4 (12 May 1983); Cf *Council of Civil Service Unions v Minister for the Civil Service* [1984] 3 All ER 935, HL. See above note 17. On the checks that will take place under the Police Act 1997 on those working with children.

possible political embarrassment. A report in 1985, however, recommended an extension of positive vetting in the security service following the case of the spy in the service, Michael Bettaney.[2] The Commission found faults in the management of the services, but the Prime Minister ruled out any Parliamentary oversight. It has also recommended the use of polygraph or lie detectors for security vetting. In 2000, the Intelligence and Security Committee conducted an Inquiry into the Mitrokhin episode which formerly would have been investigated by the Commission.[3] The essential position of the security services in the defence of the realm means that neither the Prime Minister nor the Home Secretary will answer *detailed* questions about them in Parliament. In the 1985 report which the Home Secretary referred to, the two appendices covering detailed recommendations on the internal structure of the security services were not published. Since 1992, as explained above, there has been a wider dissemination of information about the services and MI5 has its own web page (www.securityservice.gov.uk/).[4]

At present, 'national interest' demands that *operations* relating to the services are not discussed in Parliament.[5] Home Secretary Jack Straw was prepared not to seek judicial orders preventing publication of newspaper disclosures by David Shayler provided that no information about operations was contained. In July 2000, the former Secretary of State for Northern Ireland admitted that she had authorised the bugging of vehicles carrying *Sinn Fein* leaders.[6] Harold Macmillan described how security matters were for discussion between the Prime Minister and the Leader of the Opposition[7]—a convention which Mrs Thatcher threatened not to follow in 1986. The House of Commons was told as little as possible. The Denning Report revealed in 1963 that responsibility for security had rested with the Prime Minister until 1952. A recommendation from Sir Norman Brooke, the Cabinet Secretary, resulted in a directive from the Home Secretary of that year to the director-general of the security service— MI5. This stated:

in your appointment ... you will be responsible to the Home Secretary personally. The Security Service is not, however, a part

---

2 HC Debs, 3 December 1986. The Bettaney report is Cmnd 9514. See also HC Debs. vol 78, col 897 (9 May 1985). No reference was made to Sir Maurice Oldfield former Head of MI5 who had been a hyper-active homosexual.

3 Cm 4897 p.25.

4 This contains details of the MI5 Phoneline which has been in existence since 1998 for those who wish to provide information to the Service to assist in its work.

5 See *Lustgarten and Leigh* for references.

6 BBC *You Only Live Once* July 2000; *The Guardian* 21 November 2000.

7 *At the End of the Day* (1973), p 434.

of the Home Office. On appropriate occasions you will have the right of direct access to the Prime Minister.[8]

The Prime Minister continues to answer questions on 'broad issues of security' and has 'ultimate responsibility' for intelligence and security agencies[9] but, as Drewry suggests,[10] formal ministerial responsibility is rendered largely irrelevant by keeping Parliament uninformed of the detail. Indeed, the question of how far the Prime Minister is informed by the services is a major imponderable.[11] In their 2000 report, the Intelligence and Security Committee noted that the Ministerial Committee on Intelligence which the PM chairs had met very infrequently in the past two administrations. The Committee recommended it meet an least 'annually' (Cm 4897, p 9 (2000)). Apart from the inner caucus, 'ministers do not concern themselves with the detailed information which may be obtained by the Security Service' and receive only such information as is necessary for them to provide guidance. Legislative developments which are discussed below may have altered the picture — but who knows? Parliamentary questions on 'matters, of their nature secret, relating to the secret services and to security' are not in order although national security is not listed as an automatic block on questions in Erskine May[12] and there has been a relaxation to a limited extent since the beginning of the 1990s.[13] Ministerial prerogative has allowed ministers to decline to answer specific questions.[14]

Select committees of the House of Commons are unlikely to fare any better. The Employment Committee was not allowed to question certain officials when it investigated the background to the Government's

8   Cmnd 2152. There is a responsibility of the Foreign Secretary for the operation of MI6 and its Chief reports to the former. In the Zircon Spy satellite débâcle, an alleged rescue mission was launched by the Foreign Secretary and the Home Secretary for a programme ostensibly within the responsibility of the Defence Secretary (*The Guardian*, 24 January 1987).

9   T King, MP, Chairman Intelligence and Security Committee *Annual Report* Cm 4897; Drewry (1984) Public Law 370.

10   Drewry (1984) Public Law 370.

11   As evidenced by the Anthony Blunt affair: see generally C Pincher *Too Secret Too Long* (1984); and J Callaghan MP, HC 92 II (1985–6) p 223. See R Thomas *Espionage and Secrecy* (1990).

12   *Erskine May*, 22nd edn (1997), p 301-02 sets out the principles on blocked PQs. Only refusals in the same session are now noted by the Table Office to determine whether a PQ is inadmissible. A refusal to answer a PQ on the grounds of the public interest cannot be raised as a matter of privilege: Erskine May p 302. For the position of national security previously, see EM 21st ed p 292.

13   Lustgarten and Leigh loc cit.

14   Drewry (1984) *Public Law*, p 374, for 'guarded PM written answers'.

decision to ban trade union membership at GCHQ. D notices[15] and positive vetting[16] have been examined by the Defence Committee, and the Home Affairs Committee has investigated aspects of the administration and accountability of the Special Branch.[17] The Home Affairs Committee has examined the subject of *Accountability of the Security Services*[18] and in its review of the Consultation Paper and Draft Freedom of Information Bill the Public Administration Committee heard evidence from a former member of the security service.[19] The House of Commons has debated the services with reference to the Intelligence and Security Committee's (see below) annual report and the Government reply.[20] The Speaker of the House has even ruled that MPs could not see in the confines of Parliament a proposed TV programme allegedly endangering national security.[1] The House of Commons Committee of Privileges upheld the temporary ban until a full debate in the Commons could be held. The Committee rejected any removal of MPs' existing immunity from prosecution under the Official Secrets Act, or any restraint upon MPs by court injunction from disclosing information damaging to national security in the course of Parliamentary proceedings.[2] It further rejected any prohibition by ministers (through the Speaker) of an MP's right to publicise information in the House which he or she believed should be available.

In December 1987, the BBC was prevented by injunction, drafted in the widest terms, from broadcasting a Radio 4 programme discussing the security services. The programme included politicians who had held the highest offices of state and former members of the services. Information from the latter, and indeed their very identity, was a confidential matter.[3]

The potential for abuse by security service officials has been exemplified by accounts of former officials which support the claims of informed, speculative or privileged 'outsiders'. As we shall see in chapter

15 See p 197 et seq below.
16 See note 1 above.
17 HC 71 (1984-5); and see Home Affairs Committee *Accountability of the Security Service* HC 265 (1992-3) and the Trade and Industry Committee *Exports to Iraq* HC 86 (1991-2). Sir Richard Scott took evidence from members of the intelligence agencies in closed session.
18 HC 291 (1998-99) and Cm 4588 Government Reply.
19 HC 570-v (1998-99) 6 July 1999.
20 HC Debs Vol 532 col 470 22 June, 2000.
1 22 January 1987. An unsuccessful application for a ruling had been sought from the High Court.
2 HC 365 (1986–7).
3 'My Country Right or Wrong', *A-G v BBC* (1987) Times, 18 December. Subsequently works by members of the security services have been published as have works by former members of the SAS although the Government sought an injunction against one such publication which had been referred to the D Notice Committee. See *A-G v Blake* [2000] 4 All ER 385 (HL) and p 39 below.

9, the Government successfully obtained an interim injunction in the Court of Appeal and House of Lords against the reporting in newspapers of a former security official's allegations of abuse by officials, on the basis that a breach of confidence to the Crown would be perpetrated, even though a similar publication of the information had been made.[4] The court believed that the confidentiality owed to the Crown by employees and former employees of the service outweighed any public right to know of alleged shortcomings in the security service, whose papers were never put into the Public Records Office[5] and whose activities were of the 'highest sensitivity'. These arguments did not prevail before Mr Justice Powell in the Supreme Court of New South Wales, nor when the Government sought to restrict publication of *Spycatcher* in New Zealand. Indeed the Powell judgment was devastating in its critique of the Government's behaviour and actions.[6] They were also rejected in the English High Court by Scott J.—whose judgment was upheld by higher courts—when the Government sought a permanent injunction preventing reporting of the contents of *Spycatcher*. By that time the publication of the book in the USA and elsewhere had rendered protection meaningless. In a later case involving publication of a former security official's memoirs, the House of Lords established that the only ground on which publication could be prevented was where there was evidence of damage or additional damage to national security. This could take place even though the 'facts' had already been published or where the fact that it was a former official might give additional credence to the disclosures causing damage to the reputation of the services in the eyes of foreign allies.[7] In reality, numerous former security and intelligence officers, including a former Director General, have published or have sought to publish their memoirs. This in spite of a life-long prohibition on disclosures by such officers under s 1 Official Secrets Act 1989 (see ch 3). The latest episode revealed how difficult it is becoming for domestic courts to award injunctions preventing publication of former intelligence officers' work which have not been approved where the work has been published elsewhere or on the internet and was therefore in the public domain. The Court of Appeal refused to demand that editors discuss with the authorities whether work was in the public domain and editors would have to rely upon their judgement. Informal contact was 'desirable' before publication the Master of the Rolls believed. Section 12 HRA also provides an obstacle to the award of

4   See p 39 *et seq* below.
5   See now, however, ch 6 p 323 below and FOIA 2000 s 64(2) concerning records transferred to the PRO and s 2(3)(a) Intelligence Services Act 1994.
6   Especially the 'inconsistent' failure to restrict publication of C. Pincher *Their Trade Is Treachery* (1982) and *Too Secret Too Long* (1984) and Channel 4's programme, *MI5's Official Secrets* (1985).
7   *Lord Advocate v Scotsman Publications Ltd* [1989] 2 All ER 852, HL. See, however, *A-G v Blake* note 9 below.

injunctions as we shall see in chapter 9 (p 422 et seq).[8] However, in *A-G v Blake*[9] the House of Lords imposed a duty to account for profits from his book *No Other Choice* on the spy George Blake, a former member of MI6. This was a novel development for an equitable remedy for a breach of contract but conventional damages were not available and Blake was outside the jurisdiction and so beyond the reach of the Official Secrets Act. An account was ordered for payment of the profits realised from the 'very thing he had promised not to do' in his signed undertaking on entering the service. He undertook not to disclose information acquired in office, during or after his service, in book form or otherwise. 'An absolute rule against disclosure, visible to all, makes good sense' said Lord Nicholls, seeming to support, if not specifically endorsing, a life-long duty of confidentiality.[10] The Law Lords also disapproved the judgment of the Court of Appeal that the Attorney-General could prevent Blake receiving his royalties by 'public law process' and injunction. Interestingly, in spite of the life-long duty of confidentiality imposed on such agents under statute and common law Blake was not a 'fiduciary' because the information was no longer confidential – it was widely known. Lord Steyn believed that Blake was 'in a position very similar to a fiduciary' and an account was therefore appropriate.[11]

In spite of repeated Opposition requests for an 'external' inquiry into the allegations of treasonable and criminal conduct of MI5 agents beyond those adverted to above, Mrs Thatcher categorically refused to authorise such inquiries, stating that she was content with the *internal* review by the head of MI5. However, in an attempt to assuage official anxiety, in November 1987 the Prime Minister announced that a former senior civil servant was to be appointed as a 'staff counsellor' to security and intelligence personnel where their disquiet or grievances about their work could not be assuaged through 'conventional ways', ie an interview with superiors. He is to have access to all documents and all levels of management and the Cabinet Secretary. He is to report not less than once a year to the Home Secretary, the Foreign Secretary and the Prime Minister. In all, an estimated 12,000 officials in MI5, MI6 and GCHQ will be covered. The counsellor can make recommendations to heads of MI5 and

---

8   The work was written by former MI6 officer Richard Tomlinson: *The Big Breach: From Top Secret to Maximum Security.* He had been dismissed by MI6 and left the jurisdiction. He claimed that MI6 had a close association with Nelson Mandela — vigorously denied by Mandela - and that MI6 was planning to assassinate Slobodan Milosevic: *Att Gen v Times Newspapers Times,* 26 January (2001).

9   [2000] 4 All ER 385.

10 As under the Official Secrets Act 1989, s 1 and see *Scotsman Publications* n 105.

11 See *Snepp v US* chapter 2 p 77 note 11. The Law Lords assumed there was a contract in existence between Blake and the Crown vis a vis the non-publication agreement even though at the time the contract was made, civil servants were not thought to be in a contractual position re employment of the Crown.

MI6, but the Prime Minister refused to accede to a request that he be allowed to sit on meetings of the Directorate.[12] The Public Interest Disclosure Act 1998 (see chapter 4 p 192) does not apply to these agents.[13]

It is a fact that we live in a security-conscious world. Confrontation between world powers, the continuing presence of terrorism and the globalisation of organised crime dictate the necessity. The existence of a security and intelligence service is not the point. The point is to what extent should such services be rendered accountable? Who should know of their activities and responsibilities and call them to account? It is frequently claimed that simply leaving the information as a preserve of the Prime Minister and a few trusted ministers and aides is inadequate. This can allow improper influence on a Prime Minister,[14] or pressure upon the security services only to provide the information the government wishes to hear. In the 1960s, GCHQ and MI6 informed the government of how Rhodesia was able to break trade sanctions after its unilateral declaration of independence, only to be told by the Government that it did not want to know.[15] Who should know of the activities of the security services in order to vouchsafe to the public that those activities are conducted according to proper mandates and the law? Who should know of the degree of interrelationship between GCHQ and the US National Security Council[16] or the Central Intelligence Agency? The Americans appear to know more about our intelligence and security services than we do ourselves, since Congressional committees are in existence to survey the executive in this sphere of activity[17] and formal investigations by the Justice Department may be set in motion. The 1992 Maastricht Treaty contains the Third Pillar of the EU, the area known as 'judicial and

---

12   HC Debs, 2 November 1987 (WA) and 3 November 1987.

13   Industrial tribunals now cover security and intelligence officers: 1999 Employment Relations Act Sched 8; 1999-2000 AR of I&S Com Cm 4897; and see Northern Ireland Act 1998, ss 90 and 91and appeals against certificates of the Secretary of State that an act was done against an individual to safeguard national security – this followed the decision in *Tinnelly & Son v UK* (1998) 27 EHRR 249. Note also the Special Immigration Appeals Commission Act 1997 and the procedures to replace the advisory panel which heard 'appeals' from those who were subject to an order of deportation conducive to the public good on the grounds of national security. The legislation followed the ECtHR judgment in *Chahal v UK* (1996) 23 EHRR 413 (see ch 9 p 409 below).

14   The 'mystery' surrounding the resignation of Harold Wilson is often cited.

15   H Wilson's comment on the Prime Minister and national security in *The Governance of Britain* (1976) consisted of one page of text!

16   N West in *GCHQ: The Secret Wireless War* (1986) claims that at that time there was a 95% exchange of information' and an exchange of staff.

17   And note the 'Irangate' episode and Congressional committees of inquiry into the role of the President, his advisers and the National Security Council. The Congressional Committee's majority report of November 1987 recommended direct notification by the President of covert actions to the Congressional Committees, and the appointment of an independent Inspector-General for the CIA. See C Andrews (1977) 53 Int Affairs 390.

police cooperation in criminal matters'. This involves security and intelligence communities. Along with the Second Pillar on a common foreign and security policy this is an intergovernmental form of cooperation which has been a particularly secretive development in the EU (see chapters 5 and 8).

Do we need to know whether MI6 have plotted to kill Colonel Gaddafi, President Nasser, Sadam Hussein, or Slobodan Milosevic or of the 'dirty tricks' of our agents?[18] The answer is 'we do'; if not directly then there should certainly be a more extensive report and oversight than exists within the present privileged circle of communication. By insisting on too much secrecy the government will invariably engage in efforts which are counterproductive or destructive of democratic values themselves. For example, GCHQ after the union-banning fracas was raised from 'useful obscurity' to become the most notorious government HQ outside Whitehall.[19] The frequency of catastrophe within the services, from spies to internal mismanagement, makes the public expect the worst in the absence of appropriate accountability mechanisms. The brevity of past Security Commission investigations does not enhance their reports. The investigation by Lord Bridge into telephone tapping[20] considered 'all relevant documents' and the 'merits' of 6,129 tapping warrants issued between 1970 and 1984.[1] He was asked by the Home Secretary to investigate on 28 February 1985. He reported to the minister on 6 March. During that period two full days were spent by the chairman sitting as a law lord in the House of Lords. Not one 'tap' examined was unauthorised or used improperly, the Commission found. The Home Secretary declared that he knew no tap had ever been made *without* authority, in spite of the fact that a previous Home Secretary had stated that he found it impossible to know everything that the services did, let alone what they did not do.[2] What safeguards are there for the practices of the services?

Security Service Act 1989, Intelligence Services Act 1994, Security Service Act 1996 and Regulation of Investigatory Powers Act (RIPA) 2000

The most important pieces of legislative reform have been the Security Service Act 1989, which accompanied the Official Secrets Act 1989, and the Intelligence Services Act 1994.[3] To these have been added the

---

18 P Stiff *See You In November* (1986) and R Tomlinson *The Big Breach* note 8 above.
19 H Young *The Guardian*, 18 March 1986.
20 Below, Cmnd 9438.
1   The terms of reference were 'whether authorised interceptions since 1970 had been approved by ministers according to the rules'.
2   Merlyn Rees MP.
3   *Christie v UK* 21482/93 EcomHR, 78A DR 119 (1994). The Commission rejected a plea that the security and intelligence Acts contravened the ECHR.

Security Service Act 1996 and RIPA 2000. As we shall see, the Official Secrets Act did provide for a lifelong prohibition on unauthorised disclosures by security and intelligence officials and those purporting to be such officials as well as by notified officials.[4] Judicial decisions have confirmed this position under civil law. The other legislation requires a further analysis at this stage. The first two statutes do place the security and intelligence services on a statutory basis and they do provide for some form of Parliamentary oversight. In addition they set out in very broad terms the powers of the services, the necessity for warrants from the secretary of state[5] for otherwise illegal activity and they provide in each case for a commissioner and tribunal to deal with complaints about service activities and to oversee their activities. These have now been brought within RIPA 2000. The 1996 Act extended the remit of the security service as we shall see. However, compared with developments in Canada and Australia in relation to their own democratic oversight of the services, they leave a good deal to be desired. What do the statutes provide?

First of all, the 1994 Act introduced what had been rejected in 1989, namely a Parliamentary Committee on Security and Intelligence. This is a joint committee of both Houses and is charged with examining the expenditure, administration and policy of the security and intelligence services and GCHQ. There are nine members and none of these must be a minister. Members are appointed by the Prime Minister after consultation with the Leader of the Opposition. The Prime Minister may also exercise unlimited power of dismissal.[6] The Committee reports annually to the Prime Minister and may report at other times on the discharge of its functions. The annual report is laid before both Houses subject to exclusions of information which in the Prime Minister's opinion would be prejudicial to the continued discharge of the functions of the services. This subjection to ministerial veto in publication is not shared by other committees. The only safeguard against Prime Ministerial abuse is a duty upon the Prime Minister to consult the Committee about exclusions and a statement relating to the exclusion has to accompany the report. The Committee has power to determine its own procedure but not to decide if and when it goes into open session as with other committees. It cannot compel the attendance of witnesses and in this respect its powers are weaker than a Commons select committee. It may request information which shall be provided—subject to exemptions discussed below—'subject to and in accordance with arrangements approved by the secretary of state'. It will receive the key policy document setting out intelligence priorities and identifying key intelligence heads and officials. It has criticised the

---

4   Ch 3 p136 *et seq* below.
5   Or officials under certain circumstances, see eg s 3 Security Service Act 1989.
6   Section 10 (3) and Sch 3 para 1 (d). The first annual report of the Committee is Cm 3198 (1996). And see: Cm 4073 (1997), Cm 4532 (1999).

fact that it does not receive the 'confidential annexes' to the Commissioners' reports under interception and services' legislation.[7] The Committee meets in the Cabinet Office not in Westminster and is not open to the public.

Where the Committee requests presentation of information it may be refused by the relevant director/chief on several grounds, ie where it is

- sensitive information—although the director may disclose it if he considers it safe to disclose it. It is sensitive information where it might lead to the identification or provide details of sources of information, other assistance or operational methods available to the services;
- information about particular operations which have been, are being, or are proposed to be undertaken by those bodies;
- information provided by, or by an agency of, the government of a territory outside the UK where the government does not consent to the disclosure of the information.

The relevant director may nonetheless allow disclosure where the director etc considers it safe to disclose it.

Information may also be refused where the secretary of state has determined that it should be not be disclosed. He may only so decide where he would be justified in not disclosing information to a departmental select committee of the House of Commons. The secretary of state shall disclose such information if he considers it 'desirable in the public interest'. Prime Minister Blair and Home Secretary Straw have hinted at the possibility of oversight in the future by a conventional select committee.

Statutory oversight of the services became necessary both because of judicial prompting in England and pressure applied through the European Convention on Human Rights. The legislation manifested the 'Government's policy to be as open as possible about security and intelligence matters without prejudicing national security, the effectiveness of the security and intelligence services or the safety of their staff.'[8] In the passage of the Bill on MI5 in 1989, the Government accepted no amendments to the Bill and the committee stage of the Bill was a committee of the whole House. Section 1 of both the 1989 and 1994 Acts provides for the continuation of the respective services under the authority of the secretary of state. This would appear to indicate the potential authorisation of secretaries of state other than the Home or Foreign Secretary. Under the 1989 Act no reference is made to the use by the service of officers of the Special Branch or other forces, although the Prime Minister had suggested the need for additional powers for MI5

7   Cm 4897 (2000), p 14.
8   Lord Chancellor HL Debs Vol 550, col 1023.

which were announced in the Queen's Speech in November 1995. The Security Service Act 1996, makes acting in support of prevention and detection of a serious crime a function of the service and this has been taken to include computer security in Whitehall along with drug trafficking, illegal immigration rings, international trafficking in prostitutes and avoidance of excise. Arrangements will allow M15 to act in coordination with the police and 'other law enforcement agencies'. The Security Committee has expressed concern about the interrelationship between the police and the service, a concern repeated by the Security Commissioner, especially as police surveillance techniques were at that time non-statutory. They are now under the Police Act 1997 and RIPA 2000 (below). No reference is made to co-operation between British and overseas security and intelligence services or to the use of 'private' contractors or agents. RIPA speaks of those acting on behalf of the intelligence services ...

In addition to the 1996 extensions, the functions of the security service according to the 1989 Act shall be the protection of national security and in particular its protection against threats from espionage, terrorism and sabotage, from the activities of agents of foreign powers and from actions intended to overthrow or undermine Parliamentary democracy by political, industrial or violent means (section 1(2)). This leans heavily upon the erstwhile Harris definition of 'subversion' which was criticised for being far too broad.[9] 'National security' concerned 'matters related to the survival or well being of the nation as a whole, and not to party political, sectional or lesser interests'.[10] The 1989 Act contains provisions prescribing that the service shall not take action to further the interests of any political party. However all the weaknesses of the previous Harris definition survive from the perspective of civil liberties and there is nothing to prevent a Prime Minister condemning trade unionists as the 'enemy within' as occurred during the miners' strike in 1984, thereby rendering their actions 'subversive' and therefore an appropriate object of MI5 attention.[11] The same could apply to the farmers and road hauliers in their fuel protests in the Autumn of 2000. What are we to make, for instance, of animal rights activists engaging in mass non-violent protests? In the debates on the Bill the Home Secretary refused to define 'parliamentary democracy'. As Leigh and Lustgarten express the point:

> It is easy to imagine many in the service, and indeed many ministers, treating parliamentary democracy as the subjects' right to vote once every few years and their obligation to obey the rest of the time. Civil disobedience therefore becomes subversion. This

9   HL Debs vol 375 col 947.
10   HC Debs vol 143 col 1113.
11   S Milne *The Enemy Within – MI5, Maxwell and the Scargill Affair* (1995).

unsatisfactory state of affairs is compounded by the use of the term 'undermining' which imparts no limitation of immediacy or directness.[12]

The Act contains no explicit safeguards against improper instructions from ministers, apart from those of a party political nature, although the role of the staff counsellor should be recalled. The 1952 Directive authorised non-compliance with ministerial requests requiring a misuse of the Service. In Australia, where the Attorney-General instructs an inquiry to commence or discontinue in circumstances where the Director-General feels that the instructions are improper, the instruction must be in writing and copies have to be sent to the Prime Minister and the Inspector-General who oversees the service and deals with complaints. MI6 also has its functions spelt out in the statute eg 'to obtain and provide information relating to the actions or intentions of persons outside the British Islands (NI)' as well as 'other tasks' relating to such persons and such functions are exercisable only in the interests of national security 'with particular reference to the defence and foreign policies of HMG in the UK' in the interests of the economic well being of the UK—which under the 1989 Act is not qualified in any way—and in support of the prevention or detection of serious crime which is again undefined and is not jurisdictionally limited.

Both the 1989 and 1994 statutes provide for the continuation of a director-general of MI5 and chief of MI6 and director of GCHQ and it is their responsibility to ensure that only relevant information is collected by their services which is 'necessary for the proper discharge of its functions' and that information is not disclosed except for itemised functions.[13] One wonders how effective this safeguard will be given the report of the Home Affairs Committee which was extremely critical of the records handling by police forces which gave information on well in excess of 500,000 individuals to departments, agencies and local authorities in 1989. It described as 'ill defined' the power which police forces have to give information to private employers. It also found serious inaccuracies in the information produced and the Committee recommended a statutory independent agency to replace the National Identification Bureau, a recommendation realised in 1997.[14] The directors etc are responsible for ensuring the party political neutrality of their services' activities. They report on their services' activities to the Prime

---

12 Lustgarten and Leigh (1989) MLR 807.
13 Eg 1994 Act, ss 2 (2) (a) and 4 (2) (a).
14 *Criminal Records* HC 285 (1989-90). See now The Police Act 1997, Protection of children Act 1999, Care Support Act 2000 and HC 227 (2000-2001).

Minister and secretary of state annually and they may report at any other time.

Section 7 of the 1994 Act empowers authorisation by the secretary of state of acts done outside the UK which would otherwise be crimes within the UK. The authorisation is subject to safeguards. The 1996 Act makes clear that neither the intelligence service nor GCHQ may engage in property intrusive activities (burglary, trespass) within the British Islands. The security service may engage in such activities in relation to what became s 3B of the 1994 Act. This relates to warrants authorising intrusive action in relation to property where it concerns one or more offences involving the use of violence, results in substantial financial gain, or is conduct by a large number of people in pursuit of a common purpose. Alternatively, the offence, or one of the offences, is an offence for which a person over 21 with no previous convictions could reasonably expect a custodial sentence of three years or more. The Government said under the first part, the 'conduct' would relate to serious crime – 'industrial disputes cannot and do not constitute organised crime'.[15]

Both statutes also provided for commissioners to oversee the exercise of the powers in each statute by the secretary of state and the services, departmental officials and members of HM forces. These must give whatever information or documents to the commissioner as he may require to discharge their functions. These have now become the Intelligence Services Commissioner under s 59 RIPA. Under RIPA, the Commissioner's primary responsibility is to examine the issue of warrants by the secretary of state which authorise entry or interference with property or in the 1994 Act wireless telegraphy in addition to obtaining information to carry out their functions and which without the warrant would be unlawful. The Commissioner established to oversee interceptions (see below) will keep such matters under review where he is required to do so.

The Commissioner's remit also covers the performance by the Secretary of State in connection with, or in relation to, the activities of the intelligence services and of officials of the Ministry of Defence (MoD) and HM forces, other than in NI, of the powers and duties conferred on him by RIPA part I and II. These involve authorisations (warrants) for surveillance and covert human intelligence sources (see below) and investigation of electronic data protected by 'encryption' or secret keys.[16] The remit also covers the exercise and performance by members of the intelligence services (and MoD officials etc) of other powers and duties conferred on them by the same provisions. The Commissioner has to ensure the adequacy of safeguards to prevent keys obtained for understanding

15 HC Debs Vol 271 col 1054.
16 Encryption, which involves the use of 'keys' of a private and secret nature and a public key to maintian confidentiality in communications: See House of Commons Research Paper 00/25 3 March 2000 pp 47 et seq.

data from being put to wrongful use. The Commissioner also has to give the Tribunal, created by RIPA and which deals with matters arising under the Act, such assistance as the Tribunal may require in the investigation by the Tribunal of any matter or otherwise for the consideration or determination by the Tribunal of any matter (see below). 'Assistance' may include the Commissioner's opinion. The Commissioner's brief does not cover review of subordinate legislation.

The commissioner is a person of high judicial office. He makes an annual report to the Prime Minister who must lay a copy of such reports before each House of Parliament subject to exclusion of any matter 'contrary to the public interest or prejudicial to national security, the prevention or detection of serious crime, the economic well-being of the UK or the continued discharge of the functions of any public authority subject to the Crown.' A statement referring to such exclusion must be made to Parliament. Separate tribunals were established under the 1989 and 1994 legislation to deal with complaints by persons aggrieved by anything done to them or their property by the services and there was no power of cross-reference. A single Tribunal is now established by RIPA. In relation to the intelligence services (including MI5) any person may complain to the tribunal if they are complaining about a matter under s 7 of the Human Rights Act 1998 – a breach of a Convention right, especially one might add, Art 8 – by the services or persons acting on their behalf. The tribunal is the 'only appropriate' forum for such matters. The tribunal also deals with a variety of matters for which it is the 'appropriate forum' and other matters allocated to it by the Secretary of State. This refers, inter alia, to non HRA proceedings against the intelligence services or those acting on their behalf.

The tribunal is also the appropriate forum for any complaint which the complainant believes took place in relation to him, his property, any communication sent by him or intended for him, or to his use of any postal or telecommunications service or system and it was carried out by or on behalf of the intelligence services and the complaint is about their conduct. The tribunal's jurisdiction is much wider than its predecessors and covers the breadth of activities under RIPA and complaints about those activities. Proceedings may be allocated to the tribunal to the exclusion of courts or other tribunals – although they may be remitted to a court or tribunal. In making an order for a tribunal hearing, the Secretary of State has to consider the need to secure that information is not disclosed to an extent or in a manner which would be contrary to the public interest or prejudicial to national security or other matters.

The complaint is to be investigated according to relevant schedules unless the complaint is considered 'vexatious or frivolous' by the tribunal. Considering the obvious difficulty a complainant will have in obtaining relevant information, such a barrier becomes much more formidable than might appear at first sight. Under s 23 FOIA 2000, information from the intelligence services is given an absolute exemption as will be explained in chapter 6 and under s 24 information relating to national security is subject to a ministerial certificate which can only be overturned by the Information Tribunal on very limited grounds. The tribunal has power to award interim orders. The tribunal may refer to the Commissioner any case under RIPA requesting the assistance of the Commissioner or his opinion on any relevant issue. The tribunal also keeps the Commissioner informed of complaints referred to it where relevant to the Commissioner. The tribunal may report its conclusion to the PM where an authorisation given by the Secretary of State was involved. The tribunal has power to order to it disclosure of documents and information from a wide range of bodies under s 68(7). In making its determination on alleged breaches of the Convention the tribunal applies principles applicable by a court on judicial review[17] ie mistake of law, failure to consider all factors, irrationality, disproportionality and so on. A similar provision applies to other complaints but as the Convention is not involved, proportionality may not be applicable, though whether this would make much difference to the jurisprudence of the tribunal is a moot point.[18] Remedies where a breach of the act has taken place include quashing or cancelling of warrants, destruction of records obtained under warrant or held by any public authority in relation to any person and compensation. The decisions of the tribunal, and this is written in the broadest sense, are not questionable in any court of law.[19] The Secretary of State may provide otherwise by order under s 67(8). The Secretary of State has to provide for appeal for some complaints to a court under s 65. Where the Secretary of State makes an order under s 67(8), he may also establish another special tribunal to hear appeals. This will be in relation to cases where the tribunal is the 'only appropriate' or the 'appropriate' tribunal. This is a very interesting example of administrative justice and a circuitous device to comply with the requirements of the ECHR while removing the regular courts.[20] Rules may provide for the giving of reasons for its decisions.

The legislation still leaves a great deal to be covered by custom and practice. The working relationship of the Prime Minister with the services is not explained and no reference is made to direct access to the Prime Minister by the director-general in particular. In terms of service officials, the legislation only deals with reports by the heads of services and not their servants. Nor does the legislation dwell on the amount of information

---

17 These principles have developed since this formula was first used to embrace matters such as proportionality, substantive legitimate expectation and fundamental rights and not simply *Wednesbury* unreasonableness etc.

18 *R v Chief Constable of Sussex, ex p International Trader's Ferry Ltd* [1999] 1 All ER 129, HL.

19 See s 67(8). See also note 16 p 381.

20 See s 67(10)(c), however.

given to the secretary of state or the independence of the director etc from ministers, in spite of restrictions on action on party political grounds. How much of the convention survives that ministers are only informed in outline and are not given 'detailed information' but only that as may be 'necessary for the determination of any issue on which guidance is sought? (Maxwell-Fyfe Directive).

The Intelligence and Security Committee was a welcome addition but lacking the investigatory powers of select committees might, on the surface, appear a serious handicap. However, Parliamentary select committees are not equipped to investigate intelligence and security communities in the manner of Congressional committees in the USA and even these have had some notable failures including the Oliver North 'Arms to Iraq' episode (see ch 2 p 77 et seq). The general contribution of select committees has been limited although useful investigations have included the Trade and Industry inquiry into the Iraqi supergun affair. Leigh and Lustgarten for instance claim that although much of the crucial evidence only emerged when a minister let slip vital information under defence cross-examination in subsequent criminal proceedings and public interest immunity certificates were lifted in the trial, the committee had played a crucial role in helping to publicise vital if apparently unsensational evidence.[1] The movement to greater openness concerning the services has been noted and limited information has emerged during debate and in answer to parliamentary questions. Even so, information has been exceedingly exiguous and specific questions linked to operations are normally likely to be ruled out of order. Until the 1994 Act, the Comptroller and Auditor General did not audit the services and the Public Accounts Committee did not consider the budgets of the intelligence agencies. When the CAG in 1887 refused to certify expenditure on the secret service vote, a compromise was reached whereby a minister would in future submit a certificate that monies had been properly expended in 'the interests of the public service'.[2] The Committee believed that such a certificate answers 'all reasonable Parliamentary requirements...'. Control was via civil servants who by the nature of the subject would exercise very limited control. The Committee established under the 1994 Act will examine the expenditure of the services and will require access to their budget and there are provisions whereby information may be disclosed to the CAG for him to carry out his scrutiny of their expenditure.[3]

---

1   Lustgarten and Leigh (1994) p 454.
2   Ibid p 450.
3   1994 Act, ss 10 (1), 2 (3) (b), 4 (3) (b) and 1989 Act s 2 (3A) (b). See the Committee's *Interim Report* Cm 2873 (1995) and first annual report Cm 3198 (1996). See the *Annual Report 2000* pp 20-25 where among other things the Committee writes: 'Our biggest concern was the GCHQ Resource Account, which

It could be argued that, from a constitutional point of view, one of the most glaring omissions is the absence of a precise statutory code covering the powers of the services. The Acts set out their functions in very broad terms. The Government would argue, understandably, that such a code would inhibit the effectiveness of the services, especially the covert operations of MI6. 'Tight' internal controls operate so that for instance in the case of MI6, any matter of political sensitivity would require the permission of the secretary of state if a warrant were not necessary. Such a response would be more acceptable if adequate procedures existed for grievance resolution. RIPA is an improvement and far more attention has been paid to complaints but procedures remain uncertain in their scope, and they do not cover complaints relating to events before the schedules of the Acts came into effect. In any event, the 'system'—by which I mean the service and all those within and without the service who serve or assist it—is likely to seize up if there is unlawful action, in contravention of, or without, a warrant and an injured victim wishes to sue. Section 1 of RIPA provides for a tort of unlawful interception of communications, for instance. But where will the evidence come from? Where the source of information to a third party complainant is a security official, the latter will run the risk of prosecution under s 1 OSA 1989. The identity of such an official will not be kept confidential from government by investigating authorities.

It is also important to realise that these acts, given the breadth and vague nature of their contents, may not be the exclusive source of authority and power of the services. In *R v Secretary of State for the Home Department, ex p Northumbria Police Authority*[4] the Court of Appeal accepted that a prerogative power, in this case maintaining the peace, could survive a statutory enactment covering the same subject area. Traditional doctrine has it that where a statute is passed on a subject hitherto under the prerogative, the statute takes precedence unless Parliament indicates the contrary intention. There was no such intention behind the Police Act 1964, the court held. Were this reasoning to apply in the present context of security and intelligence then an ancient prerogative would be rattling its chains once more down the centuries.[5] The legislation hardly constitutes a constitutional code. The *Northumbria* decision renders uncertain the extent of the service's authority. The Home

---

showed that GCHQ had not developed a suitable system of locating, tracking and agreeing ownership of its assets.'

4   [1988] 1 All ER 556, CA.

5   See *R v Secretary of State for the Home Department, ex p Fire Brigades Union* [1995] 2 All ER 244, HL. In this case, it was established that a Secretary of State could not use prerogative powers to put a programme of criminal injuries compensation into effect in a manner which was inconsistent with statutory powers to introduce a statutory scheme under existing statutory provisions.

Secretary insisted that the 1989 legislation was 'taking an area of public policy out of the realm of the prerogative and putting it into the realm of statute'.[6] The process may have continued but the assessment may be over sanguine.

Interception of communications, surveillance and RIPA

Interception of communications has been performed by the executive since correspondence began, although until 1985 there was no legislative basis for such action. The Birkett Report of 1957 thought that the position of the law could be stated to recognise the power to intercept letters and telegrams, and 'it is wide enough to cover telephone communications as well'.[7] In *Malone v Metropolitan Police Comr*[8] the power of the secretary of state to authorise telephone taps was judicially recognised absent any other tort or criminal act. Birkett described the authority of the secretary of state as 'absolute', although authorisations were in practice issued to a limited number of listed agencies. When the European Court of Human Rights held that the British Government's guidelines on tapping were in contravention of Art 8 of the European Convention on Human Rights protecting privacy,[9] the Government produced a Bill intending to secure compliance with our obligations under the Convention. *The Times* spoke of the Bill as an act of 'dumb insolence' attempting to achieve the absolute minimum to comply with the Court of Human Rights ruling in *Malone*.[10]

The Interception of Communications Act 1985 has now been almost totally repealed by RIPA. The 1985 Act covered interception of communications by post or public telecommunications systems which includes fax and Email.[11] Since the Act was passed, the number of telecommunications companies offering fixed line service had increased from two to about 150. Mobile phones had increased in a way that was unforeseen; new services were introduced such as international simple resale. There is likely to be a rapid development of the satellite telephone market and correspondence via the internet. The Government believed that the powers of interception had to be increased to cover these developments. Furthermore, the decisions of the ECtHR on breaches of the Convention had created difficulties for the UK in relation to private

---

6   HC Debs Vol 145 col 213.
7   Cmnd 283. The Prime Minister has given a reassurance that MPs' phones will not be tapped (HC Debs, 10 December 1986).
8   [1979] Ch 344, Sir Robert Megarry VC. And see Cmnd 7873; and authorisation by the Foreign Secretary for the purposes of national security and economic well-being, Cmnd 9438, p 5.
9   ECHR, Series A, No 82, Judgment of 2 August 1984.
10   *The Times*, 6 March 1985. See I Cameron (1986) NILQ 126. Note also the report of the European Parliament of 29 May 2001 on the Echelon spying network and global eavesdropping.
11   Cm 108 para 5 and mobile phones.

telephone networks[12] and the HRA, which incorporates most of the Convention, had to be addressed in the context of interceptions.[13] The Government wished to make statutory provision for interceptions on all these forms of communications as well as to obtain 'communications data' which means information about the use of a communications service ie, the number and frequency of communications but not their content. RIPA makes unauthorised interception a criminal offence. Interception without lawful authority is also made a tort under s 1(3). Under s 1(6), controllers of private communications' services are excluded from criminal liability where they make an unauthorised intercept but their action will remain a tort unless parties are put on notice that their calls are likely to be monitored. The Secretary of State has issued regulations under s 4(2) RIPA which authorise for the purposes of RIPA the interception of telecommunications in the widest of terms for the purposes, inter alia, of monitoring business calls.[14] All reasonable steps have to be taken to inform those affected. Authority can be given by the consent of the person who made or received the communication, or where reasonable grounds exist to believe consent has been given, or by the warrant of the secretary of state. It is very rare for the Home Secretary to reject a request for a warrant[15] the highest incidence of refusals occurring in foreign affairs. The Government rejected the need for prior judicial approval for a warrant.[16]

A warrant must not be issued unless necessary for one of four specified grounds: the interests of national security; preventing or detecting serious crime; safeguarding the economic well-being of the UK; or, under the second ground in order to give effect to an international mutual assistance agreement (see s 20). The Secretary of State has to believe that the conduct authorised by the warrant is proportionate to what is sought to be achieved by that conduct. Consideration must be given to whether the information could be obtained by other means before a warrant is issued, and there are limits set for the duration and premises and persons intercepted.[17] The Secretary of State has to make arrangements to secure that disclosure of information obtained and copying of the information is limited to the minimum necessary to comply with the criteria given above, and that uncertified material obtained on an interception is not regarded or

---

12 *Halford v UK* (1997) 24 EHRR 523.

13 As well as the EC Telecommunications Data Protection Directive (97/66/EC) requiring member states to ensure the confidentiality of communications made by a public telecommunications network and telecommunication service. See Art 5(2). Section 4 RIPA incorporates Art 5(2) of the Directive.

14 The Telecommunications (Lawful Business Practice) (Interception of Communications) Regulations 2000, SI 2000/2699.

15 *Lustgarten and Leigh* p 59. In 'urgent' cases, and following statutory conditions, a senior civil servant may issue the warrant.

16 Executive authorisation was approved in *Christie v UK* (1994) ECtHR.

17 'External' interceptions are far broader than 'internal' ones.

examined. Section 6 covers those who may make applications for warrants, and as well as the Intelligence chiefs and police (largely through the National Criminal Intelligence Service) they include Customs and Excise Commissioners. Warrants must contain various details and may be modified. The Secretary of State may by order require a public postal or telecommunications service to maintain assistance in interception warrants. A Technical Advisory Board is to be established. Unauthorised disclosure of information obtained through intercepts is a criminal offence under s 19.

Authorisations must be given in order to obtain access to communications data. 'Communications data' as we have seen means information about the use of a communication service including information held by a service provider. It does not concern their content as with an intercept. The necessary grounds for obtaining such data are considerably broader than for obtaining an interception warrant. Authorisations are given by designated persons within the relevant authorities. A notice may also be given to postal or telecommunications operators to obtain or disclose data. The conduct authorised must be proportionate to the objectives of seeking the data. Codes may be issued under the Act and as of writing, three have been published for consultation.[18]

Part II of RIPA regulates the use of covert surveillance in three forms: 'directed' ie planned following of targets; 'intrusive' which involves the use of an individual in any residential premises or vehicle or surveillance devices; and the conduct and use of 'covert intelligence sources' which involves the cultivation of individual 'sources' to supply information. These definitions of directed and intrusive surveillance may be changed by order under s 47 and under s 71 codes may be issued covering covert surveillance and covert human intelligence sources.[19] Covert surveillance has to be authorised by designated authorities on specified grounds. The authorised conduct has to be proportionate. The designated authorities for intrusive surveillance are listed in s 32.[20] The Surveillance Commissioner and Chief Surveillance Commissioner possess various regulatory and appeal powers. Special provisions cover intelligence services' authorisations under Part II. The provisions under Part II add to those in the Police Act 1997, Part III and the Intelligence Services Act 1994 which regulate entry on or interference with property, or with wireless telegraphy and which were necessitated by the anticipation that use of

18 One of these includes interception. Two further codes in draft cover covert surveillance, and covert human intelligence sources. A further code will cover encryption. It has been reported that the intelligence services are seeking powers of access to all communications data and communications service providers will have to keep this for seven years: *The Guardian* 4 December 2000.
19 See above.
20 Or otherwise listed in SI 2000/2417.

secret listening devices without legal regulation was in breach of Art 8 ECHR. The decision of the ECtHR in *Khan v UK* established that there was such a breach.[1] This came after the House of Lords ruled evidence obtained by 'bugs' was admissible against the defendants and on the basis of which they were convicted of importation of prohibited drugs.[2] The Lords' judgment came before the HRA incorporated the Convention. Before the 1997 legislation and RIPA the position in respect of surveillance was governed by administrative codes.

Part III RIPA empowers authorities to demand that encrypted material - computerised and protected by a secret code - be rendered intelligible or that a key allowing it to be decrypted be handed over. It applies to such material that has come into a person's possession as a result of a statutory power of search and seizure eg Police and Criminal Evidence Act 1984, or some other lawful means. A power may be exercised by one with the 'appropriate permission' under Sch 2. A notice requiring disclosure may be served on the person who is believed to be in possession of the key. It must not be given for speculative reasons. A notice may not be required where its purpose would be defeated by being given. A disclosure request must be necessary on stated grounds and proportionate. Stricter controls apply where the key itself is required. Non disclosure when requested as well as tipping off another person about a notice where secrecy is required are punishable offences. Defences are available and a duty is imposed to safeguard keys. Breach of the duty is actionable.

RIPA establishes a tribunal which is appointed by the Crown to hear complaints not only from victims of interception of a communication either by or to them but also on a variety of topics under s 65 which was outlined above. This is where the Tribunal is the 'only appropriate' or 'appropriate' tribunal. Complaints cover conduct concerning data communications, covert surveillance under Part II, complaints concerning Part III notices and disclosure and use of keys, entry or interference with property or interference with wireless telegraphy. This will include vetting complaints. As well as being the tribunal for complaints about the intelligence services which do not fall within the HRA, the tribunal is also the appropriate tribunal for conduct under the Act which has taken place in challengeable circumstances. This means not only where there is, or purports to be, a warrant, authorisation, notice, a permission under

1   *Khan v UK* (2000) Times, *23* May. On the legality of use of foreign intercepts in English courts, see *R v P* [2001] 2 All ER 58, HL.

2   *R v Khan* [1996] 3 All ER 289, HL. Art 8 was not at that time a part of our domestic law. Under s.17 RIPA, evidence obtained from intercepts is not admissible in any legal proceedings with some exceptions in s.18 including proceedings before the Tribunal. This prohibition does not apply to the other parts of the Act although intercepted material for which keys are obtained under Part III will be covered. Section 78 PACE 1984 (below) will govern the use of such material that is not covered by the prohibition.

Sch 2, or an authorisation under s 93 Police Act 1997.[3] It also includes circumstances where there is no warrant etc but 'it would not have been appropriate for the conduct to have taken place without it' or without proper consideration of that factor. In other words, unlike the 1985 Act, the tribunal may hear complaints where action is not authorised. The Tribunals and Inquiries Act 1992 applies to the tribunal.

Rules may be made concerning the form of the hearing, the provision of information about any determination, or order etc, to be given to the complainant and on legal or other representation for complainants. Rules may provide for the giving of summaries of evidence to the complainant and giving of reasons in a manner that does not compromise sensitive information. The Secretary of State must have regard to the need to protect information from disclosure which is against the public interest, or prejudicial to national security, the prevention or detection of serious crime, or the economic well-being of the country, or the continuing discharge of the functions of any of the intelligence services.

An Interception of Communications Commissioner is appointed by the PM to keep under review the exercise of powers of warrant by the Secretary of State. The Commissioner has to assist the Tribunal in a manner similar to the Intelligence Services Commissioner. He is a person of high judicial office — Lord Justice Simon Brown. Those regulated by the Commissioner must cooperate by providing information and documents. An Investigatory Powers Commissioner is established for Northern Ireland. Scotland has its own legislation and there are various dovetailing provisions.

RIPA is a remarkable illustration of administrative justice within the inner recesses of the state. It seeks to maintain the ideals of legality and of the Convention while securing as little interference from the legal order as possible. Some of the worst features of previous legislation have gone — although much has to be provided by way of regulations and orders to realise the improved safeguards. In their place is a statute with sweepingly intrusive powers. Monitoring of private communications systems will be standard practice and authorised under regulations or by notice where users will have no choice but to use the systems. Powers are so wide that they are going to be extremely difficult to breach. Unauthorised intercepts are an offence and actionable. How is one to obtain necessary evidence when the perpetrators are likely to be cliques in the intelligence services or police? Other unauthorised action under the Act is not made 'lawful' but is not a statutory offence under RIPA. It may be actionable if tortious or an offence if otherwise criminal. It will also have to be consistent with the HRA. The Interception Commissioner and the Security Service Commissioner both reported in 1998 that there had been not a single

3   This covers authorisations to interfere with property.

successful case reported to them since they set up shop.[4] Nor are innocent targets to be notified after the intercept etc that they have been the subject of such action. This is the practice in Germany, Finland and Denmark but was too difficult in our jurisdiction.[5] The Tribunal will operate like a court hearing a judicial review and is not meant to become involved with the merits of warrants and authorisations although in HRA cases it can apply proportionality. To assist the services and law enforcement agencies, a '24 hour' National Technical Assistance Centre has been established. This will provide a central facility for complex processing and will include internet services. It will be operated by the National Criminal Intelligence Service.

Obtaining information by other means

The Police and Criminal Evidence Act substantially altered the rules of 'criminal justice' to augment police powers of entry, search and seizure. This is especially so in relation to evidence which previously may have been privileged but which is now obtainable on a warrant or order from a circuit judge and includes 'excluded material' and 'special procedure' material under the Act. Applications are made under Sch 1 of the Act which sets out conditions which must be satisfied before a judge may order production or access to the material.[6] The former covers personal, trade, professional and other records held in confidence, or human tissue or tissue fluid taken for diagnosis or medical treatment and held in confidence, or 'journalistic material'[7] held in confidence. Special procedure material is journalistic material other than excluded material[8] and material 'acquired or created in the course of any trade or other occupation or for the purpose of any paid or unpaid office' and held *inter alia* subject to an express or implied undertaking to hold it in confidence other than material subject to legal professional privilege and excluded material. Police forces have

---

4   Cm 4001para 31 (1998) and Cm 4002 para 26 (1998)]
5   See Cameron op cit note 10.
6   *R v Central Criminal Court, ex p Bright* [2001] 2 All ER 244 where the Divisional court imposed stringent safeguards on the exercise of the power.
7   Journalistic material would cover documents and eg broadcasting tapes such as those seized in the Zircon episode from the BBC studios in Glasgow under s 9 of the Official Secrets Act 1911. The Police and Criminal Evidence Act did not apply in Scotland, however. On PACE, see: M Zander *The Police and Criminal Evidence Act 1984* (3rd ed. 1995). On police treatment of evidence obtained under PACE, see *Marcel v Metropolitan Police Comr* [1992] 1 All ER 72, CA and *Hellewell v Chief Constable of Derbyshire* [1995] 4 All ER 473.
8   It would cover 'non-confidential' journalistic material. See Sch 1.

successfully used these powers to obtain a journalist's photographs of a riot.[9]

Under s 19 of the Act the law of seizure of articles has been extended to allow evidence to be seized when it might implicate virtually 'anyone in any crime'.[10] The right of seizure of computerised information is extended so that the police may require information from a computer and 'accessible from the premises' to be produced 'in a form in which it can be taken away and in which it is visible and legible'.[11]

The powers to obtain intimate body samples and fingerprints, to detain and question persons, and to tape-record the interviews constitute, on one interpretation, a serious infringement of civil liberties. The Criminal Evidence (Amendment) Act 1997 amended PACE in relation to obtaining body samples from certain groups of criminals and the Criminal Justice and Police Bill 2001 will allow the police to hold DNA samples and fingerprints where charges are dropped, where the accused is acquitted and where samples are given voluntarily. It is hoped to extend the DNA database from 1 million to 3 million within three years.[12] It is reported that the Government plans to remove confidentiality from tax files subject to Inland Revenue investigations[13] and to give greater powers to DTI inspectors. Infringements of civil liberties were also widely alleged in relation to the effective removal of the right to silence by allowing adverse inferences to be drawn from silence,[14] and the range of powers which compel those being questioned to answer questions especially in connection with financial offences.[15] The Government and police chiefs

---

9   *Ex p Bristol United Press and Picture Agency Ltd* (1986) Times, 11 November; Cf *R v Central Criminal Court, ex p Adegbesan* [1986] 3 All ER 113; *R v Central Criminal Court, ex p Carr* (1987) Independent, 5 March; *R v Crown Court at Leicester, ex p DPP* [1987] 3 All ER 654; *R v Crown Court at Lewes, ex p Hill* [1991] Crim LR 376. Nb. Contempt of Court Act 1981, s 10 and ch 9 below.

10 MDA Freeman *Current Law Statutes*, Annotation of PACE, s 84. On limitations to s 22 (2) accompanying ss 19 and 20 see, *R v Chief Constable of Lancashire, ex p Parker* [1993] QB 577. See also Proceeds of Crime Act 1995 and Drug Trafficking Act 1994 and powers of confiscation.

11 Section 20(1).

12 This was passed to reverse a decision of the Court of Appeal which ruled such evidence inadmissible although this decision was itself overruled by the House of Lords: *A-G's Reference (No 3 of 1999)* [2001] 1 All ER 577, HL.

13 See *R (On the application of Morgan Grenfell & Co Ltd v Special Comr* [2001] 1 All ER 535 (QBDDC) upheld on appeal.

14 Criminal Justice and Public Order Act 1994, ss 34-39, following the Criminal Evidence (NI) Order 1988. See *R v Cowan* [1995] 4 All ER 939, CA and *R v McGarry (PJ)* [1999] 1 WLR 1500. See *Condron v UK* ECtHR, (2000) 8 BHCR 290.

15 Sections 235 and 236 Insolvency Act 1986 and *Bishopsgate Investment Management Ltd v Maxwell* [1992] 2 All ER 856, CA; ss 431, 432 and 434 Companies Act 1985 and *Re London United Investments plc* [1992] 2 All ER 842, CA and *R v Saunders* (1995) 140 Sol Jo LB 22, CA. Note Criminal Justice Act 1987, s 2(8). These provisions have brought increasing criticism from the

regarded the changes as a necessary measure to combat increasing crime and increasingly professional and well-advised criminals. PACE was to operate under strict safeguards, some of which have had little effect.[16] The increased record-keeping, form-filling and bureaucratic detail accompanying the Act and Codes of Guidance are all meeting with increasing criticism from the police. Their complaint is that the cost of the 'safeguards' in the Act in man hours is too high. Cost is a theme I wish to return to at the end of this chapter. From the perspective of judicial safeguards the Act is pusillanimous. Section 76 concerns the admissibility of confessions at trial. Confessions are not to be admitted where they have been obtained as a result of 'oppression', which includes 'torture, inhuman or degrading treatment, and the use of threat or violence (whether or not amounting to torture)' or 'in consequence of anything said or done which was likely, in the circumstances existing at the time, to render [it] unreliable'. It is true that the prosecution must prove 'beyond reasonable doubt' that the confession was not obtained in such a manner and the court may require the prosecution to establish as much on its own motion, even if the defence has not raised the point. This loosely follows the recommendation of the Eleventh Report of the Criminal Law Revision Committee, which recommended a relaxation of the common law. The common law test was that a confession was only admissible if the prosecution could show that it was voluntary: that is, not induced by 'fear of prejudice or *hope of advantage* exercised or held out by a person in authority', nor obtained by oppression.[17] The Government rejected the test for admissibility of 'unfair' evidence proposed by Lord Scarman and accepted by the Lords, which provided a greater safeguard against unfair police practice. Under s 78, the court is only to exclude prosecution evidence if, regarding all the circumstances, including the manner in which it was obtained, its admission would so adversely affect the fairness of proceedings that the court ought not to admit it. The Court of Appeal has ruled, surprisingly, that s 78 also covers confessions.[18] British courts have generally favoured the admission of relevant evidence, even if obtained unlawfully and unfairly, on the grounds that its probative value invariably, if not inevitably, outweighs other factors.

ECtHR for breaches of Art 6: *Saunders v UK* (1996) 23 EHRR 313. See *ex p Bright* above where the court believed that English courts would follow the interpretation of the ECtHR's judgments by senior domestic courts to observe *stare decisis: see R v Hertfordshire County Council, ex p Green Environmental Industries Ltd* [2000] 1 All ER 773, HL.

16   J Benyon and C Bourn (eds) *The Police: Powers, Procedures and Properties* (1986).

17   *R v Prager* [1972] 1 All ER 1114, CA.

18   See, however, on s 78, *R v Mason* [1987] 3 All ER 481, CA and *R v Saunders* above. In *Khan* above, the House of Lords ruled that evidence obtained in breach of Art 8 ECHR was not conclusive of the decision under s 78 to admit or exclude the evidence at the trial. See *R v P* note 1 above.

Reform—some food for thought

In ch 2 we will examine the relationship between law and freedom of information overseas. Here it is pertinent to note that a 1981 Canadian report from the Commission of Inquiry Concerning Certain Activities of the Royal Canadian Mounted Police[19] (the McDonald Commission) has affirmed that the principle 'of the Rule of Law and of responsible, government in a liberal democracy' should govern the organisation of security intelligence work and policing generally.[20] The report is voluminous, and exhaustive in its investigations, which took place over a three-and-a-half-year period. It found numerous breaches of the law by security officers and deliberate withholding of relevant or significant information' from the ministers who were responsible. A crucial recommendation of the McDonald Commission was that a security agency's mandate must be 'clear and public' and must be stated in the legislation which would establish the agency. The agency's activities in relation to security and its responsibilities should be defined in statute and not 'diffuse and ambiguous' sources arising as they did from a 'melange of Cabinet directives, ministerial correspondence and unstated RCMP assumptions'. As well as arguing for more ministerial and judicial involvement in surveillance and information acquisition, the report also proposed an independent review body with complete access to the new agency's records, and a Security Appeals Tribunal to hear appeals against decisions in security screening procedures. The review body would be advisory, not executive, and would report to the Solicitor-General and to a Parliamentary joint standing committee on security and intelligence.

The Canadian Security Intelligence Services Act 1984 created the Canadian Security Intelligence Service. The director is 'under the direction of the minister'. The minister has power to give written directions to the Director, copies of which are given to the Security Intelligence Review Committee (SIRC) which was established under the Act. It has been argued that the Act falls short of the McDonald Commission's recommendations, though the service's mandate is spelt out in statute[1] and it has to report to

---

19 Ottawa: Minister of Supply, 1981. The report was in three volumes; see A Goldsmith (1985) Public Law 39; I Cameron (1985) Mod LR 201.

20 America has seen Congressional oversight, via sub-committees, of the CIA since the mid 1960s – one of the reasons why the National Security Council sprang into prominence was because it did not have such supervision. Australia has established an Inspector-General of Intelligence and Security, and in November 1986 the Federal Parliament established an all-party committee to monitor the Australian Security Intelligence Organisation.

1 Which directs the service to 'collect, by investigation or otherwise, to the extent that it is strictly necessary, and analyse and retain information and intelligence respecting activities that may on reasonable grounds be suspected of constituting threats to the security of Canada'.

and advise the Canadian government. Members of the SIRC are Privy Councillors (but not current senators and MPs). A complaints procedure is established for individuals concerning the activities of the security intelligence service, together with an inspector-general (IG) who has powers of monitoring and review, though not as wide-ranging as the SIRC's. Cabinet secrets are precluded from investigation by either the IG or the SIRC. The SIRC differs markedly from the McDonald proposals as it is not a joint parliamentary committee. It nevertheless has full powers of access to agency records, reports annually to Parliament, and reports to the minister.

The Commission under Mr Justice McDonald reported that while the security services of other liberal democracies are not a matter of public record, he doubted whether they were completely innocent of the kind of excesses the Commission recorded in the Canadian security service. Britain is a case in point.

Serious thought does need to be given to the following points: do the complaints procedures in the UK legislation need strengthening; should oversight be allowed of operational activities; should there be publication—at 10-year intervals—of details of the major activities of the services? These would include interception warrants, numbers of complaints referred to the tribunal, numbers of positive vetting referrals handled, an account of the services' opinion on threats and priorities in the relevant period; a case history relevant to the services' work from each branch; and a statement from each director etc relating to any significant changes in practice.[2] Few citizens would accept that they as individuals have a need to know the details of security operations. But that does not mean that knowledge and oversight would not be more effective, and thereby a greater safeguard for civil liberties, if they were more widely established as suggested. Such a development has taken place in Australia.[3] This followed a Royal Commission under Mr Justice Hope. Australia has a joint parliamentary committee to oversee the activities of the Security and Intelligence Organisation, and an inspector-general to hear complaints from officers. A charter spells out the powers and responsibilities of the organisation, and its director-general reports to the minister, and has to obtain the approval of the attorney-general for phone taps and other sensitive operations. The relevant Australian legislation—the Australian Security and Intelligence Organisation Act 1979—is 56 pages long; the UK legislation, excluding RIPA, is under half that length. The Act provides for legal assistance for complainants, costs, witnesses' fees and so on before the Security Appeals Tribunal which deals with security clearance. The Inspector-General of Intelligence and Security acts

---

2 ⸱ Suggested by Conservative MP, R Shepherd HC Debs col 245 (16 January 1989).
3   See below.

as an ombudsman for the public and has unlimited powers to obtain information. An agreed report may be shown to a complainant. All ministerial directions on security and intelligence must be shown to the Inspector-General.

The cost of freedom of information

National security, and the activities and oversight of those responsible for national security, is a difficult but instructive testing ground for problems associated with freedom of information. It is an area where government has made concessions to provision of more information if not openness. Cutting through the variety of arguments supporting or undermining the existing state of operations, there is one factor implicit in this or any government's reckoning. That is cost. The cost of opening up the world of security operations, it argues, even on the scale suggested above, would be destructive of our security. Giving more information, even to limited numbers of elected representatives, would increase the risk of leaks and treasonable use of information. The consequences would affect all of us. The Canadian security service is reported to be suffering a lack of morale because of the publicity given to its operations. This, the service believes, will reduce its efficacy.

In other areas of freedom of information, as we shall see, the cost factor is used as a leading argument against introduction. 'Cost' may take a variety of forms. There is the sheer financial cost. Allow access and everyone will want to see everything. This will entail indexing, and staff to deal with requests, to provide reviews, to check that exempt material is not included, to deal with litigation, to check that filing is carried out correctly. There is the cost of a loss of candour in advice when the giver or the referee knows that it may be published or shown to the subject. There is the fear of perpetual intervention when policy-makers are constantly exposed or challenged and have to justify their every move. In such a situation individuals may not wish to take risks or make innovative decisions. The cost could be a reduction in professionalism. There is the cost of inertia. There is also the possible cost of creating greater secrecy: the spectre of the file behind the file, the meeting behind the meeting, the state behind the state. There is the possible cost of 'the paperless environment' where record-keeping is minimised. As we shall see in the next chapter, overseas experience shows that the financial costs are inevitably exaggerated. The other costs are factors to consider, and will be considered throughout this book.

2 Freedom of information: overseas experience

In the previous chapter, the attempt was made to draw out some persistent themes and problems relating to control over and freedom of information. These themes were then examined in the light of one difficult area concerned with the regulation, dissemination, use and obtaining of information. This chapter will focus upon the role of legislation in other countries, as well as their political practice, in providing and protecting information, whether to or about individuals or, in the case of the USA, committees of the legislature overseeing the operation of legislation and expenditure. I will concentrate on the USA, Canada, Australia and New Zealand.[1] These are countries which in spite of their enormous differences both between themselves and with Britain nonetheless possess certain legal cultural similarities with the British system, either through common law inheritance or through direct or indirect constitutional influence. I will also look briefly at Swedish and French practices. The position in the European Union is examined in chapter 8. The examination in this chapter will allow us to assess the contribution which overseas practice has made to opening up government, and will also act as a benchmark for our own practice. While it will be argued in the next chapter that the secret state in Britain has a long and virtually unbroken tradition which legislation of itself will not remedy, the shortcomings and difficulties of overseas practice will not be overlooked. Picking up the theme of cost in the last chapter, we should note the impact of overseas legislation upon the administrative systems in which they operate.

1 Sweden and France will be referred to briefly: for a fuller analysis of civil law systems, see KG Robertson *Public Secrets* (1982) – on Sweden – and James Michael *The Politics of Secrecy* (1982). See also generally NS Marsh (ed) *Public Access To Government-Held Information: A Comparative Symposium* (1987) and R Vaughn (ed) *Freedom of Information* (2001).

USA

'Freedom of Information cases are peculiarly difficult' (*Miscavige v IRS* N0 92-8659 (11th Cir. 17 September 1993).

The USA has possessed a Freedom of Information Act (FOIA) since 1966. Previous statutes had only allowed public access to government documents if a 'need to know' was established,[2] and they allowed agencies to withhold information for 'good cause'. The Supreme Court has observed that a priority of the Act is to 'ensure that the Government's activities be opened to the sharp eye of public scrutiny.'[3] All agencies in the executive branch of the federal government, including administrative regulatory agencies, are subject to FOIA. Excluded from the operation of the Act are the judicial and legislative branches of government. So too are members of the President's *immediate personal staff,* whose sole function is to give advice and assistance to the President. State government and local and city government are not included in this legislation.[4]

The aim of the Act, as amended in 1974, is to provide public access to an agency's records if it is covered by the Act. An applicant does not have to demonstrate a specific interest in a matter to view relevant documents— an idle curiosity suffices. The legislation provides a presumptive right of access to documents and files to *anyone*—not it should be noted an American citizen. The onus is on those denying access to justify denial. In 1993, both the President and the Attorney-General made highly publicised statements emphasising their commitment to making the operation of the Act more effective to enhance openness and participation. The opposition has not been slow to laud these virtues also to enhance the role of the consumer *vis à vis* government. In 1996, the FOIA was amended by the Electronic FOIA amendments (see below).

Exemptions

Although the basic thrust of the Act is positive and supportive of openness, there are nine exemptions from the FOIA which include national defence or foreign policy information that is properly classified as confidential, secret or top secret by Presidential executive order. National

2 The Housekeeping Statute of 1789. The Administrative Procedure Act 1946 allowed inspection unless 'good cause' required confidentiality. This provision was widely invoked by agencies.
3 *United States Department of Justice v Reporters Committee for Freedom of the Press* 489 US 749 (1989).
4 Many have their own FOI laws. See P Birkinshaw *Freedom of Information; the US Experience.* Hull University Law School Studies in Law (1991).

security tends to be seen in terms of defence and foreign policy and is not as widely drawn as in the UK (see chapter 1 above). An executive order of 1982[5] reversed the trend of relaxation of security classifications and 'broadened the discretion to create official secrets'. Many of the safeguards against over enthusiastic classification were removed. So, mandatory secrecy requirements rather than permissive ones became more common, the 'balancing test' requiring the weighing of public access against the government need for secrecy was eliminated, and systematic declassification was cancelled.[6] The order allows for its own mandatory 'review requests' of classified information as an alternative to FOIA actions.[7] A new executive order took effect in October 1995 which liberalised the 1982 Reagan order.[8] This will ease the process of declassification in several ways: by shortening the period of classification in most instances to 10 years; automatic declassification has been introduced for records over 25 years old unless information is 'especially sensitive'; systematic declassification is reintroduced in other cases which establishes a programme to review classification; the balancing test is restored in amended form to 'determine whether the public interest in disclosure outweighs the damage to national security that might reasonably be expected from disclosure'. It removes presumptions against automatic classification in some areas eg foreign government information; concise reasons must be given on the documents for classification and a Security Classification Appeals Panel and a Policy Advisory Council are established. The Order will be co-ordinated by the Information Security Oversight Office under the National Security Council.[9] The White House has claimed that the NSC is a personal adviser to the President and is therefore not covered by the FOIA.[10]

Under FOIA, the internal rules and practices of an agency will be exempt but not the manuals and instructions on the interpretation of regulations. Other important exemptions include: trade secrets; commercial and financial information obtained by the government that is privileged or confidential; inter- or intra-agency memoranda or letters which are not

5   EO 12356 (47 FR 14874 – April 1982). In 1983, there were 17,141,052 derivative classification decisions made: this is the act of incorporating, paraphrasing, restating or generating in a new form classified source information
6   The National Co-ordinating Committee for the Promotion of History believed EO 12356 had caused a 'massive' restriction on previously available information.
7   There were 3,945 such requests in 1983.
8   EO 12,958.
9   US Dept of Justice *FOIA Update XVI No 2* 1995.
10   *Armstrong v Executive Office* 25 March (DC Circ 1995). On exemptions under FOIA for exports' licensing (armaments) see the Scott Report HC 115 (1995-6) para D4.5.9.

available by law;[11] information protected by other statutes especially concerning the CIA and also taxation; personnel or medical files disclosure of which would constitute an invasion of privacy; and investigatory records compiled for law enforcement purposes if disclosure would result in certain types of harm. Reliance by an agency on an exemption is discretionary and not mandatory and so exempt information may be disclosed.[12]

Challenging a refusal

Where there is a refusal to supply information, appeal procedures are specifically provided in each agency's FOIA regulations. A denial letter will inform the applicant of a right of appeal—usually within 30 days.[13] The official refusing the appeal must be identified, and the exemption and reasons for refusal must be given. The requester must be informed of his or her right to apply to the federal court where there is a complete rehearing with the burden of proof on the agency. Attorney fees are recoverable where an applicant 'substantially succeeds' and although FOIA cases no longer receive a *de jure* automatic priority in federal court dockets they do receive such treatment *de facto*.

After a Federal Court of Appeals decision,[14] trial courts may, on a motion by a plaintiff, require the government to itemise the documents, to provide a detailed justification of claimed exemptions, and to index by cross-reference the itemisation to the justification. A justification requires 'a relatively detailed analysis in manageable segments'. An itemisation must 'specify in detail' which parts the agency believes to be exempt. An index cross-references the itemisation and the justification, allowing easier identification of the information required.[15] This is particularly helpful where the applicant does not know what the content of the documents is, where classification is obscure, or where it is difficult to meet a government claim without a clearer description of the

---

11 *Department of the Interior and Bureau of Indian Affairs v Klamath Water Users protective Ass'n* US Supreme Court No 99-1871, 5 March 2001 (decided): FOIA introduced a 'general philosophy of full agency disclosure'. 'Congress had to realise that not every secret under the old law would be secret under the new.'

12 See *Chrysler Corpn v Brown* 99 S Ct 1705 (1979).

13 The 1974 Act provides for internal disciplinary measures where refusal was arbitrary or capricious.

14 *Vaughn v Rosen* 484 F 2d 820 (CA, DC, 1973).

15 See B Braverman and F Chetwynd *Information Law* (1985) for a copious treatise; RG Vaughn *Explanation of Federal FOIA etc* (1981). See also KC Davies *Administrative Law Treatise* (2nd edn, 1978), vol 1, chapter 5 and 1982 Supplement and works cited in note 1. The Department of Justice publishes a *FOI Caselist* and and a *FOI Guide* and *Privacy Act Overview* each year.

documents. Informal practices have developed whereby *inter partes* meetings will take place between applicants to discuss documents and exemptions. The process is known as an 'oral *Vaughn*' affidavit so named after the case introducing the itemised exemption practice and proceedings are used as a form of bartering or negotiation with benefits for both sides—'litigotiation' as it is called.[16]

The court can engage in *in camera* inspection of documents. If a third party wishes to stop an agency handing over information concerning him to a requestor, he may seek judicial review of an agency's decision. This is known as a reverse FOIA suit.[17] Third party practices in other jurisdictions are more sophisticated (and see chapter 8) but operated with the benefit of hindsight.

Basic requirements

Each agency covered by FOIA has to publish in the *Federal Register* details of its organisation; the employees from whom and the methods whereby information may be obtained; details of its procedures *including* informal ones; rules, policies or interpretations of general applicability; and rules of procedure and instructions as to the scope and contents of all papers, reports, or examinations. The agency cannot rely in legal proceedings upon any matter which it is bound by law to publish and which it has not, and on which the litigant has not had, 'actual and timely notice'. Agencies are also undertaking 'affirmative information disclosure' via the internet and so on whereby information is released before specific request. This has now become a legal requirement. One point that awaited final clarification is that the federal FOIA, as opposed to some state and city FOIA laws, does not spell out the types of information sources, other than documents, which are covered by the Act. However, it is taken to cover information in documents in whatever form it takes. The 1996 Electronic FOIA makes it absolutely clear that FOIA covers electronic records.[18]

General impact of the FOIA

The FOIA is often hailed as the great initiator of open government. We should not be blind to the fact that there has been considerable opposition

---

16 *FOIA for Attorneys and Access Professionals,* Att Gen's Advocacy Institute, Dept of Justice (1987) at p V 57.
17 Under Administrative Procedure Act 1946, s 10.
18 See Electronic FOIA Amendment Act 1996 and note 2 p 70 below.

to it in the USA. In 1979, Dresner[19] spoke highly of the FOIA's impact upon government accountability, scrutiny and improved decision-making, as well as on inhibiting corruption. From 1980, however, the executive presented repeated proposals for reform of the FOIA because of the cost of its administration, the quantity of case law, and because the Act was being used in ways which Congress never intended.[20] The business community has long lobbied for reform which would facilitate businesses' opportunity to challenge requests for information about them and a reform was introduced in 1987 by executive order improving the position of third parties. The law enforcement agencies were not satisfied with the exemption which covers their operations, and in 1986, 'after years of deliberation',[1] Congress passed a major FOIA reform which extends the exemption available to law enforcement practices. In fact, the 1986 Act actually *excludes* certain categories of documents from the FOIA.[2] Further, the records or information no longer have to be investigatory, and may be withheld when they *could* (not would) reasonably be expected to interfere with enforcement proceedings; could deprive a person of a fair trial; could reasonably be expected to constitute an unwarranted invasion of privacy; could reveal the identity of a confidential source which furnished information; could disclose techniques and procedures for law enforcement investigations or prosecutions; or disclosure could reasonably be expected to endanger the life or physical safety of *any individual* (not only law enforcement personnel)—which is understandable.[3]

The exemption which has been the subject of most litigation concerns inter- and intra-agency memoranda and letters not available by law. Basically, this exemption seeks to protect deliberations in the policy-making process. The exemption is meant to cover advisory opinions, not factual information, although 'pre-decisional memoranda expressly incorporated by reference in a final decision must be disclosed'.[4] Since the earlier case law the judiciary have extended the breadth of this exemption in a series of decisions.[5] In 1993, the Attorney-General

---

19 S Dresner *Open Government – Lessons from America* (1980).
20 By 'information brokers' for example, seeking commercially confidential information.
1   US Dept of Justice *FOIA Update*, Vol VII, No 4, 1986; and vol VIII, No 1, 1987, for details.
2   Section 552(7)(*c*) – 'live proceedings' and informants.
3   See *US Department of Justice v Landano* 113 S Ct 2014 (1993).
4   For the exemption to apply the documents must be protected from discovery in civil suits: *Federal Open Market Committee v Merrill* 99 S Ct 2800 (1979). In *NLRB v Sears, Roebuck* 421 US 132 (1975) the Supreme Court drew a distinction between post-decision documentation (not protected) and pre-decision documentation (protected). The exemption also protects information covered by legal professional privilege.

declared a policy guideline to the effect that this exemption should be defended in the courts only where an 'agency reasonably foresees that disclosure would be harmful to an interest protected by that exemption'.[6] Where only a governmental interest would be affected by disclosure there is a far greater scope for discretionary disclosure than in the case of personal privacy or commercial confidentiality and detailed guidance is given on factors to consider.

The 1986 Act was a major success for the Executive, and other reforms include the Paperwork Reduction Act 1980 which seeks to minimise the extent and cost of the 'paperwork burden' on small businesses and state and local government although the executive order 12356 imposing greater secrecy has been largely superseded.[7] Further, the Federal Government has employed the Espionage Act to punish unauthorised disclosure of information even though the cases did not concern spying to which it was commonly thought to have been restricted. In the past, the Executive has also taken steps to placate the British Government since Crown documents not available in the UK may well be available in the USA under FOIA. UK departments mark such documents 'UK Confidential', although this, by itself, would not ensure exemption in the USA.[8]

There are positive and well-recorded benefits to the legislation.[9] Relyea has described how a civil service acceptance of the Act has been fostered within the agencies. Specialists are responsible for FOIA requests and 'brokerage' thereon.[10] Training programmes, publications and information about the Act are first class.[11] There is a marked degree of professionalism on the government side and the requester side.[12] However, charging fees without justification, refusing to act until money is 'up-front', intentionally understaffing FOI departments, forcing litigation,

5   *Wolfe v HHS* 839 F 2d 768 (1988); *Access Reports v Department of Justice* 926 F 2d 1192 (1991); *Mapother v Department of Justice* No 95-5261 (DC Cir 17 September 1993; *Quarles v Department of Justice* 893 F 2d 390 (1990); *Petroleum Info Corp v US Department of Int* 976 F 2d 1429 (1992).
6   FOIA Update XV No 2 (1994).
7   Ehlke and Relyea (1983) *Fed Bar News and Journal*, Vol 30, No 2, p 91.
8   Examples covered documents relevant to the Sizewell 'B' proposals for a PWR nuclear generator. See incidentally *de Zeven Provincien* [1986] 3 All ER 487, HL and use of American courts in English proceedings to get pre-trial discovery of information. Embarrassment was caused when records on President Clinton relating to his residence in the UK as a student were released to the US Government in 1992.
9   Campaign for Freedom of Information *Secrets* No 22 (1991).
1 0   H Relyea 'A Comparative Review of the Access to Information Act (Canada) and the US FOIA' (1986, unpublished paper).
1 1   These include manuals published by the Department of Justice, the *FOIA Update* and also excellent publications on the use of the legislation published by Congress.
1 2   See Birkinshaw (1991) n 4 p 63.

indiscriminate censorship, and other unhelpful practices have all been well known occurrences. So too is ignoring time responses which should take 10 days for an initial response. One FOIA suit has taken 11 years to resolve through the courts.[13]

More effective procedures have been in place giving third parties notice and allowing opportunity for challenge when documents relating to them are sought. The business and commercial community were anxious for such safeguards. The commercial confidentiality exemption has placed the burden on those claiming the exemption to prove it but in *Critical Mass Energy Project v NRC*[14] the Court of Appeals upheld this rule—so that for instance if an agency states that disclosure would impair its ability to obtain similar information in the future it would have to prove such— but added a new exemption. Where information had been volunteered to agencies and was not 'customarily' made available to the public by the supplier of the information, it attracted the exemption.

The 1986 FOIA has amended the basis for charging fees for complying with duties under the legislation. Requests for commercial purposes will be charged the actual cost of document review and search time (ie employee hours involved and documents are reviewed line by line) and duplication fees, though requesters may still be entitled to a fee waiver if, for instance, their request is for information which it is in the public interest to disclose 'because it is likely to contribute significantly to public understanding of the operations of Government'. Search and review fees will be waived for educational, non-commercial scientific organisations and requesters from the news media.[15]

The FOIA has generated a vast industry in the USA among the business community.[16] Approximately 50-60% of requesters are from commercial bodies seeking information on business competitors. However, it has been stated that this does not generate any significant amount of litigation; far more significant as a generator of litigation are public interest groups' seeking information about companies' compliance with the law.[17] Next comes the public, accounting for 20-25% of requests. The press accounts for only 5-8%. In 1983, there were 262,265 requests under FOIA; in 1989, 429,936 of which approximately 57% were processed by the Department of Defense and the Department of Health and Human Services. About 80% of all requests are fully granted.[18] In 1993, there were 575,424 requests, each request averaging $189.

13 *Gulf Oil Corp v Brock* 778 F 2d 834 DDC (1985).
14 975 F 2d 871 (DC Cir 1992); cert denied 113 SCt 1579 (1993).
15 Birkinshaw n 4 p 63.
16 Relyea, op cit, n 10.
17 R Stevenson 'Protecting Business Interests under the Freedom of Information Act: Managing Exemption 4' (1982) 34 Admin Law Rev 207.
18 Relyea op cit.

Relyea has estimated that the cost of administering FOIA runs to about $60-100 million per annum. In 1994, one agency estimated that the cost of a FOIA request was an average $349.00. By 2000, this would be $544.00. In 1983, the US General Accounting Office estimated the cost of the Act in 1981 at $61 million, 'although costs cannot currently be measured with any precision'.[19] This is comparable with the price of maintaining armed services' marching bands or golf courses on military bases. Estimates of the cost of government self-promotion and public relations exercises run to about $1.5 billion per annum at 1989 prices. 'Thus, it is considerably less expensive to provide the public with the information it seeks via the FOIA than it is for the Executive to provide what it determines the public should know about agency activities and operations'.[20] One further factor factor is that government publications in the USA are not protected by copyright laws as are government publications in the UK.[1]

The FOIA is one of four major statutes facilitating open government in the USA. The FOIA is primarily concerned with individuals gaining access to agency records. Since its inception, however, a large number of professional organisations, known *inter alia* as 'data brokers or 'surrogate requesters', use FOIA to gain information which they can market and sell to those with an interest. A private foundation, the National Security Archive, is in fact used by government officials because its files are better indexed than the departments' files.

1996 FOIA Amendments

The 1996 FOIA amendments[2] expand the type of records that must be published without request to include all those that are likely to be the subject of more than one request. Agencies will also have to make many records available online; electronic reading rooms must be established in all agency reading rooms by 1 November 1997. Agencies also have to produce guides for requesters containing: an index of all major information systems of the agency, a description of 'major information and locator systems' maintained by the Agency,[3] and a handbook on obtaining information from the agency. Indexes also have to be produced of previously released records that are likely to be the subject of future requests. The traditional cameo of a paper request and a long wait for reply

---

19   The Attorney-General's estimate for 1981 was $45 million.
20   Relyea, op cit.
1   Copyright etc Act 1988, s 163. The position in the UK has become more relaxed
       on an ex gratia basis.
2   *'Recent Developments: Electronic FOIA'* (1998) Admin Law Rev 339-458.
3   Tankersley ibid p 421.

is now, because of the technology driven developments, untenable.[4] However, there has been some resistance to the index requirement by the agencies.

Agencies are given 20 days to respond to requests for documents (this was doubled from 10 days which was felt to be unrealistic). Negotiations may take place around the modification of a request. Unreasonable refusal to modify a request may justify an agency delay. However, expedited requests and responses may be made in two cases: where requesters can show that failure to obtain the records on an expedited basis will pose an immediate threat to life or physical safety of a person; or requesters who are primarily engaged in the dissemination of information to the public (press and media) where they can show that their request involves matters on which there is an urgent need to inform the public concerning 'actual or alleged federal government activity.' The agency must rule on the request for expedited processing within 10 days and provision must be made for expedited appeals. No set time limit is provided for the response which must be made as soon as practicable.

In March 2001, the General Accounting Office issued a generally favourable report on the 1996 Act and its operation. Most agencies examined had established 'electronic reading rooms' but 'data quality issues' limited the usefulness of some reports on the Act.[5]

Federal Advisory Committee Act (FACA)[6]

FACA, which is accompanied by regulations, is within the FOI mould but has its sights set more firmly on the real target of bureaucratic decision-making. The Act, enacted in 1972, has six basic objectives: to establish standards and uniform procedures to govern the creation, operation and termination of federal advisory committees; to ensure that whenever possible advisory committee meetings are open to the public and accessible; to reduce their cost; to avoid specific interest group domination and rubber-stamping of prior decisions; to keep the public and Congress advised on all aspects of advisory committees; and to ensure they remain advisory and not executive. In 1970 it was estimated that as many as 3,200 such committees existed with a membership of 22,000[7] and in 1990 there were 1,071 committees comprising 22,391 persons. There is a concern that subjective preferences of organised interests could

4   Ibid p 430.
5   US GAO 01-378 March 2001, *Information Management*.
6   BW Tuerkheimer 'Veto by Neglect' (1975) 25 *AMULR* 53; Vaughn, n 15 p 65 above.
7   HR Rep No 1731 91st Congress, 2d Sess 14–15 (1970).

easily influence official decision-makers.[8] An early indication of its potential utility was given in *FCN Inc v* Davis,[9] when a newspaper editor wished to be present at meetings between Treasury officials and consumer groups which were recommending whether labelling should be required for chemical additives in liquor. He obtained a court order prohibiting the closure of future meetings.

FACA gives a broad definition to the advisory committees, or their sub-committees or sub-groups, of agencies and departments whose members are not full-time officers or employees of the agency.[10] The Act covers such bodies if they have a fixed membership; they have a defined purpose of providing advice to a federal agency; they have regular or periodic meetings; and they have an organisational structure. Committees have a two-year lifespan and those rendered otiose are terminated. A designated official will chair the meetings or attend, and FACA requires a 'balanced representation of points of view'. In a famous example a 'task force' established to advise Hilary Clinton on health reforms and policy was held not to be a committee under the Act.[11] The Supreme Court has declined to apply FACA to the American Bar Association's Committee on Judicial Appointments which advises the President on potential nominees for federal judgeships.

Adequate advance notice of the meetings must be given in the *Federal Register,* and subject to reasonable regulations any member of the public is given the right to attend, file a written statement or make an appearance. Detailed minutes with a complete description of the discussion must be kept, along with conclusions, and they must be available for inspection and copying.

The FOIA exemptions apply with some modifications. The Agency head to whom the committee reports determines in writing whether an exemption will apply, and these have to be explained in detail. Reports have to be made out by the Agency head on the extent to which he has accepted committee recommendations as well as on the latter's activities, status and membership.

It will be appreciated that on paper the FACA could go to the nerve centre of many of the essential decisions in the interface of public/private relationships and state regulation of private interest groups. That being the case, it is not surprising that its reception was marked by 'non-administration, non-use and ingenious bureaucratic techniques of evasion'.[12] In the first year of its operation there was widespread closure

8   S Rep No 1098 92nd Congress, 2d Sess 6 (1972).
9   378 F Supp 1048, DDC (1974).
10   For meetings of these officials, see 'The Sunshine Act' below.
11   *Assoc of American Physicians and Surgeons v Clinton* 997 F 2d 898 (DC Cir 1993). This reversed an earlier decision.
12   Tuerkheimer, op cit.

of meetings, often without citation of the exemption, or with citation of exemptions which courts had ruled did not apply. Setting up of 'informal ad hoc groups' has been resorted to, although in *Aviation Consumer Action Project v Yoke*[13] the District Court ruled that an ad hoc Civil Aviation Bureau meeting with airline representatives was covered by the FACA, though not where the President consulted informally with various groups as part of a publicity exercise.[14] Other evasive tactics have included holding meetings abroad, even on a private yacht! Domination by private interest groups was not uncommon, eg the National Petroleum Council carried out much of its work in sub-committees convened without public notice and often in oil company offices.

Some of the recommendations to strengthen the safeguards—including oversight of FACA by an agency other than the Office of Manpower and Budget,[15] effective enforcement sanctions, quick and informal appellate procedures to challenge closure, and a verbatim transcript of meetings which are closed for subsequent judicial review purposes—have been accepted.

The Sunshine Act

The Sunshine Act (SA) of 1976 is an 'open meeting' law allowing access to the meetings of those agencies within its scope. Its aim is to open up to the public portions of the 'deliberative processes' of certain agencies. It does not provide a right to participate in decision-making, nor can it be invoked to insist that a meeting be held.[16]

The Act applies to all multi-headed agencies, that is 'agencies headed by a collegial body composed of two or more individual members, a majority of whom are appointed by the President, and sub-divisions of agencies appointed to act on its behalf. Certain internal advisory meetings are not covered, nor are departments headed by a single person.[17] The Act covers the deliberations of the requisite number of agency officials 'where such deliberations determine or result in the joint conduct or disposition of official agency business'.

One week's public notice of the date, time, place and topic of the meeting must be given. A named official with a publicised telephone number must be appointed to answer queries. The law requires more than

---

13 Civ No 73–707, DDC, 24 June 1974.
14 *Nader v Baroody* Civ No 74–1675, DDC, 23 June 1975.
15 OMB had stated that 15 days' notice of meetings was adequate, whereas the courts had ruled that 30 days was the requisite period. OMB works under an executive brief.
16 Vaughn, n 15 p 65 above.
17 Eg Treasury, Labor, Defense, Interior, and Food and Drug Administration.

notice in the *Federal Register*. The federal law does not, however, require the keeping of minutes or verbatim transcripts—unlike many state sunshine laws—though regulations adopted by an agency may themselves require minutes. Records do have to be kept of closed meetings. To close a meeting a majority of agency members must agree, not simply a majority of the quorum of a meeting. The FOIA exemptions, with modification, apply. The inter/intra agency communication exemption does not apply but meetings may be closed to protect information where disclosure would be likely to frustrate the implementation of a proposed agency action and to protect information concerning litigation.

Where judicial review of a closure of a meeting is sought, the burden of proof is upon the agency concerned. A failure to exhaust internal agency remedies—internal review—does not preclude the opportunity for relief via the courts. The courts will usually only interfere with a failure to pursue the procedures under the law if the breach was intentional, repetitive or prejudicial. The courts have, however, been reluctant to allow parties to use their transcript of agency proceedings under the Act to supplement the record of other agencies' decisions or rule-making in judicial proceedings. The Act provides for 'reasonable attorney fees and other litigation costs reasonably incurred' against any party (not simply the government as in FOIA) where the requesting party substantially prevails in the application.

As under the FOIA, agencies submit annual reports to Congress on the SA and the Congressional Research Service compiles an overview to discern trends for Congress as it does also for FOIA. The Administrative Conference of the United States, which is a body charged with oversight and research on administrative procedures and law for the government, Congress and the judiciary, must be consulted on regulations made by agencies implementing the Act.

The Privacy Act

The Privacy Act (PA) was passed in 1974 and has been subject to numerous amendments and a good deal of criticism. It regulates the collection, control, content, dissemination and use of certain categories of government information and focuses upon 'systems of records' established, controlled or maintained by an agency.[18] This means in those circumstances where information may be retrieved by a name or other identifying symbol. It

---

18   It does not cover information owned or possessed by private institutions, it should be noted, unless it is held by a federal body covered by the Act; cf the Data Protection Act 1998 and the UK and the 1995 EU Directive on data protection: see chapter 7.

allows individuals on whom executive federal agencies have documents, files or data to examine the documentation after a written application. A *Citizens' Guide*[19] describes in detail the procedures to follow to obtain information about oneself, and it spells out in simple terms the kinds of information that agencies are likely to possess on individuals, adding that this was 'just a fraction of the information held on individual citizens'. An individual may write to an agency head or PA official, who both have a duty to inform the individual whether files are held on him or her. Or a more thorough check may be made by consulting the compilation of PA notices published annually by the *Federal Register*. This contains details of all federal records systems, the kinds of data included, and the categories of individuals on whom the information is held. Retrieval procedures and relevant officials are identified, and the notices are available in reference, law and university libraries. The compilation is, however, poorly indexed and difficult to use.

Unlike FOI—and that Act is used frequently in conjunction with the PA—only the subject of the data or records can apply for sight of them. The subject can seek amendment of the records which he or she believes to be inaccurate, irrelevant, untimely or uncomplete. Copies of the record, in a form comprehensible to the applicant, must be provided and he or she must be told who, outside the agency, has had access. The Act provides criminal and a variety of civil sanctions.[20] There is no standard procedure for retrieval, unlike FOIA, but agency regulations prescribing procedures are common: rejections must be accompanied by a letter specifying the appeal procedures. If appeal is refused, the agency must refer to the exemption it is invoking and must also state why it is not available under FOIA. The authority for the collection of information must be specified, as must the use to which it is to be put. Information should only be collected where it is relevant or necessary for carrying out lawful duties. Information must be accurate, timely, relevant and complete, an obligation which does not apply to FOIA.

Disclosure of any record covered by the PA to a third party without the written consent or request of the subject is prohibited unless the third-party request falls under one of 11 exceptions.[1]

If an agency seeks to rely upon an exemption, however, and is challenged, a *de novo* review can take place in the courts with the burden

---

19 Report by Library of Congress, CRS 20 September 1985.
20 Enjoining access, amendment, and damages for 'improper maintenance' of the contents of records or for other breaches of the Act or regulations adversely affecting the individual.
1   Eg where records are used internally by employees of the agency in performance of their duties; 'routine' use; or where it is required and is not exempt under FOIA.

of proof on the agency to establish one of the exemptions. These fall into two categories: 'general' and 'specific'.

General exemptions cover CIA systems of records and criminal law enforcement systems of records, though the latter only cover criminal investigation records, records compiled to identify criminal offenders or alleged offenders, or compiled at any stage of law enforcement after arrest. This information is only exempt if rules state the reasons for exemption of a system of records from each provision of the PA. If an individual challenges the exemption before the courts, the courts must determine that a system of records properly falls under the exemption and that all exemption procedures have been followed.[2]

Specific exemptions cover: information classified by executive order as under the FOIA; law enforcement material not falling under the general exemption; secret service material; civil or military service employment or promotional suitability information; and information relating to suitability for federal contracts. The exemptions are discretionary, and for an agency to invoke them all necessary procedures must be followed. Under specific exemptions, an agency head may exempt his agency's records from fewer of the provisions of the Act than under general exemptions, and challenge through the courts is allowed.

The PA is one of a number of statutes protecting the privacy of personal information, including the disclosure of information identifying certain US intelligence officers, agents and sources/informants.[3] In the 98th Congress over 30 bills on privacy-related matters were introduced into Congress.[4] Such a frenzied activity may suggest that all is not well with the PA, and certainly there are apparent incompatibilities between the PA and FOIA.[5] There has also been a significant rift between the US authorities and EU institutions concerning the inadequacy of data protection in the USA when compared with the EU (see chapter 7).[6]

In 1983 Congressional *Oversight Hearings* of the PA, it was stated that the current US federal system for data protection was seriously deficient because it lacked an adequate monitoring mechanism to ensure compliance and enforcement.[7] Our own Data Protection Commissioner might come to mind in this context. There was no overall regulatory body for privacy laws in the USA. Serious malpractices such as computer

---

2   If they have not been, the records may be subject to the PA. If discretion to exempt is exercised, only a few of the Act's safeguards apply.

3   Right of Financial Privacy Act 1978; Foreign Intelligence Surveillance Act 1978; Intelligence Identities Protection Act 1982 (USA), which punishes disclosures which the authorities *have reason to believe* would harm US intelligence operations by naming officials.

4   House Committee on Government Operations: H Rep 98–455 (1983).

5   Vaughn, n 13 p 53 above.

6   Charlesworth (2000) European Public Law 253.

7   H Rep 401–59 (1983).

matching were common, it was felt. This is where whole categories of people may have their records screened to see if they belong to a separate, supposedly incompatible category such as 'welfare recipient'.[8] Computer matching amendment laws were passed in 1988 and 1990 which authorise computer matching agreements between agencies and gives the public procedural protection before agreements are finalised. In 1998, President Clinton called upon all federal agencies to take further steps to ensure privacy protection. These included identification of specific senior officials within agencies with responsibility for privacy protection and consistency in the application of privacy principles.

The USA has a constitutional background which takes privacy seriously. The First, Fourth and Fifth Amendments to the Constitution protect freedom of speech, security of property, protection against self-incrimination, and due process of law and have all been regularly invoked to protect the inviolability of an individual's privacy. A federal law protects individuals against invasions of privacy.[9] The Privacy Protection Act 1980 prohibits government agents from making unannounced searches of press offices and files if no one in the press office is suspected of a crime. As befits a privacy conscious society, many complaints are made to the Office of Management and Budget—which compiles the annual reports on PA from agencies—about agency breaches of PA provisions. It is a little surprising, therefore, that only 179 copies of the 1979 edition of the *PA Information Manual* were sold.[10]

FOI and constitutional and administrative practice

The constitutional culture of the USA has been more jealous in its protection of freedom of speech, its insistence upon informed debate and freedom of information, than has our own.[11] This was evidenced when the President bowed to public pressure to allow the investigation of the Executive and the National Security Council and their roles in illegal arms sales to Iran and unauthorised payments of sums received to

8   This is also a vexed issue in the UK.
9   Restatement 2d Torts, para 652A.
10   Maybe not: it did run to five volumes!
11   See *New York Times Co v US* 403 US 713 (1971) and the First Amendment protection of freedom of speech and the press; although see *Snepp v US* 444 US 507 (1980), where the Supreme Court held that an agreement by CIA employees not to publish *any* information acquired as an agent without specific prior approval was judicially enforceable *vis-à-vis* classified *and* non-classified information, and all profits accruing from publication were held on constructive trust for the CIA, and see *US v Marchetti* 466 F 2d 1309 (1972). See *A-G v Blake* [2000] 4 All ER 385, HL. Cf *Reading v A-G* [1951] AC 507, HL; and *Haig v Agee* 453 US 280 (1981) *inter alia*. See generally E Barendt *Freedom of Speech* (1985).

Nicaraguan rebels through the intermediation of Oliver North. Within days a Senate hearing was called to investigate[12] and to replace the internal Presidential executive inquiry. There followed investigations by Congressional committee and the appointment of a Special Prosecutor. The Special Prosecutor eventually issued a damning report which found that the Presidents (Reagan and Bush) had disregarded the law, encouraged others to do so, misled Congress and the public and that Mr Bush had engaged in a 'cover up'. Congress granted immunity to crucial witnesses hindering the prosecutor's investigation. Convictions of Colonel North and Admiral Poindexter were overturned on appeal and six high ranking officials were granted presidential immunity including the former Defense Secretary, Caspar Weinberger. Surprisingly, the President did not raise the plea of 'executive privilege' in these proceedings to protect documents, but it has been frequently invoked. It could be said that the other actions of the Presidents achieved similar objectives to privilege.

'Executive privilege' as a term was only coined in 1958, although feuds concerning the 'President's claim of constitutional authority to withhold information from Congress' go back to the eighteenth century.[13] In *US v Nixon*[14] the Supreme Court rejected an absolute claim to executive privilege by the President although the case concerned the investigation of serious *criminal* charges against senior executive officials. The courts are the final arbiters in judicial proceedings and law enforcement on what the President and his officials must produce in the interests of justice.[15]

At the height of the impeachment process against President Clinton, it was decided that government lawyers were not able to be protected by the plea of attorney-client privilege to protect their advice to the President when a Grand Jury was investigating possible commission of federal crimes.[16] As the Federal Court of Appeals said in an earlier case: 'openness

---

12   Unlike the CIA, the National Security Council had escaped Congressional oversight, see chapter 1, p 33, n 7 above. The War Powers Act 1973, as amended, required prior Congressional notification of military action or covert activity.

13   R Berger *Executive Privilege* (1974).

14   418 US 683 (1974). In *Nixon v Administrator of General Services* 433 US 425 (1977), the Court upheld as constitutional a congressional statute requiring the former President to hand over his Presidential papers to an executive agency prior to their eventual disclosure to the public. Burgher CJ and Rehnquist J dissented.

15   *US v Nixon* above, the Watergate tapes. There was an uncanny familiarity to that event when the Royal Ulster Constabulary refused to hand over their tapes recording events surrounding the shooting of two youths in Armagh in 1982 to the investigating officer, John Stalker. When pressurised into giving access, it was announced by the RUC that they had been lost. A written transcript would be made available, but only on the condition that it was not used for any report. Unlike the Special Prosecutor, Stalker never got his tapes! See J Stalker *Stalker* (1988).

16   *Re Bruce Lindsey* 148 F3d 1100 (1998 US App).

in government has always been thought crucial to ensuring that the people remain in control of their government.[17] This episode brought into dramatic focus the role of the office of independent counsel in investigating the President.

The position is not paralleled *vis-à-vis* Congressional committee demands for information. They do not have the same power as courts. Because Congress has no specific power to demand information, and because of the separation of powers doctrine as well as the equality and independence of each branch of government, Presidents have sought to refuse Congress the right to control and demand executive information. *Per contra* 'Congress as the arm of the Government responsible for making and overseeing the operation of the nation's laws, has the power to inquire into and review the methods by which those laws are enforced'.[18] Claims to such a privilege for the executive increased markedly after 1954.[19] The courts have not supported an unqualified Congressional right to demand information from the President, and Congress would have to establish a strong need to fulfil its constitutional responsibilities of oversight, and that such fulfilment was only possible with access to the President's papers, before the courts ordered access. Where such a right was claimed by a Senate Committee—in the Watergate episode—the need was not established,[20] although at that time the House Judiciary Committee possessed most of the relevant information and was about to make available its findings on impeachment proceedings against the President. A statute giving Congress the right to demand information in global terms would, in all probability, be ruled unconstitutional.[1]

In November 1982, a White House memorandum for the heads of executive departments and agencies stated that executive privilege could only be claimed 'in the most compelling of circumstances' where after 'careful review' an assertion of privilege was necessary. Brokerage between Congress and the White House would minimise the need for the invoking of executive privilege. Within a month, there was an explosive clash between the Environmental Protection Agency (EPA) and a Congressional Committee when the head of the EPA's hazardous waste programme was holding back information on toxic waste sites and their clean-up. She was cited for contempt of Congress. The Justice Department unsuccessfully sought judicial exoneration of the head as she was acting

---

17 *Re Sealed case (Espy)* 121 F3d 729 at 749 (DC Circ 1997).

18 RL Claveloux (1983) Duke LJ 1333.

19 *Berger*, n 13 above. A famous example involved President Eisenhower's refusal to cede to the demands of Joseph McCarthy who was inquiring into the army's loyalty and security programme.

20 *Senate Select Committee on Presidential Campaign Activities v Nixon* (CADC) 498 F 2d 725 (1974).

1   See *Nixon v Administrator of General Services*, n 14 above.

under the direction of the President in refusing to hand over information. The court pressed the parties for a friendly settlement without further judicial intervention.[2] The Committee eventually obtained its information.[3] Sauce was added to the fare when it was disclosed that the head of the EPA's hazardous waste programme had frequently met, informally and socially, with representatives of companies whose activities she was regulating, although similar opportunities were not offered to environmental lobby groups.[4]

It would take another book to describe the interrelationship between administrative process and law, the requirement of a full record of administrative hearings and rule-making proceedings, the opportunities for interested parties to participate in policy formulation and to be adequately informed about the subject matter, and the resort to courts for 'hard-look', or a very probing, judicial review of an agency's decisions or regulations in order to establish an adequate evidentiary basis for such decisions and regulations; that in other words an agency has taken a 'hard look' at all the evidence. And it would require a further volume to examine the reaction against excessive openness.[5] Nevertheless, safeguards combine together to put administrative policy-making through a series of tests and justifications based upon informed criticism that are largely unparalleled in the UK, although one must be careful not to exaggerate. For instance, in the desire of the White House to deregulate wherever possible, the Executive has set a cost-benefit analysis which has to be satisfied before new regulations can be passed. Executive Order 12498 instructs agencies to notify the Office of Manpower and Budget of *all* agency research with links to possible regulation. The desire to deregulate is meeting with some counterproductive consequences.[6] The movement is likely to be reinforced by electoral success of President Bush Jnr in 2000. The ascendancy of the 'New Right' in US politics has allowed a populist outcry against big government to be matched by increasing demands for information access to advance that anti-federal government movement.

2   *US v House of Representatives of the US* 556 F Supp 150 (1983). See *Congressional Quarterly*, 'EPA Document Agreement' (1983) 26 March, p 635.

3   A claim of privilege was made over the appointment of W Rehnquist as Chief Justice. The claim was withdrawn on the understanding that only senators, and not their staff, might see the relevant documentation.

4   There are specific provisions allowing access to environmental information in the US: see P Birkinshaw in E Lykke *Achieving Environmental Goals* (1992).

5   S Katz *Government Secrecy: Decisions Without Democracy* (1987).

6   AB Morrison (1986) 99 Harv LR 1059, who argues that agencies are placed in a strait jacket and the rules that do satisfy OMB tests are more easily attacked in the courts. See, ibid, p 1075, for OMB staff reply.

Canada

The Canadian constitution is a written federal constitution, but it has within its operation many features of the Westminster model of government, most notably a developed sense of ministerial responsibility and parliamentary government. FOIA in America saw a hostile executive, and direct advisers to the President are exempt from the Act although such communications may not be protected by executive privilege or attorney-client privilege (see above). The American law was generated by law reformers, good-government advocates, journalists and Congress. It is a frequently cited criticism in the USA that the FOIA laws do not apply to Congress and the judiciary and alleged connections between some members of those bodies with organised crime. In Canada, Crown privilege and Cabinet confidentiality had to be expressly incorporated into the legislation; the legislation was far from independent of executive influence, and the press impact for reform was minimal.[7] In the USA, FOIA was developed largely without executive assistance, frequently in the face of executive opposition; in Canada, the Access to Information Act (AIA) was 'drafted by the administration and developed through amendments it perfected'.[8] The AIA has eight or nine times as many exemptions as FOIA. Unlike the AIA, the FOIA did not provide for an information ombudsman or commissioner. Congressmen were jealous of their role as citizens' representatives and Americans like litigation.[9]

The AIA was passed in 1982 and is part of a broad constitutional package reflecting a wish for a new constitutional structure as Canada sloughed off the last vestige of control from Westminster.[10] Access is allowed to Federal Government records and includes: 'letters, memos, books, plans, maps, photographs, films, microfilms, sound recordings, computerised data and any other documentary material regardless of physical form or characteristics or any copy thereof.' It has been held by the Information Commissioner to apply to Email and that bodies under the Act should keep Email correspondence for two years.[11] It is specific in a way FOIA is not. An access register exists which contains descriptions of government records, their probable locations, and other information which 'will likely assist you in identifying precisely which records you

---

7 H Relyea (1986), p 68, n 10 above. The Canadian Bar Association was very proactive.

8 Ibid.

9 See RB Stewart 'Reform of American Administrative Law: The Academic Agenda vs the Political Agenda' (unpublished paper for Conference on Comparative Administration and Law, 1984). See Birkinshaw, p 63, n 4 above.

10 Canada Act 1982; Wade and Bradley *Constitutional and Administrative Law* (10th edn, 1985), pp 730–3, for a pithy and lucid account.

11 Information Commissioner *Annual Report 1994-5.*

wish to see.' Instructions are provided on how to identify, as precisely as possible, the information an applicant is looking for, how to get assistance and how to apply for access. Government departments have access co-ordinators who assist free of charge. A request must be in writing, and there is an application fee of $5 with additional fees for time in excess of five hours spent on a request and for computer processing and copying time. Originally an applicant had to be a citizen of Canada or a permanent resident.[12] In 1989, the right of application was extended to any individual or corporation present in America. An agency has 30 days to respond to the initial request, though this may be extended where a request is complicated. The head of each government institution covered by the Act must submit an annual report to Parliament on the administration of the Act. If a body claims that information is exempt, it has to justify that it is exempt. Government institutions are required to remove exempt information from disclosable information and to disclose the latter. The Act does not apply to Crown commercial organisations. As well as the provisions of the Act, information may be classified for internal security purposes under a Treasury Board Manual of 1991.

There has been evidence of official tampering of documents to hinder access; in particular to prevent access to documents relating to intrusive practices by the Canadian peace-keeping forces in Somalia.[13] It is further felt that the law lacks specific guidance on openness and that such guidance and direction needs to be spelt out.

Excluded material

Excluded material includes cabinet secrets or confidences of the Queen's Privy Council covering such items as policy proposals, background options and discussions, agenda of Privy Council meetings and minister/adviser discussions on policy briefings and draft legislation. Discussion papers may be released if *inter alia* the decision to which they relate has been made public.[14] The first Information Commissioner (IC) believed she had a right to determine whether they have become public, although the IC's decisions cannot be enforced. The Standing Committee on Justice and Solicitor-General described this blanket exclusion as unjustified. It has not been followed in all provincial access statutes.

12 See *Information Commissioner v Minister of Employment and Immigration* in *Annual Report*: Information Commissioner (1984–5), p 124, for a bizarre interpretation of this provision.
13 See Gillis chapter 8 in A MacDonald and G Terrill (eds) *Open Government: Freedom of Information and Privacy* (1998) at p 155.
14 *Or* if the *decision* was made at least four years before a relevant request, or if the papers have been in existence for more than 20 years.

Exemptions

The Act provides for mandatory and discretionary exemptions. The former include classes of documents such as: information from foreign, provincial or municipal governments; certain confidential information from the Royal Canadian Mounted Police; personal information and information supplied by outside sources *(sic)*.[15] The discretionary exemptions are extensive and include those which might harm federal/provincial affairs, international affairs, Canadian defence or the detection or prevention of 'subversive or hostile activities', lawful investigations, or those which might facilitate the committing of a criminal offence if released. If release would threaten trade secrets, legal privilege or personal safety it may be exempted. Also exempt is the 'advice or recommendations developed by or for an institution or a minister' which would disclose accounts of their deliberations and consultations apropos of negotiating plans or positions—an exemption which has the 'greatest potential for routine misuse'. Third-party information covering trade secrets, competitive ability, contractual matters or other confidential information may be waived from exemption without consent where 'the disclosure would be in the public interest and it relates to health, public safety or the protection of the environment'. Safeguards ensure third-party notice and right of challenge.

Data banks covering personal information may be made exempt where they contain exempt files which consist predominantly of personal information held for law enforcement or reasons of national security. They are made exempt under an order of the Privy Council. Use of this block exemption is carefully scrutinised by the courts.

Basic provisions

Citizens are urged to use 'existing informal channels' to obtain information and access. This may be a way of institutionalising brokerage as the access co-ordinator has responsibility for all internal aspects of the administration of the Act and has to be informed of all direct requests from the public.

Departments must introduce reading-room facilities within two years of the introduction of the Act. An Access register, available in approximately 700 libraries and 2,700 post offices, is constantly checked

---

15 Trade secrets are specifically referred to. When information relates to defence, international affairs or an 'exempt data bank'—see text—additional safeguards are adopted in the courts concerning level of judge, *in camera* proceedings and so on and are provided in the legislation: see *Reyes v Canada* (1985) 9 Admin LR 296; *Russell v Canada* (1990) 35 FTR 315 and *X v Canada* (1992) 46 FTR 206.

to ensure accuracy and that it is up to date. The register is organised in chapters, one covering each federal institution and related agencies, and each chapter contains:
1. a description of the organisation and responsibilities of the institution, including details on the programmes and functions of each division or branch;
2. a description of all classes of records under the control of the institution in sufficient detail to facilitate the exercise of the right of access under the Act;
3. all working manuals;
4. titles and addresses of appropriate officials.

The Information Commissioner (IC)

An Ombudsman—the Information Commissioner (IC)—to deal with complaints concerning access has been established and the IC has access to information which is exempt under the Act. The first IC declared her intention to construe the exemptions as narrowly as possible. Complaints must be made within a year of the initial request, and they must be in writing unless this requirement is waived. The IC's decision cannot be enforced against departments although the IC may select for judicial scrutiny points which require judicial interpretation, even when the applicant cannot afford the cost of litigation and where she has consented to the suit's proceeding after a department's refusal. Individuals have access to the courts following refusal. The Commissioner may participate in proceedings brought by others, receive information which the complainant will not—unless successful—and may be heard *ex parte* by the court.[16] Courts may review decisions on exemptions on a 'reasonableness' basis. Where the IC supports a complaint but a remedy is not negotiated, a report is made to the minister. Investigations are conducted in private.

It must be said, however, that examination of the Commissioner's annual reports produces a less sanguine perspective of the Act's operation and this tone has pervaded IC reports throughout the nineties. The IC has criticised the absence of publicity or explanations of the Act. Indeed, no clause was incorporated providing for public education and enlightenment on the Act and no funds are provided for such. The IC has reported that the 'FOIA cannot be improved upon nor can it serve a country well if its very existence is kept secret.' In the 1984-85 Report, the IC remarked that access co-ordinators were becoming demoralised and isolated and

16 Of 17 cases commenced in federal courts until 1 May 1986 alleging unjustified refusal, six were commenced by the IC 60% of all cases commenced relating to the Act (47 in the overall total) concerned third-party proceedings.

were subject to criticism from colleagues when they pursued the objectives of the Act too vigorously. Where a co-ordinator was absent, there were no temporary fill-ins, so phones and correspondence were not answered. The 1985-86 Report was even gloomier in its tone, and it noted how the most frequent users were journalists, academics and researchers although the largest group now is the business community.[17] This gloomy tone continued and in 1994/5 the IC reported how his budget had decreased by 10% since 1991 but applications had increased by 56%. In that year he dealt with 1,016 complaints. In 1998, they amounted to about 10,000 in number. He reported desultory responses from some departments but also found more constructive approaches among officials. The IC 'audits' departmental information practices. He also has four investigators who specialise in national security work and they have access to the Canadian security and information service premises and files.

The Canadian Parliament keeps the operation of the Act under review.[18] In 1993–94, the Commissioner issued a 10-year anniversary report which recommended the appointment of a Parliamentary committee to recommend reforms and he then made 43 recommendations for reform or change in government practice. He recommended repeal of the exemption which removes access rights to documents under the Act which government is under a duty to publish at a fee and for which it charged exorbitant rates (p12). He recommended that he have a binding power of decision and that there should be access to government contracts and details of bids. The role of MPs has, however, been criticised in that they have left too much to the IC and have not provided a continuing momentum for development of openness.[19]

The Privacy Act

One of the most commonly invoked exemptions under AIA is that relating to personal information. A Privacy Act was assented to in 1982 which allows access to personal individual records of scheduled government departments by the individual subjects concerned where these records are held by the department. It does not cover private sector bodies. A Privacy Commissioner (PC) shares premises and general staff with the IC, although they are different individuals and they have different legal

17 1983–4: 150 complaint files – 46 completed investigations; 1984–5: 188 complaint files – 167 completed investigations; 1985–6: 321 complaint files – 235 completed investigations.

18 Especially the 'confidentiality' clauses in existing statutes (about 30 had such); *Main Brief to HC Standing Committee on Justice and Legal Affairs*, Office of IC (May 1986).

19 See Gillis op cit p.159.

advisers because the interests of the two may clash, eg access to personal information may be sought by a 'client' of the IC and challenged by a 'client' of the PC. Personal information is given a wide interpretation and safeguards are imposed on the use, purposes, collection and dissemination of material. Personal information banks and a personal information index are published, setting out all personal information held, who has control of it, the purposes for which it is used, etc. The same criteria apply to applicants for access as obtain under the AIA. They can request correction and notice of unsuccessful requests for correction. The general scheme of the Act, including exclusions, exemptions and reviews of indexes, is similar to those under the AIA. It has carried out some useful studies on eg *Genetic Testing and Privacy* (1993 Privacy Commissioner of Canada).[20]

Most provinces have created FOI and Privacy rights in one statute and have also combined the Commissioners into one office holder. It was felt that FOI tended to dominate privacy protection.[1] Specific statutes on privacy protection are also appearing in the provinces: Ontario has introduced a Personal Health Information Privacy Act 2000.

Conclusion

In 1981, a commentator upon the FOI movement in Canada noted:[2]

> It has been the experience of public interest interveners such as the Consumers Association of Canada that regulated companies have tended to overwhelm them with information, and as a result the challenge has been to build up expertise so as to be able to interpret this mass of information. . . Is the information coming in a digestible form or in an uncontrollable manner?

This raises a general problem about obtaining information. Raw information can be next to useless. What information do we want? In what form is it most useful? Who is going to use it? For what purpose is it going to be used and how is it going to be most usable? To these points we will return.

---

20   Privacy Commissioner of Canada (1993). Success rates for complainants also differ between the Commissioners in the same subject areas. In some cases the Privacy Commissioner may be complained against in relation to the manner in which a complaint was dealt with, but the IC may not be the subject of such a complaint.
1   Gillis op cit at 151.
2   H Janisch in J McCamus (ed) *FOI – Canadian Perspectives* (1981).

The Canadian statute is less biased towards disclosure than the American one and is more mindful of past practices of confidentiality.[3] In fact, the original proponents of the FOI Bill were the Canadian Bar Association, whose Bill was far more adventurous and forthright than that which the Government accepted.[4] A review of the two Acts by the House of Commons Standing Committee on Justice and Solicitor-General has made some important recommendations on the legislation.[5] In particular, it recommended that cabinet confidences be brought into the exempt categories and that they should no longer be excluded. This was not accepted and the recommendation was repeated in the 1993/4 report of the Commissioner.

As well as the above provisions under access legislation, the Charter of Rights has been invoked to attempt to obtain government information, including that in the hands of the ombudsmen.

Australia

Official reports in Australia, prior to their FOIA, placed the blame for excessive secrecy in government on the residue of the influence of the English tradition and its association with Crown prerogative.[6] Any such residue may well have been expunged by Mr Justice Powell in the New South Wales Supreme Court when he ordered the British Government to produce details of MI5 activities in proceedings brought by the Crown against Peter Wright (see chapters 1 and 9). The FOIA enacted in 1982 has to be set against an ostensibly impressive range of reforms in Australian administrative law which straddle the Administrative Review Council, the Administrative Appeals Tribunal (AAT), the establishment of a Federal Ombudsman, and a reformed basis of judicial review of administrative action.[7] These seek to advance: openness, fairness, participation, impartiality and rationality in decision-making. In 1983, an FOI Amendment Act was passed to cover certain deficiences in the 1982 legislation, including access to documents up to five years old at the time of the commencement of the 1983 Act. Further reforms took place

---

3   J McCamus (1983) 10 Govt Publications Review 51.
4   Janisch (1982) Public Law 534.
5   *Open and Shut: Enhancing the Right To Know and the Right To Privacy* (March 1987). See specifically chapter 3 on exemptions. This report was rejected by the Federal Government in *Access and Privacy: the Steps Ahead* (1987).
6   *A-G for New South Wales v Butterworth and Co (Australia) Ltd* (1938) 38 SRNSW 195; and Report by the Senate Standing Committee on Constitutional and Legal Affairs on the FOI Bill (1978), chapter 4.
7   See, for instance, the *Annual Reports* of the Administrative Review Council; and M Partington in P McAuslan and J McEldowney (eds) *Law, Legitimacy and the Constitution* (1985), pp 199–207.

in 1986, 1988 and 1991 which introduced third party notice requirements, as well as clarifying and simplifying various procedures.

In a 1983 report on the Act by the Federal Attorney-General in Australia he spoke in hopeful tones about the benefits of the Act, which included the improvement of official decision-making, a better-informed public and a truer democratic political process as well as giving individuals information held on themselves or influencing the decisions 'fundamentally affecting their lives'. He was a little surprised, therefore, that much less use of the Act had been made than anticipated.[8] The Act has helped to strengthen and not weaken ministerial responsibility in Parliament. The Act has been the subject of a further review by the Standing Committee on Legal and Constitutional Affairs in 1987 and in 1994 the Administrative Review Council and Australian Law Commission issued a detailed discussion paper on the Act at the request of the Attorney-General with a view to publishing a final report in December 1995 recommending proposals for change or extension of the Act's provisions.[9] This followed reports from the Ombudsman who found increased departmental resistance to the Acts in the form of delays and unnecessary secrecy.

The legislation

The 1982 Act places a duty on the responsible minister to publish, not later than 12 months after commencement of the Act, particulars of the organisation he heads, its functions and powers; arrangements allowing public participation for non-official persons or groups in whatever form in the formulation of policy; the organisation's administration; the categories of its documents and details on access procedures and officers. Ministers have to publish in the *Federal Gazette* all documents—including computerised records—which may be used to make decisions or recommendations affecting rights, privileges, benefits, obligations, penalties or other 'detriments'. Every person has a legally enforceable right to agency and ministerial documents which are not exempt. A decision on access has to be given within 60 days, and refusal must be accompanied with reasons. As with Canadian and US legislation, there is a third-party notification procedure.

---

8   *FOIA 1982 Annual Report by the Att-Gen* (Aust Govt Publishing Service, 1983). The Department of Social Security anticipated 100,000 requests; it received 1177.
9   A further interim report was published in March 1995—Australian Law Reform Commission and Administrative Review Council *Discussion Paper 59.*

Exemptions[10]

The Act provides access to documents not information as such—unlike the UK code of practice on access (see chapter 5). Documents are exempt where 'disclosure .... would be contrary to the public interest', viz it 'could reasonably be expected to cause damage to: the security or defence of the Commonwealth; international relations; federal/state relations'. The AAT has formulated principles to help tease out the formulation of 'public interest' although these have not been universally acclaimed. The principles seek to protect high level communications, the policy-making process, the frankness and candour of deliberations in 'future pre-decisional communications'.[11] The Attorney-General's Department has listed a variety of features both in favour and weighing against a disclosure in the public interest.[12] The Attorney-General's Department, in fact, could find no examples of release of policy documents against the wishes of the government.[13] Cabinet and Executive Council documents are exempt, as are internal working documents where disclosure would reveal advice or deliberations relating to the 'deliberative functions of an agency or minister or of the Commonwealth Government' and would be against the public interest. A certificate from the minister covering these exemptions is conclusive evidence on the public interest. This decision cannot be reviewed by the AAT; it can determine whether there is a reasonable basis for the exemption claim. If it does not believe there is, it may *recommend* revocation.[14] The Administrative Appeals Tribunal has held that it would be cautious about entering into an unfinished course of policy-making and negotiation and the benefit of the doubt, even in cases where there were very strong grounds in favour of disclosure, would lie with the minister where he had a 'relevant reasonable ground for non-disclosure'.[15] This exemption does not apply to purely factual information, reports on scientific or technical experts expressing an opinion on technical matters, or to reports of a prescribed body or organisation *within* an agency. Other exemptions cover familiar territory: law enforcement; public safety; Commonwealth financial interests; documents the disclosure of which would involve unreasonable disclosure of personal information; legal privilege; trade secrets; disclosure which would detrimentally affect the

10 Contained in ss 32-47.
11 *Re Howard and the Treasurer of the Commonwealth of Australia* (1985) 3 AAR 169; see Terrill in McDonald and Terrill note 13 p 182 op cit at p 105.
12 Terrill p 106.
13 Ibid, p 111.
14 See Australian Law Reform Commission and Administrative Review Council *Freedom of Information* Issues Paper 12 1994, p 46 for figures; also *Re Howard etc* (1985) 3 AAR 169.
15 *Re Rae and Department of Prime Minister and Cabinet* (1986) Admin Review 136.

national economy; or which would constitute a breach of confidence. This last exemption would seem to be very wide in scope.

The Administrative Review Council found that decision-makers were unclear about how to apply the exemptions and nothing like the *Vaughn* index seems to have appeared. There are also four forms of public interest balancing tests applicable in the range of exemptions which does not make application easy. These are open unless access is contrary to the public interest; balancing of interests involved to establish where preponderant interest lies; modified—ie, disclosure in the circumstances would cause unreasonable risk or damage etc; and finally 'closed'—ie, never open.

In addition to the above exemptions, information may be refused where it relates to 'all documents, or all documents of a specified class, that contain information of a specified kind or relate to a specified subject matter' and would 'substantially and unnecessarily interfere' with the other functions of the agency or minister. Reasons must be given for refusal, but again this exemption seems to allow ample scope for refusal.

Amendment and review

Part V of the Act allows the subject of personal documents to apply to have the records amended. Part VI covers the review of the agency's or minister's decision. Departments are given 30 days to process a request—a reform introduced in 1991. An internal review will take place upon request within 14 days after the day of notification of refusal. Three months is not an unknown period. Alternatively, an application may be made to the AAT if no decision is notified within 30 days.[16] Another route is via the Commonwealth Ombudsman who, although s/he cannot investigate decisions taken by ministers, may examine the whole context of the decision. The AAT has power to make any decision that could be made by the agency or minister and can, in some cases, review whether disclosure would be contrary to the public interest.[17] Its remit is to review on the law and on the merits. *In camera* proceedings are possible for inspection of 'exempt' documents by the AAT if it is not satisfied with the minister's certificate. If a minister does not accept a finding of the AAT which is adverse to his classification, it is not binding upon him, but he must notify the applicant of his reasons and place a copy of these

---

16 As from 1 January 1987. A downpayment of $Aus 300 at that time has to be provided for registration.

17 Different departments have taken different attitudes on the same documents as to whether exemption should be claimed: *Re Dillon and Department of Treasury* and *Re Dillon and Department of Trade* (1986) Admin Review 113. Under the Act, the AAT cannot insist on access to exempt information.

before both Houses of Parliament.[18] From the AAT there is an appeal on a point of law to the Federal Court. The AAT, in spite of its introduction to reduce formality in state/citizen conflict has not escaped criticism for being over formalistic.[19]

The Ombudsman

The annual reports of the Ombudsman are notable for his own complaints that he receives inadequate funding to perform his responsibilities under the FOIA. Several persons who wished to be represented before the AAT were turned down because of a lack of funding.[20] He received no additional staff for his FOIA responsibilities. The 1983 legislation not only added the representational role to his responsibilities: he now has to monitor the Act and recommend improvements in access. He claimed that his treatment by the Government was both 'unfair and demonstrably discriminatory' and that lack of resources meant that he had been unable to monitor the Act as required. In the period after 1984-5, the position had not improved and in 1991 the Ombudsman lost the role of counsel before the AAT.[1]

The Ombudsman is beset by other problems. It has been decided that his records of complaints investigations are not exempt, under s 38[2] of the Act, from an FOIA request. All ombudsmen would invoke the protection of complete confidentiality for their investigations—a confidentiality usually protected by law—so the decision does appear anomalous.[3] To gain exemption, the Ombudsman may well have to rely upon the general confidentiality provision in the 1982 Act and other exemptions.

The Ombudsman has access to disputed documents, including those for which exemption is claimed.[4] In 1984-5 he received 142 FOI complaints, virtually double the figure for 1983-4. The Administrative Review Council has noted that the Ombudsman has not played as

---

18 A minister has responsibility for administering the FOIA, and he has access to all necessary documents. *Quaere* collective responsibility?

19 See Australian Law Reform Commission and Administrative Review Council *Freedom of Information* Issues Paper 12 1994, p 74.

20 The 1983 Amendment Act allows the AAT to make a recommendation for payment of a successful applicant's costs to the Attorney-General.

1 In that earlier period, the Commonwealth Ombudsman resigned.

2 *Kavvadias v Commonwealth Ombudsman (Nos 1 and 2)*; see CO *Annual Reports* (1983–4), pp 30–2 and (1984–5), pp 165–8. Requests came mainly from former complainants.

3 *Kavvadias* has not been followed by Victoria State *vis-à-vis* its own FOIA and their ombudsman.

4 Unless a certificate under s 9(3) of the Ombudsman Act 1976 is issued.

significant a role in FOI as anticipated[5] and in May 1995 it identified the absence of an 'advocate for FOI' to oversee the Act and monitor compliance as a deficiency.[6]

Some reaction to the legislation

The courts have ruled that the legislation is applicable to some private institutions carrying out functions in the public interest, for example a law society and universities, although documents of university council meetings have been held to be properly classified as exempt by the AAT as they were compared with cabinet documents.[7] Boldness in some areas is not reflected in others. The High Court of Australia has held that there is no general rule of common law or principle of natural justice that required the giving of reasons for administrative decisions.[8] Another judge, however, adverting to this issue and FOIA generally, spoke of the need for legislation to 'deal with the real problems and not the symbols and to preserve democratic values' of society.[9] Information rights, he argued, must extend from the public sector to the private one—a point to which I shall return. I should mention that one of the areas singled out for special attention by the ARC in its 1994 report was the extension of the legislation to the private sector, especially given the impetus for privatisation and corporatisation and government business enterprises. Coverage of private bodies performing public tasks is patchy. In the USA for instance public disclosure laws place duties on private bodies to disclose information to the public through annual inventories about designated toxic material and hazardous materials.[10] But US FOIA imposes no *direct* duties on private bodies themselves.

The Act has precipitated an increasing number of applications to the AAT, and in several years FOI applications constituted the second and third largest items respectively. In the first full year of the FOIA's operation, there were almost 20,000 requests involving 152 agencies; of these 1,105 were refused, 500 were reviewed internally and 27 formed the subject of a complaint to the Ombudsman; 168 were referred to the AAT. In 1992/3, 33, 804 access requests were made; access was granted in full in 75.2% of requests and in part in 20.6%. the bulk relating to personal information. The media have been criticised for not making

5   Tenth Annual Report, para 76.
6   Note 9 p 88 above.
7   *Re Burns and Aust NU* 1 February 1985; Cf *Sankey v Whitlam* (1978) 142 CLR 1.
8   *Public Services Board of New South Wales v Osmond* (1986) 159 CLR 656.
9   Kirby J (1986) Admin Review 1023.
10   Note 4 p 80, above.

greater use of the Act. Public interest groups are 'reasonably frequent users'. Commercial use appears to be limited. The ARC found that some agencies did not support the 'culture of openness' more than 10 years after the legislation was introduced.[11]

It is interesting to observe that departments are differing in their attitudes towards FOIA. Such differences seemed to be anticipated by the Attorney-General, who wrote to all relevant agencies in 1983 asking them to inform his secretariat of FOIA requests which were being taken to the AAT, so that *consistency* in approach could be achieved . In the early stages of the legislation there was some evidence of informal bartering by federal and provincial government to secure opposition to a federal agency's liberal attitude to disclosing information.[12] However, every state and the ACT has FOI legislation and in some cases, echoing the situation in the USA, such laws are more advanced than the federal model.

The Australian Act has been used to make some dramatic disclosures about eg, disputes before the Chief Justice and the PM Department concerning litigation involving indigenous Australians' land rights.[13] However, the fact that the Act is enforced by individuals and ultimately rests upon governmental goodwill for enforcement is seen as a serious weakness by Terrill.[14]

New Zealand[15]

New Zealand enacted an FOIA—the Official Information Act—in 1982, which bears some resemblances to the Australian legislation, although it makes provision for the publication of internal rules and has many distinct characteristics. The legislation also repealed the NZ Official Secrets Act 1951. It would be pointless running through similar provisions once more, but it is worth pointing out that an Information Ombudsman has been created, the New Zealand Ombudsman in fact, to deal with information complaints. His recommendations *are* mandatory on the minister or department concerned and take effect from the commencement of the 22nd day after the day on which his *recommendation* is made to the department, unless, originally, the responsible minister otherwise directs or decides by order in council. The Ministerial veto was replaced by a Cabinet veto by way of an Order in Council in 1987 and has never been exercised.

---

11 Australian Law Reform Commission and Administrative Review Council *Discussion Paper 59* at p 11.
12 *Re State of Queensland and Department of Aviation* (1986) Admin Review 138.
13 Terrill p 104.
14 At p 112.
15 Eagles, Liddell and Taggert *Freedom of Information—New Zealand* (1992).

There is a public interest override on some exemptions including 'the constitutional conventions protecting policy advice'.

The Act also creates an information authority. Its duties are:

(I)   to review, as a first priority, the protection accorded to official information by any Act with a view to seeing whether that protection is both reasonable and compatible with the purposes of FOIA;

(II)   to define and review categories of official information with a view to enlarging the categories of official information to which access is given as a matter of right;

(III) to recommend the making of regulations prescribing:

(a)   categories of official information to which access is given as a matter of right;

(b)   such conditions, if any, as it considers appropriate in relation to the giving of access to any category of official information.

Further duties of the Authority include reviewing of the Act and of access practices and changes in such practices; inviting public as well as official comment about the Act; making suggestions for extension of the Act; and seeking advice from and conducting investigations into all appropriate authorities. For this latter duty, access to necessary documents is given subject to veto on account of national security and to prevent crime. The Information Authority can meet in public or in private, and it reports to Parliament. It has a life-span of five years.

In 1984-5, 354 requests for investigation were made to the Ombudsman. No additional staff or resources were provided. By 1995-96, the figure was 1165. The two areas causing most difficulty in the early years were those relating to personal and private information and to competitive commercial contracts. Now policy advice is also seen as a problematic area. Exemptions most commonly relied upon were the protection of confidentiality of advice and the internal working documents exemption protecting the 'free and frank' opinions of officials. The Ombudsman has found the former exemption too expansive and has sought to restrict its scope. He heard evidence that a failure to maintain full and frank discussion neutered or hindered the civil service, and similar views had emerged from Australia.[16] Tendering for government contracts had been kept confidential, and the Ombudsman has suggested that commercially confidential information should be separated from other information in tendering.

After the Ombudsman there is the possibility of judicial review of ministers' decisions; the Ombudsman has been successfully challenged before the courts. As in Canada there is a separate Privacy Commissioner

---

16   *Report of the Chief Ombudsman*, Wellington NZ (1984) and *Murtagh v Comr of Taxation*. See *Police Comr v Ombudsman* [1985] 1 NZLR 578, on a challenge to the Ombudsman's powers.

supervising the operation of the Privacy Act and a Privacy Act of 1993 covers both the public and private sectors. Specific codes are produced which are binding and tailored to individual industries.[17] An Official Information Amendment Act was passed by Parliament in 1987 and in that year a Local Government Official Information and Meetings Act was enacted. Under s 7 of the NZ Bill of Rights Act 1990, everyone has the right to freedom of expression including the freedom to seek, receive and impart information and opinion in any kind or form.

What is interesting about the New Zealand legislation is that it concentrates attention on the public interest in disclosure rather than a class or contents exemption as is the case with the UK FOIA (see chapter 6). There are also no excluded categories of information such as Cabinet documents. *A Policy Framework for Government Held Information* (1996) has recommended greater resort to the intent of making information available in advance of FOI requests. Readers are reminded of the situation in the USA and should compare the use of publication schemes in the UK.

Sweden[18]

Outside the common law world, freedom of information took root much earlier than the mid-1960s. Sweden has had a Freedom of the Press Act as part of its constitution since 1766, and all 'official' documents are now available for inspection and copying, although public corporations, defined as commercial organisations, are excluded. Further, internal memoranda are not available until filed, ie the matter to which they refer has been finally resolved. Documents received by, or dispatched by, the authority are within the terms of the Act. There are four areas of exempt information: national security and foreign affairs; suppression of crime and illegality; protection of legitimate economic interests; and personal privacy. The statutory details concerning exempt items are contained in the Secrecy Act and refer to classes of documents and not their contents. The Secrecy Act specifies a period for which a document will be secret: from two years to 70 years. Since 1981 the emphasis has been on increasing secrecy.[19] Internal review may follow a refusal, followed by an appeal to

---

17 On the UK Data Protection Commissioner and the use of codes see chapter 7 below.

18 For a useful survey of FOI in Europe, see the memorandum of evidence submitted to the House of Lords special committee to consider the Draft UK FOI Bill: HL 97 (1998-99) at p 35.

19 Following various security-sensitive leaks.

the administrative courts. Appeal is cheap and readily available. A Data
Act of 1973 is administered by a Data Inspection Board.[20]

The making of important decisions affecting the public is generally a
secret affair, though organised interests may seek to influence membership
of commissions of inquiry, administrative and even quasi-judicial bodies,
or sponsored MPs may press for membership. The views of civil servants
and advisers do not, however, remain concealed. A very large degree of
Swedish public administration is depoliticised in so far as many,
sometimes important, decisions are not taken by political overlords, or at
least they bear no formal responsibility for such decisions. They are taken
by and are the responsibility of administrators who must place pre-
eminence upon rationality and correctness, not their political survival.
This has caused one author to suggest that secrecy lies at the troubled
boundary between politics and reason: 'Secrecy will cease at the point at
which politics ends and reason begins... Politics is the art of defining
what the problems are and reason the act of solving them.'[1] How far secrecy
goes depends on how widely the ambit of politics is allowed freedom to
range. The distinction is too pat. However, the author quoted above
suggests that in Britain, the most secret of the countries which he
examined, election manifestos of political parties were the clearest and
most detailed of those he studied.[2]

One of the interesting points about the Swedish tradition is that its
emphasis on openness may cause increasing conflict with the requirements
of EU laws on access which are not as liberal. I shall adress this question
in chapter 8.

France

The final example comes from France although information laws, not
always of an FOI variety, exist in various states of the European Union.[3]
The French law on access to administrative documents was approved in
July 1978 and has been in force since December 1978. Those served by
the French administration have access to non-'name-linked' documents.
Like the French Data Processing and Liberties Act, the 1978 Act applies
to private organisations charged by the state with operating a public
service. The Act has been criticised for its vagueness and for the terms of

---

20   J Michael *The Politics of Secrecy* (1982), chapters 7 and 9. See Petren in Marsh
      (ed) *Public Access to Government Held Information* (1987).
1   KG Robertson *Public Secrets* (1982), pp 183–4.
2   Ibid. On the 'game theory' behind parliamentary questions and answers, see Sir
      M Quinlan *Answers in Parliament* in the Scott Report para D4.61, HC 115 (1995-
      6) and p 259 *et seq* below.
3   See Commission of the EC COM (93) 191 final, for an overview and n 18 above.

its exemptions. A special commission, the *Commission d'Accés aux Documents Administratifs*, was established to supervise the implementation of the law. The general feeling was that the Act required clarification. However, the access laws are available to citizens and non-citizens alike.[4] In 1993, there were 3,200 information complaints which were sent by CADA to the Conseil d'État

It has to be explained that French administrative law, the *droit administratif,* has a very good fact-finding procedure involving officials of the *Conseil d'État,* or local courts, and the *Commissaire du Gouvernement,* who represents the public interest when there is a dispute between the state and a citizen—the public interest is not equiparated with that of the state. These officials have access to documents and files, and refusal to hand over information or to give reasons for an adverse decision will be interpreted *against* the public body and will be taken as evidence of bad faith or improper motive.[5]

Conclusion

All the above examples reveal the different approaches adopted by countries operating in a liberal-democratic tradition and at broadly similar stages of economic development. The most recent recruit to FOIA excluding the UK has been the Republic of Ireland where Official Secrets Acts still operate under the influence after so many years of former British rule.[6] The different socio-cultural and political backgrounds of the countries have ensured variations in their approaches to FOI, although all have reacted to the growth of government and bureaucracy, the escalation of information gathering and control by executive agencies— and in some cases private bodies—and the inability of democratic institutions of representative government to oversee these developments effectively, albeit in different ways.

It might be pertinent to ask whether the legislative developments constitute an acknowledgment of the failure of representative government and the first faltering steps towards a more substantial participatory form of government. If this is claimed, then the legislation we have examined has a long way to go—which has been acknowledged recently in Australia and Canada. One might say that public disquiet has been bought off rather cheaply in the countries we have examined. The legislation can only

4   R Errera in *Marsh* note 20 above.
5   N Brown and J Bell *French Administrative Law* (4th edn, 1998).
6   See A McDonagh *Freedom of Information Law in Ireland* (1998). The OSA 1963 was amended by the FOIA to prevent proper disclosure under FOIA being punished under the OSA. No such action was taken in the UK FOIA.

operate within a cultural framework which is already in existence—a governmental attitude which *might* have to undergo change as the legislation works inwardly upon it, and a public attitude which is unknowing and unfamiliar with the use of information to challenge governmental presumptions. Expectations that the legislation by itself will achieve the goals which many FOI advocates hope for are pie in the sky. Different public attitudes and different governmental institutions are necessary for the success of FOI legislation.

But we are running ahead of ourselves. We have seen how far progress has been made in other highly developed states. Some of those states in their constitutional arrangements have been directly inspired by the Westminster style of government. It is now time to account for the reasons or forces which have prevailed against such developments in the UK, and which may account for the particular features of the UK law which emerged in 2000.

The overseas legislation was also very instructive when the UK FOI Bill was first presented to the Commons Select Committee on Public Administration for the latter to scrutinise (see chapter 6). Many of the glaring deficiencies in the draft Bill compared badly with overseas legislation and the most objectionable of the provisions seemed to represent an effort to break with internationally accepted norms of conduct. The Acts in Australia, Canada, Ireland and New Zealand all possessed long titles or opening purpose clauses which afforded a central importance to openness and access in the way in which the legislation was interpreted. This was denied in the UK FOIA (see chapter 6).

3 Government and information—an historical development

Government control of information in Britain did not first emerge as a problem for government in 1889, when the first Official Secrets Act was passed.[1] Control of information had been a central preoccupation of government since government first assumed responsibility for defence, taxation and administration, and even before. The King's household, until the Tudor monarchy, was characterised by personal government on the advice of trusted counsellors who remained bound by allegiance and confidence to the Crown. Serious breaches of confidence might involve a charge of treason in the form of adhering to the King's enemies under the Act of 1351, which was extended well beyond the terms of the statute by judicial decisions.[2] High treason 'was regarded as a final denial of the divine order of things as established in the body politic and defined in the oath of allegiance'.[3]

Breaches of confidence were not always problematic in the absence of widespread printing and publishing facilities. More pressing for the power in existence was the control of the spread of seditious ideas or movements which could threaten its position. This point is vividly illustrated by the breach with the Church of Rome and the accumulation of statutes extending treason to punish *inter alios* those who 'shall by writing, printing, preaching, speech, express words or sayings, maliciously, advisedly and directly publish, set forth, and affirm that the Queen our said sovereign lady Queen Elizabeth is an heretic, schismatic, tyrant, infidel or an usurper of the Crown of the said realms or any of them... .'[4] Even

1 As first drafted, it was entitled Breach of Official Trust Bill.
2 Elton *The Tudor Constitution* (2nd edn, 1981), p 59; Cf J Bellamy *The Tudor Law of Treason* (1979).
3 Elton. op cit.
4 13 Eliz I, c I (1571).

before the advent of the Tudor dynasty, the procedure for treason trials was weighted heavily in favour of the Crown.[5] What was novel about the Tudor dynasty was the revolution in government which took place.[6]

After 1530, there 'was a rejection of the medieval conception of the kingdom as the King's estate, his private concern properly administered by his private organisation; it conceived its task to be national, its support and scope to be nationwide, and its administrative needs, therefore, divorced from the King's household'.[7] On governmental administration, the change is characterised by the individual assertion of King's advisers as opposed to the 'anonymity' of the medieval period. Almost all the available state papers from 1530-40 are those of Thomas Cromwell, Henry VIII's minister of State. A fastidious keeper of records, he also presided over an Act of 1536 'concerning the Clerkes of the Signet and Privie Seale' which enacted that no manner of writing was to pass the great seals[8] of England, Ireland, the Duchy of Lancaster and the Principality of Wales, or 'by process out of the Exchequer', unless it had first been examined by the King's principal secretary or a clerk of the signet.[9]

From the mid-1530s onwards, the Privy Council developed as an institution whose name signified 'the special "secretness" or closeness to the King of his more intimate advisers', a 'special and more important branch of the Council' based upon the exclusiveness of its 19 or so members.[10] Nevertheless, although the Council established its right to information, particularly on foreign affairs, Cromwell 'knew and insisted that serious business should be transacted in conversations with the King and himself.'[11] He acted, according to Elton, 'in practice like a somewhat despotic Prime Minister presiding over a cabinet of comparative mediocrities'. The period witnessed the emergence of national departments of state, bureaucratically organised and independent of the King's household, but responsible to the Crown. Responsibility to Parliament had yet to come, but we should note that proceedings in Parliament itself were secret, breach of secrecy constituting a serious contempt. By Elizabethan times, Parliamentary affairs were 'the common talk of tavern life',[12] however, in spite of the injunction that 'Every person of the Parliament ought to keep secret, and not to disclose, the secrets and things done and spoken in the Parliament house'.[13] Freedom of debate,

5   Elton, though see his *Policy and Police* (1972).
6   Elton *The Tudor Revolution in Government* (1953).
7   Op cit, p 4.
8   See chapter 3 of Elton *The Tudor Constitution* for a discussion of the seals.
9   The fine for disobedience was £10 – half to the Crown and half to the informer.
10   Elton, op cit n 6 above, pp 316 *et seq.*
11   Ibid, p 355.
12   Neale *House of Commons* (1949), pp 416 *et seq.*
13   Cited in D Englefield *Parliament and Information* (1980).

and freedom from the monarch's intervention, required secrecy. In 1628, it was confirmed that speeches would not be printed in the *Journal*, but by 1641 the House decided to print various notes and minutes of its proceedings to gain support in the City against Charles I.[14] In 1771, the House commenced proceedings against John Wilkes, who had published details of Parliamentary proceedings.[15] The House of Commons won its legal case, but press reporting developed informally in ensuing years. Such reporting was assisted by the growing practice of Parliament publishing its reports which brought the subject of Parliamentary privilege into conflict with the legal right right not to be defamed,[16] most famously in *Stockdale v Hansard* and subsequent litigation.[17] And yet, over 200 years after Wilkes's battles to open up Parliament, the Speaker of the House ruled in the Zircon episode in 1987 that there was information which not even MPs *in* Parliament could be apprised of.[18]

Crown, mace and information

Parliament saw secrecy for its proceedings as a necessary protection against the Crown's absolutist tendencies. An astute monarch had other ways of rendering Parliament compliant. His advisers, by courtesy of sympathetic MPs, would know what was what.

In 1641, Pym's Ten Propositions to the Lords included as number three that the King commit 'his own business, and the affairs of the Kingdom, to such councillors and officers as the Parliament may have cause to confide in'. The Nineteen Propositions of Parliament of 1 June 1642 proposed that privy Councillors and ministers be approved by both Houses of Parliament. Further, 'the great affairs of the Kingdom may not be concluded or transacted by the advice of private men, or by any unknown or unsworn councillors, but that such matters as concern the public, and

14 *Englefield.* Nb C. Parry 'Legislatures and Secrecy' (1954) 67 Harv LR 737.
15 The House still maintains its right to secure the privacy of its debates, eg in wartime. The Parliamentary Papers Act 1840 gave the protection of absolute privilege to parliamentary papers. For the position of command papers, see HC 261 (1969– 70); and Cmnd 5909, p 55. Press and broadcast reports are protected by qualified privilege: see P Leopold on 'live' broadcasting (1987) Public Law 524.
16 Unless authorised by *legislation.*
17 *Stockdale v Hansard* (1839) 9 Ad & El 1; *Case of Sheriff of Middlesex* (1840) 11 Ad & El 273. An order of the House of Commons could not override the common law of defamation. However, the courts in the second case were powerless to intervene by *habeas corpus* in the face of a statement from the House that Stockdale and two sheriffs had been committed by the House for contempt when attempting to enforce the earlier judgment.
18 HC Debs, 22 January 1987 and 26 January 1987. See D Campbell, *New Statesman*, 23 January 1987, on the Zircon satellite intelligence system. For the report from the Committee on Privileges, see HC 365 (1986–7).

are proper for the High Court of Parliament ... may be debated, resolved and transacted only in Parliament, and not elsewhere',[19] and the King should act only on the public behalf on the advice of a majority of Privy Councillors. Parliament wanted to know who advised the King, so that they could be made accountable to Parliament. How had this come to pass?

Information and accountability—the struggle

In a system of government that is monistic—that is, one which is assembled around one power base—accountability is achieved by protection of the status quo through the power of tradition, the force of custom, the influence of an unquestioned hierarchy reflecting a naturally ordained harmony: 'Take but degree away, untune that string / And, hark! what discord follows.'[20] When government is arranged around pluralistic competing forces, any assertion of a status quo maintaining the natural supremacy of one branch of public power over another is less readily justified by appeals to tradition. The emerging conflict between competing forces inevitably centres on the *nature* of accountability itself—what form does it take, to whom and by what process? Accountability is impossible in any real sense unless the body exercising power accounts to whoever asserts the right to expect an explanation, a justification for action or inaction, for acts of prerogative and for policy. Knowing who did what, and why, is the first step to rendering an institution or person accountable.

In the English tradition, the King escaped personal liability in law— the King can do no wrong.[1] Five important factors emerge on the route to constitutional monarchy: the Crown must act through a servant; a servant cannot plead in defence an unlawful command of the King; the King must be advised by councillors acceptable to Parliament; the King's will must be a matter of record; and the Commons has the power of inquiry as a necessary prelude to impeachment of the Crown's ministers.[2] Honoured as much in the breach as in the observance, these principles, their development and scope taxed the minds of the finest constitutional and legal experts of the seventeenth century as well as, with necessary modifications, their counterparts in America in more recent times.[3]

---

19 My emphasis.
20 *Troilus and Cressida*, I, iii, 109.
1   Although events as far back as 1215 testified to the view that the King could do wrong, see Art 61 of *Magna Carta*.
2   C Roberts *The Growth of Responsible Government in Stuart England* (1966), chapter 1.
3   The Watergate and Irangate, or Snoozegate, episodes, for instance and Clinton's sexual peccadilloes. See R Berger *Impeachment* (1973).

By the beginning of the seventeenth century the problem facing Parliament in controlling the King concerned control over his policies; which meant, in turn, the problem of who should advise on those policies. The claim that the Crown had a prerogative right to choose its own advisers without Parliamentary interference fell increasingly on deaf ears when the Commons from 1604 'sought to superintend a public, not a personal, administration' of the Crown.[4]

Equally important was the emergence of the Commons as *the* force in Parliament with an established political and corporate identity. The English Revolution began in a constitutional, if not material, sense when the Commons insisted on being informed of who advised the Crown so that they could be made accountable for any 'unlawful, injurious or hateful' advice and policies. Unlike the barons of previous centuries, who were content to bloody the King's nose on individual occasions by punishing his high advisers, the Commons was embarking on a process that would lead to oversight of public administration. On the eve of the Civil War in 1642, what most members wished for was 'the right to vote impeachments against ministers whose faults they could declare to be crimes, and the right to vote censures against counsellors whose advice to the King they could read in Council books'.[5] Parliamentarians and pamphleteers realised that it was of cardinal importance to discover who provided the King with 'evil counsel', not simply to punish those who followed his 'tyrannous' orders. Publicity of advice was the universal desideratum. Its realisation, of course, would run counter to every tradition of government.

The Commons wanted to know, not necessarily to nominate. The interregnum of 1649-60 was seen by many as an illustration of the undesirability of placing the executive within the legislature so that both were part of an indiscriminate whole. In that period, however, there were

> [by] the right of inquiry, of the right of interrogation, of the right of surveillance, of the right of criticism, and of the right of censure inculcated in MPs habits not even the Restoration could erase. [MPs] … questioned ministers of state. They clamoured for information. They objected to oaths of secrecy taken by their own committees. They sent committees of inquiry into the counties. They examined accounts and appropriated revenues. They investigated military failures and criticised naval designs. They opposed, condemned, criticised and censured those whom they found remiss in the performance of their duties.[6]

4   *Roberts*, p 9.
5   Ibid, p 118.
6   Ibid, p 153.

By 1667, Charles II had to accept a statutory commission with power to subpoena any royal servant and cross-examine him under oath and with access to all records *vis-à-vis* the public accounts. There was a regal reaction. Increasing use was made of special committees of the Privy Council to deal with confidential matters, eg the Committee of Intelligence and the 'Cabinet Council'. Charles promised to discuss affairs of public importance with the Privy Council at all times. A small group of confidential ministers acted as 'an informal quorum' of the Council, a trend which James II continued and reinforced:

> Throughout this century, behind the formal apparatus of councils, cabinets, committees and camarillas lay the simple, usually quite easy, relationship between the King and one or two trusted ministers.... The really important decisions were taken in complete privacy, without surviving records.[7]

A royal proclamation of 1674 forbade Charles's subjects to 'intermeddle in private discourse with state affairs, or the persons of the King's ministers'. By that date, however, the Commons had questioned his ministers on 'the innermost secrets of state', and had voted addresses to the Crown for their removal, refusing to grant supply until they were. To extract advice given to the King in his Cabinet Council, his advisers had to be brought before the Commons and intimidated. If that failed, the Commons had to resort to common fame: if a minister was known to be a party to the Council which advised the King and of which the Commons disapproved, this could form the basis of an address from the Commons that he be removed from office—but it could not form the basis of an impeachment. The enduring legacy of Court and Parliamentary battles between the years 1674 and 1681 was the voting of addresses against the King's ministers, not the voting of impeachments, which were dilatory and clumsy affairs. Having secured freedom of speech, debate and proceedings in 1689,[8] Parliament, in the Act of Settlement of 1701, insisted that important business was to be conducted in the Privy Council and councillors were to sign all resolutions to which they assented. This solved the problem of identity, but it was unworkable and was repealed in 1706.

Also repealed in 1706 was the clause of the 1701 Act which stipulated that 'no person who has an office or place of profit under the King ... shall be capable of serving as a member of the House of Commons'. As the eighteenth century unfolded, it became increasingly obvious that a most commodious partnership between Crown and Parliament could be

7   JP Kenyon *The Stuart Constitution* (1st edn, 1966), p 479.
8   Bill of Rights, I Will and Mary Sess 2, chapter 2.

built around an arrangement whereby the King appointed as leading ministers those who could control the Commons but the Commons, on their side, knew who they were. That did not mean they were entitled to know what ministers knew. Ministers might be forced to resign because of a lack of confidence among members of Parliament, but the Commons has rarely questioned ministers' right to keep confidential the innermost secrets of the cabinet, the closet or even, in the absence of an untoward event, the department of State. The Commons in its collective identity might not expect this, but others, including individual MPs, the press, the public, have. The Commons is generally content to be informed on terms laid down by the executive. At that moment when the power of the Commons to inquire into Crown business was unequivocally established, it was only operable to the extent that the power of a minister controlling a majority party in the Commons allowed it. The implications for his own position should an inquiry cause embarrassment were obvious enough. In a Parliamentary system of government, the emergence of collective and individual responsibility of ministers seemed inescapable. The irony is that the doctrines our forebears chanced upon to gain information on who was responsible for what, came to constitute the greatest barrier to a wider Parliamentary and public access to information.

By the early 1700s it was established that Parliament could inquire, investigate and criticise; but ministers initiated. And what is more, they selected the materials for investigation:

> this enquiry, Sir, will produce no great information if those whose conduct is examined, are allowed to select the evidence.[9]

Throughout the later stages of the eighteenth century and into the nineteenth century there was a growth of interest among ordinary MPs in every aspect of executive activity, initiated by concern over expenditure. With an increasing interest in social and economic problems it was inevitable that the Grand Inquest of the Nation would:

> inquire into everything which it concerns the public well to know; and *they themselves* I think, are entrusted with the determination of what falls within that category.[10]

---

9   William Pitt, II Parl Hist England 1009 (1741), cited in Berger *Executive Privilege* (1974). Berger believes that Parliament asserted an unqualified right: 'it is our duty', said Pitt, 'to inquire into every step of publick management, either abroad or at home, in order to see that nothing is done amiss' (pp 169–71). Berger's own choice of examples does not support this see p 170.

10 *Howard v Gosset* (1845) 10 QB 359 at 379–80, *per* Coleridge J. Unqualified acceptance of this dictum by Berger seems a little incautious.

As we shall see, this is a high-water mark, for they may inquire into what they want but they do not always get what they want. We should not think that the desire for a greater dissemination of information was restricted to Parliament, however.

Information and censorship

Although the demands for information and accountability formed the constitutional centrepiece of the seventeenth century, a wider audience was also involved. It was a period of prevalent censorship, although this had existed since 1408 and Archbishop Arundel's *Constitutions*. Henry VIII imposed religious censorship in 1530 before the breach with Rome, and this was augmented by royal proclamations, injunctions, Privy Council orders and Star Chamber decrees. The Star Chamber decree of 11 July 1637 was 'the most elaborate instrument in English history for the suppression of undesired publication; nothing was unforeseen except the determination with which it was defied'.[11] It became a general offence to print, import or sell 'any seditious, scismaticall or offensive Bookes or Pamphlets', and no book could be printed unless licensed, or relicensed if previously printed, and entered into the Stationers' Register.[12] The abolition of Star Chamber in 1641 left the press virtually without regulation, confirming Selden's remarks that there is 'no Law to prevent the printing of any Bookes in England, only a decree in Star Chamber'. The control over printing had been an exercise of royal prerogative . The public might write of the benefits on the alternatives of who should counsel the King in a way they had never done before, but such publication was short lived. By June 1643, Parliament passed an order which Milton described as the 'immediate image' of the decree of 1637. This order stimulated his *Areopagitica* containing his famous defence of freedom of the press and, excluding Catholics, religious toleration. The order established 'licensing, registration, signature, copyright, import control, search and seizure, arrest, imprisonment by order of Parliamentary committee and association of the Stationers in administering the order'.[13] Except for short periods in the Commonwealth, the Puritan Revolution maintained a continuous licensing of printing in England. The preoccupation of censors turned more and more to the prohibition of obscene, scandalous or scurrilous literature, which in the hands of a Walpole could be moulded into a pervasive form of political censorship, even though general censorship of the press under law by the Stationers'

11 Complete Prose Works of John Milton, Vol II (Yale UP 1958), p 159.
12 The Stationers' Company owned a monopoly of book publishing in England.
13 Berger *Executive Privilege*, p 163.

Company ceased in 1694.[14] The Spycatcher episode in the second half of the 1980s, which I examine elsewhere, at one stage threatened to resurrect a wide form of legal censorship from the seventeenth century.[15]

The executive and Parliament—the die is cast

From 1670 onwards, the Commons 'became immensely sensitive to the tactics used by the Court to circumscribe their activities or reduce their capacity for independent criticism. Naturally, they feared secret influence and they called time and time again for a statement about expenditure from the Secret Service Fund.'[16] Sir Robert Walpole was, by the 1720s, the controller of the Secret Service money and, in that capacity, was rightly regarded as the head of the Government's patronage system and thus the 'chief figure in the Ministry'.[17] He dedicated his efforts to an obsessive anti-Jacobite campaign, building up a 'vast web of counter-espionage with his own spies in all capitals and ports in Europe'.[18] He preferred to use ad hoc meetings of an inner cabinet, meeting in the houses of the chief secretaries, instead of the full cabinet which was large and unwieldy, or to have secret discussions with 'his tried and loyal supporters' or private individual interviews. 'He preferred the closet to the Cabinet', or at best a small efficient cabinet in which he could secure a majority.[19] All the while his 'love of administration, his desire to see it based efficiently on knowledge [and information] was very much in tune with the more advanced opinion of his age'.[20] It is hardly surprising that it was Walpole's use of Secret Service money for covert purposes which activated some of the most heated exchanges between Parliament and Government in this period on Parliament's right to be informed.

By the second half of the eighteenth century, the Commons could exercise its right to information in a variety of ways. A member could move that 'a return should be made to the House providing statistical or other information about a specific subject',[1] such as the collection and management of the tax revenue, public expenditure and general statistics. 'But information about the exercise of the prerogative, eg treaties with foreign powers, dispatches to and from Governors of colonies, and returns

14 Holdsworth (1920) 29 Yale LJ 841. For censorship and obscenity law, see G Robertson *Obscenity* (1979).
15 P 121 *et seq* below.
16 JH Plumb The Growth of Political Stability in England 1675–1725 (1967), p 47.
17 Plumb *Sir Robert Walpole* Vol I (1956), p 348.
18 Ibid, vol II (1960), p 41.
19 Ibid, p 330.
20 Ibid, p 234.
1   Sir Norman Chester *The English Administrative System 1780–1870* (1981). I am indebted to Chester's work for information on the following six pages.

connected with the administration of justice or the activities of one of the Secretaries of State could be obtained only by an address to the Crown.'[2] The House could not demand this information; it had to request politely.

The Government also provided information by way of reports and papers circulated by command of the Crown. This was the usual arrangement for the reports and evidence of Royal Commissions. An increasing number of reports were ordered to be printed by the Commons, not the least of which were the reports of the factory inspectors to the Home Secretary, a point seized on by Karl Marx in *Das Kapital.* These were published every six months, and 'They therefore provide regular and official statistics of the voracious appetite of the capitalists for surplus labour'.[3] However, 'let us note that England figures in the foreground here because it is the classic representative of capitalist production, and it is the only country to possess a continuous set of official statistics relating to the matters we are considering', viz capitalist economic exploitation.

Sir Norman Chester remarked how a requirement to provide returns and annual reports became a regular feature of Acts of Parliament. 'As early as 1787 an Act[4] placed an obligation on the Treasury to lay before Parliament annually an account of the produce of the duties of Customs, Excise, Stamps and the Expenses.' From 1803, the Treasury had to submit each year an account of the total revenues of Great Britain, together with an account of the Consolidated Fund and other financial details. Information was required on a regular basis on the activities of the executive in areas of current concern.[5] The requests produced an increasing workload for departments, necessitating the creation of specialised officers. In 1832, a statistical branch in the Board of Trade was agreed to by the Treasury.

Special agencies, boards or even local councils created by Parliament inevitably had to report back to Parliament, sometimes directly, more usually via a minister. Inspectors of Prisons appointed under an Act of 1835 are an example of the latter, and the Registrar of Joint Stock Companies reported back via the Board of Trade. Even where a statute remained silent on the duty of publication, practice often dictated that reports would be submitted to Parliament via the minister, eg reports of inspectors of schools and factories.

Committees of MPs could take evidence and report with recommendations, providing 'a mass of information not only to

---

2   Ibid, p 99.
3   Pelican edition (1976), vol I, p 349.
4   27 Geo III, c 13.
5   Eg the numbers employed by public departments and in public offices, as well as their salaries, 50 Geo. III, c 117: *Chester*, p 100.

Parliament but also for the Press and general public'.[6] However, these committees existed only for one session, and often could not complete their inquiries. They were not peripatetic, so witnesses had to be summoned to London. Nor was there a guarantee that a government would do anything about their recommendations. Between 1832 and 1862, 'Some 190 Royal Commissions were appointed to deal with subjects such as: Poor Relief; Municipal Corporations; Education; Military Promotions and County Courts'. They were appointed and had their terms of reference drawn up by government. Departmental committees, though not popular before 1870, were used. They comprised two or three officials, but were under no obligation to publish their reports. The Northcote-Trevelyan Report of 1854 on the civil service is a famous example of such a report which was in fact published and formed the basis of civil service reform for well into the twentieth century.

Nor were changes in government administration the only development. In 1803 the House recognised the right of the press by reserving special seats in the public gallery for the use of reporters. *Hansard* reports of debates commenced in the same year. Published debates became far more detailed; official division lists were published in 1836, thereby making it clear how particular MPs had voted. 'This made Members more consciously answerable to their constituents or to the outside groups interested in the outcome of their vote.'[7] More frequent publication of Parliamentary materials and greater availability of information became increasingly common. Parliamentary questions became more ordered and routinised, as did MPs' questioning of ministers on the floor of the House.

However, government still had ultimate control over what became public. Certain areas, while not arousing a great deal of public interest, were sensitive; these included police special branch, aliens, subversives and foreign policy. In foreign policy, dispatches and 'blue books'[8] were doctored before publication, or correspondence was simply not acknowledged. The Reform Acts of 1832 and 1867 helped to dismember the old consensus which had developed throughout the previous century between government and Parliamentary elites. The growth of the press, the emergence of strong political parties and organised party political conflict, the development of interest group politics[9] all contributed to a wider group beyond the two above which wished to be informed of public business. Until the 1830s, the battle for information had largely been fought out in a constitutional struggle between Crown and Commons, and between court and country. The reforms of the nineteenth century acted

6   Ibid, pp 102–3.
7   Ibid, pp 107–9.
8   These were despatches between the British Government, its embassies and foreign governments. I am grateful to Bernard Porter for this information.
9   SH Beer *Modern British Politics* (1982).

as a midwife to a prolonged labour for a fuller democracy. It was time for power holders not only to set the agenda for Parliament but to take active steps to prevent an unwished-for dissemination of information from departments of state.

Make no mistake, we have witnessed an enormous growth in the information business until the 1870s; government could not resist that. But information was provided on terms. The moment that compact was threatened by forces beyond the control of government and Parliament, government felt the necessity for legislation to maintain the culture of secrecy. 'As newspapers ... became almost as much a part of the political arena as the chamber of the House of Commons so most permanent officials learned to keep away from them.'[10] But not all officials or citizens wanted this isolation. Even in the eighteenth century, societies aimed at the spread of public opinion were legion[11] and included the Society for Constitutional Information. Trade and work associations emerged alongside older corporatist groups such as the church, aristocracy, country gentry, the inns of court and the universities.[12] Throughout the nineteenth century, however, a problem was developing within government departments. What if servants of the Crown broke their trust of confidentiality?

Officials and secrecy in central government

The Northcote-Trevelyan Report of 1854 recommended competitive entry to the civil service based upon examination. Sir George Cornewall Lewis wrote:

> One of the first qualities required in the clerks of a public office is trustworthiness.... The honourable secrecy which has distinguished the clerks of our superior offices ... cannot be too highly commended. But this discreet reserve depends on qualities which cannot be made the subject of examination.[13]

Much had changed in the previous years. In 1780, the typical 'Cabinet minister had the assistance of only a few clerks. The Home Office contained only four rooms and sometimes handled less than twenty letters a day.'[14]

10 *Chester*, p 108.
11 Eg Society for Supporting the Bill of Rights, the Society of the Freedom of the People (1792), the London Corresponding Society (1792).
12 Beer op. cit.
13 *Chester*, p 158.
14 Ibid, pp 282 *et seq*. The Colonial Office in nine months in 1775–6 used 2,000 pens; it employed nine officials!

The Treasury and Admiralty Boards with 'satellite and subordinate departments' were much larger. Most of the departments had a small staff who were largely engaged in copying documents and letters and other routine tasks.

By 1870, developments in administrative practice had altered departments beyond recognition. In the Treasury, the number of registered papers averaged between 2,500 and 3,000 a year in the period 1783-93; by 1800 it was 4,812. By 1820, the figure had risen to 22,288 and by 1849 it was 29,914. The Home Office was handling over 13,500 letters per annum.[15] The increasing number and routinisation of Parliamentary questions and the increasing workload of departments meant that a minister could no longer answer all questions about his department impromptu. Notice of questions was required and permanent staff prepared the answers. The Home Secretary was particularly busy.[16]

As departments grew in size, the problem of confidentiality became more acute. Older clerks steeped in the traditions of Crown service were invariably able to maintain a discreet silence about their work. The increasing number of 'outsiders' appointed to senior posts were less tractable. It was not unknown for such senior officials to espouse a cause openly, eg free trade, or to liaise with MPs, to encourage the establishment of select committees and feed them with evidence. They advised in private and advocated in public. Reform, says Chester, was what they advocated.[17]

It was difficult for ministers to perceive how such behaviour was compatible with individual ministerial responsibility. It could reveal antagonisms; it could pressurise a minister into a course of conduct which he did not favour. Peel as Prime Minister referred to Trevelyan as a 'consummate fool' for publishing departmental information in a letter to the *Morning Chronicle*. What *was* expected is caught in the following lines of Sir James Stephen:[18]

> Be assured that ... my office is, and, ought to be, that of a mere Subordinate ... [an] effective and submissive Servant to its Head ... he sustains the undivided responsibility for every decision taken here and that I am responsible only for supplying him ... with all the necessary materials for forming such decisions.

Reports to departments by their inspectors and agencies often hit a controversial tone which governments found embarrassing and which was 'inconsistent with the character such reports ought to bear'. The Home

15   Ibid.
16   The Home Secretary was responsible for prisons, the police in a general sense, poor relief, factory conditions and local government.
17   *Chester*, p 312.
18   Ibid, p 315.

Office instructed inspectors not to publish correspondence with the department or information outside the strict terms of their duties. The Education Minister censored and threatened to refuse to publish reports critical of government policy: 'It would be a mischievous principle, to lay down that the heads of each Department ... should be compelled to print indiscriminately at the public cost everything sent into them by their subordinate agents.'[19] This problem would increase as departments syphoned off executive or regulatory functions to an ever-widening range of bodies.

Parliament had expressed its desire to be informed of the contents of reports from inspectors and agencies to departmental heads. The thrust of the argument was that Parliament had a right to be kept fully informed about the administration which it was responsible for financing, and this included the ungarbled comments of those who had direct oversight over aspects of that administration. The President (Secretary of State) of the Education Department expressed a point of general principle in 1863 when he stated that it was an issue of general importance 'whether in the Education Department there shall or shall not be that discipline which exists, and is found necessary, in every Department of the State'.[20] Administration was impossible without the loyalty of 'these gentlemen'[1]

> If the House chooses to say that the Inspectors are to report directly to it of course we shall instruct them to obey the order; but if the reports are to pass through our hands, I hold it to be the first principle of official duty to enforce that sort of reticence and reserve which all official men are bound to practise ... no public Department ... can be expected to carry on its Operations with success, if it is obliged to print controversies maintained against itself by the very persons whom it employs to carry out the objects entrusted to its charge.[2]

Inspectors were thus neutered in the fashion of other officials. A select committee investigated the question of ministerial censorship and reported that ministers had exercised their powers fairly and that no objection was made by ministers to *statements of facts*. This loophole was finally to be sealed in 1911.

19   The Vice President of the Privy Council; Chester, p 318.
20   *Chester*, p 320.
1   See Robertson *Public Secrets* (1982), chapter 4.
2   *Chester*, p 320.

Legal control of information

Franz Kafka wrote that 'Official decisions are as shy as young girls'. The government did not find them as shy as it would have liked. Legislation, it asserted, was necessary and justified to protect official secrets.

A series of events from the 1830s onwards highlighted particular problems for ministers and senior civil servants over unauthorised disclosure of official information. One concerned the sale and publication of diaries and memoirs kept by officials and diplomats and the Government's attempts to prevent publication by court injunction.[3] The legal question concerned the right of property in the memoirs—usually concerning foreign affairs—and the Foreign Office was pressing for right of ownership and delivery to it of the papers. According to the records, the first case of this kind occurred in 1833, and judgment was entered for the Foreign Office. The Government was successful in other cases. Establishing a right of property in the information that was in question in these cases was bound to cause legal complexity. Absent larceny or treason, and departments could find the position heavy going. Such was the case in 1847 when *The Times* published correspondence relating to the Congress of Vienna. The Foreign Office was advised that property rights were difficult to establish and publication was not prevented, in spite of the FO's rule that materials after 1760 were not available for public inspection. In other cases larceny was charged but an essential ingredient of the offence—permanent deprivation of the article in question where there had merely been a temporary removal and copying—was missing.[4] There was no legal concept of 'official information' which was protected by the law against unauthorised dissemination thereby rendering it an 'official secret'.

By the 1870s, the large anonymous government department had been established; ministerial responsibility was faithfully accepted and party loyalty and pressure would prevent Parliamentary majorities pressing for information which could make them a nuisance. But could the ministers' servants be trusted?

In 1873 a Treasury minute on *The Premature Disclosure of Official Documents* was issued.[5] It expressed concern at what today we would refer to as civil service 'leaks' to the press. Dismissal was threatened by the Lords Commissioners of the Treasury in cases where officials were guilty of these offences which were of 'the gravest character'. The minute appealed to the civil servants' sense of honour, fidelity and trustworthiness—in short their bureaucratic professionalism. A further

---

3   See *Robertson*, note 1 above, for examples from the public records.
4   DGT Williams *Not In the Public Interest* (1965). The civil law of confidentiality was in an elementary state: *Prince Albert v Strange* (1849) 1 Mac & G 25.
5   *Robertson*, pp 53 et seq.

minute of 1875 warned civil servants of the serious consequences of close links with the press, and a Treasury minute of 1884 prohibited the publication of 'official information' without authority.[6] But neither the circulars nor minutes, nor an amendment to the law of larceny in 1861, plugged the holes. Home Office circulars of 1884 and 1896 to its factory inspectorates warned them not to disclose information to Parliamentary committees or to courts where privilege could be claimed. Robertson has shown how by 1914 Treasury minutes, memoranda and rules covered diverse matters. These included the production of information before select committees of Parliament, the political activities of civil servants, restriction of publication by officials of works from official sources, and standardisation of the rules governing publication by departments of their documents. Exceptions were made for 'internal documents, foreign relations, privacy of the individual, secret service and "scalping" and other such atrocities in war'.[7] These remained completely secret.

The Treasury assumed responsibility from the Admiralty for drafting a Bill making it an offence 'improperly [to] divulge official information'. This would cover the whole public service. After one abortive attempt, it passed into law as the Official Secrets Act 1889. The statute provided for the prosecution and punishment of unauthorised disclosure of official information by penalty of the criminal law. Details of this legislation are provided elsewhere.[8] By 1903, however, it was clear to the War Office that the legislation had incurable defects as it placed on the state the burden of proving both *mens rea* and that it was not in the interest of the state that such communication take place. Newspapers which published leaked information were not punished, and convictions could only be secured where the Government testified to the truth of the information published. An official report of 1909 recommended greater powers of arrest and search and seizure.[9] The most persuasive evidence to the committee had related to German spies, about whom there were numerous cases. Not one case had been reported by the police, although information had been provided by 'private individuals', fuelling speculation as to their identity and motives and whether they in fact existed.[10]

The committee's recommendations were aimed at espionage, and so it recommended that the Bill should be introduced by the Secretary for War

6　Ibid.
7　Ibid, p 61. Hitherto, the Treasury allowed no publication of materials after 1759; the War Office after 1830; and the Home Office after 1778.
8　Williams op cit..
9　A sub-committee on Foreign Espionage of the Committee of Imperial Defence conducted the investigation.
10　There were 47 allegations of espionage or suspicious activities by Germans in 1908, and 31 in the first three months of 1909: *Robertson,* p 64; see also D French (1978) 21 The Historical Journal 355.

and not the Home Secretary. This must rank as one of the most notable postures of disingenuousness by any government.

The Act of 1911

The Official Secrets Act (OSA) which finally emerged in 1911 did not simply strengthen the anti-espionage provisions to assist national security in s 1. Section 2 imposed the widest prohibition, on pain of criminal prosecution, on unauthorised dissemination of official information. And yet s 2 was not mentioned once in the Parliamentary debates, nor did the Government give a full explanation of the Bill. Parliament was anxious to pass the Bill to protect the security of the nation. 'There was no doubt, however,' believed Franks in his 1972 departmental report on s 2, 'that the Bill had, and was intended by the Government to have, a wider scope'.[11] Franks's own account of the circumstances surrounding the enactment of the 1911 Act is succinct, but eloquent testimony:

> It was in these circumstances that the 1911 legislation passed through Parliament with little debate. The country was in crisis and it was late summer. The debates on the Bill in the House of Lords were brief and the House of Commons passed it in one afternoon with no detailed scrutiny and virtually without debate. The debates give a clear impression of crisis legislation, aimed mainly at espionage. Closer study, and reference to official sources, reveal a different story. This legislation had been long desired by governments. It had been carefully prepared over a period of years. One of its objects was to give greater protection against leakages of any kind of official information whether or not connected with defence or national security. This was clear enough from the text of the Bill alone. Although s 2 of the Act was much wider in a number of respects than s 2 of the 1889 Act, the files suggest that the Government in 1911 honestly believed that it introduced no new principle, but merely put into practice more effectually the principle of using criminal sanctions to protect official information. At all events, the Government elected not to volunteer complete explanations of their Bill in Parliament. And Parliament, in the special circumstances of that summer, did not look behind the explanations offered.[12]

---

11 Cmnd 5104, vol I (1972), para 53.
12 Ibid, para 50.

The provisions of the Act require some general explanation. Franks pointed out that misapprehension was common; that many 'leaks' were not leaks at all, but authorised; that the signing of a declaration of notice by all civil servants and government contractors, research workers and others does not mean that express prior authorisation for dissemination is *always* required, and the declaration does not mean that it covers *all* official information. The drafting was, however, ambiguous and misleading—one must suspect deliberately so. It was often referred to as a 'catch all' provision—that it covered leaks that were harmful to the public interest and those that were harmless. Franks also indicated that s 2 did not stand alone; it supported the culture of secrecy and confidentiality that was inherent in the working of our constitution which we have examined along with vetting for sensitive posts, security classifications[13] and privacy markings. Security classifications until 1994 were: *Top Secret*—publication or disclosure would cause exceptionally great damage to the nation; *Secret*—publication, etc, would cause serious injury to the interests of the nation; *Confidential*—publication, etc, would be prejudicial to the interests of the nation; *Restricted*—publication, etc, would be undesirable in the interests of the nation. Privacy markings cover *Commercial—in Confidence*; *Management—in Confidence* and *Staff—in Confidence*. 'Confidential means secret.' As we shall soon see, security classifications were redrafted after the introduction of new official secrecy laws. The 'D notice' system covering the press and media will be examined in the next chapter, together with other devices protecting secrecy.

In 1972, Franks found the case for change 'overwhelming'. But s 2 survived until 1989. It had a remarkable durability. In December 1987, the Home Secretary, however, announced he was preparing a White Paper on 'reform'. Only once before, in 1939, had Parliament 'back-pedalled' on OSA legislation when it legislated that s 6 of the 1920 OSA, which concerned powers to obtain information in connection with offences under the OSAs, would only cover s 1 offences and not s 2 offences.[14] Section 1 is headed by the legend 'Penalties for Spying'. In *Chandler v DPP*,[15] the House of Lords held that s 1 was not restricted to spying, as was commonly thought, but also covered conspiracy to commit sabotage or enter a prohibited place intentionally, regardless of motive. In *Chandler* protestors had entered a US air base in England to demonstrate against the presence of nuclear weapons whose presence was not in the public interest, they argued. In matters of defence, the public interest was determined by the Government not by protestors.

13 The Radcliffe Report found that substantial amounts of documents were over-classified and should be downgraded, Cmnd 1681. See C Turpin *Government Contracts* (1972), p 296, n 187 and contractual clauses specifying secrecy.
14 Section 6 of OSA 1920.
15 [1964] AC 763; and D Thompson (1963) Public Law 201.

The OSA has mistakes in its drafting, its various Bill stages in Parliament have been characterised by incomplete information and erroneous explanation. It has been used to threaten an MP.[16] The legislation was among the most widely discussed of all laws in Britain and the current laws are still widely discussed.[17] Indeed, prosecution of and inability to prosecute former military, security and intelligence personnel in the late 1990s and into 2000 brought renewed attention.[18] Section 2 has now been consigned to history and repealed and its detailed provisions need not detain us but it operated to create a culture of apprehension and caution among civil servants. Such an ethos is likely to survive all but a genuine and complete relaxation of unnecessary secrecy laws.

Attempts at reform were made, including that by Mrs Thatcher shortly after taking office in 1979. This attempt was, however, sabotaged by the revelations of the Anthony Blunt affair when it was reported that the Queen's personal artistic adviser was a Russian spy and part of the unending Kilby, Burgess and Maclean saga. Had the proposed Bill been law, the press would not have been allowed to report these events prompting widespread accusations that the Bill was in fact more repressive than s 2. But change was forced upon the Government by three events which threatened to take matters out of their control.

Nevertheless use of the Acts was not abated. Before Franks reported, there had been 30 prosecutions with 26 convictions under s 2 of the Act.[19] Since 1946 there had been 20 prosecutions under s 1 of the Act for spying.[20] There were 19 convictions. By 1 August 1978, a further five prosecutions had been brought under s 2.[1] These involved three cases,

16 Duncan Sandys MP and HC 101 (1938–9) and HC 173 (1937–8). See an interesting note by AIL Campbell (1985) Public Law 212. According to Middlemas, Lloyd George was threatened in 1932 for using a cabinet document in Parliament – (1976) Pol Q 39, citing CAB 63/45.

17 D Hooper *Official Secrets: The Use and Abuse of the Act* (1987). Atomic Energy has special provisions under: the Atomic Energy Act 1946, ss 11, 13; Atomic Energy Authority Act 1954, Sch 3, s 6(3), covering prohibited places; Nuclear Installations Act 1965, s 24 and Sch 1, and European Communities Act 1972, s 11(2), covering Euratom institutions; and Radioactive Substances Act 1993, ss 34 and 39 and Radioactive Materials (Road Transport) Act 1991, s 5. See Nuclear Safeguards Act 2000. Nb Civil Aviation Act 1982, ss 18 and 23. For specific statutory provisions prohibiting the disclosure of information acquired from citizens, see *Open Government* Cm 2290 (1993) App B and P Birkinshaw *Government and Information: the Law Relating to Access, Disclosure and their Regulation* (2nd ed, (2001) Annex B.

18 The cases of David Shayler and Richard Tomlinson former MI5 and MI6 agents respectively and their publications of life inside the services: see *A-G v Times Newspapers Ltd* [2001] ECWA Civ 97, [2001] 1 WLR 885 and see p 39 n 8.

19 Many s 2 cases were tried by magistrates.

20 And Chandler.

1   I am grateful to the Attorney-General's office for the following figures.

one of which was concluded. In the same period there were six prosecutions under section 1, with four convictions, and a fifth under s 7.[2] Between 1 August 1978 and 9 February 1983, there were 11 prosecutions leading to 10 convictions under s 2.[3] There were five completed cases under s 1, three of which led to prosecution. One further case led to a conviction under s 2 alone, and another to a conviction under s 7 of the Act alone. In an additional case to the five, the police charged under s 1, but the Attorney-General did not consent to prosecution. From 10 February 1983 until 24 April 1986, there were nine cases under s 2, leading to five convictions, though one of these was subject to a successful appeal. In one further case, the Solicitor-General had authorised a prosecution. There were three prosecutions under s 1, and one authorised prosecution under section 7.[4] In 1987 and 1988 following Ponting's trial there were 23 prosecutions under s 2 before the courts bringing seven convictions. Between 1991 and 1993, there were 5 prosecutions under the 1989 Act with one conviction and 7 under the 1911 Act s 1 with 3 convictions. Between 1994-98, there were three prosecutions under the 1989 Act at Magistrates' courts, two convictions and two sentences of immediate custody.[5] These figures would not include the Shayler prosecution. These figures do not, of course, cover cases where confessions have been given *and* resignations tendered *in return for immunity,* as in the case of Ian Willmore.[6]

The OSAs are designed to operate *in terrorem.* If the Government miscalculated the public sentiment badly in the case of Ponting, it is doubtful whether the acquittal in that case would influence more than a handful of individuals to act as he did where they had a sincere, well-motivated and morally felt duty, not simply to their political overlords but to Parliament and the nation. The OSAs should be seen for what they are: the legal framework of a tradition of government which is steeped in secrecy and confidentiality which have been used 'viciously and capriciously by an embarrassed executive'.[7] In fact, it could be argued

2   Of the 1920 Act which deals with attempts, incitement etc.
3   HC Debs, 9 February 1983.
4   See HC Debs, vol 108, col 13 (12 January 1987).
5   Figures supplied by the Home Office 18 July 2000.
6   R Pyper (1985) 56 Pol Q 72.
7   See Caulfield J's memo to Franks, Vol II, p 350. On the Act's effects upon civil servants, see Franks, op cit, Vol 1, p 17; *Ponting,* pp 36–42; see also J Ward (1986) Pub Policy and Admin 11; and L Chapman *Your Disobedient Servant* (1979). NB minister to be J Aitken *Officially Secret* on *R v Aitken et al.* The absence of high judicial authority on almost any aspect of s 2 was amazing, although see *Galvin* [1987] 2 All ER 851 where the Court of Appeal quashed a conviction where a jury was not asked to consider the defence of prior dissemination of information which might have authorised its use. The courts have generally taken a strict line on information under the OSA still being secret, although in the public

that there is now a more effective regime for imposing secrecy in the Government's interests and not in the public interest (see below).

The Ponting trial

The law had been thrown into more than its usual state of uncertainty by the acquittal of the former assistant secretary at the Ministry of Defence (MoD), Clive Ponting. Ponting's trial was a sensational event. He was a civil service 'high flier' who had responsibility for 'the policy and political aspects of the operational activities of the Royal Navy'. Ponting was concerned with drafting replies and answers on the sinking of the Argentinian warship *Belgrano* by the Royal Navy during the Falklands campaign.[8] He disagreed with his colleagues on what, and how, information on the sinking should be published. His belief that the Government was positively and deliberately misleading the Commons and a select committee[9] and the public caused him to send two documents to Tam Dalyell MP. They were duly handed to the Chairman of the select committee on Foreign Affairs, who, in turn, handed them back to the Secretary of State at the MoD. Ponting was subsequently prosecuted for breach of s 2(1)(*a*). This section made it a criminal offence for a person holding office under Her Majesty to communicate official information to any person other than a person to whom he is authorised to communicate it, or a person to whom it is his duty *in the interest of the state* to communicate it. In the course of the trial 'interest' and 'interests' were used interchangeably.[10]

Both prosecution and defence accepted that Dalyell was not a person authorised to receive official information under the terms of the Act. Was an MP a person to whom it was Ponting's duty in the interest of the state to pass such information?[11] This issue was central to Ponting's defence. In the trial,[12] McCowan J consulted *Chandler v DPP* where Lord Reid observed that the term 'state' did not mean the government or the executive but 'the realm' or the 'organised community'. Lord Reid also believed that a minister or a government did not *always* have the final say on what

domain: A Nicol (1979) Crim LR 284; *R v Crisp and Homewood* (1919) 83 JP 121, though Canadian cases differ: *Boyer v R* (1948) 94 CCC 195, *per* Marchand J and *R v Toronto Sun Publishing Ltd* (1979) 47 CCC (2d) 535.

8 C Ponting, *The Right To Know* (1985). He worked with the 'Crown Jewels', which were top secret documents setting out the details of the events leading to the sinking of the *Belgrano*. Inclusion of this information meant that the jury had to be vetted.

9 The Committee reported in July 1985 and, while critical of the Government's reticence, it did not think the Government had sought to mislead it.

10 See R. Thomas, HC 92, II, App 26, for an informative analysis.

11 Cf *Ponting*.

12 [1985] Crim LR 318.

was in the public interest, although *in cases concerning the defence of the realm* a different approach would be necessary. *Chandler* was such a case.[13] McCowan J directed the jury that *'interests* of the state' (sic) were synonymous with the interests of the Government of the day, adopting Lord Reid's narrower interpretation regarding defence. The offence indicted in *Chandler* was a conspiracy to commit an act of sabotage within a prohibited place 'for a purpose prejudicial to the interests of the state' under s 1. In the context of national defence the state was the 'organised community', 'the organs of government of a national community' and responsibility for armed forces and defence fell to the Crown, viz. the Government of the day advising the Crown. This military necessity as Lord Devlin suggested, was not a blue print to suggest that the interests of the state were *always* the same as those of the Government of the day.[14] The 'duty' referred to in s 2(1)(*a*), McCowan J ruled, is an official duty under the terms of an office and authorised chain of command. It did not refer to a moral or 'public' duty. But surely this begs the question. There was ample scope to argue that this interpretation constituted a misconstruction of the provision and indeed the prosecution accepted that Ponting's leak had not adversely affected national security.

Until 1998, it remained a severe criticism of our system of government that there is no equivalent of the US Civil Service Reform Act 1978—as amended— which protects civil servants who 'blow the whistle' in the public interest from punishment by administrative disciplining. The UK Public Interest Disclosure Act 1998 seeks to protect disclosures by employees in the public interest but it does not apply to those whose work is certified by a minister as safeguarding national security. Security, intelligence and police officers are not covered by this Act. The US Act protects those servants who leak information which they reasonably believe reveals violation of the law or regulations or 'mismanagement, a gross waste of funds, an abuse of authority, or a substantial and specific danger to public health or safety'. Where the disclosure concerns foreign intelligence and counter intelligence, it must be made to designated officials who have to inform the appropriate Congressional Committee. Similar protection covers FBI agents and other officials. Reports of investigations are submitted to Congress, the President and the Complainant. These provisions were extended in 1989 following the Oliver North episode[15] (see p 77 *et seq* above and note the existence of an

13 [1964] AC 763; see above.
14 *Thomas*, p 371. And see N MacCormick in P Wallington and R Merkin (eds), *Essays in Memory of FH Lawson* (1986).
15 5 USC, ss 1206–1208, 2302. See Cripps (1983) Public Law 600; Cf use of the Espionage Act in the USA. NB the Inspector-General for the CIA and the IG's role: *Inspector-General in the CIA Compared to Other Statutory Inspectors'-General* F Kaiser CRS Report 89-679 GOV (1989).

Inspector General for CIA). That Act provides a safeguard against administrative reprisals, but not against a criminal prosecution where a crime is committed.

Additional difficulties related to the question of the *mens rea* necessary to secure a conviction and whether *proof* of intent was required, ie intent to leak *and* prejudice the safety etc of the state.

Stated in fairly dispassionate academic terms the position might seem relatively straightforward. But when the OSA is put into practice and prosecution is attempted before a jury, then unless a confession is forthcoming, as in the case of Sarah Tisdall, who leaked documents to *The Guardian* relating to the arrival of Cruise missiles, or concerns straightforward allegations of fact, it can prove to be impossible to secure a conviction. In the case of *Ponting,* failure to convict no doubt related to a jury refusing to be browbeaten by a judge, the prosecution handling the case less adroitly than it should, a feeling that the Government was actively involved in manipulating an outcome, and the Attorney-General appearing to prejudge guilt in a radio broadcast.[16] And Ponting's lawyers mounted a very successful campaign outside the courtroom.[17] Yet *all* the vital rulings in law went against Ponting. In law, the Crown (Government?) could not have asked for more, and no judge could have provided such, since juries were last imprisoned before *Bushell's* case[18] in 1670 for returning verdicts against the judge's direction. Ponting's acquittal was a resounding death knell for s 2.

The Spycatcher litigation

In terms of international notoriety this trial has only been matched in recent years by that of OJ Simpson. A former member of the British Security Service and somewhat embittered by his lack of recognition and paltry pension, Wright sought to publish his memoirs in Australia—outside the criminal jurisdiction of s 2—and these contained pretty well rehearsed allegations concerning the activities or 'dirty tricks' of the security service. The novel feature in this case was that Wright was a former 'insider', a fact which might give added credibility to his allegations. This episode and its ramifications are examined in greater detail in chapter 7 but the eventual refusal to award permanent injunctions by Scott J to prevent reporting of the allegations in *Spycatcher* and of the proceedings relating to its attempted publication, and the judge's belief that some of the

16 Bernard Ingham, the Prime Minister's press secretary, opined that he hoped a 'severe' judge would try the case!
17 *The Times*, 12 February 1985.
18 (1670) 6 State Tr 999.

original allegations deserved to be published in the public interest[19] forced the Government legal advisers to accept that the law of confidentiality would not always fill the hole left by the deficiencies in s 2 and that 'prior restraint' may not always be lightly imposed by an English court. In generally ringing terms, Scott J spoke of the strengthening of British law by the influence of art 10 of the European Convention on Human Rights which guarantees freedom of speech and dissemination of information and how the courts must hold the balance between public security and freedom of speech in a manner which did not automatically accept the *ipse dixit* of the government of the day. The courts were not justified in restraining newspaper or media reports concerning unauthorised disclosures unless there was a risk of further damage to national security. As the European Court of Human Rights subsequently established, a court may take a different attitude at different stages of the interlocutory and permanent hearings for an injunction—for that Court ruled that the original injunctions restraining newspaper coverage of events in Australian proceedings and details of the book were justified because of the possible danger to national security but that the injunctions imposed after the publication of the book in the USA were no longer justified.[20] This is actually narrower than the judgment of Scott J as stated above who felt that some of the original allegations were justified, although on this point he was *obiter*. This does no more than repeat the obvious truism that the timing of judicial proceedings is crucial in cases concerning allegedly damaging leaks of security sensitive information—the earlier the stage the greater the judicial willingness to accept the possibility of serious damage where such information is leaked. In chapter 9, I shall examine more closely the role of the courts in protecting government confidences and secrets by injunction and the extent of the public interest defence under our civil jurisdiction. This topic has now to address s 12 of the Human Rights Act 1998 which seeks to protect freedom of expression under the ECHR Art 10 as well as Art 8. As we shall see in chapters 9 and 10 (pp 379 and 454) interim injunctions preventing publication are not to be granted unless the party seeking the relief, the Attorney-General, establishes to the satisfaction of the court that he is likely to succeed in his claim at the final hearing that publication should not be allowed. Various other items have to be addressed in the case of 'journalistic, artistic and literary material' in balancing relevant interests.

Nonetheless, Scott J's decision, basically upheld in its entirety in the higher courts, indicated a new and more rational approach by the courts where government could not assume that judges would be happy to perform the executive's work on its behalf and that the only way to redress the damage was by reform of s 2.

---

19 See p 412 *et seq* below.
20 *Observer and Guardian v UK* (1991) 14 EHRR 153.

The Shepherd Bill

In November 1987, a Private Member's Bill sought to repeal s 2. It bore the same title as the Government's discredited Protection of Official Information Bill of 1979, although it differed in important respects.

Under the Bill, six classes of information or 'articles' would have been protected by the criminal law in so far as unauthorised dissemination might lead to criminal prosecution with the consent of the Attorney-General or, in some cases, the consent of the DPP. The areas covered were: defence, international relations, security or intelligence 'the unauthorised disclosure of which would be likely to cause serious injury to the interests of the nation or endanger the safety of a British citizen' (cl 1(1)(*a*) and 1(2)(*a*) information). Further classes covered information likely to be useful in commission of offences, or in facilitating an escape from legal custody or likely to impede the prevention or detection of offences or the apprehension of suspected offenders; and information supplied by an individual in accordance with any statutory requirement to do so or in connection with an application for a statutory grant or benefit or permission and where there is an express or implied duty to hold it in confidence. Other information was to be protected by administrative action, ie disciplinary proceedings.

A Crown servant was only to be guilty where he had *mens rea* in disclosing in breach of his official duties. Likewise, a government contractor would have to possess *mens rea* for an unauthorised disclosure. The burden of proof was on the prosecution. Other parties would be guilty, if with *mens rea* they made an unauthorised disclosure of information as classified above. Other offences covered wrongful detention and failure to comply with instructions as to its return or disposal. *Mens rea* had to be proved.

A defence that the information had been publicly available in the UK *or* elsewhere (cf the FOIA of the USA and elsewhere in chapter 2) was provided. A public interest defence to a criminal charge was also available if the defence could prove 'that the disclosure or retention of the information or article was in the public interest in so far as [the defendant] had reasonable cause to believe—[not conclusive proof]—that it indicated the existence of crime, fraud, abuse of authority, neglect in the performance of an official duty or other misconduct and that he had taken reasonable steps to comply with any established procedures for drawing such misconduct to the attention of the appropriate authorities without effect'.

Information under cl 1(1)(*a*) and 1(2)(*a*) had to be properly classified by a minister at the appropriate time. Classification could have been challenged by the defence. The Bill was welcomed as a relaxation of the ambit of s 2, but it was widely criticised for not going far enough in making public provision of official information.

The Bill brought a statement from Mrs Thatcher that she intended to reform s 2—although there were misgivings that such a Bill would not be a liberalising measure.[1] In fact the imposition of a life-long statutory duty of confidentiality for *all* officials, enforceable by the criminal law, was widely suggested as inspired by Government to make their eventual recommendations appear a liberalising measure. A three-line whip and invocation of the pay-roll on Tory MPs helped to kill the Bill in January 1988. The Government was emphatic that such an important subject was not suitable for backbench reform.

The White Paper on reform

The 14 pages of White Paper took 14 months to complete. It agreed with Franks that s 1 of the OSA does not provide full protection for official information and that the criminal law needs to punish leakage as well as espionage where there is a sufficient degree of harm to the public interest. The White Paper said 'nothing about the separate issue' of freedom of information because this did not arise directly out of the reform of s 2. It is therefore difficult to square with the Home Secretary's subsequent announcement that his Bill represented a 'substantial unprecedented thrust in the direction of greater openness' that it was an 'essay in openness'... 'unprecedented since the Second World War'.

The Government ultimately decided not to follow Franks but to 'look afresh at the issues', taking into account the criticisms of its 1979 Bill and the development of Parliamentary and public thinking in recent years. A closer look at such thinking would suggest that the government had been treating it less than sympathetically. Six specific areas of information were to be protected against unauthorised disclosure where the disclosure was damaging. Damaging disclosures by unauthorised recipients would be covered, but the mere receipt of official information without authority was not to be a crime unless, presumably, aiding and abetting, incitement or conspiracy could be charged. However, the White Paper dropped the idea of ministerial certificates which specified that the information was properly classified as information the disclosure of which was considered likely to cause serious injury to the interests of the nation. In Shepherd's Bill, ministerial certificates were to remain, but they were to be subject to challenge before the Judicial Committee of the Privy Council. The new requirement that a disclosure be 'damaging' was less onerous than the 'serious damage' requirement of the 1979 Bill, although in that Bill serious injury was to be established by a ministerial certificate. The White

---

1   HC Debs 12 November 1987.

Paper stipulated that there was to be no public interest defence as had been present in the Shepherd Bill, nor a defence of prior publication, even though one had been present in cl 7(1) of the 1979 Bill.

Although disclosures had normally to be proved to be damaging by the prosecution, there were four areas where the disclosure would *ipso facto* be deemed damaging, and where UK interests abroad were concerned the disclosure only had to jeopardise or seriously obstruct those interests. The first covered leaks by security and intelligence officials and notified persons of security and intelligence information. The second absolute offence concerned the disclosure of information obtained or information concerning activities under the Interception of Communications Act 1985 and what was to be the Security Service Act 1989, ie burglary and 'investigations' by MI5. It was noted in chapter 1 how the Security Service Act 1996 and RIPA 2000 were added to these statutes. These would cover Ponting, Peter Wright and Cathy Massiter, the former MI5 official who disclosed that CND's telephone lines and those of its members were being tapped.[2] The third area covered information relating to international relations. Fourthly, information obtained in confidence from other governments would be protected it seemed absolutely—as any disclosure without authority would be harmful. Information would also be protected when given in confidence to a foreign government, but only where it was leaked without authority in that state and subsequently published in the UK. The Act provided for the protection of information relating to defence and that which would be useful to criminals if disclosed without authority. These were the fifth and sixth categories of protected information.

> The government ... proposes that, when it is necessary for the courts to consider the harm likely to arise from the disclosure of particular information, the prosecution should be required to adduce evidence as to that harm and the defence should be free to produce its own evidence in rebuttal. The burden of proof would be on the prosecution in the normal way. (Cm 408: para 18)

In other words, no ministerial certificates would dictate to the jury a finding of guilt. A free trial before one's peers, recently so lauded by the remnants of the liberal press during Ponting's acquittal, was to be preserved in all its integrity. The fact that the ground rules determined that no likely defence was available for certain disclosures was beside the point. It is also a little disingenuous to state, as we shall see, that ministerial certificates have not been introduced.

---

2   *R v Secretary of State for the Home Department, ex p Ruddock* [1987] 2 All ER 518.

There were, nevertheless, certain improvements. Large areas of official information would no longer be covered by the Official Secrets Acts. For example, cabinet documents were not to be protected as a class unless they fell within one of the above protected categories. Economic information was not to be protected as a class (eg the budget), and information given to government in confidence was not to be protected *per se*. The information would have to fall within one of the six categories. The White Paper indicated that, at the same time, civil service rules and departmental rules would be amended to make new provision for internal disciplinary punishment to protect information not covered by the OSAs. New statutes would also provide for criminal offences for unauthorised disclosure as and when required. In 1993, the number of such statutes and regulations extended to 189 statutes including NI orders and 62 regulations.[3] However, it is deceptive, therefore, to assert as the White Paper does that the 'result of implementing the Government's proposals would be that only small proportions of the information in the hands of Crown servants would be protected by the criminal law' (para 71).

Classification of information for security purposes still remains, even though classification at a particular grade of secrecy is not, of itself, evidence of likely harm or damage in a court of law. Classification will continue to play an 'essential administrative role in the handling of information' within government itself and will also be relevant for internal disciplinary offences. In a criminal trial, a classification will not be evidence of the causing of damage; but the grade may be relevant 'as evidence tending to show that the defendant had reason to believe that the disclosure of the information was likely to harm the public interest'. The causation of damage will have to be proved by separate evidence. Classifications, which are reviewable internally, are as follows:[4]

- 'Top secret': the compromise of this information or material would be likely to threaten directly the internal stability of the UK or friendly countries; to lead directly to widespread loss of life; to cause exceptionally grave damage to the effectiveness or security of the UK or allied forces or to the continuing effectiveness of extremely valuable security or intelligence operations; to cause exceptionally grave damage to relations with friendly governments—what of revelations of torture in those countries; or to cause severe long-term damage to the UK economy.

---

3   Cm 2290 App B. Note the current provisions under the *Civil Service Management Code* (August 2000), Section 4 and Annex A promulgated under Civil Service (Management Functions) Act 1992 and Civil Service Order in Council 1991.

4   HC Debs 23 March 1994, cols 259-60 (Written Answers). The aim was to give departments and agencies greater responsibility for assessing the nature of the risks they face and for making decisions ... about the security measures they need to put in place.

- 'Secret' covers information or material where compromise would be likely to raise international tension or damage seriously relations with friendly governments; to threaten life directly, or seriously prejudice public order, or individual security or liberty; to cause serious damage to the operational effectiveness of security in the UK or allied forces ... or to cause material damage to national finances or economic and commercial interests.

- 'Confidential' where compromise as above would be likely materially to damage diplomatic relations ie cause formal protests; to prejudice individual liberty or security; to cause damage to the operational effectiveness or security of UK or allied forces or the effectiveness of valuable security or intelligence operations; to work substantially against national finances or economic or commercial interests; substantially to undermine the financial viability of major organisations; to impede the investigation or facilitate the commission of serious crime; to impede seriously the development or operation of government policies; to shut down or otherwise substantially disrupt significant national operations.

- Lastly, comes 'Restricted', where compromise etc would be likely to affect diplomatic relations adversely; cause substantial distress to individuals; make it more difficult to maintain the operational effectiveness or security of UK or allied forces; cause financial loss or loss of earning potential to or facilitate improper gain or advantage for individuals or companies; to prejudice the investigation or facilitate the commission of crime; to breach proper undertakings to maintain confidentiality from third party communications; to impede the effective development or implementation of government policies; to breach statutory restrictions on disclosure of information; to disadvantage government in commercial or policy negotiations with others; to undermine the proper management of the public sector and its operations.

Within government these classifications are often accompanied by descriptors which indicate the nature of the sensitivity—for example 'Appointments', 'Budget', 'Commercial', 'Contracts', 'Management', 'Policy', 'Medical', 'Regulatory', 'Staff'. Departments may add to this list to cover types of information specific to their organisation.

The burden and quantum of proof would vary as between civil servants, government contractors and civilians. Among civil servants, where the offence related to security and intelligence information, a distinction was drawn between security and intelligence officials and 'notified' officials in one group and other civil servants in another. Unauthorised disclosures by the former group are, in the absence of one unlikely defence which I will discuss below, an absolute offence. For other offences, a distinction was drawn between civil servants, government contractors and civilians.

The test of liability would depend upon the state of knowledge of the discloser, and in the case of Crown servants it is reasonable to assume that they know the value of the information received in official duties. *Mens rea* is also a component of the offence. It would be open to the civil servant or contractor to plead that they could not reasonably have been expected to realise the harm likely to be caused by the disclosure. In the case of civilians, the opposite presumption would be made, and the prosecution should have to prove that harm was likely to follow and that the discloser knew, or could be reasonably expected to know, that harm would be likely to result. The constituents of the prosecution case differ according to the category of defendant. In the case of civil servants and contractors, *mens rea* is presumed unless proved otherwise; in the case of civilians, knowledge of the damaging quality has to be established by the prosecution. In the case of information obtained under interception or security warrants, once the prosecution has established that a non-civil servant knew, or had reasonable cause to believe that, it was such information and that it was disclosed unlawfully under the Act, the offence is made out.

Reference must be made to the special treatment of classes of security and intelligence information. Because it would normally be necessary for the prosecution to present additional evidence that such disclosures were damaging to secure a conviction, the Government declared that further and possibly greater damage could be caused by adducing such information. To counter such difficulty, it was proposed that the prosecution could show that the information disclosed was of a class or description the disclosure of which would be likely to damage the operation of the services. 'This would allow the arguments to be less specific'.[5] The prosecution would simply assert that the information belongs to a class of information the disclosure of which is damaging. No *specific* supporting evidence would have to be produced although the less specific the evidence the less convincing the case. It is difficult to interpret this as anything other than a ministerial certificate by default which the White Paper had appeared to rule out. Leigh and Lustgarten have argued that this is not the same as conviction on the say so of a minister.[6] Granted that this is restricted to one category of information; nevertheless the continued classification of documents and the secret lists of ministerially designated and 'notified' officials who work in close proximity with the security and intelligence services have to be appreciated.

---

5   Cm 408, para 40.
6   Lustgarten and Leigh question whether this amounts to conviction on the 'say so' of the minister and believe the case is overstated: *In from the Cold ...* (1994), pp 238-40.

Public interest disclosure

The White Paper adverted specifically to the defences of prior publication and public interest disclosure. The Shepherd Bill had contained a public interest defence where the defendant had a reasonable cause to believe crime, fraud, abuse of authority, neglect, or other misconduct had been perpetrated. The judicially developed law of confidentiality has long recognised that there cannot be a confidence in an iniquity.[7] A duty cannot be owed to maintain as a secret that which ought, in the public interest, to be disclosed. The courts have come to accept that a disclosure may be justified not because there is an iniquity but because there is an item of information the disclosure of which is justified on the facts.[8] The public interest defence was dramatically invoked by Scott J in *Spycatcher* when he argued that the revelations of Wright's allegations, concerning the attempts to undermine the Wilson Government and the plot to assassinate President Nasser by MI5 and MI6 officials, respectively, were protected by a public interest defence (see chapter 7). Correspondingly, the press were justified in publishing this information, at least in its essentials. This was information which the concept of democracy demanded should be placed before the public. Scott J suggested that revelations by an official may also be so protected, in spite of the life-long duty of confidentiality, a point supported by the higher courts. However, since the security allegations formed a minute part of the book, Wright had been culpable in publishing the book in that particular form. What this amounted to was that, in examining the public interest defence, the court will look very carefully at the manner and method of disclosure, and the motives of the discloser. Financial gain and widespread publication may undermine the defence so that the prudent course of action might be to inform the police or Solicitor-General rather than the press. This latter point has been emphasised by Lord Donaldson MR on a variety of occasions, as well as by Lord Griffiths and Lord Goff in *Spycatcher*.

In Canada, public servants at the federal level may successfully invoke the public interest defence against disciplinary hearings.[9] The Public Interest Disclosure Act 1998 offers some protection to civil servants and

---

7   *Gartside v Outram* (1856) 26 LJ Ch 113.

8   *Lion Laboratories v Evans* [1985] QB 526. See also *Ashdown v Telegraph Group Ltd* [2001] 2 All ER 370: Article 10 ECHR could not provide a defence to a breach of copyright (a breach of confidence was also claimed) concerning reports based on a minute taken by the former Liberal Democrat leader of a meeting with the Prime Minister. Defences under ss 30 and 171(3) of the Copyright etc Act 1988 were no defence to the newspaper. Protection of property was necessary in a democratic society and an injunction preventing publication was allowed notwithstanding s 12 HRA 1998.

9   *Quigley v Treasury Board* (1987) Public Service Staff Relations Board 166-2-16866.

other employees (see chapter four p 192 et seq) but none at all to security and intelligence officers and police officers. In the case of intelligence and security officers, the House of Lords has ruled that an 'absolute ban on disclosure' makes good sense.[10] This does not seem to countenance a public interest disclosure at common law or disclosures of trivia or useless information or that already published under authority of the government as supported by Scott J. The House of Lords had to focus on the fact that Blake was seeking to profit from his wrongdoing rather than making a public interest disclosure. Where the Public Interest Disclosure Act does not apply, a public interest defence is only a defence against a civil action for breach of confidence, and the confider still retains his or her rights under the law of employment.[11] Whistleblowers tend to fare very badly.[12]

The Government refused to countenance a public interest defence which would allow juries to consider and balance the benefits of the unauthorised disclosure of information, the motives of the discloser, and the harm it was likely to cause. Several attempts to introduce such defences in the Commons and Lords failed. It was the Government's line that the object of reform of s 2 had been to introduce clarity, and that such a defence would subvert this aim. Further, the reforms would concentrate on protecting areas of information which demonstrably require the protection of the criminal law 'in the public interest'. The Government argued: 'It cannot be acceptable that a person can lawfully disclose information which he knows may, for example, lead to loss of life simply because he conceives that he has a general reason of a public character for doing so'.[13] This seems to confuse an assertion of such a defence by a defendant with its acceptance by a jury. Expressed in the Government's terms, the claim sounds startling. The public interest defence allows a defendant to plead that the disclosure has been a positive benefit to the public interest. It is not a licence for the mischievous, the woolly headed and loose-tongued. The idea is to let the jury decide where there are arguments of damage and benefit. Yet the government would not facilitate such a contest: 'the effect of disclosure on the public interest should take place within the context of the proposed damage tests where applicable.'[14] The Government's one assurance, binding in honour only, was that the Act would not be used to punish those who had embarrassed the government. However, if an offence has been committed there is no

---

10 *A-G v Blake* [2000] 4 All ER 385, HL; see also *A-G v Times Newspapers* [2001] EWCA Civ 97, [2001] 1 WLR 885.

11 *R v Civil Service Appeal Board, ex p Bruce* [1989] 2 All ER 907; *R v Lord Chancellor's Department, ex p Nangle* [1991] ICR 743 and see p 188 *et seq* below on whistle-blowing and protection.

12 Y Cripps *Disclosure in the Public Interest* (2nd ed, 1994).

13 Cm 408, para 60.

14 Ibid, para 61.

provision for juries to be instructed according to the Government's assurance. Would it be a 'perverse' jury, therefore, that saved a defendant who had acted in the public interest out of conscience. The jury that acquitted Ponting was not, arguably, perverse in that it felt, presumably, that he had acted 'in the interests of the state'. A powerful argument can be made out to the effect that for a jury to acquit in such circumstances is not a perverse action but a rational one motivated by integrity.[15] However, such a defence is no longer available. It is merely a question of the prosecutor's discretion, a matter which highlights the long-running problem over the Attorney-General's independence from Government colleagues.[16] It should also be recalled that some disclosures are *ipso facto* damaging.

The Government's continued claim that a public interest defence had no respectable precedent in our criminal law is also unfounded. As well as a generic defence of 'necessity', specific statutes may contain such defences.

Prior publication

The White Paper ruled out the necessity of a prior publication defence, arguing that the inclusion of such a defence in the 1979 Bill was 'flawed'.[17] The Government's case, also argued with success before the courts,[18] was that a further publication of information already in the public domain might be damaging, possibly even more damaging than the original publication. A newspaper story about a certain matter may carry little weight in the absence of firm evidence of its validity. But confirmation of that story by, say, a senior official of the relevant government department would be very much more damaging and deserving of prosecution. So would publication of details of 'persons in public life' in one list, even though the names and addresses were publicly, albeit not conveniently, available elsewhere.[19] Prior publication would be relevant to assess the degree of harm, and it is therefore possible to argue that the damage alleged had already been perpetrated. But prior publication would not be conclusive for the defence. In some cases, viz security and intelligence and interception and security warrant cases, prior publication would be irrelevant as the offences are 'absolute'. Case law

15 N MacCormick in P Wallington and R Merkin (eds) *Essays in Honour of FH Lawson.*(1986).
16 See *Ponting* and A Nicol (1979) Crim LR 284.
17 Cf s 180(1)(r) Financial Services Act 1986 which allowed a defence of prior publication.
18 *Lord Advocate v Scotsman Publications Ltd* [1989] 2 All ER 852, HL.
19 Cm 408, para 62.

suggests that prior publication without preventative government action may indicate that disclosure has been authorised, even though the information is still technically 'secret'.[20]

The House of Lords[1] accepted the thrust of Government thinking, when it acknowledged that the test for awarding an injunction to prevent publication in the law of confidentiality, was that if an injunction were not awarded there would be damage or further damage to the public interest. If the test is satisfied, an injunction may be awarded even where the information or document has been published on a limited basis. In the case in question it was only the Government admission that all the damage had already occurred that prevented the award of the injunction. On the other hand, Government attempts to stifle what had already been widely published had met with the rebuke from Lord Griffiths, then chairman of the Security Commission, that such awards would make the law appear an ass. As Scott J put it in December 1987, it would be part of the case for the 'absolute protection of the security services that ... could not be achieved this side of the Iron Curtain'. The metaphor maintains its potency. In 2001, the Court of Appeal refused to issue an injunction preventing publication of a book by a former MI6 officer which had been published in Russia.[2] It had entered the public domain.

In Parliament

The Bill was a faithful replica of the White Paper with one significant development concerning information relating to international relations. Although several minor amendments were made to the Bill in its Parliamentary passage, the Government refused to cede ground on any of its major objectives.

The Home Secretary rejected accusations that only allowing six days on the floor of the House to debate all 16 clauses of the Bill was 'niggardly'. Furthermore, the committee stage was a committee of the whole House. After a two and then a three line whip, the guillotine was imposed, an amendment to the Bill in committee was not incorporated for consideration at Report stage, and inconsistent answers were given on crucial points. 'The effect of the guillotine was that, while some topics received thorough discussion, others were barely considered at all.'[3]

20 *R v Galvin* [1987] 2 All ER 851, CA.
1   *Lord Advocate v Scotsman Publications Ltd* [1989] 2 All ER 852, HL; and in *A-G v Blake* (above) the duty of absolute secrecy was supported in relation to seizing profits from sales of the book. There was no question of banning a book already published.
2   *A-G v Times Newspaper Group Ltd* [2001] EWCA Civ 97, [2001] 1 WLR 885.
3   B Winetrobe *The Official Secrets Bill 1988-89* (1989) Res Note 437, HC Library.

Indeed, s 5, as we shall see, contains what could be a fatal flaw. In seeking to amend the Bill by introducing a public interest defence, Richard Shepherd reminded the Commons that, while Parliament might often pursue abuses of authority, it rarely raised them. In the Lords, Lord Hutchinson of Lullington, counsel in many OSA cases, challenged the Government view that the reform was a liberalising measure. The six areas of information saw 'even greater restrictions' introduced, and in the past 30 years all prosecutions involving leaks to the media had involved the six areas. The statutory definitions of 'damaging' were wide and vacuous, with 'weak, inexact and unreliable' criteria, 'far removed from the central issue of the security of the state.'[4]

And so it was that after 78 years, s 2 had been reformed. Reform was, of course, needed. Of that there was no doubt. Now, the Government assured us, there was to be no more talk of catch-all provisions with well over 2,000 offences. The Act would target six specific areas. Civil service codes and statutes would be used to plug other gaps as we shall see. There would be no prosecution of those who had caused only embarrassment or distress to ministers by their leaks; nor would pensions be stopped unless a conviction under the criminal law had been secured. Let me now turn to the content of these so-called 'liberalising' measures.

The Official Secrets Act 1989

The Act, which came into force on 1 March 1990, extends, with minor exceptions, to Northern Ireland and to offences committed abroad by British citizens and Crown servants (s 15). Prosecutions may only be brought with the consent of the Attorney-General or Lord Advocate, except for offences under s 4(2). This safeguard has been claimed, on numerous occasions, to be more apparent than real, as the Attorney-General is, severally, protector of the public interest, lawyer, elected politician, member of the government, government legal adviser, and Crown, ie government, prosecutor. Given the judicial endorsement, per McCowan J, in *R v Ponting* of the interests of the state as synonymous with the interests of the government of the day, it is hardly surprising that decisions of the Attorney-General have not infrequently been perceived as partial. Although ministers may be consulted, 'the final decision is his alone' on prosecutions.[5]

---

4   HL Debs Vol 504 col 1632 (9 March 1989).
5   Franks (1972) para 37.

Authorised disclosures

The distinction between an authorised and an unauthorised disclosure is central to the whole structure of the 1989 Act. The concept is also crucial for the operation of the Civil Service Codes. Some explanation is therefore required.

Throughout the 1990s and into the 2000s, it became evident to the Government that the relationship between ministers and civil servants was in need of reformulation. Civil servants had long abandoned the veil of anonymity with which their work was traditionally shrouded. A huge change in culture had taken place in the civil service brought about by the financial management initiative and a significant reduction in manpower. There were other causes and effects. The role of civil servants in leaking the Solicitor-General's letter to Michael Heseltine in the Westland saga, the confusion into which the Ponting trial and acquittal threw the Government, greater trade union activity and industrial unrest at GCHQ,[6] were all contributory factors. However, the deliberate placing of civil servants in the front-line of media and press attention by ministers was not without importance. Furthermore, by the end of the decade, the wholesale devolution of managerial responsibility to executives and line managers running executive agencies outside the ministerial/departmental structure, the increasing emphasis upon commercial enterprise and contracting out[7] and the attenuation of ministerial responsibility, all helped to place the minister/civil servant relationship under strain. The formal relationship was expressed in memoranda and Cabinet Office guidelines from Sir Robert Armstrong in 1985 and 1987 respectively. In these, he stated that civil servants were servants of the Crown. He added that the 'Crown' means, and is represented by, the government of the day whose ministers are answerable to Parliament. A civil servant's primary duty is to the minister in charge of the department in which they are serving and whom they must serve 'with complete integrity and to the best of their ability'. The maintenance of trust between ministers and civil servants, and the efficiency of government, required that the latter kept the confidences to which they become privy in their work.[8] This definition has been amended but its spirit remains intact.[9]

I shall deal with civil service codes and disciplinary proceedings later. From the above, however, it is clear that the release of information operates

6   The Government intelligence centre at Cheltenham now within the Intelligence Services Act 1994; see chapter 1 p 34 *et seq.*

7   Government Trading Act 1990; Civil Service Management Functions Act 1992; Deregulation and Contracting Out Act 1994.

8   See n 3, p 124 above, Annex A.

9   See chapter 4 p 187 *et seq* and note the former Civil Service Department's *Legal Entitlement and Administrative Practices* HMSO (1979) on compliance with the law.

under the authority of the minister. Ministers are, therefore, to a large extent, self-authorising; they do not leak, they brief. Senior civil servants are in substantially the same position,[10] the extent to which they are self-authorising depending upon their position and seniority and what is necessary for the performance of their duties. Section 2 of the 1911 Act created an offence if Crown information was disclosed to someone 'other than a person to whom [the civil servant] is authorised to communicate it, or a person to whom it is in the interests of the state [the civil servant's duty] to communicate it'. The Act did 'not explain the meaning of the quoted words'.[11] In *Ponting,* McCowan J directed the jury that the 'interests of the state' were synonymous with the interests of the government of the day. He expressed no qualification. In so instructing, he wrenched from their context dicta of the Law Lords in *Chandler v DPP* which could be used to support Ponting's case where national security was not at stake.

At the root of the problem is an inherent conflict between the governing of a country by a particular government which may abuse its powers, and the idea of the state, or specifically the Crown, as representative of a larger collective weal which is bigger than any government. 'Those whose prime loyalty is to the government of the day look to the Crown as a more enduring expression of their position within the constitution.[12] The First Division Association of Civil Servants (FDA) has argued that loyalty to the Crown included the Crown in Parliament, thereby creating a special relationship between MPs and civil servants. It is probably more accurate to look upon the 'Crown in Parliament', however, as a legislative device, not an all-pervasive functional relationship although in a sense it does describe the confusion of the executive and the legislature in both Houses.

To avoid what must have seemed to any government as metaphysical meanderings, lawful authority for a disclosure by a Crown servant or government contractor under the 1989 Act means 'if, and only if, it is made in accordance with [an] official duty'. The established view would see an official duty emanating solely from within the official chain of command, going up to, and including, the permanent secretary and minister as adviser to the Crown.

The 1989 Act provides that a disclosure by a government contractor is, tautologically, made with lawful authority if, and only if, it is made in accordance with an official authorisation, or for the purposes of the functions by virtue of which they are a government contractor without contravening an official restriction (s 7(2)). Disclosure of protected information by any other person is made with lawful authority if, and only if, it is made:

10 Franks (1972) para 18 and Treasury and Civil Service Committee *Civil Servants and Ministers: Duties and Responsibilities* HC 92 I & II (1985-6) p 5.
11 Franks.
12 HC 92 I & II para 3.2.

(a)   to a Crown servant for the purpose of his or her functions as such;
(b)   in accordance with an official authorisation (s 7(3)).

The mysteries of self authorisation will remain. A party charged with an offence under s 1–6 of the 1989 Act may prove, with the onus on that party, that at the time of the alleged offence they believed that they had lawful authority to make the disclosure in question and had no reasonable cause to believe otherwise. Their simple belief is not enough, even if mistaken.

An authorised disclosure under FOIA (see p 321) will be protected under this provision. Under s 44 FOIA, the relevant statutory prohibition is the OSA which makes a proviso for lawfully authorised disclosures.

Security and intelligence information

Section 1 protects security and intelligence information, which is defined in sub-s (9). The provision stipulates that members and former members of the services—MI5 and MI6 respectively and GCHQ employees—and 'notified' persons are guilty of an offence if without lawful authority they disclose any information, document or other article relating to security and intelligence acquired by virtue of their position as such a member/person.

In the Commons it was stated that 'carefully selected and mainly senior officials', as well as members of the armed services working in a 'few government departments' assessing intelligence information of the highest sensitivity and assisting ministers, would be notified. Also proposed for notification would be those who work on providing the services with regular professional support for their operation and activities. These will usually be Crown servants. Members of the armed forces who undertake technical communications and work alongside the services in various parts of the world will be notified, as will ministers and others 'with particular responsibilities or public duties in respect of the services'.[13] The Government insisted that a notification would be secret, so no reasons would be given though, after denial and equivocation, it was accepted by the Government that a notification would be judicially reviewable. Even with reasons, however, the possibility of a successful judicial review involving a matter of security and intelligence is extremely rare.[14] Notification will be in force for five years from the day on which it is served, though it may either be revoked within that period or indeed extended.

13   HC Debs Vol 145 cols 1128-9 (25 January 1989).
14   *Council of the Civil Service Unions v Minister for the Civil Service* [1985] AC 374, HL; *R v Secretary of State for the Home Department, ex p Ruddock* [1987] 2 All ER 518; *R v Director GCHQ, ex p Hodges* (1988) Times, 26 July. On this latter case – dismissal of a homosexual from GCHQ, see p 404 et seq below.

Section 1(2) also covers statements purporting to be security or intelligence disclosures; ie vacuous 'big talk' or idle boasts by security and intelligence officers or former officers and notified persons. Unlike the common law, there is no defence for trivia, and no public interest defence. It is not true to suggest, therefore, with respect to the Law Lords, that the OSA 1989 and the law of confidentiality are on a *par*.[15] Any disclosure within s 1(1) and (2) under the 1989 Act is presumed damaging.

It is clear that the offences of aiding, abetting, inciting etc in s 7 OSA 1920 do not apply to the 1989 Act. But there are common law offences of aiding, abetting and incitement. If these offences were invoked by a prosecutor then it would add considerable uncertainty to the position of, eg, a newspaper editor or publisher. The formless offence of conspiracy should also be kept in mind from the point of view of the recipient. Having said that, these common law offences have not been resorted to and there must be a serious risk that they would fall foul of the HRA and Art 10 ECHR if brought against reputable editors.

For Crown servants, other than members of the security services and notified persons, and for government contractors, both of which are defined in s 12, an unauthorised disclosure is punishable as an offence if it is 'damaging'. By s 1(4) a disclosure is deemed to be damaging if 'it causes damage to the work of, or any part of, the security and intelligence services'. No specific allowance is made for trivia or the public interest so that, for example, damage would be caused if a disclosure revealed that the service was engaged in murder.[16] In August 2000, when David Shaylor, formerly of MI5, was prosecuted on his return to England under the OSA, he was not prosecuted in relation to revelations of alleged MI6 plots to arrange the assassination of Colonel Gadafy. The Government also legislated via the back door for analogues of ministerial certificates to be introduced, in spite of their contrary claims—although this point has been criticised.[17] This was achieved as follows. Section 1(4) allows damage to be presumed where the disclosure is of information the unauthorised disclosure of which:

> would be likely to cause such damage [viz to security or intelligence] or which falls within a class or description of information, documents or articles the unauthorised disclosure of which would be likely to have that effect.

I have already described the impact of this provision. It will allow arguments to be 'less specific'. There would still have to be arguments and some supporting evidence but details are likely to kept exiguous.

---

15   *Lord Advocate v Scotsman Publications Ltd* [1989] 2 All ER 852, HL. And see *A-G v Blake* [2000] 4 All ER 385, HL.
16   See Lord Donaldson MR [1988] 3 All ER 545 at 603-6 esp 605d-e.
17   *Lustgarten and Leigh* p 128 n 6 above.

The prosecution will simply have to show that the information was classified under s 1(4). Once that is established, the offence is made out. The classification will be that of a minister and is evidence of its damaging quality, unlike the security classifications discussed above. Under s 8(4) OSA 1920, the public and press may be excluded from a trial under the 1989 Act (s 11(4)). Such an order excluding the press will prevent the public being informed of details.

Although the above provision has been described as an absolute offence, a defence is nonetheless available. The defence allowable under s 1(5) involves the security or other relevant officer proving that at the time of the alleged offence they did not know, and had no reasonable cause to believe, that the information or documents related to security or intelligence. One might be tempted to think that they would have to be singularly unintelligent intelligence officers to plead ignorance successfully in this context. Where the offence is not absolute, non-notified Crown servants have to prove that they did not realise that the disclosure would be damaging.

In the case of recipients, such as newspaper editors, news media or publishers, s 5 covers their unauthorised receipt and damaging disclosure of information, although I referred above to the danger of the use of common law offences of aiding and abetting offences under s 1. 'Damaging' is established in the same way as for non-notified Crown servants under s 1(4). However, the prosecution must prove in addition that the defendant made the disclosure knowing, or having reasonable cause to believe, that it is protected against disclosure under s 1. In other words, *mens rea* has to be specifically established *vis-à-vis* the recipient's disclosure; it is not presumed as in the case of Crown servants. The relevant disclosure to the recipient will, under s 5(1), be made by a Crown servant or government contractor without authority. Alternatively, it will be made after the servant or contractor has entrusted the information 'in confidence', either expressly or implicitly, and there was then an unauthorised disclosure. There are also offences covering situations where it was received by a third or fourth party and the disclosure to that party was made without authority by a person to whom it was entrusted 'in confidence'. A necessary condition for the offence is that the recipient is not committing an offence under ss 1-4 (which only cover Crown servants or government contractors). Section 5 creates the possibility of a chain *ad infinitum* from the perspective of recipients. However, *mens rea* (or a criminal intent) must be established in the case of each recipient[18] and where the disclosure without lawful authority is by a government

18 The position on *mens rea* and s 2 (1) and (2) of the 1911 Act was never satisfactorily concluded. On the position of newspaper editors and court orders to produce documents and evidence under s 9 and Sch 1 para 4 PACE 1984, see *R v Central Criminal Court, ex p Bright* [2001] 2 All ER 244, n 20 below.

contractor or by a person to whom it was entrusted in confidence by a Crown servant or government contractor, the relevant disclosure must be by a British citizen, or it must take place in the UK, Channel Islands, Isle of Man or a colony. In other words a limitation to the territorial extent of the offence is introduced.

The government accepted that, as s 5 only applies to disclosures by Crown servants or government contractors, former servants and contractors and their disclosures were not included. It should be noted that this shortcoming, from the Government's perspective, is not remedied by s 5(1) (a) (iii), which only covers a situation where an intermediary receives information in confidence. The Government may be forced to use the civil law of confidentiality in such cases. This could be a substantial flaw in the 1989 Act, since it was aimed at circumstances similar to those at stake in the Peter Wright affair. Where a newspaper does not receive information from a person who received it in confidence, which would include a former security official, a prosecution under s 5 may well flounder. And, it would not be possible to obtain an injunction under the civil law where a newspaper intended to report information received from a source not bound by confidentiality.[19]

As a concluding comment on this section it has been well observed that when everything is secret, nothing is secret. The offence under s 1 covering security officials seeks to achieve such total secrecy. It is a case of overkill and its very breadth may well prevent it meeting its objectives. Quite rightly, the question has been raised whether s 1 contravenes Art 10 ECHR guaranteeing freedom of speech. The prosecution of David Shayler in 2001 provided an opportunity for the compatibility of s 1 of OSA 1989 with Art 10 ECHR to be tested under the Human Rights Act 1998 (see pp 5-6 above). In July 2000, *The Guardian* correspondent reported that eight books had been published in recent years by former MI6, MI5, SAS or military officers.[20]

---

19 Unless it could be established that the disclosure would damage the national interest and this would be on the usual test of the balance of convenience—inevitably on the government's side in such matters.

20 27 July 2000. Approval is given by the Cabinet Secretary. The Divisional court has also spoken of the importance of fundamental rights to freedom of speech in refusing to award orders to the police to seize evidence of correspondence with David Shayler because of the stifling impact this would have on such a right and legitimate press investigation and freedom of speech. There is also discussion of the dangers of self-incrimination in allowing orders under s 9 and Sch 1 PACE 1984: *R v Central Criminal Court, ex p Bright, Alton and Rushbridger* [2001] 2 All ER 244. See chapter 1 p 56 n 6 above. The court was not prepared to accept the 'bare assertion' of the police on evidence of national security.

Defence

Section 2 of the OSA 1989 covers defence information and damaging disclosures by existing and former civil servants and defence contractors. The defendant can establish the defence that at the time of the alleged offence they did not know, and had no reasonable cause to believe, that the information related to defence or that its disclosure would be damaging. 'Damaging' is defined in s 2(2). It is a disclosure which damages or is likely to damage the capability of the armed forces of the Crown, or any part of them, to carry out their tasks. It also covers a disclosure which leads to loss of life or injury to members of those forces, or to serious damage to the equipment or installation of those forces. Last of all, it covers those disclosures which otherwise endanger the interests of the UK abroad, seriously obstructs the promotion or protection by the UK of those interests, or endangers the safety of British citizens abroad.

There were fears that the section would include within its embrace disclosures about unnecessary wastage, inefficient production and sub-standard products, especially if these affected UK economic interests abroad. Section 2(4) defines 'defence', however, to include:

(a) the size, shape, organisation, logistics, order of battle, deployment, operations, state of readiness and training of the armed forces of the Crown;

(b) the weapons, stores or other equipment of those forces and the invention, development, production and operation of such equipment and research relating to it; [This would need to be a damaging disclosure, so the jury would be correct to consider factors which diminish the damage to UK military interests abroad by, for example, revealing extravagant waste.]

(c) defence policy and strategy and military planning and intelligence;

(d) plans and measures for the maintenance of essential supplies and services that are or would be needed in time of war.

For a party who is not a civil servant or a government contractor, s 5 provides that their unauthorised receipt, or receipt in confidence, and subsequent unauthorised disclosure, is an offence where that person knows, or has reasonable cause to believe, that it is protected against disclosure by s 2 and that it has come into that person's possession as under s 5(1). The prosecution must establish *mens rea,* and that the disclosure was damaging, and that the defendant knew, or had reasonable cause to believe, that it would be damaging. Similar limits apply to a potential chain of recipients as applied in the discussion on the receipt of security and intelligence information.

This section would cover the notorious episode involving Duncan Sandys who used leaked information to reveal Britain's ill-prepared war defences prior to 1939. Apart from Parliamentary privilege for MPs, no defence would obtain to protect those who originally disclosed the information. The Sandys case prompted Sir Winston Churchill to denounce the use of the OSA to shield ministers who have strong personal interests in concealing the truth about matters from the country.

International relations and information received in confidence from states and international organisations

Section 3 is concerned with unauthorised disclosures of information relating to international relations by Crown servants and government contractors. Section 5 is concerned with the damaging disclosures of such information by others who have received the information within the terms of s 5(1). For the former defendants, knowledge of the damaging nature of the disclosure will be presumed; for the latter it has to be proved. Offences under this section include the disclosure of information relating to international relations. It also covers 'any confidential information ... obtained from a state other than the United Kingdom or an international organisation, which is, or was, in the servant or contractor's possession by virtue of their position as such'. Section 3(5) defines international relations as relations between states, international organisations (IO), or between one or more States and one or more such organisations, and 'includes any matter relating to a State other than the United Kingdom or to an international organisation which is capable of affecting the relations of the United Kingdom with another State or with an international organisation.' IO would include the European Community (EC) and Union and the UN, although Douglas Hurd expressed the view that the bulk of information from the EC was 'not confidential', and that most information received in confidence would fail the damage test.[1]

In spite of Mr Hurd's assurance, if a journalist revealed information leaked by a civil servant that subsidies were being paid to companies purchasing privatised concerns which contravened EC law, then this would concern international relations and it may well be damaging to such relations. Or, once again, a disclosure which revealed cabinet discussions and pejorative comments about the national characteristics of our EC partners and allies may be treated likewise. It could also cover the disclosure of information concerning inhumane treatment by an ally or trading partner of political opponents or minority groups. Where the broad test of 'damaging' is made out, the offence is established.

The test of damaging is to be found in s 3(2). A disclosure damages, first, if it endangers the interests of the UK abroad, seriously obstructs the

---

1   HC Debs vol 147 col 429 (15 February 1989). This is not true of the EU's second and third pillars.

promotion or protection by the UK of those interests or endangers the safety of British citizens abroad, and secondly, if it is a disclosure of information which is such that its unauthorised disclosure would be likely to have any of those effects. The breadth of this latter category can be illustrated by an example. If a document was stamped 'confidential', or was obtained in circumstances making it reasonable for the state or international organisation to expect confidentiality, which is readily presumed in international relationships, then it will be treated as confidential for the purposes of the OSA, even if it would not be considered confidential under our civil law as judicially developed.

In the White Paper, it seemed that the Government had created an absolute offence under this category. In fact, the Home Secretary and ministers were at pains to point out that the confidentiality or nature of documents might, but would not necessarily, be crucial.[2] Even though otherwise innocuous information is stamped 'confidential', a jury may infer, but is not constrained to infer, that its unauthorised leak is damaging.

Crime

Existing and former Crown servants and government contractors are guilty of an offence where they make an unauthorised disclosure of information which is or has been in their possession because of their official position, and which results in one of the following:

(a) the commission of an offence. Events in Northern Ireland concerning security leaks of information on individuals have dramatically illustrated the sensitivity of information in the possession of the police and security forces, the disclosure of which has led to the murder of IRA suspects.[3] The Government has argued that the defence available in s 4(4) (below) would protect disclosures about, for example, inefficient security systems;

(b) an escape from legal custody or the doing of any other act prejudicial to the safekeeping of persons in legal custody. One wonders about the situation where a prison officer reveals that a prison is at breaking point, or that inmates have been inhumanely treated and in consequence are on the point of insurrection;

(c) impeding the prevention or detection of offences or the apprehension or prosecution of suspected offenders.[4]

There is a general defence to these charges where the defendant can prove that at the time of the alleged offence they did not know and had no

2   Ibid cols 426-7.
3   Stevens, *The Times,* 18 May 1990.
4   Section 4(2)(a).

reasonable cause to believe that the disclosure would have any of those effects.[5]

Furthermore, by s 4(2)(b), unauthorised disclosures of information which are such that they are likely to have any of the above consequences are also an offence. A defendant may, however, show that they did not know, and had no reasonable cause to believe, that it was information to which the section applied.[6]

It is important to appreciate that police records are not given blanket protection by the OSA, although police officers are prescribed as 'Crown servants' for the purposes of the Act.[7] Where information is sold or disclosed, the law of corruption and disciplinary offences may have to be invoked against officers. It has been estimated that over one million people a year are vetted by employers with access to police records and the Home Affairs Select Committee has recommended a statutory body independent of the police to safeguard police records, many of which are currently out of date.[8]

Where 'other persons', ie non-civil servants and government contractors, receive information which is covered by the above provisions of s 4, it is an offence when they make an unauthorised disclosure of information protected by s 4 where they know, or have reasonable cause to believe, that it is protected against disclosure by s 4(2). As in the other areas of information, the prosecution must prove, and cannot simply presume, the defendant's state of knowledge.

Information relating to special investigation powers

Section 4 also applies to any information obtained under 'special investigation powers'; viz information which is obtained by warrant under the Interception of Communications Act 1985 and any related information, documents and articles, or obtained by warrant under the Security Service Act (SSA) 1989 or the Intelligence Services Act 1994. To this legislation has now been added the interception powers under RIPA 2000 as well as those matters which are carried out by the intelligence services under Part II of that Act and which require a warrant. These Acts authorise what had hitherto been practised under the prerogative powers of national security and preservation of the peace.[9] The powers of mail interception, and more latterly 'phone tapping', had

---

5   Section 4(4).
6   Section 4(5) but note this defence does not apply to s 4(2)(b).
7   Section 12.
8   *The Times,* 8 May 1990 and Home Affairs Committee *Criminal Appeal Records* HC 285 (1989-90).
9   Birkett *Interception of Communications* Cmnd 283 (1957).

always been assumed to exist, and that was felt to be sufficient justification until one plaintiff invoked art 8 of the European Convention on Human Rights (ECHR) to challenge a telephone tap. We saw the consequences in chapter 1. The provisions of the legislation were examined in that chapter.

The provisions relating to intrusive surveillance powers and encryption under RIPA and the powers under the Police Act 1997 which are not covered by this present provision may well be relevant to the preceding provision concerning crime where unauthorised disclosures are made which contravene the relevant provision, viz they impede the prevention or detection of offences, their prosecution etc.

Section 4(3) OSA 1989 makes it an absolute offence for information, as described, obtained under the Acts to be disclosed without lawful authority by a Crown servant or government contractor. In fact, 'absolute' is not strictly accurate since a defendant can make out a defence similar to the one available for security and intelligence officers under s 1 and described earlier.

Under s 5, a person, for example a newspaper editor, who received information obtained under such warrants and who knowingly discloses it without authority, is guilty of an offence. The prosecution must prove that they knew or had reasonable cause to believe it belonged to such a category to establish a criminal offence. Actual knowledge of the nature of the information has to be proved. Once proved, and in most cases it will be glaringly obvious what its nature is, the offence will be made out no matter how trivial the information is and without reference to any public interest being served by its being made public. This is the strictest provision of all for third party recipients as no damage has to be proved.[10]

The existence of this offence means that there would be no difficulty in prosecuting a Cathy Massiter, the former MI5 officer who revealed the targeting and intercepting of CND campaigners by the security service. This measure is particularly draconian and dangerous. It refuses to allow for the possibility that the rot is operating at such a high level that it is impossible to deal with it by internal devices. The investigatory and tribunal procedures under these two Acts, which seek to protect 'victims', are judicial-review proof; that is to say that they cannot be reviewed by the courts. A revelation of a phone-tap without a warrant or other unauthorised invasion of privacy would not be covered by s 4 OSA, but it may well be covered by s 1 where perpetrated by security, intelligence or other notified officials.

10 See *Lustgarten and Leigh* chapter 10.

Information entrusted in confidence to other states

The Government plugged a loop-hole by providing in s 6 OSA 1989 that the unlawful disclosure of information relating to security, intelligence, defence or international relations which has been communicated in confidence by or on behalf of the UK to another state or IO, will be an offence if two conditions are satisfied: first, if it has come into the discloser's possession, whether originally disclosed to them or another, without the authority of the state or IO, or a member of the latter; secondly, if the disclosure is not already an offence under the previous sections of the Act. Section 6 is aimed at punishing a disclosure of information which has been leaked abroad, even if already published abroad, without the authority of the state or IO to whom it was entrusted, or where the discloser otherwise has no authority. In other words, publishing a story in the UK which satisfies the above criteria and which is widely published abroad without authority, will constitute an offence. Publication with the authority of the state prior to disclosure is a defence. The prosecution must prove that the defendant made a damaging disclosure knowing, or having reasonable cause to believe, that it is information as described in section 6 and that its disclosure would be damaging.

Disclosure by recipients under s 5

We have seen how receipt of information within the terms of s 5, which is information protected by ss 1-4, and its subsequent unauthorised disclosure by the recipient, will be an offence, and how a chain of offences may be committed. We also noted the limitations and exceptions concerning an unauthorised disclosure by a Crown servant or government contractor and those to whom such disclosures are made. We need only add that an offence is not committed where such a disclosure is made by a person who is not a British citizen or takes place outside the UK, the Channel Islands, the Isle of Man or a colony.

Finally s 5 refers to s 1 of the 1911 Act which concerns 'espionage' and which has already been discussed. Section 5 stipulates that it is an offence to disclose any information without lawful authority and which the discloser knows, or has reasonable cause to believe, came into his or her possession as a result of a contravention of s 1 of the OSA 1911.

Safeguarding information

Section 8 creates a variety of offences relating to the following. Crown servants (including a notified person under s 1(1) who is not a Crown servant), or government contractors, commit an offence if they have in their possession information which it would be an offence under the Act to disclose without lawful authority and, being a Crown servant, they retain the document or article contrary to their official duty. A defence is available where they believe, and have no reasonable cause to believe othewise, that at the relevant time they were acting in accordance with an official duty. Offences also cover the failure of a government contractor to comply with an official direction for the return or disposal of a relevant document, and the failure by a Crown servant or contractor to take such care to prevent the unauthorised disclosure of the document or article as a person in his or her position may reasonably be expected to take. This latter offence criminally punishes negligence.

Any person, including a past Crown servant or government contractor, who has information which it is an offence to disclose without lawful authority under s 5, is guilty of an offence if they fail to comply with an official direction for the return or disposal of the information. Such persons are also guilty of an offence if they, in simple parlance, are negligent in looking after information entrusted to them in confidence by a Crown servant or contractor. A person is also guilty where they fail to comply with an official direction for the return of information protected by s 6. Offences also cover disclosures which facilitate unauthorised access to protected information (s 8(6)).

Miscellaneous provisions

Offences under the Act are triable on indictment or summons, although some offences under s 8 are triable by summons only. 'Trial by summons' means trial without a jury before magistrates who tend to be more sympathetic to the prosecution than juries and to be more conviction-minded. The Act contains arrest and search provisions. Although these are more extensive than under the PACE 1984, the latter Act now applies to legally privileged, excluded and special procedure material.[11] By s 11(4), the provisions of earlier secrecy legislation, allowing the public[12] to be excluded from a trial on the grounds of national security, apply to offences under the 1989 Act, although there are minor exceptions under s 8. Such orders will have to be consistent with the HRA and Art 10.[13]

Under the Act, the term 'Crown servant' includes ministers, civil servants, members of the armed forces, police officers and any other person

11   See *R v Central Criminal Court etc* above n 20 p 139. Section 11(3) of the OSA 1989 applies PACE s 9(2) and Sch 1 para 3(b) to S 9 OSA 1911.
12   *Re Crook* (1989) 93 Cr App Rep 17.
13   See *Leander v Sweden etc*

employed or appointed in or for the purposes of any police force.[14] The secretary of state may prescribe as Crown servants office holders and some or all of their staff, and the Comptroller and Auditor-General and employees of the National Audit Office have been so prescribed.[15] Such orders are subject to the affirmative resolution procedure of the House of Commons. The secretary of state may also prescribe some or all of the members of staff of a range of bodies. 'Government contractor' is defined as a person other than a Crown servant who provides goods or services for the purposes of a minister or body of Crown servants. The Act extends to Northern Ireland and to offences committed abroad by British citizens and, with minor exceptions, Crown servants.

The OSA and the question of privilege

There are bound to be problems of considerable practical importance concerning the question of disclosures in contravention of the Act and privilege. The privileges in question are of two kinds. The first is that of an MP who cannot be prosecuted under the criminal law for statements made in the House or for those which are made in the course of Parliamentary proceedings. The second concerns the privilege between a lawyer and client and the giving of legal advice during which a disclosure of information protected by the 1989 Act is made.

The Act does not add to, or diminish, Parliamentary privilege. An MP will be protected as before, though the Government resisted an attempt to allow a member of the public to be given immunity in passing protected information to an MP. The current position is that the privilege is that of the MP and no one else.[16] Similarly, the 1989 Act does not affect the operation of the law relating to legal professional privilege, contrary to the views of the Law Society as represented by the Shadow Home Secretary.[17] Where, therefore, the disclosure is made with a view to obtaining legal advice on, eg, whether it constitutes an offence, it is protected. It will not be protected where the disclosure was made to facilitate a crime to which the lawyer intended to be a party.

The Attorney-General

The role of the Attorney-General—whose *fiat* is required for a prosecution under the Act—has been described as invidious in as much as the decision

---

14   *Lewis v Cattle* [1938] 2 KB 454; *R v Loat* [1985] Crim LR 154.
15   SI 1990/200 and s 12.
16   See HC 173 (1937-8) and HC 101 (1938-9).
17   HC Debs vol 147 col 503 (16 February 1989).

to prosecute is his. Franks found no evidence of political interference with Attorneys-General in the past. Events since Franks cast doubts on the continuing accuracy of that view,[18] and in the Peter Wright episode an embarrassed Cabinet Secretary was forced to admit in open court in Australia, by the Attorney-General himself, that decisions on prosecuting, or not prosecuting, had not been the responsibility of the Attorney-General.[19] The proximity of the Attorney-General to the Government makes it very difficult for the office-holder to argue persuasively that he is an 'honest broker', regardless of his identity. The performance of the Attorney-General in the Matrix Churchill affair bestowed little credit upon the holder of the office.

Franks found that s 2 was saved from absurdity by the 'sparing exercise of the Attorney-General's discretion to prosecute', although the matter still gave rise to 'considerable unease'. Even after reform, Franks still envisaged a central place for the Attorney-General, who would retain control of prosecutions in the major areas where Franks recommended the law should operate and hopefully apply judicious discretion. An 'appropriate alternative' to legislation to protect official secrecy outside the area of espionage was difficult to conceive, the Government argued in 1972, and Franks accepted that over-reliance on voluntary forms of internal restraint by the press and media would be undesirable. They may have a 'responsibility' to publish what is in the public interest, but government has a constitutional responsibility to protect the nation, which cannot be 'abdicated on the basis that a failure to exercise them will be made good by the responsible behaviour of others'. And, as we all know, the press in particular do not always act with the requisite degree of responsibility.[20]

Local government

The most important development in our constitutional history has been the supremacy of Parliament as an institution over other governmental institutions, and the supremacy of the Crown in Parliament as a legislature. Our membership of the European Union, devolution and the HRA will put that assumption under increasing strain. Except in those areas

18 Suspicion has attended both Labour and Conservative Government interference: see *Ponting*, chapter 6 and Nicol (1979) Crim LR 284. For breaches of confidentiality proceedings and the Attorney-General's role, see HC Debs, cols 619–620 (1 December 1986). As with the Lord Chancellor, the problem attaches to a multiplicity of roles in one person: law officer, MP, minister, prosecutor etc.

19 Sir Robert gave evidence that the decision not to prosecute Chapman Pincher for revelations in *Their Trade is Treachery* was taken by the Attorney-General Sir Michael Havers. Sir Michael took no part in the decision.

20 Especially on unjustified invasion of privacy. See chapter 10 p 455 *et seq*.

occupied by Community law, the law of Parliament is supreme, and local authorities are the creature of Parliamentary statute,[1] and statute affords them wide powers to administer.

A persistent theme of relations between central and local government in this century has been the growth of centripetal tendencies as central government has removed function after function from local government responsibility, or has sought more effective control over local government spending. Today, local government accounts for approximately 25% of public expenditure (approaching £100 billion) and in 2000 employed in the region of 2.1 million people. How the money is spent, and what local authorities are getting up to, have always been high on the agenda of central government. The doctrine of 'subsidiarity' expressed in the Maastricht Treaty and reinforced at Amsterdam and the movement towards regional government will affect such centripetalist tendencies. Whether these developments will bring government closer to the people in providing greater access to decision-making and information, as opposed to simply establishing a Scottish legislative Assembly and executive and devolving powers to a Welsh and Northern Ireland Assembly and executives we shall have to see (see chapter 6 pp 327-328 on FOIA initiatives).

When central government pursues tight monetary and expenditure policies to restrict public spending, its demands for information from local government will correspondingly increase. The statute-book has seen a plethora of statutes requiring local authorities to provide information to central government and its departments, the Commission for Local Administration (the Local Ombudsman), the Auditor and Audit Commission, members and the public.[2] With the Local Government Act 1986 as amended in 1988, the Government obtained powers to prohibit and restrict the publicity exercises of local authorities.[3] Section 2 prohibits the publication of material which 'in whole or in part appears to be designed to affect support for a political party'. Section 3 restricts the use by authorities of ss 137 and 142 of the Local Government Act 1972.[4] The former authorises expenditure by authorities of a rate of 2p in the pound in a financial year, which in their opinion is in the interests of the area or any part of it, or some or all of its inhabitants, providing it is not the subject of other statutory provision. New powers on economic development are contained in the Local Government Act 2000 (LGA

1   Though cf the City of London (charter of incorporation) and note *Hazell v Hammersmith and Fulham London Borough Council* [1991] 1 All ER 545, HL.
2   Birkinshaw *Open Government: Freedom of Information and Local Government* (1986) and *Government and Information: the Law Relating to Access, Disclosure and their Regulation* (2nd ed, (2001).
3   These are being revised.
4   And their Scottish equivalents. See Widdicombe, Cmnd 9797 and his interim report *Restricting Local Authority Publicity* (HMSO, 1985).

2000). Section 142 concerns the provision of information by local authorities affecting local government. It has been held by the High Court that use of s 142 to persuade an electorate of the authority's view of the effects of rate-capping and the retention of an advertising agency to help in persuasion was invalid.[5] The section permitted explanation and factual information, not political persuasion, Glidewell J believed.[6]

The 1986 Act was prompted by the highly successful campaigns of local authorities against central government. The Act provides the belt and braces from the Government's perspective and allows codes of recommended practice to guide authorities on the content, style, distribution and cost of local authority publicity to which authorities 'shall have regard'. The code is a detailed document.[7] The strength of feeling on the Government side was expressed by a former Secretary of State for the Environment[8] when he informed a select committee that he had been at the 'wrong end of by far the most expensive publicly financed propaganda campaign ... finding that my hands were almost totally tied as to what I was entitled to do at public expense as part of my departmental duties in reply'.[9]

The 1999 LGA sought to give legal expression to a more relaxed relationship between central and local government. The provision on publicity still survives. A notorious section which the Labour Government has sought, so far unsuccessfully, to repeal is s 28 LGA 1988 which bans the promotion of homosexuality or teaching the 'acceptability of homosexuality as a pretended family relationship.'

Local government, the public and information

Since the Poor Law Reform Act 1834, a system of compulsory local authority audit has existed in England and Wales. The Municipal Corporations Act 1835 opened up the books of the corporations to inspection, in the legislature's attempts to ferret out corruption which had been rampant in the commercial oligarchies administering the cities. Duties to provide information to ministers and auditors increased as the century developed and as central government became more and more jealous of its powers of supervision over local administration. Public knowledge of local authority affairs did not appear to become an issue

---

5   *R v ILEA, ex p Westminster City Council* [1986] 1 All ER 19; and see *R v GLC, ex p Westminster City Council* (1985) Times, 22 January. See Birkinshaw *Government and Information* (2001) p 208 et seq.

6   Cf *Meek v Lothian Regional Council* 1983 SLT 494.

7   DoE Circular 20/88.

8   Patrick Jenkin MP.

9   HC 92 II, p 129 (1985–6).

until later in the nineteenth century when local government administration became more widespread and more coherent. Following a judicial decision that reporters were not allowed as of right to attend and report council meetings, an Act of 1908 was passed allowing press access to council meetings, but it could be avoided by delegating business to a committee. Nor were agendas circulated in advance under the Act. Analogies with Parliament, which had been reported freely for well over a century, were not regarded as pertinent, as Parliament is a legislative body, whereas councils and committees are executive. It was not 'practical politics' to administer in a 'goldfish' bowl.[10]

In 1960, Margaret Thatcher MP secured the passage through Parliament of the Public Bodies (Admission to Meetings) Act, which opened up council meetings to the press and public. Minutes of councils and committees[11] had to be published. Even after the 1972 Local Government Act, which opened up committees to the press and public, problems remained. The legislation did not cover subcommittees, though local authorities were urged to be open in their administration. Research conducted in the 1980s showed that while many authorities opened up their subcommittees, with exceptions, to the public, a substantial number of those who replied did not.[12] Other studies found authorities adamantly refusing to provide information which they were under a legal duty to provide.[13]

There were pronounced elements of secrecy in too many authorities which did not assist their cause at a time of highly publicised scandals relating to corruption of standards and rule by high-handed political caucuses across the political spectrum. Nor was there much evidence to show that local authorities had geared themselves to inform the public better of their rights to receive information and assistance or to make complaint or to participate in decision-making in planning,[14] urban renewal,[15] development[16] and housing,[17] to name but a few. In 1972, the Bains Report[18] urged authorities to introduce, where they had not already done so, a corporate approach to management with overall co-ordination of policy-making, which often ended up in the hands of ruling political heavyweights and the chief executive and a cadre of senior officers. The

10 DGT Williams *Not In The Public Interest*, p 121.
11 Only where they had referred powers: *Wilson v Evans* [1962] 1 All ER 247.
12 Birkinshaw, n 5 above and see: Birkinshaw, 'Open Government – Local Government Style' (1988) *Public Policy and Administration* 46.
13 P McAuslan *The Ideologies of Planning Law* (1980).
14 Ibid.
15 N Lewis and I Harden 'Law and the Local State' (1982) Urban Law and Policy 65.
16 P McAuslan *Land, Law and Planning* (1975).
17 N Lewis and R Livock (1979) Urban Law and Policy 133.
18 *The New Local Authorities: Management and Structure* (1972).

period throughout the 1970s and 1980s witnessed an increasing politicisation of local government politics,[19] at least in intensity if not pervasively,[20] with issues being fought out locally on the lines of party political allegiance reflecting, very often, national political conflict. Ruling parties, backbenchers and opposition emerged as terms of political currency. Following reports by David Widdicombe QC and a Government reply[1] the Local Government and Housing Act 1989 sought to provide for a variety of safeguards in local government administration.

Politics, members and information

The 1989 Act disqualified persons from being members of authorities where they hold politically restricted posts within s 2. By early 1991, over 36,000 had been disqualified under this provision. An adjudicator supervises and grants exemptions under the Act.[2] A monitoring officer in the authority acts as an internal 'whistleblower' and reports to the authority where s/he believes that an unlawful or 'maladministrative' act has taken place including a breach of a code within the authority. In 1988, a chief finance officer was placed under similar duties in relation to unlawful expenditure which had been or was about to be incurred and the official's duty included reporting to the auditor where necessary.[3] Controls were established over staff appointments including ensuring the confidentiality of staff records,[4] the voting rights of members of various committees and subcommittees etc; and the political balance of committees and sub committees according to political representation on the council. New controls were introduced for members' allowances and members' interests and declarations thereon were to be beefed up by regulations.[5] A new code on local government conduct was drafted which members had to undertake to be guided by and anonymity in local ombudsman reports could be removed in the case of members in certain circumstances.[6]

These controls emerged because the ante-chamber discussion became more and more closed in a growing number of authorities, and one-party

---

19 Widdicombe.
20 Birkinshaw *Government and Information: the Law Relating to Access, Disclosure and their Regulation* (2nd ed, 2001).
1   The Conduct of Local Authority Business Cmnd 9797 and Cm 433 (1988).
2   *Ahmed* v *UK* [1999] IRLR 188, ECtHR.
3   Sections 114 and 115 Local Government and Housing Act 1989.
4   Because the Local Government (Finance) Act 1982 unwittingly gave access to them it was believed.
5   LGHA s 19 and SIs 92/618 and 96/1215.
6   Where they had engaged in maladministration in breach of the revised code: see *R v Local Comr for Administration in North and North East England, ex p Liverpool City Council* [2001] 1 All ER 462, CA.

groups emerged which were often advised by, and sought the advice of, officials. Ad hoc groups, advisory bodies, working parties and the like emerged to attempt to maintain confidential discussion within political groupings. Constitutionally, this produced difficulties.

First of all, the local authority in law only knows of the existence of the council, committees, joint committees, subcommittees and officers as executive bodies. The law did not adequately reflect the political reality of administration and its organisation. In large part, the LGA 2000 in introducing new styles of 'executive arrangements' to local authority administration have sought to address some of these points as will be seen below. Secondly, the emergence of political groupings helped to increase the alienation of those who are not privy to a ruling group's policies and politics while, in urban areas at least, there had been an increasing co-option of non-elected members into council bodies, most notably from bodies who are under-represented in terms of elected representatives, eg ethnic minorities, minority groupings, council tenants, under 35-year-olds.[7] Thirdly, officers were frequently placed in a difficult situation as their duty is to advise members as a whole—not as political groups of ruling members who can shield officers by conventions such as ministerial responsibility and advisers' anonymity. Fourthly, in law members are members of the council as a whole, not members of political parties. It is around this latter point that recent legal controversy has centred. The position below relates to members' rights to council documents. This position is heavily modified in relation to the new executive arrangements.

Members of the council have a common law right to inspect the books and papers of the council. Conflicts over the scope of the right have produced an explosion of litigation.[8] Two opposing positions are present in the case law: the corporate responsibilities and duties of members of the corporation to the corporation, and the duty and responsibilities of members as representatives of a wider range of community interests which they are elected to represent.

Members do not have a 'roving commission' to examine the documents of a council.[9] They must establish a 'need to know' in order to perform their duties as councillors, and any irrelevant motivation or any ulterior, indirect or improper motive may be raised as a bar to their inspection.[10] Where a member is also a member of a specific committee, he or she has

7 To what extent were the views of those constituencies under-represented in the representative model? Nb the special position of police committees (with JPs and 'nominated persons') (cf Police and Magistrates' Courts Act 1994, s 3 and Sch 2) and education committees (with those experienced in education).

8 Birkinshaw note 20 above.

9 *R v Hampstead Borough Council, ex p Woodward* (1917) 116 LT 213.

10 Ibid and *R v Lancashire County Council Police Authority, ex p Hook* [1980] QB 603, CA.

the right to inspect the committee's documentation, barring improper motive, etc, on the part of the member, though this ought not in principle to be easy to establish on the part of the committee or council because of the strong *prima facie* right of the member to inspect.[11] Where a member is not a member of a committee, he or she has to establish a 'need to know' a committee or subcommittee's documents. The claim of such a member is not as strong as that of a member of the actual committee, although the courts will be reluctant to second-guess a council's decision to allow inspection to a non-committee member.[12] A member of a parent committee will, even though not a member of the subcommittee, usually have a right to see documents of its subcommittee, and even a right to attend the sub-committee.[13]

Case law has developed these principles. At common law it has been established that, *pace* the standing orders of the authority, which under the 1989 Act may contain items by order of the secretary of state, and which must be followed if they cover the subject area unless *ultra vires,* a ruling party can appoint *only its members* to the committees of the authority.[14] This is now altered by the 1989 Act but the restrictions on membership does not apply to new style executives. In *R v Sheffield City Council, ex p Chadwick,*[15] it was held that it was *ultra vires* for a policy committee to delegate functions to a subcommittee of ruling party members alone *simply to avoid* informing opposition members of decisions in the formulation of the budget. It was unlawful to use a subcommittee for purely party political purposes. The case involved alternatives to the actual budget recommendation that was made and could support a suggestion that a 'need to know' will cover alternative policy options. The councillor was entitled to attend the meeting and see the documents, although strictly speaking the meeting was only operating in a recommendatory capacity in settling the budget.[16] Where the leaders of a party group met informally with officers and made what in effect were decisions *on behalf of* the council, they were acting in an executive capacity and were covered by the common law 'need to know' principle. The meetings were within the formal framework of the council structure, and not outside it, and the councillor could establish a need to know and

---

11 Ibid.
12 *Birmingham City District Council v O* [1983] 1 AC 578, HL.
13 *R v Hackney London Borough Council, ex p Gamper* [1985] 3 All ER 275, subject to veto in exceptional instances. Cf *Ex p Chadwick* below.
14 *R v Rushmoor Borough Council, ex p Crawford* (1981) Times, 28 November.
15 (1985) 84 LGR 563.
16 Widdicombe recommended that recommendatory committees and subcommittees should be removed from this duty: see chapter 4 below.

a right to attend.[17] There seems no reason in principle why a 'need to know' might not exist in relation to a 'working group's', etc, papers and documents if they are council papers. It would depend upon the facts.[18]

Local Government (Access to Information) Act 1985 (ATIA)

The law relating to members' rights and the public's rights to information in particular was reformed by the ATIA. A circular accompanies the Act.[19] This Act constitutes an FOIA for local government, and there is an immediate irony in the fact that it was passed with the approval of the Government, which had steadfastly refused such legislation for itself. That legislation had to wait until FOIA 2000 (see chapter 6). Regulations heavily influenced by the 1985 Act, but with some significant alterations, apply to the new executive arrangements under the LGA 2000. The 1985 Act does apply to Oversight and Scrutiny Committees of authorities which are established under the LGA 2000 and which will have a central role in holding new style executives to account.

The 1985 Act provides for greater public access to the meetings and documents of principal councils, ie essentially county, district and London borough authorities, and regional and district authorities in Scotland and unitary authorities.[20] It opens up council, committee and subcommittee meetings to the public, and provides for access to local authority information. 'Information' in the Act includes an expression of opinion, any recommendations, and any decision taken. Meetings must be closed to the public, and information will not be available where 'confidential' items, as specifically defined, are dealt with.[1] This is where a government department provides information upon terms which forbid public disclosure. It may also be under the OSA if one of the six protected areas. It includes cases where publication is prohibited by court order or statute.[2] Under the terms of the Act, an item is not confidential simply because a party gives the information in confidence.

Information can be exempt under the Act if it falls under one of a list of categories. If exempt information is involved, the authority *may* exclude the public from its meetings and refuse access to information containing

---

17 *R v Hyndburn Borough Council, ex p Strak* (CO/918/85, 17 December 1985). If operating in a purely advisory capacity, it was doubted whether a right to attend would exist, though surely a 'need to know' may still be established for access to documents.

18 Eg officers cannot be members of committees and so on. They can now be a member of an executive p 227 et seq below.

19 DOE Circ 6/86. See SI 1986/854.

20 And the Islands. Bodies covered in England include police authorities, joint authorities and joint boards. Unitary authorities will be covered.

1   As defined by the Act, not common law.

2   It includes the Data Protection Act 1998.

such items. The list of exempt categories covers information relating to employees and office holders of the authority; tenants of the authority; applicants and recipients of any service provided by the authority, or of financial assistance in their capacity as applicants; it also covers information relating to the adoption, care, fostering or education of any child, or to the financial or business affairs of any person other than the authority unless already required to be registered under various statutes. Further exemptions protect the contractual and prospective contractual interests of the authority for as long as exemption is necessary to protect the interests of the authority and the identity of those tendering for contracts for goods or services. Labour relations are covered in certain situations. Instructions to and opinions of counsel are given a total exemption, as is 'any advice received, information obtained or action to be taken in connection with any legal proceedings by or against the authority', or 'the determination of any matter affecting the authority', or where such is contemplated. 'Determination' refers to a formal administrative ruling, for example after an inquiry. The legal opinions of officers and other information is protected when given in connection with such determinations and legal proceedings or where they are contemplated, and this would require more than a 'vague anticipation'. Exempt information covers those situations where the authority seeks to impose statutory orders or notices, especially important in the planning area and where disclosure would defeat the purpose of the order, eg a building preservation notice. Information relating to the prevention, investigation or prosecution of crime is exempt, as is that relating to 'protected informants'.[3]

Unless the 'proper officer' believes it to contain confidential or exempt information, the public will have access to officers' reports for items on the agenda of meetings and advance notice of agenda, meetings, their place and time. A reasonable number of copies of reports and agenda must be available at the meetings. The provisions requiring public notice may be waived where the chairperson is of the opinion that the item should be considered at the meeting as a matter of urgency 'by reason of special circumstances' which *must be specified* in the minutes.[4]

An important dimension to the Act concerns 'background papers', namely those documents relating to the subject matter of the report which 'disclose any facts or matters on which, *in the opinion of the proper officer,* the report or an important part of the report is based and have, *in his opinion,* been relied on to a material extent in preparing the report'

3 Whose information shows that a criminal offence, breach of statutory duty, a breach of planning control – eg s 172(1)-(4) of the Town and Country Planning Act 1990 – or a nuisance etc has been committed.

4 Does this reduce the safeguards available under the 1972 Local Government Act? Standing orders of authorities dealt with urgent business.

(emphasis added). The information is available for specified periods before and after the meeting.[5] Minutes are open for inspection. Additional information has to be published.[6] Interference with rights under the Act is a criminal offence.

The Act covers a wide range of principal councils and has been extended to cover joint consultative committees of health and local authorities and community health councils.[7] The Act also extends members of authorities' rights of access to information in the possession or under the control of local authorities and relates to any business to be transacted at a meeting of the council, its committees or subcommittees. A member does not need to establish a 'need to know' as under the common law where he or she is not a member of a specific committee, but some of the exemptions will apply to requests, especially those relating to employees, recipients of housing or services, children, contracts, the legal immunities apropos of advice and the prosecution, prevention or investigation of crime. These exemptions would *not apply* to a request at common law. However, the rights of a council member under the Act are more extensive than those of the public, as the right to go through background papers is not restricted to those papers which the 'proper officer' believes formed the basis of the officer's report to a material extent.[8]

The legislation leaves important matters of judgement in the hands of the 'proper officer'[9] and the chairman of a meeting. This includes selection of items or reports which are exempt, materials in background papers which were relied upon to a material extent, and in the case of the latter those items which as a matter of urgency require incorporation without the statutory notice of three clear days.[10] No specific procedure for challenging such decisions is contained in the statute, so it will be a matter of pressurising councillors or seeking relief via the Ombudsman or the courts.[11]

One further point concerns the fact that the Act preserves the right to exercise a power of exclusion to suppress or prevent disorderly conduct at a meeting.[12] It has been decided that a chairperson can exercise this right in advance of a meeting; this would prevent the public seeing how

---

5 Including written summaries of proceedings where exempt information is excluded from the minutes and this exclusion prevents a 'reasonably fair and coherent record of the whole or part of the proceedings'.

6 Names and addresses of councillors, rights under the Act etc.

7 Health Service Joint Consultative Committees (Access to Information) Act 1986.

8 See Birkinshaw *Government and Information: the Law Relating to Access, Disclosure and Regulation* (2nd ed, 2001) chapter 5.

9 Local Government Act 1972, s 270(3).

10 This has been amended under the LGA 2000, s 98 to allow for an extension.

11 See 2nd ed of this book, p 140 n 13 and accompanying text.

12 *R v Brent Health Authority, ex p Francis* [1985] QB 869; Cf [1986] 2 All ER 273n.

members voted when it came to a subsequent ratification of the chairperson's decision.[13]

The Government in its White Paper on *Open Government* (see chapter 5) expressed the intention of drafting a code on openness for local government which would be policed by local government ombudsmen. However, this was subject to reconsideration and guidance on good practice was issued in June 1995 by local authority associations. This will leave it up to each authority to produce its own code. (*Open Government: A good practice note on access for information* (LAAs, June 1995)). Practice in the past on complaints procedures has not been very encouraging.

The 1985 legislation will apply to committees and council meetings but the LGA seeks to reduce the number of committees. They will also apply to Oversight and Scrutiny Committees established under the LGA 2000. Local authorities will be covered by FOIA 2000 which I examine in chapter 6. Executive arrangements will fall under provisions in the LGA 2000 which are examined in chapter 4.

Some food for thought

There are numerous other statutory provisions which seek to render local government more open in its decision-making by providing information and allowing participation in decision-making. The Citizen's Charter and *Better Government* initiatives demand such and various features of this initiative have been placed in legislation for local government and education[14]. Various laws and regulations enjoin authorities to provide information to the clients of their services such as social services, housing and education[15] and now under the Best Value provisions of the LGA 1999 replacing Compulsory Competitive Tendering of the LGA 1988. The legislation and regulations were effectively restricted to local government and education until in the case of non computerised files the enactment of the Data Protection Act 1998 and FOIA 2000. Other codes such as the *National Code of Local Government Conduct* which is being redrafted for councillors[16] are in addition to standing orders of an authority and seek to prevent abuse of information and breaches of confidentiality by declarations of interest—apart, that is, from financial ones, which are covered by the law. Officers have a duty not to disclose information which

13 Ibid.
14 Local Government Act 1992; Education (Schools) Act 1992.
15 See chapter 7 below.
16 A draft *Model Code of Conduct for Members* was issued in February 2001: and see the draft Local Government England and Wales The Relevant Authorities (Model Code of Conduct) Order 2001.

would amount to a breach of confidence, unless presumably there was a greater public interest in disclosure than in maintaining a confidence.[17]

The practice of closed or secretive local government is considered in the next chapter, where an examination is undertaken of the guiding principles that inform or must be taken to be presupposed in our system of government. What promises are there, so to speak, which legitimate power, and what differences exist between EC, central and regional[18] and local government? All are operating in the public interest and have monopolies of power in important respects which are exercised on the public behalf. Is government in any of the above respects too powerful for the devices of accountability that exist? It was the Widdicombe Report's belief that, for abuses in local government, the problems would be largely resolved if members and officials were made to operate within the law. Two questions are pertinent. Firstly, is the law itself even as reformed an adequate safeguard? In relation to central government it would appear that it remains inadequate. The Scottish FOIA will be examined in chapter 6. There are widespread claims that the Scottish Parliament is operating in a very open and transparent manner, particularly with the use of petitions from citizens. We shall examine the EU in chapter 8. For local government there is fuller legal provision which is superficially easier for citizens to utilise, but its formal properties have little relevance to strengthening democratic principles, and it is these which legitimate public power. The LGA 2000 sought to address this dilemma. But, secondly, what principles are we talking about, and what does their application entail? It is time to return to the centre.

17 Chapter 9 below. The Code is an Annex to DoE Circ 8/90 and WO 23/90. See para 26 on confidential information.
18 See Ethical Standards in Public Life (Scotland) Act 2000.

4 Claims and counterclaims

The development of the secret state in Britain goes back centuries. The British have not been forced into addressing constitutional fundamentals in the face of revolution for over 300 years. The English, it has been said, had their enduring revolution in America in the eighteenth century. Constitutional upheaval in the British Islands was confined to Ireland. Incremental enfranchisement and coming to terms with the odd royal scandal involving succession have been the basic constitutional fare. One might add reviewing the veto power of the House of Lords. Nor, until Blair's Government, has the nation been compelled to undertake a reassessment of basic principles of governmental right which has forced major changes in our constitutional practice. Our union with the EC has caused a great deal of angst in influential political circles, but if anything, membership has reinforced executive control and diminished the role of Parliament. We are, constitutionally, a conservative and placid race. But we do have basic principles which governments purport to abide by in their process of rule—the Rule of Law being the most obvious. This chapter will seek to describe the operation of government today, 'the functional part', the claims for responsible government and the continuation of the practices of a secret state. In the opening chapter, a theory of communicative competence as developed by Habermas was described. What do the following pages tell us about the desirability, necessity or feasibility of that theory? Is there a systematic distortion of communication and information by government? If so, why has there not been the political will or pressure to do something to change practices? Will the Freedom of Information Act enacted in November 2000 effect such changes, or do existing practices run too deeply to be altered significantly?

Principled government

There are several sensational events which have provided an insight into contemporary governmental practice and one more systemic development which concerns government structure. The stormy episode of Michael Heseltine's resignation as Defence Secretary from Mrs Thatcher's Government in January 1986 threw into dramatic relief some of the issues relevant to the present inquiry. The factual details need not concern us now, but Mr Heseltine alleged that the Prime Minister had engineered the breakdown of constitutional government.[1] She had cancelled an agreed Cabinet meeting specifically to thwart his efforts to show that it was in the national interest that a British-owned helicopter-manufacturing company—Westland plc—was taken over by a consortium with a British component and not an American company. He claimed that the Prime Minister's conduct was in breach of collective ministerial responsibility and that his own individual ministerial responsibility necessitated that he went public on the issue. Within two weeks, the Defence Secretary's major protagonist in the Cabinet resigned because of his role in authorising[2] a leak through the Press Association of a confidential[3] letter from the Solicitor-General to Mr Heseltine. This was a major breach of confidence. The Defence Select Committee pressed for the attendance before it of the civil servants who were involved,[4] but eventually settled, albeit reluctantly, for the attendance of the head of the Home Civil Service and Secretary to the Cabinet, Sir Robert Armstrong.[5] He had conducted an internal inquiry into the leak, knowing beforehand what its conclusion would be. The whole episode was wonderful political drama. But important themes run through the episode concerning the principles of constitutional government. Mr Heseltine declared pointedly 'that the case against him was being put by "unidentified sources" '. 'We have no documents, no statements, no piece of paper that we can examine, we have

1   See M Heseltine in *The Observer*, 12 January 1986 and *Life in the Jungle* (2000) pp 535 et seq; M Thatcher *Margaret Thatcher: The Downing Sreet. Years* (2000) 423 et seq
2   HC 519 (1985–6), *Fourth Report from the Defence Committee: Westland plc: The Government's Decision-Making*. It seems he believed he had approval from the Prime Minister's Private Office for the leak; the Office certainly knew of the leak.
3   The same classification as the papers leaked by Ponting.
4   These were: the secretary to Leon Brittan; the chief press officer of the DTI; the Prime Minister's chief press and information secretary; the Prime Minister's private secretary; and a senior DTI official. To general incredulity, the Prime Minister maintained she did not know of the identities involved in the leak until two weeks after it occurred.
5   Far more accomplished than his appearance before the New South Wales court in the Peter Wright case, chapter 9 below, p 414.

just whispers on the telephone. Now, that is the way British Government is to be conducted. . . .'[6]

Michael Heseltine revealed the machinations of contemporary cabinet government, and his allegations of Prime Ministerial presidency set off a process that led to the release of more information about Whitehall's inner workings than we could normally have hoped for, although not all that the Defence Select Committee wanted. Even now, certain crucial points have not been fully clarified.[7] A court of law might have uncovered more information and have left a record of events that was more readily acceptable.[8] But this is high politics. Political survival depends upon political support which in 1986 the then Prime Minister seemed to have in abundance.

The second episode concerns the events surrounding the Matrix Churchill (MC) trial.[9] MC was an engineering company involved in exporting what transpired to be dual use equipment to Iraq which could be put to both civilian and military use. This contravened guidelines on exports made under the Import, Export and Customs Powers Act 1939 prohibiting such export and several executives of MC were charged by Customs and Excise with offences of obtaining export licences by deception. The prosecution collapsed in November 1992 when a minister, under cross-examination, admitted that the Government knew that the equipment would be used for the purpose of making armaments. It subsequently transpired that the Government had relaxed the guidelines without informing Parliament and that ministers had signed public interest immunity (PII) certificates (see chapter 9) to suppress vital evidence from the defence. On the advice of the Attorney-General these had been signed automatically in most cases without any ministerial judgement on the balance between the interests of officials and the defendants and without any real assessment by each minister of the public interest that required protection and whether such certificates were necessary.[10] (The one exception was Mr Heseltine, who had expressed to the Attorney-General

---

6   This statement was made in an interview with Brian Walden on *Weekend World*, London Weekend TV, 12 January 1986.

7   Especially regarding the knowledge of the Prime Minister. *World in Action* (30 March 1987) reported that the Prime Minister's Private Office positively exhorted the leak.

8   Leon Brittan refused to answer certain vital questions.

9   Walsh and Ridley *Under the Scott-light* (1997); A Tomkins *The Constitution after Scott: Government Unwrapped* (1998); Public Law (1996) Autumn Issue , P. Birkinshaw (1996) *Journal of Law and Society* 406.

10   'Wally' Hammond QC had played an important role in advising on the PII certificates. It was Hammond who was asked to conduct an investigation into the episode involving Peter Mandelson and the Hinduja brothers passport application, events which led to Mr Mandelson's resignation as Northern Ireland Secretary: Scott Report HC 115 (1996-97) G11.7-11, G13.5, G13.7-9, G13.88-9, J6.67]

his reservations about signing PII certificates.) Furthermore, one of the executives had also been used by the intelligence services as an informer to provide vital information. The questions raised by the MC episode go to the heart of abuse by government of secrecy; a failure to notify Parliament of changes by the executive to arms export guidelines; misleading statements to the House; failure by officials under ministerial bidding to testify before select committees investigating the 'Iraqi Supergun' affair[11] and the abuse of PII certificates in a criminal trial with a prejudicial effect on a defence.

These circumstances were the subject of a lengthy inquiry by Sir Richard Scott which was damning, but the Government took comfort from the fact that Sir Richard reported that the Government was not prepared to countenance the supply of lethal equipment to Iraq or Iran. Ministers, said the Government response to Scott, who signed PII certificates did so without 'impropriety'. There had been no 'conspiracy' to send innocent men to gaol, as alleged on Opposition benches, it was asserted. And there had been no 'deliberate' misleading of Parliament.

The circumstances in which these statements were initially made call for comment. Prior to the Government statement by the President of the Board of Trade, the Government had given itself eight days to study the report and prepare its statement. The Report, which had taken three and a quarter years to produce, ran to five volumes and was over 1800 pages in length excluding appendices. Two Opposition MPs were given three hours to study the report before the Government statement and to make their response. An offer to the Leader of the Labour Party to study the report was rejected because the terms were considered too belittling. MPs were given approximately eight minutes to study the report. MPs and press and media were bombarded with Government publicity materials. An adjournment debate was set for 10 days after the Parliamentary statement.

A closer reading revealed damning criticism of Government conduct although on the two most serious issues one minister—Mr Waldegrave—was found not to have *knowingly* misled the House and the Attorney-General was '*personally*, as opposed to constitutionally, blameless, for failure to pass on important information to the trial judge about Mr Heseltine's opposition' to signing PII certificates. In the case of Mr Waldegrave, the judge found no 'duplicitous intention in misinforming Parliament.' What was found to be duplicitous was the nature of the flexibility claimed for the guidelines which were drafted by the former Foreign Secretary, Lord Howe. While the policy of arms sales to Iraq itself may not have changed, the guidelines were relaxed and Parliament was not informed. The contention that the guidelines were not changed 'is so plainly inapposite as to be incapable of being sustained by serious

11   Trade and Industry Committee HC 86 (1991-2).

argument' remarked Sir Richard. Parliamentary answers to questions failed to inform the Lords and Commons of the current state of Government policy. Answers were 'designedly uninformative'. Their statements were 'inadequate' and 'misleading'. Mr Waldegrave, said Sir Richard, 'knew first hand the facts that, in my opinion, rendered the "No change in policy statement" untrue'. Mr Major stated that no minister would remain in office where he—that is Mr Major—judged that the minister had knowingly misled Parliament. The failure to inform Parliament of the current state of Government policy was 'deliberate' and the 'inevitable result of the agreement between three ministers' (Waldegrave, Alan Clark and Lord Trefgarne).

The Attorney-General was also criticised. The judge's recommendations for PII in criminal trials I can discuss in chapter 9 (p 441 et seq below). The Attorney-General had not even read the relevant papers from Mr Heseltine expressing his disquiet about the use of PII certificates before he gave evidence to Sir Richard. There was no conspiracy to mislead the court and secure convictions but on his failure to inform the judge Sir Richard said: 'I do not accept that he was not personally at fault'. His failure to inform prosecuting counsel of essential facts was characterised by the word 'inadequacy'. The proposition that ministers had a duty to sign PII certificates rested upon 'a fundamental misconception of the principles of PII law'. Ministers are entitled to have a view on disclosure and ought to inform the court of them. Otherwise they are, as Jonathan Aitken observed, 'mere postmen'.

The Government response to these criticisms on the application of PII certificates was that these were the views of one judge who was not an acknowledged authority in the area and the Government case had the support of leading judges and counsel. As we shall see in chapter 9, Sir Richard's analysis is more consistent with legal principle.

A week after the publication, Sir Richard made public his views that the Government were misrepresenting the content of his report by quoting highly selective extracts. In the Commons debate on the report, the Government won by one vote.

Sir Richard also made recommendations concerning government use of all intelligence material, powers to control exports, export licensing procedures, and the role of the Customs and Excise in export control and inquiry procedures. Other recommendations we can examine where relevant. Of particular interest was the fact that the Government seemed to be accepting the need for legislative change on the provision of information to Parliament and the public. The Government accepted the need for some changes in practices but lost the general election in 1997.

Sir Richard was given wide terms of reference which he could have requested the Prime Minister to extend if the former had felt this was desirable. All evidence requested was to be forthcoming, although there were some delays, and ministers and civil servants would present themselves for questioning if requested by Sir Richard. The inquiry was non-statutory and therefore could not take evidence under oath although Sir Richard was assured that any request to convert proceedings to a statutory inquiry would be met. The Inquiry was unique because it took evidence in public from a former Prime Minister, Mrs Thatcher, who was a central player in the drama and from the existing Prime Minister.[12]

The third example concerns the Bovine Spongiform Encephalopathy episode which saw variant Creutzfeldt-Jakob Disease transferred to human beings. This disease was caused by the recycling in cattle feed of cattle remains infected with BSE. Cross-contamination in feed mills led to thousands more cattle being infected. By 1995, the first recorded deaths from vCJD had occurred. By 2000, there were 85 victims (known) –80 dead – and the disease was spreading throughout Europe. The full extent and effects of the disease will not be 'discernible for many years to come.' In December 1997, the New Labour Government announced an inquiry into BSE and its development until 1996. The chair of the inquiry is Lord Phillips, a Law Lord, and his report was published in 16 volumes in October 2000.[13] What emerged from this inquiry was that there had been a suppression of the truth and an unwillingness to inform the public of known hazards. In some cases this amounted to positive censorship. Veterinary surgeons and farmers had not been alerted to the symptoms and dangers of BSE. Officials and their scientific advisers were worried about the beef export trade, the adverse public reaction to the purchase of beef and the consequences for domestic cattle farmers. 'A recurring theme in the BSE story has been the growing public suspicion and dissatisfaction that important information was not being shared and discussed openly so that people were denied proper choices in matters that deeply affected them.' A policy of openness is the correct approach, the report says. The Government must not appear to be certain where there is no certainty. 'We believe that food scares and vaccine scares thrive on a belief that Government is withholding information. If doubts are openly expressed and publicly explored, the public are capable of responding rationally and are more likely to reassurance and advice if and when it comes.' What appears crystal clear is that the Ministry of Agriculture, Fisheries and Food did not wish to lose control of the research into the diseases if universities and research institutes were informed and developed their own research. Where regulatory measures were devised, the secrecy and haste of their implementation resulted in 'unenforceable provisions.' Secrecy was counter-productive.

12 Report of the Inquiry into the Export of Defence Equipment and Dual Use Goods to Iraq and Related Prosecutions (1995–96) HC 115 V vols.
13 HC 887 (1999-00) I-XVI. See B McHenry on information and evidence gathering for the BSE and other inquiries: (1999) New LJ 1772.

At the Campaign for FOI Awards ceremony in March 1996, Tony Blair said:

> 'When a health scare like BSE occurs, the public want to know the facts, and they need to be sure that the public interest has always come first. They want to know if there was a relaxation of regulations which resulted in public safety being compromised ... the whole sorry saga of how this matter has been handled has resulted in loss of public trust in government.... The only way to begin to restore people's trust is to be completely open about what the risks are.'

It is interesting to observe that policy-making advice, prejudicing effective conduct of public affairs, information obtaining by law enforcement bodies and commercial damage are all reasons for exempting information from access under the UK 2000 FOIA which is considered in chapter 6. The Food Standards Agency was established to address some of the questions posed by MAFF's operations and proximity to the powerful food production lobby. It possesses a power to publish its advice to ministers and intends to conduct meetings in public.

The last development which has less dramatic moment than the previous episodes but which will have more lasting significance is the movement to new forms of government or public management to maintain public service or service to the public. In the late 1980s, executive agencies of central government were established to carry out the duties of departments of state accompanied by the apparent relaxation, or redefinition, of ministerial responsibility as a means of achieving accountability in the process of government. Departments will develop overall policy and will continue to be headed by a minister responsible for that policy. Agencies bound by non legally enforceable contracts established in 'framework documents' will carry out the administration—and to an unavoidable extent develop their own 'local policy' within the parameters set out by the department. Chief executives of agencies will be responsible for operating aspects and their management and for setting and meeting targets, objectives, standards and for monitoring performance. Management responsibility will be devolved within agencies and identifiable officials—employees are still civil servants—will be answerable for implementation. In several respects this constitutes a subversion of the major shibboleths of the British constitution: ministerial responsibility and anonymity of civil servants. There has been a movement to greater reliance upon the private sector to provide public sector management including the Private Finance Initiative now known as Public Private Partnerships. There has been an increased resort to 'Task forces' involving recruits from the private sector who will assist in policy development in key areas. Once again we should note that this advice will be exempt from access under FOIA 2000. A reliance upon powerful commercial interests has been noted with the Labour Government, not for private gain which was a common feature of Conservative governments under Thatcher and Major, but for the success of public projects in particular the Dome. This last example featured in the resignation of Peter Mandelson when he was accused of misrepresenting his role in assisting wealthy businessmen to obtain a British passport in return for financial support for the ailing project.

From these respective *imbroglios*[14] and managerial 'advances' how much light can be shed on the basic principles upon which constitutional government is supposedly conducted in the British state? How much information has to be given about matters of government for claims of governmental power to be legitimated? What are the leading principles of constitutional government? Are they realisable—or only idealistic or rough guides which imperfect men and women are urged to strive towards by tradition, the system or public expectation, knowing that in the world of practical politics their realisation is impossible? Are they mere shams which conceal the actual operation of power in the contemporary state and from which, like Milton's flames in *Paradise Lost,* nothing but 'darkness visible' emerged? The truth is probably a mixture of all of these.

Constitutional principles and central government

In an important work, Norman Lewis and Ian Harden have argued for an immanent critique of the actual operation of public power and government in the British tradition when set beside the *nature* of the constitutional principles which act as a talisman within our system: 'If these are your claims, your ruling principles, are you being true to them?'[15] The method of the immanent critique, very simply, is to identify the basic rules or principles which are taken as fundamental to a set of particular relationships. The question is then asked: 'To what extent are they actually observed in practice?'

The two principles on which they fasten are openness and accountability: *'With due respect to the need for confidentiality in sensitive areas of public activity,* the constitutional response must surely be to bring public business into the sunlight.'[16] Lewis and Harden's

---

14 The events surrounding Peter Mandelson's resignation and the subsequent Hammond investigation could easily be added. For a devastating report on secrecy in the NHS, see the report by Michael Redfern QC into use of bodily organs taken from children's corpses at Alder Hey hospital (30 January 2001).

15 *The Noble Lie* (1986), pp 110–11

16 Ibid, p 112. (my italics).

argument is part of a wider critique of an absence of suitable concepts of law, public and constitutional, for analytical and practical purposes. I wish to use as a springboard their belief in openness and accountability as centrepieces of our immanent or inherent, as opposed to 'real' or living, constitution. However desirable these principles are, how far do they or can they go? What counter arguments can government posit in its own defence? Lewis and Harden in the passage cited qualify the degree of openness by giving due consideration to 'confidentiality' in sensitive areas. BSE and Matrix Churchill were sensitive. Even if we accept such principles, who defines 'sensitive'? Is it the *ipse dixit* of the Prime Minister or minister? Is it Parliament? How 'sensitive' and for whom? FOIA as will be seen, places the answer firmly in the Minister's control. The government too has its own arguments. Is it open to the government to argue that openness is not one of the legitimating principles? A government strives to fulfil its manifesto pledges after a successful election. It makes public and Parliamentary statements. It acts after inquiries—whether public, as in the planning and environmental fields, or internal, as in the Westland episode itself or on alleged abuses by ministers of their public position.[17] Most of Sir Richard Scott's inquiry took place in public. It is as open as it ought to be. Any more openness would interfere with what *are* its major objectives, the realisation of which ensures legitimacy: namely, efficiency and responsiveness. Efficiency in the meeting of objectives, and responsiveness to the claims and needs of its citizens. Bentham may have asked for publicity in everything. He also asked for frugality in everything, government might assert. Too much openness would be too costly for efficiency and responsive action. Without openness, it must be asked, how do we know what objectives are and how efficiently they have been met? Without effective accountability, how can we gauge the degree of responsiveness of government?

In the last decade or so, the movement towards new styles of public management and greater reliance upon commercial and market led practice in the delivery of public services or programmes have been seen to be responsible for a degree of abuse in public office and for an appreciable increase in the sleaze factor by ministers, MPs, civil servants and ministerial powers of appointment to quasi governmental bodies. Such was the perceived level of public disquiet over the use of public office for private gain that in 1994 the Prime Minister appointed the Law Lord, Lord Nolan, to head an inquiry into *Standards in Public Life*.[18] Lord

17 Note 2, para 100 *et seq*; and note the internal inquiry by the Cabinet Secretary into the allegations of abuse of office by accepting hospitality by Jonathan Aitken as a minister. Aitken was subsequently jailed after committing perjury in a libel action against *The Guardian*.

18 *Standards in Public Life Vols I & II*, Cm 2850 (1995). Lord Nolan's successor was Lord Neill QC who in turn was followed by a former mandarin Sir Nigel Wicks.

Nolan's investigations and recommendations and subsequent reports from what is effectively a standing advisory committee to the Prime Minister will inform public service for some considerable time to come. It is instructive to spell out Nolan's seven principles of public life for these restate the desiderata of ethics in public life which must dictate the ethics of all who work in the public sector from the Prime Minister and ministers down.

His committee stated the seven general principles of conduct underpinning public life as selflessness, integrity, objectivity, accountability, openness, honesty and leadership. No one can expect a paragon of virtue. Rather, taken together, these add up to provide the following: holders of public office should take decisions solely in terms of the public interest and not for personal, family or friends' gain. They should not allow financial or other obligations to influence their decisions or public duties. Powers to award contracts (central government procurement was worth £60 billion per annum in 1995 according to HM Treasury) make appointments or bestow honours should be based on merit. They should be accountable and subject to appropriate scrutiny. They should be as open as possible in the decisions and actions they take, giving reasons for decisions and restricting information only when the public interest clearly demands. Private interests relating to public duties should be declared and conflicts removed. Lastly they should lead by example in promoting these principles. Codes of conduct should be drawn up by all public bodies incorporating these principles and internal systems for maintaining standards should be supported by independent scrutiny, and proper induction training and guidance should be given to reinforce standards in public bodies. We can examine more specific proposals as we progress although we should note that the Government has largely accepted these proposals although not until a select committee of the Commons had been appointed to advise on implementation or to assuage MPs' sensitivities.

Ministerial accountability or responsibility?

By the eighteenth century, ministerial responsibility to Parliament had become one of the focal points of constitutional attention, although the concept lacked precision and is still the subject of ongoing debate. Responsibility in a political sense is what is meant, because after 1689— and indeed prior to that date but for a liberal use of suspending and dispensing powers by the Crown—ministers were never absolved from legal responsibility for unlawful acts.[19] George I stopped attending cabinet

19 Note use of *nolle prosequi*. As Charles II observed, while his words were his own, his actions were those of his ministers.

meetings regularly from 1717, reasoning that his ministers now had to answer to Parliament for their advice to him. He could no longer protect them. The difficulties in establishing *individual* culpability led to the convention of collective responsibility of a government for its actions. If they were responsible collectively, then the government should respond and initiate, ie govern, collectively. That means unanimously. Disagreement in public could not, would not, be tolerated. It took until 1975, in the litigation concerning the diaries of the former Secretary of State, Richard Crossman,[20] for the courts to insist that, in law, proceedings within the cabinet are protected by confidentiality, at least for as long as confidentiality requires.[1] As recently as the late nineteenth century no minutes were taken of meetings, and Asquith stated in 1916 that only the Prime Minister took notes or a record for the purpose of the letter to the Monarch[2] to advise on the collective decisions of the cabinet.

Once a minister heads a ministry, and it becomes a matter of public record that an area of administration falls within the responsibility of that ministry, the minister at its head assumes responsibility to Parliament for the administration of the Ministry, and his servants, conventionally, remained anonymous. The minister has to answer the questions about the ministry's business, though s/he may not always accept the blame for what goes wrong. It depends upon the seriousness of the shortcoming and whether the minister knew or ought to have known of it and whether s/he retains colleagues' confidence. On many crucial items, the minister does not have immediate access to the research resources of his advisers, so s/he cannot ignore their advice.[3] If the minister is to be individually responsible, then s/he must be accountable to Parliament by providing information in debates and at question time[4] and by responding to investigations from select committees: 'A minister does not discharge [an] accountability to Parliament merely by acknowledging a general

20 *A-G v Jonathan Cape Ltd* [1976] QB 752; and Cmnd 6386 on publication by ex-Cabinet ministers of memoirs. The Cabinet Secretary would have the final say on information relating to national security and international relations. For background restrictions on civil servants, see K Middlemas (1976) Pol Q 39.

1   A point which was also made apropos of civil servants' information. The litigation concerned volume I. No injunction was sought for volumes II and III after it was refused for volume I. For non-security-sensitive information, Cmnd 6386 recommended a delay of 15 years, though in the case of conflict it was up to the ex-minister what to publish – subject to the possibility of an injunction. *Times Newspapers v MGN Ltd* [1993] EMLR 443 deals with the publication of material based on Mrs Thatcher's memoirs: *The Downing Street Years* without the authorisation of the newspapers who had purchased serialisation rights. Injunction refused as issue of confidentiality uncertain in hands of purchasing newspapers.

2   DGT Williams *Not In the Public Interest*, chapter 2.

3   *Ministry of Defence*, BBC 2, 9 April 1986.

4   Below.

responsibility and, if the circumstances warrant it, by resigning. Accountability involves *accounting* in detail for actions as a minister.'[5]

The Government has sought to draw a distinction between accountability and responsibility, a distinction which has been necessitated it its view by the introduction of executive agencies. Responsibility entails that a minister is directly and personally responsible for particular items eg departmental policy, for the framework through which policies are delivered, resources allocated, for such matters which s/he has to agree to under the framework documents which constitute agencies' operating manuals. Accountability it argues, refers to the constitutional duty upon ministers to account to Parliament by way of information provision for the actions of their department and its overall relationship with agencies. Responsibility may be delegated and is increasingly so. Accountability may not be delegated.[6] This is a little too pat. For example, when there is a systemic failure in an agency's programme, where responsibility has been delegated but where the minister knows of the failure, or ought to know, and fails to act—would the minister not be responsible?[7] By blaming his servants the minister may appear to have lost control of his department.

In his report into Matrix Churchill, Sir Richard Scott noted numerous instances where there had been a failure by ministers to discharge the obligation in what was then para 27 of *Questions of Procedure* (see below) 'to give Parliament, including its select committees, and the public as full information as possible about the policies, decisions and action of the Government and not to deceive or mislead Parliament and the public' (pp 1799 et seq). If responsibility were to be avoided because of a lack of knowledge or involvement then it was incumbent upon them to be 'forthcoming with information about the incident in question.'[8] The obligation of ministers to give information and explanations lies at the heart of ministerial accountability. It depends upon two vital qualities according to the select committee on the Treasury and Civil Service: 'clarity about who can be held to account and held responsible when things go wrong: confidence that Parliament is able to gain the accurate

---

5   HC 519 (1985–6), para 235.
6   Cm 2748 p 27 et seq and HC 27 I para 132 et seq (1993-4) and see Scott pp 179-180 below.
7   NB the report of the Parliamentary Commissioner for Administration on the Child Support Agency: HC 199 (1994-5). And of course the notorious events surrounding the dismissal of the Chief Executive of the Prison Service, Derek Lewis, by the Home Secretary in October 1995 following the Learmont Report on *Prison Security* Cm 3020. See *Hidden Agendas* (1997) by Lewis. On becoming Home Secretary in 1997, Jack Straw announced he was to be responsible for prison policy.
8   Paras K8.15-16 and pp 877 et seq and see text below.

information required to hold the Executive to account and to ascertain where responsibility lies'.

Withholding information means that the obligation is not discharged. This, believed Sir Richard, undermines the democratic process. His subsequent suggestion was for a commissioner to assist MPs to obtain information from ministers especially where it was refused on grounds of public interest.[9] This has not been forthcoming. The Information Commissioner under the FOIA 2000 can make a decision on the public interest but the Minister or authorised person may invoke a veto over this.[10]

The Defence Committee did not believe a full account had been given by the Government on the Westland affair, which I referred to earlier, so that doubt was cast on the conduct of civil servants whom they were not allowed to question. The Government had not been as 'forthcoming . . . as the House . . . might have expected'.[11] The same was true of the Trade and Industry Committee's investigation into the 'Iraqi Supergun' affair.[12]

We need to examine the contemporary practice of government and to compare these practices with the constitutional principles we accept. It will be necessary to look at the position of civil servants and their relationship with ministers and also at the position of Next Steps Executive agencies and how if at all they have been accommodated to the relationship. In the Westland affair, the public witnessed a minister giving information through his civil servants, as it would, he claimed, have appeared improper for him to have supplied it; a minister praying in aid the support of named civil servants; and an invitation by the select committee to the civil servants to come to the Committee to tell the story as it really was.[13] Practice confuses the division in other words. The discussion will examine the methods whereby information is provided to the press and media by officials, ministers and MP; how, in other words, the press officer, the lobby system, the Press Association and 'D notices' operate. Their collective objective is unattributable disclosure which seeks 'to influence without accepting responsibility'.[14] I will examine the relationship between government and broadcasting. The study will look

---

9   (1996) Public Law 410 at 426.
10   See chapter 6 p 320 below.
11   Note 5, para 239.
12   Above note 11 p 163. See Scott Report at para F4.61 *et seq* and see below.
13   Note 5, para 240. In the Sandline affair the Foreign Secretary Cook diverted blame for arms sales in apparent breach of a UN embargo and an Order in Council onto civil servants but insisted on questions before the FA Select Committee being put to him and not his Permanent Secretary: HC 1016 (1997-98) for the investigation by Sir Thomas Legg QC into the events. In March 2001, a former BBC reporter wrote that Cook misled the Commons three times in relation to the affair: N Jones *Control Freaks* (2001).
14   Note 5 para 168.

at the practice of quasi-government and the deliberate creation and perpetuation of obscurity in administration. I will examine the practice of local government and its resort to secrecy or openness. Throughout the chapter the discussion will assess the practice with reference to the principles.

Collective responsibility

How collective is governmental decision-making? It depends upon the Prime Minister. Ministers are given a rule-book, the *Ministerial Code,* which Lord Nolan recommended should be renamed *Conduct and Procedure for Ministers.* Its predecessor, *Questions of Procedure for Ministers* was a secret document until 1992 and cabinet secretarial staff were issued with *Talking About the Office*[15] although the latter seems long to have fallen by the wayside. The code is a non-legal statement of principles covering not just matters of collective responsibility but also ministerial responsibility to Parliament. Ministers, the *Code* states, are expected to behave according to the highest standards of constitutional and personal conduct in the performance of their duties. They must: uphold collective responsibility, account to Parliament for the performance of the policies of their departments and Next Steps agencies; give accurate and truthful information to Parliament, correcting any inadvertent error at the earliest opportunity. The Commons has resolved that ministers who knowingly mislead Parliament will be expected to offer their resignation to the Prime Minister.[16] Ministers should be as open as possible with Parliament and the public, refusing to provide information only when disclosure would not be in the public interest. This would be governed by the Code on Access (see chapter five) and by FOIA 2000 when effective. Ministers should also require that civil servants giving evidence on their behalf should be as helpful as possible in providing accurate, truthful and full information in accordance with the Civil Service Code. Ministers do not make statements on public affairs on their own behalf. The principle of collective responsibility applies.

The cabinet is supported by ministerial committees (ad hoc and standing). They seek to ensure the principle of collective responsibility.

15 The *Ministerial Code* dates from 1997. *Questions of Procedure for Ministers* Cabinet Office May 1992. See Cmnd 6386 (1976) on ministerial publications. Hennessey *Cabinet* (1986). The Select Committee on Public Administration has investigated the *Code:* HC 235 (2000-2001).

16 See HC statement Vol 292 cols 1046-7 19/3/97; Mandelson resigned because he had allegedly told an untruth to colleagues about his involvement in the Hinduja affair. This was subsequently not established by the Sir Anthony Hammond investigation and there were allegations that Mandelson had been the victim of a kangaroo court.

The Cabinet acts as a final court of appeal on interdepartmental disputes although the only 'automatic' right of appeal concerns questions of expenditure in programmes as a charge on the reserve. All efforts should be made to resolve disputes in committee. It sets out clearly the Prime Minister's authority over other ministers on a variety of subjects. The latter must consult the PM and have his authority before referring in speeches to subjects affecting the conduct of the government or before making a complaint to the Press or Broadcasting Complaints Commission and before making ministerial statements to the Commons. Parliamentary private secretaries are not members of the Government and should not be given access to secret information without the PM's permission. The restrictions on reproducing cabinet memoranda are laid out, and the record of proceedings is limited to the decision taken and 'such summary of the decisions as may be necessary for the guidance of those who have to take action'. The Cabinet Office should avoid recording the opinions of ministers. A limited circulation annex may be used for matters of special secrecy or political sensitivity. The Westland episode is recalled by the guidance on correspondence between law officers and ministers: 'When advice from the Law Officers is included in the correspondence between ministers ... the conclusions may if necessary be summarised but, if this is done, the complete text of the advice should be attached.' The fact and content of opinions of law officers, either individually or collectively, must not be disclosed outside government without their authority. However, in contradistinction to ministerial papers, written opinions of law officers are made available to succeeding administrations.

Cabinet documents, which are the property of the Crown, must be returned to a successor when required for current administration on relinquishing office and all others must be destroyed.[17] A former minister may at any time have access in the Cabinet Office to copies of cabinet or cabinet committee papers issued to him while in office. Conventions govern the use of information from one government to a succeeding one. Each minister will announce and defend his own area of interest once arrived at collectively.[18] Internal processes of reaching decisions should not be disclosed. It is no concern of Parliament or the public. Collective responsibility of ministers 'requires that they should be able to express their views frankly, in the expectation that they can argue freely in private maintaining a united front ... [T]he privacy of opinions expressed in Cabinet and ministerial committees should be maintained.' In the former editions of *Questions* it was stated that the composition, terms of reference

---

17 See the *Code* and Lord Hunt (1982) Public Law 514. A storm blew when the Churchill family sold the papers of Sir Winston Churchill for private gain when it was alleged that many were state papers. See R Brazier (1996) *Cambridge Law Journal* 65. For the position in Scotland in relation to papers of a UK Minister see: (2000) Public Law 309.

18 Only rarely will a decision be announced as a decision of HM Government.

and chairmen of cabinet committees should not be disclosed. Since 1992 and John Major's declaration of greater openness under the Citizen's Charter programme the names of cabinet committees, subcommittees and their terms of reference and membership have been published.

Previous editions of *Questions* contained rules on the *Protection against Unauthorised Disclosure of Information* and emphasised the importance of maintaining confidentiality within the 'narrow circle of knowledge' of those responsible for the formulation or execution of a particular policy. A minister's *own* views on a policy should not be publicised: 'they should put on a united front'. This is honoured almost as much in the breach as in the observance.[19] Chapter 8 concerns 'Ministers and the Presentation of Policy.' The role of the No 10 Press Office is central and virtually all speeches, interviews and presentations have to be agreed with that Office. Each department should keep a record of media contacts by both ministers and officials. Where a minister uses the lobby, the No 10 Office should be contacted. Tougher codes on briefing lobby journalists were introduced in July 1998 to deal with a growing problem of leaks by civil servants and special advisers. These were preoccupied with leaks of confidential information and making representations about privileged access to ministers and followed embarrassing revelations about Government aides.[20] Ministers are reminded of the guidelines from the Secretary to the Cabinet on advertising and publicity which were redrafted in May 1990 and on which further guidance was published in 1997 and 1999.

The remaining rules cover junior ministers, parliamentary private secretaries, statements in Parliament, White Papers, setting up committees of inquiry, public behaviour and private business while in office and restrictions on the use of civil servants for non-departmental business and use of personal advisers. These have been affected by the Nolan Report which suggested that as well as being renamed, *Questions* should contain a free-standing code of conduct drawing out the seven ethical principles which I described above. Cases of alleged impropriety by ministers should be investigated by the most appropriate method and generally advice from civil servants on such matters should not be published. Restrictions should be placed on former ministers taking up business appointments although this will be administered by the existing Advisory Committee on Business Appointments for civil servants and is advisory and moritoria apply on taking appointments. Where advice is not taken, the Committee should be able to advise the former minister to make public that advice. Waiting periods may be reduced by successful appeal to the Prime Minister. The system should be as open as possible while not compromising a minister's privacy. Departments should maintain records of gifts to ministers and

19 As in the Westland episode itself.
20 *The Guardian* 28 July 1998.

records of hospitality accepted by ministers in their official capacity and such records should be made publicly available. Most of these recommendations were accepted by the Government and have found their way into the *Code*. Lord Nolan's successor, Lord Neill, reported on 'Business Appointments' in his report *Reinforcing Standards*[1]. Following the Mandelson affair involving passport applications by the Hinduja brothers, a series of amendments to the Code seemed likely concerning ministers' contacts with lobbyists and businessmen and openness.

The Code was being examined by the Select Committee on Public Administration and changes were likely in any event after the 2001 election.[2] The Committee recommended that the constitutional status of the Code be recognised instead of it being treated as a piece of a Prime Ministerial private rule-book for the 'good fellas' club. The Committee supported Nolan's recommendation of a free-standing Code and specific highlighting of the seven principles. Neill had also reported on the Code in his sixth report and had pressed that ministers make a record of all contacts with those 'promoting outside interests'. Another recommendation was likely to be that ministers have access to an investigator immediately to examine allegations of misconduct and establish the facts to prevent Kangaroo courts dismissing them. In Mandelson's case, the role of the Chancellor of the Exchequer and Home Secretary emerged as pivotal and highly questionable. The ultimate arbiter and enforcer of the Code is likely to be the PM and this should be explicitly stated. An interesting feature to emerge was whether ministers' telephone conversations were taped. If so, a record of these would have been exempt under the FOIA 2000.[3]

The Public Administration Committee recommended an annual meeting between the PM and the Liaison Committee to discuss the Government's annual report and any breaches of the Code. This process should be included in the Code. The Parliamentary Commissioner for Standards and the Ombudsman should provide independent advice to ministers on the Code and investigate alleged breaches of the Code – a recommendation of the Committee which Neill disagreed with. The Committee stopped short of the enactment of a legal code.

Cabinet committees

The cabinet is not the only centre for decision-making. For this, or these centres, we must look *inter alia,* to cabinet committees. In November 2000

1   Cm 4557 (2000); the seven principles are not however, highlighted; Government Response to Neill: Cm 4817.
2   HC 235 (2000-01).
3   The Sir Anthony Hammond Inquiry.

it was reported that there were 34 cabinet committees and various subcommittees. In 1986 it was stated by the Government that only six cabinet secretariats reported to the Secretary to the Cabinet. In 1983 Mrs Thatcher identified four main committees. The position of the Cabinet Secretary is pivotal. It was a Cabinet Secretary who urged the Government to be fuller in their explanations for actions while stating in court that ministers and officials are necessarily 'economical with the truth.'[4]

In 1992, the Prime Minister disclosed the membership and responsibility of the main standing committees of cabinet. However, Hennessey has commented on an earlier administration that by the winter of 1985–6 there were at least 160 groups within the cabinet committee network. He identified five types of committee:[5] *standing,* ie permanent (for the duration of the Prime Minister); *ad hoc* or 'single issue';[6] *ministerial,* where civil servants do not participate; *official* for civil servants alone, and *mixed* for both ministers and civil servants.

The actual creation, administration and utilisation of such committees will doubtless vary according to the particular style of the Prime Minister. Under Mrs Thatcher the tendency had been to avoid committees, circulation of cabinet papers and cabinet debate wherever possible. Informal ad hoc groups might be stacked against an erring minister,[7] or a colleague might be asked to prepare a paper just for the Prime Minister with a back-up team of civil servants or outsider specialists. A typical follow-up would have been a meeting at No 10 with the Prime Minister and 'her team': 'a mixture of people from the Downing Street private office, the Policy Unit and Cabinet Office, with one or two personal advisers and sometimes a Treasury minister'.[8] The style is not quite presidential, Hennessey argues, but much of the 'collective spirit' of the cabinet system has been siphoned off to committees and informal groups.[9] This may be simply a more emphatic tendency in what has been happening since the end of the Second World War. Only one decision on nuclear weapons in 40 years, for instance, was approved by the whole cabinet— the decision to proceed with the 'H' Bomb. While Mr. Major was PM, a greater emphasis was placed on government through cabinet. Tony Blair deliberately pursued a strong centralised style of government while also presiding over devolved government in the UK. While he accepted the

4   Too economical in his own case. This was Sir Robert Armstrong.
5   *Hennessey,* p 31.
6   Nb Star Chamber to arbitrate on departmental bids for funding before the Expenditure White Paper, replaced by the EDX Committee and then by the PX and subsequently the PSX committee. See chapter 5 p 264 et seq below.
7   *Hennessey,* pp 102–3, cites Michael Heseltine's report 'It took a Riot' on urban deprivation. Mr Heseltine was himself accused of being over interventionist as Deputy Prime Minister in October 1995.
8   Ibid, p 102.
9   Ibid, p 11.

convention of Cabinet government, use of 'outside' advisers and reliance upon the slick presentation of policies helped create the impression of excessive 'hands-on' government and obsessive control over policy development. The No 10 Policy Unit had increased significantly in size and comprises mainly special advisers.[10] The proliferation of special task forces operating largely in secret to help the development of policy was widely criticised. These comprised special groups ('experts') and officials.[11] While some Cabinet committees were larger than the Cabinet itself, the committee dealing with the FOI Bill was an example, resort was also made to special inner committees of permanent secretaries operating outside the traditional weekly sessions of all top secretaries.[12] Government by memo, and obsessive control over style and presentation seriously undermined the popularity of Blair's first government.

The former Central Policy Review Staff (CPRS) was an attempt better to inform and co-ordinate governmental decision-making.[13] It comprised 'outside' experts and academics. The Head of CPRS had 'a seat at the table of Ministers and Ministerial Committees'. To be effective in influencing policy at this level one needs 'to have vast access to information at least as good as all the departments who are putting forward their voices as well as time and staff'. Often CPRS did not have such facilities. Their papers had a 'shallow' feel to them, the last-minute effort of a 'bright spark' which was set beside a paper on a subject prepared by senior officials and advisers who had worked on a paper for months.[14] By the mid-1980s, the Prime Minister had her own policy research unit in place of a cabinet one.

Our system of cabinet government is collective in only a very formal sense, as the information and details of policy-making are not presented to the whole cabinet, but are invariably kept within the narrowest possible range of ministers. So much is no doubt a consequence of more government and more specialisation. It is not the framework for full, free and frank discussion of government policy within the confidence of the cabinet. But it might be argued that this does not really matter. If the Government loses the confidence of the House it must go to the country. That is what is central, along with mute agreement, in collective responsibility. No minister can claim a right to know in detail what another is doing unless the matter touches upon their *own* sphere of responsibility/accountability.

10 See Public Administration *Special Advisers* HC 293 (2000-2001).

11 *Ruling by Task Force: The Politico's Guide to Labour's New Elite* A Barker and I Byrne and A Veall (1999); *In the Public Interest?* Public Management Foundation (2000).

12 D Kavanagh and A Seldon *The Powers Behind the Prime Minister: The Hidden Influence of No10* (1999).

13 Cmnd 4506 (1970), paras 44–8.

14 D Howell, quoted in *Hennessey*, p 112. See n 15 p 173 above.

Then the Minister must provide the information for Parliament to account for their *own* area of responsibility/accountability. Timing of release of information is vital, but while a minister in the cabinet, with the Prime Minister's approval, believes it best that cabinet colleagues are not informed, it is unlikely that Parliament should be. In its response to the Nolan Committee the Government while accepting most of the recommendations, did state that ministers should not be culpable unless they *knowingly* misled Parliament and furthermore ministers should have a right not to inform Parliament where it was not in the public interest that Parliament should be informed. Sir Richard Scott noted the Nolan recommendations, the addition of the qualification 'knowingly' to the duty not to misinform Parliament and then the addition of the following words to *Questions* to determine how the public interest in withholding information should be determined:

> [only when disclosure would not be in the public interest,] which should be decided in accordance with established Parliamentary convention, the law and any relevant Government Code of Practice. (HC Debs col 456 2 November 1995)

He did not feel that the qualification of 'mislead' by 'knowingly' made any material difference to the substance of the obligation on ministers not to mislead Parliament or the public. Withholding information should never be based on reasons of convenience or to avoid political embarrassment but 'should always require special and careful justification'. He also referred to the fact that the public interest could be identified from 'established Parliamentary convention'. I have noted elsewhere the numerous subjects on which by convention ministers have refused to answer questions (see p 36 n 12 above). Sir Richard believed that the justification for a refusal to answer a Parliamentary question on sale of arms or defence-related equipment to other countries should be re-examined and should be the subject of a 'comprehensive review'. 'Commercial confidentiality' should not, in short, be engaged in overkill to suppress information from Parliament and the public.

Sir Richard also points to the distinction made between 'responsibility' and 'accountability' by the Cabinet Secretary and others although it has not met with approval from all quarters. If ministers are to be excused blame and personal 'responsibility' *qua* minister

> the corollary ought to be an acceptance to be forthcoming with information about the incident in question. Otherwise Parliament (and the public) will not be in a position to judge whether the absence of personal knowledge and involvement is fairly claimed or to judge on whom responsibility for what has occurred ought to

be placed. Any re-examination of the practices and conventions relied on by Government in declining to answer, or to answer fully, certain Parliamentary Questions should, in my opinion, take account of the implications of the distinction drawn by Sir Robert between ministerial 'accountability' and ministerial 'responsibility' and of the consequent enhancement of the need for ministers to provide ... full and accurate information to Parliament. (HC 115 1995/6, p 1806)

It has been noted how the *Ministerial Code* and the resolution of the Commons provided for ministerial information to Parliament. How, and when, does Parliament get informed?

Parliament and information

As the 'Grand Inquest of the Nation' Parliament can ask questions. It was the abuse of this ability by some MPs who charged 'clients' for the privilege which was one of the major causes leading to the establishment of the Nolan Committee. Parliament can demand debates. It can summon witnesses and call for evidence before its select committees, especially the Public Accounts Committee (PAC) which receives written minutes by the accounting officer of departments where they disagree with a minister on matters relating to expenditure,[15] and the select committees which are departmentally related. By these processes it holds ministers responsible for their departmental administration. Parliamentary proceedings, like those in courts, are protected by absolute privilege.[16] The mechanisms of Parliamentary questions and debates are geared towards the provision of routine information: how many prisoners on remand; how many deportations; how many school closures?—the stuff of Parliamentary life. Others see them as opportunities for 'soundbites' and planted prompts whose usefulness will outlive any 'reform' to make

15 These powers were extended during the Nolan Inquiry to cover communications to the chair of the Public Accounts Committee by the accounting officer. They had previously been extended to allow communications to the Comptroller and Auditor-General on an extended range of concerns: *Standards in Public Life Vol II* Cm 2850 p 217 (R Sheldon) and White, Harden and Donnelly (1994) Public Law 526. See chapter 5 p 264 et seq.

16 Bradley and Ewing *Constitutional and Administrative Law* (12th ed, 1997), chapter 11. See *Prebble v Television New Zealand* [1995] 1 AC 321, PC where the Privy Council stayed an action when the defendant could not invoke evidence covered by the privilege; *Allason v Haines* (1995) Times, 25 July; and Leopold (1995) Legal Studies 204. An amendment to the 1995-6 Defamation Bill moved by Lord Hoffman allows MPs to waive the privilege and sue for defamation, thereby making an inroad into the Bill of Rights 1689: Defamation Act 1996, s 13 and *Hamilton v Al Fayad* [2000] 2 All ER 224, HL.

Parliamentary questions more meaningful, as Mr Major suggested in June 1994. The more probing investigation exercises are conducted by the select committees of MPs who can have outside specialists advising them.

There is a prevailing mood of disappointment in the work of the select committees which were created in 1979, especially apropos of their oversight over finance and expenditure.[17] They are established to oversee and scrutinise the policies, administration and expenditure of related departments, their various agencies and fringe bodies. Members are appointed by the House of Commons, and the party balance usually reflects the balance of the House as a whole, as does the division of chairmen. The Liaison Committee recommended changes in the manner in which members are appointed to Select Committees. At the time of their report this was controlled largely by party whips. The Committee highlighted good practice in select committee investigations and some innovations have included the presence of civil servants as aides to the committee to answer questions on specialised points. This practice was adopted by the Select Committee on Public Administration in its investigation into the White Paper *Your Right to Know* (Cm 3818 (1997)) and the *Draft Bill and Consultation Paper on FOI* (Cm 4355 (1999)). The Committee also noted the mixed quality of government responses to reports and suggested that the Liaison Committee itself be renamed the Select Committee Panel.[18] Select committees have power to subpoena the attendance of witnesses and to order presentation of documents. Failure to comply may be a contempt of Parliament but that is a matter for the whole House. Nevertheless a memorandum *Departmental Evidence and Response to Select Committees* exists which was revised in 1997.[19] This may not always be applicable to the Public Accounts Committee because of its unique authority (see chapter 5 pp 264 et seq). Ministers' views on withheld information must be sought. A previous memorandum supported the advice of the Procedure Committee, that:

> It would not ... be appropriate for the House to seek directly or through its committees to enforce its right to secure information from the Executive at a level below that of the ministerial head of the department concerned (normally a Cabinet minister) since such a practice would tend to undermine rather than strengthen the accountability of ministers to the House.

17 A Robinson in G Drewry (ed) *The New Select Committees* (1989, 2nd ed); V Flegmann (1985) Public Money 5; see also, John Biffen in D Englefield (ed) *Commons Select Committees* (1984).

18 HC 300 (1999-00) *Select Committees and the Executive; Government Reply* Cm 4737.

19 *Departmental Evidence and Response To Select Committees* OPSS, Cabinet Office (1997). This contains instructions on treatment of classified and confidential information and protective security markings, paras 80-87.

Officials who give evidence to Select Committees do so on behalf of ministers and subject to their directions (1997, para 37). Ministers are directly accountable to Parliament and civil servants directly accountable to ministers. This, the memorandum states, does not mean that civil servants may not be called upon to give a full account of Government policies or their own actions or recollections of events but, in doing so, their role is to facilitate ministerial accountability not to offer personal views or judgements on matters of political controversy.

Committees are advised that they are not to act as a disciplinary hearing and questions concerning the conduct of individual officials should be taken up with ministers and should not be put to officials and should not be answered without further instructions (paras 70-74). Presence of witnesses is requested rather than demanded. Ministers decide which officials are to appear. The current memorandum advises that where the presence of a particular civil servant is insisted upon, the House may enforce a formal order for attendance but this is 'unprecedented'. They, and Agency chief executives, remain 'subject to ministerial instructions as to how [to] answer questions' a point which somewhat undermines agency 'autonomy'.

Information should, the guidance explains, be provided, subject only to the terms of the guidance and what is necessary in the public interest and subject to the exemptions set out in the code on access (see chapter 5 p 238 et seq). This will have to be amended to take account of the FOIA 2000. Requests may also have to be refused where they would 'appear to involve excessive costs'. The following items should also be excluded: internal advice to ministers; inter-departmental exchanges on policy issues; the level at which decisions were taken or the manner in which a minister has consulted his colleagues; cabinet and its committees and discussions thereon; advice given by a law officer and other legal advice; information supplied in confidence; questions in the field of political controversy including Government policy; sensitive information of a commercial or economic nature, which although understandable is drafted in a very vague and potentially broad manner; personal information; conduct of individual officials; matters which are or may become the subject of sensitive negotiations with governments or *other bodies,* quasi-judicial functions or cases before the courts or Parliamentary Commissioner. These will be subject to the Code on Access and subsequently FOIA where a balancing of interests for and against disclosure is allowed. Not all exemptions are so covered.

Where a 'closed session' is held, there are guidelines on 'sidelining' or expunging classified or confidential information from the testimony. Departmental responses, on which guidance is given, should be made within two months (paras 93-110). A refusal to appear or to allow officials to appear occasioned the Leader of the House to guarantee that time will be given to debate the matter on the floor of the House. The Director of General Communications Headquarters was not allowed to testify in 1984.[20] Nor were the civil servants in the Westland case and questions were stoutly refused in the 'Iraqi supergun' investigation.[1] Scott was critical of the convention which prevented former civil servants being called to give evidence to committees because they were no longer responsible to a minister.[2] An outright refusal to appear or answer a question might constitute a contempt of Parliament; in reality a vote of censure would have to get a majority in the House, and no doubt ministers could rely upon MPs of their party at least being very careful not to encroach upon ill-defined executive privileges. Paragraph 44 now deals with retired officials and their evidence: 'retired officials cannot be said to represent the minister and hence cannot contribute directly to his accountability to the House.' Evidence should therefore be given by a minister or an official of his choosing The Government is adamant that the confidentiality of relationship between a minister and civil servant shall not be threatened by 'cross-examination' before a select committee of MPs, however much select committees might claim that they are upholding Parliamentary supremacy in contradistinction to Government's claim that committees only exist by virtue of ministerial responsibility/accountability to Parliament. It is not right, the Government maintains, to allow officials to be questioned with a view to establishing the appropriate *locus* of fault in conduct, or the conduct itself, of individual officials (paras.70-74).[3] It is claimed that committees have received more useful information from officials than ministers on occasion.[4] Pressure has been put on the Leader of the House by chairmen to obtain more information on nationalised industries and to inveigle more information out of government departments and agencies, and committees have a long-standing practice of showing papers and drafts to them for comment and further information.[5] Furthermore, lay witnesses before a select committee have pleaded the privilege against self-incrimination and effectively thwarted the thrust of the Committee's investigation.[6]

With the Next Steps executive agencies, the original Ibbs Report, which recommended their introduction to enhance management efficiency, found

20 HC 363 (1984–5).
1   Above p 163 n 11.
2   HC 115 (1995-6) para F4.61 *et seq.*
3   Cm 78 (1987).
4   *Drewry*, n 17 above, p 275.
5   HC 555 (1984–5).
6   Dramatically by the Maxwell brothers in the investigation by the Social Services Committee into the Maxwell pension scandal: HC 61 (1991-2). Edwina Curry only appeared under great protest to discuss her revelations in the salmonnella in eggs episode—had she been too liberal with the truth? HC 108 I and II (1988-89) at p 185 and Cm 687 for the Government reply.

it difficult to accommodate Parliamentary oversight via select committees with the operation of agencies. Agency chief executives are responsible for management and operational decisions and answer to select committees accordingly. Ministers are responsible for overall policy and answer to committees for that. The policy/operational divide is not clear cut, not unlike the responsibility/accountability division and it has been felt that it shelters ministers and agency chiefs to avoid appropriate levels of accountability as occurred after a series of prison escapes in late 1994 and early 1995 and in the operation of the Child Support Agency where after a highly criticised performance, including one before the select committee, the agency chief resigned.[7] The minister then responsible for the Next Steps initiative informed the Institute of Directors in 1992 that while agency chief executives operated like private sector managers, nevertheless they could be hauled before committees to answer to them. The Next Steps Initiative (NSI) has produced a wealth of information in the form of framework documents (FDs), performance indicators, reports and specific agreements between departments and their agencies, but it has been felt that committees have not pressed home to advantage the opportunities that this provision could yield and that what is missing for instance is greater interplay between the Public Accounts Committee and the departmental committees to assess the information that emerges in a less parochial fashion.[8] Agency chiefs have themselves been disappointed by not being pressed more closely by committees.[9] The Government did not accept a recommendation from the TCSC in 1994 that agency chief executives should be directly and personally accountable to select committees in relation to their annual performance agreements (which would replace key targets set for chief executives and which are announced to Parliament each year and which are agreed in the context of the business plan which is a more detailed document than the FD and which is not always published). The committee recommended that ministers should remain accountable for framework documents and for their part in negotiating the annual agreement and for instructions given to the chiefs and that all such instructions should be published subject only to personal confidentiality and necessary anonymity. The Government rejected this recommendation stating that chiefs do appear and committees have all necessary information.[10] A practice has developed after initial confusion whereby questions of an operational nature are addressed to agency chiefs

---

7   See the Derek Lewis saga, p 171 n 7 above and the running battles between Chris Woodhead of Ofsted and the Secretary of State for Education. The *Carltona* principles of delegation apply to the Chief Executive and Agency staff: *R v Secretary of State for Social Services, ex p Shirwin* (16 February 1996, unreported).
8   P Giddings, (ed) *Parliamentary Accountability* (1995).
9   Ibid p 232.
10   Cm 2748 p 31.

by members and answers are placed in *Hansard*. Obviously they cannot answer oral questions in the House (see chapter 5).

Select committees, like governments, suffer leaks. A particularly notable one occurred in the Health Committee where a draft report was leaked to the department and where pressure was allegedly exerted on the committee. The Foreign Secretary was also leaked a report before it was published by a member of the Foreign Affairs Committee in 1998 leading to the leaker's resignation. The Committee of Privileges has investigated the breach of the rule which prohibits the publication of evidence taken *in camera* or publication before report to the House, or the publication of deliberations of a committee.[11] Members of committees are 'prime misfeasants' and the code contained in the *Notes on the Practice of Lobby Journalism* is not enforced. The press show scant regard for the rules, and the House is reluctant to punish the press, as evidenced in the case of the journalist from *The Times* in 1986 who published details of a select committee's confidential report.[12] The House has power to punish a breach of privilege with imprisonment[13] or withdrawal of a press lobby or press gallery pass. The committee recommended that a pass be withdrawn for certain serious breaches.

Before leaving select committees, we should note that the Home Affairs Committee now has a role in supervising the Lord Chancellor's Department, so that the administration of the courts and prosecution policy and legal aid but not individual cases are now subject to Parliamentary scrutiny. This is true of the administration of public records for which the Lord Chancellor is responsible.[14] This Committee was involved in a notorious episode when the Permanent Secretary of the LCD was recalled before it to explain a serious inaccuracy in his evidence to the committee.[15]

MPs themselves are under a duty, by resolution of the House, to disclose private interests in debates or proceedings of the House or its committees or in their official transactions. A compulsory register has existed since 1975 although not all members chose initially to enter relevant details. In the wake of various scandals throughout the late 80s and the 90s Lord Nolan recommended improved clarity of entries and immediate updating with details of all contracts relating to the provision of services in their capacity as members—these would be available for public inspection. He also recommended a new code of conduct for

---

11 For publication of evidence of the confidential proceedings of the Committee of Privileges by a member, Tony Benn MP, see: HC 27 (1994/5).

12 HC 555 (1984-5). The journalist was not punished: HC Debs, 20 May 1986.

13 Last used in 1880. See House of Commons *Factsheet No 62*.

14 And which may cause a conflict of interest where records relate to his own actions as an erstwhile minister – eg Lord Hailsham and the Suez episode.

15 J Rozenberg *The Search for Justice chapter* 5 (1994).

members which would be overseen by a Parliamentary Commissioner for Standards of independent standing. The Commissioner would have the powers of the Parliamentary Commissioner for Administration (Ombudsman) and Comptroller and Auditor-General and would enjoy the support of a select committee and be able to initiate a complaint under his own discretion. The hearings of the committee (the Standards and Privileges Committee was established to perform this role) are usually in public. The House of Commons voted to require all MPs to disclose earnings from consultancies derived from Parliament and to impose a total ban on paid advocacy in Parliament. The recommendations for a Commissioner and code were also approved.[16] The Commissioner has engaged in some high profile investigations and the courts have ruled that the Commissioner is not subject to judicial review because his investigations are primarily for Parliament and not individuals as in the case of the Ombudsman.[17] However, when the Standards Commissioner investigated the MP and junior minister Keith Vaz for alleged breaches of the Code, the Committee criticised the obstruction which the Commissioner had met from witnesses who had not been forthcoming with evidence. Vaz had been represented by a leading solicitor in these proceedings. The episode highlighted the limits of Parliamentary self-regulation.[18] Lord Neill has also reported on a code of conduct and a compulsory register for the Lords.[19]

Ministers and civil servants

The Duties and Responsibilities of Civil Servants and Ministers has been the subject of a report from the Treasury and Civil Service Committee[20] and the general theme has featured in a variety of subsequent committee reports and government memoranda. It has now also featured in further

---

16 *Standards in Public Life* Cm 2850 I pp 43-5. Sir Gordon Downey, the former Comptroller and Auditor General became the first Commissioner. At present it is Elizabeth Filkin. The Commons also voted to register details of all contracts with the Commissioner by 31 March, 1996: HC Debs 6 November 1995. The House of Lords introduced a Members' Register of Interests. See HC 345 (1995-6) for the Commons Register.

17 *R v Parliamentary Commissioner for Standards, ex p Al Fayed* [1998] 1 All ER 93, CA; In *Hamilton v Al Fayed* [2000] 2 All ER 224, HL, the HLs disapproved dicta of the CA that the courts could entertain an action which was the subject of an investigation by the PCS and on which the PCS had reported to the Committee. This was a breach of Parliamentary privilege and Art 9 Bill of Rights. The MP had already lost the libel action which had not been stayed because of the effects of s13 Defamation Act 1996.

18 HC 314 (2000-01) paras 65-72.

19 Cm 4903 (2000).

20 HC 92, vols I and II (1985-6).

reports by the TCSC and Government responses on the future of the civil service and it was examined by Lord Nolan's Committee and by his successor Lord Neill. The background to the 1986 TCSC Report was the low morale in the civil service, the banning of trade unions at GCHQ, the *Ponting* trial, and the *Note of Guidance on the Duties and Responsibilities of Civil Servants in Relation to Ministers* issued by Sir Robert Armstrong.[1] The guidance, which 'was not intended to break new ground' and which has only been slightly modified, reasserted the tradition of civil service confidentiality and allegiance to the minister, and the responsibility of ministers to Parliament:

> Any civil servant whose loyalty is put under strain is advised to refer his complaint to his superiors, even up to his Permanent Secretary . . . but in no circumstances to seek by his own actions to frustrate ministers' policies or decisions.[2]

The Committee was surprised that principles of the 1930s were still considered adequate for the late 1980s. It was also uneasy about Sir Robert Armstrong's equation of the Crown with the government of the day. The Crown may be symbolic of the nation, the Committee ruminated, to which 'civil servants and others may owe a loyalty higher and more lasting than that which they owe to the government of the day'. The official view stated by the Cabinet Secretary was of an undivided loyalty owed by the servant to the minister. In return the minister should, Sir Robert believed, 'read, mark, learn and digest the information and advice which the Civil Service has to offer . . . and to take that seriously'.[3] Too much, the Committee believed, was left to happenstance. What was needed was a set of guidelines promulgated by the Prime Minister after consultation with other political leaders in the Commons and spelling out the duties and responsibilities of ministers to Parliament and the civil service.

The wider concerns apparent from the 1980s onwards are obviously activated by the 'low morale' which exists when senior civil servants, especially, feel their career prospects are jeopardised if they do not give *politically* acceptable advice to ministers. More immediate was the concern over the accountability of an anonymous civil servant who acted without the authority or knowledge of a minister and for whose actions the minister will not accept responsibility, and the situation where a civil servant feels obliged to reveal what his minister is doing because the latter's behaviour is not in the 'public interest', or so the civil servant

---

1   Ibid, vol II, pp 7–9.
2   Ibid.
3   Ibid, vol I, para 3.10. On the 'Crown' see J Jacob *The Republican Crown* (1996) M Sunkin and S Payne *The Nature of the Crown – A Legal and Political Analysis* (1999).

believes. On the former situation, the Committee, in agreement with the Defence Committee, believed that an internal departmental inquiry which is not fully reported to Parliament cannot qualify as accountability. The latter situation poses several problems.

In the case of a moral dilemma, Sir Robert believed a civil servant could take the matter up as a last resort with the permanent secretary of his department. The Cabinet Secretary, and through him the Prime Minister, may be consulted. The Government has endorsed and acted upon this view.[4] In the case of Ponting and Colette Bowe,[5] these procedures were found defective. Nolan found that only one appeal to the head of the Home Civil Service had been made in eight years. The First Division Association (the trade union for leading civil servants) has argued for a code of guidance to reinforce the position of the civil servant with possible redress from the Ombudsman or resort to the chairman of the appropriate select committee in the Commons or an ethics tribunal. Sir Douglas Wass has called for an 'Inspector-General for the Civil Service' who would be independent of ministers and who could hear civil servants.[6]

In its response to the 1994 TCSC report, the Government produced a draft code on ministers and civil servants which draws largely on the Armstrong memorandum in spite of the widespread criticism of that document being out of touch with the contemporary context of government. The code was amended to take account of the amendments to the *Civil Service Code* in 1996. Further revisions in May 1999 take account of devolution.[7] Civil servants in the Scottish and Welsh administrations are appointed under the terms and conditions of the Home Civil Service under the devolution Acts. Their primary duties are to 'the administration they serve.'

Where the civil servant feels that s/he is being required to act in a way which is illegal, improper, unethical, or in breach of constitutional convention, which may involve possible maladministration, or which is otherwise inconsistent with the code or raises a fundamental issue of conscience, s/he should first report the matter internally (see above). Where this path is pursued and the response in the civil servant's eyes is 'not reasonable' s/he may report the matter in writing to the Civil Service

4   Cmnd 9841. In proceedings before Scott J in which the Attorney-General sought a permanent injunction prohibiting newspaper reporting of *Spycatcher*'s contents, Sir Robert accepted the possibility, *in extremis*, of a justified leak. See chapter 9, p 412 *et seq*.

5   The chief press and information officer at the DTI who effected the leak of the Solicitor-General's letter in the Westland affair.

6   Note 3, vol II, pp 43–4. The FDA code is: *Civil Service Code of Ethics* (November 1994). On civil servants who break the law in performance of their duties, see *Legal Entitlements and Administrative Practices*, CSD (H.M.S.O. 1979). Sir Douglas Wass called for an inspector-general for the civil service: Cmnd 9841.

7   CS Code (May 1999) para 2.

Commissioners and not the Head of the Home Civil Service. Civil servants should not otherwise seek to frustrate the policies etc of ministers or disclose without authority official information received in confidence. Others claim there is widespread abuse of breaches of confidence by civil servants deliberately aimed at frustrating the policies of ministers.[8] Where the matter is not resolved by the procedures above the servant must comply with ministerial instructions or resign. Their duty of confidentiality continues after resignation and may be enforced by prosecutions under the Official Secrets Act or other statutes (see chapter 3). Nolan added a suggested amendment which would allow a servant to utilise the procedures where s/he was not personally involved and is aware of wrongdoing or maladministration—an internal whistle-blowing provision and quite significant—and this the Government accepted. He further recommended that contrary to government proposals *all successful* appeals should be reported to Parliament and not just those where the Government refused to accept the Commissioners' conclusions. This would help to ensure wider dissemination of best practice. The Government had reservations about this although it accepted that anonymous 'good practice' should be published. He also recommended an informal procedure 'a servant's friend' in each department and agency to whom servants could turn in confidence and who would not be part of line management. This was accepted.[9] The Government also rejected the proposal for ministerial *cabinets* or private offices staffed by special advisers as well as career civil servants and the minister's parliamentary private secretary. It rejected splitting up the two offices of the head of the Home Civil Service and the Secretary to the Cabinet, both currently held by one official. A conflict of interests was not seen to exist although this was the subject of investigation by the TCSC in 1995.[10]

What of leaks outside this procedure? In the *Spycatcher* trial Scott J believed there may be leaks to the press even by MI5 officers which are justified because they reveal abhorrent practices. The House of Lords has emphasised the 'absolute duty' of secrecy not necessarily to prevent publication but certainly to allow for a remedy for wrongful breach (see chapter 3 p 129). Most leaks will not cover such enormity. And it might be straining credulity in a serious matter to expect a lengthy process to be gone through and confidences kept. The Defence Committee in 1986 were adamant and probably expressed what the existing position would be:

---

8   The European Policy Forum said of 36 serious leaks that had taken place between 'the summer 'of 1994 and March 1995 and of these two-thirds were aimed at frustrating Government policies: *Financial Times* 17 September 1995.
9   For the Code see HC Deb Vol 267 col 234, 23 November 1995.
10 HC 300 (1994-5).

'Civil servants who leak information should face the sack or internal discipline', not punishment through the courts.

Nolan's recommendation, and the Government's acceptance, is a big improvement but even so until the Public Interest Disclosure Act 1998, there was nothing by way of official publication which offers scope for debate on what might be a 'justified leak' to the press by a civil servant such as is recognised in other countries.[11] The Committee appears to endorse the view that such leaks are never totally defensible, even presumably when informing of evil or criminal acts. The concluding comment in the previous paragraph reinforces what was probably the legal position on the subject of discipline and punishment. Even if the OSA could not be successfully invoked, a civil servant who communicated, in whatever form, information which would embarrass his minister, whom he believed to be acting against the public interest, would have no right to claim wrongful dismissal if sacked. For civil servants are not under a contract of employment, although such a status may be ripe for legal reassessment and the position is not free from ambiguity.[12] The Government in fact introduced a provision conferring contractual status, for limited purposes, on Crown servants in the 1988 Employment Act, s 30 and it planned to put members of the 'new' senior civil service on 'written contracts'.[13] Even if they were under such contracts, as are other employees in the public sector, it seems on the balance of authorities that it may be an implied term of a contract of employment that an employee cannot be sued for revealing the confidences of his employer if it is in the public interest to reveal such confidences and this outweighs the maintenance of confidentiality. However, such a 'defence' may not be available for wrongful dismissal. Public interest may not be invoked to

---

11 Eg US Civil Service Reform Act 1978 and 1989—the 'Whistleblower' Protection Act. The 1978 Act, strengthened in 1989, establishes the Office of Special Counsel to protect employees and receive 'leaks'. See chapter 3, pp 120-121 and the CIA. New South Wales had a Protected Disclosures Bill in 1994 to protect whistle-blowing in the public interest and in June 1995 a Bill to do likewise was presented to the Commons. To be protected, disclosures must not be made in bad faith or for reward and with reasonable grounds for believing in their accuracy. The whistle-blower would have the right to compensation, an injunction to halt threats of punishment and protection against unfair dismissal even within the two-year qualifying period. Complaints would have to be raised internally initially and would cover serious malpractice. See the Public Interest Disclosure Act 1998 below.

12 *R v Civil Service Appeal Board, ex p Bruce* [1989] 2 All ER 907, CA; *R v Lord Chancellor's Department, ex p Nangle* [1991] ICR 743; *R v Chief Constable of Devon amd Cornwall Constabulary ex p Hay* [1996] 2 All ER 711 at 724 d-g; and see Fredman and Morris (1988) Public Law 58; *The State as Employer* (1989) 61-71; (1991) Public Law 485 and Freedland (1995) Public Law 224.

13 The spy George Blake signed an agreement not to publish material gained from his employment with MI6: see p 130 above.

render a dismissal wrongful where the reason for dismissal was a breach of confidence. The defence of public interest is a defence to an action for breach of confidence whether or not contractual.[14] It will not necessarily make a dismissal wrongful which would, without that public interest, be lawful.

The law protects civil servants against unfair dismissal, but the tribunal is concerned with the 'fairness' and 'reasonableness' of the *process* of and reason for dismissal, and breach of confidentiality may well be a reasonable ground. Where an employer puts forward a relevant reason, the question then asked is 'was the dismissal fair in all the circumstances'. Similar problems attend demotion or transfer to a far less satisfactory job, in so far as such action by an employer is unlikely to constitute constructive dismissal in response to a breach of confidence by a civil servant. If a minister is abusing his or her position by deliberately misinforming Parliament, the only safe course for the civil servant may be to ask for a transfer. If he or she does inform an MP of an abuse, it could mean the minister's resignation. It is regrettable that a civil servant who has taken the necessary internal steps by appealing as prescribed without success, and who has not been transferred, should be left with damaged career prospects by following his or her conscience and going public where such a course is justified.[15] The Public Interest Disclosure Act, which is addressed below, seeks to remedy this situation.

Outright lying to Parliament by ministers may indeed be rare, but Sir Douglas Wass described the more usual practice where 'by judicious presentation and omission [the minister] gives an impression to Parliament which is not the impression which would be formed if someone had all the evidence'.[16] Presentation and timing are everything, and these are

14 Cm 2748 p 17 et seq.
15 Before the Public Interest Disclosure Act was passed, secrecy clauses in contracts have proliferated and have certainly been more widely publicised in recent years as an issue of grave public concern. They were common in the NHS and increasingly in universities, in nationalised industries and privatised industries and commercial bodies. Of crucial significance from a breach of contract perspective is whether the clause is appropriately drafted to cover a leak—many were not—and whether the leak occurred during or after the period of employment—dismissal is not possible in the latter case. The 'whistle-blower' is invariably in a weak position when in employment. In *Cornelius v Hackney London Borough Council* COIT 4376/92/LS/A an employee leaked information to outsiders—a union—and councillors and not *internally*. His dismissal was unfair but his contribution was assessed at 50%. The mode of disclosure is crucial. Doctors are to be encouraged to report on malpractices by colleagues: Vickers (1995) New LJ 1257. On disclosures by employees of health and safety information and a wider statutory protection see: EPCA 1978, s 57A. See: Cripps *The Legal Implications of Disclosure in the Public Interest* (1994 2nd ed). An action/advisory group, Public Action At Work, has been set up to assist 'whistleblowers': Dehn (1993) Public Law 603.
16 Note 48, vol II, p 42.

matters of ministerial prerogative. The minister for Open Government informed the House that government was more like playing poker than playing chess—not all the cards are placed on the table at once—a comment which caused him to be accused of authorising lying to Parliament.[17] The Prime Minister has stated that where a minister has knowingly failed to give accurate and truthful information to Parliament, they should resign 'except in quite exceptional circumstances of which a devaluation or time of war or other danger to national security have been quoted as examples'.[18]

Sir Robert Armstrong's amended memorandum and government responses promote a duty of confidence into an absolute and inflexible rule admitting of no exceptions. The civil service in the twenty-first century has changed irreversibly from the anonymous monolith of the early twentieth century—a point the Government readily accepts. Its most recent work has identified the qualities needed in the civil service to deliver its *Modernising Government* programme.[19] It has greater pressure of work because of increased and varied duties; it operates under the constant attention of the news media and the press; it is more vociferously unionised and organised around staff associations at all levels; it campaigns far more on behalf of its own causes.[20] On the government side, there is more intervention in senior appointments as well as greater resort to advertising; there have been constant demands for twenty years for more 'activist management and devolved responsibility to more junior line officials' bringing them not infrequently into the limelight.[1] There has also been an increasing resort to 'outside' advisers by government. It has been held by the EAT that special advisers are not covered by the Civil Service rules on appointments because they are not civil servants.[2]

The identity and level of responsibility of civil servants will become easier to assess, although the Cabinet Office has argued that this development starting with the financial management initiative and leading to the Public Service Agreements entered into by departments and agencies will merely strengthen ministerial responsibility or accountability. The public wants more publicity about administration,

---

17 HC Debs 8 March 1994. See TCSC HC 27(vii) and Cabinet Secretary Sir R Butler's evidence. In his evidence to Sir Richard Scott, Sir Robin Butler told the former that 'half truths' are necessary. See the evidence of Lord Howe on 'packaging' information to Parliament (HC 115 (1995-6) para D4.52).
18 Cm 2748 p 29.
19 *Modernising Government* Cm 4310 and see HC Debs Vol 341 col 219 (15 December 1999).
20 See the memorandum of Nevil Johnson, HC 92 (1985-6) Vol II, p 169.
1   Ibid.
2   *Lord Chancellor v Coker* [2001] IRLR 116. See n 10 p 178 above on special advisers.

and the civil service are asked increasingly to advise not only on policy, but on presentation of policies for public acceptance.

Public Interest Disclosure Act 1998 (PIDA)

The PIDA seeks to provide a 'framework for whistleblowing across the public, private and voluntary sectors.'[3] It amends the Employment Rights Act 1996. Where a qualifying disclosure (QD) is made, the whistleblower raising a matter of genuine concern in good faith will be protected against victimisation. A QD does not include a disclosure which is an offence eg in contravention of the Official Secrets Acts. Victims are entitled to enhanced compensation where they are not reinstated and there are no qualifying periods of employment for such rights. Interim protection orders may be sought. QDs are specified in the Act and include those made in a reasonable belief that there are actual or apprehended breaches of law, miscarriages of justice, dangers to health, safety and the environment, and includes concealing such malpractice. The Act will encourage whistleblowing procedures and will, believes Dehn, have the effect of encouraging employers to publicise employees' rights in order to minimise such disclosures.[54] Disclosure may be made internally eg, to a Minister where a civil servant is involved, employer or manager, or to an external regulator. Where a disclosure is made externally, additional safeguards must be satisfied for the disclosure to be protected. Where a cover up has been attempted, a disclosure to the press is more likely to be protected. The Act allows disclosures to others, but there must be no question of gain in such disclosures and it must be reasonable in all the circumstances and other conditions must be satisfied. This will be particularly important where a disclosure is made to the press and an order is sought seeking the identity of the source.[5] 'Reasonable' may be interpreted with regard to the identity of the person to whom the disclosure was made and the seriousness of the matter and other factors. Exceptionally serious matters may be disclosed and protected in less restricted circumstances. Confidentiality clauses seeking to prevent QDs are void. A QD may be made to a legal adviser while seeking legal advice and there is no good faith requirement in this case – the only disclosure afforded such a concession. The unavailability of the Act to the secret and intelligence services and the police was noted in chapter 1 as well as to civil servants engaged in national security work. The position of contractors is not referred to.

---

3   Dehn Current Law Statutes 1998 Vol. chapter 23.
4   Ibid.
5   See chapter 9 p 396 et seq below.

Government and media[6]

The Treasury and the Civil Service Committee believed that ministers who require their press officers to do more than present and describe their policies should make political appointments. In the run-up to the 2001 general election, Alastair Campbell the Downing Street Press Secretary was censored by the Cabinet Secretary Sir Richard Wilson for criticising the Opposition's economic policies. He was a civil servant and appeared to be breaching rules on civil service neutrality. How do governments use the media?

In 1984, a century after 'one gentleman of the press was given official permission to enter and remain in the Members' Lobby', the Lobby[7] celebrated its centenary. No formal resolution of the House authorised the event of 1884 and informal practice predated that year. The 'famous secret' of the lobby takes place twice daily, and lobby journalists see the Leader of the House and Leader of the Opposition on Thursday afternoons. Ministerial briefings of the lobby developed, some suggest, from 1926 and a visit to Downing Street during the General Strike. Regular daily briefings emerged only after 1945

The basis of the Lobby is a 'cosy collusion' whereby snippets of information will be given on the basis that the source is not identified. Even the politically uninitiated will appreciate that there are elements of a 'corporatist embrace' in the relationship in as much as the press cannot be controlled but they can be compromised if given anonymous 'confidences' by those in the know.[8] The lobby is a voluntary group which regulates itself and operates according to a convention which the Government, at least until March 2000, would not wish to cease.[9] The enforced hypocrisy has been too much for a growing number of national newspapers. However, securing reform has proved difficult,[10] even though it would only establish a more open 'on the record' form of journalism. In March 1987, the lobby voted to continue the practice of unattributable quotations and in 1991 the Prime Minister refused to countenance any alteration to the basic operation of the lobby. In March 2001, Alastair Campbell agreed to be identified by name in newspaper reports.[11] The unattributed quote is too deeply rooted to be removed by such changes.

---

6   See Seaton and Pimlott (eds) *The Media In British Politics* (1987).
7   M Cockrell, P Hennessey, D Walker *Sources Close to the Prime Minister* (1984). *Encyclopaedia of Parliament* (1968).
8   See H Young in *Inside Information* (1982), note 18 below.
9   *The Guardian*, 9 December 1986.
10   *The Guardian*, *The Independent* and *The Observer* refused for a period to publish unattributed items of government information. The lobby effectively voted for no change in its practices: *The Guardian*, 14 February 1987.
11   *The Guardian* 14 March 2000.

Outside the lobby, leaks unless authorised are subject to the usual process of law. In such cases journalists have been imprisoned for refusing to name their sources in disclosing incompetence in Whitehall.[12] In 1972, the offices of the *Sunday Times* and the *Railway Gazette* were raided because of disclosure of a DoE document advising the closure of 4,600 miles of railways. In 1973, *Newsweek* was informed that photographing an employment office was a breach of s 2 OSA. Successful prosecution followed the publication of military intelligence information by Duncan Campbell *et al* in 1978 in the ABC trial—even though the information was otherwise published. In 1987, the offices of the BBC in Glasgow were raided following publication of an article on the 'Zircon' satellite intelligence system.[13] The offices of the *Observer* and *Guardian* were objects of police requests for confiscation orders in July 2000 in order to seize correspondence from the MI5 renegade David Shayler. And so on. Powers of search under the Official Secrets Acts 1911-89 are subsumed under those in PACE 1984.

The cabinet manual *Ministerial Code* says the only safe recipients of neutered information are the lobby correspondents: 'But ministers should not at any time refer to such meetings; to do so would endanger the very special relationships with the Lobby which have been developed over many years'. In Harold Wilson's premiership, the Prime Minister had to authorise any broadcast by a minister 'in a private and non-ministerial capacity', had to be given all details of public speaking engagements, and had to give approval before a minister could write a letter to a newspaper.[14] These rules are formalised in the *Code* as was seen.

Formal rules govern the lobby and are issued by the Parliamentary lobby journalists.[15] Breach is most unlikely to lead to exclusion.[16] The lobby has often been used to discredit and to disinform, but it is a practice, notwithstanding the attribution reform in 2000, that will outlive any FOIA reform, as witness General Alexander Haig's description of his character assassination in the US by 'Reagan's henchmen' in his book *Caveat*. To achieve this, the President's men opened that 'great smithy of information'—the government—to the press. They 'escorted reporters inside in a way hitherto unknown in Washington'. The press had 'never had sources like this'—it told them everything. 'And of course, it would not risk losing these sources by offending them, so it wrote what it was given.' In the USA the press still has the matter better organised, as each

12 This followed the Vassal Tribunal of 1963.
13 Zellick (1987) New LJ 160.
14 H Young, *The Guardian*, 5 September 1985. See now p 173 *et seq* above
15 HC 555 (1984–5), pp 92–4.
16 Lobby journalists rejected a proposal that each should swear an oath of secrecy, but tied on a proposal that those who broke the confidentiality of lobby statements should be barred from the lobby.

large newspaper has a bureau at Congress. In the events leading to the fall of Peter Mandelson in January 2001, it was Alastair Campbell who described the minister as 'semi-detatched', echoing words of Bernard Ingham.[17] The Prime Minister has employed a private press spokesman since 1917. From 'around 1936', government departments 'first felt the need to possess a press officer'. 1939 saw the establishment of the Central Office of Information headed by a Minister of Information.[18] The office, but not the minister, survived the Second World War. It is now called the Government Information and Communications Service.[19] It produces an annual report. Departments have their own information officers and press officers – the Communications Directorate - to brief the press and media and present the departmental public image. Their importance in presenting ministerial policies in a favourable light has been acknowledged,[20] as has their role in press manipulation during the Falklands campaign, for example, the Gulf war and the bombing of Kosovo.[1] Weekly meetings of departmental press officers take place. The position of the Prime Minister's Downing Street Press Secretary is crucial, and there has been increasing criticism that they are used for party political and anti-Opposition purposes, and not purely governmental ones.[2] Much of this controversy concerned particular personalities. It has proven extremely difficult to prevent abuse of their position from taking place. Their 'spin' on the presentation of governments' policies has been felt to be more and more critical. There is no guarantee that it will not become counter-productive. A Government that relies on packaging and not substance will lose respect for its policies.

Government publicity has been the subject of guidance in 1985, 1989, 1997 and 1999.[3] The guidance basically states that publicity should be

---

17   Mrs Thatcher's flamboyant PS speaking about Cabinet Minister John Biffen.
18   H James in A May and K Rowan (eds), *Inside Information: British Government and the Media* (1982). The office is an executive agency seeking to 'enhance the effectiveness of government's communications': see HC 496 (1994/5).
19   Public Administration report: HC 511 (1999-00).
20   R Crossman *Diaries of a Cabinet Minister* (1975), vol I, p 497 and the Public Administration report above.
1   See *The Protection of Military Information*, Cmnd 9112 (1983). Self-censorship was emphasised but official censorship was needed, even in limited conflict. False information should be eschewed, but 'sophisticated measures' to deceive an enemy were permissible: see *The Guardian*, 13 August 1986; and D Mercer et al *The Fog of War* (1987); and *The Gulf War* BBC TV January 1996. See generally on the Press: the *Royal Commission on the Press*, Cmnd 6433, 6810–6814.
2   Especially but not exclusively in the Westland episode. In 1989, Government information officers called for a code of ethics: *The Guardian*, 19 April 1989.
3   *Government Publicity* Cabinet Office (1989), *Central Government Conventions on Publicity and Advertising: Guidance on the work of the Government Information Services* (1997) and *Guidance on the Work of the Government Information Service* (1999). See the National Audit Office HC 46 (1989-90).

relevant to government responsibilities, objective and explanatory, should not be party political and should be produced in an economic and relevant way. It should inform the public and not seek to image build. Civil service information officers are bound by the civil service code. As well as 'spin' there are constant allegations of use of public funds for party political purposes. The 1999 guidance also deals with government advertising and use of public relations consultants.[4] The British code of advertising practice exempts party political advertising from its provisions but this does not include government advertising and government or local government policy.

D Notices

Yet another corporatist embrace is illustrated by the D notice system (now known as DA notices: see The Defence Advisory Notices: A Review of the D Notice System MOD Open Government Document No 93/06). Originally established in 1912 and entitled the Admiralty, War Office and Press Committee, the relevant body is now known as the Defence, Press and Broadcasting Committee. Established on a voluntary basis and deriving no legal basis from OSA or other Acts of Parliament, its membership comprises senior civil servants from the relevant departments,[5] representatives of certain press and publishers' agencies, societies and associations, and latterly the BBC and Independent Television News. Media and press representation heavily outweighs official membership. The secretariat and expenses are borne by the government. The secretary must be fully informed of the facts behind a D notice, which is issued to limit or prevent publication of information which would be against the public interest. The secretary applies and interprets the scope of D notices, ie what is detrimental to the national security of the country. According to the memorandum of the committee submitted to the Franks Committee in 1972[6] it is not otherwise concerned with the national interest, although the secretary 'is instructed to bring to the notice of the chairman of the committee (or his deputy) any cases which lie at or beyond the border-line of the D notice system for consideration as to whether ministers should be informed of what other action should be taken.' The system is 'designed to protect national security while at the same time safeguarding the freedom and independence of the press and is based on mutual trust and confidence'.[7]

---

4   See P Birkinshaw *Government and Information* (2nd ed, 2001) pp 81-83.
5   Home Office, Foreign Office, Ministry of Defence: Cmnd 5104, vol II, pp 241 *et seq.*
6   Vol II, p 242.
7   Ibid.

There are six in operation covering eg, defence plans; defence equipment; nuclear weapons; radio and radar transmissions; cyphers (codes) and communications; civil defence and photographs of defence establishments. Ad hoc notices may be agreed and issued and more formal procedures may operate in time of war.[8] Adding addresses of ministers' second homes in the country for security reasons was discussed in 1999. They are issued personally to editors of the national and provincial press, various news agencies and relevant publishers as well as the BBC and ITV and advice is sought on their content from the secretary of the committee. However, a large number of editors said they would follow the advice of their lawyers rather than the secretary.[9] In 1992 the then secretary of the committee stated that he gave 'positive advice' urging editors not to publish about a dozen times a year. There were about a hundred inquiries a year from editors and publishers.[10] A D Notice was used in 1994 to stop publication of names of MI5 officers killed in a helicopter crash at the Mull of Kintyre; in 1999, the press were served with a D Notice to stop publication of the names of MI6 officers revealed on a website and the website address itself.

The corporatist element is emphasised in that these notices are not creatures of law but are voluntary, represent an exclusive relationship between the state and private or quasi-governmental organised interests, and are self-regulatory, although they cover some similar areas as the OSA and breach could, but not necessarily will, involve a prosecution. Indeed compliance itself is not a *legal* guarantee of immunity. This was evident in December 1987 when the Government invoked the civil law of confidentiality to prevent the broadcasting of a Radio 4 programme on the security services, although it had been cleared by the secretary to the committee[11] Failure to agree to D notices may mean exclusion from the circle of trusted recipients of information. The close interrelationship between the press and government made any significant alteration of the D notice system by the reform of s 2 OSA less than likely, though we shall have to see how it operates alongside the law of confidentiality. In fact, throughout the late 1980s the system was under strain because the Government had effectively bypassed it on several occasions.

This takes us to another facet of the contemporary state—the public/private interface and the corporatist tendencies in the distribution and exercise of power. What do we know of the networks through which contemporary government chooses to influence, and what ought we, or our representatives, to know? What are the consequences of government

---

8   *Lustgarten and Leigh* (1994) p 276 et seq.
9   Ibid p 275
10   Fairley 10 Oxford JLS 430.
11   The same allegedly occurred in the case of *Immediate Action* written by a former SAS soldier.

seeking to achieve public ends via private or quasi-public institutions? Broadcasting offers an interesting illustration.

Broadcasting, information and political censorship

Government influence and control over broadcasting is not a novel issue of concern, although it has spawned notorious episodes including the banning by the BBC of Duncan Campbell's *Secret Society* programme on the 'Zircon' information satellite system in 1987 and the prohibition by injunction of a programme on Radio 4 on the security services: *My Country Right or Wrong* and an *After Dark* programme from Channel 4 featuring Gerry Adams in 1988. Numerous cases abound of suspension of broadcasting of programmes embarrassing to the government in suspicious circumstances.[12] When Thames Television broadcast *Death on the Rock* in 1988 about the SAS shooting of three terrorists there was no hiding the Government's apoplexy. The producers were cleared by an independent inquiry chaired by a former minister and a QC of breaching the requirement of impartiality in broadcasting and of prejudicing an inquest into the deaths. There were many who associated the failure of Thames to be awarded a broadcasting licence in 1991 with this broadcast.[13] Over hostile questioning of government ministers by BBC interviewers has led to official rebuke of broadcasting in the round. Regulation and its future are important issues, but they take us beyond our brief. So too does ownership of the media and press although Tony Blair's much publicised visit to Australia for a meeting with Rupert Murdoch in 1995 and his subsequent courting of press and media magnates after 1997 bear eloquent testimony to the political importance of their influence.[14] What is of present concern is the ability of government to censor, influence or regulate the nature of political information which is broadcast. Governmental influence may

12 Preventing the broadcast about alleged financial irregularities and gerrymandering in Westminster Council because of contravention of Local Government (Finance) Act 1982, s 30; the stopping of Peter Jay's programme on the reasons for an economic slump before the 1992 general election; or of an overwillingness of the judiciary in Scotland to suspend a broadcast of an interview with the Prime Minister before local elections.

13 In September 1995, the ECtHR ruled—by a majority of one and overturning the Commission—that Britain was in breach of Art 2 of the Convention in the manner in which the terrorists were killed: *McCann v UK* (1995) 21 EHRR 97. See n 5 p 31.

14 Reward – the *Sun* advised readers to vote Labour in 2001! It also stated the general election date for 2001 should be 3 May – the PM's preferred option. This was deferred because of the foot and mouth disease. The Government White Paper on Broadcasting in December 2000 avoided any discussion of cross media ownership although it referred to 'stronger sectoral competition rules' which would be applicable to companies having 'significant market power' (para 2.1). See D Goldberg et al (eds) *Regulating the Changing Media* (1998).

not be directly exerted but may operate through the mediation of public corporations which are, ostensibly, independent.

The BBC consists in a formal, legal sense of 12 governors, appointed effectively on the 'say so' of the Prime Minister, though formally by the Queen in Council. A chairman and vice-chairman are appointed likewise. There is an General Advisory Council. Members of the Independent Television Commission which regulates commercial TV and Cable TV respectively are appointed by the secretary of state. The BBC's formal powers and responsibilities are contained in its charter of incorporation; the ITCs are contained in the 1990 Broadcasting Act. That legislation also created a Radio Authority for commercial radio. The 1996 Broadcasting Act added provisions concerning digital television. In a formal sense, both the BBC and the ITC[15] are given a wide range of discretion in their activities,[16] and are provided with minimal legal standards on quality, balance and impartiality although the ITC must ensure that accuracy and impartiality are present in news programmes and that 'due impartiality' is preserved in current political or industrial controversy or programmes relating to current political policy (s 6(1)(c)). The position with the BBC is more or less the same although changes to its charter have formalised the similarity. Both have codes and guidelines on accuracy, impartiality, taste and decency, violence and other matters. Both must refrain from editorial comment on current affairs. The Broadcasting Act 1990 places a duty on the ITC to produce a code elaborating impartiality in general broadcasting and under s 6(5) and (6) to preserve impartiality for major matters falling under s 6(1)(c) above as well as matters falling within that provision taken as a whole and a series of programmes may be considered as a whole in applying the code . These provisions are not entirely clear.[17] The word 'due' in s 6 (1)(c) has been taken to mean that it can be weighted in varying circumstances. For the BBC, impartiality may involve 'not absolute neutrality or detachment from those basic moral or constitutional beliefs upon which the nation's life rests' and it does not 'feel obliged to be neutral as between truth and untruth, justice and injustice, freedom and slavery, compassion and cruelty, tolerance and intolerance.'[18] The ITC appear to be more flexible. The BBC's duties are in its charter and guidelines. In the case of

15 The Independent Television Commission which replaced the Independent Broadcasting Authority.

16 *A-G (ex rel McWhirter) v IBA* [1973] QB 629; *R v IBA, ex p Whitehouse* (1985) Times, 4 April, CA. Cf *Lynch v BBC* [1983] NI 193; cf *Houston v BBC* 1995 SLT 1305 and the prevention of a *Panorama* programme containing an extended interview with the Prime Minister on the eve of Scottish local elections. See: *R v ITC, ex p TSW Broadcasting Ltd* [1996] EMLR 291 and *R v ITC, ex p Virgin Television Ltd* [1996] EMLR 318.

17 T Gibbons *Regulating the Media* (2nd ed, 1998).

18 BBC Charter *Annual Report etc 1985* (1986) quoted in Gibbons op cit.

advertising the ITC has a code of guidance and works in close relationship with the TV companies' representative body, the Independent Television Association.

The Home Secretary has formal powers of veto, though in the case of both the BBC and ITC they can announce that a veto has been effected and he can request the broadcasting of certain items.[19] Six veto directions of a general kind have been given, and none on a particular broadcast although one was threatened in 1972. The most famous general veto was the one issued to deny Northern Irish terrorists 'the oxygen of publicity' and to prohibit the direct sound broadcasting of the voices of members of proscribed organisations. This was unsuccessfully challenged before the House of Lords when it was held that there was no opportunity to apply art 10 of the ECHR to the interpretation of regulations where the provision in the primary legislation was clear and that proportionality was not a separate head of review in English or British law. The ban was not unreasonable. One might speculate as to whether the HRA will make any difference to this decision.[20]

The ITC has the power to issue formal directions to a broadcasting company requiring, eg apologies or corrections to be broadcast in relation to broadcasts and to revoke licences; the former IBA invariably achieved its ends informally and by influence rather than by resort to its statutory powers, or it referred to its guidelines and decisions implemented by regional officers.[1] The ITC is given more of a reactive role to suit a light touch regulation and they do not preview programmes. There is a tendency for controls on programme content to be greater in the independent sector than in the BBC as boards and executives are closer to programme makers and more knowledgeable about current operations.[2] The minister has power to revoke the licence to the BBC, and the ITC's powers of revocation etc we noted above.

Controls on good taste, sex and violence are pervasive, making TV, it has been alleged, 'the most censored form of communication in our society'.[3] Between 1959 and 1985, the BBC and the IBA[4] banned, censored, delayed or doctored 48 TV programmes. Other forms of

---

19 See generally cl 13 of the BBC's licence and agreement, Cmnd 8233, and ss 10(3), (4), 94(3) and (4) of the Broadcasting Act 1990.

20 *R v Secretary of State for the Home Department, ex p Brind* [1991] 1 AC 696. On art 10, s 92 (2)(a) Broadcasting Act 1990 and 'political' advertising on the radio, see: *R v Radio Authority, ex p Bull* [1995] 4 All ER 481,QBD. See also *Australian Capital Television Pty Ltd v Commonwealth of Australia* (1992) 177 CLR 106 on freedom of speech.

1   C Munro *Television Censorship and the Law* (1979).

2   Ibid, p 49; Channel 4 has had particular difficulty with films it wished to broadcast.

3   And see A Smith *Television and Political Life: Studies in Six European Countries* (1979); A. Briggs *The History of Broadcasting in the UK* (4 vols, 1961–79).

4   And its predecessor, the Independent Television Authority.

censorship are contained specifically in the law, and include a novel extension of the law of confidentiality.

Since 1980, a Broadcasting Complaints Commission existed to cover both the BBC and the IBA. It was appointed by the Home Secretary. The Broadcasting Act 1990 gave statutory expression to the Broadcasting Standards Council which examines standards of taste and decency and sex and violence in broadcasts and provides a code of guidance and deals with complaints about such items. Complaints may come in thick and fast on other matters which could be very convenient for government. In the first few days of the Gulf war over 4,000 complaints were received from the public complaining about the over-wide coverage of the war by the BBC.[5] The cabinet's special media committee suggested particular lines of approach in coverage[6] including preparation of public opinion for heavy losses, no doubt mindful of the USA's experience during the Vietnam war where massive prime time TV coverage of field hospitals and combat helped to turn public opinion against the war. The Broadcasting Act 1996 combined the Commission and Council into the Broadcasting Standards Commission which has to produce a code on unjust or unfair treatment or interference with privacy.[7] It has to prepare a code relating to broadcasting standards generally and the BSC has to monitor the standards of the contents of broadcasts. Sections 110-121 deal with complaints, and the BSC must publicise its findings. The broadcasting or regulatory bodies must publicise the BSC by regular announcements. The BSC publishes annual reports and any reports made to the Secretary of State.

The early history of the BBC reveals a marked element of subservience to government. In 1926 the Chairman, Sir John Reith, at the Prime Minister's prompting, refused to allow the Leader of the Opposition to broadcast. By the 1960s, a degree of independence had been firmly established, assisted without doubt by the advent of commercial TV. In 1972, for instance, the BBC resisted ministerial pressure not to broadcast *The Question of Ulster* because of the general political sensitivity of the subject. However, Stuart Hood has suggested:

> The BBC's relationship to the centres of political power in this country is government less by conspiracy than complicity; in this connection Reith's diary entry from the General Strike—'they know they can trust us not to be really impartial'—still accurately defines that relationship.[8]

5   BBC *TV AM* 25 January 1991.
6   *The Guardian* 26 January 1991.
7   See *R v Broadcasting Standards Commission, ex p BBC* [2000] 3 All ER 989; See Broadcasting Standards Commission *Codes of Guidance* and the *Code on Standards* June (1998).
8   Former Controller at BBC of TV programmes, quoted in *Munro*, p 124.

It might appear curious that such a degree of influence existed, for it was not until after 1955 that news bulletins made any reference to election campaigns. A semi-formal Committee on Party Political Broadcasting (CPPB) has existed 'in which sharing out of time takes place between delegates of all the parties with representatives in Parliament, the BBC, and ITC and party organisations'. It is chaired by the Lord President of the Council. The SDP-Liberal Alliance contested the sharing of time to achieve balance and impartiality in news and current affairs coverage on the BBC. After an inconclusive court hearing,[9] the BBC promised to produce a pamphlet explaining its rules and procedures for achieving such balance and to give *limited* publicity to results of monitoring of its practices. Political broadcasts covering elections are formulated through the CPPB.[10]

Since 1937, BBC staff, on appointment or promotion, have been politically vetted by MI5. This was a negative form of vetting; the subject is not informed and cannot therefore correct false or inaccurate information. In April 1986,[11] the BBC undertook to restrict the extent of vetting to security-sensitive posts.

For Northern Ireland, internal and external censorship by the government is vigorous, if not always respected by the respective broadcasting authorities.[12] In an attempt to maintain 'impartiality', ie the status quo, they must not show scenes which might encourage republican sentiment, and must not criticise the armed forces. On this and on all subjects in the UK, political impartiality must be maintained, so that if one suggested a school was falling down this would not be impartial unless a government spokesman could say it was not.[13]

The Northern Ireland (Emergency Provisions) Act 1991 prohibits collecting, recording, publishing or attempting to elicit any information concerning the police, army, judges, court officials or prison officers, which is likely to be of use to terrorists. It is an offence to collect or record any information which is likely to be useful to terrorists in carrying out an act of violence, or to possess any record or document containing any

9   *The Times*, 15 July 1986, following *R v Broadcasting Complaints Commission, ex p Owen* [1985] QB 1153. Cf the copious scope of review by the Conseil d'Etat over the French Broadcasting Authority: (1986) Public Law 155.

10 See Gibbons note 17 above; and A.Boyle (1986) Public Law 562. Nb s 93 Representation of the People Act 1983; *X and Association Z v UK* Application 4515/70 (1970) and the ECHR.

11 *The Guardian*, 16 April 1986. Guidelines on vetting generally were revised in 1990 and 1994 – see ch 1 p 34 note 1 above. In 1989 the Home Affairs Committee was informed that 508,942 'checks' were made to the National Identitification Bureau on national security grounds: HC 285 (1989-90). See the unsuccessful application of Isobel Hilton and the E Commission of HR: Application No 12015/86.

12 See p 199 above.

13 See *Wilson v IBA* 1979 SC 351.

of these types of information. The Act, as drafted, would cover ordinary journalistic practices, although the consent of the Northern Ireland DPP is required to bring a prosecution. A defence of lawful authority or 'reasonable excuse' may be made out.

The Prevention of Terrorism (Temporary Provisions) Act 1989 applies to the whole of the UK. Section 18 provides that persons are under a duty to disclose to the police any information which might be of material assistance in preventing an act of terrorism or in apprehending, prosecuting or convicting someone suspected of terrorism.[14] The Attorney-General has previously threatened to adopt a hard line under this section (under the 1984 Act) after reporting by BBC crews in Northern Ireland. It was invoked in March 1988 after the murder of two British soldiers at a Republican funeral. Both these statutes were repealed by the Terrorism Act 2000 but s 19 of the latter achieves the same effect as s 18 of the 1989 Act.

These legislative provisions, understandably, help to maintain an ethos of caution, but authorities would not wish to be seen to be using them oppressively. There are more subtle forms of political persuasion. The Foreign and Commonwealth Office has close and informal contacts with the BBC World Service, and every day delivers a 'selection' of cables it has received. The World Service is bound to 'plan and prepare its programmes in the national interest' according to the BBC licence, and its hours and languages of broadcast are prescribed by the FCO. Under cl 13(5) of the licence, the World Service has to obtain and accept from the FCO 'such information regarding conditions in, and the policies of Her Majesty's Government towards countries' in planning and preparing its programmes. Any complaints from foreign governments about broadcasts are invariably made to the FCO, which duly presents them to the BBC while maintaining to complainants that the BBC is independent. Many complaints come from authoritarian regimes with whom our Government has important diplomatic or commercial arrangements.[15] Closer to the home front have been studies indicating pro-Government bias in the news programmes covering the miners' strike of 1984-5[16] and overt pressure on the IBA and TVS not to rebroadcast in their existing form a series of programmes on the Greek civil war of the 1940s, or to sell them overseas.[17] The interpretation offered of the war was not favourable to the 'establishment' version, it was claimed. The inquiry into the

14 And note *DPP v Channel 4 Television Co Ltd* [1993] 2 All ER 517. See Terrorism Act 2000, s 19.
15 *The Guardian*, 31 August 1985.
16 G Cumberbatch *et al*, *TV News and the Miners' Strike*, Broadcasting Research Unit (1986). Syndicated tapes are widely used by government departments for promotional purposes on local radio.
17 *The Guardian*, 5 July 1986.

complaints was not made by the Broadcasting Complaints Commission but by Channel 4 itself internally, 'because of the seriousness of the allegations'. The issue centred on the alternative versions of the truth emerging from historical events.

In 1972, the Irish Government banned the appearance of members of illegal organisations on the media, a ban which has been revoked. The Annan Committee Report rejected such a move in the UK, arguing that 'these organisations are a political force in Northern Ireland; and it would be unrealistic for the broadcasters not to recognise them'. The prohibition on direct voice broadcasting was noted above and this was lifted with the peace initiative in Northern Ireland in 1995. In 1985, however, the BBC governors postponed the screening of *Real Lives,* a programme concerning members of Northern Irish para-military organisations after the board of management had passed the programme for screening. The governors had reacted, it seemed, to overt pressure from the Home Secretary and senior officials, and for the first time vetted a programme before it was broadcast. The decision was taken shortly after the Prime Minister had spoken publicly of the need to starve terrorists of publicity. Only one BBC governor dissented. The Home Secretary believed that, while censorship under the criminal law would be wrong, he should be allowed to convey the Government's view of the public interest to the BBC. The chairman of the governors was approached directly by the Home Secretary after the board of management, largely comprising directors of the BBC, decided not to show the documentary to the governors, fearing that the board's 'editorial independence' might be undermined. The Home Secretary was adamant that it was *not* a question of not maintaining balance, but of the undesirability of broadcasting the committed and extreme views of terrorists from both sides of the division in Northern Ireland. Under the charter, the governors carry legal responsibility, are the ultimate management authority and are the 'independent' judges of programmes on the public behalf. It will be recalled that they are appointed by the Crown on the recommendation of the Prime Minister.[18] A less guarded approach was witnessed when the BBC broadcast in October 2000 the names of four men in connection with the Omagh bombing which killed 29 people. A court order preventing the broadcast was unsuccessfully sought by the Northern Ireland Human Rights Commission[19]

General De Gaulle once said, 'They have the newspapers, I have the television.' A former director[20] of the BBC asked why the Prime Minister should have both. This is now unfair to the press who on balance have given greater support to the Opposition since 1997 than to the

18 See Lady Faulkner in *The Listener*, 8 August 1985, maintaining their independence.
19 *The Guardian* 10 October 2000. Those named lived in the Irish Republic.
20 A Singer *The Listener* 8 August 1985.

Government. It is also unfair to the media, both publicly and privately owned. However, whether the governors acted from good motives or bad in the *Real Lives* saga, the episode has left a damaging taint on the BBC's image. The functional confusion of the roles of governors and managers, and the BBC's dependence on the acceptance of an appropriate licence fee, ie their income, by the Home Secretary, leaves a situation ripe for political exploitation. By law the Home Secretary had a power of veto; was this not the appropriate route in the situations above rather than via the back door, which compromised the governors?[1] Other episodes suggesting covert pressure have followed[2] as well as complaints by the Conservative Party chairman about anti-Conservative bias—complaints which were made on behalf of consumers and co-ordinated use of the press and Parliamentary pressure to cower broadcasters. The Labour Party also has made its complaints of unfair treatment and overly hostile questioning – more stridently since it returned to power.

Annan found the erstwhile IBA position more clear-cut. It contracts out and then supervises; the position of the ITC is similar although it is deliberately less interventionist in its powers. The BBC has a confusion of roles. What is required is a clear division between governors and management. The governors have few friends and their continuation has been under threat. The board of management should manage; the governors should vet standards in the public interest, and the licence seeks to ensure that appropriately experienced individuals are appointed. Here lies the snag. How representative of the community are the governors? How far afield does the Prime Minister's search go? What safeguards are there to prevent the packing of allies and like-minded souls on the board? If the example of the erstwhile Public Appointments Unit is anything to go by, precious little. This was maintained in the Cabinet Office and keeps a central list of the 'Great and the Good'. The criteria for admission to the list, and the fact that it was open to self-proposal, were not made public.[3] Information about the operation of the unit has been denied on the ground that it was 'purely a matter of internal efficiency'. In May 1995, it was reported that fewer than 6% of relevant appointments to quangos were made from persons recommended by the Unit.[4] These weaknesses generally in public appointments were addressed by Lord Nolan's report on *Standards in Public Life*. His recommendations led to the

---

1   The Home Secretary moved to the Department of Trade and Industry shortly after this fracas.
2   The enforced settlement of a libel action against the BBC brought by two right-wing Conservative MPs of allegedly 'extremist' views and the attack by the Conservative Party chairman on BBC's 'left-wing bias': HC Debs, 4 November 1986.
3   See A Davies in A Barker (ed) *Quangos In Britain* (1982), chapter 10.
4   *Financial Times* 18 May 1995.

establishment of the Public Appointments Commissioner to oversee public appointments in specified areas. These were added to in October 1998.[5] An argument has been made that the governors should be elected by an electoral college appointed by viewers and listeners and that their deliberations be made public.[6] Even the National Heritage Committee has accepted that the governors are unrepresentative of viewers.[7]

The Peacock Committee Report on the Financing of the BBC[8] recommended a greater reliance on pay-as-you-watch TV and on the auctioning of commercial sector broadcasting contracts/licences. The Broadcasting Act 1990 introduced the latter with certain thresholds for quality and 'basically' success for the highest bidder.[9] The dangers in choosing wealth as the most significant factor in public broadcasting are all too obvious as regards the overwhelming support that such a criterion is likely to create for one political party and political creed. When Fox's Libel Act of 1792 placed power in the hands of juries and not judges to decide not only the facts, but whether the facts amounted to libel in charges of seditious libel brought by the Crown, the Crown managed quite nicely without the assistance of the offence. Newspaper owners had become the friends of government and less likely to publish seditious libel.

TV represents the most immediate and effective mass persuader and conveyor of information in our culture. In the era of direct satellite broadcasting of transmissions from overseas and the encouragement of an integrated European TV system, the need for vigilance to ensure proper political balance is as great as ever, possibly greater.[10] It is as great as the

---

5   First Report Public Administration Committee (1997-8) and Government Response; Neill Report Committee on Standards in Public Life Cm 4557 vol I (2000); the remit of the Public Appointments Com'r was extended to utility regulators, boards of nationalised industries and public corporations and advisory NDPBs from October 1998.

6   *The Future of the BBC: Commerce, consumers and Governance* IPPR (1995).

7   *The Future of the BBC.* National Heritage Committee *Second Report* (1993-94).

8   Cmnd 9824 (1986).

9   See note 16 p 200 above on litigation involving the contract allocation process.

10 Censorship by the test of obscenity was introduced in the Cable and Broadcasting Act 1984 and then in the Broadcasting Act 1990; and nb the Video Recordings Act 1984 and the role of the British Board of Film Classification and Criminal Justice and Public Order Act 1994, ss 88-91. The BBFC has been described as the most powerful body of film censors in Western Europe. In 1994, 10 of 13 members were replaced, three stating they had been dismissed and were barred from speaking out: *The Guardian* 14 April 1994. For pornography transmitted via satellite see: 'Red Hot Television' Coleman and McMurtrie (1995) 1 European Public Law 201 and *R v Secretary of State for National Heritage, ex p Continental Television BV* [1993] 2 CMLR 333; affd [1993] 3 CMLR 387, CA. See the Broadcasting Act ss 43-45 and use of nominal licences and controlling discs and ss 177-79. The Broadcasting Act 1996 begins to address the question of cross-media ownership.

need to maintain standards of taste and decency. Government and money must not have the only word on settling those issues.

In the UK, as early as 1995 the Director General of Telecommunications has added that 'the traditional regulatory distinction between broadcasting and telecommunications will be difficult to sustain' indicating the global nature of the subject.[11] The interdependence of broadcasting and communications since then has increased dramatically. Computer magnates are purchasing shares in cable networks; global satellite enterprises are being established by media magnates. Radio spectrum management is subject to increasing demands.[12] The White Paper *A New Future for Communications* of 2000[13] failed to address cross-media ownership and control. It recommended an overarching regulatory body to provide a 'clear and fair ... modernising' form of regulation but its remit will be essentially national. The issue is truly global. It will produce a code on content and will take a role in privacy protection. Although the regulator will bring the BBC within its ambit, the White Paper also gave a reprieve to the governors and the BBC will have to spell out its public service remit via the governors who will seek to maintain the BBC's impartiality and editorial independence. The governors are to lose some powers including those over taste and decency which are now to assessed in the light of 'acceptable community standards.' Political advertising will remain banned.[14]

Government, non-departmental bodies and private organisations

Openness and accountability are two of the legitimating principles of our governmental system, though they have to be weighed against other principles such as efficiency, responsiveness and security. Collective and individual ministerial responsibility are predicated upon the former. If we set these claims upon which legitimacy is dependent against actual practice, the constitutional principles are invariably suborned. Democracy is based upon voting and representation for all those whose personal attributes do not disqualify them. In order to vote meaningfully, I must know what I am voting for. My representative must convey what the Parliamentary elite have done in their stewardship of the 'gubernatorial power' and what, in return, he or she has done, or the legislative assembly

11 OFTEL *Beyond the Telephone, the TV etc* (1995) para 1.4.4.
12 Wireless Telegraphy Act 1998.
13 Cm 5010. See the critical comments of Gerald Kaufman on the position of BBC governors HC 161 I (2000-2001).
14 Party political advertising is exempt from the Advertising Standards Code, above p 197.

has done, to investigate that stewardship. It comes to this: we cannot guarantee that we will know all that is relevant, and the system of government has not been devised in which we could. But we can ensure that vigilance and suitable pressure have been applied to ask the right questions, and get the best answers.

Openness and accountability cannot be taken as absolutes, because we do yield to countervailing pressures which are present in appeals to efficiency, responsiveness and security and which are duties of government. In the fictional TV series *Yes Minister*, Sir Humphrey's advice to young Bernard, a junior civil servant high-flier concerning open government, 'My dear boy, it's a contradiction in terms. You can be open, or you can have government,'[15] is far too strong, but there is a scintilla of uncomfortable truth for the advocate of open government. The lines between openness and accountability, and efficiency, responsiveness and security, represent clashes between degrees of participatory and representative forms of democracy. But make no mistake, they are clashes over forms of democracy. The lines are always shifting as encroachments are made on the nature of the government prerogative and its assertion of the absolute supremacy of executive power and politics and policy in government and administration. The encroachments demand justification for the exercise of collective power in the purported furtherance of the public interest through reasons, rational explanation, debate and institutional structure. That area of pure politics will never disappear entirely; far from it unless we require stultifying uniformity and oppressive, perhaps irresponsible inertia. Our present task is to confine it to its legitimate realm and not to allow it to rule arrogantly and rudely where it does not belong.

The chapter so far has concentrated on Whitehall. What about government beyond Whitehall which is not subject to the democratic pressure of our high politics? We all know who can vote; less easy to assess is on what issues we can vote.

The points which follow are complex, but they involve the following themes.[16] Outside the formal and constitutional structure of government emerge bodies which are created by government/Parliament by a variety of devices. We saw in chapter 3 how governments have in the past sought to control and censor such agencies. These bodies are responsible for particular areas of administration which fall outside a department's specific responsibility to administer directly, but which might be under the direction or guidance of a ministry which can be achieved by a variety of

15 'Open Government' in the BBC TV series *Yes, Minister.*
16 See: Birkinshaw, Harden and Lewis *Government by Moonlight: the Hybrid Parts of the State* (1990).

devices.[17] Ministerial power of appointment is an obvious means of control and one that has caused sensational press and media coverage in recent years. This was an area which was addressed by Lord Nolan who made a variety of recommendations to deal with appointments to quangos. It must be said that the FOIA 2000 has as one of its distinct and positive features an enormously broad remit of bodies covered by the duties on access. To these bodies which are in Schedule 1 of the Act and which include many advisory bodies and non-departmental executive bodies may be added bodies designated by the Secretary of State to be covered by the Act's provisions. This may occur where they perform public duties or provide public services under contract with a public authority and it is appropriate to designate them as a 'public authority' (see chapter 6 p 293 et seq). They will of course be protected by the Act's exemptions.

If public expenditure is involved, either by way of grant in aid from the sponsoring department or by direct vote from Parliament, then the Comptroller and Auditor-General (CAG) would have the duty of scrutiny and inspection of accounts.[18] In their evidence to Nolan the CAG and chairman of the Public Accounts Committee outlined difficulties they had encountered with non departmental bodies and the CAG provided a list of bodies whose accounts he did not audit. A report from the PAC detailed shortcomings in financial regularity concerning many non-departmental bodies and executive agencies 'representing a departure from the standards of public conduct which have mainly been established during the past 140 years.'[19] Among the faults identified were poor monitoring of expenditure, failure by departments to establish effective monitoring of non-departmental public bodies which they fund and sponsor, failure to obtain information by those in authority, infrequent meetings which were improperly recorded, concealing information, and failure to secure arms' length relationships with private sector consultants.[20]

What concerns us is that these bodies themselves become repositories of vast amounts of information, and secondly they establish relationships with sponsoring departments which are not on the record of any public document. The subject of nationalised industries in the past and the public corporations which manage them, and indeed the boards of privatised industries, and the relationships of these bodies with ministers, is a case

---

17 Issuing codes of guidance, statutory regulations, departmental regulations or by allowing an appeal or complaint to be made by an aggrieved party to the secretary of state; see Birkinshaw *Grievances, Remedies and the State* (1994), chapter 4.

18 See chapter 5 below p 264 *et seq* and White etc n 1 p 271.

19 *The Proper Conduct of Public Business* HC 154 (1993-4).

20 £318 million had been spent on consultants' fees for privatisation and market testing since 1979, according to one calculation: *The Guardian* 18 September 1995.

in point. The relationship between these bodies and ministers is of a confidential nature, and it is impossible to fathom whether such bodies are under a greater degree of political control than the arm's length statutes establishing them would suggest. In 1995 for instance the Director-General of Electricity—the electricity regulator—held off announcement of a price rise in electricity until after the Government sold shares in two generating companies! It may have been coincidental. The privatisation of British Rail spawned a plethora of regulatory and managerial bodies the complexity and opacity of which in their relationship with each other and with the Secretary of State has done much to bring the industry into unqualified disrepute. Accident investigation reports are likely to be protected under FOIA exemptions. The response to a series of serious accidents was not to hold an inquiry which would publish its results but to threaten prosecutions for corporate manslaughter. Convictions for this crime are notoriously difficult to secure.

When a monopoly industry is privatised, as in the case of British Telecommunications (BT), the Government establishes a regulatory body which, as with BT, supervises the licence which the Government has issued to BT to provide telecommunication services to the consumer.[1] There are now numerous telecoms providers and there is far more competition in the industry. In 1984, the National Consumer Council wrote:

Without a clear statutory definition of whose interests the Office of Telecommunications is supposed to be looking after there is a danger that OFTEL will take whichever side can make life easier for OFTEL; this is unlikely ever to be the consumer.[2]

In 1995 on two occasions price increases were ordered by the regulator in industries only months after a previous price increase, fuelling widespread belief that the Regulator had not obtained all relevant information. Was he sure he had obtained such on the second occasion? The procedures for enforcing licensing conditions are cumbersome. In spite of improvements and legal duties to provide information OFTEL will have to rely upon BT for much of the information which it requires for effective regulation—'it is not in BT's interests to be open and frank'. In an early annual report[3] the Director-General of OFTEL stated his discontent over BT's licence terms, which provide only for the corporation to supply information on specific request. He would like to be supplied with information on a regular basis. It is worthwhile examining how the

---

1   See C Graham *Regulating Public Utilities: A Constitutional Approach* (2000).
2   NCC *Controlling Public Utilities* (1984).
3   *Annual Report 1985*, HC 403 (1985–6).

legal relationship has developed. Consumer bodies do not have a right to demand information from the industry but will have to rely upon the Director-General supplying them. The powers of the DG and to some extent consumer representative bodies were beefed up by the Competition and Services (Utilities) Act 1992 which inter alia provided a legal duty to provide complaints procedures for privatised industries' consumers. Section 53 of the Telecommunications Act 1984 empowers the DG to require, on notice, information or the production of documentation, as in civil proceedings and creates a new criminal offence of failure to comply with a request for information or of deliberately tampering with or concealing information. It was noted that the total number of staff working for the audit department of BT was larger than the total complement of the DG's staff. Under the 1992 Act, these powers may be exercisable by the DG in relation to complaint resolution under that act. By s 55 the DG is under a duty to publish an annual report of his activities and a general survey of developments including the reports of his advisory bodies. Restrictions are placed on the disclosure of information collected by him. Under the 1992 Act, regulations may be made by the DG prescribing 'such standards of performance in connection with the provision of relevant services' as in the DG's opinion should be achieved. Consumer bodies have to be involved in the consultation leading to these rules and research has to be conducted with representative samples of persons likely to be affected by the rules. The operator may be placed under a duty to advise persons of their rights under this section. Compensation will be paid where standards are not met.

The DG is under a duty to collect information with respect to compensation paid, the levels of overall performance achieved by designated operators and the DG may collect information on compensation paid in realtion to each standard of service. Failure to provide is a criminal offence. The DG is under a duty to arrange for the publication of the information provided but he has a discretion in what to publish or not publish. The idea is to allow the DG to assess performance against prescribed target levels of service. The Government hoped that that it would lead to greater understanding by customers and more informed public debate. Operators are under a duty to publish information for customers about levels of performance achieved and the DG has power to ensure that it is published in a meaningful manner. Unlike s 48 TA 1984, this places the duty primarily on the operator and not the DG.

The DG's have come under a great deal of criticism because of their own modus operandi.[4] They achieve results by negotiation with the industries and these are conducted in informal, closed sessions especially concerning licence modification and informal enforcement of the licence

---

4   C Veljanovski *The Future of Industry Regulation in the UK* (1993).

and in establishing crucial definitions of 'business' for auditing purposes. Such a wide discretion is devoid of appropriate control. This upsets not only consumer groups who take no effective part in policy development but also, in telecommunications, BT's competitors. In 1995 the DG gave a speech on 'interconnection' of competitors into the BT network. In the consultation process, BT asked to make informal confidential and not formal open submissions to OFTEL. The DG 'felt he could not refuse to respond ... the result, however, has been a lack of transparency, a lack of understanding by the rest of the industry of what BT's position is and frankly the suspicion of an OFTEL/BT deal in a closed room ... The rest of the industry has no real opportunity to respond to BT's arguments. As a result I am seriously considering procedures and rules for the future to ensure that the consultation process is open and visible ... unless a test of material commercial harm was met.'[5] The licence modification included accounting separation and publication of regulatory accounts on a regular basis for the first time to achieve a clearer picture of true costs for BT. This would involve 'unbundled standard charges showing details of how cost are derived'; this would be published and audited according to stiff standards; and greater investigatory powers *vis à vis* cross-subsidy and BT's accounting procedures.

It is interesting to compare this method with the one that obtains in the USA where there is a far more legalistic regime of regulation and where the provisions of the FOIA and Sunshine and Federal Advisory Committee Acts operate with fuller and more formal rights of public participation (see chapter 2). Interestingly, the DG's of all industries will fall under the provisions of the Government code on openness and so they will have to respond to requests for information under the terms of that code which I examine in chapter 5. They will also be covered by FOIA as will the industries although not their purely private businesses. However, the OFTEL DG was sceptical of more information for information's sake and was also wary of a burgeoning legalism in regulation: 'More lawyers and more accountants will reduce the pace, reduce the flexibility and worsen the quality of decision-making.

OFTEL proceeded to develop consultation procedures whereby parties were allowed to comment upon the submissions of others. 'Confidentiality' was not *per se*, a ground for refusing access and parties were warned of this. The practice bore a resemblance to the better rule-making procedures which agencies follow in the US (see chapter 2 p 80 et seq). The Food Standards Agency is also planning to hold meetings in public. The Government has produced a Code on consultation which will be examined in chapter five. The Utilities Act 2000 has also sought to

---

5   *Financial Times Conference* 8 February 1995. In November 1995, open hearings were held under a neutral chair to discuss OFTEL's operations. In July 1995, The DG announced that a register of enforcement findings was to be published.

bring more openness in the energy sectors. This legislation was originally planned to cover telecommunications and water but was confined to gas and electricity because of pressure from the telecoms and water industries to be excluded! The idea was to converge the regulatory regimes for the principal utilities. This it was felt would help produce greater fairness for consumers as well as meet wider social and environmental objectives. Only gas and electricity are now covered by the Act which has a combined regulator as well as a combined consumer council: the Gas and Electricity Markets Authority and the Gas and Electricity Consumer Council. These bodies are placed under increased duties to publish more information, to assist consumers and to name and shame reluctant energy companies and to protect vulnerable consumers such as the disabled or chronically sick, those of pensionable age or residing in rural areas.

In the non-departmental sector the use of gagging clauses in contracts of employment has been staggering. This is true in the NHS where the select committee on the Parliamentary Commissioner for Administration has examined the question and the Government has even produced an ambivalent code on whistle-blowing which acknowledges the right of employees to go to MPs and the media—although in the latter case it warns that disciplinary action could follow where internal procedures are not pursued.[6] Prior to the sale of British Gas and other privatisations its employees were warned by an internal circular not to talk about the sale to 'outsiders'. Use of such clauses has spread through universities. The modification of the BT licence contained detailed provisions covering five pages of A4 paper on the subject of 'confidentiality agreements' between an operator and licensees ie those connecting to the network. The CAG reported to Lord Nolan that he often has employees in the bodies he audits contacting him with information but rarely will they wish to go on the record. To do so would be career-wrecking. The Government have extended the disclosure provision concerning an accounting officer in bodies audited by the CAG so that they may send their note of disagreement with a minister to the chair of the PAC directly and not simply to the CAG on more serious differences. However, in NDPBs many of the managers will be the accounting officers. The process of contracting out has seen 'commercial confidentiality' stamped liberally over the details of the public/private interface. The Public Interest Disclosure Act which was examined above will help in these areas. But to repeat, whistleblowers rarely emerge unscathed.

If, for example, a government hives off to an independent agency executive powers to regulate, license or control an aspect of commerce or finance in the public interest, how do we or our representatives know that the public interest is being maintained? Indeed, does the government know

---

6   EL (93) 51 Dept of Health. Such matters would now fall within the Public Interest Disclosure Act 1998.

that the public interest is being maintained? In deciding whether to assume a responsibility for regulation or supervision of a sector or activity, the government has to make a political decision. These decisions are made through the traditional channels of government decisions, followed by legislation, Royal charter or whatever.

Government then has to decide how to carry out its programme. Is management best achieved—in the case of an industry—by a minister or a manager or a board? Is privatisation best achieved by complete sale, by retention of shares, or by a partnership with the private sector, the much acclaimed Public Private Partnerships which in the case of the London Underground showed how they can take myriad forms?[7] Is regulation best achieved by a government department or by an independent body—if so, how independent[8]—or by an organised interest already in existence with which the state can enter into bartering relationships and which can speak on behalf of a client group? In this latter range of questions, it has been suggested, the government is acting more as a legal agent.[9] It has to choose the instruments through which its objectives can best be achieved. Very often this will be through law. The legislation is invariably facilitative: authorising various things to happen, allowing others to happen. It is usually widely drafted. It lacks specificity. It does not provide answers, nor does it help to pinpoint responsibility. It does not insist on publication of details and it rarely gives public interests, eg the consumer, an opportunity to be fully informed or to make a meaningful contribution.

Inevitably, in the case of formal institutions established by government, there is a duty to inform the minister on whatever he directs; to present accounts to him or to the Comptroller and Auditor-General; and to make reports, in the case of statutory bodies inevitably to Parliament. But Parliament has itself found it difficult to break through hollow ministerial answers, or in the case of nationalised industries to obtain corporate plans.[10] Where the government or its agencies collect information in the course of inspections, refusal to publicise information is far from rare. The Ministry of Agriculture, Fisheries and Food refused to allow public examination of the detailed information on the 400 pesticides already approved for use in Britain, and no timetable has been set for safety review. The Health and Safety Executive for years refused to

---

7 See Greater London Authority Act 1999, Pt IV, chapter VII on PPPs in London. M Freedland (1998) Public Law 288.
8 If it is a private body acting as a surrogate for the state, the courts may hold it susceptible to judicial review: *R v Panel on Take-Overs and Mergers, ex p Datafin plc* [1987] 1 All ER 564, CA; *R v Panel on Take-Overs and Mergers, ex p Guinness plc* [1989] 1 All ER 509, CA and so on.
9 P Nonet and P Selznick *Law and Society In Transition: Toward Responsive Law* (1978), p 112.
10 The responsibilities of the former Select Committee on Nationalised Industries were assumed by departmental select committees in 1979.

establish a public register of companies licensed to handle hazardous chemicals and to release details of firms convicted of breaking regulations[11]—the result of a misinterpretation of provisions under the Health and Safety at Work etc Act 1974. There is no publication of accident 'near misses' or other dangerous situations.[12] In the NHS 'accountability is generally limited to inspection and reports, which for the most part remain firmly within the system' and which are not regularly reported in the reports of health authorities.[13] A code of practice on openness has been produced for the NHS under the open government initiative and we can examine this in chapter 5. The NHS will be covered by the FOIA 2000. We shall see that the nature of the exemptions from access under FOIA may help prevent openness. But closed practices are coming under increasing pressure from, among others, the courts. The inquiry into Dr Harold Shipman's murders which the Secretary of State wanted to be conducted in private had to be held in open. To do otherwise was irrational and deprived the relatives of their rights under Art 10 to freedom of speech.[14] The secret practices involving use of body parts were facilitated by a culture of secrecy and not just the activities of several rogue consultants.[15] Even the Health and Safety Executive reports fail to give details of the criteria of standards adopted by inspectors in investigations.[16] The National Rivers Authority was charging £150 per sheet of A4 sized paper after the introduction of the *Code on Open Government* which operated as an effective barrier to access. They were passing on the cost of gathering information which they were under a duty to collect to the requester—a practice which was probably ultra vires. The former Monopolies and Mergers Commission investigated in private and does not hold press conferences and it has singularly failed to define the 'public interest' in relation to mergers and monopolies. Will the Competition Commission fare any better? The secretary of state does not have to accept a report of the Commission and does not have to give reasons for this and he does not have to publish a report of inspectors examining those proposing takeovers and mergers.[17] In 2000, the

11 It agreed to do so. There have been attempts to pass Bills allowing access to registers of those served with enforcement notices on environmental grounds. Details of 'almost accidents' within hospitals are to be published for the first time.

12 'Confidential' reports on the lack of safety on railways had to be leaked from Railtrack in September 1995.

13 A. Harrison, J. Gretton *Health Care UK* (1985) CIPFA.

14 *R (Wagstaff) v Secretary of State for Health* [2001] 1 WLR 292; see chapter 9 below.

15 Report by M Redfern QC into Alder Hey Children's Hospital, 30 January, 2001.

16 Notes 11 and 12 above.

17 See: *R v MMC, ex p Argyll Group plc* [1986] 2 All ER 257; *R v MMC, ex p Matthew Brown plc* [1987] 1 All ER 463; *R v MMC, ex p Air Europe* (1988) 4 BCC 182 for judicial tests of fairness of MMC procedures. Cf. DTI *Mergers Policy* (HMSO,

Secretary of State announced that he would publish Office of Fair Trading advice on mergers. The Secretary of State's role in mergers is being reduced.

For the more 'apparent' of public outposts, the Cabinet Office and Treasury published in 1996 a guide for departments.[18] This is a detailed document setting out four main criteria: rigorous examination of proposals to establish new NDPBs; comprehensive review of existing bodies and advisory bodies at least every five years to assess whether they are still needed or whether the function can be privatised or contracted out; clearly define the relationship between a department and a NDPB which supports an appropriate degree of delegation and independence and propriety and value for money in financial management; winding up unnecessary bodies. Departments should ask whether the private or the voluntary sector could perform the tasks under consideration. While establishing an NDPB implies a degree of independence from ministerial control,

> the responsible minister is answerable to Parliament for the degree of independence which an NDPB enjoys, for its usefulness as an instrument of government policy, and so ultimately for the overall effectiveness and efficiency with which it carries out its functions.

The guide is voluminous in its *internal* controls, eg the necessary information-flow between public bodies and ministers for meeting objectives and realisation of roles, keeping statements of accounts, and providing information which is consistent with the Treasury's financial information system[19] effective corporate planning systems and management systems and applying next steps principles to NDPBs. Its public dimension was originally meagre but was extended in 1996. The chapter concerned with 'Public Disclosure of Information' was one of the shortest in the guide, concentrating on annual reports, remuneration and expenses, and the information that should be provided to select committees—are they 'related bodies' for the purpose of select committees? The test is whether there is a significant degree of ministerial responsibility but surely this confuses the Government's own distinction between responsibility and accountability. Accountability is what is meant here because the whole point of a NDPB is to break with ministerial responsibility. Their publications should 'as far as possible' be supplied to the House of Commons library. The *Government Publicity and Advertising Conventions* do not formally apply to NDPBs and they may

---

1988) and *Abuse of Market Power* Cm 2100 (1992) and the Competition Act 1998. See also *R v ITC, ex p Virgin Television* [1996] EMLR 318.

18 *Non-Departmental Public Bodies – A Guide for Departments* (Cabinet Office 1992 revised 1996); I. Harden (1987) Public Law 27.

19 Ibid, chapters 5 and 6.

justify expenditure on publicity that would not be appropriate for a department. The provisions were added to in 1996, to take account of the Code on Access to Government Information (revised 1997) as well as complaints from the public. The Nolan Committee's Standards of Best Practice for Meetings and Publications is also referred to. The report only deals with public bodies in a formal sense; it does not cover bodies or interests with which the government enters into private concordats and which in legal terms are private enterprises.[20] Although there is a reference to advisory bodies a good deal of the report will not have much relevance to the subterranean world of advisory committees and their usual confidential mode of operation. These are often advisory in name only, possessing *de facto* executive powers.[1] They report in confidence to the minister, and their meetings and minutes are not public. The US Federal Advisory Committee Act should be recalled at this point (see chapter 2). Where these are providing public services or or performing public tasks, then they will be covered by FOIA 2000 in the UK. The Code on Consultation published in 2000 (see below) will also be of relevance. It has also to be said that the Cabinet Office guidance on *Quangos* and a subsequent report have made important suggestions for change (below). These, however, have no relevance to the task forces which have been a pronounced feature of Blair's administration.

When the state enters into close working relationships with private concerns, the problems posed for the constitutional 'watcher' include establishing what has been devolved on to the private body by way of public responsibility. A classic case of this kind was the administration of the civil legal aid scheme by the Law Society now devolved onto an NDPB. A further example is the state's reliance upon the accountancy profession to formulate appropriate standards of good practice in the keeping of accounts and the supervision of audits. A prolonged process of bartering involved the Government's desire to extract undertakings from the Institute of Chartered Accountants that the latter would take a much more active role in ensuring that its members provide information to the Bank of England on the financial affairs of banks and financial institutions whose books its members audited. The profession initially managed to avoid the incorporation of these duties in legislation on the undertaking that satisfactory *internal* criteria were met.[2] A series of

---

20 See note 8 p 215 above and *ex p Datafin*, especially Donaldson MR and Lloyd LJ. The issue of fact and degree of compenetration of public and private will necessitate individual assessment of each institution – see eg *Law v National Greyhound Racing Club Ltd* [1983] 3 All ER 300 and *R v Jockey Club, ex p RAM Racecourses Ltd* [1993] 2 All ER 225 and de Smith, Woolf and Jowell *Judicial Review of Administrative Action* (5th ed, 1995 and Supplement) paras 3.023 et seq.

1 Where their advice forms the basis of the decision.

2 Section 47 of Banking Act 1987 and SI 1994/524.

scandals including the BCCI collapse and the subsequent Bingham Report have forced the Government to place these duties in statutory regulations.[3]

Who makes decisions? How? Where? Under what controls? With what publicity? If we do not know what is going on, we cannot hope for answers. It must be conceded that this is not so much a right for individuals, unless their lives are directly affected by such decision-making, as for Parliament. Parliament knows little of what goes on in this twilight world—indeed, one of the benefits of privatisation from the Government's perspective is that Parliament's interest ought thereby to be reduced. In his second report on *Standards in Public Life*[4] Lord Nolan observed how in local public bodies such as Training and Enterprise Councils there was invariably too much 'hands on' control by central government.

It is quite clear that in dealing with mighty client groups, not even the government is always fully informed. The CAG has commented adversely upon the failure of the companies within the armaments industry to supply adequate information of profit levels and pricing to the Treasury. Many of the important contracts are not open to competitive tender.[5] The Review Board for Government Contracts—a joint non-statutory CBI/Ministry of Defence nominated body—reviews the appropriate profit formula for non-competitive contracts every three years. Its recommendations are used as a basis for discussion between the CBI and the government. It also reviews individual contracts referred to it. The CAG has criticised the industries for failing to reveal the details behind the information which they provide to the Board: 'I question whether this denial of information is consistent with the government's responsibility to Parliament to account for the basis on which they have accepted the recommendation.' The Treasury did not know how to get this information while still retaining the 'co-operation' of the industry.[6] It is a big money-earner and a big employer. It cannot be told, it has to be persuaded, to adopt suitable approaches after *quid pro quo* bartering. It is impossible to know whether this is in the public interest. Steps have been taken to make armament procurement more efficient and cost-sensitive from the government's perspective but not even the Public Procurement Directives of the EC apply to such contracts so none of the

---

3 See also Auditors (FSA) Rules 1994, SI 1994/526 and Financial Services Act 1986 s 109; and note SI 1994/449 and a similar duty in relation to insurance companies under ss 38-45 Insurance Companies Act 1982. See: *A Statutory Duty on Auditors in the Regulated Sector* HM Treasury and DTI, March 1993 and the *Response of Public Concern at Work* to this report (August 1993). Also, the Cadbury Report *The Financial Aspects of Corporate Governance* December 1992. See now Financial services and Markets Act 2000 ss 341-346.

4 Cm 3270 I and II.

5 National Audit Office MoD: Profit Formula for Non-Competitive Government Contracts (1985).

6 HC 390 (1984/85), para 26.

advertising publicity and non-discrimination or 'transparency' provisions apply.[7]

A similar theme concerns the Department of Health and the Pharmaceutical Price Regulation Scheme which is regulated by the department and is non-statutory. Companies which are not exempt from the scheme have to submit accounts and production and sales figures to the officials. Companies may be asked to reduce *overall* profit rates if these are considered too high. There is no enforcement but 'negotiation'. The PPRS does not apply to individual drugs but to overall levels of profitability, which allows a variety of accounting sleights of hand by drug companies to distort the real profit level. The department lacks adequate information and inside knowledge on costs and did not know 'whether they had played a good hand or had been the victim of a bluff'.[8] The chairman of the Public Accounts Committee has asked officials whether 'the Department . . . [is] really serious about wanting to get a good deal for the taxpayer'.[9] The PPRS was revised in 1999, but it has not properly addressed the problem of obtaining adequate information from the drug companies.

What is really at issue here are the methods by which government governs. Anyone with an interest in freedom of information and open government must understand that the topic is not exhausted by allowing individuals to have access to public documents. It is centrally concerned with knowing how these dense networks operate. Only when we know this can we hope to know what questions to ask and who to put them to.

In *Quangos: Opening the Doors*[10] the Government set out its proposals for about 1,100 NDPBs spending over £22 billion pa. There should be annual public meetings 'where practicable and appropriate' and other public meetings where these would help consultation. Where practicable, they should release summary reports of meetings. Evidence should be invited from members of the public to discuss matters of public concern and widespread consultation should be exercised by such bodies. There should be consideration of bringing more bodies within the jurisdiction of the Parliamentary Commissioner for Administration (Ombudsman). The FOIA would apply where relevant (see chapter 6). Select Committees should have oversight and codes and registers of interests should apply

---

7   The MoD has undertaken to publicise details of every major contract just signed or going to tender. The minister undertook to notify the Chairman of the Public Accounts Committee of security-sensitive defence contracts in excess of £250 million. He was not informed of the Zircon satellite system, which was estimated at £500 million. The £250 million threshold has been reduced to £25 million.

8   P West in *Health Care UK 1985*, note 13 p 216 above; see HC 551 (1983–4).

9   HC 551 (1983–4), Chairman PAC.

10   Cabinet Office (1998) following earlier consultation paper *Opening up Quangos* November 1997.

for members. They should publish annual reports and possibly efficiency reports and make greater use of the internet. Bodies will be removed where no longer required and will be subject to periodic reviews. The remit of the Public Appointments Commissioner will be extended. The Select Committee on Public Administration recommended that there should be an annual publication covering all bodies 'carrying out its policy' possibly accompanying the Government's annual report. It recommended a greater role for select committees, including receipt of minutes of meetings between Ministers and NDPBs and audit of all executive NDPBs accounts by the CAG although this would have to be considered by the Public Accounts Committee. Local bodies should report to scrutiny committees of local authorities as a condition of any funding agreement. Regional structures of accountability should exist for those bodies which operate regionally or locally. Any vacancies to be filled on boards should be placed on the internet as should reports from the Prior Options Reviews which examine whether a function should be exercised by a NDPB.[11] As will be explained in the next chapter, FOIA will cover bodies which are not exercising devolved powers in Scotland and Wales. Special provisions apply where the Secretary of State designates a body which will operate in Wales or Northern Ireland. The devolved regimes will produce there own provisions for FOI as explained in chapter 6.

Local government

Openness and accountability apply equally to local government as to central government. The arguments a propos of the ascendancy of those principles over efficiency, effectiveness and responsiveness have already been addressed and need not be repeated here. The latter group implies the former. It must be borne in mind that local government does not embrace problems which affect national security unless civil defence and emergency planning[12] and police affairs outside the metropolitan area are included. 'Policing' is a sensitive topic in those localities where police committees of local authorities and police authorities wish to be informed about policing policy and operational items relating to the police. Traditionally chief officers of police refuse to cover such matters in any detail in their reports to such authorities or to be drawn into answering detailed questions.[13] Information addressed to the chief constable from

---

11 HC 209 I and II (1998-99) and Government Response HC 317 (1999-00).
12 L Hilliard (1986) Mod LR 476.
13 Birkinshaw *Grievances, Remedies and the State* (1994) p 228 *et seq* and Police and Magistrates Courts Act 1994, Part I, chapter 1. See for the police authority etc in Greater London, Greater London Authority Act 1999, Part VI.

the Home Office in confidence is not addressed to the authority, nor is it in the authority's possession, and his position as an officer of the Crown probably means that members of the authority have no right to demand and receive it.[14]

In the previous chapter, the legal requirements for the openness of local government were noted. The Local Government (Access to Information) Act 1985, which amends the Local Government Act 1972, has opened up to council members and the public the opinions and advice of officers at all levels. The Conservative governments from 1979-1997 used the ideologies of openness and accountability for their own purposes: to claim that they has assisted in open government—at the local level alone. This was particularly pointed when it restricted the Access to Personal Files Act and accompanying regulations to local authorities, excluding its own administration which impinged directly on individuals. Government might claim that it rectified an abuse of democratic government by making local government more fully answerable to its electorate and taxpayers, especially business ratepayers.[15] Many remain convinced that the real problem lies within central and quasi-government. Until FOIA comes into effect, only codes of practice affected these latter areas.

Nevertheless bureaucratic conflicts, as well as ideological political conflicts, are a pervasive feature of local government administration. How can these features foster a secrecy or lack of information which militates against openness in the public interest? What follows looks at some of the more closed practices of authorities in response to legislative duties to open up administration. It must be said that the 'fault' is sometimes that of the legislature or the government—its legislation does not cover the real problem or it missed its target. Secondly, authorities might see in legislation which affects their procedures and powers the heavy hand of 'some bright spark in Marsham Street'.[16] Resistance is geared more towards a perceived unwarranted interference by central government in local government's affairs. Be that as it may, local authorities are there to govern and administer, and as such their responsibilities are built upon openness and accountability. But to what extent?

Three basic kinds of information can justifiably claim the protection of confidentiality in local government. The first relates to a political group

---

14 He is not in the analogous position of senior officers who are servants of the authority. Such officers must ultimately work through committees of members, unless power is delegated to them under s 101 of the Local Government Act 1972. Such a conflict between governmental secrecy and local authority pressure to be informed would make an officer's position untenable. See further *R v Secretary of State for the Home Department, ex p Northumbria Police Authority* [1988] 1 All ER 556, CA. See also Police etc Act 1994 at n 13.

15 Section 65 Local Government Finance Act 1992; and cf s 6., Education (No 2) Act 1986.

16 As it was put to me by a chief housing officer.

formulating policies outside the structure of official channels and *before* it constitutes council business. Such a protection must be carefully circumscribed as I point out in chapter 6 under FOIA 2000 and chapter 10. A second concerns information on individuals, the disclosure of which to others would amount to an unwarranted interference in their privacy. A third category covers information where the local authority is acting in a business or regulatory capacity, or is taking legal advice and where disclosure would harm or prejudice its legitimate management or destroy legal immunity. The 1985 Act deals with the latter two categories directly, and indirectly with the first. The Local Government Act 2000 (LGA) was devised to address some of the key problems identified with the first.

The courts have contributed to the party political contest which dominates in some local authorities where old political understandings have been upset by the arrival of third parties and politicians prepared to use local political fora in a contest with central government or to repeat national conflict at a local level. In *R v Sheffield City Council, ex p Chadwick*[17] the High Court held that a member of the city's Policy Committee was entitled to see the reports of alternative budget proposals which were before its subcommittee. The subcommittee had been appointed purely on leading party political lines. The exclusion of the applicant, a member of the opposition party, was unlawful because party political reasons for drawing up subcommittees were invalid[18] and the member had a right to know by virtue of his membership of the parent committee. It was accepted by the court that there could be information which was so sensitive that a member of the parent committee would not be entitled to see it. This would be very rare, however.[19] It seems that, at common law, if ruling parties wish to propose alternative strategies and discuss political points confidentially, they must organise *outside* the formal structure of council, committees and subcommittees.[20] The Widdicombe Report deplored this, arguing that it should be possible to have recommendatory non-executive committees to which the public and council members who are not members of the committees in question would have no access and no right to information. His point is that it will

17 (1985) 84 LGR 563.
18 See chapter 3 above, p 154.
19 Ibid.
20 They will also be outside the terms of the 1985 Local Government (Access To Information) Act. This is a difficult issue, as an authority only has formal power to create committees and subcommittees, whether joint or individual. Creation of an ad hoc working party would have to be effected informally and it would possess no executive powers. Even then, its genesis would be looked at with scrutiny to see what it really was: *R v Eden District Council, ex p Moffat* (15 April 1987, unreported) (Crown Office List), held that a working party could be established under s 111 of the Local Government Act 1972, but not as an executive body: see also *R v Broadland District Council, ex p Lashley* (2001) Times, 20 March.

have to be referred back to appropriate committees or the council for resolution, at which stage the provisions of the 1985 Act come into play. Widdicombe's solution to exclusion was to suggest that the standing orders of a local authority should stipulate that the constitution of decision-taking (not deliberative) committees should reflect *as far as practicable* the balance of political power in the authority. The chief executive would be responsible for the detailed application of the rule and for deciding which information councillors could see.[1] The Government's response was to ensure that committees, subcommittees and joint committees reflected the political balance on the full council and to impose mandatory requirements in standing orders.[2]

The Government accepted that voting rights of non-members should be curtailed but did not accept the case for 'deliberative committees' of an authority.[3] Such bodies should operate informally outside the council structure and may be advised by officers but not where non-members are present. This facility should be open to all parties, the Government believed, and should be governed by local conventions and regulated by the chief executive or chief officer. So the practice continues that if the political party in power or in opposition wishes to discuss matters informally, it must do so *outside* the formal structure of the council. Establishing a need to know at common law is going to be difficult where it is a non-executive, informal group.[4] The ideal must cede to the practical reality of party politics. If the group is advised by officers, a member's right to know will be similarly established; is it information in the possession or control of the council or is it an informal, off-the-record opinion to individuals constituting a political group, but not a formal committee or subcommittee? Widdicombe's suggestion that if this facility is provided to one party, it should apply to all, has merit.[5] Among the other recommendations, the provision of a question time for the general public at the end of council meetings and the opposition right to place items on the agenda have been standard practice in more advanced authorities for well over a decade.

Where powers are delegated to an officer, Woolf J has stated 'that in respect of decisions taken by officers the rights of councillors to be informed' (at common law) also depended upon the need to know. Under the terms of the 1985 Act, an officer's decision will come back to the record of a committee, etc, and come within that Act. Decisions cannot be

---

1   This might reduce members' rights to information, but would improve pro rata rights of membership on committees.
2   Cm 433 (1988) and Local Government and Housing Act 1989, ss 15-17.
3   Local Government and Housing Act 1989, s 13.
4   P 153 et seq above.
5   See *Leicester City Council v District Auditor for Leicester* [1989] RVR 162, CA.

delegated to one member alone.[6] (Recommended by Widdicombe not accepted by Government). An increasing number of authorities are delegating to an officer who must consult with the leader or a committee chair before deciding. The need-to-know provision applies, as does the statute. Where the officer reports 'what he is told to write' and this is all that is presented to a committee before a decision, or where a report is written that is tendentious and omits facts and alternative possibilities, what then?[7] Files often contain contrary evidence from sources that are not presented in a report. *Chadwick* would suggest that members can ask for and receive alternative proposals; under the 1985 Act they ought to form part of the background papers which the public can see if not exempt. Some authorities have adopted the following standing order:

> Officers preparing reports for members have a duty to take into account all relevant information. This must include any arguments that are counter to those expressed in the report. Any background documents that do not support the arguments expressed in the report must be mentioned along with those that do.[8]

A preserve on information is, in local government as in other forms of government, a means of securing influence, allowing the 'right' conditions for the exercise of decision-making to prevail, courting political favour with the electorate by knowing where to go for results, and diminishing the efficiency of the opposition by exclusion. Local government has been subjected to legally imposed processes of open decision-making which have invited judicial intervention in a way that other areas of our public administration have not. This is not to say that such intervention has been pervasive or necessarily influential. It is in stark contrast to the position in central government and its agencies and client groups.

Nonetheless, stories about evasion of the 1985 Act are legion. These do not simply involve members as described above. Below is an extract from a memorandum to all members of a council which is not untypical of the devices used to circumvent the Act:

> To All Members of the Council: as you will be aware the above Act places onerous new responsibilities on Local Authorities with regard

6   *R v Secretary of State, ex p Hillingdon LBC* [1986] 1 All ER 810.
7   In the passage of the Local Government (Access To Information) Bill, a city council's assistant solicitor informed a committee that the provision of 'background papers' would cause endless difficulties; he did not inform the members that he had opinions to the contrary from other authorities.
8   Cf *Associated Provincial Picture Houses Ltd v Wednesbury Corpn* [1948] 1 KB 223; *R v Liverpool City Council, ex p Professional Association of Teachers* (1984) 82 LGR 648.

to the availability of information to the press and public. Consequent upon this issue it is encumbent on a Local Authority to provide, in connection with any report considered, a background list of information which has been relied upon to a material extent in compiling the report. For practical purposes this list of information will, in most instances, need to be supported by a copy of the document concerned and kept available with the papers for the statutory period of four years.

This requirement, however, only applies to reports which are considered by the Authority through the Committee process and whilst matters are dealt with in this manner there is no alternative other than to abide by the requirements of the Act.

In considering the Health and Housing Committee Agenda a number of items on which reports arise are likely to present considerable problems to officers in compiling the information. I refer particularly to the following:

(a)   Housing Progress Report.

(b)   Progress Report—Council House Sales.

(c)   Housing Rent Arrears Statistics.[9]

Whilst they do not relate to written reports, it is also relevant to consider in this context the under mentioned items:

(d)   Home Improvement Grant and outstanding commitments.

(e)   Housing Waiting List.

(f)   Housing Stock Figures.

As these items are of course purely informative in nature and prior to the Council Meeting . . . the Chairman and Vice-Chairman of the Committee have exercised their delegated powers to authorise that in future they are no longer dealt with through the Committee system. Instead updated situation reports will be sent direct to Members for their information and they will then be able to take up any queries privately with the Officers concerned.

Further devices include: calling bodies a working party or group and not a committee or subcommittee; charging excessive fees; and taking no steps whatsoever to publicise the existence of rights to access.

---

9   These could be exempt under the 1985 Act.

The LGA 2000 and new executive arrangements for authorities

In *Modern Local Government: In Touch With the People*,[10] the Government set out its plans for modern local government and appropriate forms of executives for such authorities. Such executives were to be built on a 'culture of openness and ready accountability.'[11] Pointing out the pathetically low turnout at local elections, the paper believed that councillors did not sufficiently reflect their communities (only a quarter of councillors were women) and that the structures within which local authorities operated were the result of nineteenth century legal philosophy. The committee structure, which has been examined above and in chapter 3, was 'inefficient and opaque', with councillors spending 'too many hours on often fruitless meetings.'[12] 'Above all, the committee system leads to the real decisions being taken elsewhere, behind closed doors, with little open, democratic scrutiny and where many councillors feel unable to influence events.'[13] It set forth an agenda for change involving new organisational frameworks to run councils, the creation of opportunities for giving local people a greater say in the running of the council and its service provision – by establishing 'beacon councils', improving local services, reforming business rates, improving local financial accountability, capital finance and providing a new ethical framework. The subject of standards and organisation had been heavily influenced by the Nolan Committee on Standards report on local government.[14] These themes were developed in *Local Leadership: Local Choice*[15] and are now in the LGA 2000 and regulations.

The way forward was for councils – which under new arrangements will remain single legal entities — to consult the local community on how they wish to be governed with referenda on whether there should be a directly elected mayor as in London. Detailed guidance on local consultation has been provided.[16] This referendum could be initiated by a petition of 5% of the electorate or a proposal from the Council. Statutory guidance would provide details on content and timing of referenda and

10 Cm 4014 (1998).
11 Para 1.2.
12 Para 1.15.
13 Ibid.
14 Cm 3702 (1997).
15 Cm 4298 (1999).
16 *Modern Local Government: Guidance on Enhancing Public Participation*. DETR (1998). *The Local Government Act 2000 New Council Constitutions – Guidance Pack* DETR (2000) has further guidance on *Consultation Guidelines for English Local Authorities*.

regulations would contain the rules of conduct for a referendum paying regard to the Neill report (Nolan's successor) on party political funding.[17] A majority decision in favour of change would be binding on the council. If the proposal is not supported, it cannot be implemented.

The three new models of management are: a directly elected mayor with a cabinet; a cabinet with a leader; a directly elected mayor and a council manager. These models will seek to provide a 'clearly identified and separate executive to give leadership and clarity to decision-taking' and 'powerful roles for all councillors to ensure transparency and local accountability.'[18] Such forms of governance will provide for a separation of the executive and will be efficient, transparent, and accountable. 'All councillors will have powerful roles, acting together in the council, or as members of the executive or powerful overview and scrutiny committees. People will know who is responsible for decisions, and communities will have a clear focus for leadership. Decisions will be scrutinised in public, and those who take them and implement them will be called publicly to account for their performance.'[19] *Consultative Drafts of proposed Guidance and Regulations on New Constitutions for Councils* were published in May 2000.[20]

The details on these points are contained in Part II of the LGA 2000 and include the minutiae of executive functions and their discharge. They will be supplemented by regulations and guidance.[1] A resolution of an authority is required in order for the executive arrangements which must be available for inspection at principal offices for public inspection.[2] Standard provisions apply in terms of notices in two newspapers circulating in the area providing the details of arrangements.

Before adopting its new constitution, a council should address a variety of themes relating to the model of its new constitution and the executive's functions and whether they should be limited. All councillors will agree or approve key plans and decisions. Regulatory responsibilities such as licensing and planning will not be functions of the executive but will be carried out by the full council or delegated to committees.

All new forms of local governance must have one or more overview and scrutiny committees (OSCs: see LGA, s 22). They are to have the same political balance as the full council and will in public with the current rules on public access (see above p 155 et seq) applying. Details on size, number etc would be for local choice. They would be required to cover

---

17   Cm 4057 (1998).
18   *Local Leadership etc* para 3.1.
19   Para 3.3.
20   DETR , May 2000. See also *Modular Constitutions for English Local Authorities* DETR (2000).
1   See note 16 above.
2   LGA 2000 s29.

all aspects of the executive's responsibilities. The constitution would provide for details such as co-opted members (non-voting) and chairs, and requesting a full debate in council before a decision is taken or implemented. Constitutions of authorities will be required to provide that OSCs would be: able to require members of the executive and officers to attend their meetings and to invite others to attend; required to meet and examine these people in public (the current rules on access to meetings and information to apply); able to have all necessary support and information and training to discover what their local community wants and to represent them effectively; required to ensure the standing orders protect minority interests on the committee to get their concerns onto the agenda.

The executive is the driving force of new arrangements and will take the lead on all policy and strategy issues, including the budget, searching for best value under the LGA 1999 (see chapter 3 above p 158) and decisions on resources and priorities. The executive will be the focus for forging links and partnerships outside the council. The expected size will be 15% of the council or 10 councillors whichever is the smaller. They may be smaller but where there is a cabinet with a leader or elected mayor there should be at least three members. The constitution would set out membership but the executive would not usually reflect the political balance on the council – unlike other committees and sub committees of the authority. It will comprise majority or coalition members. Specific members would be given portfolios — this was the preferred option with the government because it 'speeds up decisions and clarifies responsibilities, improving accountability.'[3] Decisions would either be taken by the whole cabinet, in sub-groups, as individuals or as combinations of these. In a cabinet with a leader, appointments would be made by either the leader or the council and in the latter case it would by majority vote decide the make-up of the cabinet under its constitution.

Formal co-option would not be allowed but a mayor could benefit from a political adviser paid for by the council in addition to those advisers serving the three largest groups. S/he could attend but not vote at executive meetings. Where there is an elected mayor, policy would be implemented via a council manager – 'typically' the chief executive.

Executive meetings and access to information

It is envisaged that 'at a minimum' any provisions on access to information will need to comply with FOIA (see chapter 6). An executive must ensure that a record of all decisions taken, and the reasons for those decisions is produced, and that record, along with factual and background papers

3   Para 3.41 ibid.

(excluding that information which is currently exempt under Sch 12A LGA 1972 (see chapter 3) relating to those decisions must be made public. Once a decision is taken by an individual, the record of that decision and the reasons for the decision and additional items must be made public. In the case of executive decisions and decisions by individuals ('individual decisions') officers must ensure the public availability of the record of the decision and the reasons for it, any alternative options considered and rejected (note the FOIA chapter 6) and other matters such as an interest in a decision. The 1972 legislation (as amended by the 1985 Local Government (Access to Information) Act) will continue to apply to meetings of the full council, committees and sub-committees including the overview and scrutiny committees (OSC). The same provisions on openness that apply to committees will apply to cases where the executive consults with an OSC. OSC will also have the right to see, but not make public, any information relating to their responsibilities which would be exempt to the public by virtue of Sch 12A LGA 1972 although the regulations spelt out qualifications (see below). The OSC is under the provisions on access set out in the amended 1972 legislation and is also within the provisions of s 15 Local Government and Housing Act 1989 (duty to allocate seats in relation to the size of representation of political groups. Political advice to the executive remains private. Meetings of the executive may be open to the public [or press] or private (see below and s 22(1) LGA 2000).

As explained above, the OSC would have the right to demand the attendance of the mayor or leader, along with members of the executive or council officers to answer questions or to contribute to a debate on policy with an implied right to call for papers from those parties. The Government was originally minded to make advice from officers public along with factual material. This would have created an anomalous position vis a vis the FOIA 2000 (see p 312 et seq below). The Government realised that officers might be placed in a sensitive position when it was seen that their advice was not being followed and the regulations excluded access to their advice. Reports and background papers will be provided as explained below. The duty to create a record of decision and the reasons would lie on an officer when it is the decision of all or some of the executive. If made by an individual member of the executive, it is their responsibility to create the record and to make it available to the proper officer who is under a duty to ensure it becomes publicly available as described above and failure to create or make it available is a criminal offence. OSC will also be able to ask for any additional factual information they require to support their work.

In s 22(1) of the LGA 2000, meetings of the executive or its committees, joint committees and sub committees may be held in public or private. The decision on openness is taken by the executive. This seems at first to cut across the thrust of the 1985 legislation on access but that legislation has been used as a basis for the regulations on openness and access (see below). A written record must be kept of *prescribed* decisions made by executives and their committees held in private and by individual members which must include reasons for decisions. Prescribed suggests obviously not all. These records, together with 'such reports, background papers or other documents 'as may be prescribed' must be made available to the public in accordance with regulations made by the Secretary of State. These bear some similarities with the provisions in the 1985 legislation. They would, however, have to be consistent with FOIA 2000. The whole or any part of a document may be held back on specified grounds. The regulations may make provision as to the circumstances in which meetings are to be held in private in whole or in part; the information to be included in written records; on the reasons to be included; those responsible for the records; on the requirement that such records may be made available to members of authorities and to the OSC; their availability by electronic means; on the regulations' ability to confer rights on members of the public, members of local authorities or OSC in relation to records or documents; and to create offences in respect of rights or 'requirements' under the section. Further regulations may be made concerning access to joint committees or written records where held in private etc (see s 22(12) LGA 2000).

Draft regulations made under this section[4] while containing rights for the public to see papers relating to forthcoming decisions require executive meetings or part of meetings to meet in public when taking 'key decisions' and on three other occasions. These cover the situation where an officer is present during a discussion but not where the officer is present for the 'principal purpose' of giving advice to the meeting, and also where items in the Forward Plan (below) are to be discussed and a decision will be made on such items within 28 days of that meeting.[5] The requirement for a public meeting is subject to reg 21 concerning confidentiality and other matters (below). Meetings held in public must have reports, agendas and background papers published three clear days in advance.

'Key decisions' is a pivotal feature of these arrangements and these are basically decisions which in the opinion of the decision-taker are likely to result in significant financial implications. In determining 'significant' regard shall be had to guidance issued by the Secretary of State. The intention may be good but the regulation (reg 8) bristles with

4   Local Authorities (Executive Arrangements) (Access to Information)(England) Regulations 2000, SI 2000/3272 (coming into effect 9 January 2001).

5   'Principal purpose' may be interpreted in the light of guidance issued by the Secretary of State. The third ground involves a situation where a reg 15 notice has been given concerning a key decision and the matter is 'impracticable' re inclusion in FP.

subjective judgements. This does not prevent *discussion* of key decisions by executives in secret (a 'private meeting') where the officer is not in attendance or is offering advice. Executives will decide what is a key decision. Where it is not a key decision, or otherwise not within reg 7, the authority can meet in private and papers will not have to be available in advance. Key decisions may be delegated to individuals and only discussed at meetings and this will produce less publicity although reports on decisions taken by individual executive members must be publicly available in advance for at least three clear days before making a key decision. The member or officer shall ensure it is publicly available as soon as possible after the member or officer receives it. This is subject to confidential and other items in reg 21 (see below). Background papers must also be available for reports or part of reports in sufficient number. In Standing Committee, the Minister stated that 'an executive may meet as a group of executive members, each of whom will have personal responsibility for an area of decision taking'.[6] If a decision is based on a *draft* report are these excluded from the publicity provisions? One would expect that a decision based on a *draft* report converts the report into a final report. The regulation states that 'report' does not include a draft report and 'document' does not include a draft document. Reports submitted to an individual executive member or officer with a view to it being considered when he makes a key decision must be sent by the person submitting the report to the Chair, or every member in the absence of the former, of a relevant OSC.

Executives must publish 'Forward Plans' (FPs) with details of key decisions due to be taken in the coming four months (reg 13(2)) the documentation available about them, and the proposed consultation arrangements. A plan, other than the first plan, shall have effect from the first day of the second month for which the immediately preceding plan has effect – they are updated on a monthly basis. Regulation 14 concerns the contents of plans. These include the matter in respect of which the decision is to be taken, details of individual decision takers, dates or periods of decisions, all those to be consulted and the means of such consultation, steps and details to be taken by those who wish to make representations to the executive about decisions to be taken, and a list of documents submitted for consideration to the decision-taker but not those only available in draft form.

The taking of a 'key executive decision' must be preceded by the publication of a regulation 12 notice. Regulation 12 provides for an instruction to be given to the proper officer to publish a notice of key decisions, that a FP with particulars of those decisions has been prepared, the period for which the FP is to have effect, that the FP may be inspected

---

6   Standing Committee A, 23 May 2000, col 269.

free of charge and at all reasonable hours at the authority's offices, that the FP contains a list of documents submitted to the decision takers for consideration in relation to the matters in respect of which decisions are to be taken, addresses from which copies of listed items are available, that other relevant documents may be submitted, procedures for requesting those documents (if any) as they become available, the dates in each month in the following 12 months on which each FP will be published and made available to the public at the local authority's offices. This must be published in one newspaper circulating in the authority's area not later than 14 days before the first day on which the forward plan is to have effect.

There is a general exception to this requirement in reg 15 – where publication is 'impracticable' – but, subject to reg 16, no decision shall be taken until the decision-taker, either an individual or a chairman of a body, has informed the Chair of a relevant OSC or each member thereof of the matter to which the decision is to be taken (reg 15(1)(a)). Various formalities must be complied with. There is also an exception on the grounds of 'urgency'. Once again, a variety of safeguards exists to attempt to prevent abuse of the provisos. Where an executive decision has been taken and it was not treated by the decision maker as a key decision, the OSC may require a report to be submitted by the executive to the local authority within such time as specified. This must include details of the decision and reasons for it, the body or individual who made the decision, and reasons for the executive's opinion that it was not a key decision. The executive leader or appropriate person must submit a quarterly report on decisions taken under reg 16 in the preceding three months, the number of such decisions and a summary of their subject matter. Obstruction of rights of public access is an offence (reg 23)

In the final stages of the LGA Bill (24 July 2000) the Government made it clear that executives would be open to the public when discussing 'key decisions' made by authorised individuals and not simply when making a collective decision. They will be open unless the public are excluded under reg 21(1), ie whenever it is likely that if the public were present, confidential items would be disclosed to them in breach of the obligation of confidence. The definition of confidentiality is that available under the Local Government (Access to Information) Act 1985. The public may be excluded by resolution from an executive meeting whenever it is likely, in view of the nature of the business to be transacted or the nature of the proceedings, that if members of the public were present during that item there would be disclosure to them of exempt information. The public may be excluded where advice is given by a political adviser/assistant. The public may also be excluded to maintain public order. Further provisions on resolutions, public notice ('three clear days' and see p 157 n 10 below) and public attendance and facilities for 'duly accredited members of the press echo those in the 1985 legislation. These provisions also cover meetings of committees of executives.

Regulations make provision for the inspection of documents after executive meetings of authorities and executives' committees, as well as inspection of background papers, additional rights of access to documents for members of local authorities which are similar to some of the provisions contained in the Local Government (Access to Information) Act 1985. Nothing in the regulations confers a right of access to confidential or exempt information or to 'advice provided by a political adviser.' (reg 21). Where a copy of a report or part of a report accompanying agenda items at a meeting is withheld, the report shall be marked 'not for publication' and a statement to that effect specifying that it contains confidential information, by reference to the descriptions in Sch 12A of the Local Government Act 1972, the description of exempt information applicable to that report; or that the report contains advice of a political adviser or assistant. The public may be excluded from meetings on similar grounds as above by resolution which has to identify the part or parts of meetings from which the public are excluded. Records and reports must be publicly available for six years beginning on the date on which the decision relating to the record or report was made. Background documents are available for four years from the date of the meeting; any longer period is discretionary.

The additional rights of members to access covers 'any document, which is in the possession, or under the control of the executive of a local authority and contains material relating to any business to be transacted at a public meeting' other than a document which is in the form of a draft (see reg 2). Certain exemptions under Sch 12A are grounds for refusing access to documents and parts of documents and are the same as under the rights of members for access to committee documents under the 1985 Act. The above rights are in addition to any other rights, eg common law, or under the 1985 Act. The discussion of the common law above (p 152 et seq) should be recalled.

The regulations add a new exemption: 'advice from political advisers'.[7] Although such advisers may participate in discussions of political groups, they can take no role in formal meetings. As the Campaign for FOI state the point, 'by formally encouraging the involvement of political advisers – but allowing all traces of their advice to be deleted from the published record – the government may be undermining its own claim that the new arrangements will provide greater transparency and accountability than at present.'[8]

7   Regulation 7(3)(c) and see s.9 LGHA 1989.
8   *Local Government Bill: Briefing for Report Stage,* Campaign for FOI (2000).

Conclusion

These are ambitious plans which I can only pass over. Their public dimension improved as they progressed through Parliament but they are going to be labyrinthine in their operation and comprehension. In previous legislation involving housing and education, governments have attempted to get citizens more actively involved in details of service provision.[9] Work attempting to reveal how successful these attempts had been very often revealed poor results. It would be easy to say that in spite of these reforms to get the public and members more involved, rights to be informed and to make contributions to the actual decisions affecting people's lives must give way to executive will, especially in the pursuit of economic objectives. But deeper lessons lie in the history of the earlier legislation. To be informed, to be consulted and to participate is meaningless unless we actively develop the skills required to assess and analyse information; to use information to press a case or a point of view; to use information through processes which are not closed or foreshortened, in which alternatives will be seriously considered, and which do not constitute a distortion of communication in Habermas's sense. Unless we give pressing thought to these points, public decision-making will remain the private concern of elite politicians and their trusted confidants. In some circumstances, this is inevitable; as a pervasive practice it sets the framework for a 'fraud on the majority'. The biggest threat to democratic standards comes when privatisation is proffered as a form of accountability in itself.[10] Its proponents argue that we can vote with our feet. A monopolised or oligopolised market offers little alternative direction in which to aim our feet. The arguments that the vote is the quintessential feature of democracy, and that to vote between alternatives one must be informed on what the alternatives have done and propose to do, are weakened by the simple expedient of reducing those issues on which we can vote by declaring them private. Regulation will then replace democratisation. This realisation in the USA was the impetus behind the Administrative Procedure Act of 1946 and the FOIA movement. If bodies are not elected democratically, then where they impact upon the public and public interest they must be subject to appropriate degrees of openness and access.

Central government's invitation to private enterprises to provide initiatives, or combine in joint efforts with the centre, to combat urban decline and revive public services has been one of the major features of politics since 1980. Use of the private sector has been seen as a way of

9   See the discussion of housing and education legislation in *Freedom of Information: the Law, the Practice and the Ideal* (2nd ed, 1996).
10 From 1980–3, the London Docklands Development Corporation, an NDPB replacing local authorities, reported only once to Parliament, the GLC alleged.

reducing the role of local government in planning, housing and development, education and commercial initiatives. The various assortment of task forces, action teams, the Financial Institutions Group, Inner City Enterprises Limited and the urban development corporations witnessed a movement away from the role of local government and the spearheading of private initiatives with central government pump-priming or financial support. The Labour Government has pursued such partnerships with enthusiasm in the form of education and housing action areas and PPPs. A private management company is planning to take over responsibility for the management of public sector schools. Needless to say, this takes us into the public/private interface where democratic forms of accountability or rights to information as in the 1985 AIA, the 2000 LGA and the FOIA are absent. The 'commercial confidential' escape route will be invoked to ensure that all but a minimum of information about the real nature of decision-making is reported to the public and Parliament. Indeed, an annual report of the former London Dockland Development Corporation spoke well of its consultation processes while deprecating the duty to attend public inquiries because of the cost in terms of directors' time.[11]

The Government has argued that the local authority is incapable of adaptation for effective operation in a business environment. Speed and confidentiality are required, along with flexibility of recruitment. Widdicombe noted how criticism of local public/commercial enterprise centres on an absence of openness and accountability.[12] Where local authorities had established such private sector companies, on their initiative or at government insistence,[13] Widdicombe proposed more specific legislation and articles of association, better reporting provisions and audit provisions, and a majority of councillors on such companies.[14] Parts IV and V of the 1989 legislation introduced new provisions for companies 'controlled' by authorities. What *degree* of openness will be generated, however?

11 Annual Report LDDC 1983/84.
12 *Widdicombe*, pp 202–3 (n 1 p 152 above).
13 Eg Transport Act 1985, transferring passenger transport executives to private-sector companies, or by use of s 137 of the Local Government Act 1972.
14 See DoE Consultation Paper 1988 Local Authorities' Interests in Companies.

5 Openness as a practice or non-practice

Our discussion so far has centred on the creation and maintenance of secrecy in government and public administration. A major governmental prerogative concerns its power to control the flow and timing of information. How does government provide information? The previous two chapters have discussed the emergence and contemporary practice of the secret state. Now we must look at the converse side and examine how much information is provided, and on what terms. The examination will involve legislation and practice outside the FOIA 2000 which is examined in the following chapter. A wide range of statutes allows government to release information at its discretion:[1] a 1994 statute allowed public access to information on a register maintained by the Coal Authority relating to coal mining operations, for instance.[2] In 2000, it was decided to publish house prices from 1 April 2000. My first aim is to examine the most significant development concerning access to government information that we have witnessed, namely the *Code of Practice on Open Government* which emerged under the Citizen's Charter initiative. This is likely to be in operation for several years to come as the 2000 Act is phased in—probably over several years. It also applies in Scotland pending legislation. I shall then inquire into the circumstances in which government has to declare its position and provide information through political pressure to legitimate its exercise of power. There is an overlap here as it was originally envisaged under the White Paper on *Open Government* that the information available to the public would be that

1 White Paper on Open Government Annexe B Part II, Cm 2290. See also, Birkinshaw *Government and Information: the Law Relating to Access, Disclosure and their Regulation* (2001) Annex B.
2 See eg Coal Industry Act 1994, s 57 though s 59 concerns information that must be kept confidential.

available to MPs via Parliamentary questions although this restriction was not placed in the code. Government intervention and regulation have spawned a wide range of fora through which decisions and proposals can be challenged or objected to, in addition to the traditional legal and political structures. This chapter will examine the practices and procedures of open and closed government and to what extent they are advanced or negated by informal networks of relationships within a complex institutional framework. The 'corridors of power', it has been confidently asserted, 'are studded with doors' through which the public, Parliament, the Ombudsman, academia, the press, etc, 'pour in'.[3] What do governments give, and what are they made to give?

Central government

The White Paper and Code on Open Government and Access to Information

The movement by the Government towards more open government was a necessary development from the Prime Minister's Citizen's Charter initiative in 1990. Under the Charter and its annual reports, the Government had celebrated its achievements in providing more information to the public on the objectives of bodies providing public services, on their success in meeting targets of performance and on publishing service charters which would provide information to the consumers who pay for the services through taxes. Having tightened up secrecy laws to make them more effective, if less scattergun in impact, and having consistently argued since 1979 that there was no need for a freedom of information statute, it became hard for the Government to justify the absence of provisions opening itself to greater scrutiny when its policies were insisting on greater accountability and openness in other spheres of public service. By 1993, the Government had become convinced that 'Open government is part of an effective democracy' (White Paper para. 1.1) and that citizens had to have adequate access to the information and analysis on which government business is based. While the Government accepted the need for ministers and their servants to explain policies, actions and decisions to the public there was also a need for some secrecy and protection of personal privacy.

The Government based its approach on three themes:
* handling information in a way which promotes informed policy-making and debate and efficient service delivery;
* providing timely and accessible information to the citizen to explain the Government's policies, actions and decisions;

3   Lord Bancroft, HC 92 II (1985-6), p 252. On the time-consuming nature of pressure groups, see D Hurd, reported in *The Guardian*, 20 September 1986.

- restricting access to information only where there are very good reasons for doing so. (ibid, para 1.7)

Its exemptions from access take up the major part of the Code which was introduced in 1994 (revised in 1997)[4] and can be examined in a moment but some novel features of an access to information regime, some might say startling, must first be analysed.

Some novel arrangements

First of all a code meant precisely that—it was a non-legal instrument and not enforceable through the courts, unless one were to use arguments of the code creating a legitimate expectation and judicial review and so on. Legislation was cumbersome and unnecessary, the Government felt, and a code offered greater flexibility. I know of no other country which has introduced FOI and which has not done so by law, where the provisions are ultimately enforceable through the courts or a tribunal. After devolution Scotland continued to operate a code based on the UK model. Wales also introduced a code on access (see chapter 6 p 327). Secondly, the Code would not provide for access to documents—which once again is the standard practice overseas as we saw in chapter 2. There would be access to information which would be selected /filleted and presented by officials—'people ... find it easier to describe the information they seek rather than the documents they wish to see ' (ibid, para 4.8).

In addition to information available on request and assuming that it is not exempt there will be information made available on a voluntary basis which includes the facts and analysis of the facts *which the government considered important and relevant* in framing major policy proposals and decisions—usually to be made available when decisions are announced. The White Paper also undertook that government would provide information following 'reasonable requests' for factual information relating to the policies, actions, and decisions of departments subject to charges for additional work.[5]

The second group concerns explanatory material including departments' internal guidance on dealing with the public and guidance on rules and procedures and administrative manuals 'as will assist better understanding of departmental action in dealing with the public' except where such information should be withheld under the confidentiality provisions. In the DSS and its related agencies, for instance, there were 175 internal guidelines in January 1996, a list which did not include

4   *Guidance* on the *Code* was also re-issued in 1997.
5   The Code referred to 'specific' requests and dropped the requirement of 'factual'. Details of publications and charters under the Citizen's Charter are at: *The Citizen's Charter: The Facts and Figures* Cm 2970 (1995) pp 132 et seq.

customer leaflets, consultation documents and 'technical manuals'. Twenty guidelines were not published and a further 33 were under review for possible publication.[6]

The third group relates to information concerning reasons for decisions, which would be available to those affected, except discretionary decisions concerning selection for honours, promotions or appointment, or a decision not to prosecute or *where there is an established convention or statutory authority not to give reasons for a decision.* There is no general duty in English law to give reasons for decisions and areas covered by statute are really the tip of the iceberg.[7] The FOIA 2000 will affect this area as will be seen in the next chapter. The courts have made dramatic steps forward in terms of giving of reasons for adverse decisions (chapter 9 p 424 et seq).

The last group concerns information relating to standards of service, targets, objectives, and performance audited against such standards: to cost, complaints procedures, and full and comparable information about what services are being provided elsewhere. The Code added a fifth group: the release following a specific request for information relating to their policies, actions and decisions and other matters relating to bodies' areas of responsibility.

The third novel dimension will require some attention. Because the Government had not created a legally enforceable regime they had to have some device to legitimise the operation of the Code beyond their own internal complaints procedures (see below); there had to be some independent element to police the Code and to act as a pressure point for consumers. The adopted instrument was to be the Parliamentary Commissioner for Administration—the Ombudsman.

From the Government's perspective use of the Ombudsman was something of a master stroke. It was seen in chapter 2 how ombudsmen frequently appear in FOIA schemes—although not in the USA—but they are usually the precursor to a judicial or quasi-judicial enforcement body. To remove any taint of 'legalism' from their new scheme not only was there to be a non-legal instrument operating under the discretion of officials but the scheme was to fall within the traditional operational conventions of British government. This meant that ultimately a minister was to be responsible or accountable to Parliament for the operation of the Code and the decisions of his officials. Where information was refused under the exemptions, a requester could ultimately bring a complaint to an MP who could refer the complaint to the Ombudsman, who would examine the complaint in a modified manner. The modifications included

6   *Open Government* HC84 (1995–6) pp 75–81.
7   Tribunals and Inquiries Act 1992, s 10.

the fact that a complainant would not have to show identifiable injury or injustice; 'It would be enough ... that the person or persons concerned had not been given information which, in accordance with the Code of Practice to which the Government is committed, they believed they were entitled to have.'

Furthermore, as the Ombudsman provision is tacked onto the 1967 Act which governs the operation of the Ombudsman it is, obviously enough, operable within the terms of that Act. This means that the Ombudsman may only investigate complaints into those information requests refused by bodies within his jurisdiction: the Cabinet Office, the Prime Minister's Office and the Bank of England, to name a few, are not within his jurisdiction and neither are MI5, MI6 or GCHQ. However, the Next Steps executive agencies of central government departments are within his jurisdiction and so too are 'functions' carried out on behalf of a department or public body by contractors. Furthermore, there are a wide variety of subjects into which the Ombudsman may not pursue a complaint, including commercial and contractual matters, personnel matters, prosecutions and civil proceedings, international relations, extradition, criminal investigation authorised by the secretary of state and national security, the prerogative of mercy, and so on. These are outside his information remit. The Ombudsman, like virtually all other ombudsmen, has no power of enforcement or coercion: he recommends. Interestingly, the White Paper did not see this as a disadvantage because 'there is a very high level of compliance with his recommendations'. The Ombudsman is not allowed to question a decision on the merits of the exercise of a discretion unless there is maladministration in the way the decision was made. One reason for maintaining Parliamentary oversight on these complaints via the Ombudsman was because fine questions of judgement are involved in disclosing and withholding information and it was more appropriate for Parliament to be the forum in which these matters were resolved. Parliament is a forum dominated by the government.

Where information is refused because the department alleges that it is against the public interest to disclose it because damage or harm would be caused, will that be construed as a decision on the merits and therefore beyond the Ombudsman's jurisdiction in the absence of maladministration? Where information is refused, the departmental officials and even the minister may be summoned before the Select Committee on the Parliamentary Commissioner for Administration and in such cases they were promised a 'roasting' by the Committee; but why the Committee should be any more effective on information complaints

8   See para 4.22.

than any other select committee is unclear and all committees are under the guidance of the Osmotherly rules concerning appearances and questions.[9] What the White Paper envisaged was a 'constructive, persuasive and informal dialogue with departments with the free services of the Ombudsman whose staff complement was considerably increased to deal with an anticipated rush of cases. The White Paper was however correct to emphasise the very considerable information-gathering and investigatory powers of the Ombudsman, who has complete power to go into departments and to look at the books subject only to the limits on his jurisdiction and to the express exclusion of cabinet and cabinet committee documents. It is also interesting to observe that many investigations by the Ombudsman before the code came into operation involved complaints about information.[10] Under s 11(3) of the 1967 Act the minister may embargo the passing of information from the Ombudsman to any other body or person (see below). While a convenient power for government, this power has never been used in information complaints.

What was interesting was the development of a 'living law' underneath these formal legal provisions. The Government seemed to suggest that the Ombudsman would invariably have the matter under his control if he disagreed with a department's decision not to release. He has also stated that in information complaints, he may well disagree with a departmental decision on the merits (see chapter 6 p 304 et seq). This approach is reinforced by his ability in exemptions where a disclosure is damaging to recommend a disclosure in the public interest unless the public interest in so doing is outweighed by the public interest in maintaining secrecy.

The White Paper suggested that charges for information requests would fall into two categories: departments may wish to consider 'standard charges' for 'simple requests' and additional charges for 'complex requests'. These matters can be addressed when we look at the operation of the Code which came into effect on 4 April 1994. The White Paper was a paper on open government and it made various other recommendations for greater openness including those relating to public records (see below), statutory rights of access to personal records (see below) and to health and safety at work information—quite why these items should be embraced by statutory provisions but those in the code should not was never convincingly explained—and a review of statutory provisions which prohibit unauthorised disclosure and impose criminal sanctions (see chapter 4).

9   These are published as *Departmental Evidence and Response to Select Committees* Cabinet Office, 1994 and were revised in 1997. See chapter 4.

10   See p 257 *et seq* below.

The provisions of the Code and its operation

The Code does not require departments to acquire information they do not possess, to provide information which is already published, to provide material which the government did not consider to be reliable information—whether or not it has been relied upon by the government and this exclusion is totally within the government's discretion—or to provide information which is part of an existing charged service other than through that service.[11]

Target response rates are 20 working days from receipt of the request although this may be extended where 'significant search or collation of material is required'. Departments, agencies, etc will make their own arrangements for charging—which in some cases has led to scandalously high charges and the two-tier system outlined above was adopted.

Exempt information

There is *Guidance on Interpretation to the Code* which observes that classification of information is not a prerequisite of exemption and nor does classification mean that information is automatically exempt.[12] The Code sets out in just over one page what will be disclosed and in almost five pages it sets out what will be exempt! Information whose disclosure would cause harm or prejudice to the public interest is exempt but there is an important proviso in the Code that where harm or prejudice would occur or might reasonably be anticipated upon release, then 'it should be considered whether any harm or prejudice arising from disclosure is outweighed by the public interest in making information available'. This has been interpreted by the Ombudsman to allow a balancing of public interests to take place allowing disclosure where the public interest is best served thereby.[13] The Code further stipulates that exemptions will not be interpreted in a way which causes injustice to individuals. Some of the exemptions require no evidence of harm or prejudice. The exemptions are:

11 The Information Commissioner in Cananda had noted a tendency to make information available under statutory provisions other than the access legislation and to charge far higher rates for access than under the former. Information was not available under the access laws. The Commissioner has also complained about Crown copyright in Canada and the 'owning' of statutes by government in right of the Crown. Who is the Crown if not the people? Canadian Information Commissioner *Annual Report* (1991-2). FOIA 2000 allows for this but unreasonable charges may be subject to complaint to the Information Commissioner.

12 Open Government Code of Practice on Access to Government Information; Guidance on Interpretation, Cabinet Office 1994, para 10.

13 Case A8/00 HC 494 (1999-00), Case A31/99 HC 21 (1999-00).

- information whose release would cause damage to defence, national security or international relations as well as that received in confidence from foreign governments, foreign courts or international organisations;
- disclosure which would harm the frankness and candour of internal discussion,[14] including:
  - proceedings of cabinet and cabinet committees;
    internal opinion, advice, recommendation, consultation and deliberation;
  - projections and assumptions relating to internal policy analysis; analysis of alternative policy options and information relating to rejected policy options;

  This is an exemption which seeks to protect the candour of the policy-making process but its understandable objective is written in the form of overkill. This is not as narrow as the exemption which the Labour Government has included in FOIA (see p 312 et seq). It should be noted the Code has exempted all the information which would allow meaningful assessment of the merits of adopted policies and their alternatives. The Code added information relating to policies following a specific request but the exemptions remove much of the significant material. Although 'factual' information will be supplied—subject to its non-rejection—the exemptions ensure maximum discretion for the government. The Government has stated, informally, that the exemption only seeks to protect *specific* information where release would cause damage. The Ombudsman has ruled that factual information cannot be withheld under this exemption which only protects advice.
- confidential communications between departments, public bodies and regulatory bodies;
- communications between ministers and members of the Royal Household—no harm is required;
- any disclosure of information which would prejudice law enforcement and legal proceedings and legal/judicial administration. This is drawn in very broad terms eg 'information whose disclosure would prejudice security of any building or penal institution'—what of requests concerning ill-treatment being practised, being improperly guarded and so on? Or information whose disclosure would harm public order? Remember that the PCA may exercise a balancing test.

---

14 The first reference to 'internal candour' protection in case law is *Smith v East India Co* (1841) 1 Ph 50 at 55 according to Eagles et al *Freedom of Information in New Zealand* (1992). See Lord Upjohn in *Conway v Rimmer* [1968] 1 All ER 874.

- information relating to legal proceedings including tribunals, inquiries or formal investigations;
- information covered by legal professional privilege;
- information whose disclosure could endanger the life or physical safety of any person or identify the source of information or assistance given in confidence for law enforcement or security;
- information whose disclosure would increase the likelihood of damage to the environment;
- information concerning immigration and nationality was given a complete exemption and was startling in its breadth. In 1997, information could be provided where there was 'no risk' that disclosure would prejudice the effective administration of immigration controls or other statutory provisions. Presumably, the public interest test applies, but will be weighed more firmly in favour of retention. There will be no access to personal information under this concession.
- where disclosure would harm the management of the economy or lead to improper gain or harm effective collection of tax. Under the 'improper gain' exemption it should be recalled that a scandal broke when OFELS delayed the announcement of a price review in electricity until after the flotatation of the electricity generating companies' shares in early 1995;
- disclosure which would harm effective management and operations of the public service which includes harming negotiations or the effective conduct ... of commercial or contractual activities. At a sweep this could exclude so much of the new form of government by contract from the Code's provisions;
- information relating to public employment, appointments and honours;
- voluminous or vexatious requests or those requiring 'unreasonable diversion of resources';[15]
- information whose publication would be 'premature' a propos of an announcement;
- information relating to incomplete analysis, research or statistics— but has it been used for policy formulation and would its disclosure undermine an adopted policy? If so, is it not in the public interest for this to be known?
- unwarranted invasion of personal privacy (including that of a deceased person);
- information including commercial confidences whose unwarranted disclosure would harm the competitive position of a third party. Such

15 The *Guidance* describes an answer to Parliamentary questions as 'disproportionate' at £450, para 9.2. This has been raised to £500 and £550.

an exemption applies in the USA and elsewhere but the case has to be proved by the person claiming the exemption on a strictly applied judicial test. Also covered is information concerning discretionary grants and this seems unduly broad: 'the exemption includes payment schemes covered by the Treasury's general guidelines on ex gratia payments in *Government Accounting* which make clear that rules governing ex gratia payments should not be published;[16]

- information given in confidence where there is a statutory guarantee of confidence, where the person is under no legal obligation to supply it and has not consented to its disclosure or where disclosure without the consent of the supplier would prejudice the future supply of such information; and medical information;

- information protected by any law or international agreement or whose disclosure would amount to a breach of Parliamentary privilege.

The Guidance says that departments should establish contact points from which requesters can obtain information on making requests, charges, internal review procedures, redirecting requests, as well as logging and monitoring progress on requests. This Guidance should be requested by those seeking information and contact points in departments can be obtained by contacting <http://www.homeoffice.gov.uk/opengov2.htm> and requesting the Code and Guidance on the Code. It advises that information requests should be as specific as possible. A non-returnable fee may be demanded on application to the department; in the case of the Home Office this was initially £15. There may be additional charges. There is no commitment in the Code to release 'pre-existing documents'.

The Ombudsman has published regular reports under s 10 (4) of his Act which have been concerned solely with the Code and complaints under it.[17] He provided observations on the exemptions relevant to his investigations, holding, for example, that the exemption protecting the frankness and candour of the internal deliberations of officials cannot operate in perpetuity. Where a relationship between a department and another body contained negotiating positions the 'competitive position and contractual commercial exemption did not justify withholding information about other relationships of a different character'. The fact that discussions had taken place between a department and third parties may not need to be protected, but identities might under exemption 14. He made five preliminary observations:

- The Code allows members of the public 'genuine benefits' in terms of obtaining information but the public needs to be better informed of its rights (see below).

16 Ibid, para 7.10.
17 The most recent is HC 126 (2000-2001).

- To achieve vital consistency in interpretation, the Office of Public Service and Science must disseminate the Ombudsman's reports and interpretations to departments and information officials.
- His investigations had taken on average 15 weeks—his target was 13.
- More information was being released voluntarily.
- Officials must notify requesters of review rights where information is refused and of rights to have a complaint referred to the Ombudsman via an MP.[18]

He has also recommended that documents themselves be disclosed where this is the easiest way to comply with a request and that a letter between the Department of Transport and the European Commission be disclosed in spite of departments' reluctance to disclose communications between themselves and the Commission. He has been reluctant to release information which might prejudice the receipt of future information by a department. The Ombudsman has been critical of the dilatory and obstructive approach taken by officials to code requests.[19] It was observed how several exemptions were thrown together in a 'scatter-gun' approach hoping one would hit the target.[20] In 1999, a large number of NDPBs and advisory bodies were added to the Ombudsman's jurisdiction.

The Office of Public Service and Science originally produced an annual report on the Code.[1] Responsibility passed to the Home Office who took over FOI in July 1998. The 1999 report is a very helpful and informative document carrying the contact points within bodies for code requests and relevant internet addresses. This follows the helpful practice adopted in the US by the Department of Justice. In 1999, there were 4,863 code requests. The figure in 1998 was 23,754 but over 20,000 of these were 'rogue' requests which were improperly counted. In 1994, the figure was 2,493. In 1997, the figure was 3,772. The source of requests is MPs and Peers — 1.4%; charities and lobbyists – 1.6%; academics – 4.8%; media – 4.8%; business – 17.2%; individuals – 30.6%; and 'others' – 39.6%. These are approximate figures. 28.8pc of requests in 1999 were refused compared with 7.3% in 1998 although this figure was distorted because of the error reported above. From 4,863 requests in 1999, there were 48 internal reviews, the Ombudsman received 36 complaints (39 in 1998) and he agreed to investigate 15 and he issued 20 reports (including 10 from the 15). 'Code' requests are registered as those which identify the Code, those for which a standard fee is levied and those for which information is refused under one of the exemptions. Departments were

---

18 HC 91 (1994-5).
19 Parliamentary Ombudsman *Annual Report 1995* pp 50-51.
20 HC 845 (1997-98).
1   Code of Practice on Access to Government Information 1994 Report.

meeting code request periods of response targets in 91.8% of cases. The exemption invoked most frequently was for internal discussion and advice (10) followed by law enforcement and legal proceedings (8). The 1999 Report has details on applications to departments and how they are processed and charging schemes. Information was also published on information volunteered by departments and agencies. *The Guidance on Interpretation* of the *Code* says that departments should not charge for the provision of information which it is necessary for the public to have 'as part of fair and accountable performance of their functions.' This includes: benefits, grants, rights and entitlements; standards and availability of services; reasons for administrative decisions made in an applicant's case; ways in which a citizen may exercise rights of appeal or complain about decisions; regulatory requirements affecting affairs of a business or commercial interests; the main points of existing departmental policies or initiatives. (paras 72-73) The Ombudsman may deal with complaints about charging.

Charges made by departments are listed in the annual reports and also listed are the contact points in departments for Code requests—a useful catalogue and one that was initially developed in US departments under FOIA as seen above. In the first eight months of the Code the Government spent £51,000 publicising the Code in contradistinction to £542,000 publicising the Citizen's Charter in the first nine months of its existence and almost £2 million on sending the Parent's Charter to all schools. There was no media advertising. The Data Protection Registry spent between £400,000 and £750,000 pa publishing the rights and obligations of the computer users under the 1984 Data Protection Act. Training sessions on open government have been organised by the Civil Service College. All departments have produced 'internal guidelines'.

The Ombudsman gave evidence to the Select Committee on the operation of the Code. The most interesting point related to his reference to the ministerial veto under s 11 (3). He reported the Chancellor of the Duchy of Lancaster saying that the Ombudsman had it in his hands to publish information where a permanent secretary was against release and he cited an answer to a Parliamentary question from the Prime Minister to like effect—it was in the Ombudsman's hands to publish. With respect this is not the law. No one had complained of charges even though the NRA had charged £100 per page for photocopying, the Public Health Service Laboratory £2000-3000 for naming any local authority in any reported incident, the Health and Safety Executive £45 per hour, for example. The Ombudsman cannot take questions from an MP about his own complaints. Finally, he was not prepared to 'pontificate' at this early stage on the criteria employed in deducing 'public interest' in recommending disclosure. The Ombudsman had set about this work in a spirited fashion.

The Campaign for Freedom of Information in their evidence commented upon the fact that it had asked for information from the Lord Chancellor's Department arising from the *Pepper v Hart* decision in 1992[2] which held that in appropriate circumstances the courts could refer to ministerial statements in the House to help in the interpretation of legislation. This was denied on the ground that this was cabinet information although this only became clear on the Ombudsman's report to their MP because initially the Department had refused access on grounds of internal advice under exemption 2.[3] Interestingly, all exemptions containing a damage test would appear to have a discretionary override, as I explained above; however, the exclusion of cabinet documents to the PCA under the 1967 Act prevents the public interest in disclosure being assessed by the PCA. As discussed elsewhere, this exclusion seems outdated now and was recommended for removal in 1978 by the select committee.[4] In 1992, as part of John Major's move to openness, the existence of cabinet committees, their membership and terms of reference were made public. The FOI Campaign and other consumer groups have highlighted the delay in requests, redirected requests, the refusals and difficulties in their own experience but have urged citizens none the less to use the Code. The Ombudsman has criticised the tendency for some departments to use every argument that can be mounted to deny access, a posture which he found over defensive.[5] In 1998, he wrote how some departments still adopted a 'scatter-gun' approach and 'pepper their response with a range of Code exemptions many of which are of no relevance to the case under consideration.'[6] In the 1993 White Paper the Government spelt out its commitment to legislate to allow access by individuals to their personal records held by government departments and public bodies and to provide access to health and safety information. This had to wait until FOIA enacted in November 2000 comes into effect. Codes were also produced for the NHS and local government. The NHS Code does not apply to pre-existing information whereas the above code does—the latter does not cover pre-existing *documents*. The relationship between the local government code and the Local Government (Access to Information) Act which I examine elsewhere

2   [1993] 1 All ER 42, HL.
3   Evidence of the Campaign for Freedom of Information to the Select Committee on the Parliamentary Commissioner for Administration, 20 March 1995. See the interesting evidence from the Treasury: HC 84 (1995-6) p 82.
4   See P Birkinshaw *Grievances, Remedies and the State,* chapter 5 (1994). A Cabinet Office review of public sector ombudsmen was being undertaken in 2000-2001: see Select Committee on Public Administration HC 612 (1999-2000).
5   PCA AR 1995 pp 50-51.
6   HC 845 (1997-98).

was not explained (p 155 *et seq*). Both these codes were to be supervised by the relevant ombudsmen. In the case of local government, refusal by authorities to accept their decisions runs at about 6% of investigations. It was noted in chapter 3 that the Government have back-pedalled on producing a code for local government. Local government will be covered by FOIA and new provisions on executive arrangements (see chapter 4 p 227 et seq)

In the White Paper the Government stated that it was having discussions with the pharmaceutical industry to produce a voluntary code on disclosure. In 1993, the Government opposed a Private Member's Bill allowing access rights to safety and efficacy information concerning pharmaceutical products subject to an exemption for commercially confidential information.[7] As of writing, s 118 of the Medicines Act 1968 makes it a criminal offence for an official to reveal without consent any information obtained by the licensing authority in the course of its duties. This includes safety data, advice of government expert committees and reasons behind licensing decisions. Information has therefore frequently held back on pharmaceutical products. At the committee stage, opposition to the Bill was expressed by leading pharmaceutical companies claiming the Bill would cause lasting damage to the industry. In fact there had at the time of the White Paper been no formal discussions merely one 'informal meeting'. The Government argued that British companies should not be placed at a disadvantage compared with continental competitors—the former had threatened to obtain approval through European countries. The Government stated its intention to promote greater openness in European licensing. From early 1995, two new European pharmaceutical approval schemes came into force. Under a 'centralised procedure' which is co-ordinated by a new European Medicines Evaluation Agency products may be licensed throughout the European Union. Under the 'decentralised procedure', a licence is obtained in one member state but must be subsequently recognised in other member states unless they raise an objection which will be dealt with by binding arbitration. Under the former, a summary assessment of its safety and efficacy will be made public. But this procedure is compulsory only for genetically engineered and some 'high tech' products. The vast majority seem likely to be licensed under the latter procedure which has no disclosure although in the distant future more openness has been promised following EC legislation. So s 118 and unbridled discretion prevails. FOIA 2000 will provide very wide exemptions for trade secrets and disclosure which could damage commercial interests. These will have a wide application in areas concerning pharmaceuticals.

7   See Frankel (1994) *Chemistry and Industry* 1016.

Public Records Act

The first point to make is that government documents are available, after selection, 30 years after they came into existence.[8] A recommendation may, however, be made for extended closure. The FOIA 2000 will align FOI and the public records regimes as administered by the Public Record Office (PRO) (see chapter 6, p 323 et seq). Government inquiries frequently produce information in advance of this date which would otherwise remain undisclosed in any detail—the Franks Inquiry into the causes of the Falklands War is an example.[9] The White Paper stated the Government's intention to make as many records as possible available after 30-years. Under the Act the thirty year period may be shortened or lengthened by decision of the Lord Chancellor. Scotland and Northern Ireland are not covered by the legislation but administrative arrangements parallel those in England. Each department has a departmental records officer who is responsible to the minister in charge of a department. His responsibilities under the Act cover papers from their creation until they are transferred to the PRO. The PRO possesses 91 miles shelf space of documents.

The subject of public records was examined by the Wilson Report of 1981.[10] This found that many documents were not available when administrators or researchers needed them. It was impossible to know whether this was by accident, bad judgement or design. About 99% of public records are destroyed because they are regarded as unimportant.[11] Sir John Donaldson MR criticised Government apathy.[12] Wilson found 'maximum destruction' at the first review of documents after five years, and only at the second review after 25 years were historical factors considered. The WP stated that historical grounds were considered at the initial review. The White Paper stated that in the 35 largest government departments some 155,000 feet (30 miles) are given First Review and 23,000 feet (4$^1/_3$ miles) are subject to second review. The PRO takes in about one mile each year. In 1962 it was estimated that departments created 100 miles of documents each year. Because only one department, Defence, had established a body of academic experts to assist its selection,

---

8 Public Records Acts 1958 and 1967. See M Roper in Chapman and Hunter (eds) *Open Government* (1987). This legislation does not cover Scottish records. See further A McDonald in *Open Government: Freedom of Information and Privacy* eds A McDonald and G Terrill (1998) and see the Select Committee report on the Draft FOI Bill: HC 570 II (1998-99).

9 Cmnd 8787 (1983). Or the Scott Report.

10 Cmnd 8204, *Modern Public Records: Selection and Access*; Government reply, Cmnd 8204.

11 *Timewatch*, BBC 2, 1 January 1986.

12 See Sir John Donaldson's apprehension on Government apathy: Public Record Office, 26th Annual Report (1985). The Master of the Rolls is chairman of the advisory committee.

the Public Records Act established an Advisory Council on Public Records consisting of lawyers, MPs, senior civil servants and historians. It does not advise on selection; departments do: 'Therefore its members have no means of knowing which records have been withheld, and why.' Where a department is asked for papers which it has retained, and it refuses, the Committee may be approached on an informal basis. From 1993, more than 90,000 documents were released by departments.[13] Security papers are not usually transferred. Sensitive information on national security is scrutinised by a Cabinet Office committee.

Papers which are recommended for extended closure[14] under present practice include: 'exceptionally sensitive papers' whose disclosure would be against the public interest; documents containing information supplied in confidence, the disclosure of which would, or *might,* constitute a breach of good faith; personal documents whose disclosure would cause distress or embarrassment to living persons or to their descendants. In 1971, papers of 'political or commercial sensitivity' were added.[15] Departments may also retain records within the department for administrative reasons eg 'in constant use' and secondly those 'whose sensitivity is such that no date can be put on their potential release' (para 9.23). These include blanket coverage and cover security and intelligence, personal records of civil servants, and various other caregories under review or to be placed under review.

The Lord Chancellor has responsibility for public records, and his department is now answerable to a departmentally related select committee.[16] In 1992 he set in motion a review of the closure criteria. This concluded that disclosure after 30 years should be allowed unless there was harm to national security, international relations, defence, or the economic interests of the UK or its release would distress or endanger individuals and descendants and the information was given in confidence. The protection of documents supplied in confidence to government was added where disclosure might constitute a breach of good faith. *Actual harm* to those interests would have to be proved. Detailed guidance was to be given to departments. For the first group, closure will be reviewed 10 years after the 30-year period. For the remaining categories, 75 or 100 years is the recommended period of closure generally for sensitive personal information. In future an outline reason for closure or retention will be given eg 'administrative', 'national security' etc together with appropriate

---

13   HC 570-II (1998-99) pp 24 et seq.
14   For such periods as the Lord Chancellor designates.
15   The White paper does not refer to these.
16   This was the reason ostensibly why the LC was called to give evidence to the Select Committee on the White Paper *Your Right to Know* Cm which preceded the FOI Bill. He was questioned far more broadly than on Public Records: HC 398 I (1997-98) pp 80 et seq.

information providing that will not put the information at risk. The Advisory Council set up under the Act will give advice on applications from departments for retention as well as closure. The White Paper also gives examples of documents released under new relaxed provisions of John Major's Government.[17] These provisions will apply until the FOIA takes over. The idea, as we shall see in chapter 6, is to align the discretionary regime as it now exists with the provisions of FOIA.

Where a Lord Chancellor has been a member of a government whose papers are eligible for release, a conflict of interest can arise.[18]

Government statistics

Before we proceed, something should be said about government statistics. Great controversy was caused among the 'chattering classes' when an article due to appear in *Social Trends*—the social statistics bible—was excluded, reportedly by order of the head of the Government Statistical Service. The article highlighted growing inequality in social trends and objection was taken to its political tone. The question of government statistics has been even more controversial. The index on unemployment has been changed 31 times, for instance, and in May 1995 plans were afoot to scrap the 'longer leading indicator' on the economy which by all accounts made depressing reading. The official size of the population was two million at least below the real figure. Figures on trade statistics were unreliable, NHS figures were completely misleading; and so it continued.

The Central Statistical Office—renamed the Office for National Statistics in early 1996—is a Next Steps agency which reports to the Chancellor of the Exchequer.[19] The Rayner cuts in the civil service in the early 1980s led to a reduction in staff at the Office from 9,000 to 4,000 and emphasis changed, it was claimed, to the collection of information which government needed rather than that which was collected for a broader public interest, eg housing statistics were aimed only at right-to-buy public sector tenancies not on rent levels and information on school repairs and housing repairs was stopped. It was claimed that Britain had the worst details on production statistics in the developed world—only 400 items were collected (the Treasury said 900) while in the USA it was 11,000. The Royal Statistical Society recommended an Independent Statistical Commission upholding the belief elsewhere that effective

17 The papers of Winston Churchill were sold as a private collection and not as state papers: see R Brazier (1996) Cambridge Law Journal 65.
18 As occurred in 1986–7 *vis-à-vis* Lord Hailsham and Suez.
19 It provides statistics to the UK Government and to EC institutions under EC legislation.

statistics publicly available are a prerequisite of democratic government. The Government was 'reluctant to provide a market researcher for private companies'. Huge numbers of figures are published under the Citizen's Charter initiative and its successor, but not to make up deficiencies in central statistics.

Your Right to Know (1997), which set out the New Labour plans for FOI legislation, spoke of steps to enhance the reliability of national statistics. In October 1999, a white paper outlined plans for the publication of a Framework for National Statistics and the appointment of an independent Statistics Commission and a National Statistician.[20]

The cabinet

There are conventions restricting the disclosure by the government of the day of the papers of a previous government within the 30-year rule without the consent of the previous Prime Minister concerned and the consent of the Queen.[1] Such matters are now going to be governed by FOIA and its exemptions (see chapter 6) but the Cabinet and the Cabinet secretariat are not a government department and are therefore not within FOIA – ie they are excluded.[2] The Cabinet Office is included. A practice also exists whereby government in office denies itself access to a previous government's papers if of a different political party. The conventions on release to third parties cover ministerial minutes, and other documents written by a former minister in the course of his duties are not publicly available unless under the terms of FOIA. The convention on government access to previous papers covers advice to ministers from their officials. Information in the public domain, such as letters to trade associations, trade unions and MPs, is not included in the government's self-denial, nor is information known to a foreign government nor the written opinions of law officers. Lord Hunt believed that common sense would bridge the gap between this convention and the need to keep present ministers informed where 'continuity of knowledge is important', although clearly

20   Cm 4412.
1   Lord Hunt (1982) Public Law 514. Five previous Prime Ministers were consulted in seeking access to documents relevant to Franks' inquiry into the Falklands war. The inquiry had access to all the secret intelligence papers it required. The Cabinet Secretary has access to the papers of a previous administration.
2   A government department in s 84 FOIA includes 'any body or authority exercising statutory functions on behalf of the Crown'. The definition is inclusive. These bodies do not exercise *statutory* functions on behalf of the Crown and they are not mentioned in Sch 1 of FOIA 2000.

the fact that civil servants must possess such continuity of knowledge affords them a certain degree of superiority over ministers.[3]

If it were felt that a previous minister's cabinet papers should be disclosed to his successor, the permission of the former would be sought. A strong plea has been made for an incoming administration to be supplied with sufficient 'information on potential immediate problems and on the difficulties of implementing specific proposals to ward against initial errors during its first year in office'.[4] Difficulties have been caused over specific projects, eg Concorde, or constraints of forward commitments on public expenditure and economic policy.[5] It was felt that greater contact should be encouraged between officials and opposition parties than is practised at present, which is usually restricted to discussion of the machinery of government. Any wider practice has been regarded as 'taboo' although in 1995 civil servants briefed the Opposition leadership on matters arising from their adopted policies more than 18 months before a prospective election.

Members of the Cabinet do not receive a full and unabridged set of Cabinet minutes as does the Queen.

The departments

Tradition in Whitehall dictates that a minister and not an official must answer inquiries from MPs—although the status of the MP may well be commensurate with the ministerial status of the reply.

All departments and agencies must publish annual reports detailing achievements, targets, output and performance and financial information. This was formalised after the cessation of the January Public Expenditure White Paper which had played a crucial role in the budget cycle. Their primary role is to inform Parliament of general performance and expenditure. In addition, framework documents (FDs) and agreements on performance between departments and agencies are published together with other agreements but corporate plans are not usually published. In 1992 the minister in charge of executive agencies refused to inform

3 A pointed episode involved the allegations of MI5's undermining of Harold Wilson's Government by Peter Wright. The allegations were investigated in 1977 when James Callaghan was Prime Minister. On the conventions just described, Margaret Thatcher denied herself access to the papers. The 'link man' between the Home Office and MI5 at the relevant time was Sir Robert Armstrong, claimed H Young (*The Guardian*, 19 March 1987). Not so, claimed Sir Robert – the Cabinet Secretary – *The Guardian*, 20 March 1987. The 'link man' was the permanent secretary, who was deceased. On the Scottish Executives' treatment of UK Ministerial papers, see (2000) Public Law 309.
4 Dr W Wallace and Dr W Plowden, HC 92 II (1985–6), p 383.
5 Ibid.

Parliament which agencies had had their FDs amended and seems unusually defensive.[6] Public service agreements are published.

Since the early 1980s, departments have developed ever more detailed information as part of internal management structures. This began with the DoE which introduced MINIS—the Minister's Information System—to provide the minister with information on departmental performance. It only gave information on about 1% of annual expenditure in the DoE. MINIS concentrated upon:

> systematic annual reviews of objectives, tasks, costs and performance measures; much greater precision in the definition of tasks; much more precise performance measures; more specific attribution of costs and staff numbers to tasks and management functions, presentation of the results to ministers ... and publication of the results. The system or its equivalent should be used in departments and made available for public inspection and sent to the public for small cost.

Financial management initiatives (FMI) for departments concentrated upon informing managers within departments on the meeting of performance objectives and costs to help ensure their responsibility for the performance of programmes. They originally had little public dimension apart from being within the purview of departmentally related select committees. The Treasury and Civil Service Committee has argued the case vehemently for departmental annual reports to explain policies and provide sensible performance indicators and information on FMIs as a back-up for the general annual reviews. As we saw above, this has now been done.[7] The latest development has seen Public service agreements which are said to be 'at the cutting edge of of a revolution in the way public services are managed.' These concentrate on outcomes rather than inputs and funding is tied to results. Clear targets for performance have to be set; their realisation will result in extra investment. Targets include information on access to information and citizen redress and electronic delivery of public service.[8]

Although the Government has published more and more details of its policies and priorities in the form of White Papers[9] and more speculative Green Papers before drafting and publishing Bills where necessary to implement programmes, its efforts are, naturally enough, geared primarily to informing Parliament. In 1977, the then head of the Home Civil Service,

---

6   HC Debs Vol 209 col 685—William Waldegrave then responsible for open government.
7   See 13th Report of Committee of Public Accounts, *Financial Management Initiatives* (1986–7).
8   See ND Lewis (2000) European Public Law 201.
9   There are about 350 command papers each year.

Sir Douglas Allen, issued what is known as the Croham Directive urging the publication of more background information on departments' decisions. The directive had some success,[10] although it was restricted in its objectives as it excluded policy matters, and it was regarded as a dead letter by the incoming Thatcher administration. Our attention must in any event focus upon the Code on Open Government and the FOIA.

Parliament has to assist it the Parliamentary Commissioner for Administration (PCA), who investigates cases referred to him by MPs alleging maladministration in the conduct of a department's affairs where the complainant concerned has been affected, and as a consequence hardship or injustice has been caused. The Cabinet Office has set in motion a review of the public sector ombudsmen to see whether they should be brought into one office or Commission. His role in information complaints has already been noted above. The Parliamentary Ombudsman has also frequently investigated cases involving a failure to give advice, or to give inaccurate advice and such errors have been identified as maladministration.[11] He conducts the investigation in private and has access to all the relevant files and documents; he can interview witnesses and demand information, even from a minister, and he can take evidence on oath. Where a minister believes, and issues a notice, that disclosure of information either in content, or as a class of information or documents, would be prejudicial to the safety of the state or otherwise contrary to the public interest, the PCA must not disseminate the information beyond himself and his officers.[12] He is not allowed access to documents of cabinet proceedings or of cabinet committees. A certificate from the Cabinet Secretary approved by the Prime Minister is conclusive. We shall see that case law has given judges more scope than the Commissioner, although his powers were to be equal to those of judges *vis-à-vis* investigation and examination. The Commissioner is unlikely to require access to cabinet papers in any event in his usual complaints role, since his office is shaped to cater for the more routine grievances. But that is not a good reason for excluding such papers from his responsibilities under the Code (above). On one occasion the Government has found it necessary to issue a certificate on cabinet documents. This arose out of the Commissioner's

10 C Bennett and P Hennessey *A Consumer's Guide To Open Government* (1980).
11   See his *Annual Report* (1993) para 7, HC 290 (1993–94) and P Birkinshaw *Grievances, Remedies and the State* (2nd ed, 1994) pp 203–204.
12 One reason for insisting that his officers are civil servants. An interesting example of the power of the Commissioner was seen in relation to the NIPCA (Northern Ireland), who took over a complaint made originally to the Fair Employment Agency who were debarred from inquiry because of a ministerial certificate. The NIPCA was not so barred by the certificate and investigated: NIPCA *Annual Report 1984* HC 419 (1984–5), para 19, though cf Parliamentary Commissioner Act (NI) 1969, Sch 2(2): cf *Johnston v Chief Constable RUC* [1986] 3 All ER 135, ECJ and *Tinnelly & Son Ltd v UK* (1998) 4 BHRC 393 (ECtHR). See ch.1.

investigation into the *Court Line* episode, which concerned misleading statements made by the secretary of state in the Commons. The certificate was limited under s 8(4) of the Parliamentary Commissioner Act 1967 to the actual transactions of a cabinet committee and did not include drafts of its papers. He was informed of the outcome of the cabinet committee's discussions and the minister was interviewed.[13] A case involving the local ombudsman, who operates under a very similar regime to the Parliamentary ombudsman although there is direct access to the local ombudsman, has an instructive lesson on the powers of information-gathering given to the ombudsman. In a case involving irregularities in a planning decision in Liverpool where councillors with an interest had voted on a recommendation, one of the reasons why the court of appeal allowed an investigation by the ombudsman to stand, in spite of the fact that there was the possibility of a remedy in a court, was because of the ombudsman's access to information and documents. The ombudsman had the means to investigate serious allegations and ordinary litigants were unlikely to be able to acquire the evidence that would be necessary to support a successful application for review.[14] There are various bodies which the Parliamentary ombudsman may not investigate including the Cabinet Office and the Bank of England. His powers in relation to those performing services for departments under contract ie 'contracted out' were noted above. It was also seen that there are a wide variety of functions which he may not investigate.

Although successive Commissioners must be criticised for their limited use of the media and press and the scant publicity which their reports have received, more recent Commissioners have shown a more innovative, indeed combative, approach. He has used his powers to publish reports under s 10 (4), which allows for a special report on a single subject; some of these complaints have related to failure to provide accurate advice or to provide information—and this was before the code on *Open Government* was operational. The most famous of these was *Barlow Clowes*.[15] The Commissioner has also produced special reports on his access to information investigations. He also publishes a report where a department or agency fail to accept or act upon his recommendation and where an injustice caused to an individual by maladministration has not been, or will not be, remedied. Such a report was published in 1995 and dealt with the subject of complaints arising from the Channel Tunnel and blighted land adjoining the various approach routes to the tunnel from London.[16]

13 HC 498 (1974–5).
14 *R v Local Comr for Administration in North and North Easy of England, ex p Liverpool City Council* [2001] 1 All ER 462, CA.
15 HC 76 (1989) for the Barlow Clowes affair.
16 Under s 10 (3): HC 193 (1994-5). The Government subsequently showed signs of relenting: HC 819 (1994/5).

Investigation reports are presented to the MP who sponsored the complaint, the departmental or agency head, and the person alleged to have taken the action complained of.[17] The Commissioner presents an annual report before both Houses of Parliament. He compiles quarterly volumes of reports of select cases which are published. These reports contain a large amount of information on the day-to-day workings of the departments of state and agencies and non departmental bodies under his jurisdiction.[18] The FOIA has allowed the Information Commissioner established by that Act and public sector ombudsmen to hand information to each other gathered from their respective investigations in order to facilitate their respective investigations.[19] For most individuals, the information in the ombudsman's reports will be of little interest, although it could be of use and an examination is under way to see whether the reports need to be published in a new format to help accessibility. The information is vital for MPs on the Public Administration select committee which was formerly the Select Committee on the PCA. The reports of this body and the select committees which we examined in the previous chapter and the Public Accounts Committee provide information that would not be published but for their existence. 'For centuries, Parliament has been at the centre of the nation's information network', even if it is not the only centre.[20] How adequately is Parliament informed in order effectively to perform its responsibilities?

Parliament and information

We have looked at select committees before. The comments of Sir Richard Scott on provision of information to Parliament and ministerial accountability were noted in the last chapter. Parliament as an 'information centre' requires further treatment. In the UK, there are up to 40,000 parliamentary questions (PQs) put to ministers in a session in Parliament: 'the House debates 7-8 hours a day, five days a week for some 36 weeks a year. The magnitude of information in Hansard is apparent.'[1] MPs are informed by constituents, by civil servants via parliamentary questions and select committee appearances, by lobbies and interest groups and by their own political parties, by employers and trade unions, by all-party subject groups of which they are members, and so on. MPs have limited

---

17 The Head will see the report in draft and will doubtless recommend significant changes, where he feels it is necessary, in the drafting.
18 Cmnd 9563.
19 Chapter 6 p 326.
20 D Englefield *Parliament and Information* (1980), p 1.
1   Englefield.

resources for back-up staff and so the assistance of the House of Commons library is invaluable:[2]

> There are too many questions and too few staff to guarantee that more than a small number of answers are checked by others before they go to a member. This is in stark contrast to most large organisations, such as the Civil Service or nationalised industries or regulatory authorities where information sent to Parliament will have been vetted several times.[3]

Questions may be refused an answer on a wide variety of grounds including those involving 'disproportionate cost'. In response to a question from Mr Tony Banks MP on cost Mrs Thatcher had this to say:

> It is for ministers to decide whether to decline to answer a question on grounds of disproportionate cost. Any question likely to cost more than £200 is referred to the responsible minister before significant cost resources are committed.

Mr Banks asked the Prime Minister how many questions she had refused to answer since 1979 on the grounds of disproportionate costs. The Prime Minister replied that this information could be supplied only at disproportionate cost.[4] Once a ground for refusing an answer is established, it sets a binding precedent, a practice which Sir Richard Scott found baffling.

Reports of the Public Administration Committee have detailed the practice of blocking questions. The position was relaxed in relation to questions which have been asked and answered or not answered in the same session of Parliament. The former may not be asked again within the same session and the latter must wait for three months to elapse unless in either case the circumstances have changed.[5] Where information was refused on grounds of confidentiality, too many departments were not giving reasons under the Code (above) which is to be replaced by FOIA.[6]. The Table Office, responsible for processing PQs, published a memorandum each year itemising PQs blocked by ministers' refusal to answer them. This is published by that select committee. The major 'blockers' in 1998-99 were the Ministry of Defence, the Attorney-General

2   Ibid, pp 20–49.
3   Ibid, p 28.
4   HC Debs Vol 121 cols 358-9 (29 October 1987). See M Frankel in N Lewis, (ed) *Happy and Glorious* (1990). The current cost has risen to £550.
5   See Public Administration Committee HC 61 (2000-01).
6   HC 820 (1997-98) para.15 and HC 61 (2000-01)

and the Church Commissioners. The lowest was Education and Employment.

The Speaker is the final authority on the admissibility of questions.[7] It might be claimed that the 'obligation of the minister answering to the High Court of Parliament is exactly that of a witness before the High Court of Justice: to tell the truth, the whole truth and nothing but the truth',[8] but the analogy is not exact. Parliament, the highest court in the land, is essentially a legislative assembly and a 'talking shop' not a court of law, and while ministers who mislead or deceive can be treated severely (see chapter 4 p 173), a minister who answered in total candour would be regarded as politically naive. Among the devices used to curtail the whole truth are: refusing to answer; bland, inconsequential or partial answers; declaring that the information is not available in its requested form or that statistics as required are not kept; timing the answer to avoid embarrassment in the media and press, eg on the eve of a recess; or replies such as 'I shall write to the Hon Member' or 'I shall place the document in the Library'. One example cited by Christopher Price was a question to the Environment Secretary on (a) current and (b) total expenditure of every local authority in England in 1981/2 showing its estimated final block grant entitlement and any penalties to be imposed.[9] The minister replied that he would write, and sent the raw print-outs from the DoE computer.[10] Price has argued that a system of rapid assembly of information in parliamentary questions in a form in which it can be extracted and used has not been maintained. Neither MPs, the library nor specialist lobbies have yet assembled the resources to utilise effectively the more informative answers to parliamentary questions. This point has been repeated by the director of a public relations company, who wrote that 'there had been no systematic review of how citizens can obtain information from either their legislature or executive', although the Code on Open Government must now be included.[11]

A development of real significance occurred with the use of select committees to engage in pre-legislative scrutiny of draft bills in addition to White Papers. The FOI bill and consultation paper were examined by this process. Another development has seen the publication of draft Bills with the White Paper. This occurred with the Human Rights Bill and the Local Government Bill enacted in 2000.[12] The Public Administration

---

7   *Erskine May* (22nd ed, 1997) p 294.
8   C Price *Public Money*, December 1984, p 26.
9   Ibid.
10 Ibid.
11 P Luff *Public Money*, September 1985, p 12.
12 Although there were several Bills that went through pre-legislative scrutiny from 1997 onwards, there are similar practices going back to the 1970s.

Committee had two months to engage in pre-legislation scrutiny of the FOI Bill in the Spring of 1999.

The Commons library contains official documents which are not published outside Parliament, eg in the past these included the *Instruction Book for the Guidance of the Metropolitan Police* and the *Governors' Handbook* for prison governors. Certain facilities of the library are available for members of the European Parliament. Peers have their own library.

Englefield[13] has studied Parliamentary proceedings to assess their role in extracting information from government spokesman on, for instance, the stages of a government Bill through both Houses and the relevant standing committees, government and opposition motions, adjournment debates, the variety of parliamentary questions[14] and ministerial statements. During the Committee stage of Bills, it had become usual for MPs to be supplied with more information than previously in the form of notes on clauses. These will not include arguments drafted by civil servants, but they will contain explanations of clauses. The House of Lords has experimented with special standing committees which take written and oral evidence within a period of 28 days after the second reading of a Bill in the Lords. After that period the Commitee becomes a public Bill committee considering Bills clause by clause. This is particularly suited to uncontentious Bills of a technical nature or Law Commission proposals.[15] Special standing committees may also be used in the Commons but they are rarely appointed. Deregulatory orders under the Deregulation and Contracting Out Act 1994 have special procedures given their constitutional novelty.[16]

Ministers are likely to face oral questions about once every four weeks, although every week the Prime Minister has one session of Parliamentary questions, lasting about 30 minutes. There is a tendency for 'constitutional watchers' to downplay the practical importance of parliamentary questions, that it is all part of a theatrical display with little real impact in terms of information provision. Much information is provided by questions and one of the most serious abuses of public office which led to the Nolan inquiry was the payment of MPs by lobbyists to ask questions.

In 1970 Parliament discussed the introduction of a computer-based information-retrieval system in the Commons Library. A scheme was introduced in 1980. The Parliamentary on-line computer-based indexing system (POLIS) which is in the library is a database which is accessible

---

13 *Whitehall and Westminster: Government Informs Parliament* (1985).
14 See *Erskine May* (22nd edn, 1997), pp 291-306; and also House of Commons Factsheet No 46 *Questions* (1997).
15 See Parliamentary Procedure and the Law Commission, Law Commission November 1994 and Hansard Society Report from the Hansard Society Commission on the Legislative Process (1992).
16 HC 238 (1993-4).

through the Parliamentary intranet. The database is updated daily and covers parliamentary questions, private notice questions, debates, Bills, statements, reports, evidence, Treaty series papers, deposited papers from ministers, departmental publications (both HMSO—the Stationery Office—and non-HMSO) and EC official publications and unpublished papers. POLIS is used increasingly by external organisations subscribing to its services.[17] The House of Commons Public Information Office uses PRESTEL.[18] The Information Committee of the House of Commons has supported a relaxation of copyright laws covering Parliamentary publications and greater use of free access via the internet. Commercial licensing should be allowed.[19] As with government, Parliamentary use of the internet has increased dramatically.

A growing number of lobbyists from commercial and voluntary organisations have obtained passes to gain access to the Votes Office and Sales Office of the House of Commons and Lords for documents not published by HMSO, and this has led to fears of favouritism and abuse. The following improvements were suggested:

1. a list of types of documents whose publication and general availability would be beneficial should be agreed;[20]
2. a sales point, outside the Palace of Westminster, should be established, where all these documents would be available to personal callers, or for telephone or mail order;
3. the sales point should publish a list of all daily documents available which would itself be available on a subscription basis—a significant expansion of HMSO daily lists.

While these would not solve every problem, these suggestions would, it is submitted, be a useful addition. Publications are protected by Crown or Parliamentary copyright under the Copyright etc Act 1988 unlike the situation in the USA. This could prevent placing statutes, bills and official papers on the internet. The spirit of the Act of Settlement 1700, s IV 'and whereas the Laws of England are the Birthright of the People thereof ...' needs to be placed in its modern context. Such a relaxation has occurred and Bills, statutory instruments and official documents are on the internet.

Broadcasting of Parliamentary proceedings has taken place, in one form or another, since 1968 and in February 1988 the House of Commons voted to allow an experimental period of TV broadcasting of its proceedings. A select committee has been established on the televising of Parliament and a code containing tight guidelines has been produced

17 However, these services are very costly and materials are covered by Crown and Parliamentary copyright. Many materials are now available free on the internet.
18 See Appendix V of *Englefield* (1985) for a list of reports and accounts laid before Parliament and ordered to be printed.
19 HC 328 (1995-6).
20 Note the House of Commons *Factsheet* series.

for broadcasters. This instructs cameras immediately to switch to the Speaker in the event of any disorder. Also banned are: close up shots of members' or officers' papers, shots of press and public galleries, officials and visitors' boxes, the area behind the Speaker's chair and the Speaker receiving advice from a clerk.

Parliament and expenditure—a case study

The role of departmental select committees—with the exception of the Treasury and Civil Service Committee (renamed the Treasury Committee)—in examining the expenditure programmes of related departments has been viewed as disappointing. The accusation has been made that the examination of finance requires painstaking discussion of detail and analysis, and that most MPs do not care about and/or are not very good in this role.[1]

Government requires money—lots of it. This is true of UK government, as well as devolved government. Separate arrangements now exist for Scotland, Wales and Northern Ireland, I will concentrate on the UK.[2] The most effective way to oversee government is to know how much it is spending and on what. Constitutional fundamentals,[3] such as they are, have dictated that Parliament should authorise and oversee expenditure and the raising of revenue. Long before Parliament is presented with information, there is a secretive budgetary process undertaken between the Treasury and departments known as PES which since 1976 has been more concerned with control of expenditure than planning of expenditure by devices such as cash limits or the fixing of expenditure for three years in advance under a comprehensive spending review and the setting of performance targets. Departmental plans are agreed to in the form of public service agreements between the Treasury and departments. There is also annual managed expenditure which involves annual review. Membership of the EMU will involve strict controls over annual and overall deficits as well controls over inflation.

The Comptroller and Auditor-General has agreed that the lay person who wishes to be informed of expenditure in central or local government should be assisted by way of reports and explanations. However, the prime recipient should be Parliament or elected members of local government.[4]

---

1   See chapter 4 above, n 17 p 181 and D Wass, *Government and the Governed* (1984).
2   Prosser and Mullen (2001) European Public Law Issue 2 for the position in Scotland following the Public Finance and Accountability Act 2000.
3   Eg Bill of Rights 1689, art 4. Supply procedure is primeval.
4   As well as the secretary of state and members of the new style of executives in local government.

For MPs, there is a 'mountain of estimates, accounts, reports and other material produced in ever-increasing volume on all aspects of public business'.[5] However, the Comptroller and Auditor-General has written that 'the quantity of information made available is frequently not matched by its quality', nor is it made available at the right time; there is 'a significant lack of analysis and statement of objectives, and those to whom information is directed often have neither the will nor the organisation to make the best use of it'.

Since 1998, the Chancellor of the Exchequer has employed a Code for Fiscal Stability. This is a code for the long-term framework for fiscal stability. It is based on s 155 of the Finance Act 1998 and the code has been approved by resolution of the House of Commons. It commits the government to the pursuit of the principles of openness, transparency, stability, responsibility, fairness and efficiency in its policies concerning fiscal and debt management. This is a helpful start given the ultimate obscurity of many of the powers and practices of the Treasury which takes the executive lead on economic and fiscal policy.

Accountability, either by way of *ex ante* control or *ex post facto* scrutiny, depends upon information.

> The fundamental requirement is the provision of the right information, at the right time, to the right people, as a basis for timely and effective action. In this context there is little benefit in information for its own sake. It has value only where it is provided for a clear and defined purpose. Clear objectives are needed both by those supplying the information and by those receiving it.[6]

From this the then Comptroller, Sir Gordon Downey, believed two questions flowed: Does Parliament get the information it needs? Does Parliament make effective use of the information it gets—or could get? There are four basic documents covering the first question:

1. the Chancellor's budget statement to Parliament: from December 1993 this was a unified budget bringing together tax and expenditure proposals. A consultative pre-budget report has been produced for Parliament since 1997. A statistical supplement was published early in the New Year. The statement provided the details on departmental allocations of expenditure which have been agreed during the Public Expenditure Survey (see below). Before this reform tax and expenditure decisions were taken separately leading to a great deal of criticism. It was decided to respond by bringing forward the budget from the Spring to a date in December and tax and spending charges

5   G Downey Public Money, June 1986, p 35.
6   Ibid.

would be dealt with together. The unified budget was accompanied by the financial statement and budget report, an analysis of departmental spending plans for the next three years, a statement of the government medium-term financial strategy, a short-term economic forecast, detailed material on the likely out-turn for the public finances in the current year and the revenue forecasts for the year ahead, a description of the main tax and NIC measures and their revenue consequences and information on the cost of tax reliefs. The attempt by the Major Government to unify taxation and expenditure in the unified budget was not entirely successful. From 1998, the budget has reverted to March preceded by a pre-budget Autumn statement. The Code of Fiscal Stability (above) and changes in accounting from accruals to resource accounting and budgeting aim to bring closer the relationship between taxation and expenditure to facilitate analysis. The Code aims to make the Government spell out more clearly the context of its expenditure decisions through a pre-budget report and the financial statement and budget report now split into two documents containing a budget judgement, short-term outlook, and an explanation of proposed fiscal measures. The second report is the economic and fiscal strategy report dealing with longer term financial strategy. Under the Code, transparency is defined as providing sufficient information to allow for a scrutiny (by Parliament and the public) of fiscal policy and the state of public finances. Provision of information is subject to a range of provisos not unlike the exemptions under the FOIA 2000 (chapter 6).

2. the main supply estimates – approved by resolution and subsequently enacted in the Appropriation Act in July — presented to Parliament by ministers in March for the former to approve, which they always do. These are derived from the Public Expenditure Survey and the budget statement. A vote on account[7] is required in the previous November to pay for expenditure before the following April – July and before the Appropriation Act.

3. departmental reports which will contain detailed information on expenditure for the next three years and which are published from February;

4. the appropriation accounts, showing how actual spending has compared with the Estimates approved. These are audited by the Comptroller and may include CAG reports.

The accusation has been made that the estimates have ignored 'incalculable capital assets and other resources acquired and paid for in recent years'. Proposed changes to the method of accounting will give a

---

7   About 45% of current government expenditure for the approaching year

clearer idea of how money has been spent, the Chancellor of the Exchequer has claimed, and will take effect from 1998.[8] The accounts will reveal a purely technical overspending of voted expenditure—however small. They will leave Parliament ignorant on, for instance, the effects on health care of hospital spending of almost £10 billion per annum. The changes will involve a shift from resource accounting and budgeting, now confirmed by the Government Resources and Accounts Act 2000. These replaced systems based on cash accounts and budgets. While the latter were far easier to follow and use they were far less reliable as indicators of a financial position: they did not include contractual obligations, made no distinction between capital and current expenditure and took little account of capital assets. From 1994, departmental reports have included information on capital assets, and environmental performance. The answer was in more and better information from departments and agencies themselves which has taken place to a considerable extent in the shape of annual reports. This would better inform not only Parliament, but the public who wished to know. The Treasury proposed changing the format of supply estimates from 1995/6. These are in three parts, Part II containing detailed information under subheads. These seek better integration and coherence on government's spending plans. Important information will concentrate on the objectives and achievements of expenditure in departmental annual reports rather than in estimates and by providing better alignment between information in the two sets of documents, though this change was largely dictated by administrative cost-cutting. The legal authority for spending is the vote which goes forward for incorporation in the Appropriation Act each year. The number of votes – individual supply estimates — has decreased significantly since 1996-97 thereby ostensibly affording Parliament less opportunity to scrutinise estimates effectively. New 'requests for resources' for major blocks of expenditure were therefore agreed within the new votes. The Public Accounts Committee had the following note of warning:[9]

> We consider that Parliament's scrutiny of government spending plans could be impaired if the alignment of estimates and departmental reports is not clear, if important detail is lost in the transfer from estimates to departmental reports or if reports are not available at the same time as estimates. And the usefulness of departmental annual reports might be eroded if standards and presentation are allowed to drift ...

8   Better Accounting for Taxpayers' Money, Cm 2929 (1995).
9   HC 386 (1993-4) pp v-vi.

The Committee was also concerned about the loss of information by way of disappearing subheads. Some of these were used to provide 'interesting information' on sub-programmes, projects and significant items of expenditure 'which is useful when voting funds'. Ideally, the necessary information will be in reports but the Committee was most concerned that the Treasury had not spelt 'out in more detail the principles and rules about what information should appear in departmental reports and take steps to ensure departments adhere to them. Furthermore the information lost from the subheads will also be lost from the appropriation accounts 'and will not therefore be subject to audit or validation by the Comptroller and Auditor-General.'

In general, introductory notes to votes in the estimates were bland or vapid. An absence of figures in volume terms, *how much* service is provided, meant that assessment of levels of service was impossible from the estimates alone. Members would have to consult the departmental reports and we noted the misgivings of the Public Accounts Committee (PAC) above on the new style of estimates. Yet Parliament based its supply on assumptions of levels of service, and 'it is arguable that it should also receive systematic out-turn information on the levels actually received'. The Government would argue that such information is now in annual reports and its proposed auditing changes which were introduced in 1998 will improve matters.

Research commissioned by the National Audit Offices[10] to investigate Parliamentary use of the estimates and appropriation accounts found that select committees did not find it generally worthwhile or productive to perform systematic scrutinies of the main estimates and only the PAC seemed to use accounts positively in consideration of the Comptroller and Auditor-General's reports. Methods used to select estimates for scrutiny varied from consultation between clerks and specialist advisers, to direct lobbying after a reduction in service.

From the reports there emerges a general agreement that not only was more information required for Parliament but MPs were not using that which they receive as efficiently as they ought if they take accountability seriously.

Behind this information and its shortcomings lies the secretive public expenditure survey. This concerns the wrangling and horse-trading within and between departments and the Treasury over prospective items and levels of expenditure.[11] The process ends up with the PSX or Public Expenditure Committee of the Cabinet chaired by the Chancellor of the Exchequer with the Chief Secretary of the Treasury in attendance. The Committee has become less of an arbitrator of contested bids, more the

---

10   By A Likierman.
11   See I Harden and N Lewis *The Noble Lie* (1986), pp 120 *et seq.*

formulator of departmental spending decisions within an agreed total. The completed results will contribute to the budget report.

Daintith and Page[12] have analysed the new system of presenting estimates in relation to one department, the Lord Chancellor's Department. They compared the main vote for estimates approved in 1991-92 with that of the new scheme in 1996-97. The latter form three pages of text instead of nine and the budget covering in 1996-97 legal aid, and the addition of magistrates' courts, is much larger — £2.2 billion as opposed to £397 million. In 1991-92, the vote was split into eight sections with 34 sub-heads. The 1996-97 vote had three sections, plus one each for legal aid and magistrates' courts. 'There is less information, but what there is is designed to be more significant in economic terms, and to present the cash provisions which Parliament is invited to grant by way of supply [money] in a way which is consistent with the expenditure plans emerging from the PES process by way first of the Financial Statement and Budget Report, giving the global expenditure picture, and then through the departmental reports which translate it into departmental plans.'[13] However, as the CAG feared, information in the departmental reports is far from consistent in the way it is presented resulting in disparities in information supply to Parliament. Daintith and Page conclude that the Treasury's own highly developed computerised Financial Information System may be developing as a substitute for formal Parliamentary oversight.[14] Could this not be available to Parliament to assist in its scrutiny and investigation of expenditure? The former CAG suggested that the internal departmental financial management initiatives should be available to Parliament.

In many respects the following criticism is more serious. On Parliament's ability to handle the information, the former Comptroller was equally pessimistic. Supply debates were rarely used for supply itself, and even 'the relatively recent change to link debates with certain nominated estimates does little to provide any coherent coverage of the aims, purpose and objectives of the major funds involved.... A Parliament which *de facto* gives up its control of supply gives up much of its constitutional control of government and accountability.' Parliament as a whole lacks the resources and expertise to use the information it can extract. But this is to overlook the Committee of Public Accounts (PAC). This draws on the work of the National Audit Office (NAO) and its 750 or so staff. Under the National Audit Act 1983:

> The NAO has direct and independent access to documents, records and information in all government departments, and produces a

12 *The Executive in the Constitution: Structure, Autonomy and Internal Control* (1999), p 162 et seq.
13 Ibid p 163.
14 Ibid p 164.

series of analysed reports dealing with the efficiency, economy and effectiveness with which departments have used their resources. There has been some controversy over the 'Not for the eyes of the Comptroller and Auditor General' tag applying to some files and documents barring access to departmental papers (see below).

The PAC is the most developed form of *ex post facto* accountability of departmental administration that we possess, the Comptroller and Auditor-General believed. It will be examined shortly.

Local government is not covered by the 1983 National Audit Act, but by the Audit Commission Act 1998 amending and consolidating the Local Government (Finance) Act 1982. The 1982 Act established the Audit Commission which now also audits the NHS bodies with modifications.[15] Nor are nationalised industries under the 1983 Act or bodies of a commercial nature. In the past, the position of nationalised industries was very unsatisfactory and privatisation has not removed problems of accountability because, eg, of enormous state subsidies paid to private rail companies. What is included and what excluded from CAG audit has been a source of considerable difficulty and controversy. Under s 9 Government Resource and Accounts Act 2000, the Treasury have to prepare for each financial year a set of accounts for bodies which appear to the Treasury to exercise functions of a public nature or which are entirely or substantially funded by public funds. The Treasury will have control over the information to be contained in such accounts and s 10 gives the Treasury wide powers to demand information from designated bodies. For Welsh bodies, the information may be sent to the Welsh Assembly. Accounts prepared under s 9 shall be sent to the CAG.[16] The National Audit Office has been critical of expenditure papers in the past on the following grounds. There is no distinction between aims (high-level) and objectives (specific planned achievements), and these terms are used interchangeably. Objectives tend not to be qualified, although some are targeted, eg the Department of Transport's target that 90% of driver vehicle licensing applications should be processed within 10 days. Targets concentrate on manpower rather than target *achievement*. Aims and objectives are not complete, eg not all functional lines within departments are covered and only 46% of functional lines have sections of text which contain aims and objectives. Lastly, even where aims and objectives are well defined, it can still be difficult to relate these to the programme structure. Departmental reports have addressed many of these points and the impact of the *Citizen's Charter* and its successors have

15   See the Government Resource and Accounts Act 2000 and NHS bodies.
16   Section 11; and see s 25. See the Public Finance and Accountability (Scotland) Act 2000.

been beneficial in so far as more reliable information on performance has been produced.

The Comptroller and Auditor-General (CAG) and the Public Accounts Committee (PAC)

The primary responsibility of the CAG is to examine the accounts of designated bodies and to issue reports for the PAC of the House of Commons. During the first round of hearings by Lord Nolan's Committee, the Government announced that where a minister was minded to overrule an accounting officer's – usually the permanent secretary or agency chief executive — opinion on the prudent and economical use of public funds the officer could inform the Chair of the Public Accounts Committee.[17] Previously officers informed the CAG and Treasury where they were overruled in more serious matters by a minister involving 'propriety or regularity'. In the Pergau Dam episode in 1994, which concerned the conferral of overseas aid to the Malaysian government in terms which were subsequently ruled *ultra vires*, there was felt by the civil servants to be no question of irregularity and so the overruling was not communicated to the CAG.[18] He uncovered it when conducting a value for money audit of the Overseas Development Administration. Following this episode, the Government accepted that all overrulings would be communicated to the CAG without delay; there then followed the further concession to the PAC. In the course of the inquiry, it was disclosed that 1,500 Whitehall files were given 'Not for NAO [National Audit Office] eyes' status. This was stopped as a practice after the Labour Government came to power in 1997. These included ministerial private office files containing cabinet or cabinet committee papers or minutes and files dealing with the conduct of business with the NAO or PAC usually while they are current. This limitation has been developed from the interpretation of s 8(1) National Audit Act 1983 which allows the CAG to have a right of access to all such documents as he *may reasonably require* for carrying out an examination and to require the person holding or responsible for a document to give such *information and explanation as are reasonably necessary*. Clearly such a limitation is open to abuse.

Section 8 of the Government Resource and Accounts Act 2000[19] provides that the CAG shall have rights of access at all reasonable times

---

17 White et al (1994) Public Law 526. See also White and Hollingsworth *Audit, Accountability and Government* (1999).

18 *R v Secretary of State for Foreign Affairs, ex p World Development Movement Ltd* [1995] 1 All ER 611: the secretary of state was found to have acted unlawfully in giving £234 million to the Malaysian government to build a dam as a part of our overseas development programme.

19 See Hollingsworth and White (2001) Public Law 50.

to any of the documents relating to a department's accounts. Those holding or controlling such documents must give the CAG any assistance, information or explanation required. Under s 25, it is provided that s 8 will apply where the accounts of a body are to be audited by the CAG by statute or by agreement ie, they are not government departments or agencies.

As we have noted, the reports of the CAG have been accused of being 'unambitious', 'constrained' and 'coded', and of failing to explain causes and effects. The CAG cannot examine 'policy' itself, only the impact and expenditure implications and value-for-money (VFM) aspects of departmental programmes. VFM audits are a vital feature of CAG investigations concentrating on wider concerns of economy, efficiency and effectiveness of public expenditure and not simply the exchequer audits of accounts. Instead of reporting boldly, giving substantial reasons, 'the CAG has preferred to work discreetly, through informal pressure within departments, and to give time and opportunity for people to remedy the weaknesses themselves'. The CAG responded[20] that his reports were checked by departments and had to avoid political controversy in their tone. They were prepared for the PAC, which is a formal and business-like body with more extensive powers than any other select committee. The accounting officer has to appear before it, and it has access to all necessary information providing the department possesses it.[1] In defence procurement and pharmaceutical production, the departments do not have all the information that the PAC would like, as we have seen elsewhere.[2] The flow of information often relates to the symbiotic relationship between the department and the trade association or manufacturing company. Elsewhere the PAC has criticised the Ministry of Defence, in particular, for failing to give information on the accounts of bodies in advance of a proposed privatisation.[3] This takes us to a further problem.

Alice in Quangoland

Governments do not exist in splendid isolation. They stand at the apex of the administrative structure of the state. They have to rely upon others in the public and private sector to help promote, administer and deliver

---

20 Public Money, September 1984, and reply, Public Money, December 1984, p 10.

1   A controversy arose when Peter Levene became head of Procurement Executive for the MoD on terms that he dissociate completely from his former employer with the consequence that he could not answer the committee's questions relating to the placement or operation of government contracts with the company: HC 390 (1984–5), p v.

2   See p 219 *et seq* above. See National Audit Act 1983, s 8.

3   See McEldowney [1991] MLR 933.

governmental programmes. In the case of resort to public corporations to administer or regulate an area of activity, the statute usually does not reveal the real relationship between a minister and the chairman of a management board of a nationalised industry or other corporation, a relationship which operates behind the scenes. The same is true of a corporation established by Royal charter, although the charter is invariably supposed to recognise and preserve a body's independence from government. The charter will describe and define the body's objects, constitution and powers to govern its own affairs although, as we saw in the previous chapter with the BBC, the formal terms of the charter may not reflect the reality of its operations.

Advisory bodies are usually set up by administrative/ministerial *fiat*, and although the 'minister concerned should inform Parliament of his action in establishing an advisory body; a written answer to a parliamentary question is usually sufficient.'[4] Legislation will be necessary where advisory bodies will require significant continuing government funding. They inevitably advise in confidence. In chapter 4 it was seen how the Government has become more conscious of the need for safeguards over advisory bodies and how a large number were added to the Parliamentary Ombudsman's jurisdiction in 1999 following reports on *Quangos*.[5] Royal Commissions are advisory bodies of a formal and prestigious nature appointed by Royal warrant of the Crown issued through the appropriate secretary of state. The reports are published as command papers laid before Parliament. The reasons for establishing such a body are diverse.[6] Functions can be hived off by creating a corporate body under the Companies Acts, although Parliamentary approval should usually be sought before departmental responsibilities are hived off in this way. 'Departments will need, in the absence of legislation, to devise suitable arrangements to ensure that ministers have sufficient information about, and control over, the companies' activities.' This has been true in some privatisation programmes which have seen sponsoring ministers retaining a significant degree of influence over companies via the memoranda and articles of association and special holdings of 'golden shares' and the like.[7] The last category concerns bodies which are private but which enter into close and detailed working relationships with the state. Trade associations, the Confederation of British Industry, multinational and national companies, professional associations, trade unions and pressure groups come to mind. Under the terms of the

4   *Non-Departmental Public Bodies* (Cabinet Office 1996 update), para 3.2.1.
5   See the Code on Access *1999 Annual Report.*
6   TJ Cartwright *Royal Commissions and Departmental Committees in Britain* (1975). The bodies may be seen as expert and pre-eminent, independent and/or representative, a cover for the fact that a decision has effectively been made or a way of putting off a decision, etc.
7   Graham and Prosser *Privatising Public Enterprises* (1991).

Deregulation and Contracting Out Act 1994 the process of contracting out government functions to private bodies has been facilitated easing the provision of public services through such bodies. The means adopted by government to achieve its policy objectives are of crucial significance.

The Public Private Partnerships (formerly Private Finance Initiative) are a striking illustration of this development where a government funded company, Partnerships UK, has taken over responsibility for encouraging, advising and promoting PPPs. In chapter four the role of the Task Forces under Blair's Government was noted.

If, however, a non-departmental advisory body is acting as a *de facto* executive body, details of the arrangements will rarely be forthcoming. The relationship is one of confidentiality between the minister and his advisers. Important features of the operation of such bodies will not be within the formal terms of reference of ministerial responsibility/ accountability. More secluded will be the operations of such bodies and their relationships with organised interests and the network of multi-layered pluralistic or corporatist relationships which sprout from their existence. Government needs advice, assistance and information from specialist professional, commercial or industrial concerns. It might seek 'sponsorship' from business. This latter topic was investigated by Lord Neill's Committee on Standards in Public Life.[8] It needs their know-how and financial strength. In return, a trade-off may be bartered around degrees of self-regulation and administration and exclusive rights to enter into certain areas of exploitation, or utilisation of resources may be offered. Government deem this to be in the public interest. The point is, if, for instance, wealth creation is the only or the pre-eminent criterion of public interest, do we know that wealth is actually being created where information is not forthcoming or adequate? If 'private' bodies operating in the public interest are not subject to the pressures of democratic accountability, because they do not have to account for what they are doing on the public behalf,[9] are forms of accountability based upon commercial practice and accountancy practice adequate? These might inform us of financial accountability. But what of social and political accountability?[10] Who should know, and how much should they know? It will be seen in the next chapter that commercial interests is a ground for exemption from the FOIA as well as information which if disclosed in the reasonable opinion of a qualified person 'would otherwise prejudice, or would be likely to prejudice, the effective conduct of public affairs.'

---

8   Ch 8 Cm 4557-I (2000).
9   If the body in question is considered to be a private body, and not a public one, for instance: see chapter 4, p 215, n 8 above.
10   See Baldwin and McCrudden (eds) *Regulation and Public Law* (1987).

In the field of competition policy we have the Office of Fair Trading (OFT), the Competition Commission (CC – formerly Monopolies and Mergers Commission), and the Secretary of State for Trade and Industry. In the late 1980s, the City Panel on Take-Overs and Mergers was ruled to be susceptible to judicial review even though ostensibly a private body in form, but the impact of that decision is marginal to our present concern. The OFT would like to possess fuller powers to get at the books and obtain information from the business concerns it investigates and keeps under review and discussions go back on this topic for well over two decades before there was any reform.[11] The 1998 Competition Act allows the CC to carry out formal hearings by groups in private with power to allow interested parties to be heard and to be represented, to allow cross examination or 'otherwise to take part' in proceedings.[12] The CC may also conduct a variety of appeals when it acts as a tribunal which allow for pre-hearing reviews and for appeals to be heard in private if against the public interest or if commercial information or information concerning private affairs falling within s 56 is to be heard. Appeals lie on a point of law from its decision. Schedule 9 allows for a variety of procedural matters including a power to order disclosure between parties or production of documents.[13] The CC is covered by the FOIA but not in its capacity as a tribunal. Prior to the 1998 Act, the MMC had been the defendant in court proceedings when it proposed to give documentation to the take-over target of the bidding company's proposed merger, including that part of the latter's confidential submission dealing with future financing plans and tactics apropos of the take-over bid.[14] It was 'entirely unprecedented for a company to have to hand over such documentation to the bid for company for the latter to comment upon'. A sniff of this sensitivity was repeated when a report by the Stock Exchange into the share-dealings surrounding the takeover of Westland plc in early 1986 was not published, even though the report might have been instrumental in formulating new Stock Exchange rules.[15] Much of the work of the Office of Fair Trading

11 Cf *IRC v Rossminster* [1980] AC 952 and tax investigations and P Ely *An Independent Enquiry into the Powers of the Board of Inland Revenue to Call for the Papers of Tax Accountants* 1994 (Inland Revenue), and note s 255 Finance Act 1994 and ibid, ss 187 and 23-5; see Review of Restrictive Trade Practices Policy, Cm 331 (1988) and Cm 2100. Reforms were again proposed in early 1996 and the Competition Act (CA) emerged in 1998. This sets an EC framework to much of our competition law.

12 See CA 1998, s 45 and Sch 7 para 19 and: *R v MMC, ex p Elders IXL plc* [1987] 1 All ER 451; *R v MMC, ex p Matthew Brown plc* [1987] 1 All ER 463; *R v MMC, ex p Air Europe* (1988) 4 BCC 182. On giving information to an unwelcome bidder, see *City Takeover Code* rule 20.2. See Part VI Companies' Act 1989.

13 Sections 46 and 48 and Sch 9 para 9.

14 *Ex p Elders plc*, above. See also *Smith Kline & French Laboratories Ltd v Licensing Authority* [1989] 1 All ER 578, HL.

15 Note 12 above.

and CC is geared towards putting the government in a good bargaining position to extract undertakings from private and indeed public bodies to avoid open proceedings in court. The scene is set, in other words, for off-the-record deals to pursue the public interest. This was never more clearly illustrated than in the events surrounding the struggle for the takeover of Harrods when the secretary of state refused to publish the report by inspectors into one of the rival bidders and refused to give reasons for his decision not to refer the matter to the MMC for them to investigate. It would have been a brave court that ordered disclosure and the giving of reasons but the subsequent events seemed to vindicate the position of the unsuccessful bidder.[16] The Secretary of State has also undertaken to publish OFT advice on mergers.[17]

What government wants is information, knowledge or favours; what regulated bodies or those on exclusive licences receive is suspected of favouritism in the absence of appropriate degrees of transparency. Is the trade-off really in the public interest? How do we know? What quality of information have we got? What should we strive for? Where does political responsibility begin and market responsibility end? This is of lasting significance regardless of whether government seeks to privatise public markets and assets as at present, or whether it seeks the co-operation of vested interests in the economy such as employers or trade associations or trade unions and the like, or whether it buys out essential industries in the private sector while still seeking to gain the benefits of commercial confidentiality and official secrecy in their undertakings. The UK FOIA has a far broader reach than comparable FOI statutes insofar as it covers private bodies performing public functions or providing public services and only to the extent of those public functions. The exemptions are, however, extremely broad and confidential information is what is referred to as an 'absolute exemption' (see chapter 6 pp 296 and 298).

The problems relating to the trade-offs on information and power were identified with the government and interest group interface in a classic passage from Beer's *Modern British Politics*:[18]

... The needs of the class or interest in question should be considered not simply because they are legitimised by the design of the good

---

16 The 'subsequent events' were the revelations involving the Fayed brothers: *Lonrho plc v Secretary of State for Trade and Industry* [1989] 2 All ER 609, HL; and see *Fayed v UK* (1994) 18 EHRR 393, E Ct HR; note the important *R v Secretary of State for Health, ex p United States Tobacco International Inc* [1992] 1 All ER 212 and the handing over of reports of a scientific nature prepared by a specialist committee for the secretary of state in reaching a decision concerning the manufacture of nicotine substances involving the applicant's commercial interests.

17 See pp 216-217 above.

18 Pp 72-3.

society, but also because this element (whether stratum or lesser community) carries out a function important to the social whole. This justifies giving it power to protect itself ... it also means that the knowledge of those performing this function may well be necessary for the good governing of the wider community. They have special skills, experience, expertise which government must have at hand if it is to understand and control the complex and interdependent social whole ... a special emphasis is given to this need by the conditions of government in modern industrial society. As control extends into the complex and technical affairs of the economy, government must win the cooperation of crucial sectors and show sensitivity to their values and purposes. Not least, it must elicit their expert advice. These sectors are the seats of technical, professional, and scientific knowledge indispensable to effective policy making... . For the proponents of functional representation in modern times, this contribution is especially 'knowledge'.

A particularly significant example of this was apparent in the way the Government wished to use the accountancy profession not simply as guard dogs but as bloodhounds and retrievers for the Bank of England when checking the books of banks and other financial institutions in their audit. The Government originally settled for a non-statutory scheme whereby the profession would inform the Bank of England of any irregularities. This would take the profession outside its usual 'confidential' relationship with its clients. It was notable that contemporaneously the profession sought legislative immunity from negligence suits in respect of its members' auditing of books.[19] The collapse of the BCCI bank produced dramatic evidence of the breakdown of audit, a lack of adequate information for regulators and a failure to learn from past lessons.[20] The duties are now contained in the Financial Services and Markets Act 2000, ss 341-346.

The Government's action was originally prompted by the collapse of a merchant bank and the initiation of new financial markets after the relaxation of restrictive practices in the Stock Exchange and elsewhere.[1] The British Bankers' Association remonstrated with the Government, pointing out that it was wrong for the Bank of England to pass on information it received to government departments other than the Treasury. 'Customers are entitled to expect their affairs to be kept secret

---

19 See note 3 p 219 above.
20 See the report of Sir Thomas Bingham HC 198 (1992-3) into the BCCI affair.
1   See, inter alia, Financial Services Act 1986 (now Financial Services and Markets Act 2000) and Building Societies Act 1986.

unless there are cogent reasons to the contrary.'[2] Similar protestations were uttered by the City's support for Government proposals to limit the amount of information that has to be given on a shareholders' or members' register.[3] These are documents which are difficult to obtain and invariably obscure.[4] The registrar, usually a clearing bank, is inevitably reluctant to allow even cursory glances at the register without a reference to the secretary of the company in question. Certainly requests to take notes or subject the information to detailed scrutiny would have to be accompanied by detailed reasons in writing. The law merely requires a fee, which is discretionary, and 10 days' notice. One request about British Telecom revealed that 28% of share capital was held by unnamed corporate bodies.[5] A Department of Trade and Industry paper has suggested the end of annual returns to Companies House, and only those shareholders with more than 1% of share capital should have to register.[6] Non-statutory bodies frequently distribute information on behalf of the government. A typical example was the non-statutory training and enterprise councils which are established by industries and which disseminated information on training schemes and reported on various activities, often in close alliance with government departments and local authorities. These have been particularly secretive in their practices and refused to hand over information to the Nolan Committee when requested.[7] Conversely, the Director-General of Telecommunications has a duty to encourage the preparation of codes by associations to help safeguard customers' information.

Nirex, which will not be covered by FOIA, is a private body responsible for advising the nuclear power industry on the disposal of nuclear waste has produced a very detailed code on access to information and also a panel to deal with disputes where there is a refusal to allow access for reasons usually of public interest or commercial confidentiality. It seems a remarkably well developed scheme.

Several important developments have either been undertaken or are promised and in the pipeline in addition to FOIA. First of all, Lord Nolan made some important recommendations to counter abuse of ministerial patronage in the appointment of political supporters to quangos. Ministers

2   *The Guardian*, 14 February 1986 and see DPR reports and the Jack Report Cm 622 (1989) and the 'Good Banking' Code of Practice: see DPR Annual Report 1994, p 19. For the duty of confidentiality owed by a bank to a client, see chapter 10 below, note 13 p 461.
3   Companies Act 1985, ss 352–62 and regulations; and nb ss 198–219 and regulations and Companies Act 1989 Part IV and ss 125-7, 134, 143 and Schs 3-8 inclusive.
4   Registers are usually kept in a clearing bank.
5   *The Guardian*, 14 February 1987.
6   See Part XXIII Financial Services and Markets Act 2000.
7   *The Guardian*, 30 September 1995.

would retain power of appointment—although many bodies being purely private would fall outside that degree of ministerial patronage—and public appointments would be governed by the overriding principle of merit and balanced representation. Selection should be made from a number of skills and backgrounds and criteria should be made explicit. All appointments to NDPBs and NHS bodies should be made after taking advice from a panel which includes an independent element—amounting to about a third of its membership. A Commissioner for Public Appointments has been appointed who may be one of the Civil Service Commissioners. Departmental appointments procedures would be monitored and regulated by the Commissioner. The Commissioner would publish an annual report and the Public Appointments Unit would come under the Commissioner's control and not the Cabinet Office. All secretaries of state would have to report annually on public appointments made by their departments and candidates would have to declare 'significant political activity' in the previous five years—but what about political contributions?—and the Commissioner would draw up a code (in fact guidance) for the operation of relevant procedures and reasons for departure from the Code on the grounds of 'proportionality' should be documented and capable of review. The government should after a review seek to produce a more consistent legal framework governing propriety and accountability in public bodies. A code of conduct for members of public bodies and their staff should be mandatory and compliance should be a condition of appointment. The role of NDPB and NHS accounting officers should emphasise formal responsibility for all aspects of propriety. The Audit Commission should be authorised to publish public interest reports on NHS bodies at its own discretion. A member of the board of the NHS executive body should act as a complaints officer for internal complaints from staff raised confidentially and outside the usual management structure. Anonymity should be guaranteed.[8] Others have suggested a role for select committees in approving appointments.

In 1998, the Commissioner's remit was extended to cover nationalised industries, public corporations, utility regulators and advisory NDPBs, although the procedures would not be applied with full rigour in the case of the latter because many of the positions are unpaid. The remit does not extend to task forces (see ch 4). Lord Neill examined the operation of the Commissioner and task forces in his report in 2000 and found a concern over 'disproportionality' in the way the procedures worked in the case of non-remunerated appointments and posed the question whether 'expert' positions should be occupied by reference to criteria that might not concentrate on competition, balance and fairness.

---

8   See the former Public Service Committee: HC 168 (1995-6).

Codes on openness were recommended for NDPBs and in April 1995 a code on openness was produced for the NHS. This builds on the progress made by the Patient's Charter and applies to health authorities, NHS trusts, the Mental Health Act Commission and community health councils. It also covers family doctors and dentists *inter alios*. The NHS must respond positively to requests for information and the code[9] seeks to ensure that people have access to available information about the services provided by the NHS, its cost, quality and performance against targets; that they are provided with explanations about proposed service changes and have an opportunity to influence such changes; are aware of the reasons for decisions and actions affecting their own treatment; know what information is available and where to get it. This is all very welcome; rather than trawl through the provisions in detail, other than saying that procedures must be established for dealing with requests and charging should be 'exceptional' the code has been criticised by an authoritative source on four major grounds. Firstly, in case of commercial or contractual activities the NHS allows information to be withheld where disclosure could, not *would* as in the central government code, 'prejudice such activities'. Secondly the code appears to have no retrospective application and applies only to information held after 1 June 1995. Thirdly, the public interest override in the government code has no application here, so it appears. Fourthly, the NHS ombudsman will police the code. The two codes may apply to the same complaint and may be undertaken by the Commissioner in two separate guises.[10]

FOIA and the Data Protection Act 1998 will provide a more uniform basis for access and will replace the codes and various promises for statutory reform which had not been met. One area where laws were passed was in relation to the environment. This followed an EC Directive.[11] As will be seen in chapter 6, the Aarhus Convention will have to be implemented into UK law and will govern access to environmental information and participation in decision making and not FOIA.

The regulations implementing the directive allow public access to environmental information held by a large number of environmental agencies although the advent of the Environment Agency (and the Scottish EA) will help rationalisation.[12] A presumptive right of access

9   *Code of Practice on Openness in the NHS* NHS Executive Body (1995).
10 As Parliamentary and Health Commissioners. The NHS Ombudsman has had his jurisdiction extended and has been given greater powers to disclose information: Health Service Commissioners (Amendment) Act 1996.
11 90/313/EEC; SI 1992/3240 and SI 1998/1447.
12 See previous note. No specific enforcement procedures are provided other than the courts. The Government in the White Paper on *Open Government* did suggest an enforcement agency or body not unlike the Data Protection Registrar for safety information and its provision. As FOIA does not apply to this area, the enforcement mechanisms under FOIA will not appear to be available. See Environment Act 1995, s 113. The EA is under FOIA.

with a broad range of exemptions is included and covers information held about the quality of the environment, polluting activities or administrative and other measures to protect the environment. Confidential information is given a wide exemption. It includes that which may be treated as such, including commercially confidential information and that which must be treated as such, including that supplied by a person who was not under an obligation to supply it and the person holding the information was not under a duty to provide it to the public apart from the provisions in the regulations and the supplier has not consented to its being disclosed. It also gives mandatory protection to information which is subject to a 'secrecy agreement'.[13]

The regulations also advert to provisions to supply information under other legal provisions the most important of which are under the Environmental Protection Act 1990, the Water Act 1989 as amended and the Environment Act 1995. The former provides for registers and where pollution is regulated an authorisation must be obtained by the polluter. The register will contain and will disclose to the public applications for authorisations to release pollution, the authorisation itself, results of pollution monitoring and enforcement action taken. Information may be withheld where it relates to national security and commercial confidentiality although the authority must place on the register a statement specifying whether or not there has been compliance with any relevant condition of the authorisation. In the original Bill the disclosure provisions were limited but these were extended in the Bill's passage and commercially confidential information was originally to be exempted indefinitely. The period of exemption lasts for four years subject to renewal, and provision of a register for public nuisances was rejected. Applications to discharge must be accompanied by information on environmental impact and proposals for monitoring. The public are not in a favourable position when it comes to applications for discharge consent, or variation of conditions, and have to rely upon notice in press announcements. Notice and comment provisions apply and appeal hearings following a refusal may be public with those making comments invited to attend. These follow an inquiry process although it is hoped that informality will apply in the procedure. The procedure will be determined by the inspector and participation of third parties is at the inspector's discretion subject to the principles of fair procedure/natural justice.[14]

---

13 In the USA legislation covers access to information about and precautions concerning hazardous substances: Emergency Planning and Community Right to Know Act 1986. The Toxics Release Inventory requires 30,000 manufacturers to reveal to the public information about routine emissions of about 350 toxic chemicals into the land, air or water. This is in addition to the FOIA laws: see chapter 2.

14 See Birkinshaw in E Lykke *Achieving Environmental Goals* (1992).

Registers relating to water pollution[15] are maintained by the Environment Agency (EA) under the Water Act 1989. The Water Supply Regulations 1989[16] require water undertakers to maintain records relating to the quality of water in their supply zones and to make this available free of charge to the public. The EA is advised by an advisory committee for each regional undertaker—to which nothing like FACA will apply— although advisory committees will be subject to Nolan's recommendations and will be subject to FOIA provisions. The committee represents the views of consumers but its meetings may exclude the public and press following a resolution under the Public Bodies (Admission to Meetings) Act 1960.[17] Meetings of the EA and regional water boards are not legally required to be open to the public. The corporate plans of the regional offices of the former National Rivers Authority which were sent to the national board were not published except in summary form, in spite of the fact that they contained environmental and public health improvement notices. The EA is now covered by FOIA. There is also often a considerable delay between a pollution event and publication of relevant information. While companies are under a duty to inform the local authority of a polluting event they are not so obliged to inform the public. And so on.[18] Use of registers and general provisions relating to them seemed far from adequate with minimal use of computers to extract worthwhile information. The Director-General of Water Services also maintains a register open to the public. The public may also participate in the making of water quality objectives by a process of notice and comment.[19] One should observe, however, the large number of different registers available at different locations.

Two further points are relevant. While there have been major developments in local government and consultation exercises, a People's Panel has been established comprising 5,000 members to advise on public services across the spectrum. Located in the Cabinet Office, it was established after advice and professional support from the marketing company MORI.[20] Secondly, a Code of Practice on written consultation has been produced by the Cabinet Office. A register of the 'main' written current consultations will be produced on the internet (UKOnline.gov.uk) The code seeks to safeguard those without access to the internet – it does not say how – and builds on good practice. Particularly interesting are a requirement for proper feedback from government after consultation including an explanation of why particular options were, or were not,

15 SI 1989/1160.
16 SI 1991/3699.
17 On a very indulgent judicial interpretation of this Act see *R v Liverpool City Council, ex p Liverpool Taxi Fleet Opreators' Association* [1975] 1 All ER 379.
18 Burton (1989) Journal of Environmental Law 192.
19 Water Act 1989, s 106.
20 *People's Panel* Cabinet Office, Issues 1-8 (1998-2001) ongoing.

favoured. There is also a requirement for departments to establish 'machinery' to police compliance. This is not quite the American 'hard-look' doctrine but it is welcome. It will be evaluated after two years.[1]

Local government

Local government is local, elected and increasingly under statutory obligations to be open to the public and the press.[2] Where central government gives information, it has invariably done so as an act of grace and favour or instrumental necessity; even the Code on Access is a code not law. The FOIA breaks with this tradition. In the world of quasi-government, there is no elected representation, no public voting and no political accountability, and very rarely are there duties to inform the public in even the most exiguous of terms of what is being carried out on the public behalf. The recommendations of the Nolan Committee have been described. It is worthwhile noting these points when we consider the range of non-departmental bodies the government has created, and the close links it has attempted to forge with organised interests, usually of a commercial, financial or engineering nature, to rejuvenate the economic infrastructure; to ensure responsibility for education programmes; to exploit the removal of planning restrictions, and eg, to administer housing schemes and even schools. Democratic involvement has not been a notable feature, and indeed the democratic nature of local government has been a reason for that tier of government being excluded from governmental responsibilities if it will not operate as a business manager. As one chief executive expressed it: 'We are being pressed to become like commercial organisations, yet what commercial organisations are being pressed to become as open as local authorities?' The PPPs which have been very extensive throughout local government have not been a beacon of openness.

Local government will not disappear. New forms under regional control may well develop.[3] In our constitutional design it poses very particular problems of openness and information. Its record, as we saw in chapters 3 and 4, is mixed. The new executive arrangements were introduced to redress some of the excesses of one party political domination and secrecy in local government. We should not assume that all senior officers and leading members of local government are advocates of open government. A chief executive expressed the quintessential conflict between serious open political debate and public access to meetings as follows:

1 *Code of Practice on Written Consultation* Cabinet Office Nov 2000. It does not cover oral consultations.
2 See chapters 3 and 4 above.
3 See Regional Development Act 1998. In England these were largely under central government initiatives involving departments operating regionally.

I have serious reservations about the current craze for so called 'open government'. It is my considered opinion, and I believe it is the opinion of many of my colleagues, that the quality of debate and the quality of decision-making in local authority committees has fallen very very considerably ever since, with the coming into operation of the Local Government Act 1972, the press and public have been admitted to committees. There is no doubt whatsoever that not only do members play to the gallery and spend far more time scoring cheap political points off each other than ever they did before, but perhaps even more importantly officers are reluctant now to come out with ideas and to enter debate with the same freedom that they were prepared to do when the committee was closed, and there was no risk of seeing a headline in the local paper 'Chief Executive Clashes with Opposition Leader etc.' I also believe it is true to say that as a result of this so-called open government, far more decisions are now in fact taken in private than ever was the case before.

This raises the question of the cost of freedom of information legislation, which was alluded to in chapter 1. The quality of decision-making falls as rational input from professional officials declines and politicians engage increasingly in point-scoring and being seen to be effective by sectional interests whom they represent, rather than by the community as a whole. The chief executive quoted above described a climate which was not conducive to the giving of advice in public with commitment and candour. Decisions were becoming less influenced by professionals and were far more frequently the result of informal agreement between political heavy-weights in group meetings. As a consequence, the quality of decisions had dropped enormously. This was the price of openness. There was less real or meaningful debate of the underlying issues, interests and implications in decisions. The views of the chief executive deserve respect. In other words, efficiency was deleteriously affected. It is well to remember, however, that in the period before committees were opened to the public there were widespread examples of corruption in local government, and countless examples of arbitrary decisions riding rough-shod over local views where secrecy assisted unresponsive government. In the 1990s, well-catalogued dramas and auditors' inquiries in local government have highlighted egregious abuse of local power;[4] the Government directed Nolan into the area of local government—to deflect

---

4   The events surrounding Dame Shirley Porter and the case of Westminster City Council and the ruling group's use of public housing stock for gerrymandering purposes according to the auditor's report: see *Porter v Magill* [2000] 2 WLR 1420.

criticism from itself some observers have suggested.[5] The present Government announced with its Local Government Act 1999 a new era of cooperation with local government, especially in terms of financing local government. Cooperation was needed to fulfil its ambitious plans for linked-up government in service provision.[6]

There are numerous and important statutory duties imposed on authorities to provide information to central government, the Audit Commission, the Local Government Ombudsman, members of authorities and the public.[7] The new arrangements for an authority for London repeat many of the general provisions that we have seen as well as providing for some statutory innovations such as the mayor's annual report, the annual state of London debate and a People's Question Time, the PPP arbiter and his powers to require information from any party to a PPP, public participation in the 'spatial development strategy', the mayor's environment report and numerous provisions. The Local Government Act 1992, now amended by the Audit Commission Act 1998, requires publication of information as to standards of service by authorities under the direction of the Audit Commission so that comparison may be made between different authorities and between different years. The information is open to public inspection by local electors. Auditors' reports under these provisions must be considered at a public meeting from which the public may be excluded under the terms of the 1985 Local Government (Access to Information) Act. The Audit Commission is given wide powers to publicise relevant matters including contravention of the duty to collect and publicise information. These of course flow from the Citizen's Charter but similar legal duties do not affect central government.[8] Such provisions are unlikely to generate much public feedback.

The Local Government Act 1999, which introduced 'Best value' in the provision of public service in local government, envisaged widespread local consultation with local communities in establishing 'best value'. New executive arrangements will follow consultations and voting by affected communities (see chapter 4). Detailed guidance on best consultation practices has been produced by the Government for local authorities to follow when consulting.[9] One chief executive put the point eloquently in expressing his frustration at the lack of public feedback:

---

5   See the Nolan Committee on local government: Cm 3702 I&II (1997).
6   See *Modernising Government* Cm 4310 (1999).
7   See chapter 4 of Birkinshaw *Government and Information: the Law Relating to Access, Disclosure and their Regulation* (2001).
8   The provisions which do apply here are internal and administrative.
9   DETR *Guidance on Enhancing Public Participation in Local Government* (1998); V Lowndes and N Rao *Enhancing Public Participation in Local Government* (2000).

I think we are all a bit cynical of the worth of the information in terms of public consumption. I would dearly love to receive searching questions from the public about information contained in our annual report ... but in the three years we have been publishing a report I have received no feedback from the public whatsoever.

In the past, criticism was made that central government was simply picking on an easy target in the public sector and one it disliked. There had been no real effort to sort out what the public wants to know; no real attempt to break down unresponsive bureaucracy where it exists in local government. It was, in short, political buck-passing. If the intention to open up government had been serious, then more work should have been carried out to test the market, by the authorities concerned and by independent assessors. The comments on previous legislation from chief executives are pertinent for any subsequent FOIA involving central government:

There are scant minimum requirements for disclosure of information by encouragement or discouragement. For the most part the problem is about interpretation, practice, attitudes or defensiveness on the part of councillors as well as officials. Few local authorities have systematically set out to research the market to test the demand for more information, or its quality. [As] far as I know none has really taken a conscious decision to aim information at the broadest group of people, and to employ all available skills and resources to that end in the way that a newspaper does, or TV or radio do. In many areas where there are ethnic minorities, the problems of communication are particularly acute. Legislation is largely irrelevant. Will and attitude are far more important.

Has central government avoided these mistakes in establishing new regimes for local government and for itself?

There were numerous examples of open practices and provision of information in local government irrespective of statutory or common law duties.[10] There were community forums, citizen juries, user groups and the like for services and facilities, advisory panels, opinion polls, referenda, local hearings. Community and parish councils were given a fillip. To these were added a myriad of statutory duties to consult, allow participation, allow appeals and provide information in housing, planning, education, social services. Hardly an area of local government activity was untouched by specific legislation. All were covered by general

10   See 2nd ed of this book at p 242 et seq.

provisions that we have examined. One was left with the distinct impression that while so much of the legislation was welcome, its success in creating greater openness depended upon will and official attitude – creating the right culture and ethos. Where these were lacking, the legislation could be used as a bureaucratic barrier by concentration on technicalities, formal provisions and strict compliance with the letter of the law.

Beyond the scope of duty

We examined the effects of the Local Government (Access to Information) Act 1985 in the previous chapter. Some authorities had gone further than the provisions of the Act and are still more open than the Act enjoins. Some of this is due to the influence of the Citizen's Charter and the *Better Government* initiative. But much of it predates the Charter. The Association of London Authorities has asserted that decisions based on inadequate reasoning or information must be open to scrutiny and challenge and has insisted that greater openness enhances equality of opportunity by paving the way for greater public participation, particularly for those who have historically suffered discrimination.[11] Members of the public, it continues, should have internal rights of appeal where information is refused; the public should be allowed to ask questions at council meetings and make deputations to the council, and the timing and location of meetings should take account of the needs of all sections of the community, particularly those disadvantaged because of special needs. Personal manual files should be available, as are computer files, although here events have been partly overtaken by the Data Protection Act 1998 which we examine in chapter 7. Authorities should have a complaints procedure for any grievance raised by a member of the public which should include a right of appeal to a body with a preponderant councillor component. Information on the local government ombudsman, the Data Protection Commissioner and Tribunal (see chapter 7) should be readily available and well publicised. As well as urging the use of plain language the Association enjoins all members and chief officers to complete a comprehensive declaration of interests from which authorities will compile a public register of interests. Some boroughs and authorities require declarations of pecuniary and personal interests beyond legal requirements. In the case of committees, refusal to comply means members will not be appointed to sit on committees. This had led to litigation where the stipulation was held *intra vires*.[12] However, such 'superrerogatory'

11 *Charter for Open Government* ALA (1996).
12 *R v Newham London Borough Council, ex p Haggerty* (1986) 85 LGR 48. This decision was reversed by legislation.

requirements were themselves forbidden by s 19(5) of the Local Government and Housing Act 1989. Elsewhere, authorities have established methods to review performance in service areas, to gauge satisfaction or otherwise and to improve performance, an exercise which is based on being fully informed of what is happening in a service area.[13]

A National Code of Local Government Conduct was revised in 1990 following the Local Government and Housing Act and deals, *inter alia,* with the disclosure of pecuniary and other interests.[14] A power to issue a new code on conduct was conferred on the Secretary of State under s 50 Local Government Act 2000. A draft Code for consultation was issued in February 2001.[15] This deals in its draft form with general principles, scope of the Code, general obligations, declarations of interests, registers of interests, gifts and hospitality and dispensations. The appendix deals with the categories of financial interests to be registered. Principles governing the conduct of local government members may be specified by order under s 49. These build on the general Nolan principles and the 1990 Code and were developed in a 1998 White Paper and a consultation document issued in July 2000.[16] Authorities will have to produce their own codes of conduct which are to be available for inspection. Authorities must also establish Standards Committees to promote high standards of conduct by members and co-opted members. A Standards Board is established for England to promote and maintain high standards of conduct and to refer cases to ethical standards officers for investigation. There are detailed provisions on investigations and reports. Cases may be referred to an Adjudications' Panel. In Wales, the functions of the Standards Board are performed by the Local Ombudsman and there is a Welsh Adjudications Panel.

The law provides for the disclosure of pecuniary interests by members—the 1990 Code seeks to cover other interests which may interfere or conflict with a councillor's public duties. Rule 6 says: 'As a councillor you necessarily acquire much information that has not yet been made public and is still confidential. It is a grave betrayal of trust to use confidential information for the personal advantage of yourself or anyone you know.' Breach of the Code could constitute maladministration.[17] Section 19 of the Local Government and Housing Act 1989 introduced a compulsory register for members' pecuniary interests but not other

13 See Audit Commission *Charting a Course* (1993).
14 DoE 8/90; Welsh Office 23/90. On an authority's powers to discipline members under ss 101 and 111 LGA 1972, see *R v Broadland District Council, ex p Lashley* (2000) 2 LGLR 933, (2001) Times, 20 March.
15 *A Model Code of Conduct for Members* DETR 2001.
16 Cm 4014 (1998) and *General Principles of Conduct in Local Government* (2000, DETR)
17 And see Cmnd 5636 and Cmnd 6524.

interests.[18] The draft 2001 Code seeks to widen this. Section 19 has now been replaced by s 81 of the 2000 Act and s 82 empowers the Secretary of State to issue by order a code for local government employees. The power to surcharge those responsible for unlawful expenditure or for failing to bring an item of expenditure into account has been repealed following the Nolan recommendations on local government.

So much preceded and survives FOIA 2000. That Act must now be examined.

---

18 Reversing *Haggerty* note 12 above. The draft 2001 Code states that Ministers believe that members should declare membership of freemasons and 'similar organisations': para 5.6. This will be contentious.

6 The Freedom of Information Act 2000

On 30 November 2000, the Freedom of Information Bill was given Royal Assent to become the Freedom of Information Act 2000 (FOIA). The Bill had been before Parliament for over a year. Prior to that the White Paper on Access to Information and then a draft bill and consultation paper had been scrutinised by the Select Committee on Public Administration in the Commons as well as, in the case of the latter, by a special committee of the House of Lords.[1] Since 1974, and throughout the long years of opposition, the Labour Party had supported numerous Freedom of Information bills.[2] These would have created a right for an Information Commissioner to enforce the disclosure of information and would also have amended the Official Secrets Act along the lines suggested in chapter 3.

Reluctant support was given to a Private Member's bill in 1979 by Prime Minister Callaghan immediately before the loss of office to Mrs Thatcher. Neil Kinnock stated in 1992 that a FOI Bill would be among the first Bills of an incoming Labour Government. For Tony Blair freedom of information legislation (FOI) was essential to bring about a culture change in British government. It would be a signal of a 'new relationship' between the people and government. 'This fundamental and vital change

---

1 For the Commons Committee: HC 398-I and II (1997-98), HC 570-I and II (1998-99)and HC 78 (1999-00); for the House of Lords special committee of the House of Lords: HL 97 (1998-99); the proposals had also been before the Lords Deregulation Committee to consider powers delegated under the Bill: HL 79 (1998-99).

2 See chapter Eight of the second edition of this work and also P Birkinshaw and A Parkin 'Freedom of Information' in R Blackburn and R Plant eds *Constitutional Reform: The Labour Government's Constitutional Reform Agenda* (1999) chapter 8.

in the relationship between government and governed'[3] would be at the heart of his reforms on access to information. The new government was over two years into power before a FOI Bill was published; its publication had been subject to numerous delays — in spite of the fact that many western democratic states had models which could act as inspiration for the British model. A wealth of experience had been acquired on FOI regimes overseas.

There was a prevailing sense of disappointment, indeed outrage, on the publication of this Bill in May 1999. Why should this be so? Generally, there was a widespread and pervasive sense that underlying the provision of a right to information held by public bodies, the Bill was characterised by numerous devices whose deliberate objective was the maintenance of secrecy. After two years in power the initial declarations of building a new constitution fit for a new millennium had been tempered by caution, even defensiveness. The government had suffered embarrassing leaks and publications of sensitive information.[4] More particularly, the Bill, which was part of a consultation package, was seen as a wholesale abandonment of the liberal principles contained in the White Paper (WP) on *Your Right to Know*[5] which was published along with an enthusiastic endorsement by the Prime Minister in December 1997.[6] The WP was widely acclaimed for offering a completely new vista on how government should be run in the future, turning its back on unnecessary secrecy in British public life: the WP would introduce a legal right of access to information across the public sector, a sector which was to be broadly defined. 'This will be a radical change in the relationship between citizens and their government' it proclaimed. Too radical, it seems, for the minister responsible for the WP was sacked in the Cabinet reshuffle in July 1998 after press revelations of his being humbled by senior ministers and responsibility for the Bill was handed to the Home Office, never a ministry to experiment with radical innovation in Government.[7]

3   *Your Right to Know: Freedom of Information Cm* 3818 (1997), *Preface* by the Prime Minister.
4   These included the Ecclestone affair; events surrounding publicity for the arrest of Jack Straw's son; the McPherson report on the death of Stephen Lawrence Cm 4262 I and II (1999) published in Scotland by the press before official publication and then the discovery that addresses of witnesses had wrongly been published; press publication of Cabinet minutes of the Dome project, the press story about Mandelson and the Hinduja brothers' passports and so on.
5   Note 3.
6   See above.
7   The Home Office headed a league table of departments in which inquiries into leaks were conducted. It headed the list with 9, followed by the Department of Health and Northern Ireland Office with 7, Ministry of Defence 5, Cabinet Office 4 and the Scottish Office with 1: *The Guardian* 14 February 2000.

The WP promised that there would be a legally enforceable right to information, which included documents,[8] held by public bodies. In particular, the WP stated that in all but one area - policy formulation - the test for withholding information would be where its disclosure would cause 'substantial harm' — a more demanding test than any other FOI statute. The Information Commissioner (IC) would have power to decide on where the greater public interest lay — in publication or in withholding information. The Commissioner's decisions would be enforced through the courts. There would be no ministerial override to prevent disclosure. Exempting interests would number seven and not 15 as under the 1994 Code of John Major (see chapter 5). While almost universally acclaimed, the WP had possessed some problems at its core. The relationship between access to personal documents and to other official documents was not clearly thought through. The subject of access to personal records under FOIA and other provisions is taken up in chapter 7. In the case of personal documents the law would have to conform with the provisions of the EU Directive on data protection, implemented by the Data Protection Act 1998.[9]

Several areas of information were excluded from the Bill – meaning the proposed law would have no application whatsoever to those items of information. These included the security and intelligence services and also functions relating to the investigation, prosecution or prevention of crime or the bringing of civil or criminal proceedings by public authorities. Public authorities would be excluded from provisions allowing access to their personnel records by employees. Legal advice and that protected by legal professional privilege were to be excluded.[10]

As well as these difficulties which were criticised by the advocates of open government, there were criticisms of a different persuasion. It was also felt by some that the tone of the WP was hopelessly optimistic especially for instance in setting the damage test as one of 'substantial harm' and that not enough was present to prevent administrative over-load, especially given the wide range of bodies covered by the WP many of whom would have no expertise in dealing with access to information claims.[11] This is a wonderful White Paper, opined one eminent Australian judge, but, he added, it won't see its way into law! The WP also had its detractors in influential circles among the senior ranks of the civil service although others were supportive.

8   The 1994 Code only covers information not documents although the Ombudsman has suggested that the easiest manner in which to comply with the Code may well be by supplying documents.

9   EC Council Directive 95/46 ([1995] OJ L281/31). See chapter 7.

10   The report of the Commons Select Committee on Public Administration on the WP is HC 398 I&II (1997/98).

11   See the evidence of Professor Hazell to the Select Committee HC 570— v (1998/99) Q.485.

The Bill and its contents

It is necessary to describe the draft bill and its Parliamentary amendments to give an understanding of how the Government altered its position of almost a quarter of a century and in order to assess why it was so heavily criticised. The bill, which also deals with amendments to the public records legislation, makes information held by public authorities available as a legal right unless it is exempt or otherwise access is qualified, or where the public authority is excluded from the bill's provisions, ie it is not named in the schedule. Authorities must respond 'promptly' to requests, which have to be in writing, and in any event within 40 days, although this was subsequently reduced as we shall see.[12] There is no undertaking to produce indexes of information held by authorities, a reform introduced in 1996 in the USA (see chapter 8). The law relating to EU documents allows for the establishment of a register (see chapter eight). Full indexes would help the task of requesters enormously. They would assist them to establish what documents they wished to see.

Public authorities

The bill and the Act, following the WP, cover an extremely wide range of public and private bodies making it unique in the world FOI landscape. A very large corpus of non-departmental public bodies and advisory bodies is included in Sch 1 of the FOIA. It includes the ombudsmen and the Information Commissioner. It covers all government departments, the House of Commons and House of Lords (unlike the USA where Congress is not included), the Northern Ireland and Welsh Assemblies and the armed forces of the Crown.[13] In brief it covers local government, although the relationship between existing and new local government provisions was never thought through (see chapters 4 and 5), the NHS, educational bodies funded by the state including universities, the police including British Transport and Ministry of Defence police. The Act provides that bodies created by the Royal prerogative or enactment or by ministerial fiat or by a government department or the Welsh Assembly and whose members are appointed by the Crown, a minister, a government department or the Welsh Assembly may be included.[14] The minister may designate private

---

12 The period in the 1994 Code is 20 days for 'simple requests'. The forty day period was a cause of complaint by many. Reforms in 1996 in the USA to its FOIA have set a time limit of 10 days to respond to expedited requests in two subject areas.

13 But not the special forces or those assisting GCHQ; see chapter 1.

14 They do not have to be scheduled. Could the IC presume they were public authorities?

bodies as public bodies for the purposes of the Bill where they are performing public functions as well as bodies under contract with public authorities to deliver public services. In the case of the former, privatised utilities spring to mind although not all their functions are public. It covers 'publicly owned companies'[15]. Public authorities may be listed as bodies to which the Act has limited application. It will not apply to non-public affairs. This was of particular concern to privatised industries. Bodies not included in the schedule or which are not designated or otherwise covered are excluded: eg the Cabinet secretariat, the Cabinet. The Bank of England is scheduled but not in relation to monetary policy, financial operations supporting financial institutions to maintain stability and the provision of private banking and related services.

Because of this breadth of coverage, the Bill's provisions do not have to be implemented for five years in order to allow those bodies who have no expertise in access requests to acquire that expertise. Central government would be brought under the Act within eighteen months – they had been used to operating under the Code on Access. Provisions on access to personal documents would be effective from October 2001. In March 2001, it was reported that the Act would not come into effect in relation to Government departments until at least July 2002 because many files were missing or unlocated.[16] But this date would only cover publication schemes; rights of individual access would come later.

Publication schemes

Authorities will have to draw up publication schemes detailing the information that they will publish and the manner in which it will be published and whether it is available free of charge or for a fee. The scheme may be published in such manner as the authority thinks fit. Schemes are to be approved by the Commissioner who may produce model schemes. While these give significant powers of influence to the Commissioner, she is not given any power to compel the inclusion of specific items. She may simply refuse to approve the scheme or she may revoke approval given – with notice and reasons. The publication schemes could be of enormous value if, for instance, they published information about internal manuals, guidelines, rules and procedures which are used to determine individual cases. In the USA, information requested on two previous occasions is automatically published under mandatory provisions as is that for which there is likely to be a substantial demand. It was envisaged at an early stage that information about government decisions and the

15 Sections 3(1)(b) and 6.
16 *The Guardian* 7 March 2001.

facts and analysis behind them would be made available under such schemes. Schemes could usefully include information about government contracts (contract price, unit prices, performance targets) or returns to a consultation document and information about specific contracts. The public interest in making information available would have to be considered by authorities as well as a general provision on giving reasons for decisions. Originally, it was envisaged that the IC could award a practice recommendation against an authority that was not complying with its scheme but this now appears unlikely as such recommendations are linked to matters covered in a code of practice and the draft code says practically nothing about schemes. An enforcement notice may be served by the IC to ensure compliance by an authority with a scheme (see below).

Public interest disclosures and exemptions

The clause dealing with public interest disclosures where an exemption applies was originally cl 14. This provision was subject to considerable amendment as it progressed through Parliament. It was a barometer of the changing nature of the Bill: was it becoming a true measure of openness with ultimate power in the Commissioner, or was it yet a further grace and favour measure under the ultimate control of the executive? The end result is a mixture of both of these positions. Although in the original bill authorities have to have regard to the public interest when exercising this discretion (see below), the decision on disclosure was *their* decision and there was no public interest override in the bill enforceable by the Commissioner. This was considered to be a substantial compromise of the spirit of the WP. In the case of a minister, s/he can account to Parliament for a refusal to disclose. For public bodies not headed by a Minister, this option was not available. The bill was subsequently amended to allow the Commissioner to order the disclosure of information but this was subject to what amounts to a veto power in various parties to stop disclosure. The veto power which the WP rejected was therefore resurrected in various respects (see below).

But this failure to give the Commissioner final power of decision in public interest disclosures was just one of numerous alleged compromises contained in the bill. It has to be said, however, that several of the excluded categories were brought in as exemptions. First of all the number of exemptions has grown from seven in the WP to over 30. In the final bill as enacted it amounts to 23.[17] The test for withholding information in those

17 This does not include sub-divisions of exemptions within sections. Excluding retrospective exemptions, the Campaign for Freedom of Information numbered all of them at 31: *FOI Briefing* 20 April 2000.

areas where a contents exemption applied is where disclosure 'prejudices' or 'is likely to prejudice' one of a number of identified interests. The qualifying use of 'substantial' has gone. Many exemptions are class based, ie they do not have to be justified by a claim of prejudice or any other form of harm although most of these are still subject to the discretionary test of public interest disclosure.[18] However, as well as these exemptions, and the exclusion of those bodies not listed in the Schedule,[19] there are also eight exemptions which are 'absolute'. There is, in other words no discretion to allow a public interest disclosure by the authority and the Commissioner cannot order (even though subject to the veto) disclosure. I deal with these below.

Some of the exemptions are outrageously broad, eg those covering policy advice and policy formulation and criminal and civil investigations and commercial interests. These clauses were again subject to considerable amendment as we shall see. Authorities are given widespread powers allowing them not to be covered by (excluded from) the duty to confirm or deny the existence of documents under section 1 covering numerous exemptions.[20] In other words, they are allowed not only to deny access but to play the deadest of bats in response to a request. The response of the 'inscrutable face of the Sphinx'!

Novel features

But the novel developments, not only in terms of withdrawal from the spirit of the WP but also from any known FOI regime, included the fact that requesters could be asked why they want the information and would

---

18 Those which are not so subject include security service etc information, court records and information relating to legal proceedings as well as, arguably, national security information when correctly certified. The Act does not apply to courts. The contents/class basis of withholding information resembles the position in public interest immunity although following the Iraqi supergun report (the Scott Report) the Government undertook not to make class claims and this was supported by the incoming Labour Government: HC Debs Vol 287 col 949 and HL Debs Vol 576 col 1507 (Dec 18, 1996) and HC Debs Vol 297 col 616 (July 11, 1997). It had been held that police may make such claims in certain cases: *Taylor v Anderton (Police Complaints Authority Intervening)* [1995] 2 All ER 420 distinguishing *R v Chief Constable of the West Midlands Police, ex p Wiley* [1994] 3 All ER 420, HL.

19 Ie the Security and Intelligence Services, the Cabinet, the Bank of England, Nirex and bodies which are private in form and not within FOIA ss 4-6 and so on.

20 In the USA, this is restricted to intelligence and law enforcement information: Exec Order No 12,958 s 1.8(e) and 5 USC s 552 b (7) especially (C). Aspects of criminal law investigations may be excluded totally from the USFOIA: 5 USC s 52(c)(1), (c)(2) and (c)(3).

have allowed the authorities to have placed restrictions on its use.[1] This is unique and remarkable and comes close to making the provisions a discretionary 'need to know' regime, not one built on a 'right to know'. Furthermore, the Home Secretary was given power to add to exemptions retrospectively — surely another example of a *de lege* veto power which the WP had rejected? Clause 37 of the draft bill is another remarkable — a word easily used and not an exaggeration in the context of this bill — provision which allows the authority to deny access to information where that information when pieced together with other information, which may not even be disclosable under the bill or otherwise, could make the information as a package fall within one of numerous exemptions.[2] This provision known as the 'jigsaw' provision has its provenance in the USA where the courts developed the possibility of a 'mosaic' basis to deny access initially to security and intelligence information. It was extended by administrative *fiat* in 1986 to law enforcement information although whether this would be successfully invoked has never been tested in the courts.[3] In other words its use in the States has been strictly confined and is subject to judicial control. After searing criticism from the Commons Select Committee and from the Lords' Committee, all the above clauses were removed.[4]

1 Again in the USA, this practice would be unlawful and the Supreme Court has ruled that placing any restrictions on the use of information obtained would be unlawful: *Schiffer v FBI* 78 F 3rd 1405 (9th Cir 1996).

2 Clauses 21(1) defence, 22(1) international relations, 23(1) relations within the UK, 24(1) the economy, 26(1) law enforcement, 28(3) collective responsibility, 30(1) health and safety and 34(2) commercial interests. It is interesting that it did not apply against clause 25 (s.30 on investigations and proceedings), presumably because that clause is so extensive it does not require a jigsaw. A broad swathe of investigations were removed from what was cl 25 on amendment including investigations into accidents. This information may be protected under other provisions.

3 *Halperin v CIA* 629 F 21, 144 (DC — 1980) and *FOI Guidance and Privacy Act Overview* US Department of Justice, Sept 1998 p 93.

4 One further provision from the many should be mentioned. Under cl 44(7) of the Draft Bill the Commissioner may be denied access to information where it would lead to self-incrimination by a public authority. This is remarkable because it extends a right possessed by an individual against self-incrimination to an authority. Such a right — akin to a human right and protected under the ECHR - should not be of benefit to institutions operating on behalf of the public welfare thereby protecting wrongdoing in the service of the public. It is difficult to see how the authority can invoke this provision without in some way compromising its position and the provision could invite duplicity. How for instance would an authority respond to an individual request for information which could incriminate the authority and which could be protected against disclosure to the Commissioner but not to a requester? It is not one of the exemptions. It is not otherwise unlawful to disclose the information because it is at most privileged not prohibited. The reason for this provision, it was stated, was that the Crown and Crown bodies were not subject to the criminal process and would not be liable to self-

We have seen that where a damage test has to be satisfied to withhold information, the test in the WP of substantial harm had been reduced to prejudice. The test in the WP had met with almost universal support.[5] The test introduced in the bill met with universal criticism but was explained away by the Home Secretary who in Parliament stated that the prejudice would have to be 'real, actual or of substance' and it referred to a probability of prejudice not a possibility and that in interpreting 'prejudice' in specific cases, officials could invoke his statement in support of such an interpretation under the rule in *Pepper v Hart*.[6] This is problematic for a variety of reasons. First of all if the provision is one requiring *real* prejudice why not say what the law means in the legislation? Secondly the reference to the case is misleading: it only applies where there is an ambiguity in a statutory provision which the reference to Hansard may clarify. There is no need to seek elucidation on the word 'prejudice' — its meaning is clear enough. It is certainly not the same as 'serious' or 'substantial' prejudice. Lastly, the people who will be most in need of guidance are officials making decisions on access at the coal face as it were. They, unlike courts of law, do not need to seek authorisation under the rule in *Pepper v Hart* to refer to the Home Secretary's words.

Arguably, what officials need is a purpose clause to give the necessary support for greater openness. The absence of such a clause was a further criticism in the bill: it contained no purpose clause setting out the pursuit of greater openness and provision of information as an overriding statutory objective to influence the decisions of officials who have to interpret the eventual Act. Such provisions are common in other FOI statutes: in Australia, Canada, New Zealand and most recently in Ireland.[7] Indeed they are not uncommon in domestic provisions. A recent and outstanding example is seen in the Civil Procedure Rules 1998, r 1.1.[8] This states that the rules are a new procedural code 'with the overriding objective of enabling the court to deal with cases justly.' What this means is spelt out

---

incrimination! Therefore the privilege should apply to all bodies covered by the bill — a sort of even playing field. This only emerged when questions were put to the civil servants present at the Public Administration Committee throughout its investigation to assist the Committee with technical points of drafting and background information. Here as elsewhere the obfuscatory device of the Crown in British government and administration is witnessed.

5   See for instance Richard Shepherd MP cross-examining the Home Secretary at HC 570— (1998-99), p 5 et seq.

6   [1993] 1 All ER 42, HL.

7   See respectively: s 3 of the Australian Act, s 2 of the Canadian Act, s 4 'Purposes' of the New Zealand Act and the long title of the 1997 FOIA (Ireland). Purpose clauses are well known in an English context: s 1(1) Children Act 1989, s 37(1) Crime and Disorder Act 1998, and Civil Procedure Rules 1998, SI 1998/3032, r 1.1. See HC 570-I (1998-99) paras 55 et seq.

8   SI 1998/3032.

in r 1.2 and includes ensuring the parties are on an equal footing, saving expense, dealing with cases in a manner which is proportionate, expeditiously and fairly and that it receives a proper allocation of a court's resources. Lord Woolf, the inspiration for the rules, in his evidence to the Select Committee supported the case for a purpose clause saying:

> 'As I understand it, one of the things that the Government is seeking to do, and on which they should be complimented, is that they are seeking to change the culture with regard to freedom of information and I think that in that sort of situation a signpost at the beginning as to the general intent of the legislation can be very important.'[9]

The official response was that such a clause would cause confusion and the solution, as provided in the Bill it was felt, was in a clear expression of rights and exemptions which are set out clearly. The clause setting out the right to information (originally cl 8, now s 1), proclaimed Jack Straw, *was* a purpose clause. As the Select Committee on Public Administration pointed out, however, a purpose clause would do more than tip the balance in favour of disclosure where a discretion was involved under cl 14 – the public interest clause; it would colour attitudes generally in favour of access and openness at every level of discretion.

The difficult question of 'third party rights' is also dealt with in a problematic manner in the bill. This concerns the situation where a requester seeks access to information about another person or body. It most often applies to commercial information but can also cover personal information.[10] The Government were disinclined to build in legal duties to consult such parties; it would be too onerous. A code of practice would set out good practice on consultation. The law of confidentiality, it was felt, would protect those whose legal interests were being infringed. This is all rather happenstance and is reminiscent of the situation in the USA before a special procedure was introduced by executive order to notify third parties of claims for information covering their, usually, businesses (see chapter 2). The order was necessitated by the chaos caused by the absence of any safeguards. Nor will the law of confidentiality be adequate where all that can be claimed is damages after an allegedly wrongful disclosure where consultation did not take place.[11]

The WP's promise of a duty to give reasons for administrative decisions has not resulted in a clause directly in the bill but will be placed in an

---

9   Lord Woolf Q.889, HC 570—ix (1998/99).
10 Personal information may well be covered by the Data Protection Act 1998.
11 The Act seeks to give an immunity for breaches of the statute, but this would not cover breaches of confidentiality or negligence: see now s 56.

authority's publication scheme.[12] The authority is to 'have regard to the public interest .... in the publication of reasons for decisions made by the authority.' This is another example of how what would best be placed in statutory duties has been reduced to a discretionary practice. The Commissioner will have to be vigilant in approving schemes to ensure among other things that appropriate provisions apply to the giving of reasons for administrative decisions — perhaps a matter for the 'model publication schemes' that the Commissioner may produce — and that the authority comply with its own schemes. The clause and the bill originally said nothing about duties on authorities to give reasons for decisions either to unsuccessful applicants for information or to the Commissioner on an investigation where exempt information has not been forthcoming. If the Commissioner is not told the reasons for refusal and how the public interest is exercised, her position is otiose. Amendments did provide for the giving of reasons as we shall see. More will be said on this point under 'enforcement' below.

Many of the essential administrative practices under the FOI regime will be contained in a code of practice issued by the Secretary of State (there will also be a code issued by the Lord Chancellor for public records aspects) which will set out desirable practice for them to follow on inter alia: the provision of advice to requesters and complaint handling (and also third parties as noted above). Breaches of the code may result in the award by the Commissioner of a practice recommendation to the authority.[13] Under the bill, a practice recommendation (PR) may have been awarded in relation to a failure to comply with the publication scheme. This was dropped from the Act and PRs are awarded in relation to the code. The code may cover any item in Part I. As seen above, the draft code made no reference to schemes. Many essential details on practice will be contained in the code and publication schemes, provisions which elsewhere would be in law.[14] At the Report Stage in the Lords, an amendment was added (now s 16) which stated that public authorities were under a duty 'so far as it would be reasonable to expect

---

12   In the 1997 edition of John Major's Code, bodies covered by the Code had to give reasons for decisions except in those few areas such as certain monopoly and merger cases and enforcement action where there was a well established authority against giving reasons.

13   The Home Office say a practice recommendation is enforceable by judicial review. Breaches are subject to public law controls of legitimate expectation and the contents of the code are relevant criteria to address in exercising a discretion.

14   In the States for instance, manuals, decisions, formal and informal procedures etc are all provided for in primary legislation. Under the 1996 reforms, where information has previously been requested on a certain number of occasions, it will automatically be published: see p 294 above.

the authority to do so' to provide advice and assistance to requesters. This was satisfied by complying with the Code.[15]

Basically, it was felt that the bill had been the outcome of a pact between forces of darkness in government and an extremely clever if somewhat context blind — in terms of openness — draftsman. This pact had undermined the major principles of the WP by removing the power of the Commissioner to make binding decisions on bodies covered by the bill so that release of information should be enforced where a greater public interest was served by disclosure than by secrecy, confidentiality or privacy. There were rumours of enormous lobbying by commercial and utility interests. It was reported that the bill was given the particular support of Tony Blair in that it made various concessions for the first time to legal rights of access, but it left absolute control with ministers in every crucial area. The Select Committee in the Commons believed that what the bill sought to introduce was a discretionary Open Government framework in the tradition of successive British governments starting with the Croham Directive of 1977 and culminating in John Major's 1994 Code. All good intent but no real substance. This was in contradistinction to a FOI statutory regime proper where information was available as a right and where exemptions were subject to independent scrutiny and arbitration so that the *ipse dixit* of the minister did not prevail. It has to be said of course that 'open government' elsewhere does not have this meaning but means opening up a wider range of official decision-making processes to external scrutiny under legal constraint (see chapter 1, p 27 et seq.).

Civil servants and ministers were both blamed for the about-turn and the Cabinet Committee which deliberated the bill was the only such committee to have more members than the Cabinet. Everybody wanted to attend to protect their patch.[16] This was reflected in the numerous class exemptions which protect information on a blanket basis, although in most cases it will be subject to a public interest test, as well as the other unusual aspects of a FOI provision.

Open points

At the Campaign for FOI Awards Ceremony in June 1999, at which the Home Secretary was guest of honour, and on his first appearance before the Select Committee to give evidence on the bill and consultation Paper, Jack Straw expressed deep surprise at the hostility aimed at the bill. Putting

15 A draft Code has been published: Home Office *Draft Code of Practice On the Discharge of the Functions of Public Authorities under Part I FOIA 2000.*
16 See Peter Hennessy's evidence to the House of Lords committee: HL 97 (1998/99) Q.391.

the bill in the context of wide-ranging constitutional reforms, he clearly felt that many criticisms had been grossly exaggerated, misinformed or simply inaccurate.[17] Wasn't any praise due for allowing a legal right of access? There are indeed some good points to the bill. It has removed all but one of the exclusions that were in the WP. It is retrospective unlike the WP. It provides a legally enforceable right to information via the powers of the Commissioner who may impose a series of notices ordering disclosure under s 1, and enforcing obligations under Part I of the bill or enforcing access by herself to contested information. It is not entirely clear what the position will be in regard to access to information covered by absolute exemptions.[18] Where the Commissioner challenges the basis for claiming whether such an exemption is established (see below) access will be crucial. The bill applies to a wide range of public bodies and covers functions and services as was indicated above. Unlike the 1994 code, contractual and commercial matters are not excluded by virtue of the Parliamentary Commissioner's governing statute.[19] It unifies the Data Protection and FOI regimes as the Select Committee suggested in its report on the WP and thereby avoids the confusion of roles between the two Commissioners that the WP seemed to offer, although the result is very technical and will prove very difficult for officials to deal with.[20] It covers the police and is not restricted to their administrative functions but the exemptions are excessively broad. The Government has maintained its intention to set about the repeal of unnecessary secrecy clauses in previous statutes[1] and to make alteration etc of documents to prevent disclosure a criminal offence. The Government left open the possibility of including Parliament itself in the bill's coverage and both Houses were subsequently included in amendments.[2] The charging structure 'up to

17 For a critical account see the evidence of the Campaign for Freedom of Information: HC 570—i (1998/99) p 15 et seq.
18 The IC may issue an information notice to obtain access. The relevant section, s 51, does not exclude absolute exemptions. A notice may be subject to appeal to the Tribunal.
19 The ombudsman is prohibited from investigating complaints about commercial or contractual matters. This is by virtue of the Parliamentary Commissioner for Administration Act 1967, Sch 3, para 9. Public services delivered by private contractors are within the scope of the Act where maladministration is present in delivery. The *Guidance on Interpretation* on the Code stated: '[Para 9] should not impair his ability to investigate complaints about non-disclosure of information relating to the functions delivered through contractors.' Part IV. See eg HC 572 (1998-99) p 17.
20 Basically, access by data subjects to their own files etc is via the Data Protection Act. Access to files on another is via the FOIA. See chapter 7.
1   The White Paper *Open Government* Cm 90 (1993) Annex B Part I contains a list of statutory prohibitions on disclosure. Part II has a list of statutory provisions conferring powers to disclose. See Annex D on release of papers especially intelligence papers and also courts martial.
2   Quite what this will achieve is unclear but there was a feeling that imposing a duty on other public bodies but excluding Parliament itself might look like hypocrisy.

10% of the marginal costs of providing information' and the full cost of disbursements appears quite liberal.[3] The maximum charge will be £50 for marginal costs. Where the marginal costs exceed £500 (subsequently increased to £550), the information will be exempt. In the Act, information may be disclosed even though exempt because the cost of compliance exceeds the appropriate limit, but a different scale of fees may be provided in regulations for such disclosures (s 13). This was an amendment introduced in the Lords. Regulations may also provide that in the case of multiple requests from one person or from different persons who appear to the authority to be acting in concert or in pursuance of a campaign, the estimated cost for dealing with any request is to be taken as the estimated cost of complying with all of them.

The Home Secretary and concessions

On his second appearance[4] before the Commons Committee to give evidence on the bill, the Home Secretary did not display the complete confidence that had characterised his first appearance before the Committee. He also seemed prepared to consider reforms on some key questions including cl 25 and investigations and cl 37 and the 'jigsaw' or mosaic. Perhaps the level of criticism had got to him. There appeared to be the possibility of a concession on the powers of the Commissioner in relation to the discretionary information under cl 14 in so far as she would be given a power of recommendation but not an override. The latter would, he believed, give an enormous political power to an unelected official. But is this not true of judges in public interest immunity litigation (see chapter nine p 441 et seq)? The need for a purpose clause was not conceded by the Home Secretary. These points, including the power of recommendation under cl 14, in fact formed central features of the Commons Select Committee report and the Lords Committee agreed on many points with the Commons committee although on some points the Lords Committee differed from the Public Administration Committee.[5] The Government responded.[6] There is no doubt that the bill gained enormously from the scrutiny of the white paper and the draft bill particularly in the case of the input from the Commons committee which alone scrutinised the WP.

---

3   'Marginal costs' includes staff costs and computer processing. 'Disbursements' includes copying, postage, computer discs etc.

4   HC 570—xii (1998/99) 21 July 1999.

5   On purpose clauses, and on national security, the Lords differed from the Commons Committee.

6   Public Administration Committee *Fifth Special Report* HC 831 (1998-99) and see HC 925 (1998-99) and HC 78 (1999-2000).

Progress was clearly being made. But a major weakness in the bill concerned the central question of independent enforcement and its absence where the government wishes to resist disclosure.

Denying the Commissioner the ultimate say

The failure to provide a power for the Commissioner to enforce her decisions (the first Commissioner will be Elizabeth France the Data Protection Commissioner) where disclosure is discretionary on public interest grounds, ie where it is protected by an exemption but not an absolute exemption, was one of the most criticised aspects of the bill. Although the WP was widely, indeed enthusiastically praised by many, under the WP the Commissioner did not possess an overriding power on the public interest which she could enforce directly. She had to go to the High Court seeking a contempt order for failure to comply with a disclosure order. Her decision on 'disclosure' was subject to judicial review. This was not a very coherent approach.

Under the 1994 Code, the PCA effectively seized an opportunity and claimed the power to disclose and the then Prime Minister acquiesced.[7] Although the PCA could not enforce his recommendation he could say to an authority:

'nevertheless my judgement is different from yours; it is that the balance of advantage in the public interest is thus rather than thus, and that has been accepted[8]

Under the Act, the Commissioner can enforce the production of information under s 1 which, presumably, it is 'not otherwise unlawful to disclose.'[9] Section 58 DPA, which extends to FOIA, prevents any legal

7   See Case A 12/95 para 8 and evidence of William Reid to the Select Committee on the Parliamentary Commissioner for Administration 8 March 1995, HC 84 (1995-96) Q.41.

8   HC 570—ii (1998/99) Q. 101. Under s 11(3) of the PCA Act 1967, the minister has the power to prevent the Ombudsman handing information to anyone else: see above p 242.

9   The original cl 14 included these words but they were omitted from s 2. The lawfulness of the IC's decision may be challenged before the Tribunal and then before the courts. Section 78 states that nothing in the Act takes away existing powers to disclose information. The biggest barrier to disclosure would be the Official Secrets Act 1989; see s 58, as amended by FOIA, in the text. Some of the wording of the exemptions leans heavily on the 1989 Act. The IC could not give information obtained from an information notice to a claimant, it is submitted and acting pursuant to a notice will be deferred pending exhaustion of any appeal. Under s 59 DPA as amended by Sch 19 FOIA the IC is prohibited, along with former IC's and staff and former staff and agents, from disclosing information about an identified or identifiable individual or business unless made under lawful authority: see DPA, s 59(2) for lawful authority.

barrier to disclosure in other legislation or rule of law precluding an individual disclosing information the IC. The OSA cannot be preyed in aid, for instance where the information is necessary for functions under DPA or FOIA. She can, according to the Home Office, enforce the steps that are to be taken by authorities in producing their publication schemes although she cannot write the schemes for authorities. If an authority fails to publish information as set out in its schemes, can the Commissioner respond to a complaint on such a matter and issue a decision or enforcement notice? These may be appealed to the Information Tribunal. FOIA appears not to confer power to award a decision notice in relation to a scheme as these seem related to 'requests for information' under s 1 and other matters. An enforcement notice may be served where the IC is satisfied that an authority has failed to comply with any of the requirements in Part I which includes s 19 dealing with schemes. Where the code of practice issued by the Secretary of State is not followed by an authority that can be remedied by a practice recommendation. Quite what this will do is not clear.[10] The ability of the Commissioner to issue a variety of notices to authorities to make decisions and to enforce them is backed up by a power to issue information notices under s 51 which allow the Commissioner to gain access to information. The information notice is also subject to exclusions concerning legal professional privilege. The Commissioner also has considerable powers of entry, inspection and seizure under a warrant issued by a circuit judge which again are subject to excluded items.[11]

The role of the Commissioner was also assisted by the addition of duties on public authorities to provide reasons for claiming that the public interest in either maintaining the exclusion of the duty to confirm or deny (see below) it holds information or withholding information outweighs the duty to disclose that it holds the information or to disclose the information. The balance is in favour of disclosing where the scales are even; this reversed the position in earlier versions of the bill. In either case, the authority under s 17 has to provide reasons for its decision and as will be seen, the Commissioner will have access to all relevant documents. Gaps in reasoning will be quickly exposed. In refusing information under s 1(1), the authority must not only state which exemption applies, but also state why the exemption applies. Reasons also have to be given where an absolute exemption is claimed but not so as to compromise the exemption.

10 See n 13 p 300 above for the Home Office views on judicial review where a practice recommendation had not been complied with under the original Bill. This is an area where the back-up of a Parliamentary Committee to support the Commissioner would be vital.

11 Information exempt by virtue of ss 23(1) and 24(1) ie the intelligence services and national security and matters protected by legal professional privilege arising under the Act: Sch 3.

Responding to a request

Requests have to be made in writing and this may include electronic form providing it is clear. The Code advises on assistance where a request is not in writing. The authority are under a duty to inform the requester for information in writing whether it holds information of the type specified in the request. If they do then they must communicate the information – which means information recorded in any form – by means of a copy in permanent form, or another form acceptable to the requester. Communication may be made by allowing inspection or by providing a digest or summary of the information in permanent form. The authority must as far as reasonably practicable adopt the chosen means of communication although the authority may have regard to the question of cost involved in a chosen means of communication. An authority may reasonably request further information from a requester in order to identify and locate information. The information is that held at the time of the receipt of the request although amendments or deletions may be made where they would have been made regardless of the request. They must not be made *because of* the request. A request does not have to be complied with until any fee in a fees notice served on the applicant has been paid. The requester has three months from the date the notice is given to pay the fee. Regulations may waive fees in prescribed cases and set maximum fees (see above) as well as provide for their manner of calculation. The authority must comply with the request promptly and in any event within 20 days of receiving the request. This period may be extended to 60 days by regulations and may also prescribe different days in relation to different cases and confer a discretion on the Commissioner. However, any period during which a requested fee is not paid delays the computation of the 20 day, or presumably other, period.

There is no specific power to redact or censor papers or documents before handing them over but an applicant may request information in summary form. An authority may comply with a request by communicating information by any means which are 'reasonable in the circumstances.'

The exemptions

Central to any FOI regime is the existence of exemptions. A frequent question is: 'With so many exemptions what's the point of having a FOIA? A brief answer is that it allows access to information otherwise not available and most regimes place the burden of justifying non-disclosure on those seeking to withhold it. While the UK FOIA contains many exemptions that are similar to those present in overseas laws, there are some peculiar characteristics of the UK law. There are 23 exemptions[12] including s 12 which covers the situation where the cost of compliance exceeds the appropriate limit[13] and s 14 which deals with vexatious or repeated requests. Apart from these two exemptions, all the others are in Part II of the Act. Seventeen are on a class basis.[14] In a class exemption, disclosure of any document within the class is *ipso facto* damaging although public interest disclosures may be made under s 2 where they are not absolute exemptions. In the case of the other exemptions where 'prejudice' or damage would be caused by the disclosure because of their contents, an exemption may be claimed on the basis of the prejudice caused. However, the Commissioner may make a judgement on whether 'prejudice' exists and whether, if it exists, it is *de minimis*. This judgement is not subject to the veto under s 53, but it is subject to appeal by the authority to the Information Tribunal.

I will deal very briefly with the corpus of exemptions and then concentrate on the more controversial.

In addition to ss 12 and 14 above, the exemptions are: information which is reasonably accessible to the applicant other than in accordance with s 1 even if a payment is required. This will cover information which has to be communicated under any enactment. It will also cover information contained in a publication scheme and any payments required are contained in that scheme. It does not cover information which an authority may release upon request.

Information which is held and intended for future publication by the authority or any other person is exempt. A notorious event may have the sting temporarily drawn by authorising an internal inquiry to report to the PM. This will then allow the exemption to be invoked to prevent disclosure. When the former Treasury Solicitor was summoned from retirement to investigate the events surrounding the intervention by Peter Mandelson's private office in the Hinduja affair (see chapter 4 p 176 above) this provided a convenient excuse not to disclose information

12 Where all the subsections within sections are counted the total is larger; see n 17 p 295 above.

13 Under s 13 the authority may disclose such information under a fee structure peculiar to s 13. This was a late amendment to allow for expensive disclosures regardless of s 12.

14 These are information accessible through other means; where information is intended for future publication; information supplied by, or relating to, security and intelligence bodies; national security, although a ministerial certificate stating as much is subject to limited challenge in the Tribunal; investigations and proceedings conducted by public authorities; court records; Parliamentary privilege; formulation of government policy; communications with Her Majesty and conferral of honours; environmental information (though this will be available under other provisions); personal information (available under DPA); confidential information; that protected by legal professional privilege; trade secrets; information subject to other legal prohibitions on disclosure.

about the affair and in particular whether there were recordings of conversations by the former Northern Ireland Secretary. This information may also have been exempted under the 'prejudice to the effective conduct of public affairs' exemption (see below). It does not matter whether the date for publication is determined or not. The information has to be held with a view to such publication at the time of the request and in all the circumstances of the case it is reasonable that information be withheld until the future date. This exemption contains a provision which I shall refer to hereon as the non-application of the duty to confirm or deny. Basically, the duty to confirm or deny that the authority holds information does not arise where compliance with s 1(1) would involve the disclosure of information (whether or not already recorded) falling within the exemption, in this case s 22(1). In the USA this is restricted to intelligence and criminal law enforcement. This is because of the sensitivity of information relating especially to informers and where confirming or denying whether such information is held could arouse suspicion among the criminal fraternity. Its repetitive refrain throughout this Act suggests overkill.

The next exemption comes under Part II and concerns information supplied by, or relating to, bodies dealing with security matters. The bodies themselves are excluded from the provisions of the Act because they are not identified in the Schedule to the Act. It is exempt if it was supplied to the public authority directly or indirectly by such bodies or the information relates to any of the following bodies: the Security Service; the Secret Intelligence Service; the Government Communications HQ and the special forces.[15] The duty of confirmation or denial does not apply. A minister may certify that information covered by the certificate relates to, or was supplied by, the specified bodies and this is conclusive evidence subject to an appeal to the Information Tribunal under s 60 by the IC or applicant on the grounds the information was not exempt information.

Information not falling within s 23 is exempt if required for the purpose of safeguarding national security. The duty of confirmation or denial does not apply where exemption from s 1(1)(a) is required for the purposes of safeguarding national security. This is the old favourite and ministerial certificates shall be conclusive evidence although an appeal may again be made to the Information Tribunal.[16] Information may be identified in a 'general sense' and a certificate may have prospective effect. Appeal

15 Other bodies are: the tribunals established under s 65 Regulation of Investigatory Powers Act 2000, s 7 Interception of Communications Act 1985, s 5 Security Service Act 1989, s 9 Intelligence Services Act 1994, the Security Vetting Appeals Panel, the Security Commission, the National Criminal Intelligence Service and its Service Authority.

16 See s 25. A certificate may only be issued by a member of the Cabinet or the Attorney-General, Advocate General or NI Attorney-General. See also Sch 4.

empowers the Tribunal to quash a certificate where it finds 'on applying the principles applied by the court on an application for judicial review, the minister did not have reasonable grounds for issuing the certificate'.[17] This formulation in other legislation was examined in chapter 1 (p 48).

Further exemptions cover disclosures which would, or be likely to, prejudice defence or the capability, effectiveness or security of any relevant forces and international relations. The duty to confirm or deny does not apply in both exemptions. This exemption could be used to prevent disclosures of tests on eg depleted uranium shells and bombs, controversially used in Kosovo, where widespread and serious after effects were reported and treated. Section 27(1) sets out what is meant by international relations. Information is also exempt information if it is confidential information obtained from a state other than the UK or from an international organisation or international court.[18] It is treated as confidential if it was obtained on terms requiring confidentiality or where the circumstances on which it was obtained make it reasonable for the state etc to expect confidentiality. This will be the norm in international communications that are not meant for public consumption.

Section 28 makes information exempt where its disclosure would, or would be likely to, prejudice relations between the government of the UK, the Scottish Administration, the Executive Committee of the Northern Ireland Assembly or the National Assembly for Wales. The duty to confirm or deny does not arise. An important development has taken place in the form of 'concordats' contained in memoranda of understanding 'a multilateral arrangement involving the different devolved administrations as well as the UK Government.'[19] Rawlings has written that although the concordats are published, they operate in secrecy and confidentially under UK domination. They result in a lack of transparency and a rule by cooperation which allows Whitehall the upper hand. Essential information is given by Whitehall on the basis that it is treated in confidence. This could prove to be difficult given the different approaches to FOI being adopted in Scotland and Wales which is discussed below.

Further exemptions cover information whose disclosure would, or would be likely to, prejudice the economic interests of the UK or any part of the UK, or the financial interests of any administration in the UK as set out in the preceding paragraph. The duty to confirm or deny does not apply. The matters excluded in relation to the Bank of England were noted above (p 294).

17 See s 60(4).
18 See s 27(5) for state, international court and international organisation.
19 See R Rawlings 'Concordats of the Constitution' (2000) LQR 257 and Cm 4806 on the *Memorandum of Understanding* between the UK Government, the Scottish Executive, the Welsh Assembly and the Northern Ireland Executive Committee.

Information held by authorities for the purpose of any investigation as defined or criminal proceedings is exempt on a class basis as is information obtained from confidential sources relating to investigations and proceedings as described. I will deal with this exemption in more detail below. The duty to confirm or deny does not apply in relation to information exempt under this section. Section 31 exempts information the disclosure of which would, or would be likely to, prejudice law enforcement as defined. This includes the prevention or detection of crime, the apprehension or prosecution of offenders, the administration of justice, assessment or collection of tax or duty, immigration controls, maintenance of security or good order in prisons or other places of lawful detention, and the exercise of functions for the purposes enumerated in sub-s (2),[20] various civil proceedings, and inquiries under the Fatal Accidents and Sudden Deaths Inquiries (Scotland) Act 1976. The duty to conform or deny does not apply on the usual basis.

Information is exempt if held by a public authority and it is contained in documents filed with or otherwise placed in the custody of a court for proceedings or created by a court or its administrative staff for the purposes of a particular cause.[1] Similar provisions cover inquiries[2] and arbitrations. The duty to confirm or deny does not apply in relation to information exempt under this provision. Under s 33, information held by a public authority for the purpose of audit and VFM functions which it carries out in relation to other authorities is exempt on the usual basis of prejudice. The duty to confirm or deny does not apply. Section 34 exempts information where disclosure would breach Parliamentary privilege. The Speaker's certificate, or that of the Clerk of the Parliaments in the case of the Lords, is conclusive.[3]

I pass over for the time being information exempt because it relates to the formulation of Government policy or information the disclosure of which, in the reasonable opinion of a 'qualified person', would prejudice the effective conduct of public affairs. These are controversial measures deserving fuller treatment (see below).

---

20 These include the purpose of ascertaining whether any person has failed to comply with the law; whether any person is responsible for any conduct which is improper; whether regulatory action is justified; ascertaining a person's fitness for corporate management or performance of any profession; causes of accidents; protecting charities; securing health, safety and welfare of persons at work; and protecting persons other than those at work against risk to health of safety arising from the actions of people at work. This exemption is on a contents basis and is subject to the public interest test.

1 At present, presiding judges do have discretion to allow access to documents filed with the court subject to confidentiality or non-disclosure orders. See Sir Richard Scott HC 570-ix (1998-99), Q.893.

2 See s 32(4) for 'court' etc. It includes any inquest or post-mortem.

3 Section 34(3) and could not be challenged in any other place by virtue of the Bill of Rights 1989.

Section 37(1) protects information concerning communications with Her Majesty, other members of the Royal Family or Household as well as any conferral by the Crown of any honour or dignity. The duty of confirmation and denial does not apply. Information is exempt if its disclosure would, or would be likely to, endanger the physical or mental health of any individual or their safety. The duty to confirm or deny does not apply. Environmental information which the authority has to disclose under s 74 is exempt and will be explained below. Personal data is also exempt and will be dealt with in detail in chapter 7. FOIA has amended the Data Protection Act 1998 to extend the definition of data to cover 'recorded information' held by a public authority not falling within existing definitions of data. This is known as 'unstructured personal data'. Access to personal data thus extended is made under the DPA by the data subject where s/he is requesting his or her own data. Access to information about others takes place under FOIA but subject to various DPA safeguards and exemptions. This area is covered in chapter 7.

Information whose disclosure would constitute an actionable breach of confidence is exempt. This covers information from any other person including another public authority.[4] A special exclusion covers the duty of confirmation or denial. Exemptions also cover legal professional privilege, commercial interests and that information whose disclosure is prohibited by law. These latter two are dealt with in fuller detail below.

Specific exemptions

Investigations and proceedings conducted by public authorities

The first of the exemptions to cause concern because of its breadth was that set out above and is in s 30. In the WP the prospect was set out of law enforcement being given an exclusion from the Act. In evidence to the Select Committee in 1998, the Home Secretary stated that if an exemption were substituted for an exclusion it would be so wide as to make it tantamount to an exclusion. Section 30 provides that information held by a public authority is exempt information if it has at any time been held by the authority for the purposes of: any investigation which the public authority has a duty to conduct with a view to its being ascertained whether a person should be charged with an offence or whether a person charged with an offence is guilty of it; where it has been held for any

---

4 Section 81 states that 'each government department is to be treated as a person separate from any other government department.' However, this does not allow one department to maintain that disclosure of information by it would be an actionable breach of confidence by another department in order to claim the exemption. The 'Crown' owns the information in any event.

investigation which is conducted by the authority and in the circumstances may lead to a decision by the authority to institute criminal proceedings which the authority has power to conduct; or, any criminal proceedings which the authority has power to conduct. This is a class exemption and does not relate to any interference with the process of justice or any prejudice to any person, litigant or defendant. The fact that it falls within the exemption is sufficient. It covers information held *at any time*. It is subject to the public interest provisions but the protection for s 30(2) appears limitless when read with the public records provisions on access (see below).

Information is also exempted where it relates to any such investigation or criminal proceedings as set out above, any investigation conducted for the purposes of s 31(2) (below) under prerogative or statutory powers, or civil proceedings brought by the authority arising from such investigations *and* it relates to information obtained from confidential sources ie informers.[5] The duty to confirm or deny does not arise in relation to exempt information. The section defines those who may institute or conduct criminal proceedings in very broad terms and criminal offences includes a variety of military disciplinary offences.[6]

Law enforcement

This is provided for by s 31. Enough has been said about this exemption above, save where information is not protected by s 30, it will be exempted by this section where its disclosure would, or would be likely to, prejudice the matters listed above. It requires prejudice and is not as questionable as the exemption under s 30. It now contains the provision on information relating to accidents, which would cover notorious railway and other accidents, preventing information about causes and shortcomings being disclosed until official 'blessing' had been given to its format.

Formulation of Government policy

This section – 35 - and s 36 were the most heavily criticised exemptions in the Act. Section 35 exempts information held by a government department or the National Assembly for Wales if it relates to (note the looseness of that terminology) the formulation or development of policy; ministerial communications; advice or requests for advice by the law

---

5   Who are always afforded special protection by the courts: *Marks v Beyfus* (1890) 25 QBD 494; see *Swinney v Chief Constable of Northumbria* [1996] 3 All ER 449.
6   Section 30(5).

officers;[7] or the operation of any ministerial private office.[8] The duty to confirm or deny does not apply to such exempt information. Once a decision has been taken, statistical information 'used to provide an informed background' to the formulation of government policy or which relates to ministerial communications may be disclosed. Under a public interest disclosure involving this exempt information which is covered by s 2(1)(b) or 2(2)(b), authorities shall have regard to the particular public interest in the disclosure of factual information which has been used, or is intended to be used, to provide an informed background to decision-making. It says nothing about factual information not used and which may have militated against the policy decision.[9] There is nothing about the disclosure of rejected options. Whether publication schemes will cover this information and in what form remains to be seen.

Policy advice, whether from civil servants or special advisers, is not included specifically in this section but it will be covered by s 36. It is difficult to see how advice will not be covered by formulation of government policy where advice is central. There is nothing about legal advice from others apart from law officers in the formulation of policy or other expert opinion. The BSE episode which was examined in chapter 4 (p 165 et seq) brought home the enormity of this provision whereby information about the government response to the episode would be protected by this exemption as well as other exemptions. The criticism this attracted was noted. Policy itself could be destroyed or seriously undermined by premature publication but this section extends way beyond such protection. Government policy includes the policy of the Executive Committee of the Northern Ireland Assembly and the National Assembly for Wales. I return to this question in chapter 10.

It has to be said that this exemption contradicts the plea made by the Prime Minister in *Modernising Government* for extensive consultation with 'others' ie outsiders as early as possible in policy making.[10] Furthermore, the Food Standards Agency and the Advisory Committee on Pesticides both publish advice to ministers, in the former case under statutory authority.[11] These points are equally valid under s 36.

7 Norman Lamont when Chancellor of the Exchequer was given advice by the law officers when he had inadvertently leased premises he owned for use as a brothel.
8 Section 35(5) defines this as 'any part of a government department which provides personal administrative support to a Minister of the Crown' and NI Ministers and equivalent support for Welsh Assembly First and Deputy Secretaries. It was a crucial feature in the Peter Mandelson episode leading to his resignation.
9 Remember how in local authority executive arrangements alternative options may be disclosed; chapter 4 p 229 et seq.
10 Cm 4310 para 6. See *R v Secretary of State for Health, ex p United States Tobacco International plc* [1992] 1 All ER 212, and the duty to hand over scientific information from a specialist committee to a consultee.
11 Food Standards Act 1999, s 19(1)(a). On pesticides, see Pesticides Act 1998.

Prejudice to effective conduct of public affairs

Section 36 exempts information not protected by s 35 and which is held by a government department or 'any other public authority'.[12] It is exempt if in the reasonable opinion of a qualified person disclosure of the information under the Act would, or would be likely to, prejudice:

(a) the maintenance of the convention of the collective responsibility of Ministers of the Crown, or

(b) the work of the Executive Committee of the Northern Ireland Assembly, or

(c) the work of the executive committee of the National Assembly for Wales.

What is so precious about collective responsibility? In the formulation of the policy and in drafting the bill on FOI there were widely publicised disagreements between ministers about the appropriate content of the bill and who should have ultimate responsibility for the Bill. No harm was done to the eventual outcome.

The section continues: [where disclosure] would or would be likely to, inhibit the free and frank provision of advice or the free and frank exchange of views for the purpose of deliberation. Clearly there are legitimate reasons why a public authority may not wish to divulge advice before a decision is made. Timing could be crucial; early release might sabotage a tactical advantage or a decision itself or might cause damage. People feel inhibited from giving their honest advice if subjected to the glare of publicity and if unpopular or controversial – the government in the goldfish bowl syndrome. The official 'advice' aspect has always been a sensitive issue for FOI reform because it was seen as running the risk of focusing attention on individual civil servants which could lead to 'retribution' by incoming governments who were hostile to such policies on which they had advised. It might also lead to embarrassing publicity where it was clear there was a division between advice and advisers and ministers. To what extent will the authority claim that even after a decision is made releasing such advice or deliberation, the disclosure will inhibit future decisions because civil servants will be identified and disagreements between them and ministers will be made public putting them in an impossible position? Last of all, it is exempt where disclosure would otherwise prejudice, or would be likely otherwise to prejudice, the effective conduct of public affairs. Potentially, this could cover just about everything and is truly reminiscent of the spirit of the OSA. All the exemptions are made out where 'in the reasonable opinion of a qualified person'[13] disclosure would cause the prejudice specified. In the case of

12 The 1997 WP seemed to confine this exemption to 'government' meaning central government. It was soon developed to have a wider application.

13 Section 35(5) lists the 'qualified persons' for the purposes of the section.

statistical information this requirement does not justify exemption so the authority in this case would have to establish the damage that could be caused by disclosure. 'In the reasonable opinion' connotes an objectively justifiable decision and not the *Wednesbury* test of leaving a decision alone unless so unreasonable that no reasonable person could come to such a conclusion.

The duty to confirm or deny does not arise if in the reasonable opinion of a qualified person compliance with s 1(1)(a) would or would be likely to have any of the effects in sub-s (2). Qualified person is defined in sub-s (5) and includes the Houses of Parliament where the certificate is conclusive. Where a public authority is not listed it means a minister of the Crown, a public authority authorised by a minister or any officer or employee so authorised. Authorisations may relate to specified person(s) within a specified class, may be general or limited and may be conditional.

Environmental information

I noted above how environmental information is exempt from access under FOIA where the authority is obliged to disclose it under regulations made under s 74. There is in existence a regulation on access to environmental information which implemented an EC Directive[14] as well as numerous other provisions concerning access to statistics on pollution.[15] The regulation basically applies to any information concerning the environment which is held by a relevant person. There is an obligation to disclose such information to a requester subject to a confidentiality exemption which is given a broad coverage. Section 74 concerns the implementation of the Aarhus Convention on Access to Information, Public Participation in Decision-making and Access to Justice in Environmental Matters signed on 25 June 1998.[16] The information provisions are in Art 4 together with Arts 3 and 9 which concern access to justice. Articles 6, 7 and 8 deal with public participation. The Convention sets out harm tests for refusing disclosure and the public interest in disclosure of exempt information must also be considered. The Secretary of State may implement the information provisions by regulations made under s 74(4). Regulations may provide for charges to be made to make information available; provide that the obligation to make information

14 90/313/EEC and SI 1992/3240 as amended.
15 See P Birkinshaw *Government and Information: the Law Relating to Access, Disclosure and their Regulation* (2nd ed, 2001), *chapter* 8.
16 Cm 4736 (2000). See HC 570-II (1998-99) p 30 et seq for a submission by the Friends of the Earth on the compatibility of the Draft FOI Bill with the EC directive on Access to Environmental information and with Aarhus. See also HL 9 (1996-97) *Freedom of Access to Information on the Environment*.

available is to apply notwithstanding any contrary rule of law; and make provision for the publication by the Secretary of State of a code of guidance.

Commercial interests

Information is exempt where it constitutes a trade secret. This is a common and unexceptional provision in FOI regimes. There is considerable divergence in the various legal systems as to the legal definition of 'trade secret'. 'Trade secret' is a legal term of art and has been stated by the Law Commission to cover information which is not generally known, which derives its value from that fact, whose owner has indicated expressly or by implication the wish to maintain it as secret and probably the information is used in trade or business.[17] An amendment in the Lords sought to define a trade secret as: 'confidential trade information which if disclosed to a competitor would cause harm to its owner.' This was unsuccessful.

The second part of s 43 is drawn in extremely broad terms. It states that information is exempt if its disclosure under this Act would, or would be likely to, prejudice the commercial interests of any person (including the public authority holding it). The duty to confirm or deny is excluded. 'Commercial interests' is very broad – the more usual formulation is commercial confidences, at least implying some degree of confidentiality. Could commercial interests block access to information about utilities cutting off customers who cannot pay bills? What amount of contractual pricing, tenders, penalty clauses and so on might it cover? What about claw back provisions, or information on overpayments where the authority has made a bad deal? The Commissioner would have to be satisfied that prejudice would or would be likely to be caused and a threshold would have to be crossed. The Parliamentary Commissioner for Administration has conducted numerous investigations under the Code on Access where commercial confidentiality has been raised by officials as an objection. So for instance, tenders or pricing decisions should not be disclosed where that would clearly interfere with the commercial position of an authority. But once contracts were finalised, there would appear less good reason why tenders should be protected by confidentiality unless it could be proved to interfere with future competition against the public interest.[18] This is likely to be an important exemption in contracting out arrangements, under public private partnerships or otherwise. Powerful

17 Law Commission *Misuse of Trade Secrets* (1997) No 150 para 1.29. See also *Commercial Confidentiality* NCC (1998).
18 See the Parliamentary Ombudsman in Case A9/94, Case A5/96 and Case A1/95.

contractors are likely to stipulate what is to remain exempt in the terms of the contracts. Unless they are designated as public authorities, the duty to disclose, if any, is on the public authority not the contractor.

It is also interesting to note that provisions in other domestic laws protect information where disclosure could *prejudice to an unreasonable* degree the commercial interests of any person. No such qualification applies here.[19]

Prohibitions on disclosure

The last of the difficult provisions concerns legal prohibitions on disclosure. These will cover court orders and statutory restrictions. It also includes Community obligations. This latter carries with it some complications because the Regulation made under Art 255 EC Treaty seeks in its Commission Council formulation to give precedence to Community obligations on secrecy over member state provisions. In some member states, eg the Scandinavian, the traditions are much more open than in others including the UK. This could be a source of conflict. This point is addressed in detail in chapter 8.

Public interest disclosures

The real problem occurs with exempt information and the exercise by the authority of its discretion to disclose when it considers the public interest under s 2. This clause was upgraded from cl 13 (then 14) to follow the duty to disclose information under s 1. The authority's discretion operates beyond the exemption, as it were. The exemptions which were discussed above are contained in Part II of FOIA—apart from ss 12 and 14. The Commissioner can determine whether the test for exemption is made out, ie whether the 'prejudice' actually exists or is fanciful or *de minimis* or whether a class exemption is established. This has been described as a question of fact although it is in reality a question of law or jurisdictional fact. Once the prejudice does exist, or the class exemption is made out, then the duty in s 1(1)(a) to inform the applicant whether the authority holds information does not apply where an absolute exemption applies or 'in all the circumstances of the case the public interest in maintaining the exclusion of the duty to confirm or deny' outweighs the public interest in disclosing whether the authority holds the information. The duty to communicate the information under s 1(1)(b) does not apply where once

---

19 Clean Air Act 1993, s 37; Control of Major Accident Hazard Regulations 1999, Sch 8, para 18 and so on.

again the information is subject to an absolute exemption or in all the circumstances of the case the public interest in maintaining the exemption outweighs the public interest in disclosure.

The wording of the two clauses which allow for a weighing of public interests was amended in the Lords Report stage to make sure that where the public interests in disclosure or non-disclosure were evenly balanced or likewise exclusion or non-exclusion of the duty to confirm or deny the holding of the information, the scales would come down on the side of disclosure or non-exclusion. Previously the bias was the other way.

The absolute exemptions which I indicate below are in ss 21 (information accessible by other means); 23 (information supplied by or dealing with security matters); 32 (information contained in court records which is broadly defined); 34 (information protected by Parliamentary privilege); 36 (information whose disclosure would be prejudicial to the affairs of the House of Commons or Lords); 40 (which covers certain features concerning personal information (see chapter 7); 41 (information provided in confidence); and 44 (information whose disclosure is prohibited by legal obligation). In the case of absolute exemptions, the authority possesses no discretion to disclose under the statute[20] and the Commissioner cannot override a decision not to disclose where such exemptions apply. The Commissioner may, however, make a decision on whether the factual basis of an absolute exemption has been established, ie that it is not 'confidential' or prohibited by law

The power of veto comes as an immunity against the enforcement powers of the Commissioner which I discuss below. Under s 17, an authority which to any extent relies upon a claim that an exemption in Part II of FOIA applies in response to a request for information, ie to exclude a confirmation or denial of holding information or to justify non disclosure, has to give the applicant a notice. This must state the fact of their reliance, specify the exemption in question and state (if that would not otherwise be apparent) why the exemption applies. The notice must also contain an estimate of when a decision on the public interest involving exemptions which are not absolute exemptions will be made. The reasons for claiming a public interest balance in favour of maintaining the exclusion or non-disclosing must be stated either in the notice or another notice, although not in a manner which compromises any exemption. Along with some other matters, a notice must contain details of internal complaints procedures within authorities and particulars of applying for a decision notice from the Commissioner (below). Although the Commissioner may make a decision on the public interest which differs from the authority's, specified authorities may be protected by a veto (below).

---

20 But at common law a public interest disclosure of such information may still be made; see chapter 9, p 419 et seq.

Enforcement

A person wishing to complain about the manner in which an application has been dealt with may apply to the Commissioner for her decision on whether their request has been dealt with in accordance with 'the requirements of Part I'. This will include the general rights of access as well as public interest disclosures under s 2.[1] The Commissioner must specify the steps that have to be taken by an authority, and the time within which they must be taken, to comply with the requirements of s 1 as well as ss 11 and 17 of the Act. Section 17 concerns the situation where an authority relies upon an exemption under Part II as explained above when responding to a request for information. A statement of compliance or non-compliance will be made by way of a decision notice. The complainant must first exhaust any internal complaints procedure. The IC will have to be satisfied that there has been no 'undue delay' in making the application, that the application is not frivolous or vexatious and that it has not been withdrawn or abandoned. If the Commissioner makes no decision, this fact must be notified to the complainant together with 'his grounds for not doing so'. Where a decision notice is made, both the complainant and public authority must be informed together with notice of rights of appeal under s 57. Any period specified in a decision notice for taking action shall not operate so as to interfere with any rights of appeal. This is also true of steps required to be taken by enforcement and information notices (below).

The Commissioner may issue, where satisfied that an authority has failed to comply with any of the requirements of Part I of the Act, an enforcement notice requiring the authority to take such steps as are specified within a timescale as specified. The EN must contain a statement of the requirement(s) under Part I which the Commissioner is satisfied have not been complied with and her reasons for so finding as well as particulars of a right of appeal. This seems to have a wider remit than a decision notice and could cover publication schemes as discussed above.

The Commissioner may also serve an information notice under s 51. This is a formal requirement to provide information as requested to the Commissioner in relation to applications under s 50, or which is reasonably required for the purposes of determining whether a public authority is complying with any of the requirements under Part I, or to determine whether an authority's practice in relation to functions under the Act complies with the codes of practice under ss 45 and 46. The notice may include 'unrecorded information'. It must also contain particulars of any rights of appeal and information does not have to be handed over until an

---

1 Complaints may also include: fees, compliance time, failure to provide particulars of refusal and other matters.

appeal is exhausted. It may not cover information protected by legal professional privilege in relation to obligations, liabilities or rights arising under the Act or in connection with or in contemplation of proceedings arising under the Act. Other information protected by privilege is not so excluded but it will be exempt and subject to the public interest test. Schedule 3 confers powers of entry and inspection on the Commissioner after a warrant from a circuit judge but not in relation to those items protected by privilege.

Where the authority fails to comply with any of the above notices, the Commissioner may certify that failure by referring the matter to the High Court for it to punish as a contempt. Failure includes knowingly making a false statement or recklessly making a statement which is false in a material respect. The authority and requester may appeal to the Tribunal against a decision notice and the authority alone may appeal against an enforcement and information notice. The Tribunal has very extensive powers to reverse the Commissioner on appeal.[2]

The veto

Where the Commissioner serves a decision or enforcement notice which concerns request(s) for exempt information and where the authority neither confirms nor denies its existence, nor communicates the information, ie the authority believes the public interest in withholding the information outweighs the disclosure of the information, the authority may resist that notice. In other words, the power of the IC added as the bill progressed through Parliament to enforce a decision on the public interest instead of merely recommending an outcome was compromised by a veto. The provisions are in s 53. The veto was confined in the passage of the bill to an 'accountable person' who is a Cabinet minister or the Attorney-General (or Scottish or Northern Ireland equivalents) and special provisions apply to Northern Irish and Welsh bodies. Bodies covered by the veto are government departments, the National Assembly for Wales and any public body designated by order of the Secretary of State. Special provisions relate to consultation where designated bodies are Welsh or Northern Irish public authorities.

Basically, the accountable person may serve on the Commissioner a signed certificate stating that s/he has on reasonable grounds formed the opinion that there was no failure to comply with duties of disclosure in

2   The grounds of appeal are: the notice was not in accordance with the law; or a notice involved an exercise of discretion by the Commissioner and she ought to have exercised discretion differently ie, a merits appeal. Any finding of fact on which a notice is based may be reviewed.

relation to request(s) for information. The certificate must be served within 20 working days of the effective date.[3] Although the Commissioner's powers under the Act are terminated by such a certificate, it is not entirely clear whether the Commissioner or the complainant can seek a judicial review of such a veto (see below). Nor is it clear whether alongside the statutory framework, the information could be sought under common law and general powers of disclosure. Under s 78, it is provided that nothing in FOIA is to be taken to limit the powers of a public authority to disclose information held by it. These may be statutory or common law powers. At common law, an authority can disclose whatever it is not unlawful to disclose, which begs questions about self-authorisation which were examined in chapter 3 in relation to the Official Secrets Act (p 134 above) or what it is not against the public interest to disclose. It would take a very brave judge to prevent a department disclosing what it had decided to disclose within its sphere of responsibility, as Lord Woolf pointed out in *ex p Wiley*.[4] In evidence to the Commons Select Committee, the Home Office felt that the decision of the authority on the public interest under cl 14 – which in the Act has become s 2 — could be subject to a judicial review. This was because the clause merely dealt with an existing discretion to disclose. Given the detailed treatment of the discretion in cl 14, the existence of the Commissioner as a remedial device under the bill and the role of the court on contempt, it is difficult to see what role would be left for a judicial review if the statute were the exclusive route to information.[5]

Under s 53(6), a complainant has to be given reasons for the accountable person's opinion that a veto should apply it should be noted, although not in a manner which would disclose exempt information. The Commissioner is only entitled to the s 53 certificate but she will have access to the information itself and to the background to the decision-making process, so she will be in a good position to assess whether the certificate is supportable. Copies of the certificate have to be laid before both Houses of Parliament and where relevant before the Northern Ireland Assembly and Welsh National Assembly.

The view of the public interest clause under the original clause, cl 14, differed between those who felt they were virtually toothless (Campaign for Freedom of Information, Lord Lester QC) or 'illusory' (Data Protection Registrar) and others, especially the Government side, who felt the powers

---

3   Section 53(4) for effective date: either the day on which a notice was given, or if
     there is an appeal the date of its determination.
4   *R v Chief Constable of the West Midlands Police, ex p Wiley* [1994] 3 All ER 420
     at 438 b-c.
5   See HC 570—xii (1998/99) Q.1068.

here were considerable.[6] The clause developed to provide firstly a power of recommendation in the IC, amended to allow a decision by the IC on the public interest subject to veto, but not a veto that may be made by all bodies under the Act.

The Commissioner would have access to the information herself and so would be in a much better position to judge the cogency of the reasoning and decision of an authority under s 2 than would say a reviewing court which is usually operating in the dark or at best twilight. The Select Committee's view was that cl 14 should be amended so as to include a specific provision coming down in favour of disclosure 'unless there is a compelling argument to the contrary'. This is what s 2 now does. Authorities would have to give to complainants (but not to the IC) reasons for their decisions refusing access under s 2. Complainants might use these to seek judicial review because no other avenue is open to them where a veto is entered. Could the IC seek judicial review of a veto, arming herself with the details gathered in her investigation?[7] There seems nothing in principle to rule out such a possibility. The IC was denied the power of litigating on behalf of a complainant. The Home Office believed this would impair the IC's impartiality. Can she not properly be regarded as an advocate for openness? She does have advisory and promotional responsibilities under the Act. There seems no reason in principle why she cannot seek a judicial review.

The opportunity to seek a ruling under s 54 on contempt would offer no comfort to the Commissioner because s 54 only applies to notices that are not complied with, and these cannot be issued in relation to s 53. The veto is a trump card to that extent. The contempt provisions were originally presented as a central means of enforcing the Act. They will now only be called upon where there is a failure to comply with a notice. Under s 54(2) the making of false statements by an authority in response to an information notice is taken as non-compliance. Section 54(3), which deals with inquiries by the court where there is an alleged failure to comply with a notice, seems to envisage some judicial investigation into the action of the authority and the court would appear to be able to do more than simply accept the bare assertion of the accountable person. It is not likely that the court would be able to open a window into the mind of that person, however. Section 77 creates an offence of altering, concealing, destroying etc records which have been requested and where there is an entitlement to see them.

---

6   For Patrick Birkinshaw's evidence to the Select Committee on this point, see HC 570—v (1998/99) Q515 et seq.
7   The Lords committee believed there should be an override power in the Commissioner or at least a power to publish an opinion on the merits that a refusal to disclose on the public interest was wrong. This was before the veto was added to the bill in the Lords.

The Government came a long way from the original cl 14 to what is s 2. In the USA judicial deference has been shown to the executive in sensitive areas. In Australia, the minister may issue conclusive certificates in the public interest denying access. These are not reviewable by the Administrative Appeals Tribunal although it may make a recommendation. The position in relation to New Zealand and Canada was noted in chapter 2. Every system of FOI allows the executive to have the final say on the most sensitive of points or affords the executive the greatest deference in such areas; all others, however, do not make the final task of denial as easy for the executive as this Act encompasses. For Jack Straw, to allow the Commissioner the final say would not be 'our way of doing things'. And this in a constitution fit for the new millennium!

Public records

The WP envisaged that the provisions concerning access to public records would be brought within the FOIA regime and inconsistent provisions in the Public Records Acts would be repealed. The system for dealing with public records was explained in chapter 5. When a record reaches the end of 30 years after the year in which it was created, it becomes an 'historical record'. They are disclosed, usually to great press attention at the beginning of each year. However, under existing practice, records may be retained in departments and not transferred to the Public Record office. The basic idea was that as many records as possible should be disclosed once they are 'historical records' – if they have not been disclosed before under FOIA. Exemptions in ss 28, 30(1), 32, 33, 35, 36, 37(1)(a), 42 or 43[8] have no application to historical records. Informing an applicant whether it holds historical records is not to be taken to have any of the effects referred to in ss 28(3), 33(3), 36(3), 42(2), or 43(3) – ie prejudicing any of the matters contained in those sections by acknowledging their existence. In the case of s 37(1)(b) – conferring any honour or dignity by the Crown — the period after which the exemption evaporates is 60 years. In the case of s 31(1) which lists information relating to the prevention or detection of crime and other matters,[9] compliance with s 1(1)(a) in relation to *any* record is not to be taken to prejudice any of the items in the section after a period of 100 years.

---

8 Relations within the UK, investigations and proceedings conducted by public authorities, court records, audit functions, formulation of Government policy, prejudice to effective conduct of public affairs, communications with Her Majesty etc, legal professional privilege and commercial interests.

9 Apprehension or prosecution of offenders, administration of justice, assessment or collection of tax or duty, operation of immigration controls etc.

Information contained in a historical record in the PRO or PRO (NI) cannot be exempt under ss 21 – accessible by other means — or 22 – information intended for future publication. In the case of any information within a historical record in the PRO or PRO(NI) falling under the exemption in s 23(1) – information supplied by or relating to the security and intelligence etc services — a public interest disclosure may be made of such 'historical documents' notwithstanding s 2(3) making it an absolute exemption. Where the records are not in the PRO, and most are unlikely to be, the absolute exemption still applies. However, where an absolute exemption is contained within s 2(3) and information is not otherwise provided for as above, the period of closure is indefinite.[10]

Consultation has to take place with the LC and appropriate NI Minister before a request is refused for an historical record which is a statutory public record held by the authority which is subject to an ordinary exemption. This does not apply to records transferred to the PRO, PRO(NI) or other authorised place of repository designated by the LC.[11] Under s 66, disclosure of *any* information contained in such records other than 'open information'[12] where there is an exemption other than under s 2(3) must be made by the public authority after being consulted by the PRO etc. Further provisions cover consultation with the LC and NI Minister where the record is a transferred public record.

For the position on public records in Scotland, *An Open Scotland*[13] envisaged no significant changes to PR management north of the border, which are unaffected by the Public Records Acts.

The Tribunal

The role of the Tribunal was added at the bill stage and was not present in the WP. It will take over the role of the DP Tribunal. It will be able to take appeals against ministers' 'classifications' under ss 23(2) and 24(3) concerning classification of security and intelligence and national security but the ground of appeal in the latter case is very narrow.[14] The tribunal will be built on traditional tripartite models, ie a legally qualified chair and two wing persons to represent the interests of authorities and users. The fact that no legal aid will be available will act as a deterrent to those

---

10 This includes ss 34: Parliamentary privilege; 40: personal information; 41: confidential information; 44: disclosure prohibited by order; and s23(1) where not in the PRO.
11 And see s 15.
12 This is a designation made by the responsible authority.
13 Scottish Executive SE/1999/51.
14 The Tribunal finds, applying the principles applied by a court on an application for judicial review, the Minister did not have reasonable grounds for issuing the certificate.

wishing to appeal[15] and the position is not remedied by refusing to allow the Commissioner the power to assist the appellant where the decision notice was in the applicant's favour. This role for the Commissioner is allowed in other jurisdictions. The Commissioner will be allowed to conduct an audit of an authority's practice in relation to FOI where the authority consents to her doing so. There is no right for the Commissioner to do this on her own initiative as a result, for instance, of unfavourable press reports.

The Data Protection Commissioner as Information Commissioner

This is far from an easy regime to comprehend. It is complicated by the fact that the Government fastened various provisions of this scheme onto the Data Protection provisions. In fact that Act seems to have set the mould for the FOIA. The use of the Data Protection Registrar (now Commissioner) as the Information Commissioner does raise an important point of principle. In her evidence to the Select Committee in its examination of the WP, she saw herself very much as the champion of privacy — hardly surprising given her role as DPR as she then was. The question is will she come with a preconceived attachment to privacy protection rather than towards freedom of information and openness? In her evidence on the Bill, the DPR expressed the view that perhaps the Bill was weighted too much in favour of privacy. She will be responsible for both areas. In other regimes where both posts have been held by the same person or where there are two separate posts, the privacy brief has dominated, although this is not an invariable rule and owes a great deal to force of personality it seems.[16] The FOI brief is a much wider brief than the DPA field. Where the provisions of the DP Directive apply then there is no option but for the FOI provisions to cede pride of place. The DPR has already indicated areas where there may be problems by an overlap and where access to the 'public' aspects of an individual's life may not be sufficiently open under the FOI provisions. There is a danger that the DPA provisions may make a file 'secret' where a person's name is attached to it but it is not sensitive or personal information. As we shall see in the following chapter, such a case has arisen under a clash of EU access laws and data protection.[17]

The Commons Select Committee was alive to the inherent difficulties here and suggested that they should interview any prospective

15 *Freedom of Information Background Material* Annex. A, para 26.
16 See R Hazell in A McDonald and G Terrill (eds) *Open Government: Freedom of Information and Privacy* (1998).
17 *R v Ministry of Agriculture, Fisheries and Food, ex p Fisher (t/a TR & P Fisher)* Case C-369/98 (2000) Times, 10 October.

appointment to the IC's office and that the IC should report directly to that Committee rather like the Ombudsman. Certainly that Committee has been a considerable bulwark to the PCA over the years and the IC is likely to need considerable support in tackling such a wide range of bodies. The Commissioner is appointed under letters patent by the Crown, in reality the Prime Minister, and while she enjoys security while in office, her tenure is for five years up to a maximum of 15. An effective Commissioner may not be re-appointed after the first five-year period.

There is also likely to be considerable overlap between the Information Commissioner, the PCA, the Health Service Commissioner and local ombudsmen. In the Lords, this overlap was provided for by the powers of the public sector ombudsmen and the IC to exchange information which is relevant to their respective investigations.[18] There is likely to be ample scope for constructive co-operation and support. Many ombudsmen investigations involve complaints about inadequate or inaccurate information.

Throughout the events chronicled in this chapter, no-one had spoken against FOI. To that extent it shows how far we have moved since the orthodoxy of the Thatcher years when legislation enjoining greater openness on central government was regarded as apostasy. The main points of complaint were that the bill did not go far enough. The possibility dawned that perhaps in the face of serious difficulties in both chambers, the Government might drop the bill. There were enough difficult constitutional bills to be presented without the prospect of a bill that could cause significant rebellion in the Government's own party. Its legislative timetable seemed strained as it was. Various witnesses had expressed the view that this was a bill with good points and more pertinent could easily be made into a very good bill. Ronnie Campbell MP hit an appropriate note when he said that basically the bad stuff had been put in so that much of it could be taken out in order that the Government could take the credit.[19] Sir Richard Scott felt that it was a FOI bill but it required 'stiffening up'. It is, as Tony Wright the Commons Committee Chair said, a bill that can quite easily be unpacked of some of its undesirable qualities. Lord Woolf's advice to the Committee was basically: 'sometimes one has to be happy with what one can get'.[20] This advice may not have been universally welcomed within the FOI community but the point was reached in proceedings where it was felt that too much opposition to the bill could kill it off. It would be unlikely to reappear for some considerable time.

My view now is that it is better that this bill, with all its faults, was enacted than that it fell. Considerable concessions were made although

18 Section 76 and Sch 7 FOIA.
19 HC 570—i Q.41 (1998/99) 22 June 1999.
20 HC 570—ix (1998/99) Qs 916 and 920 respectively, 14 July 1999.

not on some of the central features which were seen by Government as undermining 'our way of doing things'. On some vital aspects the bill (now Act) will need further work or thought on its implications. This was true in the area of its application within a devolved structure of government in the UK and also in relation to its charging policies. Both of these points emerged from the background document that was published after the bill's publication.[1]

FOIA and devolution

In the case of FOI covering devolved functions in Scotland and Wales, Scotland's executive produced plans in *An Open Scotland*[2] for a very ambitious FOIA which would give compulsory powers of disclosure to an Information Commissioner subject to a collective decision of the Scottish ministers.[3] Information received 'in confidence' from the UK government and departments would be subject to the UK FOIA. The test for withholding information covered by the legislation would be one of 'substantial prejudice' where it was a contents exemption. Class exemptions would be subject to the public interest override. In some areas, such as criminal investigation and enforcement, Scottish law would have to gel with UK law. These plans were published in 1999 and, early in 2001, the Scottish bill was published. This has maintained the 'substantial prejudice' test but it has also been inspired by the UK Act. Absolute exemptions are included as in FOIA. The veto as discussed above will apply in some cases of class exemptions but the veto is to be exercised by the First Minister after consulting other ministers. However, there is to be no tribunal in Scotland making the Scottish IC the means of enforcement, although the IC's decision will be subject to judicial challenge – as in the original WP although the Scots have opted for an appeal and not a review. In the meantime, a code of practice on access, like the one described in chapter 5 will apply in Scotland and is policed by the Scottish Parliamentary Commissioner.

In Wales, a Code of Practice has been produced by the Welsh Assembly implementing s 70 of the Government of Wales Act 1998 and Standing Order 17. Part I outlines the provisions under which the Assembly will operate and Part II sets out exemptions. The Code undertakes to operate under a presumption of openness and sets out information it will publish automatically (see www.wales.gov.uk). The response rate set by the Code is 15 working days. Where 'harm or prejudice' are referred to as a ground

---

1   See *Background Material* in note 15 above at pp 37 and 18 et seq respectively.
2   See note .. above.
3   See The Scotland Act 1998 (Modifications of Schedules 4 and 5) Order 1999, SI 1999/1749 amending the Scotland Act 1998, Part II, Sch 5.

for not allowing disclosure, these may be outweighed by a greater public interest in disclosure. There are nine categories of exempt information.

Conclusions

The history behind FOI bills going back over 25 years in the UK and the amount of work and preparation that went into the present Act are remarkable. The bill was a focal point of attention from numerous groups all of which benefited from the extended Parliamentary scrutiny of the WP and the draft bill. The Campaign for FOI, newspapers, environmental and consumer and other pressure groups all advocated vigorously the case for reform. The bill was before Parliament for over a year and even on report back to the House of Commons after it passed the Lords, 118 amendments were tabled causing the Home Secretary to apply the guillotine. It is common to have antagonistic sectional interests in the lead up to legislation – think of hunting, abortion or privatisation. No group spoke against FOI publicly. Lobbying was behind the scenes.

The turnaround from the WP produced a vehement sense of betrayal expressed by so many interest groups in a manner not often witnessed in response to bills. Some of this may well have been due to the fact that the information in FOI is 'owned' by the public; it is information about us, or for us or concerning us and our future. It is 'us'. It simply happens to be in the government's possession on trust, as it were.[4] An FOIA is a necessary component in the progress towards a proper participatory democracy. That seemed to be present in the incoming Government's rhetoric after Blair's victory in 1997. Since then, of course, the harsh realities of executive power have brought home the necessity for a balance between openness, privacy and confidentiality, or so it is claimed. New Labour was seen to be protecting and benefiting from old practices.

The Government was accused of abandoning internationally recognised standards of conduct in producing its draft bill. Jack Straw denied the existence of such international norms and asserted that the British tradition of government was far more compliant with legal norms than most others. There is truth in both sides' assertions. A good deal of the criticism was exaggerated. The idea of FOI received the highest of judicial endorsements. The bill and the Act contain elements which could too easily lead to over-protection. The disputes over the bill were not confined to the usual Government/Opposition/Parliamentary dimensions but produced a clear split in the Cabinet at the highest of levels. There were ministerial scalps. This Government's path to FOI provided more than its fair share of drama.

---

4   Sir Richard Scott refused to be drawn into a question of ownership of government information which was a 'philosophical question'.

The episode confirms in our mind what has been written for many years: information and its collection and control are the life-blood of government. It always will be as long as we have *government* and the movement towards commercialised, off-loaded, privatised and hybrid government merely compounds the problem — hence incidentally the danger of the breadth of the protection for commercial information in this Act which has been outlined above.

The extraordinary contents of some clauses of the draft bill were highlighted in the Committee hearings before both Houses — the pre-legislative hearings which are a novel feature of Parliament under this New Labour Government. In the legislative process, Government is invariably in charge but the pre-legislative scrutiny offered enormous opportunities for feed-in at an open and pretty accessible level. The Government deserves credit for this. Was the turn-around all a ploy as Ronnie Campbell suggested to the Home Secretary? Bad bits had been put in so that many could be taken out and the Government would get all the credit while leaving it with an Act which clearly left ministers in charge. The Act is much better than the original bill. The swing towards greater emphasis on public interest disclosures was balanced by the introduction of absolute exemptions – these are effectively exclusions—and the veto.

Influential figures in the Public Administration Select Committee decided not to fight against exclusions and wide exemptions for security matters. This was not a battle they would win. The stinging criticism from that committee was very effectively directed against highly dubious provisions forcing the Home Secretary to promise that he would go away and take a further look. He did, and the bill was significantly improved. If the more offensive provisions had not been removed, the Blair Government would have compromised much of what it had said about the new relationship between government and governed in the new millennium. Had a collective veto been introduced instead of one by an 'accountable person' – how one may ask are they to be made accountable other than by vapid answers to questions in Parliament? – that would have made the Act more acceptable if accompanied by an order and public statement. That would have left some very wide exemptions which are not necessary in their existing breadth to protect the public interest. We shall have to see what the IC and possibly the courts make of the 'prejudice' test and what degree of probative material will have to support withholding of information on a contents basis.

Would the bill have been dropped had there been too much opposition? Who would have been the loser if it had been dropped? We would be left with the 1994 Code which although heavily criticised at the time of its introduction gained sudden respect indeed affection when compared with the provisions in the draft bill.[5] Newspapers have started

5 The Select Committee in its report on the Draft Bill compared the provisions of the Bill and the Code: HC 570 I (1998-99) p lxxxv et seq.

to use the Major Code more frequently and allege they are finding opposition from Government in its use. With some amendments the bill was worth saving. Had it been lost, it is unlikely that it would have been reintroduced in any form for many years. It is now up to others to make the most of it. Further remarks are made about the FOIA in chapter 10.

Access to information legislation began in local government as we have seen. It was introduced by FOIA into central government and public authorities generally. The next step will be in regional government where codes currently exist. The new style Greater London Authority has novel features on publicity and availability of the mayor's strategies,[6] and provisions on openness which involve the 1985 LG(ATI) Act, information schemes on matters relating to London,[7] annual reports by the mayor, an annual state of London debate and a People's Question Time.[8]

The interesting question will be to what extent the more liberal regimes operating in devolved government, particularly Scotland – although Scotland's draft legislation has been heavily influenced by the UK model – and Wales will help to act as a counterweight to Whitehall hegemony and its concentration on secrecy and confidentiality. We have to see what will happen in Northern Ireland. The role of confidentiality, as was seen, features prominently in the new concordats between London and Edinburgh and Cardiff. What opportunities will there be for constitutional pluralism in openness and access?

Some of the most popularly used provisions in FOIA will probably relate to access to personal records. This will involve knowledge of the Data Protection Act 1998. It is to this that I now turn.

6   GLA Act 1999, s 43.
7   Ibid, s 397.
8   Sections 46, 47, and 48.

7 Access to personal information

For almost 30 years British Governments have presented Bills to
Parliament which have allowed access to personal information by the
individuals on whom the information is kept—the 'subject'. The most
far-reaching has been the Data Protection Act 1984 now superseded by
the Data Protection Act 1998. The 1984 Act dealt with computerised
personal information. The 1998 Act, as we shall see, is not so confined.
The 1998 Act subsumes the legislation and regulations which covered
the topic of subject access to paper files in health, education (schools),
social services and housing as well as consumer credit. The 1998 Act
appeared a comprehensive provision but it has been amended by FOIA
2000. Until the 1998 and 2000 Acts, demands for laws covering paper
records held by employers on employees had been stoutly resisted in spite
of notorious episodes concerning abuses by self-styled private vetting
agencies. One of these had 30,000 manual files on 'left of centre'
individuals and had 2,000 companies as clients.[1] The Government has
supported the possibility of private security firms selling information such
as criminal records to employers even though the private security industry
was not at that time regulated.[2] In 1993, the Government promised
legislation to allow access to personal paper files held by public bodies
which it said would be regulated by a figure such as the Data Protection
Registrar. This would not of itself have stopped trade in such documents.

---

1   The Economic League was such a body; it was disbanded in 1993 but operatives
    were to continue in the business of selling information about employees. See
    generally: R Norton Taylor *Blacklist: the Inside Story of Political Vetting* (1988).
    A company specialises in collecting information about police officers who have
    been or are the subject of complaints from the public and which they market. See
    now s 3 Employment Relations Act 1999 and 'black lists'.
2   See now Private Security Industry Bill (2000-01).

The Department of Health sells information on its database which records patient reaction to pharmaceuticals.[3] The possibilities involving unregulated use of genetic information are startling as indeed are the implications of commercial patenting of such information. The Metropolitan Police, for instance, had refused to destroy 3,500 DNA profiles taken from people questioned but subsequently ruled out of police investigations.[4] Before examining the 1998 Act as amended by FOIA, it is important to realise what might be achieved under common law and what the ECHR has achieved.

The common law witnessed some interesting developments in relation to applications for records where legislation did not apply. In *ex p Martin*[5] a person suffering from psychiatric problems applied to two medical authorities for the disclosure of his medical records to establish more information about specific incidents in the past. Because the records were not on computer and were made before 1991, they were not subject to the existing statutory provisions. The first authority refused to make disclosure stating it lacked authority to do so. The second authority was prepared to make disclosure subject to conditions that an assurance had to be given by the applicant that no litigation was contemplated by him. This assurance the applicant refused to give. The second respondent subsequently refused access after the responsible consultant psychiatrist determined that disclosure to the applicant was not in his best interests and would be detrimental to him. After applying for a judicial review of this decision, the second respondent's solicitor wrote stating that the applicant's nominated medical adviser could have access to the documents to decide whether and to what extent disclosure could be made to the applicant without causing him harm. The Court of Appeal upheld the High Court's decision to refuse access stating that access could be denied by the owner of the patient's records (the authority) if it was in his best interests not to see them, ie where reading them could be detrimental to his health. The Court felt that on the facts, the offer by the authority was a complete answer to the request and it was, one might add, a generous

---

3   See *R v Department of Health, ex p Source Infomatics Ltd* [2000] 1 All ER 786, CA. A company wanted pharmacists to supply it for payment information about the prescription details of GPs with any personal information anonymised. In cases involving personal confidences, anonymised information, even if not in the public domain, would not be protected where there was no breach of confidence or privacy. The patients did not own the information or documents in question.

4   See *A-G's Reference (No 3 of 1999)* [2001] 1 All ER 577, HL where the House of Lords ruled that such DNA material unlawfully retained was admissible as evidence subject to s 78 PACE. Note the Criminal Justice and Police Bill (2000-2001).

5   *R v Mid Glamorgan Family Health Authority, ex p Martin* [1995] 1 All ER 356; see *Sidaway v Bethlem Royal Hospital Governors* [1985] 1 All ER 643, HL and *McInerney v MacDonald* (1992) 93 DLR (4th) 415, Canada.

offer. Because the respondent had done all that was necessary to comply with their duty, judicial review was rightly denied. One might suspect that had the offer not been made, the approach of the Court of Appeal may have been less generous to the authority. Nourse LJ for instance stated that a health authority, no more than a private doctor, does not have an absolute right to deal with medical records in any way it chooses and has at all times to act in the best interests of the patient. 'Those interests would usually require that a patient's medical records should not be disclosed to third parties; conversely, that they should usually be handed on by one doctor to the next or made available to the patient's legal advisers if they are reasonably required for the purposes of legal proceedings in which he is involved.' [6]

Where personal information is held by 'holders' and is not protected by legislation, and where the possession by such individuals of such information is not otherwise prohibited by the law, it will be well to remember that the possibility of a breach of confidence, trespass or wrongful interference with personal property (documents) under the Torts (Interference with Goods) Act 1977 may have occurred in the manner in which the information was obtained or in which it was used. There may be a breach of copyright involved or some other aspect of intellectual property law. It is of course well to remember the impact of the Human Rights Act 1998 on this area and the application of Article 8 protecting family life and privacy. In spite of age-old resistance to the creation of a law of privacy in our case law, the courts are getting closer to creating a right to privacy protection. [7]

This was evidenced by the litigation involving film stars Michael Douglas and Catherine Zeta-Jones where they signed an exclusive right to use photographs of their wedding with a publishing group. A rival publisher published the photographs depriving the parties of the benefit of their agreement. The Court of Appeal felt that their right to privacy had been invaded unjustifiably but an injunction was not awarded to prevent wrongful publication because damages would be an adequate remedy. [8] In *Venables and Thompson v Newsgroup Newspapers Ltd* [9] the High Court was prepared to protect the identity of the murderers of James Bulger after their release from prison in very extensive terms under a combination of arts 2 (guaranteeing a right to life), Art 3 (right not to suffer torture, inhuman or degrading treatment) and art 8 ECHR (right to

6   *Martin* at p 363j.
7   See notes 8 and 9 below but note *Kaye v Robertson* [1991] FSR 62 and *R v Broadcasting Complaints Commission, ex p Granada Television Ltd* [1995] 7 LS Gaz R 36.
8   *Douglas, Zeta-Jones and Northern Shell Ltd, Douglas v Hello! Ltd* [2000] 2 All ER 289.
9   *Venables and Thompson v News Group Newspapers Ltd* [2001] 1 All ER 908.

privacy). Serious and sustained threats had been made against the youths and the press wanted to reveal any new identities they were given and their whereabouts after their release in accordance with their right to freedom of speech under HRA 1998 and Art 10 ECHR. Both cases can be explained on the grounds of established principles of confidentiality.

Decisions of the Court and Commission of Human Rights in Strasbourg have placed limits on a public body's power to refuse access to personal documents or have allowed access to documents in order to make meaningful rights under Art 8 and these include the famous decision in *Gaskin v UK*[10] where the absence of an independent arbitration to determine requests for access which were contested by the record holder constituted a breach of Art 8, but not Art 10. In *Guerra v Italy*,[11] the European Court of Human Rights held that not informing local residents of the dangers of a local chemical plant interfered with their right to enjoyment of privacy and family life under Art 8 but not their rights under Art 10 to freedom to pass on information. Article 10 did not provide a positive right to be informed. The Commission disagreed on this point. Likewise in *McGinley and Egan v UK*[12] where the UK authorities had exposed servicemen to nuclear test explosions, the authorities' failure to provide an effective and accessible procedure to allow parties to seek all relevant information and papers constituted a breach of Art 8. Art 10, however, does not allow a positive right to state held documents. It prevents the state placing unjustified limits on others passing on information and expressing themselves freely. A committee of experts is examining previous recommendations of the Council of Ministers on access to official documents with a view to revision.[13]

Further, the dealing with inaccurate information which causes harm – financial or physical/emotional – could on the facts amount to negligence as well as defamation. The proximity of the holder to the subject ought to be sufficient to satisfy a duty of care situation in the law of negligence[14] – in spite of recent attempts to limit the range of victims.[15] However, it has to be said that the comprehensive nature of the DPA will make the residual role of the common law less useful in seeking access. But the common

---

10 *Gaskin v UK* (1989) 12 EHRR 36; also, *McMichael v UK* [1995] 2 FCR 718, ECtHR. *Gaskin* concerned social welfare files: see Children Act 1989 ss 22 (4), 26 (2)(d), 26 (3) and SI 1990/2244; and the Butler Sloss Report Cm 412 (1988) and *Working Together* HMSO on consulting and informing in child care.
11 (1998) 4 BHRC 63.
12 Case No 10/1997/794/995-996 (1998) 27 EHRR 1.
13 Rec No R(81)19. I Harden (2001) European Public Law forthcoming.
14 *Spring v Guardian Association plc* [1994] 3 All ER 129, HL duty between referee and job applicant
15 See also Malicious Communications Act 1988.

law will have a greater role to play in protecting information and its publication.

It must be emphasised that before the Access to Personal Information Act 1987 was passed by Parliament, the British Association of Social Workers, the National Council for Voluntary Organisations, individual authorities, education authorities and schools had supported or accepted voluntary access procedures. Some hospitals carried out an informal practice of notifying patients of the contents of their files, and an unexpected consequence was that doctors' notes were more carefully written, honest and straightforward. However, the British Medical Association[16] voted in June 1986 to maintain the confidentiality of doctors' files, consultants showing themselves especially protective of confidentiality. The BMA also pressed for reversal of the General Medical Council guidance that broke the complete confidentiality owed by doctors to their patients. This concerned girls under 16 seeking contraception, after the Court of Appeal ruling in the case of *Gillick* held that doctors must notify the parents.[17] When an inquiry into an alleged medical malpractice is held in public, the GMC has warned participants not to use confidential files on patients in evidence in public, but only *in camera*. This was the GMC ruling even though it seemed that patients were happy to have the evidence examined in public.[18] The inquiry was held in public at the request of the person investigated to avoid a 'cover-up', although usually such inquiries are internal.[19] The inquiry into the notorious murderer Dr Harold Shipman was held in public after a judicial ruling that a private inquiry would be a breach of Art 10 ECHR.[20] In other circumstances inquiries into tragedies, such as child deaths, have been roundly condemned *because* they were heard in public.[1]

While protection of personal information is becoming more of a preoccupation, legislation is increasing the range of duties that exist to disclose information on convictions and especially in relation to children

16 It is essentially a professional association and not a governing body. In July 1987, it voted to 'Aids test' patients without their consent where a doctor felt this to be necessary; the BMA's ruling council subsequently blocked this move.

17 Reversed in *Gillick v West Norfolk and Wisbeach Area Health Authority* [1985] 3 All ER 402 , HL. Confidentiality for Aids victims must be maintained: and note *X v Y* [1988] 2 All ER 648. On police removal of AIDS/HIV information on victims identified on the Police National Computer, see DPR *Annual Report 1995* pp 29-30, HC 629 (1994/5).

18 *The Guardian* 13 February 1986. The case concerned the obstetrician Dr Wendy Savage. For alleged GMC equivocation on this point, see W Savage, *The Guardian* 3 June 1987.

19 Dr Savage wanted an open inquiry to avoid a 'cover-up' she claimed. An internal report for the health authority said the inquiry should not have been held: *The Guardian* 9 July 1987.

20 *R (Wagstaff) v Secretary of State for Health* [2001] 1 WLR 292.

1 As with the notorious case of Tyra Henry in 1986.

and in law enforcement generally.[2] There are also statutory provisions on information relating to child abuse[3] and copious case law on child protection registers.[4]

The Data Protection Act 1998

In the literature of political science there is a phrase which describes the rationality crisis when the state can no longer cater for all the tasks which its regulation has created. This was known as 'administrative overload'. The Data Protection Act 1984 (DPA) might be described as Parliament's first step to deal with 'information overload'. The Act is only concerned with personal information or data.

It has to be emphasised that although the DPA covers both computerised and manual personal information, computerised information generally is subject to the same control and availability as manual information. It does not involve additional security measures. If within a government department there is computerised data covered by the Official Secrets Acts and its disclosure is not exempt from prosecution by virtue of the DPA, unauthorised disclosure could result in prosecution. If it is a question of Parliament being informed of the data held by government or its agencies, whatever limitations apply to Parliament's ability to obtain information from the government will apply here also. Data constitutes property, although the complexities involved in the legal classification of concepts conveying appropriate rights and protection have caused, and will cause, legal disputation of a more than usually complex nature.[5]

The DPA was passed primarily to incorporate into British law the provisions of the European Convention on Data Protection 1981.[6] Had the Convention not been incorporated, the flow of data into the UK from other signatory states might well have been prohibited. By 1993, several signatory states had not established data protection laws. In July 1995 an

---

2   Rehabilitation of Offenders Act 1974; Part V Police Act 1997 and the Criminal Records Agency; Protection of Children Act 1999 and Care Standards Act 2000. See Birkinshaw *Government and Information* (2nd ed, 2001) pp 314-15.

3   Children Act 1989, ss 19 and 47 and also s 26. See *Re EC (Disclosure of Material)* [1996] 2 FLR 725; *Re V (Sexual Abuse: Disclosure)* [1999] 1 FLR 267.

4   *R v Norfolk CC Social Services Department, ex p M* [1989] 2 All ER 359; *R v Harrow LBC, ex p D* [1990] Fam 133; *R v Devon CC, ex p L* [1991] 2 FLR 541; *R v Lewisham LBC, ex p P* [[1991] 3 All ER 529; *R v Hampshire CC, ex p H* [1999] 2 FLR 359.

5   C Tapper *Computer Law* (1989); I Lloyd *Information Technology* (3rd ed, 2000); Copyright (Computer Software) Amendment Act 1985.

6   There was a commercial necessity in the incorporation by the UK Government of the Convention. See Austin (1984) Public Law 618.

EU Directive was adopted on data protection which sought to harmonise laws throughout member states on access to personal data.[7] By virtue of Art 286 EC and Regulation (EC) 45/2001, the Directive applies to Community institutions. In 1997, a directive was passed on the processing of personal data and the protection of privacy in the telecommunications sector.[8] A new telecoms Data Protection Directive is being prepared.

The basic idea behind the Directive and Act is that data subjects should have access to data, subject to exemptions, controls should exist over the use that is made of information in personal data and there should be impartial supervision of data holders. The directive applied to both computerised and manual data and allowed trans-border transfer of electronic personal data to countries without data protection laws where certain conditions were fulfilled. The Directive applied to public and private sector holders of personal information, as did the 1984 Act, and is closer to a privacy protection law than anything that operated in the UK in that positive duties to inform subjects of the use of data will be established along with rights to object by the subjects to the holding of data. The Directive had to be implemented within three years of adoption. The implementing measure was the DPA 1998. The Directive was subject to considerable hostility both here and in the USA where opposition continues.[9] The Home Office commissioned studies suggesting that compliance costs will amount to £2 billion. The Directive was accused of being a part of the stifling EU bureaucratic over-regulation.

What the Act does

Basically, the DPA creates a very wide right of access to personal data by the subjects of the data – much wider than under the 1984 Act. If inaccurate, the subject may apply to the court for it to correct, block, erase or destroy the data. There are exemptions from access on the grounds of national security, in relation to crime and taxation and other matters. Data controllers (DCs) will have to register ('notify') with the Data Protection Commissioner (to be re-named the Information Commissioner under FOIA 2000) although there will be exemptions from notification. Failure to register where required will be a criminal offence. Subjects will have rights to compensation where there are breaches of the Act. The subject has a right to give notice to a data controller to order them to stop processing data which is likely to cause 'substantial damage' or 'substantial distress' to the subject which is unwarranted. These terms are not defined and there

7   Directive 95/46/EC: OJ L 281/31, 31 November 1995. See D Bainbridge *EC Data Protection Directive* (1996).
8   Directive 97/66/EC. See I Lloyd *A Guide to the Data Protection Act 1998* (1998).
9   A Charlesworth 'Clash of the Data Titans' (2000) European Public Law 253

are provisos. There is also a right to prevent processing for the purposes of direct marketing.

'Data' and related matters

Section 1 of the 1998 Act defines 'data' and related terms. 'Data' means personal information which is being processed by means of equipment operating automatically in response to instructions given for the purpose – basically computerised; secondly, information which is recorded with the intention that it should be processed by such equipment; thirdly, information which is recorded as part of a relevant filing system or with the intention that it should form part of a relevant filing system.[10] This embraces 'structured information' which is stored by reference to a code or identifying number for instance. This information covers manual or paper files. The precise scope of what manual files are included has led to conflicting interpretations with the DPC interpreting the provision more broadly than the Government.[11] Does it cover a file on which the subject's name is on the front but the information in loosely assorted papers is not readily extractable? If not part of a 'set' it could fall under the personal data added by the FOIA rather than under this heading. It seems it will cover card indexes, rollerdex, microfiche. The last definition under the unamended 1998 DPA covers manual information not covered above but which forms part of an accessible record under s 68 DPA. This covers health records, educational (school) records as defined in schedules and accessible records as defined in Sch 12 which covers housing and social services records.

The FOIA additions

The FOIA s 68 adds to the definitions *recorded* information held by a public authority which does not fall within any of the above provisions, ie it is not computerised or organised in such a way as to be covered by the definitions in the DPA. By this means DPA rights of subject access and data accuracy are extended to all personal information held by public authorities as defined. The first four categories however, apply regardless of whether the data is held by a public or private body. The latter only

10 Although not operating automatically, the information is structured, either by reference to individuals or by reference to criteria relating to individuals, in such a way that specific information relating to a particular individual is readily accessible. These would include, as well as filing systems, card indexes.

11 See the DPC's *Introduction to the 1998 Act.* This was the view of the DPC when she gave evidence to the Select Committee on Public Administration in its inquiry into the White Paper *Open Government*: HC 398 I (1997-98) Qu 220.

applies to data held by a public authority covered by the FOIA. By this means, the wider areas of personal information covered by FOIA are not extended to private holders of such information.

Data Protection Act and Freedom of Information Act

While the FOIA states that all personal information held by public authorities is included within the DPA, it cancels all the effects of being within the DPA for this last category of information apart from subject access rights and accuracy so that the full impact of the DPA will not apply. Even access rights and accuracy will not apply to non-designated functions of public authorities – those basically which are not of a public nature — and personal information held by those bodies falling under this last group of information. This means therefore that the DPA applies to public authorities' non-automated records even though they are not part of a relevant filing system and not part of an 'accessible record' as defined in the Act. 'An example of this might be incidental personal information on a policy file, or in loose papers.'[12] Section 68 FOIA adds a further qualification to subject access rights to the group of personal information introduced under FOIA. Where the information is, although not part of a relevant filing system or part of an accessible record, nonetheless structured to a certain extent by reference to individuals eg 'a case file about an individual which contains correspondence about a number of matters relating to that individual and is indexed by reference only to the dates of the correspondence'[13] it is treated for subject access purposes as any other personal information under the DPA.

Where it is not 'relatively structured', ie 'relatively unstructured', additional conditions are imposed on access requests. First, unstructured personal data will not be given unless the information is *expressly* described in the request. Requests for information covered by the DPA will usually be met by giving the subject all of their data without them having to specify any part of it. 'No part of the residue of relatively unstructured personal information, however, will be included in response to a subject access request unless the data subject has expressly described it.'[14] It should be recalled that under FOIA generally, requests for additional information may be made by public authorities. Requests by applicants will therefore have to be more specific for this kind of information. Secondly, the authority may refuse an access request in so far as it relates to that information where to allow it would cost more than is provided for in a 'prescribed cost ceiling' (see chapter 6).

12 *FOI Consultation on Draft Legislation*, para 169, Cm 4355, (1999).
13 Ibid, para 170.
14 Ibid.

The effect of s 69 is to deprive data subjects on whom personal data covered by the 2000 FOIA is held of all the substantive rights under the DPA to the group of personal information introduced under FOIA apart, as we have seen, from subject access and inaccuracy. It further adds that the extension of access and accuracy rights does not apply to personnel records within that group of information held by public authorities and this follows the FOI White Paper of 1997. Employees do not have rights of access to their personnel records under FOIA provisions

The DPA provides that where there is a statutory duty to provide information to the public it is exempt from subject access, accuracy and certain other restrictions on disclosure. This is because such access provisions eg marriage, births, death registers and the Land Registry,[15] make their own detailed provisions. If the provision stood without more, it would also embrace and thereby exempt those duties under FOIA. FOIA is therefore not included within these provisions. If this were not the case, rights under FOIA would override those under the DPA.

Personal data, sensitive personal data and 'special purposes'

Personal data means data which relates to a living individual – the data subject – who can be identified from that data (or from that data and other information in the possession of the holder of information, or which is likely to come into the possession of the data controller) including an expression of opinion about the individual and any indications of the intentions of the data controller in respect of the individual. Previously where opinions on employees were processed and were not exempt they would have to be disclosed to the employee, but not the intentions of the employer, ie to dismiss or to promote. Such data will now be disclosable.

A new category of data known as 'sensitive personal data' is provided for by s 2. This includes: the subject's racial or ethnic origin, political opinions, religious beliefs or 'other beliefs of a similar nature', whether a member of a trade union, physical or mental health or condition, sexual life, commission or allegation of any offences, any criminal proceedings or sentences against the subject. This is information which is likely to be tradeable and abused.

There are also 'special purposes' relating to journalism, artistic purposes and literary purposes (including biographies) which are important in order to ensure added protection to data controllers (below) using data covered by the DPA for these purposes. Basically, such DCs may use personal data for such purposes so as not to allow privacy protection to impede freedom of expression (see below).

---

15 The price of residential property will be made public after 1 April 2000.

The data controller and processing

The controller and processor of data is referred to as the 'data controller' (DC) and 'data processor' (DP). The DC means a person who either alone or jointly or in common with others determines the purposes for which and the manner in which any personal data are, or are to be, processed – it covers an intention to process data.[16] Data may be controlled by an individual, in tandem with others via an intranet as a part of a group using groupware[17] A DP is 'any person' who processes the data on behalf of the DC – but it does not include a DC's employee. An example of such a person is an independent contractor.

Processing in relation to data or information means obtaining, recording or holding the information or data or carrying out any operation or set of operations on the information or data, including

(a) organisation, adaptation or alteration of the information or data,
(b) retrieval, consultation or use of the information or data,
(c) disclosure of the information or data by transmission, dissemination or otherwise making it available, or
(d) alignment, combination, blocking, erasure or destruction of the information or data.

This is a much wider definition than under the 1984 Act and includes obtaining and recording data.[18] Processing no longer has to take place with reference to the data subject as under the 1984 Act. 'It is a compendious definition and it is difficult to envisage any action involving data which does not amount to processing within this definition.'[19] The s 1 definition was also necessary to circumvent the decision of the Law Lords in *R v Brown*[20] which held that where a defendant was charged with using personal data, then accessing or retrieval of information on a computer so that it could be read either on screen or by means of a print-out was not 'using' the information but simply transferring the information into a different form prior to possible use being made of it, ie passing it on to a third party.

General points

DCs have to comply with the Data Protection Principles (DPP) in relation to all personal data over which they are the controller (see below). The

---

16 Section 1(1).
17 A Charlesworth *Annotation to Data Protection* Act Current Law Statutes 1998 chapter 29.
18 Section 1(2) and (3).
19 Data Protection Commissioner *Introduction to the 1998 Act* chapter 2.
20 [1996] 1 All ER 545, HL.

Act applies to DCs established in the UK, and DCs outside the UK and EEA who use equipment inside the UK for processing the data 'otherwise than for the purposes of transit through the UK.'

The Act renames the Data Protection Registrar the Data Protection Commissioner and also establishes the DP Tribunal. As we have seen the FOIA renames these bodies the Information Commissioner and Information Tribunal. A chairman will be assisted by a person representing the interests of information (including data controllers) holders and information (including data subjects) requesters.

Duty of notification

Under the 1984 Act a DC had to register with the DPR. This has been replaced by a duty to notify the Commissioner that they wish to be placed on a register of those intending to process personal data. There are exemptions from notification and fees are payable.[1] The register will contain registrable particulars from the DCs application. Even though a DC is not registered because of either a breach of the statute or an exemption, DCs will nonetheless be liable for breaches of the Data Protection Principles. Data may be processed without registration where it is not 'assessable' under s 22 – ie processing likely to cause substantial damage or distress to data subjects or otherwise prejudice the rights and freedoms of subjects and for which special provisions apply — *and* the processing is not by means of equipment operating automatically in response to instructions given for that purpose or data were not recorded with such an intention, ie it is manual data. Section 17(3) allows the Secretary of State to exempt the DC from notification where he believes that data may be processed within a particular category of processing which will not prejudice the rights and freedoms of data subjects. Exemption from notification may also be claimed where a DC has a reliable system of self-regulation. This is consistent with the aims of the Directive. A register entry will last for 12 months unless notification regulations vary this period. Even where data are exempt from the notification process, s 24 stipulates that a DC must make 'relevant particulars' available in accordance with s 16(1) to any person making a written request within 21 days free of charge.

The Commissioner has to make publicly available at all reasonable hours information on the register free of charge in 'visible and legible' form. A fee may be required for a copy.[2] DCs must ensure entries are as up to date as possible and processing in breach of a registration requirement

---

1   See SI 2000/188.
2   The register is available on the DPC's homepage at n 4 below.

is a criminal offence. Entries will include the name of the DC and their address or that of their nominated representative, a description of data to be processed and categories of data subjects to which it relates, purpose(s) of processing, recipients of data and non-EEA countries to which data are or may be transferred. The register will allow subjects to assess, in general terms, whether a DC is likely to hold information upon them as eg, an employer, retailer or client, customer and so on. The subject may then ask the DC whether the DC has information covered by the Act on the subject. If this is the case, then subject to exemptions and payment of any fee,[3] the subject has right of access.

Rights of appeal to Tribunal

There are rights of appeal against notices served on DCs by the Commissioner. The Tribunal will be renamed the Information Tribunal. It will have a legally qualified chair with one wing person representing the interests of subjects and one representing DCs – but not one for data processors.

The Commissioner's duties[4]

The Commissioner has a variety of duties under the Act including the promotion of good practice by Data Controller's (DC and see infra) and to promote the observance of the Act by DCs. She shall arrange for the publication of information about the Act and good practice as well as advice as appears appropriate. She shall also prepare and disseminate to such persons as she considers appropriate codes of practice for guidance on good practice. This may be done by order of the Secretary of State or at the Commissioner's discretion. This will also follow consultation with trade associations, data subjects and their representatives as she considers appropriate. The Commissioner may encourage the making of codes by trade associations for their members and she may consider any code after consulting with data subjects or representatives and may advise whether the code promotes the following features of good practice.[5] No doubt many such codes will be produced but one of special interest relates to *Users of Closed Circuit TV*[6] which sets out, inter alia, rights of subjects,

3   Section 26 and n 13 p 358 below.
4   The home page for the Commissioner is: http://www.dataprotection.gov.uk.
5   See eg the Code of Practice for Fire Brigades. Codes are being prepared by ACPO, the Association of Chief Probation Officers and the DPC is preparing a code on employment relations.
6   See Wadham (2000) New LJ 1173 and 1236.

ie those caught on security camera and access to data by third parties. She may disseminate certain EC matters and information on processing outside the EEA. She may, with the DCs consent, assess processing of personal data to see if good practice is followed. The DC will be informed of the results. She may charge for services provided. Annual reports and other reports shall be laid before each House of Parliament as well as any codes prepared under s 51(3).

The data protection principles

The principles which govern the holding etc of data are set out in the DPP. A central feature of the DPA is the protection afforded to data subjects. The DPP are central to this task. The DPP are contained in the first schedule to the Act and are to be interpreted in accordance with Part II of that schedule. Unless a DC is exempted from the DPP (under s 27(1)), they are bound to comply them with in accordance with s 4. The DPP are as follows:

(1) Personal data shall be processed, fairly[7] and lawfully and shall not be processed unless (a) one of the conditions in Sch 2 is met and in the case of sensitive personal data, one of the conditions in Sch 3 is also met. The conditions are set out below.

(2) Personal data shall be obtained only for one or more specified and lawful purposes and shall not be further processed in any manner incompatible with that purpose(s).

(3) Personal data held shall be adequate, relevant and not excessive in relation to the purpose(s) for which they are processed

(4) Personal data shall be accurate and, where necessary, kept up-to-date.

(5) Personal data processed for any purpose or purposes shall not be kept for longer than is necessary for that purpose or those purposes.

(6) Personal data shall be processed in accordance with the rights of data subjects under this Act.

(7) Appropriate technical and organisational measures shall be taken against unauthorised or unlawful processing of personal data and against accidental loss or destruction of, or damage to, personal data.

(8) Personal data shall not be transferred to a country or territory outside the EEA unless that country or territory ensures an adequate level of protection for the rights and freedoms of data subjects in relation to the processing of personal data. Contravention of this Principle will be an offence and subject to the Commissioner's remedies. It should be noted however, that there is no power for the Commissioner in the

---

7   See the DPR's Annual Report for 1999 pp 58-66 for a report of an appeal to the tribunal concerning Midlands Electricity plc and processing unfairly in that the company was using information about customers without their consent.

1998 legislation to issue a Transfer Prohibition Notice preventing the transfer out of the UK as under the 1984 Act. In fact under the 1984 Act only one TPN was issued by the DPR.

How are the principles interpreted?

Under Part II of Sch I in relation to the first principle, when determining for the purposes of the first principle whether personal data were obtained fairly, regard is to be had to the method by which they were obtained, including in particular whether any person from whom they are obtained is deceived or misled as to the purpose(s) for which they are processed.

Subject to para 2 below, data are treated as obtained fairly under the first principle if they consist of information obtained from a person who:
(a) is authorised by or under any enactment to supply it; or
(b) is required to supply it by or under any enactment or by any convention or other instrument imposing an international obligation on the UK.

Any disclosure authorised by such statute, or required by such convention or instrument shall be disregarded in determining whether information was obtained fairly.

The DPC will need to consider all the circumstances behind the obtaining of information to assess whether it was obtained unfairly. Was there a full explanation by the user to the subject of why information was required and how it was to be used, in response to questions or otherwise? Could the subject reasonably have been expected to understand the explanation etc? Intended uses and disclosures should be disclosed. The DPC has expressed the hope that codes of practice prepared by users will encourage the provision of full and helpful explanations to individuals.

Subject to para 3, for the purposes of the first principle in the case of data obtained from the data subject, data are not to be treated as processed fairly unless the subject has information specified in sub-para 3 (which states the identity of the DC or his representative, the purpose(s) or intended purpose(s) of processing or any further information which is necessary in the circumstances to allow processing to be fair) or (b) the subject is provided with it, or it is made readily available to him 'so far as practicable' and in any other case, the DC ensures as far as practicable that before the relevant time or as soon as practicable after that time the data subject has, is provided with or has readily made available to him specified information (in sub-para 3). The sub-paragraph spells out the relevant time. In relation to (b) above, where the provision of that information would involve a 'disproportionate effort' or the recording or disclosure of information is required by a legal provision binding on the DC except one imposed by contract the provisions of sub-para 3 do not apply.

Special provisions apply to personal identifiers.

In relation to the second principle, Part II states that the purpose(s) for which personal data are obtained may be specified in a notice from the DC to the subject or in a notification given to the Commissioner under Part III DPA. Regard is to be had to the purpose(s) for which personal data are intended to be processed by any person to whom they are disclosed in determining whether any disclosure of personal data is compatible with the purpose(s) for which the data were obtained.

In relation to the fourth principle, Part II sets out when the fourth principle is not to be regarded as contravened by reason of inaccuracy in personal data which accurately record information obtained by the DC from the subject or a third party ie the DC has taken reasonable steps to ensure the accuracy of the data having regard to the purpose(s) of obtaining and further processing the data, and the subject has notified the DC of their inaccuracy and the data indicate that fact.

In relation to the sixth principle a person is to be regarded as contravening the sixth principle if, but only if, he contravenes provisions of ss 7, 10(1) and (3), 11(1), 12(1)(2)(b), (2)(a) or (3). These concern rights of access, processing for direct marketing as well as processing data for automated decision-taking.

In relation to the seventh principle which concerns levels of security appropriate to the degrees of harm that might follow from the events in the seventh principle, the nature of the data to be protected, the DC has to ensure the reliability of employees, ensuring reliability of data processors and forms for contracts for processing and the stipulated terms ie compliance with the seventh principle.

In relation to the interpretation of the eighth principle criteria are set out on adequate levels of protection for data transferred out of the UK and include the nature of the personal data. The protection is one which is adequate in all the circumstances of the case having particular regard to: the country or territory of origin of the information of the information contained in the data; the country or territory of final destination of that information; the purposes for which and period during which the data are intended to be processed; the law in force on the country or territory in question; international obligations of that country or territory; any relevant codes of conduct or other enforceable rules in that country or territory; and any security measures taken in respect of the data in that country or territory.

Schedule 4 describes situations where the eighth principle does not apply. It covers consent by the subject to transfer and necessary transfers.

Section 33 makes provision for data processed for 'research purposes' which includes statistical or historical purposes. Such data are exempt from certain of the Data Protection Principles. The purpose of the research processing must not be in the form of measures or decisions targeted at particular individuals and the processing does not cause harm or distress. Where the 'relevant conditions' are complied with, processing for the above purposes is exempt from the second DPP, the fifth DPP, and they are exempt from s 7 (access rights). The research must be made available through results in a way which does not identify individuals.

Conditions for lawful processing

Schedule 2 sets out conditions relevant for the purpose of the first principle and one of these must be satisfied for the lawful processing of personal data – they are pivotal in spite of being buried away in a schedule. They list the case where the subject has given his consent; and also where the processing is necessary for a variety of grounds such as the performance by the DS of a contract, compliance by the DC with legal obligations other than under a contract, for the vital interests of the DS, for the administration of justice, the performance of a wide range of public functions (statutory, Crown, ministerial or departmental) including those performed in the public interest or for the pursuit of the legitimate interests of the DC or a third party except where disclosure is unwarranted because of prejudice to the rights, freedoms or legitimate interests of the DS.

Schedule 3 sets out conditions for the first principle and sensitive personal data (and see SI 2000/417). The subject must have given his *explicit* consent to the processing and processing is necessary for a variety of reasons or is carried out for 'legitimate activities' or eg legal proceedings. The list is very detailed and includes the situation where processing is necessary for 'medical purposes' and duties on the DC in relation to employment subject to specified exclusions or further conditions, to protect vital interests of the DS or another where consent has not been given or has been unreasonably withheld, and to protect the legitimate activities of non profit bodies which exist for religious, trade union, political, or philosophical purposes and subject to further conditions including the consent of the DS to third party disclosure. It covers the situation where processing is necessary for the administration of justice or for the purposes of central government. The Secretary of State is given power by order to provide for additional safeguards.

Rights of data subjects and others

For data subjects the test of a successful data protection scheme is whether it provides adequate safeguards and rights for the subject. These include rights of access and correction. These rights are contained in Part II of the DPA. Basically, under s 7(1)(a), an individual is entitled after making a request in writing and paying the prescribed fee, to be informed by any data controller whether personal data of which that individual is the data subject are being processed by or on behalf of that data controller. If so, then they shall be given by the DC a description of:

(a) personal data of which that data is the data subject
(b) the purposes for which they are being or are to be processed
(c) recipients or classes of recipient to whom they are entitled to be disclosed.[8]

The subject is entitled to have communicated to them in an intelligible form

(a) the information constituting any personal data of which that individual is the data subject (see s 8(2)), and
(b) any information available to the DC as to the source of those data, and -

under s 7(1)(d) the subject is entitled to know the logic involved in decision-making (although this will not cover a trade secret) where the data is processed automatically and is likely to form the sole basis for any decision significantly affecting the subject such as work performance, credit-worthiness, reliability or conduct.

A DC is not obliged to comply with the request under this section unless the DC is supplied with such information as they may reasonably require in order to be satisfied as to the identity of the requester and to locate information which that person seeks.[9] Where disclosure to a requester would allow disclosure of information about another individual who can be identified from that information, the DC does not have to comply unless the other person consents to that disclosure to the requester or it is reasonable in all the circumstances to comply with the request without consent [10] Another individual can be identified from the information being disclosed 'if he can be identified from that information, or from that and any other information which, in the reasonable belief of the DC, is likely to be in, or come into, the possession of the data subject making the request.[11] A request must be complied with promptly and in any event before the end of the prescribed period beginning with the relevant day. The prescribed period is 40 days or such other period as may be prescribed by regulations (it is interesting that 40 days was the original period specified in the draft FOI bill). A court may order a DC to comply with the request. Regulations under s 8 may state that if a DC receives a request for information under s 7(1) he must also supply other pieces of information

---

8   Section 7(1)(b).
9   Where personal data added by the FOIA is requested the onus on the requester to provide additional indentiying criteria is greater (see above p 339).
10 See s 7(5) on supplying information where the identity can be omitted; see s 7(6) on factors to consider in assessing 'reasonable'.
11 Section 8(7).

described in s 7(1) as well. There are safeguards against repetitious requests. Data supplied must be that held at the time the request is received subject to any deletions or amendments between that time and the time of supply that were going to be made regardless of the request. Section 9 contains modifications to s 7 requests where the DC is a credit reference bureau and covers requests under s 159 Consumer Credit Act 1974.[12] It is possible to detect the similarity between some of these provisions and those that found their way into the FOI bill and Act.

Section 10 provides a right to the DS to give a notice to a DC requiring the DC at the end of a period which is reasonable in the circumstances to cease, or not to begin, processing etc data of which the DS is the subject where the processing etc is likely to cause or is causing substantial damage or substantial distress to him or to another which is or would be unwarranted. This provision does not apply where any of the conditions in paras 1-4 of Sch 2 is met or in cases prescribed by regulations. Within 21 days of receipt of the written notice, the DC must give the person sending the notice their own written notice stating that he has complied or intends to comply with the DS notice or stating reasons why the DC regards the notice as unjustified and the extent to which he intends to comply with it. The court may take such steps as it thinks fit to ensure compliance with a notice served on a DC where there is a failure to comply. This is likely to be very important in cases of 'blacklisting' and may have special relevance to sensitive information under s 2.

Section 11 confers a right on an individual to prevent or to cease processing for the purposes of direct marketing by serving a written notice and the court may take such steps as it sees fit to enforce the notice where satisfied that the DC has failed to comply. 'Direct marketing' means the communication (by whatever means) of any advertising or marketing material which is directed to particular individuals.[13]

Section 12 deals with the individual's right to prevent decisions taken by the DC which significantly affect that individual being based solely on the processing by automatic means of personal data in respect of which that individual is the DS. This involves evaluations of the subject's performance at work, creditworthiness, reliability or conduct. These matters are specifically referred to but are not exclusive. It has been pointed out that under the 1984 Act, such processing was 'effectively controlled'[14] and although widely known in relation to credit-worthiness, the less known but increasing use of psychometric testing for employment decisions is covered.[15] The individual has the right where such a decision

---

12 This was an early statutory access right. It is now brought within the DPA.
13 Section 11(3).
14 *Equifax Europe Ltd v DPR* (unreported, 1992, Data Protection Tribunal).
15 Charlesworth *Data Protection Act 1998* Current Law Statutes 1998 chapter 29, 29-21.

has been made by such processing to require the DC to reconsider or take a new decision 'otherwise than on that basis'. This may be enforced by the court. There are time limits of 21 days from receipt of the notice to set out the steps taken by the DC to comply with the DS notice. These provisions do not apply to exempt decisions. These exemptions cover decisions as specified which satisfy certain conditions or are otherwise prescribed by regulations. The specified conditions are those decisions relating to the entering or performing of a contract with the DS, those authorised or required by any enactment, and the effect of the decision is to grant a request of the DS, or steps have been taken to safeguard the legitimate interests of the DS by eg allowing representations to be made.

Individuals who suffer damage by reason of any contravention by a DC of any of the requirements of this Act are entitled to compensation from the DC for that damage. This is much broader than the right under the 1984 Act. The Act further provides that distress by reason of any contravention by a DC of any of the requirements of this Act is also compensable by the DC if the individual suffers damage by reason of the contravention or the contravention relates to the processing of personal data for the special purposes. A defence is available to a DC that he took such care as was reasonable in all the circumstances to comply.

Where a court[16] is satisfied on the application of a DS that personal data of which the applicant is the subject are inaccurate, the court may order the DC to rectify, block[17], erase or destroy those data and any other personal data in respect of which he is the DC and which contain an expression of opinion which appears to the court to be based on the inaccurate data. This applies whether or not data accurately record information received from the DS or a third party. Where it does accurately record such information and Sch 1, Part II para 7 is satisfied[18] then instead of making the above order the court may require the data to be supplemented by such statement of the true facts relating to the matters dealt with by the data as the court may approve (s 14(2)(a)). Where any provisions in para 7 are not complied with it may make such an order to secure compliance with or without the above statement. Courts may also take steps to prevent further contraventions of the Act. DCs may also be required to notify third parties to whom they have passed inaccurate personal data, where it considers it reasonably practicable – ie the extent of the numbers involved (s 14(6)), of any rectification etc.

16   The jurisdiction is exercised by the High Court or county court in England and Wales and the Court of Session and sheriff court in Scotland. The court has wide powers of inspection but not of disclosure to applicants pending the determination of that question in the applicant's favour.

17   'Blocking' is not defined. It seems to suggest that data is made inaccessible although it may be held: see R Jay and A Hamilton *Data Protection Law and Practice* (1999).

18   This concerns the fourth principle: see above.

FOIA exemptions and the DPA

The DPA is a comprehensive code but it is subject to exemptions. However, personal information is exempt under FOIA and this subject has to be addressed before dealing with the DPA's exemptions.

As explained in chapter 6, access to personal data/documents under FOIA is exempt from the provisions of FOIA if it is data covered by the DPA. This is because access to such documents by a data subject has to be made under the DPA in accordance with that Act's provisions and the exemption under FOIA is absolute. This will include access to data added by FOIA. Access to records about others has to be made under FOIA. But an exemption applies under s 40 FOIA. This exemption is absolute where it constitutes data falling within paras (a) – (d) of the definition of data within s 1(1) DPA and disclosure to a member of the public would contravene any of the DPP. There is also an absolute exemption in the case of data added by the FOIA where disclosure to a member of the public would contravene any of the DPP but for the exemption in section 33A DPA (added by FOIA s 70). This only applies to manual data introduced by FOIA and held by public authorities. Where a request is for personal data not covered by the DPA or FOIA, it is not exempt. Where it is data covered by the DPA and FOIA as described above, but it is exempt from s 7(1)(c) DPA by virtue of any provision in Part IV of the same, it is then exempt from disclosure under FOIA, but the exemption is not absolute. It is subject to the public interest test (see chapter 6 p 317). Where data falls within section 1(1)(a)-(d) DPA and is exempt from disclosure under s 10, it is exempt under FOIA but the exemption is not absolute.

Exemptions

Exemptions from the DP provisions are contained in Part IV of the Act. Part IV has to be read in conjunction with Sch 7. The Secretary of State also has power to make additional exemptions under s 38 although wider exemption making powers were removed from the Bill in the Lords.[19] Personal data may be exempted from either: subject information provisions and the non-disclosure provisions.

Subject information provisions. These contain two basic features. Firstly, that data may only be treated as processed fairly when certain safeguards are followed – disclosure to the DS of the DCs identity or that of his representative; the purposes for which the data are to be processed;

---

19 Yet another example of how the DPA influenced the FOIA draft Bill. It was interesting that a device to protect privacy should have been seen as acceptable for FOI provisions. This clause in the FOI bill caused serious disquiet.

and any such information as would be required to make the processing fair. Where the DS has supplied the data the DC has to provide this information. Where the DS did not supply the data, the information must be supplied to the DS before the data are processed or disclosed to a third party. Secondly, the DS has the right of access to the personal data.

The non-disclosure provisions have three basic features: that personal data may only be treated as processed fairly if any disclosure of that personal data does not infringe the disclosure restrictions contained in Sch 2 and 3; that any disclosure of personal data must take place in conformity with the second to fifth DP principles (see above); that any disclosure of personal data must take account of the right of the DS to object to processing likely to cause damage or distress, the right of the DS to have inaccurate personal data of which he is the subject rectified etc (see above) and to have third parties to whom the data have been notified informed of that rectification etc.

The exemptions cover national security which is exempted from the DP principles, Parts II (rights of DS), III (notification) and V (enforcement and see section 28(11)) and section 55 which concerns criminal offences of unlawfully obtaining etc personal data). The exemption of national security is in fact an exclusion from the Act where all the exemptions apply. A certificate signed by a minister of the Crown stating that the exemption from all or any of the above provisions 'is or at any time' was required for national security shall be conclusive evidence of that fact. The certificate under sub-s (2) may identify the personal data to which it applies by means of a general description and may have prospective effect.[20] The person affected by the certificate may appeal to the Information Tribunal and that body, applying the principles applied by a court on an application for judicial review, may allow the appeal and quash the certificate if it finds that the minister did not have reasonable grounds for issuing the certificate. One should note the similarity to the FOIA, ss 23 and 24 which were discussed in chapter 6. It should be noted how circumscribed the powers of the Tribunal are.[1] One could not share the view of a former DPR that in the face of a certificate the courts are powerless. Their powers are clearly circumscribed since the statute stipulates that the certificate is 'conclusive evidence' of the fact that data is exempt for the purpose of safeguarding national security. Recent pronouncements by the courts that a bare assertion of national security by the executive is not sufficient to bar judicial inquiry are not to the point as the certificate is 'conclusive' evidence. However, the certificate must be related to the statutory purpose; and it must not bear illegality upon its forehead, ie bad faith, abuse of process or ulterior intent. Could

20   Note the similarity to the FOIA, s 24(4).
1   See SI 2000/206 and SI 2000/731.

one add a disproportionate judgement by the executive? As the facts are completely within the control of the executive, judicial intervention is unlikely except in the most blatant of cases (see p 48 above).

Any other parties may appeal to the Tribunal against the alleged effects of a certificate in relation to general descriptions of data applying to personal data. The Tribunal may determine that the certificate does not so apply. The power to issue a certificate must be exercised by a member of the Cabinet or Attorney-General or Lord Advocate.[2]

Where data are processed for the purpose of:

(a) the prevention or detection of crime
(b) the apprehension or prosecution of offenders
(c) the assessment or collection of any tax or duty or of any imposition of a similar nature

then the data are exempt essentially from the subject information provisions and the non-disclosure provisions. It also allows for the disclosure of such data to bodies like the police performing their statutory functions so that they can process it free from the subject access provisions. Further provisions cover housing benefit and council tax.

Section 30 covers exemptions for health, education and social work. The Secretary of State may by order exempt from the subject information provisions, or modify those provisions in relation personal data consisting of information as to the physical or mental health or condition of the DS. Similar provisions may be made covering school pupils including past pupils. Exemptions may also cover social work in relation to the data subject or other individuals conducted by government departments, local authorities or voluntary bodies.

Listed relevant functions of a regulatory nature under s 31 may also be exempted from the subject information provisions. These cover items such as financial loss due to dishonesty, malpractice or other seriously improper conduct by or unfitness or incompetence of persons in banking, insurance, investment or other financial services or in the management of corporate bodies. Relevant functions include: any statutory function; any function of the Crown, minister of the Crown, government department or 'any other function which is of a public nature and is exercised in the public interest.'[3] The public sector ombudsmen and Director General of Fair Trading are likewise provided with exemptions.[4]

In the case of 'special purposes' concerning processing data in connection with journalism, literary and artistic purposes and publications for those purposes, exemptions are allowed from various DPPs where the DC reasonably believes that the publication would be in the public

---

2   See also s 28(8) and (9).
3   Section 31(3)(c).
4   And see s 233 Financial Services Act 2000.

interest and where compliance with the provisions is incompatible with the special purposes. The aim is to protect freedom of speech: it will require an appraisal of the relationship between Arts 8 and 10 ECHR. In a general sense, neither is absolute and a wide range of factors will have to be considered in seeking a balance. The Act, however, seeks to ensure that the courts cannot be used to obtain a prior restraint against publications using such material by staying proceedings until either the DPC has determined that the processing of data is not taking place for the special purposes or the claim is withdrawn (see s 45).

Where data consist of any information which the DC is obliged to make available to the public by or under any enactment, which includes an 'enactment passed under the DPA' (s 70(1)) and whether by publication, inspection or otherwise and whether free or by charge it is exempt from the subject information provisions, the non-disclosure provisions and the fourth DP principle and s 14(1) to (3). This section is amended by s 72 FOIA so that 'enactment' does not include FOIA. This was to prevent access rights dominating over data protection rights. A constantly reiterated fear was that the latter would dominate the former (see chapter 6 p 325). Such a problem arose in *ex p Fisher*.[5]

The Ministry of Agriculture, Fisheries and Food refused to supply information to a farmer from a database which was set up under an EC Regulation related to what was known as the 'set-aside' scheme. The data had been supplied by a previous owner of the land in question and identified the fields which had been set aside. This, it was claimed, was covered by the DPA 1984. The farmer was penalised by MAFF for farming the fields in question even though MAFF had the information under its exclusive control which would have allowed the farmer to make correct claims had he been so informed. The ECJ felt that it was not possible to apply a rule that stated that data could not be disclosed without the consent of the person who supplied it. The legitimate interests of the applicant for information should be considered. No damage was done to any fundamental interests, rights or privacy of the data provider. Relevant criteria for balancing the interests involved could be found in EC Directive 95/46/EC on data protection. The Court said:

> 'Article 7(f) of that Directive authorised the disclosure of data if it was necessary for the purposes of the legitimate interests pursued by a third party to whom the personal data were disclosed, except where such interests were overridden by the interests or fundamental rights and freedoms of the data subject which required protection.'

5   Case C-369/98 *R v Minister of Agriculture, Fisheries and Food, ex p Fisher* (2000) Times, 10 October, ECJ. See I Harden (2001) European Public Law forthcoming.

Fisher would not have any right under s 34 DPA as amended because it excludes FOIA. He might have rights under s 35. This provides that personal data are also exempt from the non-disclosure provisions where the disclosure is required by or under any enactment, any rule of law or court order under s 35. They are also similarly exempt where disclosure is necessary for the purposes of or in connection with any legal proceedings (including prospective legal proceedings) or for the purpose of obtaining legal advice or 'is otherwise necessary for the purposes of establishing, exercising or defending legal rights.'

Where data are processed by an individual only for the purposes of that individual's personal, family or household affairs (including recreational purposes) they are exempt from the DP principles and the provisions of Parts I and II. We have already noted that s 38 confers powers on the Secretary of State to make additional exemptions. Schedule 7 contains further miscellaneous exemptions.

Confidential references given by the DC are exempt from s 7 if given for: education, training, employment of the DS including prospective; appointments to an office; provision of any service by the DS.

Where disclosure of personal data would be likely to compromise the combat effectiveness of any of the armed forces of the Crown they are exempt from the subject information provisions. Personal data processed for assessing suitability for judicial appointments including QCs and conferring any honour by the Crown are exempt from the subject information provisions. Personal data processed for the purposes of Crown employment and appointments to offices by the Crown, ministers or NI departments may be exempted by order from the Secretary of State from the subject information provisions.

Management forecasts to assist in business or other activity are exempt from the subject information provisions and corporate finance are exempt from the subject information provisions where the application of those provisions would be likely, or would have, respectively specified consequences. Further exemptions cover: prejudicing negotiations; examination marks,[6] examination scripts; data which could be subject to a claim of legal professional privilege or where disclosure would lead to self-incrimination for an offence other than one under the DPA.

---

6   This provision is to prevent access before results are published. Some universities have stopped publication of class lists unless those included have consented. This is to avoid receiving notices that processing such data may cause substantial damage or distress in releasing, eg an individual's whereabouts.

Data Protection (Subject Access Modification) Orders

A variety of access modification orders has been approved by Parliament. These modify access in relation to health records. Social work, education and miscellaneous subject access are also provided for. These provide exemptions from subject access or access by others on the subject's behalf on a variety of grounds.

Transitional relief

Schedule 8 contains very detailed transitional relief by way of exemptions.[7] The aim is to provide a smooth transition from the existing regime to the new one. The transitional exemptions only apply to processing systems under way immediately before 24 October 1998 (the 'eligibility criterion') but this qualification does not apply to data covered by s 1(1)(d) DPA 1998. If there is something different about the processing after that date it might not qualify as 'processing under way immediately before' that date and will not be eligible for transitional relief. These exemptions can apply in *addition* to the other exemptions discussed above. Historical research data are covered by separate provisions.

The first transitional period (FTP) lasts until the end of 23 October 2001. The second transitional period (STP) is available between 24 October 2001 and 23 October 2007. Both automated and manual data may benefit from the FTP. Only qualifying manual data which is actually processed immediately up until 24 October 1998 and DPA will benefit from the STP. To these, however, have been added personal data under FOIA 2000. The FOIA personal data are exempt from most of the DPA in any event. They will have additional exemptions under the STP. Where access rights have been transferred from other legislation (Consumer Credit Act 1974, Access to Personal Files Act 1987 and Access to Health Records Act 1990) those provisions will cover transitional access rights. The end result is that 'eligible manual data' (which means eligible data which are not 'eligible automated data', which means eligible data falling within paragraphs (a) or (b) of the definition of data in s 1(1)), are exempt from the DP principles and Parts II and III of the DPA during the first transitional period. The details of relief are very technical.[8]

The DPC has advised that where her decision on eligibility differs from a DC's, 'the Commissioner will give the DC ample opportunity to make representations before deciding whether to take enforcement action.' She

---

7　The DPC has produced guidance on this topic: *Introduction to the 1998 Act*, (1998) *chapter* 6. There is a helpful table setting out the transitional relief in *Charlesworth* n 31 above.

8　See Birkinshaw *Government and Information* (2nd ed, 2001) chapter 7 for details.

will consider whether the effect on individuals and whether damage or distress has been or is likely to be caused before taking enforcement action. This does not preclude pursuit by individuals of remedies via the courts.

Enforcement

Yet another influence of the DPA on FOIA may be seen in the area of enforcement. The Commissioner, where satisfied that a DC has or is contravening any of the data protection principles, may serve on that person an enforcement notice (EN) (s 40(1)). This requires that person to take or refrain from taking, specified steps within a certain period and/or to refrain from processing any personal data or specified data or processing them in a manner, or for a purpose and after such time, as specified. The DPC must consider, in deciding whether to serve an enforcement notice, whether the contravention has caused or is likely to cause any person damage or distress. In relation to breaches of the fourth principle, the EN may require rectification, erasure, blocking or destruction of other data held by the DC which contains an opinion which appears to the Commissioner to be based on the inaccurate data. Third parties may have to be informed by the DC. An EN must contain various details. Steps may have to be taken as a matter of urgency. There is a period of informal negotiation, and following that oral or written representations may be made before service of an EN. The DPC has indicated her approach to ENs in the transitional periods. She will allow representations and negotiation and seek to establish whether any distress is likely, or has been caused. An EN may be cancelled or varied by written notice. The DPC may receive a request under s 42 by or on behalf of any person who is directly affected by any processing of personal data to make an assessment of whether any processing is being carried out in compliance with the Act. The DPC may also, as under FOIA, serve an information notice (see chapter 6) as well as a special information notice. The latter is used in connection with requests under s 42 as well as in relation to special purposes as set out above, ie journalism etc. Section 42 allows the DPC to carry out an assessment on a person's request but it is subject to a number of conditions and procedural requirements.[9]

A party to actual or prospective proceedings involving special purpose data may apply to the Commissioner for assistance in relation to those proceedings under several provisions of the Act.[10] The case must involve

---

9 The DPC may require information to satisfy herself as to the requester's identity: another provision which influenced the FOI Bill. Here, however, we are dealing with *personal* information. There are a variety of factors that the DPC has to consider. This is an ombudsman function.

10 Under ss 7(9), 10(4), 12(8) or 14 'or by virtue of s 13.

'a matter of substantial public importance.' Appeals may be made against notices to the tribunal as well as determinations on special purpose data under s 45. The grounds of appeal are similar to those to the tribunal under FOIA and it is now to be known as the Information Tribunal. Appeal lies on a point of law to the High Court or Court of Session. The DPC may apply for search and seizure warrants to a circuit judge under Sch 9 including an authorisation to test and operate equipment. As well as offences involving DCs where they process data without complying with registration or notification requirements, s 55 makes disclosure of data or information therein without the DCs consent an offence. Mens rea is required. Section 56 contains restrictions on enforced access – forcing others to gain access to their own information to hand it to the 'enforcer'.[11] The former DPR had noted an increase in enforced subject access whereby subjects are compelled by prospective employers to gain access to criminal and national insurance records to disclose any period spent in prison or other items. Official figures show that there were 11,500 subject access requests to the Police National Computer in the year ending March 1994, 12,500 requests for national insurance records—in both cases it was felt that in excess of 90% of these were enforced subject access.[12]

Any term or condition in a contract will be void insofar as it seeks to require an individual to produce all or part of a record obtained under data access rights by that individual and which contains information about that individual's mental or physical health made by a health professional in the course of caring for the individual (s 58).

Fees have been set by regulations. These are set at a maximum of £10 for applications under s 7(2)(b)[13] except where the request comes under regs 4, 5 and 6 of SI 2000/191. A schedule is attached setting out rates for written documents according to page lengths. The maximum that may be charged is £50.[14] The Act binds the Crown. Each government department shall be treated as a person separate from any other government department. Each will have to notify the Commissioner of their processing. Government departments shall not be liable to prosecution under the Act but Crown servants may be prosecuted for various matters: unlawfully obtaining and disclosing personal data, unlawfully procuring the disclosure to another person of information contained in personal data, or selling unlawfully obtained personal data.

---

11 See ss 112-13 and 115 Police Act 1997.
12 Police National Computer *Annual Report 1994*.
13 See SI 2000/191 and SI 2001/187.
14 Regulations cover *inter alia* notification by DCs and fees: SI 2000/188; Processing of Sensitive Personal Data SI 2000/417; functions of designated authority; and designated codes of practice SI 2000/418 (as amended).

The DPA is not an easy Act to comprehend. It is accompanied by numerous regulations. It will still place primary emphasis on self-regulation and internal audit – the latter are provided for by s 23. Satisfactory schemes of self-regulation may allow for exemption from the notification provisions discussed above. The DPA has replaced the Access to Personal Files Act 1987, the regulations under that Act as well as other access statutes including the Access to Medical Files Act 1990 and the Consumer Credit Act, s 158. These concerned paper files only and were selective.[15] It does not replace the Access to Medical Reports Act 1988 which confers a right on an individual to have access, in accordance with the provisions of the Act, to any medical report relating to that individual which is to be, or has been, supplied by a medical practitioner for employment purposes or insurance purposes.

The DPC has written about the dangers of computer matching by government and public bodies, for which there is growing statutory authorisation, in the era of joined-up government.[16] Her annual report for 2000 is also of interest because of the Commissioner's concern with the increasing interface of telecommunications and computers and the implications for access to personal data via emails for instance. We saw in chapter 1 how regulations made under RIPA will allow the widest of interceptions of domestic phones and also computer communications. The EC Telecommunications Directive addresses some of these points.[17] The state's growing fascination for privatisation and contractualisation has brought an increasing interest in snooping.

Conclusion

The Government was at pains to point out as the DP bill was going through Parliament that it was not seeking to introduce a privacy protection statute through the back door. The DPA is a privacy protection measure, or perhaps a privacy regulation measure because it does not introduce privacy protection laws as known in the USA. The extensive nature of the rights to access it provides both in the public and private sectors has produced virulent opposition to the EC Directive in the USA. The DPA does not provide the right to 'be left alone' as privacy has been famously

---

15 The Human Fertilisation and Embryology Act 1990 is excluded by order from the Act's provisions: see s 38(2) DPA 1998.

16 *Modernising Government* Cm 4310; See the DPC's *Annual Report 2000*. And Birkinshaw *Government and Information* (2nd ed, 2001) chapter 7, p 313 et seq.

17 EC Telecommunications Directive 97/66/EC (implemented by the Telecoms Regulations 1999 SI 2093 which came into effect on 1 March 2000) deals with the processing of personal data and protection of privacy in the telecommunications sector. New regulations are being prepared.

described. It provides safeguards in the use of personal information. It was feared that privacy protection would outweigh the rights of access to information and that politicians in particular would be able to use the Human Rights Act and Convention rights to prevent access to personal information that it was in the public interest to know. The amendment to s 34 DPA by s 72 FOIA was noted above. Special provisions were built in to protect freedom of speech in the DPA and the HRA where artistic, journalistic or literary uses are involved.[18] Rights to access and rights to privacy have to be balanced and the courts have shown that neither is absolute and that freedom of publication and the right to pass on information must not be used to damage an individual's reputation without justification. Any interference with freedom of speech must be shown to be necessary. The courts have been more and more aware of the importance of this overriding protection for a fundamental human right.[19] But it is not an absolute. Perhaps the approach is not as robust as that adopted in the USA where those in the public limelight are not given the full protection as others in the law of defamation for instance thereby allowing inaccurate comments to be made about politicians for instance with impunity providing they are nor knowingly or recklessly inaccurate.[20] For the foreseeable future, the British are not likely to develop a full-blown law of privacy protection as in the USA. We shall make do with non-statutory codes on privacy for the press and media.[1]

What protection should be afforded to private personal information? To allow *all* personal information to be protected by the law of confidentiality and perhaps privacy would be going too far. It would undermine a genuine public interest in knowing.[2] Once the principle of subject access had been accepted with the Data Protection Act 1984, it seemed unnecessarily cautious to restrict access by individual subjects to manual files containing personal information about them. The EC

---

18 The 'special purposes data' under s 3 (see above) and s 12 of the HRA 1998.

19 See eg *Kelly v BBC* [2001] 1 All ER 323. See *R v BSC* below.

20 Compare *New York Times v Sullivan* 376 US 254 (1964) and *Reynolds v Times Newspapers Ltd* [1999] 4 All ER 609 where the House of Lords refused to adopt under English common law a qualified privilege of 'political information'. See p 457 et seq. Note the use in the US of discovery in such trials: 'The trade-off for the more extensive defence has been the requirement of full disclosure by way of extensive and onerous pre-trial discovery' per Lord Hobhouse at 659e.

1 See chapter 4 p 202 et seq and *Codes of Guidance* Broadcasting Standards Commission June 1998 and the *Code of Practice* ratified by the Press Complaints Commission, December 1999. In relation to the Broadcasting Standards Commission, the Court of Appeal has ruled that the code's protection of privacy extends to a company regardless of the position under the ECHR: citing *Niemietz v Germany* (1992) 16 EHRR 97. The case concerned surreptitious filming of sales of allegedly second hand goods as new in Dixons: *R v Broadcasting Standards Commission, ex p BBC* [2000] 3 All ER 989, CA.

2 For laws enjoining the reporting of information see eg s 11 Public Health (Control of Diseases) Act 1984.

Directive on Data Protection recognised this as does the 1998 legislation as amended. The use of misleading, inaccurate or irrelevant personal information by wielders of power and influence, whether professional bodies or employers or institutions, is a widely documented abuse of power.[3] One area which has caused particular problems has been health records. As well as the 1998 Act there are undertakings in the Patient's Charter to provide information to patients and guidelines were reviewed in 1993 on informing those patients who may be at risk of infection from doctors and other medical staff with the HIV virus or Aids. Authorities and NHS trusts are under a 'duty' to inform patients of this information. Laws also enjoin public authorities to report information concerning contagious diseases to appropriate authorities. The DPC has returned to this theme in her 2000 Annual Report noting the recommendations in the Caldicott report.

Numerous reports have criticised the chaotic state of hospital records and the poor practice relating to patients' rights to records or to be informed. The Association of Community Health Councils reported that many record holders were not conversant with the Access to Health Records Act's provisions and refused to receive requests from patients or those entitled under the Act or engaged in inconsistent practices eg allowing or not allowing next of kin to have access.[4] This is in spite of the Act and the better known Patient's Charter which requires access. The Audit Commission reported that almost half the patient case notes examined by the Commission were disorganised and too bulky to work with. One out of six files was missing at the start of out-patient clinics. Hospitals have different records systems or no system at all in spite of calls for consistency from more than 30 years ago. Incomplete case notes were far too common a feature.[5] The Caldicott Committee Report on *Patient Identifiable Information* (December 1997) made 16 recommendations for good practice. The report in 2001 by Michael Redfern QC into the use of children's body parts without consent at Alder Hey hospital revealed, as have other reports, how patients are deliberately kept uninformed of the details of medical practice affecting them. Sunlight is the best of disinfectants!

Finally, the dangers in inaccurate data forming the basis of decisions on individuals has been accentuated as we have seen by the increasing provision for computer matching of personal information in statute,[6] the explosion and novel use of personal information through

---

3   The use by private bodies of information on the political affiliations of prospective employees has been highlighted: HC Debs vol 110, col 1176.

4   Access to Health Records Act 1990, Association of Community Health Councils May 1994.

5   *Setting the Record Straight* Audit Commission, June 1995.

6   See Birkinshaw *Government and Information* (2nd ed, 2001) n 16).

telecommunications systems – a problem addressed by the DPA and the EC Directive on Telecommunications and implementing regulations[7] and the increased range of duties to provide information to the authorities. More basically, as was explained in chapter 1, the Commons Home Affairs Committee has pointed out that the personal records on the Police National Computer which will be relied upon by the Criminal Records Bureau to provide checks on those working with children contain errors in 15-65% of records.[8]

7   DPA *Annual Report for 2000*; the Directive is addressed in n 17 above.
8   HC 227 (2000-01) covering both minor and major errors.

8 Secrecy and access in the European Union

Introduction

British practice of over secrecy in government at least has the excuse of being age old. As a part of our international commitments, there are the provisions of Recommendation No R(81)19 of the Committee of Ministers of the Council of Europe concerning access to information held by public authorities and Arts 8 and 10 of the European Convention on Human Rights. These, as is well known, protect privacy and family life and freedom of speech including receiving and imparting information. With the coming into effect in October 2000 of the Human Rights Act 1998, the articles are now part of domestic law and are not solely a part of our international legal obligations.[1]

The European Community or European Union which makes binding laws for the UK is often criticised because it has effectively enhanced the powers of the national executives *vis à vis* democratic assemblies. Its origins as an international organisation, whatever Community jurists may say of the contemporary order, have ensured that maximum secrecy and sensitivity would attend its diplomatic relationships. In its own operations and practices it displays a 'democratic deficit', it is commonly alleged, in so far as the directly-elected European Parliament does not have overall control of the legislative process, although its position has been enhanced by procedural changes introduced by the Maastricht revisions to the Treaty of Rome.[2] The absence of effective oversight of EC laws by national assemblies[3] has been a further cause of concern as the legislative

---

1 See n 14 of old text (OT).
2 The co-decision procedure introduced under Art 251 EC.
3 Birkinshaw and Ashiagbor (1996) 33 Common Market Law Review 499; Kerse (2000) European Public Law 81; Amsterdam TEU Treaty Protocol No13.

impact from the EC assumes ever-growing importance in terms of domestic influence as witness, in the present discussion, the Directive on Access to Environmental Information which has been implemented in the UK (see chapter 5) and the Directive on Data Protection (ch 7).

Transparency and Maastricht

'Transparency' has been a central theme in Community administration for some years, but this is a much wider expression than access to information. The record of the EC on openness has not been strikingly good.[4] In 1992, for instance, a proposed Council regulation[5] would have introduced security classifications for information in a manner which bore some resemblance to the wider excesses of the Official Secrecy Acts of the UK. Article 296 [223] (EC) provides that no member state shall be obliged to supply information the disclosure of which it considers contrary to the essential interests of its security. In the *Zwartveld* case[6] the Commission refused to supply a Dutch investigating magistrate investigating a case of fraud with reports drafted by Commission officials. They relied upon provisions stating that archives of the Community were 'inviolable', which were based upon a Commission decision and a Council directive which entail that Community documents which have come from national governments must not be disclosed even if available in a member state under its legislative provisions. The court paid no heed to such arguments stating that it was incumbent upon Community institutions actively to assist national legal proceedings by way of documentation or appearance of Commission officials in national proceedings. The Commission fiercely resisted such enforced openness.

In the Declarations to the Maastricht Treaty the Conference proclaimed that 'transparency of the decision-making process strengthens the democratic nature of the institutions and the public's confidence in the administration' and recommended that the Commission submit to the Council no later than 1993 a report on measures designed to improve public access to the information available to the institutions. The Birmingham European Council in October 1992 and that in Edinburgh in December 1992, respectively emphasised the 'need for better informed public debate' on the Community's activities and measures to support this, eg 'open debates on Presidency and Commission work programmes, on major community issues and on the first stage of legislative proposals; the publication of Council voting records whenever a formal vote is taken'

---

4   Deckmyn and Thompson (eds) *Openness and Transparency in the European Union* (1998).
5   92/C 72/16 COM(92) FINAL.
6   [1990] ECR I-3365.

and better background information. The European Council in Copenhagen reaffirmed the necessity of greater access to information. The Commission was making greater use of green papers and consultation and publication of its annual work programme by October 1993. In a report in 1993,[7] the Commission discussed measures designed to encourage public access to Community institutions' information. In early 1995, the EC Parliament for the first time questioned the 20 members of the new Commission in a public session. The European Parliament has, however, also experienced difficulties in obtaining information about subjects where it should be regularly informed.

The Joint Code on Access

Council meetings were not open to the public, except those falling under Art 6 of its 1993 Rules of Procedure. These are policy debates on the six-monthly work programme and if appropriate the Commission's annual work programme. Following an agreed code on access, the Council reached a decision on 20 December 1993 on public access to Council documents and the Commission published its own decision likewise on 18 February 1994 implementing a code on access.[8] The decisions and the Code allow public access to Council and Commission documents—meaning any written text whatever its medium—providing the written application is sufficiently precise and with due regard for provisions governing the protection of classified information. Article 2 contains the following: 'Where the requested document was written by a natural or legal person, a Member State, another Community institution or body, or any other national or international body, the application must not be sent to the Council but direct to the author'. The Code contains a similar provision for the Commission. Many documents received by public bodies in FOIA systems allow access to such documents subject to exemptions. This provision seems to exclude them completely from the provisions on access to Council documents. The exemptions cover the usual subjects viz protecting public security, international relations, monetary stability, court proceedings, individual privacy, commercial and industrial secrecy, protection of the Community's financial interests and protection of confidentiality as requested by the supplier of the information in the document or as required by a member state's legislation from which the information came. These are very wide exemptions and the Code states access *will* be denied where disclosure *could* undermine

---

7   COM (1993) 258 FINAL.
8   93/731/EC OJ L 340/43 (31 December 1993) and 94//90/ECSC, EC, Euratom: OJ 46/58 (18 February 1994).

the above, ie it is a mandatory provision. A further provision gives a discretionary exemption where the Commission or Council seeks to protect the confidentiality of its proceedings.

The articles set out procedural steps for applicants and time limits. The applicant may apply for a refusal to be reconsidered—'a confirmatory application'—within a month. Where this is refused the applicant shall be notified within a month and given the reasons together with details of the contents of Art 195 EC [138e] and 230 [173] of the Treaty of Rome concerning referral to the Ombudsman (appointed July 1995) and judicial review by the courts of the decision. The code on access came into effect by 1 January 1994. The code will be implemented in full compliance with provisions concerning classified information.

Since the introduction of the Code there have been several episodes revealing a less than open approach by the Council where it has refused to reveal the voting decisions of members of the Council because it might upset relations between member states were such information revealed. Likewise, there have been refusals and 'mistakes' where minutes were released or applied for which showed disagreements between national positions on legislation, revealed concessions for member states and jeopardised confidentiality. A decison on refusal to disclose the minutes was successfully challenged in the Court of First Instance of the ECJ but only in terms that the Council had wrongfully exercised its discretion to regard documents as confidential without regard to the particular merits; the court made no statement about access rights in general.[9] The court adverted to the fact that confidentiality was stated to be necessary because members are sometimes forced to move away from 'national instructions' from Parliaments, publicity for which would cause embarrassment. By October 1995, a change in the code would allow access to minutes and declarations made by member states in Council meetings when acting as a legislator.[10] 'Exceptional circumstances' may require secrecy and will be decided on a straightforward majority. The Council has also adopted a register of documents allowing Council documents drawn up after 1 January 1999 to be identified.

The means adopted by the Council and Commission to allow access, ie via a Code, was also challenged by the Dutch government under Art 173 EC Treaty because it was treated as an internal procedural matter and not one creating rights for community citizens. This was unsuccessful.[11] The Code was backed by legally binding decisions, the ECJ reasoned. It

---

9   Ministers of member states were inclined to include statements about the national position on draft laws which were incorporated in the minutes and it was not wished for these to be made public: *Carvel v EU Council* Case T-194/94 [1996] All ER (EC) 53, CFI.

10   PRES/95/271 'Transparency of Council Proceedings'.

11   *Netherlands v EU Council* C-58/94 [1996] ECR I-2169, ECJ (30 April 1996).

appeared that the ECJ had failed to rise to the challenge of the Advocate General who argued for a legal, indeed a constitutional right of access in that 'the basis for the individual's right to information should be sought in the principle of democracy, which constitutes one of the cornerstones of the Community edifice.'[12] The right of access to official documents constituted part of the democratic principle. Interestingly, the ECJ noted the fact that many member states' domestic legislation now incorporates rights of access to official information and documents. It amounted to 'a progressive affirmation of individuals' right of access to documents held by public authorities.' A full-blown constitutional principle may not have emerged but the penny was dropping.

Under the Code, over 90% of requests were granted and there were 29 confirmatory applications after a refusal in 1998 (44 in 1997). The Code was amended slightly in 1996. By 1998 there had been 10 complaints to the EU Ombudsman about the Code as well as some case law (see below). The Commission believed that the Code had a 'relatively limited impact on the public' although it 'was clear ... that people make less use of access at Community level than at national level largely for language reasons, given that the documents are not available in all EU languages.' In 1998, requests in descending order came from public authorities (20.8), academics (20.4) lobbyists (19) and industry (15.4%).[13]

Deficiencies and judicial decisions

However, the Code was seriously deficient in vital respects; there was no reference in the decisions and Code to the Second and Third Pillars for instance covering common foreign policy and security and justice and home affairs (now police and judicial cooperation in criminal matters). The European Council was not included. Crucially, it only covered the Council and Commission. A vast array of other institutions and satellites emanating from these institutions were not included. These included bodies under the Schengen Agreement between, originally, the Benelux countries, France and Germany which opens up borders between the countries with special effect on international aliens, refugees and criminal law. An executive committee was established under the agreement with binding powers for members. Meetings were closed to the public and decisions adopted in the committee were not very often made public even

12 Advocate General Tesauro, Opinion 28 November 1995, op cit point 19. See Epilogue below.
13 European Commission Secretary General 18 March 1999, SEC/1999/449 p 23. There are also figures for requests from member states. Belgium (30.4%) was the highest, Portugal and Greece the lowest (0.5%). The UK was second highest. Could geography matter?

though they may affect the laws in Schengen states. Schengen has now been widely extended under the terms of the Amsterdam Treaty and brought within the EC and EU Treaties.

Some of the deficiencies in the Code and Decisions were dealt with by the Court of First Instance (CFI) in decisions which usually turned on technical points of law rather than bold development of principle but which increasingly made significant inroads into institutional secrecy. The CFI has ruled that the Code and decisions prevail over specific provisions in regulations enjoining secrecy in relation to investigative missions in Bangladesh.[14] In *WWF UK v EU Commission*[15] the Commission was ruled to be acting unlawfully when it failed to give proper reasons for refusing access and to follow correct procedures. Blanket reasons for refusal have been ruled unlawful where these were not justified.[16] The CFI has ruled that it has jurisdiction over Third Pillar documents in the possession of the Council[17] (a point made by the Ombudsman also) and subsequently that it had access to Second Pillar documents – in both cases subject to exemptions.[18] A pressing concern was over the status of 'comitology' documents. This term refers to the numerous informal committees serving the Commission very often comprising national civil servants and representative or specialist private concerns.[19] The CFI held these documents were covered by the Code.[20] Partial access may be allowed where exempt items are concealed.

When investigating complaints, the EU Ombudsman has wide powers of access to documents in the possession of Community institutions and also to documents originating in a member state. There are saving provisions where documents are classified by the member state as secret. In other cases the member state has to be informed of a request. The Ombudsman may request information from a member state via the permanent representatives of member states to the EC and they are obliged to provide it, subject to their secrecy laws or other measures 'preventing its being communicated' (art 3, Statute of the European Ombudsman, OJL 113, 4 May 1995, p 15). Article 193 [138c] EC empowers the European Parliament to establish temporary committees of inquiry to investigate alleged breaches, or maladministration, in the implementation of Community law and Art 194 [138d] allows the petition of the European Parliament by 'any citizen of the Union'. The Ombudsman has in fact

14 *JT's Corpn Ltd v EU Commission* Case T-123/99 (2000) Times, 18 October.
15 [1997] ECR II-313, CFI.
16 *Kuijer v EU Council* Case T-188/98 [2000] 2 CMLR 400, CFI. The case concerned asylum seekers.
17 *Svenska Journalistförbundet v EU Council* Case T-174/95 [1998] ECR II-2289
18 *Heidi Hautala v EU Council* Case T-14/98, [1999] 3 CMLR 528, CFI.
19 See R Pedler and G Schaefer *Shaping European Law and Policy* (1996).
20 *Rothmans International BV v EC Commission* Case T-188/97 [1999] ECR-II 2463, CFI.

attacked secrecy in the EU with missionary zeal.[1] All institutions not covered by the Code, including the court, eventually accepted that they should adopt their own practices in relation to access which were based on the Code. Without such a practice, they would run the risk of being found guilty of maladministration.[2] The Ombudsman has also produced *A Model Code of Good Administrative Procedure* expressing the view that institutions should produce information on request subject to permissible exemptions. This has been adopted by several Community institutions. The Commission has produced its own code of practice. The Ombudsman has also been instrumental in interpreting powers in the Code in a manner which is citizen oriented.[3]

International organisations have brought about their own downfall in the past because of excessive secrecy.[4] The United Nations has adopted a very open policy for meetings and documents although the Security Council has adopted more private preliminary meetings. In 1946, a Resolution of the United Nations General Assembly stated: 'Freedom of information is a fundamental human right and is the touchstone for all freedoms to which the United Nations is consecrated.'[5] This is a remarkably prescient statement setting access to information as a human right, which the EU and domestic systems have been reluctant to accept, and a theme to which we shall return in chapter 10.

Amsterdam, Article 255 EC and the Regulation on Access to Information

The Amsterdam treaty in Art 1 of Title 1 TEU stated as one of the general principles of the European Union that 'This Treaty marks a new stage in the process of creating an ever closer union among the peoples of Europe, in which decisions are taken *as openly as possible* and as closely as possible to the citizen.' The italicised words were added at Amsterdam. They herald a greater emphasis on openness as well as subsidiarity – decision taking at as local a level as possible. The immediate development came in an amendment to the EC Treaty and Art 255 which provided for the introduction of a regulation on access to documents covering the Council, Commission and Parliament. It is restricted to those institutions. The Regulation, which is to be prepared in draft by the Commission, must be adopted by 1 May 2001 after completing the procedure in Art 251 –

---

1   See the FIDE Report 1998 and the general rapport by the EU Ombudsman *The Citizen, the Administration and Community Law.*
2   *Annual Report of the EU Ombudsman* 1999 p 245.
3   See I Harden (2001) EPL forthcoming.
4   Curtin and Meijers (1995) CMLR 391 at 395.
5   Resolution of 14 December 1946, 65th Plenary Meeting.

the co-decision procedure. Each institution must also establish specific provisions regarding access to its own documents in its rules of procedure.

There is one very controversial provision in the Recital (No 12) which has caused considerable concern and which can be picked up below. This states that: 'member states shall take care not to hamper the proper application of this Regulation which is binding in its entirety and directly applicable in all member states'. Could this undermine the more liberal regimes which exist in some member states, traditions which the Commission acknowledged?

In accordance with Art 255, any citizen of the Union and any natural or legal person residing or having its registered office in a member state will enjoy the right of access. A reason, or a case, for access does not have to be made out. The Regulation will cover all documents held by the three institutions and will not be restricted to documents produced by them.[6] By virtue of Arts 28(1) and 41(1) of the TEU, it will cover Second and Third Pillar documents. It will also cover ESC and Euratom documents.[7] Access to a document received from a third party will not be allowed if the document is covered by an exemption in Art 4 of the Regulation. The third party will be consulted and the holder of documents will make its own decision where the third party does not respond. Access to third party documents will only cover documents received after the Regulation comes into effect.

The definition of document is broad: any document on a topic falling within the institution's remit excluding those expressing an individual opinion or reflecting free and frank discussion or provision advice as part of internal consultations and deliberations as well as informal messages such as email 'which can be considered the equivalent of telephone conversations.' To which one might add: not if they are saved. The discussion on ss 35 and 36 of the UK FOIA in chapter 6 should be recalled (p 312 et seq).

The Explanatory Memorandum of the Commission stated that specific rules on access giving persons a particular interest in confidential documents will not be displaced by the general provisions in the Regulation, but such special provisions will need to be revised in the future 'in the light of general principles of transparency.'

The draft Regulation contains a number of exceptions to access. These are based on a harm test if there were disclosure which means disclosure will be allowed unless disclosure 'might significantly undermine certain specific interests, which are spelled out in Art 4.' This signifies a test that has to be made out to justify exception to access and might incorporate a proportionality test where there is a public benefit to be conferred by access. Disclosure may undermine an interest but does it do so

6   Declaration 35 of the TEU Amsterdam Treaty supports this wider remit.
7   By virtue of *Deutsche Babcock* Case 328/85 [1987] ECR 5119.

'significantly'? Documents may be redacted to comply with an exception and the abridged version may be handed over.

Requests for documents must be in writing and must be sufficiently precise for the institution to identify the documents. Further details may be requested by the institution to help identify documents. The duty to hold a register will be invaluable. Applicants may be consulted where there are repetitive requests or where large (voluminous) files are sought. Access may be had by either consulting documents 'on the spot' or by receiving a copy and the cost of access may be charged to the applicant. Documents will be supplied in the available language version, account being taken of the applicant's preference. A document received may not be reproduced for commercial purposes or exploited for any other economic purposes except with the prior authorisation of the interested party.

The time limit for replies on action to be taken – one month – may be extended by one month. Reasons for the extension must be provided. Where a request for confirmation has been made, ie an applicant has challenged refusal, no reply equals consent to disclose. Institutions are given one month to reply to such a request. This may also be extended for one month with reasons and advance notice. The grounds for refusing access must be stated along with rights of challenge. Registers of documents will be maintained – a big advance on British plans under FOIA – and staff should be trained for the tasks involved in access requests and existing procedures for registering, filing, archiving and classifying documents. The institutions must also take steps to inform the public of their rights. While the Commission has taken great steps to inform the community of its policies, actions and plans there is no equivalent of publication schemes as under UK law to provide information on a voluntary basis (see Epilogue below). Until such time as specific rules are made by each institution implementing the Regulation for access to its documents, the Regulation cannot be applicable.

These rules on implementation are very important because the Regulation is not effective until they are made and they will deal with items such as the confidentiality of their own proceedings. In a Council Decision of 14 August 2000, the Council amended its Decision of 93/731/EC (on public access to Council documents) and Decision 2000/23/EC (on improvement of information on the Council's legislative services and the public register of Council documents) and incorporated the effects of the Decision of the Secretary General of the Council on classification of documents.[8] This allows for the classification of documents as 'top secret', 'secret', 'confidential', 'restricted' and various internal references for information; this information and these documents are not to be publicly available. Where documents are in the first three classifications

---

8   Decision of 27 July 2000, OJ 2000/C 239/01

and they concern 'military and non-military crisis management within the framework of a strengthened European security and defence policy' they shall be excluded from the provisions allowing access under the Decision. They are automatic mandatory exclusions.[9] Further, to protect classified information 'it is .. necessary to provide that a Council document from which conclusions may be drawn regarding the content of classified information put out by a natural or legal person, a Member State, another Community institution or body or any other national or international body may be made available to the public only with the prior written consent of the author of the information in question, (para (4)).[10] The public register will contain no reference to the information classified in the manner stated above. This has attracted a good deal of criticism, not least because it was passed effectively in the summer recess.

The draft Regulation spells out what precisely it means by the institutions of the EU that are covered: for the Council, the Permanent Representatives Committee, working parties and departments and committees set up by the Treaty or by the legislator to assist the Council; Commission includes members of the Commission as a collective body, individual members and their private offices, Directorates General and departments,[11] representations and delegations together with committees set up by the Commission and committees set up to help it exercise its implementing powers. This would cover the Comitology committees which have become an object of considerable academic interest.[12] It would not cover the agencies created for a variety of specific purposes. A list of such committees of both the Council and Commission shall be drawn up in implementing measures.

Article 4 establishes the exceptions or exemptions. The Regulation states:

'The institutions shall refuse access to documents where disclosure could[13] significantly undermine the protection of:
a)   the public interest and in particular:
  –   public security,
  –   defence and international relations,

---

9   The action of the Council is being challenged in cases C-369/00 and C-387/00.
10   OJ L 212, 23/08/2000 p 0009.
11   There are 35 directorates general together with 20 commissioners at present.
12   See R Pedler and G Schaefer (eds) *Shaping European Law and Policy: the Role of Committees and Comitology in the Political Process* (1996).
13   In *Svenska* above, the CFI said that 'could' meant 'is likely to.' The test for damage at that time was 'undermine'. 'Significantly' has been added making it a stricter test cf the FOIA in the UK in chapter 1. These words imply a balancing exercise which is susceptible to judicial or EU Ombudsman appraisal, ie it must be a proportionate decision. See Epilogue below.

- relations between and/or with the Member States or Community and non-Community institutions,
- financial or economic interests,
- monetary stability,
- the stability of the Community legal order,
- court proceedings,
- inspections, investigations and audits,[14]
- infringement proceedings, including the preparatory stages thereof,
- the deliberations and effective functioning of the institutions;

b) privacy and the individual and in particular:
- personal files,
- information, opinions and assessments given in confidence with a view to recruitments or appointments,
- an individual's personal details or documents containing information such as medical secrets which, if disclosed, might constitute an infringement of privacy or facilitate such an infringement;

c) commercial and industrial secrecy or the economic interests of a specific natural or legal person and in particular:[15]
- business and commercial secrets,
- intellectual and industrial property,
- industrial, financial, banking and commercial information, including information relating to business relations or contracts,
- information on costs and tenders following award procedures;

- confidentiality as requested by the third party that supplied the document or the information

or as required by the legislation of the Member State.'

It should be observed that there is no public interest override allowing the courts or the Ombudsman to allow access where a greater public interest is served by disclosure than by secrecy. The institutions will have to prove that disclosure could significantly undermine the protection of: the public interest and specified subject areas, privacy, commercial and industrial secrecy and confidentiality as requested by third party suppliers

---

14 This would only cover the duration of an inspection etc and would not prevent a public report it is submitted.

15 This is very broad. The third indent makes no reference to secrecy or confidentiality but it would have to be read in the light of c) which refers to secrecy and to the general balancing test in 'could significantly undermine'

or the legislation of member states. 'Could' has been interpreted by the ECJ to mean 'is likely to' and 'significantly' must connote to a considerable extent.[16] This seems to invite the prospect of a refusal being proportionate and the proper weighing of balancing considerations. A simple rejection will not be sufficient in law. The courts and the Ombudsman will require reasons for refusals which make plain the basis on which refusal is being maintained. If these are inadequate, it is to be hoped that the courts and Ombudsman will adopt a strict approach and, if adequate reasons cannot be provided, order disclosure. This is fully consistent with decisions of the ECJ and EU Ombudsman. The Regulation is somewhat lame in this respect and only imposes the duty to 'state the ground' of refusal. This may be taken as an invitation to repeat the words of the exception.[17] The Regulation (No 6) states that an applicant has to be informed of rights to challenge under Arts 230 (173) and 195 (138e).

The reaction to the Regulation

The EU Ombudsman has been very critical of this Regulation.[18] In a valuable report, the House of Lords Committee on the EU reported on this draft Regulation.[19] It was critical of the Commission's failure to consult before the adoption of the draft Regulation. 'Extensive external consultation would have demonstrated a commitment to openness.' (para 46) It criticised Recital 12 which states that 'Member States shall take care not to hamper the proper application of this Regulation.' It was seen as going far beyond the requirements of cooperation in Art 10 EC and seems to impose a requirement on member states FOI laws not to be more liberal than the EC regime. Sweden and Scandinavian countries pride themselves on their openness and many member states are seeing the benefits from greater transparency. The 'Community system should not create any unnecessary restrictions, especially where national FOI regimes are more liberal.' (para 53).

The Committee was critical of the exclusion of documents under Art 2(2) — those which are available under other provisions. Applicants should have the benefit of both provisions. The Committee felt unease about excluding texts for internal use such as 'discussion documents,

16 See n 13 above.
17 Reasons have to be given in EC law both under the Treaty in relation to legislative measures and also as a general principle of law: Art 253 and *UNECTEF v Heylens* Case 222/86 [1987] ECR 4097. The ECJ has held that reasons do not have to be given by a national legislature when implementing EC law: *Sodemore* Case C-70/95 [1997] ECR I-3395.
18 See *Wall Street Journal* 24 February 2000, p 11 and reply from Romano Prodi same journal 9 March 2000.
19 HL 109 (1999-2000) *Sixteenth Report*.

opinions of departments and also excluding informal messages.' These should be subject to Art 4 exceptions so that access and denial could be balanced under eg the effective functioning of the institution. This exclusion also raises the question of what documents should be listed in the register (paras 77 and 85). Emails should be covered to the same extent as other paper communications. One would add the obvious fact that this only covers those that are saved. The committee further believed that the mandatory nature of the exceptions — ie 'shall refuse...' should be reformulated to 'may refuse access to documents whose disclosure *would be likely to be harmful'* setting a test which is 'objectively necessary and proportionate in a democratic society.' (para 102) The long list of exceptions seems to go against 'greater openness and transparency' (paras 143 and 145). The Committee recommended that the publication of details about the new access regime should be in a new edition of the *Citizen's Guide* (para 168). Finally, the Committee recommended that detailed implementation by the Rules of Procedure should be an open exercise and accompanied by appropriate levels of consultation. There had been serious mistakes in the failure to consult in the production of the draft Regulation and such errors should not be repeated.

The Regulation has been the subject of considerable amendment in the European Parliament, but whether these amendments – which relate both to the substance of the Regulation and its coverage – will survive the Council's own proposals in the co-decision procedure under Art 251 EC remains to be seen. The Regulation was also the basis of the article on access to documents (Art 40) in the Draft Charter of Fundamental Rights of the EU to be incorporated into the Treaty after Nice. Access was restricted to documents of the Council, Commission and Parliament.

The major amendments introduced by the Parliament[20] include a right to information on the activities of the institutions of the EU which should be produced automatically and which should be built on Art 2 EU which sets out the principle of transparency and Art 6 EU which states that the Union is founded on the principle of democracy. A right to information is not enough. Information should be supplied voluntarily. Setting out information in publication schemes as in the UK or under mandatory provisions as in the USA comes to mind (see chapters 2 and 6). This will include all legislative proposals, common positions and final decisions as a legal obligation; at present this 'is not always the case with second and third pillar documents'. Documents should be available automatically in a register on the internet including: Parliament reports, Commission white and green papers, annual reports and preparatory

---

20 European Parliament Final A5 – 0318/2000, 27 October 2000 and Final A5 – 0318/2000 Part 2 3 November 2000, the Cashman Report.

documents of internal bodies in the institutions. This will cover all pillars as well as activities under ECSC and Euratom.[1]

Secondly, all the institutions and bodies covered by Art 255 should be expressly stated in the Regulation (as in UK FOIA) and should include not only committees and working groups but all agencies created by the institutions. This should include Europol, albeit with a transitional period. Those institutions not covered, eg the Central Bank, should be reminded that as a matter of good administration[2] they could follow the principles of this Regulation.

Thirdly, in principle, all documents should be accessible and exceptions to the right should be limited as far as possible. The harm test should be applied on a case by case basis. Where third party documents are sent to the institutions with a request for confidentiality there should, where necessary, be an arbitration procedure between the third party and institution concerned. This might involve the ECJ, the EU Ombudsman or the data control authorities in the institutions. Documents on security from eg NATO cannot be treated in the same way as company documents. However, the EP was critical of the security reviews on classification made by the Council in the summer of 2000 which was referred to above and the Regulation will repeal the Council decision on classification. Specific rules on confidentiality eg Schengen should be repealed. And those of Europol must give way to the Regulation, as must those rules which seek to provide confidentiality in competition, state aids, fraud investigation, application of Community law, archives and environmental information as well as personal data. While being consistent with the Regulation, they should also be subject to periodic review. Where documents are not available to the public they will be available to the European Parliament on the basis of an inter-institutional agreement. Parliamentary participation would nonetheless preserve confidentiality where necessary.

Fourthly the term 'document' should be interpreted broadly, the various committees of the EP believed. This will include internal documents of the institutions although 'informal documents' ie purely personal documents involving personal opinions and 'brain-storming' will not be included. This provision if enacted will be difficult to operate but it has not caused overwhelming problems in eg the USA where the distinction is made. The Commission proposal actually reduces access to internal documents the EP committees felt.

Fifthly, modes of access should be made as easy as possible especially in the case of legislative documents. The register should contain 'mostly the documents relating to the legislative procedures and including all

1   Articles. 28(1) and 41(1) TEU and *Deutsche Babcock* Case 328/85 [1987] ECR 5119.
2   Article 41 EU Charter of Fundamental Rights.

proposals, opinions, working documents, agendas, documents for discussion at formal meetings, minutes, declarations and positions of member states.'[3] Classified documents should also be listed so that a challenge may be made to their classification as non-public. Information officers should replace secretary-generals as the arbiter on access for confirmatory decisions. Electronic versions of the Official Journal and of internal registries should be available in reading rooms everywhere in the Union. Under Art 10 EC (co-operation) local authorities could be asked to arrange this facility. Access should be user friendly.

Lastly, where a member state is asked for documents of an EU institution, national rules should prevail subject to a spirit of loyal co-operation entailing that member states should inform institutions of the request and fully take into account their views. It is important not to prejudice the development of Community policy.

When the EP and the Council failed to reach a common position, the Cashman report, which is the name given to the EP proposals, became the adopted position of the EP. By late March 2001, resort to the Conciliation Committee under Art 251 EC – the co-decision procedure – seemed inevitable.

For the final version of the Regulation approved by the EP, see the Epilogue below.

Conclusion

While these proposals significantly affect the Commission draft Regulation, it is 'incumbent upon the European institutions to deliver a real right of access for citizens' the report states. The amendments do improve the Regulation and it may prove difficult for the Council to resist a measure enhancing openness for the citizen. The whole episode of openness in the EU has been a grudging experience whereby the Council and Commission have had to make concessions after opposition to their practices and proposals: in the courts, before the Ombudsman and now from the EP. It is interesting that Art 255 EC did not emerge from a section of the Amsterdam Treaty on rights of citizens but from a section entitled 'Provisions Common to Several Institutions'. We shall have to see whether the incorporation of a right of access in the Charter of Rights of the EC Treaty will have any impact in changing attitudes. A final observation is that at the behest of Her Majesty's Government, the Charter is not a legally enforceable part of the Treaty!

---

3   Ibid, n 20 above at p 172.

9 Openness, information and the courts

The future role of the courts in helping to create a more open society is going to be vital. It has been said that the success of the HRA depends upon the mutual cooperation of the executive, Parliament and the courts. The same could be true for development of greater openness. The courts' role in FOIA is likely to be limited given the establishment of the Information Commissioner and Tribunal, deliberately introduced to diminish the role of courts. But as we saw, courts could be called upon to make crucial decisions on review. Proceedings in the *Spycatcher* litigation before Powell J in the New South Wales Supreme Court, and before Scott J in the English High Court where the Cabinet Secretary was subjected to detailed cross-examination, suggested the potential for the insights that may be gained into the inner workings of government.[1] We have seen the extra-judicial contribution of judges in famous inquiries into *Matrix Churchill* and *Standards in Public Life* by Scott LJ and Lord Nolan.[2] We do not possess a rich case law of decisions debating citizens' rights to governmental information, which is not in the public domain, because the common law interprets such claims in terms of property holding and quasi-proprietorial rights; or it interprets the claims in the face of statutory prohibitions, such as the Official Secrets Acts. If you do not own the information, or the documents on which it is expressed or placed, or you cannot claim the protection of confidentiality, you have no claim in law although it has been considered that a health authority does not have an absolute right to treat patients' documents as it pleases and must always

---

1   A-G v Guardian Newspapers Ltd (No 2) [1988] 3 All ER 545. The worldwide *Spycatcher* litigation is published as M Fysh (ed) [1989] *The Spycatcher Cases* European Law Centre.
2   Nolan, Cm 2850 I & II; Scott Report HC 115 (1995-6).

act in the best interests of the patient.[3] One has to rely upon release of information at the government's will to our representatives or to the public at large by the devices we have discussed unless information is being withheld in breach of a statutory discretion.[4] The High Court has stated that it cannot create a freedom of information statute.[5] Parliament has now created one, and we await the judicial reaction where the Commissioner proves powerless. There is no doubt that after years of indifference, English courts have displayed a greater awareness of the benefits to be gained from openness and freedom of expression. The common law was recognising such a fundamental right – and not simply a state concession — and it has been boosted by the HRA 1998 and s 12's emphatic instruction that the 'Court must have particular regard to the Convention right of freedom of expression ...' in order to ensure a free press unhampered by unnecessary restraints.[6] To add to these remarkable developments the decision of the Privy Council in *Lewis v Attorney-General of Jamaica*[7] where death sentences were overturned because there had been a failure to disclose materials to petitioners for mercy should be added.

One qualification must be made. Since 1967 courts, following earlier administrative concessions, have been prepared to assist litigants in dispute with state institutions in England and Wales, to the extent that, on exacting conditions, they will allow access to documents in the possession of state bodies or allow cross-examination of official witnesses. This topic, discussed in more detail later in this chapter, is known as public interest immunity.

When discussing openness and the courts, it must be appreciated that the theme is subject to various interpretations. It may refer to the openness of courts themselves: their being open to the public, their proceedings

---

3   *R v Mid Glamorgan Family Health Services Authority, ex p Martin* [1995] 1 All ER 356 , CA. Was there a breach of art 8 ECHR? What of information held by departments and passed on to other departments? See DPA 1998, s 63 and FOIA 2000, s 81. See *R v Blackledge (No 2)* (1995) Times, 8 November, CA and *Butler v Board of Trade* [1971] 1 Ch 680; *Re Arrows* [1993] Ch 452, CA and [1995] 2 AC 75, HL; or to individuals *Re Application Pursuant to R 728 of the Insolvency Rules 1986* (1994) BCC 369 placing restrictions on an insolvency consultant searching the Bankruptcy Register; note *Melton Medes v SIB* [1995] 3 All ER 880—no action for breach of 'restricted information' order by the SIB. I am grateful to Cosmo Graham for raising this point. See also *Re G (a minor)(social worker: disclosure)* [1996] 2 All ER 65.

4   See the remarkable decision of the Divisional Court in *R v Secretary of State for Trade and Industry, ex p Lonrho plc* (1989) 5 BCC 266.

5   *R v Secretary of State for Defence, ex p Sancto* (1992) Times, 19 September.

6   *Derbyshire CC v Times Newspapers Ltd* [1993] 1 All ER 1011, HL, *R v Secretary of State for the Home Department ex p Simms* [1999] 3 All ER 400, HL and Lord Steyn in particular; and *Kelly v BBC* [2001] 1 All ER etc.

7   [2000] WLR 1785 PC.

being in the public domain—the ultimate form of openness being live broadcasts, which the OJ Simpson trial in the mid 1990s did much to discredit;[8] their proceedings being open in the style and manner of their argument and the accessibility of their discourse. In a second sense the phrase can refer to the role of the courts in helping to achieve openness or fuller provision of information: by insisting on information being provided as evidence supporting an assertion, or by way of reasons being afforded for decisions which affect our lives, or by giving greater access to those claiming a right to information. A further element in this second sense would involve the role of the courts in advancing freedom of speech; protecting and enhancing our civil liberties such as demonstrating peaceably; developing without unjustified interference our intellectual and personal lives even in the absence of a first amendment entrenching a right to freedom of speech as in the USA.

A third sense of the expression can refer to the role of the courts in resolving disputes between parties over property rights in information or over the use of information acquired in a variety of circumstances. Typically, a confidential relationship creates certain obligations and entitlements over the use of information. While the courts have developed the law of confidentiality,[9] especially in the realm of government information, it has remained for the legislature to give fuller definition to the law relating to copyright and patents, [10] and copyright of information held on computers and computer misuse.[11] Our law on intellectual property still awaits systematisation. Defamation would also be relevant.[12] I touch on this third sense in this chapter, but my overriding concern is with the first two senses. I will not be able to deal in any detailed manner with freedom of speech or demonstration or censorship. These are detailed topics and are well provided for elsewhere.[13]

---

8   There has been discussion of live broadcasts of trials but not those involving juries or magistrates. See *BBC, Petitioners (No2)* 2000 SLT 860 and broadcasting of the Lockerbie trial. Broadcasts of proceedings in Scottish courts have been allowed to a limited extent.

9   See p 419 below and nb the Law Commission's report suggesting, *inter alia*, a new tort of breach of confidence: Cmnd 8388 (1981).

10   Copyright, Designs and Patents Act 1988.

11   Computer Misuse Act 1990; see also Copyright (Computer Software) Amendment Act 1985 and nb *Intellectual Property and Innovation*, Cmnd 9712 (1986). See generally J Phillips and A Firth *Introduction To Intellectual Property Law* (3rd edn, 1995), WR Cornish *Intellectual Property* (4th ed, 1999).

12   See most recently the Defamation Act 1996.

13   E Barendt *Freedom of Speech* (1985); G Robertson *Obscenity* (1979); Public Order Act 1986 *Current Law Statutes Annotation*, vol 4, chapter 64 T. Gibbons; Criminal Justice and Public Order Act 1994; D Feldman *Civil Liberties and Human Rights* (2nd ed, forthcoming), J Beatson and Y Cripps (eds) *Freedom of Expression and Freedom of Information* (2000).

The 'Golden Met-wand'

Publicity for the law, and public information about the rules of conduct of society which are to be implemented through its courts and which may account for deprivation of liberty, property, and until 1965 in the UK one's life,[14] are vital components of the rule of law.[15] So too is a judiciary free from executive or other interference. Developed markets and commercial and financial enterprise require an extended law of property; contract; corporations law; patents; securities and investment law. The fact that most of dispute resolution, guidance through rules or standards, or the establishment of dispute procedures and policy-initiating bodies, does not involve the use of courts, is not to deny the fact that courts are ultimately the final arbiters of law. Unless, that is, Parliament has definitively and successfully excluded the courts from a province of decision-making,[16] or where practice has effectively excluded the courts.[17] Deliberate exclusion by Parliament is comparatively rare, and usually jealously scrutinised by the courts. What goes on in the courts is public business, even if it concerns private parties. Screening of security or undercover officials giving evidence may take place as an alternative to *in camera* proceedings.[18] And what is said in court is protected by absolute privilege in any subsequent defamation proceedings.

There is no rule of law as such that judges must give reasons for their decisions although the expectation has been growing that they should.[19]

---

14 The death penalty still survived for treason and some military offences until the Human Rights Act 1998, s 1(3), Sch 1, Part III. It may be revived in time of war or imminent threat of war, ibid.

15 Harden and Lewis *The Noble Lie* (1986).

16 *Anisminic Ltd v Foreign Compensation Commission* [1969] 2 AC 147 is a famous example of the enforced casuistry in which the courts engage to insist upon all errors of law being of a jurisdictional nature. Cf *Page v Visitor of the University of Hull* [1993] 1 All ER 97 , HL. In *R v Security Service Tribunal, ex p Harman and Hewitt* QBD 14 February 1992, Kennedy J questioned the efficacy of the provision seeking to prevent judicial review of decisions of the Security Service Tribunal, s 5(4) Security Service Act 1989.

17 Especially in the field of government contracts, where even formal arbitration is rare. The EC Procurement Directives have made some difference and note the Local Government Contracts Act 1997.

18 See M Gilbert (1990) Public Law 207 and 'secret witnesses'. See also *R v Lord Saville of Newdigate, ex p A* [1999] 4 All ER 860, CA and anonymity of witnesses at the 'Bloody Sunday' Inquiry.

19 *Flannery v Halifax Estate Agencies Ltd* [2000] 1 All ER 373, CA. 'The duty to give reasons was a function of due process and, therefore, of justice in all cases, however, transparency should be the watchword.' Henry LJ. Cf s 10 Tribunals and Inquiries Act 1992. Poor reasons are likely to be a ground for successful appeal.

Nor is there any administrative stricture or exhortation.[20] Yet judges operate within a tradition spreading back as far as the common law which *insists* that the reasons for their decisions are, unlike juries, publicly expressed or published. Their decisions have to fit into the body of established precedent and be reasoned to conclusions which will be publicly contested and rigorously analysed in academic work and subsequent judicial proceedings. A good judge feels the pressure of his peers to 'pass muster'. If he does not, his reputation as a lawyer, though not his judicial salary,[1] will suffer. Indeed, the alleged secrecy of Star Chamber proceedings was the cause of one of several vitriolic attacks on that body in the seventeenth century. The attack was politically motivated by common lawyers, but it struck a deep and pervasive chord of sympathy in influential circles.[2] The law must be known after hard argument and testing. Being allowed to utter forth truthfully on the law without a reck as to consequences is one thing and has a centuries' old tradition behind it. Being instructed, on the other hand, that certain matters are reserved issues for politics alone, is another tradition and one that has been deeply engrained in our political and legal consciousness. This is why case law has featured so little in our discussions to date. Freedom of governmental information has been reserved business. Unlike freedom of speech or right to life, it has not been perceived as a human right. Even when confronted with cases concerning freedom of speech, courts traditionally disclaimed any constitutional dimension to their decisions, holding that the prevention of a meeting or a public address was simply a corollary of the police apprehending a breach of the peace, a concept which has been stretched to breaking point.[3] The wind of change has made its presence felt. In *Derbyshire County Council v Times Newspapers*[4] a novel departure

---

20 The advice of Lord Mansfield CJ to magistrates was not to give reasons for while their decisions would doubtless be correct their reasons would often be wrong and thus reviewable.

1 Prospects of promotion will doubtless be blighted if there is an ostentatious record of successful appeal.

2 Both Elton in *The Tudor Constitution* (2nd edn, 1981) and Kenyon in *The Stuart Constitution* (1966) believe that Star Chamber was much maligned and unjustly so: it administered 'the Common Law by means of a different procedure', including written depositions, exchange of evidence and cross-examination of the accused under oath (*Kenyon*, p 117). Allegations of secrecy were fabrications. For criticism of the view that it was the Privy Council in another guise, see W Holdsworth *History of English Law*, vol V, chapter IV.

3 Eg *Duncan v Jones* [1936] 1 KB 218; *Thomas v Sawkins* [1935] 2 KB 249; *McLeod v Metropolitan Police Comr* [1994] 4 All ER 553, CA; Viscount Dilhorne in *British Steel Corporation v Granada Television Ltd* [1981] AC 1096; and Lord Diplock in *Secretary of State for Defence v Guardian Newspapers Ltd* [1984] 3 All ER 601, HL. For graphic evidence on the 'right' to demonstrate and its development under common law and ECHR Art 11, see *DPP v Jones* [1999] 2 All ER 257, HL.

4 [1993] 1 All ER 1011, HL. On the Convention, see *Castells v Spain* (1992) 14 EHRR 445; *Jersild v Denmark* (1994) 19 EHRR 1.

was seen among the ranks of our senior judiciary when the House of Lords unanimously ruled that a local authority, and indeed even central government, could not sue for defamation. Such an action for the 'organs of government' would be contrary to the public interest because it was of the 'highest public importance' that a public body should be open to uninhibited public criticism and a right to sue would place an undesirable fetter on freedom of speech. What was striking was that the House of Lords chose to make their ruling on the basis of the common law and not under the provisions of art 10 of the European Convention on Human Rights which was a prime factor in the Court of Appeal's decision denying such an action.[5] The Law Lords' decision is a particularly robust assertion of the role of the common law in protecting human rights and it probably has presaged a longer term change in judicial sentiment. This change was evident before the HRA 1998 came into effect and it is worthwhile repeating Lord Hope's words from *DPP v Kebelene*[6] where he said that 'it is now plain that incorporation of the ECHR into our domestic law will subject the entire legal system to a fundamental process of review and, where necessary, reform by the judiciary.' In *ex p Simms*, the Law Lords ruled that it was unlawful to interfere with a prisoner's right of access to a journalist who was interested in writing an article about the possibility of a wrongful conviction. The journalist had declined to sign an undertaking not to publish such an article. The interference, which regulations could not justify in the absence of specific authorisation in legislation, amounted to an invasion of the prisoner's 'fundamental or basic right' to freedom of expression.[7] Lord Steyn emphasised the point graphically: 'freedom of speech is the lifeblood of democracy. The free flow of information and ideas informs political debate. It is a safety valve....'[8] Article 10 lay behind the decision to open up the inquiry into Dr Harold Shipman, the mass murderer, to the public – a secret inquiry would have interfered with freedom of expression and a right to pass on information.[9]

---

5   *Oberschlick v Austria* Case No 1990/197/257 (1991) 19 EHRR 389, E Ct HR; see *Re W* [1992] 1 All ER 794, CA and allowing publication of an article about a ward of court because of a real public interest in the case which involved two homosexual male foster parents: Art 10 invoked in support and *Kelly v BBC* [2001] 1 All ER 323. On use of criminal libel, see *Lingens v Austria* (1986) 8 EHRR 407 and *Oberschlick* above; and *Prager and Oberschilick v Austria* (1995) 21 EHRR 1.

6   *DPP v Kebelene* [1999] 4 All ER 801 at 838h-j. Not all are happy with this prospect of what John Griffith's has described as 'celestial jurisprudence'.

7   *R v Secretary of State for the Home Department, ex p Simms* [1999] 3 All ER 400, HL.

8   At 408d.

9   *R (Wagstaff) v Secretary of State for Health* [2001] 1 WLR 292.

Various international declarations seek to protect freedom of expression, opinion and information. The European Convention on Human Rights, art 10, proclaims that:

> Everyone has the right to freedom of expression. This right shall include freedom to hold opinions and to receive and impart information and ideas without interference by public authority and regardless of frontiers.[10]

But the right, because it carries duties and responsibilities, is subject to qualifications: 'as are prescribed by law and are necessary in a democratic society, in the interests of national security,[11] territorial integrity or public safety, for the prevention of disorder or crime, for the protection of health or morals, for the protection of the rights, authority and impartiality of the judiciary.'[12] This body of qualifications has to be seen in the context of case law of the European Commission and Court of Human Rights, which has stressed that the restrictions *must be* prescribed in law,[13] are *necessary*, are proportionate to legitimate objectives and subject to strict interpretation. The restrictions must be predicated by a 'pressing social need'[14] which is proportionate to the means of safeguarding it; in short, the authorities must not engage in overkill or exaggerated reaction. We saw a balancing or rights under Art 10 and under other Convention articles, especially Art 2 and the right to life in *Venables and Thompson* – the notorious murderers of Jamie Bulger (see p 333 et seq below). Furthermore, the Convention allows judges to strike a note of fundamentalism which had been absent from our legal traditions until the last decade. In *Handyside,* for instance, it was noted how:

> Freedom of expression constitutes one of the essential foundations of a society, one of the basic conditions for its progress and for the development of every man [sic]. Subject to paragraph 2 of Article 10, it is applicable not only to 'information' or 'ideas' that are favourably received, but also to those that offend, shock or disturb

---

10 Article 10 (1).

11 I Cameron *National Security and the ECHR* (2000).

12 Article 10 (2). Cf *Leander v Sweden* (1987) 9 EHRR 433, A 116 and *Z v Austria No 10392/83* (1988) and *VW BLUF v Netherlands* (1995) 20 EHRR 189. See DJ Harris et al *Law of the Convention on Human Rights* (1995) chapter 11. See *Hadjianastassiou v Greece* (1992) 16 EHRR 219 and *Informatsionverein Lentia v Austria* (1993) 17 EHRR 93. See *Goodwin* p 402 below and Harris etc above.

13 Not necessarily statute or statutory instrument, but in a body of *published* rules considered binding: *Silver v UK* (1983) 5 EHRR 347 and discussion of the proviso in Art 8(2); *Sunday Times v UK* (1979) 2 EHRR 245. See *R v Advertising Standards Authority Ltd, ex p Matthias Rath BV* (2001) Times, 10 January.

14 The *Sunday Times* case, above.

the State or any sector of the population. Such are the demands of that pluralism, tolerance and broad-mindedness without which there is no democratic society.[15]

An absence of a constitutional culture, an absence of government guaranteed freedom of speech, and a repetitive failure seriously to question executive right, have in the past all helped to ensure that far from questioning *raison d'état,* the British judiciary would afford it, with very few exceptions, every endorsement. The common law may be enjoying a revitalised vigour, to which the HRA will give enormous encouragement. Together, these might prompt from the judiciary a new approach in the defence of civil liberties which *is* surely needed in the UK, without making them unaccountable defenders of entrenched conservatism. This latter position may be encouraged by the closed nature of judicial appointments.[16]

Judicial appointments[17]

The process has ensured that only the 'safe and the sound' will be promoted to the Bench. For an appointment to the High Court, a barrister is expected to have displayed the necessary ambition and dedication not only to have mastered the most difficult briefs, but to have mastered the system. For appointments to QC, level of income is important though no longer described as 'decisive'. Any injudicious, intemperate or outspoken public statements would doubtless be damning. Boat-rockers do not reach the top – unless perhaps one is Lord Chancellor. Lord Irvine's comparison of himself to Cardinal Wolsey and his widely publicised invitation on his official headed paper to senior lawyers who were Labour supporters to contribute to the Labour Party coffers brought home the dangers of so much power of appointment being confused with political powers in the hands of one individual.

15 *Handyside v UK* (1976) 1 EHRR 737, *Silver,* n 115. In *Leander,* n 12 above, refusing access to information on a national security register was neither a breach of Art 8 – right to privacy – nor Art 10, the Court held; see *Rotaru v Romania* 8 BHRC 449 and failure to provide redress where security services hold erroneous information about individuals. See *Kelly v BBC* [2001] 1 All ER 323 for an example of the influence of Art 10.

16 J. Rozenberg *In Search of Justice* (1994) chapter 2 for a readable account.

17 See the Lord Chancellor's Guidance and the *Independent Scrutiny of the Appointment Processes of Judges and QCs* Sir L Peach December 1999, LCD; and Sit T Legg (2001) Public Law 62. C Thomas and K Malleson *Judicial Appointments Commissions: the European and North American Experience and Possible Implications for the UK* (1997).

The background of the vast majority of individuals concerned and the remarkable absence of notoriety among the judiciary, certainly the higher judiciary, testify to that.[18] Data information on judicial appointments is one of the protected items under the Data Protection Act. There are 12,000 files on successful and unsuccessful applicants for judicial office in the Lord Chancellor's Department. In 1992 when the Chairman of the Bar suggested that he and his successors should see the file of a disappointed applicant for office in order to plead his case; the request was refused.[19] Feedback on the tenor of comments is now given. Judicial appointments to the High Court were by invitation only. The Lord Chancellor's *Policies and Procedures* on all judicial appointments emphasise open procedures based on merit 'irrespective of ethnic origins, gender, marital status, political affiliation, sexual orientation, religion or disability. Appointments still follow the cosy informal process of sounding out, so beloved of the British tradition although procedures are now spelt out in the Lord Chancellor's guidance. Such soundings are still regarded as an important part of the process according to the Peach Report in 1999. Class is not referred to. It is likely to be a big barrier to *entry* to the profession and practice. Safeguards exist against 'blackballing' of individuals by one person as individuals are given a chance to comment. Information is collected by the 'Judicial Group' in the Lord Chancellor's Department and interviews include a lay member on the panel who is 'specially selected and trained.' Sir Leonard Peach found that there was no independent oversight of the system and recommended in his report a judicial appointments commissioner and deputy commissioners to act as an audit and ombudsman and to make recommendations to the Lord Chancellor. In early 2001, the Lord Chancellor, stung into response by his confusion of roles and a report from the Office of Fair Trading, announced that interviews were taking place for a commissioner.[20] This would cover appointment of QCs and tribunal chairmen. A Judicial Appointments Board or Commission has been refused – although not completely off the agenda – as have Senate-style hearings into prospective justices of the Supreme Court in the USA where their personal and political proclivities are investigated with relish by their opponents.

Individuals are recommended for senior appointment by the Lord Chancellor to the Prime Minister. Circuit judges, who have usually served as recorders, are recommended by the Lord Chancellor, as are High Court

---

18 In recent years the participation of Lord Hoffman in the *Pinochet* case when he had an interest with one of the litigants and the pressure on Harman J to resign have been the highlights of judicial notoriety.
19 Lord Williams QC, *The Guardian,* 24 May 1994.
20 HL Debs. 21 February 2001. The first Commissioner is Sir Colin Campbell Vice Chancellor of Nottingham University and former legal academic. He will head a team of up to 10 deputy commissioners.

judges.[1] Appointments are by the Crown. In 1994, circuit and district judgeships were advertised in the press for the first time in terms described as a model of political correctness. Since Lord Irvine's tenure as Lord Chancellor in 1997, advertisements have been placed in the press for applications to the High Court. Much criticism has been made of the white male domination of the Bench. In 1998-99, from 634 judicial appointments, 76.5% were male, 23.5% were female and of those 92.9% were white. 5.4% were 'other ethnic origin' and 1.7% were 'not known'.[2] The Royal Commission on Criminal Justice has recommended that judges should receive far more training than is currently the case; for those trying cases under the Children Act 1989 a training programme has been claimed to have been a great success. A Judicial Studies Board provides what has been termed 'management for judges by judges'. In April 2000, the Scottish Executive proposed a Scottish Judicial Appointments Board.

Once in office, judges no longer serve under a 'voluntary' code of silence known as the 'Kilmuir Rules'. These were written in 1955 by the then Lord Chancellor stating that generally judges should not make public utterances on subjects in the media.[3] Their application was relaxed over the years as Law Lords appear to have been excluded from their provisions. In his first press conference as Lord Chancellor, Lord Mackay announced that the 'Kilmuir Rules' were ripe for reform. He would encourage more discretion on the part of judges so long as interviews did not prejudice their judicial work.[4] Measured judicial comments have become more overtly critical of Government policies and legislative reform. Lord Woolf has attacked the removal of a right of appeal in the Asylum Bill which had existed for over 21 years. The former Lord Chief Justice, Lord Taylor, criticised the Criminal Justice Act 1991 for attempting to restrict judicial discretion in sentencing and his predecessor spoke out against reform of the legal profession. On this latter point, the

1   Circuit judges may be sacked by the Lord Chancellor on the ground of 'incapacity or misbehaviour'. One former recorder has threatened the Lord Chancellor with judicial review for failing to renew an appointment; between 1981 and December 1986, 27 expired appointments had not been renewed: HC Debs vol 107, col 431 (16 December 1986). The author was informed in 1996 that more recent figures in the Lord Chancellor's Department were not computer-accessible! The relative insecurity of recorders has become an important issue under the HRA 1998 and Article 6 ECHR: see in Scotland and temporary sheriffs *Starrs v Ruxton* 2000 SLT 42, HCJ. High Court judges hold office during good behaviour subject to removal by the Queen on an address from both Houses of Parliament to the Queen: Supreme Court Act 1981, s 11(3). Similar provisions cover Law Lords. The former Lord Chancellor Lord Mackay was credited with introducing an enlightened approach to judicial appointments.
2   See Legg above for the senior judiciary and H Genn *Paths to Justice: what people do and think about going to law* (1999).
3   (1986) Public Law 384.
4   *The Guardian* 4 November 1987.

judiciary collectively went on strike in 1989.[5] Lord Taylor appeared on *Question Time* and delivered the Dimbleby lecture on TV. Press conferences have been called by Lord Taylor and Lord Woolf, in the latter case on a subject—imprisonment—which drew a fierce retort from the Home Secretary and which prompted the Lord Chief Justice to write to all High Court judges advising them to think twice before speaking to the media. Sir Richard Scott's engages with the Government after the publication of the *Matrix Churchill* Report are particularly notable. There have been very interesting judicial observations in academic and professional journals on the waning of judicial independence, including in the latter case an attack on the previous Lord Chancellor for seeming to interfere with the independence of the President of the Employment Appeal Tribunal, Wood J.[6] In May 1995 *The Times* reported a clash of opinion between the Lord Chancellor and the Lord Chief Justice over a change in the law which would allow research to be conducted on how juries reach their decisions, the former being in favour of such a change and responsible research.[7] Such open comments are bound to attract public attention and possibly criticism. There are numerous judicial comments of a less weighty nature which have placed the judiciary in a very poor light or put them on a par with 'new wave comedians'.[8] The contribution made by greater openness has been welcome but the words of Viscount Kilmuir had some sound advice: 'So long as a judge keeps silent', opined Kilmuir, 'his reputation for wisdom and impartiality remains unassailable.' By greater openness, they expose both strengths and weaknesses. They will also lay themselves open to increased accusations of prejudice.

What of the openness of the courts themselves?

In *Scott v Scott*[9] it was stated as a general principle that justice should be openly administered, although proceedings in chambers were an exception. In 1998, however, the High Court ruled that even though proceedings were in chambers, that did not mean that a judgment had to be secret: 'The concept of a secret judgment is one which I believe to be inherently abhorrent' declared Jacob J.[10] Secrecy would depend upon the

5   *Rozenberg* above pp 71-2.

6   Sir F Purchass 'Lord Mackay and the Judiciary' (1994) NLJ 527.

7   *The Times* 1 May 1995. And see Lord Taylor's comments on the Home Secretary's proposals to increase prison sentences: *The Times* 12 October 1995 and 24 May 1996.

8   Judge Pickles describing Lord Lane CJ as a 'dinosaur': *The Guardian* 28 November 1990.

9   [1913] AC 417; see *Re X* [1975] Fam 47 and *Re Z* [1995] 4 All ER 961, CA. See *Storer v British Gas plc* [2000] 2 All ER 440 and *R v Bow County Court, ex p Pelling* [1999] 4 All ER 751, CA. I am grateful to Joe Jacob for giving me details of this last case and *Forbes and Hodgson* below.

10 *Forbes v Smith* [1998] 1 All ER 973; and see *Hodgson v Imperial Tobacco Ltd* [1998] 1 WLR 1056.

nature of the proceedings and their subject-matter. The openness of the courts is not to satisfy public curiosity or to stimulate debate, but to keep the 'judge while trying under trial'.[11] Trials concerning prosecutions under the Official Secrets Acts and security-sensitive information have been the obvious occasions where secrecy has been invoked,[12] as are cases where justice itself would be defeated. In cases concerning the Adoption Act 1976, the court has exercised its inherent power to suppress information, ie a birth certificate in the hands of the Registrar-General where there was a risk of serious injury to a person named therein in spite of an apparent absolute duty to disclose.[13] It has also ordered restrictions on disclosure of information placed on a register where not to do so may bring about a real risk of serious injury to a child.[14] The Court of Appeal has also prevented the publication of the identities of witnesses (former paratroopers) involved in the Bloody Sunday shootings in Derry in 1972 when they gave evidence to the inquiry under Lord Saville.[15] Sufficient weight had not been given to the safety and right to life of the former soldiers by the tribunal.

The Woolf reforms on civil procedure led to a new rule under Part 39 Civil Procedure Rules 1998. This provides under r 39.2 that 'the general rule is that a hearing (trial) is to be in public.' Special arrangements do not have to be made for accommodating members of the public. Hearings, or parts of hearings, may be in private where, inter alia, publicity would defeat the object of the hearing, the matter involves national security, confidential information, or it is necessary to protect the interests of children or patients. A private hearing may also be held where the court believes this is necessary in the interests of justice.

Contempt of court

It was thought that the Contempt of Court Act 1981[16] put most of the law of contempt on to a statutory footing. Conduct which tends to interfere with the course of justice in particular legal proceedings, regardless of intent to do so, may be treated as a contempt. This rule of 'strict liability' only applies to proceedings which are 'active' under the terms of the Act at the time of a publication[17] which creates a 'substantial risk that the

---

11 *Per* Lord Diplock in *Home Office v Harman*, below.
12 As in parts of Clive Ponting's trial; OSA 1920, s 8. Public Interest Immunity (below) was not claimed in Ponting's trial, but was in *Matrix Churchill*.
13 *R v Registrar-General, ex p Smith* [1991] 2 All ER 88, CA.
14 *Re X* [1994] 3 All ER 372, CA.
15 *R v Lord Saville of Newdigate, ex p A* [1999] 4 All ER 860.
16 See *A-G v Times Newspapers Ltd* [1974] AC 273 and the Phillimore Report, Cmnd 5794 (1974).
17 Schedule I for 'active' and s 2(1) for 'publication'.

course of justice in the proceedings in question will be seriously impeded or prejudiced'.[18] A TV company has been prevented by the Court of Appeal from broadcasting nightly dramatised courtroom events from a trial on the same day because this might 'adversely affect the public view of the judgment.'[19] A defence is available where 'if at the time of publication (having taken all reasonable care) [the publisher] does not know and has no reason to suspect that relevant proceedings are active'.[20] A person will not be guilty of contempt under the strict liability rule in respect of a fair and accurate report of legal proceedings held in public, published contemporaneously and in good faith.[1] The court has power under s 4(2) to order postponement of publication for such periods as it thinks necessary to prevent a substantial risk of prejudice to the administration of justice in those proceedings, or any other proceedings, pending or imminent.[2] Knowledge of the order must be proved to establish contempt (and see below).[3] A further defence is available under s 5. This protects publication 'made as or part of a discussion in good faith of public affairs or other matters of general public interest'. When 'the risk of impediment or prejudice to particular legal proceedings is merely incidental to the discussion' it is not to be treated as a contempt of court under the strict liability rule.[4] Even where contempt proceedings have not been brought, prejudicial statements in the course of a trial by the Secretary of State which were reported in the media and which had special relevance to the defendants necessitated quashing of convictions.[5]

The Attorney-General's *fiat* is required for issue of contempt proceedings or they can be issued 'on the motion of a court having jurisdiction to deal with the matter'. The exercise of this judgement is inviolable.[6] The Act leaves to the common law publication or behaviour which interferes with the *general* administration of justice[7] and preserves

18 *A-G v ITV News Ltd* [1995] 2 All ER 370; *A-G v Guardian Newspapers Ltd* [1992] 3 All ER 38; *A-G v MGN Ltd* [1997] 1 All ER 456; *A-G v Birmingham Post and Mail Ltd* [1998] 4 All ER 49.
19 *Re Channel 4 TV Co Ltd* (1987) Times, 18 December.
20 Section 3. The burden of proof is on the defendant to make out the defence. The distributor is also afforded protection.
1   Section 4(1) and *A-G v Times Newspapers Ltd* (1983) Times, 12 February.
2   *Re Central Independent Television plc* [1991] 1 All ER 347: court postponed all TV and radio reports so the jury would not hear news items; the Court of Appeal said this was 'overkill'. See also *Ex p Telegraph plc* [1993] 2 All ER 971.
3   *Re F* [1977] 1 All ER 114, CA and *Re L* [1988] 1 All ER 418; cf *A-G v Leveller Magazines Ltd* [1979] 1 All ER 745, HL.
4   *A-G v English* [1982] 2 All ER 903, HL, *A-G v TVS Television Ltd* (1989) Times, 7 July.
5   *R v Cullen* (1990) 92 Cr App Rep 239, CA: Government minister Tom King criticised the right to silence in a Parliamentary statement at the time of the trial of defendants for conspiracy to murder *inter alios* himself and who had exercised the right.
6   *R v A-G, ex p Taylor* (1995) Independent, 31 July, QBD.
7   Defaming judges as incompetent or biased: see *Prager etc* on Art 10 ECHR and comments about judges, above, n 5, p 383.

as contempt that which intentionally impedes or prejudices the administration of justice.[8] In *A-G v Newspaper Publishing Ltd*,[9] the Court of Appeal overruled a decision of the Vice-Chancellor and held that publication by a third party of material covered by an injunction not to publish and which was not binding on that third party could amount to a contempt of court where publication would destroy the confidentiality in material which the earlier court had sought to protect.[10] This would be established where the party was shown to have published with knowledge that the material was subject to a court order prohibiting publication and that it was the subject matter of a pending action. The substance of this decision was subsequently confirmed by the House of Lords[11] and *contra mundum* orders have been used by the courts to restrain the 'whole world' from prejudicing the court's orders.[12] This is an extremely convenient gagging device for government and represents one of the only unqualified victories from the *Spycatcher* episode from which this ruling emerged. In *A-G v Punch Ltd*, the Court of Appeal ruled that an intention to interfere with the *purpose* of the judicial order had to be established.[13] Where orders were very broad or where there was insufficient evidence to establish that in the case of national security there was knowledge that the materials had not been previously published a contempt would not be established. A split decision of the Court of Appeal ruled that any other approach would introduce censorship by the Attorney-General in breach of Art 10 ECHR. This seems to have reined in the excessive breadth of earlier decisions. The court also reminded the A-G of the possibility of proceeding against the publisher for aiding and abetting a breach by the subject of the injunction of that order.

Section 8 of the Act protects the confidentiality of jury deliberations by making breach of such a contempt.[14] Section 9 of the Act prohibits the use of tape-recorders unless the leave of the court is obtained,[15] although these recordings must not be published in any way. Section 11 allows the

---

8   *A-G v Sport Newspapers Ltd* [1992] 1 All ER 503. Section 6(*c*). Eg bribing or intimidating jurors; see also: *Raymond v Honey* [1983] 1 AC 1. Nb *A-G v Newspaper Publishing plc* [1987] 3 All ER 276.
9   [1987] 3 All ER 276.
10 The *mens rea* required was specific intent not recklessness as to whether the administration of justice would be impeded or prejudiced.
11 *A-G v Times Newspapers Ltd* [1991] 2 All ER 398.
12 For *contra mundum* injunctions: *Re X County Council v A* [1985] 1 All ER 53; *Venables and Thompson v News Group Newspapers Ltd* [2001] 1 All ER 908. Nb *Punch* below.
13 *A-G v Punch Ltd* [2001] 2 All ER 655, CA. This involved publication of Shayler's allegations. Simon Brown LJ felt the publisher had the necessary *mens rea* because the publisher assumed responsibility for determining whether national security was risked, thereby thwarting the court's intention.
14 *A-G v New Statesman and Nation Publishing Co Ltd* [1981] QB 1; *A-G v Associated Newspapers Ltd* [1994] 2 AC 238, HL.
15 Codes of guidance exist.

court to give directions prohibiting the publication of names or evidence where these were not disclosed in open court. The section does not give instruction on when such matters may be withheld.[16] The widespread use of the section to protect the anonymity of witnesses, decisions which cannot be directly reviewed, has led to challenge in the European Commission of Human Rights and a right of appeal was provided against s 4 (2) and s 11 orders and other orders restricting publication of reports of trials on indictment and access to such trials and ancillary matters.[17] Brooke J has urged caution in accommodating the legitimate interests of the media and that judges should 'think long and hard' before banning contemporaneous reporting under section 4(2);[18] courts had a discretionary power to hear representations from the press or media before considering whether to make a section 4(2) order and they ought normally to hear representations when a request for such was made and the court anticipated that their representations would be of assistance.[19] The Court of Appeal has ruled that a judge should only withdraw into chambers to consider a section 4(2) order where this is appropriate and s/he must resume sitting in open court 'as soon as it emerges that the need to exclude the public is not plainly necessary'.[20] It has also ruled that the court must be satisfied that in reporting the proceedings a substantial risk of prejudice to the administration of justice is present and if so whether it was necessary to make an order postponing publication in the circumstances of the case. Secondly, the court must balance the considerations which supported the need for a fair trial by an unprejudiced jury and the requirements of open justice and a legitimate public interest on the other.[1] Judges should also not be over protective of juries and must credit them with intelligence.[2] Nonetheless, the *New Law Journal* has claimed that in the Central Criminal Court up to 20% of all cases 'on some days' are covered by section 4(2) orders.[3]

Some statutes allow the names of witnesses and other evidence to be withheld,[4] and courts have a common law power to withhold identity

---

16 *R v Evesham Justices, ex p McDonagh* [1988] 1 All ER 371; and *R v Westminster City Council, ex p Castelli* [1996] 2 FCR 49.
17 Section 159 (1) Criminal Justice Act 1988.
18 *A-G v Guardian Newspapers Ltd* [1992] 3 All ER 38.
19 *R v Clerkenwell Magistrates' Court, ex p Telegraph plc* [1993] 2 All ER 183.
20 *Re Crook's Appeal* [1992] 2 All ER 687.
1   *R v Beck, ex p Daily Telegraph plc* [1993] 2 All ER 177 , CA.
2   *Ex p Daily Telegraph* (1993) Guardian, 15 March. See (1992) New LJ 957.
3   Above.
4   Eg Children and Young Persons Act 1933, ss 39 (amended by s 45 Youth Justice and Criminal Evidence Act 1999) and 49; Administration of Justice Act 1960, s 12; Sexual Offences (Amendment) Act 1976; Magistrates Courts Act 1980, ss 8 and 71; see Children Act 1989 s 97 (as amended by the Access to Justice Act 1999): see *Kelly v BBC* [2001] 1 All ER 323 and the impact of Art 10 ECHR;

and information where its revelation would frustrate the cause of the action, such as breach of confidence or patent. The subject headings of contempt have been developed by judicial precedent, and as they are based upon 'the broadest of principles' they can occasionally be put to novel and unexpected use. We saw such a development in the *Spycatcher* case above. In 1980, a prisoner named Williams sued the Home Office for false imprisonment in the control unit in Wakefield Prison. His claim was based on the argument that the control unit was established without specific legal authority and in breach of the Prison Rules.[5] The unit concentrated on particularly severe forms of isolation, deprivation and discipline. To help establish Williams's case, the Home Office had been ordered, after an application for discovery (now disclosure), to hand over to Williams's solicitors at the National Council for Civil Liberties documents relating to the establishment and operation of the unit. These constituted a voluminous bundle of documents, many of which were read out and examined in open court. A reporter for *The Guardian* asked Williams's solicitor if he could borrow the documents for a feature article on the case and its background. Without any improper motive on her part,[6] the solicitor allowed sight of the documents which had been obtained on discovery. The Home Office had released the documents by order of the court on the basis that they were used for the litigation and not for other general purposes of the NCCL.

The House of Lords held by a 3-2 majority, upholding the High Court and Court of Appeal, that the solicitor had been guilty of civil contempt by breaking an undertaking to the court.[7] 'The case', fulminated Lord Diplock, 'is *not* about freedom of speech, freedom of the press, openness of justice or documents coming into the "public domain" ... nor does it call for considerations of any of those human rights and fundamental freedoms' contained in the European Convention for the Protection of Human Rights and Fundamental Freedoms. The case was about discovery of documents in litigation, the compulsory handing over of documents in their possession or control between the parties in a lawsuit for inspection and copying and which 'contain information that may, either directly or indirectly, enable that other party either to advance his own case or damage the case of his adversary or which may fairly lead to a chain of inquiry which may have either of these two consequences'. It is an 'inroad' into privacy in the name of justice which requires safeguards against

---

Criminal Justice Act 1988 and rape victims; and Criminal Justice and Public Order Act 1994, s 44 which repeals s 8(8) Magistrates' Courts Act 1980. JPs cannot withhold their own identities from the public: *R v Felixstowe Justices, ex p Leigh* [1987] QB 582.

5   *Williams v Home Office (No 2)* [1981] 1 All ER 1211.
6   Though cf Lord Denning in the Court of Appeal [1981] QB 534.
7   *Home Office v Harman* [1983] 1 AC 280.

abuse.[8] Had the reporter copied all the evidence given in court orally as the trial proceeded, no breach of law would have ensued as long as the public were admitted.[9] He could also have 'bargained privately' to obtain a copy of the mechanically recorded speeches in court. He was a feature article writer, not a reporter producing an accurate account of the proceedings for the quality press,[10] so his sight of the documents was not *de minimis* and a mere breach of technicality, but a serious contempt, the majority held.

Lords Scarman and Simon believed that once documents had been read out in open court, the obligation of protection of confidentiality ceased; potentially inadmissible documents should be filed separately; anything else marked as exhibits should be available for inspection as part of the public record, as occurs in the USA, whether read out or not. The documents had become public knowledge, and after objecting to discovery the Home Office had not subsequently objected to publication on grounds of 'public interest immunity'. Lord Scarman favoured the American practice of a judicial record and a public right to 'complete information' as a common law right.[11] *Per contra,* Lord Roskill observed that, at that time, we had no FOIA in this country.[12] The decision to hold in contempt the solicitor who handed over the documents, from which evidence had been given publicly, seems vindictive. But the story does not end there.

The case was taken to the European Commission of Human Rights,[13] and in June 1986 the Government announced that it intended to amend the law of contempt after reaching a friendly settlement before the Commission, rather than persisting to the full opinion of the Commission and judgment before the European Court of Human Rights. The provisional opinion of the Commission and the terms of the settlement are confidential. A formal report with detailed findings and opinions is

8   It is peculiar to common law systems. The Civil Procedure Rules 1998 now provide for disclosure and inspection.
9   800 pages of documents were read out. Counsel have been required to restrict the length of oral proceedings in civil cases by increased use of written submissions a process encouraged by the Civil Procedure Rules 1998.
10 Which might involve some question-begging!
11 See *Re Application of NBC, USA v Meyers* 635 F 2d 945 (1980); *US v Mitchell* 551 F 2d 1252 (1976); *Nixon v Warner Communications Inc* 435 US 589 (1978). See Lord Hobhouse in *Reynolds v Times Newspapers* [1999] 4 All ER 609, HL.
12 And he made some unsupported assertions that discovery (disclosure) was more widely available (as a practice?) against government departments since *Conway v Rimmer*; but see eg Lord Cross in *Alfred Crompton v Customs and Excise Comrs (No 2)* [1973] 2 All ER 1169 at 1185d. Note the Scott Report HC 115 (1995-6) paras G18.43 *et seq.*
13 After an inquiry by Bingham J was scuppered.

not issued, but a four-page report which gives outline statements and which is published with little publicity is published. In many previous friendly settlements, the press had not noticed the reports that were issued, and the Home Office had not made an announcement about those unnoticed. The Government's increased use of friendly settlements marks an interesting development away from confrontation and towards informally bargained confidential outcomes involving the European Convention. In February 1987, the Lord Chancellor's Department produced a draft memorandum suggesting that judges should have an unfettered discretion to decide whether a document 'given in evidence' in open court should remain confidential.[14] This became the RSC Ord 24, r 14A which governed this matter until the new Civil Procedure Rules came into effect following the recommendations of Lord Woolf. Part 31(22) Civil Procedure Rules governs the subsequent use of disclosed documents. The court still has the power to order the restriction or prohibition of the use of a document which has been disclosed, even when read to or by the court or referred to in a public hearing. The courts, however, have shown a greater degree of flexibility in establishing when documents have entered the public domain.[15] Unlike the amended rule in 1987, the 1998 version will have to be read in the context of Art 10 ECHR: that freedom of speech should only be restricted where there is a pressing social need or to advance some other important objective. The frequent use of sections 4(2) and 11 of the Contempt of Court Act by judges to prohibit reporting of proceedings caused apprehension *vis-à-vis* the exercise of the proposed discretion in 1987.[16] The climate has changed.

14 Supreme Court Rule Committee, 6 February 1987; and see RSC Ord 24, r 14A.
15 *SmithKline Beecham Biologicals SA v Connaught Laboratories Inc* [1999] 4 All ER 498, CA; In *McCartan Turkington Breen v Times Newspapers (NI)* [2000] 4 All ER 913, HL the House of Lords held that a press conference called on private premises was a 'public meeting' for the purposes of attracting qualified privilege under legislation. It did not decide that the public had a right to attend. What limits may be placed on journalists on information imparted at such meetings being further disseminated because it is argued it is confidential? Lord Bingham said at 922 c-d 'It is very largely through the media, including ..the press, that [citizens] will be informed. The proper functioning of a modern participatory democracy requires that the media be free, active, professional and enquiring.' But what if they overstep the mark – what protection does an innocent victim have?
16 Pannick, *The Guardian*, 6 March 1987.

Protection of sources of information in litigation[17]

Section 10 of the Contempt of Court Act states:[18]

> No court may require a person to disclose, nor is any person guilty of contempt of court for refusing to disclose, the source of information contained in a publication for which he is responsible unless it be established to the satisfaction of the court that disclosure is necessary in the interests of justice or national security or for the prevention of disorder or crime.

This section gives an immunity from contempt proceedings to those who do not reveal the identity of a source of information contained in a publication for which they are responsible, unless the person seeking the identity proves to the court that disclosure is *necessary* for one or other of the stated grounds. This is a crucial provision in relation to leaks of information which result in 'publications' because if the identity of the 'leaker' is revealed the full wrath of the 'injured' party will be visited upon the former. At common law, courts may order an individual to reveal the identity of a source of information and this involved a straightforward balancing exercise.[19] Under s 10 the court may not order disclosure unless one of the grounds is made out and even then it must exercise a discretion before ordering disclosure and must regard a broad array of factors. These may include the means of obtaining the information, and the public importance of disclosing the information from the source when balancing competing claims.[20] Disclosure of the source must be necessary, not desirable or conducive towards one of the four stated objectives, before the discretion is exercised.[1] Of especial importance is the need to maintain confidentiality of the source of supply *inter alia,* of information to the police,[2] voluntary or public bodies promoting the welfare of vulnerable individuals,[3] or licensing or regulatory authorities promoting the public interest.[4] Prior to s 10 being enacted, the courts had given no immunity

---

17 See the Johannesburg Principles on National Security, freedom of expression and access to information adopted by the NGO Coalition (1998) 20 HRQ, No.18: protection of national security may not be used as a reason to compel a journalist to reveal a confidential source.

18 See Y Cripps (1984) Camb LJ 266, for the history behind s 10.

19 *Alfred Crompton*, n 12 p 394 above, whether or not contained in a publication.

20 *X Ltd v Morgan Grampian (Publishers) Ltd* [1990] 2 All ER 1, HL.

1   Ibid.

2   *Marks v Beyfus* (1890) 25 QBD 494; Cmnd 6542, para 287. See *ex p Wiley* [1994] 3 All ER 420 , HL.

3   *D v NSPCC* [1977] 1 All ER 589, HL.

4   *R v Gaming Board for Great Britain, ex p Benaim and Khaida* [1970] 2 QB 417; *Rogers v Secretary of State for the Home Department* [1972] 2 All ER 1057.

to protect the revelation of a source of information where national security was allegedly involved.[5] Nor had courts given much succour to claims of immunity where the 'interests of justice' *are* advanced by disclosure,[6] though immunity may be given where investigation of crime, or its possibility, is advanced, as in the case of police informers or where information relates directly to law enforcement, eg collection of customs and excise revenues, or taxes.[7]

It was the litigation concerning the 'mole' in the *British Steel* case[8] which constituted the leading judicial discussion of immunity from revealing a source of information in the interests of justice before the enactment of s 10. The chairman of the British Steel Corporation had been involved in an industrial dispute with the steel unions over wage levels and redundancies. An employee at the Corporation handed a substantial number of documents to Granada TV, which was making a documentary on the dispute. The thrust of these documents, it was suggested, was that, far from being caused by inefficient workforce practices, the ills of the nationalised industry were more closely related to mismanagement and too much political interference in the Corporation's affairs from successive ministers. Informed by these documents, the interviewer subjected the chairman of British Steel to a 'disgraceful' and 'unfair' cross-examination for *seven* minutes of prime viewing time.[9] To pursue an action against the unidentified 'mole', BSC required Granada TV, which by its actions had become implicated in the wrong, to reveal his identity. This Granada refused to do, claiming that there was a public interest in informing the public of the behind-the-scenes activity in a major nationalised industry whose fortunes had a direct bearing on the well-being of the national economy.[10] It was urged on Granada's behalf that, by analogy with the 'newspaper rule' which protected newspapers from revealing the source of information in a publication that was the subject of possible defamation proceedings, the media should be likewise protected for breaches of confidence which were in the public interest on one or other of various grounds.

Granada's argument was not successful at first instance, nor before the Court of Appeal. Lord Wilberforce in the House of Lords did not think

---

5   *A-G v Mulholland*, and *A-G v Clough* [1963] 2 QB 477 and [1963] 1 QB 773 respectively.

6   *Norwich Pharmacal Co v Customs and Excise Comrs* [1974] AC 133, a case involving discovery against a third party. Note also *Ashworth Hospital Authority v MGN Ltd* [2001] 1 All ER 991 (below). See, incidentally, Consumer Safety (Amendment) Act 1986, s 1.

7   *Alfred Crompton*, n 12 p 394 above.

8   *British Steel Corpn v Granada Television Ltd* [1981] AC 1096.

9   *Per* Lord Denning in the Court of Appeal.

10 *Per* Lord Salmon.

the analogy with defamation was exact, although before the House of Lords the main argument of Granada turned on technical aspects of their defence and not on whether the balancing of the public interest on either side was required. '[This] brings out the limitations of the reasons we are required to give', Lord Wilberforce believed. Both appeal courts accepted in principle the possibility of an immunity from disclosure, but not on the facts before them. The conduct of the TV producers was reprehensible and unfair in the context of a 'trial'—but this was the first time the documents had been made public, and short of a 'leak' they would not have been made available to the public or to Parliament. Lord Wilberforce thought there was a public interest in the free flow of information, the strength of which will vary from case to case. In some cases it may be very weak; in others very strong. He did not believe there was 'iniquity' on the part of management or the politicians, and he did not believe the public interest was such that the source of the information should be protected. Viscount Dilhorne did not think the case concerned the freedom of the press,[11] despite 'the resounding rhetoric' to the contrary. This is, quite frankly, baffling, as Lord Salmon suggested in his dissenting judgment. The story of 'woe', the latter believed, had to be known in the public interest.[12]

This, then, was the background to s 10 of the Contempt of Court Act. The section introduced a rule of law concerning disclosure of sources of information in addition to the judicial balancing of competing interests which appeared previously to be the case. The section was considered *in extenso* in the litigation[13] involving the *Guardian* newspaper and the arrival of cruise missiles and, as it transpired, Sarah Tisdall.

A 'secret' memorandum was prepared by the Ministry of Defence relating to the installation of cruise missiles at a Royal Air Force base in the UK. A copy of the memorandum was sent to the Prime Minister, and six copies were sent to senior members of the cabinet and the Cabinet Secretary. A junior civil servant photocopied the memorandum and anonymously handed it to *The Guardian,* which subsequently published the memorandum. The Secretary of State for Defence was furious[14] and demanded the return of the documents in order to identify the source of the leak from markings on the copy and to take appropriate action. The claim of the Crown was basically that it was their property and they were

---

11 Aspinall *Politics and the Press 1780–1850* (1973).

12 See *A-G v Lundin* (1982) 75 Cr App Rep 90, and an acknowledgement by the court of a possible 'public policy' protection of an informer's source of information at common law.

13 *Secretary of State for Defence v Guardian Newspapers Ltd* [1984] 3 All ER 601, HL.

14 He had hoped to outflank the Opposition by revealing the information to Parliament at the last possible moment.

entitled to its return under the Torts (Interference with Goods) Act 1977 in an undamaged form. Although successful in the lower courts, this point did not succeed in the House of Lords.[15] The Crown also argued that recovery was necessary in the interests of national security. While publication of this particular document was not a security risk, but merely a political embarrassment since its publication warned the Opposition in Parliament of the time of arrival of the missiles, the fact remained that a civil servant in a position of trust and confidence had betrayed a loyalty to the minister, and this did constitute a security risk for future, more important potential leaks. Section 10 was prayed in aid by *The Guardian*.

The House of Lords established that s 10 places the onus of proof on the party seeking the order of disclosure of identity, viz the Crown. Identity will remain a secret unless the court is satisfied that 'disclosure is necessary in the interests of justice or national security or for the prevention of disorder or crime'. Lord Diplock was emphatic that the discretion involved in balancing the interests between the public interest in being informed of events of public importance and the public interest in maintaining a confidence did not occur. The immunity applied *until and unless* one of the four grounds of release was established on the balance of probabilities to the satisfaction of the court. This is a question of fact, not a question of discretion or of 'constitutional right', an evocative phrase which Lord Diplock would repudiate:

> if it is intended to mean anything more than that in ascertaining the extent of the rights which it confers the section should give a purposive construction and, that being done, like other rights conferred on persons by statute, effect must be given to it in the courts.[16]

It is important to appreciate that the case came to the Law Lords as an appeal against an interlocutory order, ie a preliminary procedural point. By the time the Law Lords had to decide the construction of s 10 and its application to the case, the identity of the 'leaker', Sarah Tisdall,[17] had become an issue of national notoriety. The Court of Appeal and three of the Law Lords thought that the affidavit evidence of the principal establishment officer of the Ministry of Defence, to the effect that disclosure of the document was necessary to discover the source of the

---

15 Griffiths LJ did not concur on this point with the majority in the Court of Appeal. See Cripps *The Legal Implications of Disclosure in the Public Interest* (2nd ed, 1994) at pp 284-5 on the effect of s 8(4) and (5) of the Official Secrets Act 1989.

16 Cf Lord Scarman, below. See *X Ltd v Morgan Grampian (Publishers) Ltd* n 9 below where the Law Lords held that a balancing of interests will take place even after it is established that revelation is necessary.

17 A junior clerk in the registry of the private office of the Foreign Secretary.

leak, established that disclosure was necessary in the interests of national security. This was further supported by the affidavit evidence of the editor of *The Guardian*[18] and, for the Law Lords, the notorious events concerning Sarah Tisdall, who pleaded guilty to a charge under s 2 of the OSA 1911, and of which judicial notice could be taken. Taken together, these factors *just about* established the case for the Crown. As Lord Diplock noted, however, there was evidence in existence *at the time the affidavit from the principal establishment officer was presented to the High Court* which would have put beyond all doubt that it was necessary to establish the identity of the leaker. Two Law Lords, and the judge who heard the application for the order of disclosure, did not think that the Crown had made out their case at the time of the application under s 10. The two dissenting Law Lords did not think that it was permissible to take judicial notice of events subsequent to the application. It is not unknown for judges to give instruction to officials on how they *should have* drafted affidavits to put forward a more plausible case in order to avoid such difficulties in the future.[19] This Lord Diplock obligingly provided,[20] as well as applying 'the necessary mental gymnastics' in order to feel satisfied that the interests of national security required the release of the document to establish the identity of the source. 'The evidence', said Lord Fraser to the contrary, 'may have caused a little political embarrassment to the Government', but it contained nothing of military value. 'Without more information than he had, the judge could not properly have been satisfied that disclosure' by *The Guardian* was 'necessary'—not necessary and expedient, but necessary in the interests of national security. Any other interpretation, agreed Lord Scarman, would not have done justice to the rule which in its structure 'bears a striking resemblance' to the way in which the articles of the European Convention are drafted, viz 'a general rule subject to carefully drawn and limited exceptions which are required to be established, in case of dispute, to the satisfaction of the European Court of Human Rights .... It is no part of the judge's function to use his common sense in an attempt to fill a gap which can be filled only by evidence.'[1] On the contrary, Lord Bridge's common sense dictated, 'it is surely unthinkable that the Government should have embarked on the present litigation without taking the elementary step ... of an internal interview' to establish the identity of the 'leaker'. And Lord Bridge could infer from his involvement in governmental responsibilities[2] that a lack

---

18   He destroyed some security-sensitive information.
19   See eg Lawton LJ in *R v Lemsatef* [1977] 2 All ER 835.
20   See pp 608 h–j and 610 g–h.
1   The evidence of danger to the security system, he believed, was 'meagre and full of omissions'.
2   As Chairman of the Security Commission?

of urgency in the Government's demand for the document[3] was not due to sloth on its part. Judicial notice could be taken of the fact 'that important decisions in Government are rarely taken without time-consuming consultation and deliberation'.[4]

On one point, however, the Law Lords rejected the Crown's arguments, accepted by the judge at first instance and the Court of Appeal by majority, that its right of property in the documents and information thereon defeated *ipso facto* the immunity from disclosure under s 10. The Crown could not use its proprietorial claim to get access to information from the document, thereby allowing it to pursue its contractual, tortious or equitable claims against the 'leaker' in order to pursue the 'interests of justice':

> Having regard to the emphatic terms in which s 10 of the 1981 Act is cast, I have not found it possible to envisage any case that might occur in real life, in which, since the passing of the Act, it would be necessary *in the interests of justice* to order delivery up of the document... .[5]

on a proprietorial basis alone. In more fundamental terms, Lord Scarman declared:

> [Since] it is in the 'interests of all of us that we should have a truly effective press' (per Griffiths LJ) rights of property have to yield pride of place to the national interest which Parliament must have had in mind when enacting the section.

This might seem to cover the situation in the *British Steel Corpn* case,[6] encouraging the view that it might well be decided differently today in favour of Granada TV.[7] 'In the interests of justice' meant identifying a source of information to advance the actual administration of justice, and not justice in an abstract sense of vindicating a speculative claim in law or that which is relevant to determine an issue before the court. 'The public

3   The story was published on 31 October; proceedings were commenced on 22 November.
4   Cf Lord Bridge's review of telephone taps, chapter 1 above, p 41.
5   Emphasis added; see below. Nb *X v Y* [1988] 2 All ER 648 annd s 8(4) and (5) OSA 1989.
6   P 397 above, where a contractual or tortious claim is pursued ie, breach of confidence.
7   Cf *Maxwell v Pressdram Ltd* [1987] 1 All ER 656, CA. A journalist has been refused immunity from revealing sources of information relating to *fraud* in the City in a DTI inquiry, *Re an Inquiry under the Company Securities (Insider Dealing) Act 1985* [1988] 1 All ER 203, HL. The journalist was fined £20,000 for contempt when he refused to identify the 'leak'.

interest which s 10 … serves is therefore the preservation of sources of information and ensuring that they come forward.'[8]

However, in subsequent case law the Court of Appeal and the House of Lords have ruled that 'in the interests of justice' meant nothing more august than vindicating a right by pursuing an action[9] opening up the possibility of the section being used to assist a breach of confidence action. This occurred in a case concerning a journalist named Goodwin who had obtained confidential information about the financial position of an engineering company and who sought the comments of the company for its views. It responded by obtaining a breach of confidence injunction against Goodwin and by seeking an order for the disclosure of his source. This would clash with a journalist's first commandment—'Do not reveal your sources'. Both the Code of Practice of the Press Complaints Commission and the Code of Conduct of the NUJ state the moral obligation of a journalist to protect sources. The company convinced the courts that the information must have come from a stolen copy of a company document and it needed the source's identity to obtain further protective injunctions and to trace the thief and take appropriate action. The source had been involved in a serious breach of confidentiality, the Law Lords believed, and the interests of justice outweighed the statutory protection. There had been no 'iniquity' on the part of the company and there was no great public interest value in the information and the company could suffer serious damage if unable to identify who had passed secrets to the press. The journalist was subsequently fined £5,000 for failing to obey a court order.[10]

Although the Law Lords appeared to conduct some sort of balancing exercise, this is a worrying precedent for independent and investigatory journalism because it does seem to place a premium on proprietorial rights over the ethical considerations of a journalist. Robertson and Nicol have suggested that a possible amendment might restrict the exception to the 'interests of criminal law'. In 1994, the European Commission of Human Rights ruled by 11 votes to 6 that the court order in *Goodwin*'s case was in breach of the ECHR, art 10. The Government has suggested that a possible solution before the European Court would be to argue that journalists should offer sources a warning before receiving information: 'I must warn you that anything you say or give …'.[11] Subsequently, the Commission's view of *Goodwin's* case was upheld by the European Court

---

8 *Per* Parker LJ in *Maxwell*.
9 *X Ltd v Morgan Grampian (Publishers) Ltd* [1990] 2 All ER 1, HL. On website service providers: *Totalise plc v Motley Food Ltd* [2001] NLJR 644.
10 He was lucky not to have been imprisoned.
11 See *Broadmoor Hospital v Hyde* (1994) Times, 18 March: information of no great importance and no attempt internally to establish the identity of a 'leaker'; disclosure not ordered.

of Human Rights by an 11–7 judgment. The rulings of the English courts were not necessary in a democratic society in the interests of justice – they were disproportionate.[12] This judgment appeared to necessitate the reform of section 10 of the Contempt of Court Act. Goodwin was awarded legal costs and expenses but received no compensation. His story never ran. Under the HRA s 2(1), the Court of Human Rights judgment will now have to be taken into account by domestic courts.[13] The Court emphasised that protection of journalists' sources was vital for press freedom. The absence of such protection would have a 'chilling' effect on sources and would undermine the 'vital public watchdog role of the press.' Their ability to provide accurate and reliable information may be adversely affected.[14]

The decision was followed by the Court of Appeal's judgment in *Camelot*[15] where the national lottery operator wished to obtain disclosure orders to establish the identity of an employee who had disclosed documents to a journalist. Fearing, the plaintiff claimed, that future leaks could involve the disclosure of the identity of a lottery winner, the Court awarded the orders for disclosure as there was no overriding public interest involved in exposing a 'spin on accounts.' A source, Schiemann LJ believed, would always have to run a risk in disclosure. The Court of Appeal subsequently came down on the side of the journalist and the public interest in protecting the confidentiality of his sources and these outweighed any legal professional privilege that might apply. The case involved the leak of a barrister's draft opinion. The chambers had not assisted themselves in that they had failed to conduct an internal inquiry to try and establish the identity of the leaker. LPP did not outweigh the interest in protecting the source on the facts of the case.[16] However, where a case has no merit, and confidential information about a patient is leaked in unjustifiable circumstances, the Court of Appeal has been swift to order disclosure of the source. Any 'chilling effect' was worthwhile the court believed.[17] The protection of confidential patient information was 'vital' and the case was 'exceptional'.

The House of Lords has ruled that prevention of crime meant crime in general, not a specific crime, in denying a journalist the immunity.[18] Other case law has established that 'in order to prevent crime' meant that a crime had to be possible or be likely to be committed and not a breach of confidentiality.[19] Doctors and journalists have codes of practice

12　*Goodwin v UK* (1996) 22 EHRR 123, ECtHR.
13　As will the jurisprudence of the Commission and Council of Ministers.
14　Ibid, at para 39.
15　[1998] 1 All ER 251; see, however, *Saunders v Punch Ltd* [1998] 1 All ER 234, ChD.
16　*John v Express Newspapers plc* [2000] 3 All ER 257.
17　*Ashdown Security Hospital v MGN Ltd* [2001] 1 All ER 991, CA.
18　*Re an Inquiry etc.*, n 7 above.
19　*X v Y* above, n 5.

protecting the identity of confidential information and sources of information in the latter case and the problem is not going to disappear.[20]

Readers should be reminded of the wide powers to demand information under PACE 1984 and Sch 7, para 3 of the Prevention of Terrorism (Temporary Provisions) Act 1989 (see chapter 1 and see the 1996 Prevention of Terrorism (Temporary Provisions) Act). The 1989 provision (now replaced under the Terrorism Act 2000) featured in a sensational case involving a Channel Four documentary broadcast alleging large-scale collusion and conspiracy between members of the Royal Ulster Constabulary and loyalist terrorist groups in Northern Ireland resulting in over 20 murders and numerous conspiracies to murder. When the journalists refused to hand over material under a court order because it would reveal a source who had been promised anonymity and the identity of a junior researcher whose life would be endangered, contempt proceedings were initiated. The programme could easily be labelled as unreliable because it relied heavily on the evidence of one uncorroborated and unidentified witness, but it was in the best tradition of investigative journalism. The Divisional Court achieved a compromise of sorts because it recognised the 'moral stance' of the journalists impelling them not to reveal identities and the court did not impose sequestration orders as sought by the Attorney-General which would have bankrupted the respondents, but imposed a fine of £75,000. In future, however, companies would not be treated so leniently.[1]

Now we can look at the role of the courts in insisting upon, if not complete openness, then at least the provision of information. Our first consideration continues the discussion of national security.

The courts as guarantors of openness

National security

For years before the *Zamora* case[2] and for years afterwards courts accepted unquestionably the sentiments of Lord Parker that

> Those who are responsible for the national security must be the sole judge of what the national security requires. It would be obviously

---

20 See Public Interest Disclosure Act 1998, s 43G and stringent conditions for protection of disclosures to the media.
1   *DPP v Channel Four Television Co Ltd* [1993] 2 All ER 517; cost to company £750,000. See incidentally: *Hunter v Mann* [1974] 1 QB 767 and s 168(2) Road Traffic Act 1972.
2   [1916] 2 AC 77, though nb the comments of Lord Scarman in *Guardian Newspapers* above.

undesirable that such matters should be made the subject of evidence in a court of law or otherwise discussed in public.

In that case, however, the order for angary of a cargo in the Prize Court by the Government failed because the judge did not have evidence before him that the goods were needed in the *national interest*. As evidenced by *Chandler v DPP*, although the courts might not associate ineluctably the interests of the state with the interests of the government of the day,[3] on national security matters they were ready to defer to the judgment of the Crown and would not allow evidence on national security from its witness to be shaken in cross-examination. In the *Hosenball* litigation, deportation of an American citizen in the interests of national security precluded the usual tenets of fair play and knowing the details of the case that one's accusers were making. 'In national security cases,' declared Lord Denning, 'even natural justice must take a back seat.'[4] National security 'is par excellence a non-justiciable question' said Lord Diplock. These are familiar fare to the public lawyer, given added interest by judicial decisions in which the national security blanket has been spread over executive action.

The first such judicial decision concerned the controversy surrounding events at General Communications Headquarters. The Government in January 1984 announced that it was banning trade union membership among civil servants at GCHQ at Cheltenham.[5] There had been minor disruptions through industrial action at GCHQ, the last occasion being in 1981, and for some years the Government had been conscious of the sensitivity of serious disruption in the information-gathering responsibilities of GCHQ. The Government was studying the possibility of lie detectors (polygraph security screening) on the staff at GCHQ, and the Cabinet Secretary told union leaders, prior to the Government's announcement about banning unions, that there would be further consultation after the results of pilot schemes were known. In the event, the right of the GCHQ civil servants to belong to a trade union was taken away without any consultation with their representatives (the right was restored in 1997). On the Government side it was claimed that what was done was performed on the grounds of national security. A contrary belief

3   Cf McCowan J in *R v Ponting* [1985] Crim LR 318 chapter 3 above, p 101 *et seq.* See *A-G v Punch Ltd* n 13 p 391.

4   *R v Secretary of State for the Home Department, ex p Hosenball* [1977] 3 All ER 452; the 'Three Advisers' who were resorted to have now given way to procedures under the Special Immigration Appeals Commission Act 1997: see chapter 1 above, p 40 n 13. Sedley J had ruled that in refusing admission of an alien to the UK on grounds that presence was 'not conducive to the public good' the applicant must be given the opportunity to make representations: *R v Secretary of State for the Home Department, ex p Moon* [1996] COD 54.

5   For GCHQ, see chapter 1 above, p 34 *et seq.* The decision was not announced to the cabinet.

is that the Prime Minister wished to implement lie detectors without any objection from unions and that the Government had acted under pressure from the US Government. The claim of a threat to national security was not made in substance at the hearing in the High Court when the Council of Civil Service Unions challenged the legality of the Government's action. It was argued on the Government's behalf that consultation upon matters affecting national security would be so circumscribed as to be practically useless. Glidewell J rejected this, holding that the decision was one that should be taken fairly, and that the failure to consult rendered it unfair and a denial of a legitimate expectation of consultation because of the serious implications involved in depriving an individual of union membership.[6] The Court of Appeal accepted the Government's claim that consultation *could* have interfered with the interests of national security, and so did the House of Lords,[7] holding that, on the facts, consultation was not necessary as a matter of law.

In the House of Lords much attention was given to the role of the courts in assessing claims involving the invocation of national security. Courts, the Law Lords unanimously believed, were ill-suited to assess the national security requirements of state affairs. However, if action affecting individual rights, interests or legitimate expectations were based upon national security, whether in consequence of a statutory or prerogative power, the courts would look for *evidence* to support a claim that the action was, as in the instant case, for the purpose of avoiding disruption injurious to the national security. The court must act on evidence, said Lord Scarman. 'Evidence', reiterated Lord Roskill, 'and not mere assertion must be forthcoming.'

The evidence relied upon was an affidavit of Sir Robert Armstrong, the Cabinet Secretary, sworn on 6 April 1984. His affidavit recorded the apprehension that consultation would have caused disruption. Two months prior to this, the Foreign Secretary, in giving evidence to the Commons Foreign Affairs Select Committee, did not mention this matter, but spoke of the necessity of keeping the activities of GCHQ out of the public eye.[8] Nor was the matter mentioned in legal argument at first instance before Glidewell J. It may be, as Griffith has suggested, that the real reason for banning union membership without warning was one of

---

6   [1984] IRLR 309.
7   *Council of Civil Service Unions v Minister for the Civil Service* [1984] 3 All ER 935, HL. To the limited extent that courts require some evidence of possible injury to national security when action affects individual rights, they have accepted that such issues are justiciable, ie susceptible to the judicial process. Usually such topics are catered for and allocated by a constitution: *Baker v Carr* 369 US 186 (1962) esp Brennan J. See also Lustgarten and Leigh *In from the Cold* chapter 12 (1994).
8   See JAG Griffith (1985) Public Law 564.

political expediency and not national security.[9] Certainly, the courts accepted without question the affidavit evidence. It was not tested; it was not probed; it was not examined. The case was an application for judicial review, and this procedure is not meant to be a process for clarifying disputes of fact by allowing cross-examination of the witnesses—the Prime Minister, the Foreign Secretary, the Secretary to the Cabinet—nor allowing frequent applications for discovery of documents.[10] The courts wanted evidence of a national security risk; the evidence had to be more than a bare assertion; but the court was not prepared to weigh it. Some evidence was given, and in the circumstances it would take a brave person to predict that disruption injurious to national security would not have occurred had the unions been forewarned.[11] One may suspect the duplicity of the Government, but, as our law stands, it would be difficult to come to a conclusion other than that decided if one were put into a neutral seat and asked whether was there a possibility of such disruption, and if so would it be likely to affect adversely national security? The argument is not against the outcome of the GCHQ decision, though the Government's case should have been pressed more severely; the argument is against the manner in which courts are structured in Britain to avoid asking the most pressing questions in cases affecting the public interest, and in which the prerogative of national security happens to be one example. Should we require evidence of a clear and present danger to national security? The argument also concerns the issue of whether we need to give fuller definition to what the 'national security' actually is.[12]

On other occasions the courts have refused to accept that national security deprives them of jurisdiction but they have been reluctant to do anything which would resemble either a challenge on the merits of a decision made on the grounds of national security or to investigate a procedure leading to a decision concerning national security where the very procedure itself was adopted on grounds of national security. In *ex p Hodges* an employee at GCHQ had his positive vetting security clearance withdrawn when he revealed to his supervisors that he was a sexually active homosexual. He had volunteered full details of his activities. So while the courts would not contest the merits of the decision itself they would investigate the question of his being denied access to the notes of interviews, although his challenge here was unsuccessful.[13]

9   Ibid.
10 See below for discovery (now disclosure), p 440 *et seq.*
11 The European Commission of Human Rights rejected as inadmissible an application from the union under art 11(2): App No 11603/85, Decision 20 January 1987.
12 See chapter 1, above p 30 *et seq.*
13 *R v Director of GCHQ, ex p Hodges* (1988) Times, 26 July; see Ruddock below.

In *Cheblak*[14] the Court of Appeal virtually abandoned all but the most exiguous forms of controlling the Home Secretary's power of deportation on the grounds of national security and assumed that the latter had acted in good faith unless the contrary were proved and as he was under no duty to give any reason other than deportation was on the grounds of national security this was an impossible task. In fact this area generally is one where courts in other countries are reluctant to tread.[15] It is interesting therefore to assess the impact of EC law in a domestic case concerning discrimination in employment.

In *Johnston*[16] a woman police officer challenged a non-renewal of a contract of employment because of a policy in the RUC not to allow women to be armed on service which meant they could not perform 'general police duties'. In the industrial tribunal where she alleged a breach

14   [1991] 2 All ER 319. See also *Chahal* [1995] 1 All ER 658, CA where a deportation order was served on the applicant because his presence was deemed by the Home Secretary not to be conducive to the public good. He applied for political asylum. Under the relevant provisions of the Geneva Convention a refugee requesting asylum could be deported where their presence was a danger to the security of the host nation. The Home Secretary so decided. The court could not review the evidence on which the Home Secretary based his decision although it was satisfied that he had balanced the welfare of the refugee and national security.Chahal successfully applied to the European Court of Human Rights which established a brreach of Art 6 ECHR; see n 20 below. Under the Special Immigration Appeals Commission Act 1997, a new procedure was introduced to circumvent the problems posed by the *Chahal* decision in the Court of Human Rights. See, however, *Secretary of State for the Home Department v Rehman* [2000] 3 All ER 778, CA.

15   See Lustgarten and Leigh and their discussion of *Australian Communist Party v Commonwealth* (1951) 83 CLR 1.

16   *Johnston v Chief Constable of Royal Ulster Constabulary* [1986] 3 All ER 135. In *R v Secretary of State for the Home Department, ex p McQuillan* [1995] 4 All ER 400, Sedley J stayed proceedings involving a challenge to an exclusion order under the Prevention of Terrorism (TP) Act 1989 pending the outcome of other references before the ECJ on the question of the impact of Art 8a(1) of the EC Treaty and Art 9 of Directive 64/221 which allows derogation from freedom of movement (Art 48) with safeguards: *R v Secretary of State for the Home Department, ex p Adams* [1995] All ER (EC) 177. The applicant claimed his right to life was threatened by residence in NI. Although the courts would usually scrutinise executive action and evidence which threatened such a right 'that was not possible if the interests of national security were such as to prevent the court from knowing the Secretary of State's reasons for making the order.' This was despite the fact that the reason advanced by the Secretary of State appeared to be of a public interest immunity nature—protecting sources of information—and not of national security. In *Gallagher* the ECJ found that in the case of the Irish nationals the UK was in breach of EC law because of the absence of an independent competent authority to hear the deportee's appeal: *R v Secretary of State for the Home Department, ex p Gallagher* [1996] 1 CMLR 557 and SI 892/1996, introducing a right of interview for the deportee with persons nominated by the Secretary of State.

of domestic laws outlawing discrimination a ministerial certificate was issued stating that the action was taken in the interests of national security and public order effectively barring further inquiry by the tribunal. It was argued that this denied her rights under the Directive on the implementation of equal treatment under EC law. The European Court of Justice held that even though stated to be conclusive evidence of the reason for derogation from the Treaty, the certificate nonetheless sought to deprive an individual of her rights and to deny the principle of effective judicial control over the power of derogation. On the facts of the case the derogation was not justified because it did not confer a general proviso covering all measures taken for reasons of public safety and had to relate to specific factors which were not made out by the chief constable and Government. The impact of a European presence was also felt in *Tinnelly & Son Ltd v UK*[17] where a certificate had been issued under the Fair Employment (NI) Act 1976, s 42 barring a claim to judicial review of a decision to reject a tender on grounds of national security. Such a certificate was deemed conclusive evidence. The plaintiffs were Roman Catholic building contractors who had lodged a complaint with the Fair Employment Agency that they had been the subject of religious or political discrimination. They complained to the ECtHR that the certificate prevented them exercising their rights of access to a court under Art 6 of the Convention for the determination of the merits of its complaint of unlawful religious discrimination. They were successful.[18] Finally in *Svenska Journalistförbundet* the Court of First Instance of the EC ruled that the Council's reliance on public security to deny access to documents by Swedish journalists was unlawful as there had not been a proper reliance on Art 190 and its requirement to provide a reason for a decision. The case was important for stating that Third Pillar documents were within the scope of the Decision and Codes of the EC on access and that public order was not an automatic ground for excluding judicial examination.[19] The procedures involved in the *Chahal* case where Chahal was detained subject to decisions on his status as an asylum seeker whose presence was not deemed conducive to the public good were examined in chapter 1 (p 40 et seq). Although the High Court refused to intervene in that case, the EctHR found breaches of Arts 3 (degrading and inhuman treatment) 5 (detention without judicial authorisation) and 13 (lack of an effective remedy in relation to Art 30) because the procedures involved in the UK

---

17 (1998) 27 EHRR 249.
18 As noted in chapter 1 above p 40 et seq. This decision led to the introduction of new procedural safeguards in NI.
19 Case T-174/95 [1998] All ER (EC) 545.

only allowed an exiguous form of review of such an important matter.[20] As we saw, these decisions in *Tinnelly* and *Chahal* led to legislative changes in the UK (p 40 et seq). In *Chahal*, the Court of Justice stated that national authorities cannot be free from 'effective control by the domestic courts whenever they choose to assert that national security and terrorism are involved.'

The allegations by Ms Massiter, to which reference was made, led to judicial proceedings in England when representatives of CND[1] sought a declaration that the phone of its deputy director was unlawfully tapped on the authority of the Home Secretary. It was alleged that this was done to gain information to embarrass CND as a Conservative Party ploy prior to the 1983 general election. The judge required evidence of the 'highest order' to establish these claims and was satisfied that the deputy director's membership of the Communist Party, and Communist infiltration of CND, was a legitimate reason for the tap.[2] However, he rejected the Government assertion that, because the Government maintained silence on telephone taps in the interests of national security, the court should do likewise: 'To do so would be to say that the court should never inquire into a complaint against a minister if he says his policy is to maintain silence in the interests of national security.'[3] The facts of this case emerged before the Interception of Telecommunications Act (and now RIPA 2000) took effect; but that Act would have made no difference to the outcome, because the tribunal applies judicial review principles to authorised warrants. The case suggested that even in cases involving national security, the courts will not refuse to ask questions. But what sort of answers or reasons do they insist upon to justify the exercise of power? In *Cheblak*[4] where an

---

20 *R v Secretary of State for the Home Department, ex p Chahal* [1995] 1 All ER 658 and *Chahal v UK* (1996) 23 EHRR 413; see *Smith v UK* (1999) 29 EHRR 493 where the threshold for judicial review in a case involving Art 8 ECHR was set at too high a level therefore breaching the right to an effective remedy right under Art 13 ECHR. Cf *Vilvarajah v UK* (1991) 14 EHRR 248 and the recent decision of *Kingsley v UK* Application No 35605/97 (2001) Times, 9 January: judicial review was not a fair hearing for purposes of Art 6 ECHR where an applicant was alleging bias on the part of a supervisory board. The court could only question the quality of the decision making process rather than the merits of the decision.

1   *R v Secretary of State for the Home Department, ex p Ruddock* [1987] 2 All ER 518; see I Leigh (1987) Public Law 12.

2   CND was not at the relevant time regarded as subversive; it had been when 'communist dominated' in the 1960s. The warrant would have been one of those examined by Lord Bridge, see chapter 1, p 41 above, a fact noted by Taylor J (Leigh).

3   Any change in guidelines on tapping should have been publicised, Taylor J believed.

4   Note 14. See *R v Ministry of Defence, ex p Smith* [1995] 4 All ER 427: exercise of the prerogative power in defence of the realm was justiciable in all but the rarest of cases, ie those involving a clear issue of national security where in addition

alien was deported on grounds of national security in the Gulf war—in background circumstances which proved to be highly unsatisfactory— the Home Secretary refused to give reasons for his action beyond stating that the person had links with an organisation which could take terrorist action against Western targets in favour of Iraq. Further details could not be disclosed because of national security. The court of appeal held that a statement that the deportation was on the grounds of national security was a sufficient reason to fulfil statutory requirements under immigration regulations and no further notice was required. His detention was lawful and the decision valid. In other litigation, it has been held that banning homosexuals from the armed forces had nothing to do with national security, and the ban was a justiciable matter, and national security could prevent judicial protection only in those cases where a court was out of its depth.[5] The High Court has queried whether seeking to protect evidence from being given in court was really not a matter of public interest immunity rather than national security. However, the invocation of national security prevented the court from further inquiry even though fundamental rights were involved.[6] However, even in these decisions, a failure to follow a fair procedure may be upbraided by the courts. Once again, the HRA will be felt even in these sensitive areas. Where fundamental human rights are involved, the Court of Human Rights has expected a more probing procedure to test the case and this has had its impact on national courts. But the courts have been limited nonetheless because of the inherent limitations of judicial review as a remedy; it can only examine form and legality and not substance and merits. The Court of Human Rights has held in the past that judicial review in England was an effective remedy under Convention law, Art 13.[7] But that decision must be subjected to sustained analysis now that judicial review was seen as an inadequate remedy for purposes of Convention law where bias was alleged.[8] If bias, why not unfairness, or irrationality, or breach of principles of legality? The only ground which should prevent judicial investigation is where there is a real likelihood that their investigation is damaging to national security. One should not forget the power of the courts to go into private session.

A few more points on the use of 'national security' to preclude examination in the courts of matters of public interest are apposite.

---

the court lacked expertise or material for a judgment *per* Simon Brown LJ. On appeal [1996] 1 All ER 257.
5   *Smith* above. Cf *Vilvarajah v UK* (1991) 14 EHRR 248 and *Kingsley* above.
6   *McQuillan* above. See *A-G v Punch Ltd* n 13 p 391.
7   Cf *Vilvarajah v UK* (1991) 14 EHRR 248. Art 13 is concerned with the provision of an effective remedy.
8   *Kingsley v UK* (2001) Times, 9 January (ECtHR) App 35605/97.

A Wright mess

Peter Wright was a former member of the British security services who wished to publish his memoirs.[9] In these he made serious allegations against senior officers of MI5 of treasonable wrongdoing and criminal activity.[10] The allegations were based on 'confidential' material gained while in Crown employment. He sought to publish his book in Australia. The English Attorney-General sought to restrain publication by commencing proceedings in New South Wales. He also commenced proceedings in England against the *Observer* and *Guardian* newspapers, which had published details of the affair which they claimed to have received from other sources as well as the author. Further proceedings were commenced against other newspapers. In the English proceedings,[11] the Attorney-General sought injunctions restraining further publication. This is referred to as 'prior restraint'. Its use in the USA is heavily circumscribed because of the First Amendment to the Constitution guaranteeing freedom of speech.[12] It had a much wider scope in England, where courts were not so prepared to allow publication, while reminding the 'injured' party that he may sue for damages. This position has now been altered by the HRA 1998, s 12 (see below). The absence of 'prior restraint' may, conversely, help freedom of speech; it can also be easily abused by a powerful and irresponsible press.

No one suggested in the case of the *Observer* or the *Guardian* that they were acting irresponsibly.[13] In fact they gave an undertaking that they would exercise their own judgment carefully before publishing anything relating to the security service. This would permit, said Sir John Donaldson, 'the disclosure or publication of information whether or not in the public domain, about serious criminal misconduct or other serious wrongdoing by members of the British security services'. This was too much. While accepting that there was a public interest in knowing of grave malefactions by senior officers, there was a competing public interest in maintaining a confidentiality which was not simply a private 'contractual'

---

9   See *A-G v Observer Newspapers Ltd* [1986] NLJ Rep 799, CA upholding the order of Millett J. Approval must be given for publications of memoirs by civil servants. For CIA agents, see *Snepp v US*, chapter 2, n 11, p 77, above.

10 Many details of which had already been published – see chapter 1, above.

11 See n 9 above and for later interlocutory proceedings: *A-G v Guardian Newspapers Ltd* [1987] 3 All ER 316, Ch D, CA and HL. For the European Convention and confidentiality of state secrets, see: Application 4274/69 *X v Germany* 35 Recueil 158, and 9401/81 *X v Norway* 27 DR 228 and *Leander* and *VW BLUF!* p 384 above.

12 E Barendt *Freedom of Speech* (1987).

13 The allegations had also been published elsewhere. *The Independent*, 27 April 1987, and other papers published extracts in defiance of the injunction. The Australian courts had issued orders restraining publication of the book pending the trial.

confidentiality but a confidentiality relating to 'public secrets':[14] 'The Attorney-General is not personally the beneficiary of the right to confidentiality which he asserts, nor is the executive. His claim is made on behalf of the state, that is the general community.' When assessing the competing public interests of knowing, and maintaining a duty of confidentiality by preventing the public from knowing, it 'might lead a court properly to conclude that, in the context of the confidentiality of the work of the security service, the proper approach is that the conflict ... should be resolved in favour of restraint unless the court is satisfied that there is a serious defence of public interest which is *very likely*[15] to succeed at the trial'. It *was* in the public interest to discover wrongdoing in the security service, and the greater the wrongdoing, the greater the right to know; but Sir John could not agree that, given 'a sufficiently serious *allegation'*, publication of the allegation with a view to forcing an investigation[16] 'was justified'.[17] Sir John reasoned:

Where there is a confidentiality, the public interest in its maintenance has to be overborne by a countervailing public interest, if publication is not to be restrained. In some cases the weight of the public interest in the maintenance of the confidentiality will be small and the weight of the public interest in publication will be great. But in weighing these countervailing public interests or ... those countervailing aspects of a single public interest, both the nature and circumstances of the proposed publication have to be examined with considerable care. This is sometimes referred to as the principle of proportionality—the restraint or lack of restraint proportionate to the overall assessment of the public interest. Thus it by no means follows that, because the public interest in the exposure of wrong-doing would justify the communication to the police or some such authority of material which has been unlawfully obtained, it would also justify wholesale publication of material in a national newspaper. [18]

Publication through a newspaper, 'the widest and most indiscriminate' form of publication, was not justified. However, the papers were free to

---

14 *A-G v Jonathan Cape* [1976] QB 752. See *Fairfax* p 420 et seq below.
15 Emphasis in original. This was questioned in particular in the Court of Appeal in *Spycatcher No 2* by Bingham LJ.
16 Chapter 4, p 189 *et seq* above.
17 In the NSW proceedings to restrain Wright's book, the British Government accepted the truth of the allegations for *those* proceedings to avoid examination of those issues. This tactical ploy backfired, forcing the Attorney-General and the Solicitor-General to make a press statement: see *The Guardian*, 16 August 1986.
18 [1986] NLJ Rep 799 at 800. *Unlawfully* here means in breach of confidence.

publish accurate reports of legal proceedings in New South Wales (although the House of Lords subsequently enjoined such discussion) or England, or proceedings before Parliament. One matter which had not been enjoined was a TV programme by Ms Cathy Massiter—a former security official—which contained an appearance by Mr Wright. No action was taken against Ms Massiter in England, yet it was taken against Mr Wright in Australia. In those latter proceedings, the British Government admitted the veracity of Wright's allegations as a tactical ploy to avoid a confrontation with Mr Wright and Ms Massiter.[19] This left the British Government with the unenviable task of persuading an Australian court that it was in Australia's national interest to maintain Wright's confidence to the Crown. Public interest immunity of documents was sought by the Crown for relevant documents in the New South Wales proceedings. This was refused, and the Crown's case was presented in evidence by the Secretary to the Cabinet, who was subjected to rigorous, indeed hostile, cross-examination. His performance was poor. He had to take the witness box a second time to retract a statement alleging that the decision not to prosecute previous 'leaks' of MI5 secrets was taken by the Attorney-General. It was not so, Attorney-General Sir Michael Havers stated in Parliament. The senior civil servant who had performed so adroitly before the Defence Select Committee in the Westland episode[20] was made to look implausible and totally unconvincing. The New South Wales court refused the injunction sought by the Crown, undermining all the Crown's assertions unequivocally.[1] The court also criticised Sir John Donaldson's judgment preventing by interim injunction reporting in newspapers in England of allegations of unlawful conduct. A different view of such matters was taken in Australia.[2] The Court of Appeal of New South Wales rejected the Government's appeal. 'National security' did not allow the Government to conceal that it had acted without honour and capriciously. The High Court of Australia also rejected the appeal.[3]

In the GCHQ saga, the feeling remains that such a concealment was maintained. More probing, more testing, would have vindicated the role of the courts as guardians of our liberties. Even if it is not for the courts to make decisions on the 'national security', they should convince us that they are not over-willing to be sold the 'dummy pass'. And we all have a right to know what national security means. Is this not appropriate for statutory definition? This would involve judicial supervision of criteria approved by Parliament, not judicial second-guessing.

---

19   Note 17.
20   HC 519 (1985–6).
1   See n 1 p 378 above. He who comes to equity ... !
2   *Commonwealth of Australia v John Fairfax & Sons Ltd* (1980) 147 CLR 39. See n2 p 420 below.
3   See M Fysh (ed) *The Spycatcher Cases* [1989] European Law Centre.

The injunctions issued against the *Guardian* and the *Observer* were subject to further proceedings when three English newspapers published extracts from Peter Wright's memoirs. Sir John Donaldson in his judgment had warned that other newspapers were not free to republish, and the Lord Chancellor had chipped in with his own warning. In proceedings initiated by the Attorney-General, Sir Nicolas Browne Wilkinson held that a contempt of court for breach of the precise terms of an injunction could only be committed by a party enjoined by the injunction—the *Guardian* or the *Observer*—or by a party who has aided and abetted those bound by the injunction.[4] In the absence of such elements, it would only bind those who were parties to the initial litigation: it operated *in personam* not *in rem*. Sir Nicolas was at pains to dissociate himself from the necessity of the law protecting a public secret as a public right, as Sir John had endeavoured to do. '[T]he basic right protected by the 1986 injunction was exactly the same as the right of a manufacturer to stop an employee disclosing trade secrets or of one spouse to restrain the other from revealing "pillow talk".' It was for Parliament and not the courts to create a public law remedy protecting public rights to confidentiality of state secrets, he believed. This, however, is what Scott J did but not in terms which extended the law.

This reasoning did not prevail in the Court of Appeal, which overturned the Vice-Chancellor's decision, paving the way for contempt proceedings against the respective newspapers. However, the judgment of the Master of the Rolls was particularly receptive to some of the Vice-Chancellor's criticisms. The case was not about national security, nor about a state interest (as he had formerly suggested), but about confidentiality protecting an employment relationship, he believed. The Attorney-General was now seeking to protect a right to confidentiality by contempt proceedings against publication which was 'intended or calculated to impede, obstruct or prejudice the administration of justice'. Publication would destroy that most evanescent of rights, confidentiality. The courts, and no one else, would decide to what extent the right should be protected, regardless of who asserted it.[5] This seems understandable in basic principle. But its similarity to a 'gagging writ' should not be overlooked, especially where, as in Wright's case, the publishers allege that the Government acquiesced in prior publication of similar 'confidential' information. As we noted above the House of Lords effectively endorsed this judgment in subsequent proceedings.[6] The position of s 12 HRA would today have to be considered.

4 *A-G v Newspaper Publishing plc* [1987] 3 All ER 276. See n 13 p 391 above.
5 [1987] 3 All ER 276 at 289. See *Re X* [1984] 1 WLR 1422.
6 [1991] 2 All ER 398, HL. On the worrying implications of the interlocutory and contempt proceedings from *Spycatcher* see Lord Oliver writing extra judicially at: 'Spycatcher, Confidence, Copyright and Contempt' (1989) 23 Is LR 409. See n 13 p 391.

Wright's case became a matter of international notoriety. After publication of his book in the USA, and further publication of extracts in the *Sunday Times,* the Government's attempts to protect the confidentiality of information acquired by its servants appeared forlorn. Government efforts concentrated on seizing the profits emanating from Wright's breach of duty, as well as maintaining the injunction. That such a confidentiality existed was accepted, though it was unclear whether it was a private or public law right protecting public or private confidences. That, however, did not prevent the House of Lords from upholding the interim injunction, and even extending it to cover legal proceedings in New South Wales concerning Wright's allegations.[7] The real motive of the majority of the Law Lords appears to have been the desire to use an injunction against the newspapers to punish Wright and to deter other security officers, rather than to protect a confidence. The public could not read reports of what was publicly available. Two of the dissenting Law Lords, Lord Bridge and Lord Lloyd, both addressed the judicial freneticism in the English litigation with some considerable degree of foreboding. Lord Bridge, former Chairman of the Security Commission, believed that for the first time in his life he had seen the necessity of the incorporation of the European Convention of Human Rights into English law given the executive excesses he had been witness to.[8] In further proceedings, the BBC was enjoined from broadcasting a serious discussion on the security services on Radio 4.[9]

As I have remarked elsewhere, a contract enforceable at common law did not appear to exist between Crown servants and the Crown at the relevant time, though matters in this respect have moved on—the Government accepted that civil servants would be contractually bound to provide evidence to Sir Richard Scott's inquiry. That is no reason why an express stipulation of confidentiality and a subjection to vetting of memoirs for approval before publication might not be incorporated into the relationship.[10] The law of confidentiality is not dependent upon the law of contract. As we saw in chapter 2, CIA agents may publish memoirs, but only after vetting has been performed and approval given. The Government would not have approved Wright's request to publish his memoirs. A right of appeal to an independent body would therefore be

---

7   The injunction was lifted in the High Court, restored with amendments in the Court of Appeal and extended in the House of Lords in a 3–2 judgment, *A-G v Guardian Newspapers* [1987] 3 All ER 316. Cf the First Amendment to the US Constitution and *New York Times Co v US* 403 US 713 (1971) and nb *US v Progressive Inc* 467 F Supp 990 (1979). On prohibition of library loans of *Spycatcher,* see *A-G v Observer Ltd, Re Application by Derbyshire County Council* [1988] 1 All ER 385.

8   [1987] 3 All ER 316 at pp 346-7.

9   *A-G v BBC* (1987) Times, 18 December.

10 See A Cavendish, *The Guardian*, 24 July 1987, and *Inside Intelligence*.

necessary. The Civil Service Management Code stipulates that work written by civil servants may contain Crown copyright material and the approval not only of the departmental head but also of HMSO may be necessary.

Some judicial sanity was restored to these events when Scott J refused to award a permanent injunction against the newspapers at the suit of the Attorney-General. In a judgment distinguished by its clarity and grasp of legal principle, the judge held that the secret was out and the public interest dictated it be reported upon. Any damage to the public interest had been done; a court order was unnecessary and not justified. Confidentiality was not the same as copyright in the case of the newspapers.[11] The Government appealed unsuccessfully to the Court of Appeal and to the House of Lords.[12] The court upheld the right of the press to report on what was in the public domain. Two appeal court judges agreed with Scott J that the newspapers were correct to publish the initial serious allegations because it was in the public interest that they should be reported and this was supported in the House of Lords. This would seem to go against the thrust of the House of Lords majority judgment in the interlocutory proceedings. Neither Wright himself nor his agents or servants could publish his book because this remained a serious breach of confidence.

It is now reasonably clear that should the Attorney-General seek an injunction to protect confidences owed by officials in security or intelligence or related civil servants or indeed others the court will only award an injunction to prevent publication by a third party where there is a risk of *additional* harm to national security or public order or to the public interest where that information is already in the public domain. The duty owed by security and intelligence officers themselves is life-long unless it falls within the iniquity category recognised by Scott J and which was given some degree of support by two of the Law Lords and the Court of Appeal in the *Spycatcher* litigation or where possibly, as Scott J suggested, it is no longer confidential or comprises trivia. In *Lord Advocate v Scotsman Publications*, however, the Law Lords accepted the

---

11 *A-G v Guardian Newspapers Ltd (No 2)* [1988] 3 All ER 545, ChD, CA and HL. In the House of Lords, Lord Griffiths dissented on two points from the other judges including on the question of the *Guardian's* breach of confidence in reporting Australian proceedings; he felt they were in breach of confidence.

12 See Lords Goff and Griffiths giving qualified support to the general proposition although there was no public interest in Wright's disclosures concerning operations of the service. Lord Goff doubted whether Wright could be prevented from publishing the book but he was alone on that point. Scott J raised the point of whether in equity the Crown owned the copyright to the book because it recorded events which took place while he was in Crown service; see Lords Griffiths and Jauncey in *Guardian Newspapers (No 2)*. This point has been taken up in subsequent proceedings.

duty of confidentiality owed by such officers was life-long and it was assumed that that was the holding in *Spycatcher*. Is the duty life-long irrespective of the material or is it only life-long where the material remains confidential? The latter accords with better sense.

But even where disclosure may be justified, the means adopted must be appropriate. Publication may take place where the matter is 'trivia'— but who is to judge, and it may well be an offence under the OSA—or where publication is duly authorised. Where information is published by third parties where the source is a security or intelligence official there may well be criminal offences under the Official Secrets Act 1989 (see chapter 3). Where all possible damage has been done an injunction will not be issued to prevent third parties publishing. That may well be the case at an application for a permanent injunction as in the proceedings before Scott J but on an application for an interim injunction different considerations are bound to come into play. There the court is concerned to hold the ring and to ensure that no damage is done to either party in what are often uncertain circumstances. It does not require that damage be proved. With two competing versions of the public interest it would be a brave judge who preferred the word of an editor or whoever against that of the Government on where the public interest lay. Even the European Court of Human Rights held in *Spycatcher* when that case inevitably made its way to Strasbourg that the original injunctions were not in breach of art 10 of the ECHR; it was only after publication in the USA that the continuation of the injunctions constituted a breach of that article.[13] While s 12 HRA may make a crucial difference in applications for orders prohibiting interim injunctions in the future (see pp 397 and 454) where serious evidence of possible damage to national security is present, no court will second guess the government's claims. Section 12 will help root out the clearly bogus claims.

The emergence of the internet and the globalisation of publishing make the efficacy of prohibition orders all the more questionable. In July 2001, the High Court dismissed an application by the Attorney-General to prevent publication by a 'renegade MI6 officer' Richard Tomlinson of extracts of his book '*The Big Breach: From Top Secret to Maximum Security*' because of publication elsewhere in the world (in this case, Moscow).[14] The Master of the Rolls also held that the editor may decide what is in the public interest to publish without seeking the prior approval of the authorities. Consultation was 'desirable' but the A-G's permission was not required.

---

13 *Observer and Guardian v UK* (1991) 14 EHRR 153, ECtHR.
14 *A-G v Times Newspapers Ltd* [2001] 1 WLR 885. See *A-G v Punch Ltd* above n 13 p 391 on publication of Shayler's allegations and contempt proceedings and disapproval by Lord Phillips of the A-G as censor. See, however, Simon Brown LJ.

The House of Lords in *A-G v Blake*[15] gave the Government cause for hope in this area when it ruled that MI5 and MI6 officers and former officers do owe a life-long duty of confidentiality to the Crown ('an *absolute* rule against disclosure, visible to all, makes sense'). Furthermore, if such officers do publish in contravention of their written undertakings under the OSA not to divulge any material acquired in the service in the press or in book form, and which is not otherwise confidential or damaging to the public interest to disclose, such officers must account for any profits acquired from the breach of the undertaking. As Blake was an escaped prisoner outside the jurisdiction and not amenable to the criminal courts and an indictment for breaches of s 1 OSA 1989, nonetheless, Blake's position, if not a fiduciary in relation to this information, was analogous to a fiduciary and an account of profits was the appropriate remedy, the court believed.[16] Armed with this decision, it was subsequently argued that Tomlinson also had to account for profits in that in addition to the breach of undertaking, he had assigned copyright to the Crown.

There was no need for the Law Lords to rule on the compatibility of s 1 OSA with Art 10 ECHR (see pp 5-6 above) Furthermore, *Blake* does not decide that information from a source such as Blake cannot be published. It decides that the wrongdoer in breach of his promise will have to account for ill-gotten gain.

Judges and confidences

The law recognises a duty to maintain a confidence which has arisen from a contractual relationship, or in circumstances where information is acquired and from which an obligation of confidence can be inferred. In the absence of an express or implied contractual undertaking, most common in employment and trade secrets cases, the law looks for some relationship where it would be inequitable not to protect the confidences or 'secrets' which exist within a relationship.[17] The fact that information is stamped 'confidential' does not make it so for legal purposes, nor is every secret protected by the law.

In the Crossman diaries litigation[18] it was held that the law of confidentiality could protect by injunction not only domestic or trade/commercial secrets, but 'public' secrets, that is information emanating from state or public business, not information which has been made

15 [2000] 4 All ER 385, HL.
16 Lord Hobhouse dissented; in the Court of Appeal the A-G's claim was upheld on 'public law' grounds to prevent Blake profiting from his wrong. This was overruled in the House of Lords.
17 *Argyll v Argyll* [1967] Ch 302. See Sedley LJ in *Douglas v Hello! Ltd* [2001] 2 All ER 289, CA.
18 Ch 4, p 170 above.

public.[19] The case concerned cabinet and cabinet committee discussions, which are buttressed by the convention of ministerial collective responsibility, a convention which the court saw it as its duty to maintain to protect the confidentiality owed in law to cabinet discussions and details of decisions. The period of time for which it had to be maintained was a matter of judgment on the facts of the individual case. The litigation involved the diaries of the former cabinet minister, which revealed information about cabinet business while in office obtained from other cabinet ministers and civil servants. The Crown was seeking to restrain publication by injunction—by prior restraint. On the facts, an injunction was not necessary, because the events happened over 10 years before the litigation.[20] As we have seen, the concept of public secrets was extended in the Court of Appeal decision prohibiting the publication of memoirs by Peter Wright, the former MI5 official,[1] to protect the confidentiality of the 'public secrets' attaching to operations of the security services. In his judgment, Scott J and higher courts were very influenced by an Australian decision in which the Australian government sought to prevent publication of a book containing confidential government information.[2] In an appreciably eloquent passage, Mason J explained how the equitable principle of confidentiality was fashioned to protect personal, private and proprietary interests of the citizen 'not to protect the very different interests of the executive government.' Equity will protect government information but it has uppermost in mind that government is operating in the public interest not in a private interest.

> It may be a sufficient detriment to the citizen that disclosure of information will expose his actions to public discussion and criticism. But it can scarcely be a relevant detriment to the Government that publication of material concerning its actions will merely expose it to public discussion and criticism. It is unacceptable in our democratic society that there should be a restraint on the publication of information relating to government when the only vice of that information is that it enables the public to discuss, review and criticise Government action... Unless

---

19 Though damages or an account of profits would then be appropriate if disclosure followed a breach of the obligation. The Wright episode led to some startling measures from the courts to protect information already in the public domain or public knowledge – see n 3 above and G Jones (1970) LQR at 466–70; and further (1990) 42 Current Legal Problems 48.

20 An injunction was not sought to prevent publication of volumes II and, especially, III. Since then, publication of ministerial memoirs has become the norm.

1 *A-G v Guardian and Observer* (1986) Times, 26 July and [1987] 3 All ER 316. An injunction was upheld in England to prevent distribution of *One Girl's War* by former MI5 officer, Joan Miller, but was lifted in the Irish Republic on 2 December 1986; see *A-G v Turnaround Distribution Ltd* [1989] FSR 169.

2 *Commonwealth of Australia v John Fairfax and Sons Ltd* (1980) 147 CLR 39.

disclosure is likely to injure the public interest, it will not be protected.

The judge continued:

> If, however, it appears that disclosure will be inimical to the public interest because national security, relations with foreign countries *or the ordinary business of government will be prejudiced,* disclosure will be restrained.[3]

This sets out quite clearly the different tests to be applied in private and public ie state relationships. Confidentiality remains a protean but uncertain concept protecting information. When the courts are concerned with relationships between individuals and a legal remedy is sought to protect confidentiality, the courts are on more familiar territory where they can assimilate the concept with property—though this can be taken too far. This is especially important for trade secrets and freedom of trade, and according to the majority opinion in the interlocutory *Spycatcher* litigation for secrets acquired in Crown service.[4] The law is on more difficult ground where it seeks to protect confidences arising from relationships when breach of confidence would allegedly be inequitable. Difficult perhaps, but far from impossible. Confidentiality alone is insufficient reason to withhold information where the interests of justice require its release.[5] In sex and race discrimination cases, for instance, the tribunal chairman can examine papers on other employees to assess whether discrimination has taken place against the plaintiff in promotions or appointments.[6]

In cases involving public bodies, the public interest is advanced by healthy debate and criticism of government. Measures inhibiting freedom of speech and freedom of the press move on thin ice. The courts have held that the 'public interest' may justify a leak which would constitute a breach of confidence or copyright, and a defence to an application for an injunction could be made by establishing that it was in the public interest for the public to know, for instance, that the police were using unreliable

3 Ibid.
4 See eg *Faccenda Chicken Ltd v Fowler* [1985] 1 All ER 724, and [1986] 1 All ER 617, CA which deal with the position of 'trade secrets' in employment. See Jones (1970) LQR 463; and the Law Commission's Report n 9 p 380 above. In *Wright's* case, the Crown sought to vindicate a right *in personam* to the profits of his breach of confidentiality and a right *in rem* to the confidential information itself, above. See also *A-G v Blake* n 15 above; and *Re Z* [1995] 4 All ER 961 and ss 1(1), 3(1) and 8(1) Children Act 1989.
5 *Alfred Crompton*, p 394 above, n 12. See the curious decision in *Woodward v Hutchins* [1977] 1 WLR 760.
6 *Science Research Council v Nassé* [1980] AC 1028; note *West Midlands Passenger Executive v Singh* [1987] ICR 837.

instruments to assess the level of alcohol in motorists' blood, as in *Lion*.[7] However, to be protected, one has to show that the breach was in the public interest and not merely interesting to the public, and that the chosen method of publication is appropriate. Illegal or other wrongdoing which is effected by a breach of confidence may be more appropriately published by informing the police or respective authorities, rather than by detailing the contents of a conversation, obtained by an illegal tap, in the national press.[8] In *Lion,* the Court of Appeal believed that plaintiffs seeking an injunction prohibiting publication would have to establish that the defendant could not show that there is a serious defence of public interest which *may* succeed at the trial. In *Lion* the plaintiffs could not establish this, so the injunction was refused.[9] Where a defence of public interest can be raised, the courts can involve themselves in a familiar balancing act of weighing the public interest in maintaining confidentiality, against the public interest of informing the public of matters of *real* public concern. Donaldson MR has insisted that there should be a 'moral imperative' to publish openly, rather than informing the authorities before an injunction restraining publication would be refused. In the *Spycatcher* case, Scott J believed it was of real public concern that there should be reporting of allegations of serious misconduct by MI5 officers. Section 12 HRA should be recalled and how this will place the onus on those who are seeking to prevent publication. Applicants have to establish that they are likely to win their case at full trial when seeking to prevent publication and the judge is instructed to have regard to a range of factors including the importance of freedom of expression (see pp 379 and 454 below). The courts have also developed confidentiality to protect the identity of the murderers of Jamie Bulger as their right to life and avoidance of maiming by those intent on harming them outweighed the freedom of the press to report on their new identities and addresses.[10] Contrariwise the police were correct to inform the owner of a caravan site that two occupants were convicted paedophiles, information which caused the owner to order the two occupants to leave. The police had disclosed the information in the public interest to protect local children and 'vulnerable' adults. The

7   *Lion Laboratories Ltd v Evans* [1984] 2 All ER 417, CA. This was not a publication of a wrongdoing as such.

8   *Francome v Mirror Group Newspapers Ltd* [1984] 2 All ER 408.

9   Nb the test on the defendants in *A-G v Guardian and Observer*, above, pp 412-413. Cf *Schering Chemicals Ltd v Falkman Ltd* [1982] QB 1. See *Bonnard v Perryman* [1891] 2 Ch 269; *Gulf Oil (GB) Ltd v Page* [1987] 3 All ER 14. See Cmnd 8388 and remember that bribing employees eg to disclose information is a crime: Prevention of Corruption Act 1906 and 1916. And see *Raising Standards and Upholding Integrity* Cm 4759 with suggestions for a revamping of the law relating to corruption. See Supreme Court Act 1981, s 72, and self-incrimination in intellectual property cases.

10   *Venables v News Group Newspapers Ltd* [2001] 1 All ER 908.

information was already in the public arena. Although it would have been desirable to have interviewed the two occupants before disclosing the information, a course which the police did not adopt, the police had not acted unlawfully because any information provided by the occupants would have made no difference to the situation.[11] Laws have placed increasing obligations upon sex offenders to disclose their wrongdoing in order to warn the public but we have not yet adopted the practice of some US states whereby the names of such offenders are publicly displayed.[12]

The law will protect a confidential, original and commercially promising idea. There can be no breach of copyright in a creative idea unless it is reduced to material form and used without permission. It is beyond the scope of a work such as this to describe the emerging law relating to intellectual property, copyright and patents.[13] Judicial law is inadequate to provide appropriate protection to such ideas and information and has given way to a succession of unsatisfactory statutes.[14] A White Paper of April 1986 proposed he establishment of a patent office which will be a non-Crown, non-departmental body, appointed by the secretary of state.[15] An advisory group, the 'Whitehall Liaison Group', will be established to improve the Government's knowledge and understanding of intellectual property. The Patent Comptroller and Performing Rights Tribunal will be given extended jurisdiction over disputes. As well as incorporating relevant European Conventions, further proposals cover employee inventions; industrial designs; levies on blank audio tapes; restrictions on educational broadcasts; the addition of perpetual copyright and the introduction of lifelong 'moral rights' for authors; boosting of criminal sanctions against bootleggers and formalisation of civil remedies. In 1985, the Copyright (Computer Software) Act was passed.[16] Computer software piracy ran to about £150 million in 1984, a figure readily extendable because of the ease with which computer programs can be broken into and copied. The Act extends the Copyright legislation to computer programs with necessary 'adaptation' of programs and to include storage within a computer as forms of 'reproduction in … or reduction to

11 *R v Chief Constable North Wales Police, ex p AB* [1998] 3 All ER 310, Home Office Circular 39/1997; *Woolgar v Chief Constable of the Sussex Police* [1999] 3 All ER 604;cf *Hellewell v Chief Constable of Derbyshire* [1995] 4 All ER 473]
12 Known colloquially as 'Megan's law'. Under the Police Act 1997, Pt V, the Protection of Children Act 1999 and the Care Standards Act 2000 there are compulsory vetting and disclosure provisions relating to those who work with children and other activities.
13 J Phillips and A Firth, *Introduction to Intellectual Property Law* (1995) WR Cornish *Intellectual Property* (4th ed).
14 The first copyright act was passed in 1709.
15 Cmnd 9712.
16 See DT Bainbridge (1986) MLR 214.

a material form'. Many key terms and phrases, eg 'Computer', 'Computer program', are not defined.

The Copyright, Designs and Patents Act of 1988 was passed incorporating many of the above features. There were fears that it would unjustifiably extend authors' proprietorial rights in a manner which would substantially interfere with freedom of speech. As an end-note it is interesting to observe in the *Fairfax* decision referred to above, although the court issued a judgment which became the basis of the present law concerning the inapplicability of the private law of confidentiality to the world of government, publication of the work in question was prevented by injunction because it breached copyright.[17] Courts in England have also held that the public interest defence under copyright law is not as broad as under confidentiality and Article 10 ECHR is no defence against a breach of copyright.[18] While Art 10 is not an absolute, there is a danger exercise of property rights may defeat a 'fundamental right'.

Reasons for decisions[19]

Another Australian court has upheld the long-standing doctrine of English common law which holds that public bodies are not required to give reasons for decisions in the absence of statutory requirements.[20] It may be that we are witnessing an assault on this bastion of inscrutability although until recently one would hesitate to call it full frontal. In *Stefan v GMC* the Privy Council said although there was no presumption of reasons for decisions and no general statutory requirement, it noted the trend towards the giving of reasons for decisions and this was consistent with current developments towards an increased openness in matters of government and administration.[1] Since 1963,[2] the courts have developed a more pronounced sense of fair play in novel institutional settings by extending the concept of natural justice which insists on a hearing before an unbiased decision-maker before being condemned or suffering a detriment. Fair procedure and legitimate expectation in fairness have been significantly extended; and acting unfairly, or acting unreasonably, or deviating unexpectedly from a settled, consistent or promised state of

17 Note 2 p 420.
18 *Hyde Park Residences Ltd v Yelland* (2000) Times, 16 January; and *Ashdown v Telegraph Group plc* [2001] 2 All ER 370.
19 A LeSueur (1999) 52 CLP 150 and G Richardson (1986) Public Law 437.
20 *Public Service Board of New South Wales v Osmond* (1986) 63 ALR 559. Nb s 13, Administrative Decisions (Judicial Review) Act 1977 (Aus).
1   [1999] 1 WLR 1293, PC. And see the powerful decision in *R v CICA, ex p Leatherland* (2000) Times, 12 October.
2   *Ridge v Baldwin* [1964] AC 40. And note Lord Reid in *Anisminic* [1969] 1 All ER 208 at 214, HL.

affairs before making a decision, have all been met with censure from the courts and have been regarded as unfair administrative decision-making. A very flexible range of standards and tests has been invoked and developed to protect individuals who face administrative decision-making which might be adverse to their interests or expectations, as well as legal rights. So that, for instance, being forewarned of allegations or accusations,[3] being allowed a reasonable time to prepare one's side of a case or argument,[4] being allowed an oral hearing and legal representation as a right *where the circumstances warrant it* because of the difficulty of the charges or proceedings,[5] being allowed to probe the evidence against one, if necessary in a form that maintains confidentiality for the person who gave the information leading to the adverse decision—are considered necessary elements of fair procedure.[6] Perhaps the high water mark was the decision in *ex p Al Fayed*. Under s 44 British Nationality Act 1981, nothing required the relevant authorities to give reasons for decisions, nonetheless it was a requirement of 'fairness' that the applicant was provided with 'sufficient information' relating to any concerns or anxieties that the Home Secretary may have about the application. This was subject to any reasons in the public interest why information should not be disclosed.[7] The move from natural justice in a legal/judicial forum to fair procedure in a broad range of administrative processes has been one of the success stories in the development of our administrative law. Another recent example of the growing recognition of the importance of openness in decision-making came in the Privy Council's decision in *Stefan v GMC* (above). But certain irrational limits have been set. If reasons for decisions are not demanded by the courts, then this constitutes a barrier to fairness, an attack on openness, and it helps to pre-empt legitimate challenge to arbitrariness and inefficiency.

In Britain courts are loath to meddle too frequently or too pervasively in public administration. The success with which the autonomy of law has been perceived in a British setting has rested very obviously on judges operating within their allotted areas and not trespassing into politics or into areas of administration for which there is ultimate political responsibility. Too frequent an incursion would arouse suspicion of political bias or at best would result in accusations that judges were setting

---

3   Cf *Furnell v Whangrei High Schools Board* [1973] AC 660; *Rees v Crane* [1994] 1 All ER 833, PC.

4   *Lloyd v McMahon* [1987] 1 All ER 1118, CA and HL; and being allowed all necessary documentation: *R v Department of Health, ex p Gandhi* [1991] 4 All ER 547.

5   *R v Army Board of the Defence Council, ex p Anderson* [1991] 3 All ER 375 and *R v Secretary of State for the Home Department, ex p Anderson* [1984] QB 778.

6   *Re Pergamon Press* [1971] Ch 388. Cf *Kingsley v UK* above.

7   [1997] 1 All ER 228. After this decision Jack Straw announced he would give reasons for nationality decisions.

themselves up as administrators.[8] The notorious reluctance of the British judiciary to apply tests of proportionality to challenge public decisions is an obvious illustration. The HRA will make this test inescapable and will introduce more exacting review of decisions where fundamental principles are applicable to protect an individual 'victim'. We have seen as much in asylum cases in relation to Art 3 of the ECHR where a more rigorous review of the factual basis of the decision was undertaken by the court than would have been the case previously.[9] The more substantial the interference with human rights, the more the court will require in justification to be satisfied that the decision is reasonable. However, a refusal to insist on giving good reasons for decisions or non-decisions,[10] a general failure to ensure full information about a decision or to allow informed challenge to public decision-making, might be equally political in favour of the status quo and vested interests, a presumption as to the adequacy of existing arrangements for debate or discussion of proposals and decisions, or an assumption that those who make decisions always know best. There is a residue of 'It is of course always to be presumed that the executive will act honestly and that its powers will be reasonably exercised'.[11]

The judicial record on these points has not until the late 1980s been a venerable one. It took Parliamentary legislation in 1958 to reverse the impact of judicial decisions which held that reasons did not have to be forthcoming after an appeal had been made to the minister in an environmental matter and after an inspector had conducted an inquiry and made recommendations to the minister. Nor was the appellant allowed sight of the recommendations.[12] It was the 1958 Act which imposed a statutory duty to give reasons for decisions on a range of scheduled tribunals and ministerial decisions following public inquiries.[13] The courts have settled for an approach which would suggest that for tribunals which are under an obligation to give reasons for decisions, a failure to give reasons, or adequate reasons, is not *per se* a reason for allowing an appeal for an error of law from the tribunal.[14] The failure to supply a sufficient reason would appear bad enough, but to provide no reason would

8   See *Grievances, Remedies and the State* (2nd ed, 1994) chapters 1 and 6. Nb *The Judge Over Your Shoulder* (1987) Tr Sol Dept and the less dyspeptic 1994 edition.

9   *R v Secretary of State for the Home Department, ex p Turgut* [2001] 1 All ER 719; this was anticipated by *Bugdaycay v Secretary of State for the Home Department* [1987] AC 514.

10   For a novel judicial recognition of 'non-decisions', see Lloyd LJ in *Ex p Datafin* [1987] 1 All ER 564.

11   Lord Reading in *R v Governor of Wormwood Scrubs Prison, ex p Foy* [1920] 2 KB 305.

12   The Franks Report, Cmnd 218 (1957), and its exhortation of 'openness, fairness and impartiality' for inquiries and tribunals.

13   Now Tribunals and Inquiries Act 1992.

14   *Crake v Supplementary Benefits Council* [1982] 1 All ER 498; *Mountview Court Properties Ltd v Devlin* (1970) 21 P & CR 689.

seem to fly in the face of the requirement that reasons shall be given and is today questionable.[15] The arguments in favour of this restrictive approach centre on the proposition that the appellant must show that the process of decision-making itself was vitiated by erroneous legal reasoning. Keeping a decision record to a minimum, and giving exiguous reasons, would make successful challenge less than likely, and probably deliberately so. In *Crake v SBC*, Woolf J adumbrated a test which, while not automatically stating that a failure to give adequate reasons is conclusive proof one way or the other on whether a tribunal has erred in law, suggested: 'in practice I think that there will be few cases when it will not be possible, where the reasons are inadequate, to say one way or another whether the tribunal has gone wrong in law. Courts, he felt, are now more readily persuaded that inadequate reasons, or reasons which show a failure to consider relevant factors, may lead to an *inference* that a decision was bad in law. If it is impossible to make this inference but doubt exists, the court can remit the case to the tribunal for reconsideration. When considering the reasons, the court will have the benefit of the chairman's notes in deciding whether, although the reasons are inadequate, the decision-making process was itself sound.[16] Where it is impossible to discern from the surrounding evidence what the reasons for the decision of the tribunal are, and where the subject-matter of the decision is important, eg it involves the liberty of the subject,[17] or severe physical injury,[18] the court may be more willing to quash the decision for an error of law in as much as the decision does not comply with the statutory duty to give reasons.[19] This is consistent in cases where the courts have applied a more probing and exacting test of review of a decision concerning fundamental rights. The influence of the jurisprudence of the Court of Human Rights has been apparent where that court has decided that the traditional basis of judicial review in England does not provide an

15　*Re Poyser and Mills' Arbitration* [1963] 1 All ER 612.
16　Note 13 above. Social Security Commissioners, who hear appeals from local social security tribunals, and other special appeal tribunals, have generally taken a stricter approach on the requirement to provide reasons for decisions (Richardson, op cit, note 19 p 424).
17　*R v Mental Health Review Tribunal, ex p Pickering* [1986] 1 All ER 99, challenge by certiorari; *United Kingdom Association of Professional Engineers v ACAS* [1979] 2 All ER 478, declaration under private law.
18　*R v Vaccine Damage Tribunal, ex p Loveday* (1985) Times, 20 April, or where they defer to the expertise of 'experts', *Daejan Properties Ltd v Chambers* (1985) 277 Estates Gazette 308.
19　In the area of an individual's liberty the courts have insisted upon *sufficient* reasons being made out to their satisfaction to detain a person on grounds of illegal entry into the UK: *Khawaja v Secretary of State for the Home Department* [1984] AC 74; cf *Bugdaycay v Secretary of State for the Home Department* [1987] 1 All ER 940, HL, and *Ex p Singh* [1987] Imm AR 489. See also *R v ADHAC etc, ex p Brough* (1986) 19 HLR 367. See *ex p McQuillan* and *ex p Smith* notes 16 p 408 notes 4 and 20 p 410 above.

effective remedy where Convention rights are in question precisely because it does not allow the court to excavate below the surface of the decision.[20]

It is possible to see, however, that the courts might impugn failure to give adequate reasons where they construe that the duty is a part of the *conditions* for the exercise of power and Parliament intended it to be such a condition. This appears to be the case in planning and environmental cases where a traditional right of property is being interfered with or effectively restricted. Here, because the property-owning developer needs to be informed of the reasons for an adverse decision so that he may amend a future application to the planning authority, failure to provide adequate, intelligible reasons has been fatal.[1] Indeed, the courts have gone further, holding in some cases that a failure to provide factual support for the reasons given could also prove fatal to the legality of the decision.[2] It is difficult to know how to reconcile these decisions,[3] although one can point to the fact that the tribunal cases generally refer to statutory rights of appeal[4] whereas the environmental cases involve a statutory application to quash.[5] But not all distinctions are thus explicable. Distinctions on procedural points are the stuff of law in any system, but it is lamentable that such important issues of principle are obscured by an over-technical debate. Latterly the courts have shown more latitude to a secretary of state and where 'a lack of particularity' in the reasons following an inquiry into proposed demolition of listed buildings in the City of London under the town and country planning legislation did not reveal a flaw in the decision-making process serious enough to justify quashing the decision the legal requirement to give reasons was satisfied.[6] The onus was always on the applicant to satisfy the court that s/he has been substantially prejudiced by a deficiency of the reasons and only when that is the case might a court quash the decision. The degree of particularity is variable according to the context and the minister etc was not to be judged harshly where there were flaws because s/he had access to legal advice.

However, there are signs of reassessment by senior judiciary so that where the courts have previously not insisted on the giving of full reasons

---

20 See note 20 p 410 and note 8 p 411 above. See *R (on the application of Holding and Barnes plc) v Secretary of State for the Environment* [2001] UKHL 23 [2001] 2 WLR 1389 and Art 6 ECHR and planning appeals.

1 *Fairmount Investments v Secretary of State for the Environment* [1976] 2 All ER 865, HL; *French Kier Developments v Secretary of State* [1977] 1 All ER 296.

2 Eg *Coleen Properties Ltd v Minister of Housing and Local Government* [1971] 1 WLR 433; *Prest v Secretary of State for Wales* (1982) 81 LGR 193, CA.

3 See also *South Northamptonshire Council v Secretary of State* (1995) 70 P & CR 224.

4 Under the Tribunals and Inquiries Act 1992, s 11, on a point of law.

5 Eg s 288 of the Town and Country Planning Act 1990.

6 *Save Britain's Heritage v Secretary of State for the Environment* [1991] 2 All ER 10, HL.

by the Parole Board, chairmen of local review committees, or the Home Secretary, in more recent cases involving refusal to grant a prisoner release on licence or in decisions recalling a prisoner on licence[7] such holdings have been brought into question. In *Doody*, the Law Lords in a notably combative judgment by Lord Mustill held a mandatory life prisoner is entitled to know the period recommended by the trial judge for deterrence and retribution—the penal period—and the right to know what factors the Secretary of State would take into account in deciding upon the penal element in his sentence of life imprisonment and the right to be given reasons why the Secretary of State had departed from the judge's recommendation. He would not be entitled to the entirety of the documents on which the judge based his decision. This is to ensure that the prisoner may put to the Secretary of State reasons why the penal period should be reduced—thus triggering referral of his case to the Parole Board which might recommend release on licence—and that his submissions were based on informed argument and not idle speculation.[8] Furthermore, in *ex p Wilson* a discretionary life prisoner was entitled 'as a matter of fairness' to have disclosed to him reports to be presented to the Parole Board on the forthcoming review of his case.[9] Applicants for immediate release on parole should be informed of material which might militate against their release.[10] Convicted prisoners were entitled to have disclosed to them fresh evidence revealed by police inquiries on behalf of the Home Secretary after they had petitioned him to refer their cases to the Court of Appeal and they should be given a specific opportunity to make representations on that evidence. The specific level of disclosure to be made was sufficient disclosure to enable the petitioner to present his best case effectively.[11] These decisions have been prompted to some extent by decisions of the European Court of Human Rights, such as *Weeks v UK*, which found the UK in breach of art 5(4) when a prisoner on parole did not have the benefit of full disclosure of adverse information in the possession of the Parole Board on decisions affecting recall or review.[12] But there has been a more subtle awareness of the requirements of fairness among the judiciary and in a non-prison context the decision in *ex p Cunningham*[13] will have broad analogical potential.

---

7 *Payne v Lord Harris of Greenwich* [1981] 2 All ER 842; *R v Secretary of State, ex p Gunnell* [1985] Crim LR 105, CA. Cf *Weeks v UK* (1987) 10 EHRR 293, and *The Guardian* and *Wilson's* case, 28 March 1985. And see: *R v Parole Board, ex p Mansell* (1996) Times, 21 March.

8 *Doody v Secretary of State for the Home Department* [1993] 3 All ER 92 , HL.

9 [1991] 2 All ER 576 , CA.

10 *R v Parole Board, ex p Georghiades* [1992] COD 412. And see Criminal Justice Act 1991, ss 32–51 on changes concerning parole ss 32-51.

11 *R v Secretary of State for the Home Department, ex p Hickey (No 2)* [1995] 1 All ER 490.

12 (1987) 10 EHRR 293; and *Thynne v UK* Case No 23/1989/183/241-243 (1990) 13 EHRR 666.

13 *R v Civil Service Appeal Board, ex p Cunningham* [1991] 4 All ER 310, CA.

Here the Civil Service Appeal Board found that a civil servant had been unfairly dismissed and assessed compensation at under half the amount that would have been awarded by an industrial tribunal. The Board's refusal to give reasons for its decisions was held to be a breach of natural justice and while this was partly explicable by analogy with industrial tribunals which were under such duties it was also related to the duty of the Board to act judicially. A growing realisation of the desirability of explaining decisions of a judicial or administrative nature is manifest particularly where the decision is apparently inexplicable or begs an explanation or suggests unfairness. So where the aldermen of the City of London were entitled to 'blackball' one of their brethren—an ancient right going back to Richard II—they had to give reasons for their decision to prevent an elected alderman taking office.[14] As well as giving reasons the courts have shown themselves more willing to allow access to documents and to allow cross-examination when this is demanded by fairness.[15] However, consistency is not always immediately apparent so that Sedley J, who has made significant contributions towards our developing sensitivity in public law, has held that a body making academic judgments relating to the research assessment of a university department which would have a significant impact on its future funding was not under a duty to give reasons because of the Delphic nature of academic peer judgments.[16] No such considerations apply to a line of cases decided in the Court of Appeal and the House of Lords which reveal a questionable over-sympathy for administrative expedience at the expense, it is felt, of human dignity in the areas of immigration and housing the homeless. It may be that different considerations would apply today and the statutory details have changed since the time of the decisions.

The decision of *ex p Swati*[17] concerned the refusal of entry to this country of visitors—essentially those from the new Commonwealth. Briefly, such visitors had, via the intercession of relatives or friends who were already in the UK, sought to delay their removal by invoking the assistance of an MP[18] or applying for leave for judicial review. The Home Office responded to the former practice by restricting the opportunities to contact MPs. The Court of Appeal dealt with the latter practice by holding that the standard reason for refusing leave of entry was a sufficient *ex facie* reason to refuse entry. This allows the officer to state baldly that he or she is not satisfied that the visitor is 'genuinely seeking entry for the period of the visit as stated'. To go any further, Parker LJ believed,

---

14   *Financial Times,* 19 August 1995.
15   *R v Army Board of the Defence Council, ex p Anderson* [1991] 3 All ER 375.
16   *R v Higher Education Funding Council, ex p Institute of Dental Surgery* [1994] 1 All ER 651.
17   [1986] 1 All ER 717. See also *Abdi v Home Secretary* [1996] 1 All ER 641, HL.
18   Use of MPs to prevent removal has provoked the Home Secretary to heated comments and various amendments to the procedure.

was to seek 'not reasons for refusal, but the reasons for the reasons for refusal'. If such a reason is *ex facie* good, leave will not be given to apply for judicial review unless the applicant has further information that the officer's decision is unlawful. If the officer does not have to give a reason of any more substance than the above, the applicant will have nothing to shift the burden of proof from his shoulders.

The second case is a House of Lords decision which suggests that, in cases where local authorities are challenged by individuals claiming various rights under the Housing (Homeless Persons) Act (subsequently amended), the decisions of fact are for the local housing authorities, and courts should be reluctant to interfere with their decisions and decision-making processes. Their decisions should be viewed with latitude, and a loose framework, ie no safeguards, should not be taken to mean that improprieties existed on the authorities' part.[19] In these circumstances, individuals are going to find it virtually impossible to substantiate allegations of unfairness or abuse of discretion. As Lord Denning once suggested: welfare legislation should not become the 'happy hunting ground of lawyers'.[20] When the courts want to keep out, they can easily allow processes to remain closed. When they wish to intervene, they can construe a duty to give reasons strictly or establish that findings are unsubstantiated by the facts.[1] Too often, predictability is reduced to a guessing game.

There are judicial dicta that might have encouraged a rationalising tendency far earlier than might be the case. In *Padfield*, Lord Upjohn suggested that a failure to give reasons for a decision *could* lead a court to presume that no good reasons in law existed for the decision, which would then be invalid and subject to possible redress in the courts.[2] Such a piece of *obiter dicta* was bound to be interpreted by later courts as a momentary lapse from judicious caution, simple exaggeration or confined to a particular statutory context.[3] It is sobering, therefore, to consider that in France it has been a presumption of law in *droit administratif* that no reasons for a decision constitute 'bad reasons' for a decision in law and

---

19 *Puhlhofer v Hillingdon LBC* [1986] AC 484; see Birkinshaw (1982) Urban Law and Policy 255; see s 14(2) of the Housing and Planning Act 1986.

20 *R v Preston SB Appeal Tribunal, ex p Moore* [1975] 1 WLR 624; and *R v Deputy Governor of Camphill Prison, ex p King* [1984] 3 All ER 897, CA.

1 *Secretary of State etc v Tameside MBC* [1977] AC 1014; *Wheeler v Leicester City Council* [1985] AC 1054; and perennial reliance for contradictory outcomes on *Associated Provincial Picture Houses v Wednesbury Corpn* [1947] 1 KB 223 as witnessed in *Nottinghamshire CC v Secretary of State for the Environment* [1986] 1 All ER 199, HL; *Hammersmith and Fulham LB v Secretary of State for the Environment* [1990] 3 All ER 589, QBD, CA and HL.

2 *Padfield v Minister of Agriculture, Fisheries and Food* [1968] AC 997.

3 *British Airways Board v Laker Airways* [1985] AC 58, specially Lord Diplock.

this has been reinforced by a legislative duty to provide reasons.[4] French public administration works in a very different manner and cultural framework from our own, but surely there is a lesson to be learned. And from a common law jurisdiction, the right to have a decision, or rules expressing policies based upon 'reliable, probative and substantial evidence', under the Administrative Procedure Act (APA) of the USA, has helped to promote the expectation of fully reasoned decisions as a matter of course. The requirement has assisted in cutting down the use of administrative procedures as opportunities for closed bartering between regulatory overlords and powerful regulated interests.[5] The fact that FOIA legislation was required testifies to the fact that the APA was not, in itself, a panacea for closed or cosy brokerage between powerful groups but— and this is the important point—the US legislation and judicial interpretations of it have shown an awareness and insight of the realities of administrative and commercial power which have, as yet, been denied to our law and lawyers, even if a period of retrenchment has existed in the USA latterly.[6] And so too in the Antipodes.[7] The Charter of Fundamental Rights of the EU contains an obligation for administrative authorities to give reasons for decisions as do the Commission and EU Ombudsman's codes of good administrative practice. The ECJ has created a right to the giving of reasons for decisions following the more limited right in Art 253 EC to reasons for legislative decisions.[8] What is required in a British setting is a greater provision of statutory duties to give reasons which stipulate the consequences of failure to comply, and which specify the items which should be addressed in the reasons. The failure of British judges until recently to adopt a more vigorous approach to the giving of reasons for the exercise of discretionary power bears sad testimony to their lack of appreciation of the requirements of constitutionality. This is all the more regrettable considering the judiciary's extra-judicial support for such constitutional safeguards, and their tendentious application of them in practice.[9] Things may be changing; judges tell us they are but there are reverse as well as forward gears.

---

4   See R Errera's discussion of *Ministre Des Affaires Sociales* (1987) Public Law 119.

5   With modifications in the field of social security administration, see J Mashaw *Bureaucratic Justice* (1983) and *Due Process In the Administrative State* (1985).

6   M Garland (1985) 98 Harv LR 507; Morrison (1986) 99 Harv LR 1059 and CR Sunstein *After the Rights Revolution* (1990).

7   Although the contribution of the new administrative law of Australia to public law jurisprudence has been remarkable: see Lewis and Birkinshaw *When Citizens Complain: Reforming Justice and Administration* (1993).

8   *UNECTEF v Heylens* [1987] ECR 4097; this did not extend to measures of a national legislature implementing EC laws: *Sodemare* Case C-70/95 [1997] ECR I-3395.

9   Eg Denning *Freedom Under the Law* (1949), pp 91–2.

As was seen in chapter 6, the UK FOIA carries with it a variety of duties to provide reasons for decisions against the applicant's request or interests. In publication schemes, authorities will be under a duty to have regard to the public interest in the publication of reasons for decisions made by the authority. They shall publish their schemes in such manner as they deem fit. This is not the full enthusiastic endorsement of a duty to give reasons that one might wish for. It is hedged in by discretion and a lack of specificity. It gives no encouragement to discuss why reasons should be given, what form this should take and in what sought of detail they should be made.

Foreclosing discussion

In a way, some of these arguments are thrown into greater relief by looking at challenges to administrative decision-making which are not centred on individuals being given reasons for decisions, but which are attempts to put an alternative view to those who make decisions which will have a pronounced impact upon the collective weal. We therefore find in relation to public inquiries that, while obtaining reasons for a decision is important for a property holder whose land is affected,[10] when we come to broader-ranging inquiries where a policy proposal is more obviously in issue, limiting the issues on the agenda is as crucial and as important as the giving of reasons, if not more so. The courts, for instance, have ruled out the necessity of any discussion of the policies or merits of a proposal to build a road, for example, at an inquiry. Furthermore, discussion of the factual basis supporting a proposal, eg the traffic flow predictions for future years, has been held to be an unsuitable topic for discussion at a public inquiry.[11] These matters are better suited to discussion within the department, and between the department and local authorities, rather than being debated in public.[12] For broad policy concerns the minister can answer to Parliament.[13] Rules for inquiries, which were recast in 2000, invariably stipulate that where a representative of the minister is obliged to appear, s/he is not required to answer questions on the merits of policy. The inquiry is into objections, not the merits of proposals.[14] Nothing prevents a department opening up a large inquiry to debate the need and

10   P 428 above.
11   *Bushell v Secretary of State* [1981] AC 75; cf Lord Diplock at p 96 C–D.
12   See Purdue (1985) Public Law 475. See also the *Greenpeace* litigation at [1994] 4 All ER 329 and 352 and the added dimension of EC law in planning matters: *R v Durham City Council ex p Huddlestan* [2000] 1 WLR 1484, CA.
13   *Bushell*; Franks, n 12 p 426 above, paras 273 and 288. Nb the use of a standing committee of MPs to hear objections in to the proposals for the Channel Tunnel.
14   SI 2000/1624. Cf Franks, para 317.

merits for a proposal if it so wishes, and the Sizewell 'B' inquiry into the Central Electricity Generating Board's proposal to build Britain's first pressurised water reactor at Sizewell is a case in point. The Department of Energy, but not other departments, allowed questions on the merits of policy.[15] However, although the Department of Energy allowed a pressure group to use 'misappropriated' internal documents, it refused their requests for more up-to-date figures which might have thrown light on that document; nor would the same department reveal 'as a matter of practice ... internal departmental working documents'.[16]

The difficulty with inquiries into major proposals is that it is often impossible to discern where policy begins, and pure fact or details behind the proposals end. The House of Lords decision in the 1980 *Bushell* case is illustrative of such a problem.[17] It was also evident in litigation where the Department sought to exclude the question of the *principle* of levying tolls for the Severn Bridge from the scope of the inquiry into objections against a proposal to raise the tolls.[18] Objections on the specific application of the policy had been made at the inquiry, but had not formed part of the inspectors' recommendations. The department argued that the principle of raising tolls *per se* involved government economic policy.[19] At first instance, the judge disagreed, holding that this was not a matter which was unsuitable for discussion. While ministers had power to remove from discussion matters that were not suitable for an inquiry, it was not simply a matter of their *ipse dixit* but depended upon whether the minister would be assisted by discussion,[20] or whether he was already committed *lawfully* to a policy which could only be upset at the cost of considerable disruption.[1] That was not the case here, since the objectors wished their views on the *specific application* of policy to be raised in the inspector's report. The Court of Appeal unanimously overruled the judgment to quash the secretary of state's decision.[2] The inspector had been perfectly correct not to allude to the policy objections, because they related to 'general policy matters' and his views would be of no more significance than those

---

15 *Purdue* n 12 at 477, and (1987) Public Law 162.
16 *Purdue* (1985) Public Law 475 at p 487. The FOIA is unlikely to make any difference to this approach.
17 Note 11 above, and Birkinshaw *Grievances, Remedies and the State*, chapter 2.
18 *R v Secretary of State for Transport, ex p Gwent CC* [1986] 2 All ER 18.
19 Making users pay would reduce the overall level of government subsidy, reducing the PSBR and taxation.
20 In *Bushell*, the court accepted, the minister would not have been assisted by a discussion of traffic-flow predictions and the inspector's recommendations thereon.
1   Again in *Bushell*, the commitment to motorway interconnections. On issues that were relevant for discussion the minister must not have precluded alternatives, as this would run the risk of being an unlawful fettering of his discretion. Motorways and bridge building would now be prime candidates for Public Private Partnerships.
2   [1987] 1 All ER 161.

of any other 'member of the public'. Furthermore, the court was satisfied that the secretary of state *had* considered the gravamen of the objections on policy in his department, deciding nonetheless to increase the tolls. All in all, fairness had been achieved.[3] The House of Lords have recently ruled that the planning system in which a Secretary of State with an interest in an outcome decides a planning appeal is not in breach of Art 6 ECHR.[4]

An inquiry has to be fixed into a continuing time process through which new information will emerge. It was clear in *Bushell* that where such information emerges from *within* the sponsoring department *after* the inquiry, natural justice does not dictate that this has to be presented to the objectors at a new inquiry. Inquiries rules under statute[5] only provide for the position where, after the inquiry, new evidence or facts[6] are considered and *as a consequence* the minister is minded to disagree with the inspector's recommendations. This rule seemed to have been given a strained interpretation when an inspector was unhappy about environmental safeguards surrounding an application to build an aerodrome in the London Dockland. He recommended conditions to be attached to the grant of permission. The secretary of state took evidence from another department *after* the inquiry and gave permission for development without reopening the inquiry. The court held that the minister had not disagreed with the inspector's recommendations but had merely amplified and clarified them,[7] so therefore the safeguard in the rules was not triggered.

Some more positive developments should be noted where the courts have acted creatively to establish a public hearing into public access to a footpath on private land where there was conflicting evidence as to whether there had been a dedication to the public. A good deal of documentary evidence supported the claims of those seeking to establish a public dedication contrary to the claim of the former owner that it had not been dedicated. The Court of Appeal held that where there was

---

3 A department is unlikely to do anything other than confirm its own policy or inclination. Without testing of their position, how fair is their review likely to be?

4 Ie in a 'call-in' procedure: *R (on the application of Holding and Barnes plc) v Secretary of State etc* [2001] UKHL 23 [2001] 2 WLR 1389. Legality could be challenged in the courts

5 Eg Town and Country Planning (Inquiries Procedure) Rules 2000, SI 2000/1624. In *Bushell*, the minister *accepted* the inspector's recommendations.

6 But not where he disagrees on a matter of policy and its application: *Lord Luke of Pavenham v Minister of Housing and Local Government* [1968] 1 QB 172. See Cm 43 (1986) and Government observations on major inquiries; and see the Energy Committee's criticism of draft rules restricting objectors' rights at inquiries into proposed electricity stations (HC 310 1987–8). See now the 2000 Rules n 5 and the additional procedural safeguards.

7 *R v Secretary of State for the Environment, John Mowlem & Co plc, Londn Dockland Development Corpn, ex p GLC* [1986] JPL 32. Informal meetings and discussions did take place.

conflicting evidence as in the present case, the Secretary of State who had rejected an appeal by the supporters of a public dedication claim must act fairly. This meant that a public hearing to which there was a legitimate expectation even though the statute had not allowed for an inquiry in these circumstances but had provided for one at a later stage, should be held. To follow the strict letter of the statute without regarding the 'peculiar facts of the case' was unfair. The common law was supplementing the statute not supplanting it.[8] The inquiry into the murders by Dr Shipman was made to sit in public to comply with the requirements of Art 10 ECHR.[9] However, following the rail crash at Hatfield in October 2000 which led to several fatalities and major disruption of the national rail network because of serious faults with the quality of rail maintenance, the Secretary of State refused to hold an inquiry which might reveal the underlying cause of systemic problems but decided to prosecute individuals for specific criminal offences.

One final point concerning the restriction of the agenda, and the effect this restriction has on information provision, concerns the former Transport Users Consultative Committee (TUCC) and closure of passenger railway lines. Different provisions now apply under the Railways Act 1993 which is unlikely to alter the following practices in any real sense but at the relevant time public hearings had to take place before the TUCC. These hearings could examine the economic case for closure. At the hearings into the prospective closure of the Settle-Carlisle railway line, counsel for British Rail accepted that the economic case was the sheet anchor of their case, but the hearing was precluded from discussing this item. The Committee's report criticised this exclusion vehemently.[10] The Court of Appeal has, moreover, held that the procedure at these truncated hearings is at the chairman's discretion, so that he was within his powers to refuse cross-examination of BR witnesses or to allow final submissions from counsel for the objectors.[11] The body was making recommendations, not determining a justiciable issue. This is a lame excuse if *fairness* is not seen to be done. It is a question of balance, and too often the balance is heavily weighted in favour of administrative convenience.[12] Where an

---

8   *R v Secretary of State for Wales, ex p Emery* [1996] 4 All ER 1and cf s 302 Highways Act 1980; upheld on different grounds by the Court of Appeal: [1998] 4 All ER 367 and which disapproved of the judge at first instance's decision on the holding of an inquiry. It has to be said that although perhaps welcome as an exercise in fairness, the first instance decision did appear to break with conventions of statutory construction. But therein lies the problem.

9   *R (Wagstaff) v Secretary of State for Health* [2001] 1 WLR 292.

10 The chairman was subsequently not reappointed in March 1987.

11 *R v London Regional Passengers Committee, ex p Brent LBC* (1985) Financial Times, 29 November.

12 See *R v Rochdale Health Authority, ex p Rochdale MBC* (1992) 8 BMLR 137 and s 5(2) NHS and Community Care Act 1990. The Secretary of State may hold a further round of written consultation after the first round of consultation to establish

authority held a public meeting to discuss a school closure in an ethnically mixed inner city area the fact that not every group had a translator provided did not vitiate proceedings in law. This would create an impossible burden, the Divisional Court held.[13] And the court has held that where a statute states that information is to be provided, it need only be provided in English.[14] The Citizen's Charter and its successor advert to the need for information to be provided in minority languages and the subject has been treated with greater sensitivity by administrators than by courts.

Information and the conduct of legal argument

In January 1985, an Australian Royal Commission under the chairmanship of an Australian High Court judge began the first day of its sitting by lambasting the British Government for its refusal to hand over information concerning the testing of nuclear weapons by the British Government in Australian deserts and the Christmas Islands in the early 1950s. The papers covered medical reports and monitoring the effects of the explosions, including the effects on servicemen who took part.[15] Many of these claimed they had been exposed to radiation with inadequate protection. The Government released over a period of time three and a half tons of documents. These revealed that such monitoring had taken place at the time but had remained secret.

Technically, the Government was not bound to give any information to the Commission. The episode is interesting because of the robust manner in which a judge criticised government secrecy, and for the fact that a considerable degree of evidence was forthcoming eventually. When it comes to the crunch, what will a British court insist on a British public body disclosing? This has to be seen in the context of the adversarial process, which is the method adopted by British, and common law, courts to establish facts and obtain information. It is to be compared with the inquisitorial process, which is the method of inquiries, commissions and

---

a health trust. He may supply consultees with further information but the mere fact that the responses included objections based on a perceived absence of information about part of the proposal does not of itself oblige him to do so.

13 *R v Birmingham City Council, ex p Kaur* [1991] COD 21.

14 Woolf LJ in *R v Governors of Small Heath School, ex p Birmingham City Council* (1989) Independent, 30 June.

15 An estimated 20,000. See *Pearce v Secretary of State for Defence* [1988] AC 755 and the interpretation, in the servicemen's favour, of s 10, Crown Proceedings Act 1947. According to *The Guardian*, the Crown sought an assurance that its witnesses would not be proceeded against for perjury after the Royal Commission's hearings: 6 December 1985. A Royal Commission does not have power to take evidence on oath. Cf Crown Proceedings (Armed Forces) Act 1987. See the EctHR judgment in *McGinley and Egan v UK* (1998) at p 334 n 12 above.

civil jurisdictions. The distinction between the two has been explained by Lord Devlin:[16]

> The essential difference between the two systems is apparent from their names: the one is a trial of strength and the other is an inquiry. The question in the first is: are the shoulders of the party upon whom is laid the burden of proof, the plaintiff or the prosecution as the case may be, strong enough to carry and discharge it? In the second the question is: what is the truth of the matter? In the first the judge or jury are arbiters; they do not pose questions and seek answers; they weigh such material as is put before them, but they have no responsibility for seeing that it is complete. In the second the judge is in charge of the inquiry from the start; he will of course permit the parties to make out their cases and may rely on them to do so, but it is for him to say what it is that he wants to know.

This distinction was at the heart of Lord Howe's attack on the unfairness of the inquisitorial technique used by Scott LJ in his inquiry into Matrix Churchill (see chapter 4). Civil servants who were not used to that kind of 'inquisition' were not adequately protected given the seriousness of the issues. In fact an assurance had been given before the inquiry began that civil servants would face no criminal or administrative repercussions for anything said at the inquiry. The matter had reached a stage, Whitehall felt, where the safeguards of an adversarial system were required, especially full notice of 'charges' or a case to answer and legal representation. Sir Richard Scott has explained what he believed the content of fairness to be at an inquiry of the sort conducted into Matrix Churchill and when it was desirable to hold proceedings in public. His primary objective was to marry fairness and efficient progress.

The courts provide, in an adversarial system, on the surface at least, a forum within which an equal debate can take place. It is up to the parties involved to present their cases as fully and completely as possible. The judge can then adjudicate. It is a contest which operates within procedural restraints imposed by the rules of evidence and the rules of procedure, as

---

16 *The Judge* (1979), p 54. See *Mahon v Air New Zealand Ltd Airways* [1984] AC 808 and procedural protection where inquiries become 'accusatorial'. Sir Richard Scott has explained for the rationale for his adopted procedure in the Matrix Churchill inquiry: (1995) LQR 596. It is an extended commentary upon the Salmon Commission *Tribunals of Inquiry* Cmnd 3121 (1966). See also HC 115 (1995-6) pp 19-48 and 1753-8. After the Report, the Lord Chancellor's Department conducted a review of inquiry procedures. Note also the attacks by Keith Vaz's solicitor on the procedures adopted by the Parliamentary Commissioner for Standards in her investigation of allegations of breaches of the code of behaviour for MPs: HC 314 I & II (2000-01).

well as substantive restraints. These latter are contained in the law itself. To give a simple example, a tenant facing eviction at the suit of an allegedly rapacious landlord may see his 'problem' relating to a whole series of social, economic and possibly political factors. These could be unemployment, indigence, the favouritism or otherwise shown to property-holders over the propertyless, reduction of publicly supported accommodation. The law cuts down the substance of these issues by asking does, or does not, the landlord have a legal right to possess the property? Everything else is irrelevant in law. Law narrows the range of debate. The procedure narrows the issues which are legally relevant by insisting that they be presented in a particular way, ie that only admissible evidence is entered and that hearsay evidence is not.[17] The fundamental reforms of the civil justice system introduced following Lord Woolf's recommendations may actually limit still further the nature of legal debate as litigation becomes strictly managed by judges who are expected to take a far more directorial approach to the conduct of litigation to save time and costs. The overriding objective in r 1.1 of the Civil Procedure Rules 1998 is enabling courts to deal with cases 'justly': this includes saving expense, and dealing with cases in a way which is 'proportionate' to a variety of issues including the amount of money involved, the importance of the case, the complexity of the issues and the financial position of each party. While ensuring that parties are on an equal footing, the court's resources, and expeditious but fair treatment, are also referred to.

The received tradition of the adversarial process, then, is of a two-cornered fight between the parties before the judge.[18] In public law cases, it is difficult to justify this approach when the 'public interest' or constitutional issues are involved. The courts may recognise such an interest, although there is frequently a reluctance to describe matters involving individuals as constitutional, as opposed to legal.[19] There is increasing reference to 'fundamental' common law rights even before the HRA came into effect. The restraints of law, both substantive and procedural, have ensured that courts have not, in a British system, been used to prise open closed government or widen the debate about political right against our governors. Unlike the situation in the USA, the British courts are not sympathetic to extended *amicus curiae* briefs or class actions which allow a wider range of interests to be represented in a legal

---

17 Though the very range of the exceptions to the hearsay rule in criminal trials, especially *res gestae*, testifies to the tensions between narrow formalism and a fuller procedural justice: *R v Andrews* [1987] 1 All ER 513; and *R v Kearley* [1992] 2 All ER 345 , HL.
18 See eg the Court of Appeal and majority judgment of the law lords in *Air Canada v Secretary of State for Trade (No 2)* [1983] 1 All ER 161 and [1983] 2 AC 394.
19 See eg p 382 *et seq* above.

case. Conversely, locus standi has been given a fairly generous treatment by the courts in England.

When parties are involved in litigation, the court does not give them an unbridled right to invade each other's privacy. Questions can be asked before and during the proceedings which are relevant to those proceedings. In a trial between private parties, discovery or disclosure as it is now called and inspection of documents in the possession, custody or power of either may be ordered to the other. There is 'standard disclosure' which is the usual form of disclosure where there is an order for disclosure, and such orders are not automatic and 'specific disclosure' which is directed.[20] Pre-action protocols will also contain important guidance on disclosure. In some circumstances, the courts may even award an Anton Piller or search order[1] where, if there is a danger that relevant documents will be destroyed, the court will allow the other party to enter the relevant premises to seize them for the purposes of the litigation for 'such relatively short period' as is reasonably necessary to copy them.[2] It is hardly surprising that the subject of discovery of documents should have spawned a wide-ranging body of case law on the extent of a third parties' duty to disclose documents to a party in litigation;[3] being allowed to use a skilled co-ordinator who was a third party to collate and conduct discovery in an action involving over one million documents requiring a multiplicity of scientific skills;[4] whether documents discovered in one action may be used against the same party in other litigation;[5] the extent of the immunity of legal professional privilege, especially where the party claiming it has accidentally allowed access to such 'privileged' documents;[6] whether a party is in 'control' of documents and how far down its corporate hierarchy a company must go to establish the existence of documents which have to be handed over on

20 Civil Procedure Rules 1998, Part 31.
1   Section 7 Civil Jurisdiction Act 1997.
2   *Anton Piller KG v Manufacturing Processes* [1976] Ch 55, CA; and cf *Columbia Picture Industries Inc v Robinson* [1986] 3 All ER 338; *EMI Records Ltd v Spillane* [1986] 1 WLR 967; *IBM United Kingdom Ltd v Prima Data International Ltd* [1994] 4 All ER 748; *Tate Access Floors Inc v Boswell* [1990] 3 All ER 303; and Practice Direction [1994] 4 All ER 52.
3   *Lee v South West Thames RHA* [1985] 2 All ER 385; *Norwich Pharmacal*, above; *Wilden Pump Engineering Co v Fusfield* [1985] FSR 159, CA; *Ricci v Chow* [1987] 3 All ER 534 and attempted discovery from a mere witness; *Ashworth Hospital Authority v MGN Ltd* [2001] 1 All ER 991, CA; cf Newspapers etc Repeal Act 1869, Sch 2.
4   *Davies v Eli Lilly & Co* [1987] 1 All ER 801, CA. Cf *Blyth v Bloomsbury HA* (1987) [1993] 4 Med LR 151.
5   See M Dockray (1986) NLJ 219 at 221.
6   Lee, above. *Lord Ashburton v Pape* [1913] 2 Ch 469; *Goddard v Nationwide Building Society* [1986] 3 All ER 264; *Guinness Peat Properties Ltd v Fitzroy Robinson Partnership* [1987] 2 All ER 716; *British Coal Corpn v Rye (No 2)* [1988] 1 WLR 1113; *Hoechst UK Ltd v Chemiculture Ltd* [1993] FSR 270.

discovery.[7] Reforms in the Civil Procedure Rules 1998, Part 31 are unlikely to remove such problems.

Our pressing concern is with public interest immunity. This somewhat arcane subject, unknown to any but a small band of litigation and academic lawyers, was projected into public notoriety by events surrounding the collapse of the Matrix Churchill prosecution where 'gagging orders', as the press and media called them, were slapped onto documents which proved to be essential for the defence. It was a central subject in Sir Richard Scott's inquiry and report where a detailed analysis of the law is contained (see chapter 4).

Public interest, immunity and information

A public body[8] a term now given an identification in FOIA 2000,[9] may wish to withhold documents, or not to have officials answering questions in a court, because the public interest demands that the information should not be made public. A claim used to be made, misleadingly, for Crown privilege.[10] The Crown possessed a prerogative immunity at common law against orders for discovery of documents. This was abolished by s 28 of the Crown Proceedings Act 1947, subject to two provisos: any rule of law survived which authorised the withholding of information in the public interest because disclosure would be injurious to that interest;[11] and disclosure of the very existence of a document was not to be enforced if in the opinion of the minister it would be injurious to disclose whether it existed.[12] The first proviso related to the doctrine of Crown privilege, which was given extensive definition by a unanimous House of Lords in 1942,[13] whereby, having regard to the contents of the particular document(s), or if the document belongs to a class which, on the grounds of public interest, must as a class be withheld from production, they should be withheld. This grouping of documents was used in FOIA 2000 as was

---

7   *Stanfield Properties v National Westminster Bank* [1983] 2 All ER 249.
8   While it is clear that public interest immunity may be invoked by bodies which are 'private' in a legal sense to protect the confidential aspects of work which they perform on the public welfare *D v NSPCC* [1978] AC 171, the courts will circumscribe the circumstances in which it may be invoked: *SRC v Nassé* [1980] AC 1028. In another context see: *Re D* [1995] 4 All ER 385 , HL, *Re G (a minor)* [1996] 2 All ER 65.
9   Sections 3-7 and Sch 1.
10 'Privilege' is misleading in so far as the minister, and court, are under a *duty* not to allow disclosure of information *injurious* to the public interest.
11 RSC Ord 24, r 15 now Civil Procedure Rules 1998 Part 31.3(1)(a).
12 RSC Ord 77, r 12(2) now CPR Part 31.19.
13 *Duncan v Cammell Laird & Co Ltd* [1942] AC 624, *per* Viscount Simon.

seen in chapter 6. The judgment of the minister sufficed although Viscount Simon insisted that the minister must exercise a proper judgment.[14]

Administrative concessions were made by the Government, and in 1968 the House of Lords overruled the wider aspects of *Duncan v Cammell Laird* in *Conway v Rimmer*[15]. Against the claim of the Crown that the candour[16] of communications between officials required protection, the Law Lords maintained the court's right to inspect the documents for itself; to make its own judgment on whether they should be protected; and if not, whether they should be disclosed to the other party if relevant. The decision was regarded as epoch-making, albeit daunting. Judges were to be the arbiters of the public interest in what could be highly sensitive areas of official confidentiality. Professor de Smith thought that if 'There are some things that English judges are poorly equipped to do', this was certainly one of them.[17] Examination of the judgments in *Conway v Rimmer*[18] shows how cautious the Law Lords were. Cabinet documents were excluded, as were diplomatic dispatches and even the non-disclosure of papers coming before junior ministers concerning advice and formulation of policy at a low level met with judicial approval. 'The business of government is difficult enough,' opined Lord Reid, 'and no government could contemplate with equanimity the inner workings of the government machine being exposed to the gaze of those ready to criticise without adequate knowledge of the background and perhaps with some axe to grind.'[19] These were all examples of 'class documents'.

On the contrary Lord Keith, in the *Burmah Oil*[20] decision, believed such an opening up might lead 'not to captious or ill-informed criticism, but to criticism calculated to improve the nature of that working [of Government] as affecting the individual citizen'. In *Burmah Oil*, the House of Lords held that a certificate from a Secretary of State that the documents were of a high-policy content, and related to ministerial discussions with

14 The *breadth* of the decision was not supported by previous authorities, and was not accepted totally in Scotland or the Commonwealth (for the US, see *US v Reynolds* 345 US 1 (1952)). The 'contents' claim was used extensively after 1947, especially to protect inter- and intra-departmental communications and communications between outsiders and officials.

15 [1968] AC 910. A judicial reaction had already set in against the full impact of *Duncan*; see DGT Williams, *Not In The Public Interest*. On statutory privileges for information, see I Eagles (1983) Camb LJ 118; see *Sethia v Stern* (1987) Times, 4 November.

16 Confidentiality by itself is not an adequate ground to prevent discovery: *Alfred Crompton Amusement Machines Ltd v Customs and Excise Comrs (No 2)* [1973] 2 All ER 1169, and cf *SRC v Nassé*, n 8.

17 *Judicial Review of Administrative Action* (4th edn, 1980), p 40, n 57.

18 Above n 15.

19 In *Burmah Oil*, below, Lord Wilberforce declared that 'it is not for the courts to assume the role of advocates for open government'.

20 *Burmah Oil Co Ltd v Bank of England* [1980] AC 1090.

senior officials,[1] was not conclusive. The courts could balance the public interest of preventing harm to the state or the public service by not ordering disclosure, and the public interest of doing individual justice in the courts by ordering discovery if that would assist a litigant to vindicate his claims in law. If necessary, the court could examine the documents if they appeared likely to be relevant to the cause in action.[2] The case extended the principle of *Conway v Rimmer* and was doubtless influenced by case law in Australia and the USA.[3] The Law Lords' insistence that courts had a power to review the certificate of the minister concerning documents of a 'high policy content' in the highest levels of government, subject to national security or considerations of an equally important dimension,[4] is quite startling, albeit welcome. The impact of this approach can be seen in a case such as *Williams v Home Office*,[5] where discovery was ordered to a former prisoner of discussion documents between high-level officials and a minister on the merits of the control unit at HM Prison Wakefield. The plaintiff did not win his eventual action, but the documents revealed a clash at the highest level on the merits and propriety of the form of punishment implemented within the unit, and confusion in the aims of penal policy. Its impact was seen also in litigation concerning haemophiliacs who had been infected by HIV-contaminated blood purchased by the NHS from the USA. In their negligence action they successfully overcame Government arguments seeking to withhold necessary documents because the latter claimed they related to the formulation of Government policy of self-sufficiency in blood products by ministers and briefings for ministers for which the department claimed public interest immunity.[6]

But *Burmah Oil* was perhaps too emphatic. The grounding of the argument by some of the judges in terms of the rhetoric of constitutional principle could not, at that time, remain unamended.[7] A 'more considered' approach characterised the majority ruling in the *Air Canada* litigation.[8]

1 And communications with the senior officials of the Bank of England.
2 They did examine but decided that they were of no assistance to Burmah Oil's claim for an unconscionable transaction.
3 *Sankey v Whitlam* (1978) 53 ALJR 11; *US v Nixon* 418 US 683 (1974); *Env Defence Soc v SPA Ltd* [1981] 1 NZLR 146; *Auditor General of Canada v Minister of Energy Mines and Resources* (1985) 23 DLR (4th) 210. In the first two cases, evidence was required for criminal proceedings. See also de Smith *Judicial Review of Administrative Action* (5th edn, 1995) p 70 *et seq.*
4 Eg diplomatic and foreign affairs.
5 [1981] 1 All ER 1151; cf *R v Secretary of State for the Home Department, ex p Herbage (No 2)* [1987] QB 1077, CA.
6 *Re HIV Haemophiliac Litigation* [1990] NLJR 1349.
7 The reaction in some quarters was not unlike the response to the education of the children of the masses in the nineteenth century: the expletives were now written closer to the ground!
8 *(No 2)* [1983] 2 AC 394.

This concerned the test judges should apply before they examine documents and before they make their balancing decision on disclosure or confidentiality. Air Canada and other airlines complained of the exorbitant landing and user charges at Heathrow Airport. It was claimed on their behalf that the charges imposed by the British Airports Authority were *ultra vires* in as much as they were not exacted for the purposes contained in the statute,[9] but to pursue an ulterior Governmental economic policy of reducing public sector borrowing.[10] On general discovery[11] the minister refused to disclose documents which comprised communications passing between Government ministers and the preparatory drafts used by Ministers of their meetings, and which related to the formulation of Government policy regarding BAA and the limitation of public sector borrowing. Public interest immunity was claimed. At first instance the judge ordered production, subject to his inspection, even though the documents might not assist the plaintiff's case *because* the information 'would substantially assist the court to elicit the true facts regarding the plaintiffs' case' and would thereby affect the court's decision. This was a sufficient public interest justification for their discovery, subject to judicial inspection and exhaustion of appeals before inspection by the applicants. This decision was overruled in the Court of Appeal and by majority in the House of Lords.[12]

The majority decision of the Law Lords held that, before a judge exercises a discretion to examine documents for which immunity is claimed, plaintiffs must establish that they will assist their case or damage their adversary's, and that they are necessary for disposing fairly of the case or saving costs. Not only is the onus on the applicant to convince the judge that they will assist the applicant, but s/he will also have to convince the judge as to *how* they will assist. If a requester cannot be precise on this point, stating with conviction and specificity what they will contain, then the danger is that the arguments will appear speculative and part of a fishing expedition. In cases against a public authority, Fox LJ held in the Court of Appeal, a plaintiff must have *prima facie* evidence of his own without the aid of discovery, 'save in the most exceptional of cases'. The case must be able to take off without assistance said a Law Lord. The 'interests of justice', the majority held in the House of Lords, meant that the task of the court was to decide the case fairly on the evidence before it, and 'not to ascertain some independent truth by seeking out evidence of its own accord'. The minority felt that the court could inspect where disclosure *might* assist the plaintiff, or defendant, *or the court,* in

---

9   Airports Authority Act 1975.

10   By setting strict financial targets for the British Airports Authority to meet.

11   Which involved the exchange of lists of relevant documents. The certificate was actually signed by a senior civil servant.

12   Lords Scarman and Templeman dissented.

determining the issues, with the onus of proof on the applicant for discovery. If this onus is discharged, then there is strong authority to suggest that even cabinet documents can be inspected by the judge to establish whether disclosure to the applicant is necessary.[13] Without a doubt, the onus on the applicant to get the judge to inspect is a very heavy one. The more probing a judicial inquiry is, the more likely it is that there will be material to establish *ultra vires* or unlawful considerations or action. Courts are not there to inquire, they are there to decide on the basis of what the applicant can give them.

This is especially true of judicial review cases, which are meant to be speedy and expeditious and, save in rare circumstances, a review on the affidavits as filed and not by way of discovery and cross-examination of witnesses.[14] Case law has suggested that discovery should only be allowed where there is a mistake or something unsatisfactory in the affidavits.[15] It is unlikely that the limited approach has altered with the replacement of Order 53 by Part 54 of the Civil Procedure Rules which now deals with judicial review and which is no longer exclusively available in London. What is under consideration is the surface of the decision-making process, not the contents of documents or the decision maker's state of mind. The Law Commission had favoured greater liberalisation here but was not in favour of amending the relevant Rules of the Supreme Court.[16] The Bowman Report on the Crown Office List recommended that judicial review should not attract a general power of disclosure, with or without leave to proceed to a hearing for review. Disclosure should only take place under the direction of the court 'and only to the extent that it is necessary to dispose fairly of the case.' However, the report acknowledged that cases brought under the HRA might require more frequent applications for disclosure in order to ascertain whether action was 'necessary under Art 8 or 10 ECHR'.[17] It might also prove necessary to establish an effective remedy under Art 13 ECHR which although not part of the Convention incorporated under the HRA, is nonetheless a potent factor in the Court of Justice's assessment of alleged breaches. The Court has demanded more rigorous and exacting scrutiny where human rights are involved.[18] A claim

13 See Lord Fraser in *Air Canada* for the majority. He referred to cases of 'serious misconduct'.
14 Lord Wilberforce in *Zamir v Secretary of State* [1980] AC 930; Lord Scarman in *IRC v National Federation of Self Employed and Small Businesses* [1982] AC 617; Lord Diplock in *O'Reilly v Mackman* [1983] 2 AC 237, and cf *R v Liverpool City Council, ex p Coade* (1986) Times, 10 October and *R v Secretary of State for the Home Department, ex p Gardian* (1996) Times, 1 April. See the *Bowman Review of the Crown Office List* LCD (2000) which led to Civil Procedure Rules 1998 Part 54.
15 *R v Secretary of State for Foreign Affairs, ex p WDM Ltd* [1995] 1 All ER 611.
16 Order 53, r 8 (1).
17 This would appear to be reinforced by the cases in note 18 below.
18 See *Smith and Chahal etc* above note 20 p 410. Note *R v Secretary of State for the Home Department, ex p Turgut* [2001] 1 All ER 719, CA.

for review would contain all the information formerly in form 86A.[19] It has been suggested that the applicant is put in a less advantageous position in the new Part 54 than the defendant – the public authority.[20] John Griffith has asked that as judges are required 'to make policy decisions in the public interest, they should equip themselves with the means to gather all the relevant information. That is an indispensable necessity for all decision-makers.'[1] His comment came after a critique of the pusillanimous approach of English courts to testing ministers' claims that they were acting in the interests of national security, or in judicial interpretation of complex statutes affecting social policy without referring to White Papers, policy documents or debates in the House explaining the intention of the legislators.[2] The courts may now examine the record of proceedings in the stages of a Bill in certain circumstances to assist in interpretation and there has been far greater reference to legal academic literature but the general criticism still holds.[3] Arguments have been advanced before for a British equivalent to the Commissaire du Gouvernement and rapporteur system in France, who have access to the files within public authorities and who enters into public law cases to argue for the 'public interest' as identified by a non-combatant where that interest requires representation. As Sir Harry Woolf has said:

> The position of the public in general must be taken into account [in judicial review] since ... public law is designed to protect the public as a whole as well as the individual applicant. The public has a very real interest in seeing that litigation does not necessarily and unduly interfere with the process of government both at a national and a local level.[4]

In judicial review cases, Sir Harry continued, the court is not concerned with a fact-finding exercise and 'in practice applications for discovery and cross-examination are very rare ... I have no doubt ... that justice is served by the present approach'.[5] It has been seen how human rights

---

19   Which accompanied an application for judicial review and which identifies the authority/person challenged, decision etc challenged, the grounds of challenge and the relief sought.

20   T Cornford 'The New Rules of Procedure for Judicial Review [2000] 5 Web JCLI http://webjcli.ncl.ac.uk/2000/issue5/cornford5.html.

1   (1985) Public Law at 582.

2   He concentrates upon the *GCHQ*, the *Guardian Newspapers* and the GLC 'Fares Fair' litigation. See also *R v Secretary of State for Trade, ex p Anderson Strathclyde* [1983] 2 All ER 233.

3   *Pepper v Hart* [1993] 1 All ER 42, HL; and there is far more reference to the work of living authors. See also on EC measures *Three Rivers District Council v Bank of England (No 3)* [1996] 3 All ER 558.

4   (1986) Public Law at 230.

5   Ibid, p 231.

review has changed the approach. Nevertheless, he had misgivings about the adversarial approach adopted, even in judicial review cases, and suggested a Director of Civil Proceedings for public law litigation, sufficiently independent of, but answerable to, a minister of the Crown or the Attorney-General. The Director would take references from the public and would proceed where he thought necessary in the public interest, assuming the expense and responsibility. He would monitor cases before the court on judicial review,[6] and would intervene with an argument on behalf of the public which is not catered for by the parties before the court. The initiative would be with the Director not the court, 'and would depend upon the special expertise which the Director would build up as a result of his ability to consult the relevant government departments and special interest groups'.[7] He would have access to the papers and books of public bodies,[12] as the Ombudsman does and as the IC does. The Ombudsman, as we saw, is not allowed access to cabinet documents. The IC is not so expressly barred although the Cabinet and its committees are excluded bodies under FOIA – the Cabinet is not a government department. This barrier ought not to apply to the Director, although Sir Harry was silent on the point, especially as he envisaged the Director advising the courts on discovery or disclosure of documents and we have seen that these might include cabinet documents. Lord Woolf has reiterated these points more recently and in a judicial capacity he gave the leading judgment in the *Wiley* decision which reversed previous authority and held that information in documents collected in the course of an investigation by the police complaints authority is not protected by a class immunity although they may attract a contents immunity.[8]

In cases that do not raise issues of a sensitive politicised nature, the courts have suggested a possible liberalisation of the test for discovery on judicial review, aligning it with the same test for private law actions.[9] So where a prisoner contested the conditions of his confinement, discovery of all medical and psychiatric reports was allowed.[10] A decision of the Court of Appeal[11] could have a bearing on giving of information and

---

6   The Commissaire du Gouvernement is not restricted to judicial review cases, but also participates in what we would refer to as private actions involving public bodies. On public law litigation and constitutional issues in the USA, see Chayes (1982) 86 Harv LR 4.

7   Note 342, p237.

8   Cf *Ex p Wiley* [1994] 3 All ER 420 , HL and *Taylor v Anderton* [1995] 2 All ER 420, CA, where the investigator's report was protected.

9   See Lord Diplock: *O'Reilly v Mackman* [1983] 2 AC 237. Cross-examination was allowable on the same basis as a private action commenced by originating summons, *not by writ*.

10   *R v Secretary of State for the Home Department, ex p Herbage* [1987] QB 872, QBD.

11   *R v Lancashire CC, ex p Huddleston* [1986] 2 All ER 941; and see *R v Secretary of State for Transport, ex p Sherriff & Sons Ltd* (1986) Times, 18 December.

reasons for decisions by public bodies. The court accepted that public bodies who are challenged over the matter of the exercise of a discretion or power can expect that the burden of establishing a case will be upon the applicant; however, once the case is accepted for hearing, it becomes the duty of the respondent council 'to make full and fair disclosure'.[12] It is, said the Master of the Rolls, 'a process which falls to be conducted with all the cards face upwards ... and the vast majority of cards will start in the authority's hands'. It won't do for the authority to assert that it acted within the law and that the applicant must prove to the contrary:

> If the allegation is that a decision is *prima facie* irrational and that these are grounds for inquiring whether something immaterial may have been considered or something material omitted from consideration, it really does not help to assert boldly that all relevant matters and no irrelevant matters are taken into consideration without condescending to mention some at least of the principal factors on which the decision was based.[13]

The authority should set out fully and fairly what is required to meet the challenge by way of explanation.[14] Having promised so much, the court then backed down entirely and did not allow review even where such explanations were not forthcoming. If courts do not go all the way, they should not tease. When the courts do decide to go through the books of public authorities on application for discovery, they will inevitably find what they are looking for if they wish to intervene. In the Fares Fair litigation,[15] which involved the pursuit of a manifesto pledge to reduce fares on the London Transport system by increasing public subsidy financed by a rate increase, while Griffith attacked the courts for failing to examine the background information on urban transport enterprises and systems,[16] it is clear that the Court of Appeal and House of Lords went through the internal documents of the Greater London Council with a fine-tooth comb to establish procedural and substantive errors in the decisions of the GLC. This is particularly apparent in the influential and pivotal judgment of Oliver LJ: 'In the GLC's bundle of documents there is *another* significant document... . It is a report of a transport policy committee running into over 100 pages.'[17] In a discussion, a lawyer working for the GLC informed the present writer of the extent of the order

12　Not by disclosure, but by a 'voluntary' explanation of events.
13　Cf the inconsistencies in this approach and those in *Ex p Swati* and *Puhlhofer* [1986] 1 All ER 717 and [1986] AC 484 respectively.
14　Note 11.
15　*Bromley LBC v GLC* [1982] 1 All ER 129.
16　Note 1 above.
17　[1982] 1 All ER at p 147a.

of discovery against the authority and his surprise at its ambit. When the judges wish to intervene, they know the weapons: get reasons and insist on fuller information. In themselves, these are desirable objectives of a democratic and civilised government; it is therefore regrettable that the judicial record has been so inconsistent and, at times, pusillanimous.[18]

A decision which revealed the spirit of openness among some of the senior judiciary, *Wiley,* was referred to above. The practical application of this decision will have the following effect. Under earlier decisions police complaint investigation documents were protected by a class immunity and a complainant could not see the complaint documents and report since these were protected. The complaint itself was not protected, so the officer complained against could commence a defamation action over the complaint.[19] Where an officer was sued after a complaint, it was common for the officer's counsel to have the statements of the complainant, but not vice versa. Indeed, the chairman of the Police Complaints Authority complained of the unfair use by the police of witnesses' statements to the investigating officer, which the chairman cannot publicise other than in anonymous summary form. The Home Secretary and the police were not so restricted.[20] Now the information will be available although an immunity may cover investigation reports.[1] In this case they should not be used by either side if earlier authorities are followed. The chairman of the Authority has stated that he would like to have powers to make full publication, subject to the legitimate needs of confidentiality.[2] The Police Complaints Authority is covered by FOIA 2000, but the exemptions in sections 30 and 31 would have effect.

The case law on PII is legion and represents one of the most delicate areas of judicial judgment in contemporary law. Out of the abundance, three points can be made briefly. One is that it has been extended to criminal cases which could cause extreme difficulties for the defence. The courts and the Attorney-General have given guidance on such cases.[3]

---

18 Eg *Tameside,* where the minister did not have adequate information to be satisfied that the LEA was acting 'unreasonably', and *R v Secretary of State for the Environment, ex p Hackney LBC.* (1985) 84 LGR 32, CA, where the court held, in refusing to rule as unlawful the rate support grant report, that 'a disclosure of thinking behind the principles of the guidance in the report was not required'.

19 *Conerney v Jacklin* [1985] Crim LR 234, CA.

20 And have used the evidence publicly to discredit complainants. On various notorious cases the closing of ranks has prevented the Police Complaints Authority obtaining essential identity information of officers.

1   See *Wiley* and *Taylor* note 8 above. In which case they should not be available to either side: *Ex p Coventry Newspapers Ltd* [1993] 1 All ER 86 and see *Ex p Wiley* in the Court of Appeal: [1994] 1 All ER 702.

2   See HC 307 (1985–6). See s.98 PACE and restrictions on disclosure of information.

3   (1981) 74 Cr App Rep 302. See *Disclosure* Home Office Cm 2864 (1995) and *R v Ward* [1993] 2 All ER 577; *R v Keane* [1994] 2 All ER 478; *R v Brown (Winston)* [1994] 1 WLR 1599.

Where a defence is jeopardised by PII the prosecution should surely withdraw charges. Nevertheless, the Court of Human Rights has ruled that where the prosecution withheld information from the defence without informing the trial judge, a subsequent review of the evidence by the Court of Appeal in the absence of the defence lawyers did not remedy a breach of Article 6(1) and (3)(a) and (b) ECHR.[4] Scott's recommendation for use of PII certificates in criminal trials was that they should not be used on a class basis to protect information. '[I]f PII class claims are sanctioned, Whitehall departments will inevitably seek to bring within the recognised classes an increasing range of documents. I do not believe that the instinctive Whitehall reaction to seek to withhold Government documents from public inspection is likely to change.' Only a contents claim should be made and if the evidence is relevant and material and may, the court believes, be of assistance to the defence, it should be disclosed. If there is a risk of the public interest being seriously damaged by disclosure, then the trial should be halted. In that respect, Sir Richard did not believe it was correct to talk of a balancing of interests as had previous cases—the public interest of doing justice as against the public interest of protecting public security. Justice demanded the provision of information or the withdrawal of charges.[5] He made recommendations on prosecution procedures including documents held by other departments.

New procedures were introduced by the Criminal Procedure and Investigations Act 1996, Parts I and II along with a code of practice. This Act gives a remarkable discretion to the police as to what is 'relevant' and 'sensitive' material and what is referred to court for disclosure to the defence. Clearly, abuse of the discretion would run the risk of breach of Article 6 under the HRA, but one first has to know that the material exists and what it contains. Here, the FOIA will be of little use, given the exemption in sections 30 and 31 (pp 311-312). Indeed, public authorities generally are likely to view information for which a FOIA disclosure is requested with a view to possible litigation causing them to invoke an exemption.

Secondly, it emerged in Matrix Churchill—and largely from a judgment of Bingham LJ—that ministers were advised by the Attorney-General to sign PII certificates virtually as an automatic response without considering whether such was really required. On the contrary, it is up to the minister to exercise his own judgment. The fact that a judge makes the ultimate decision on disclosure does not absolve the minister of his

---

4   *Rowe and Davis v UK* 2890/95 (2000) 30 EHRR 1 and see *Hugh Jordan v UK* ECtHR 4 May 2001 and breaches of Art 2 where there were inadequate investigations into the shooting of Catholics in Northern Ireland. This included use of PII certificates and inadequate provision of information.
5   HC 115 (1995-6).

duty.[6] Last of all, where national security is impleaded the courts will rarely wish to look behind the minister's appropriately drafted certificate although there must be a residuary discretion in the court.[7]

Sir Richard Scott was critical of the use made by the Attorney-General of PII certificates in his report into the *Matrix Churchill* trial. He was clearly of the view that Ministers must read the certificates for themselves and formulate their own opinion and not simply act as a rubber stamp, an approach which is neither 'necessary nor appropriate'. He followed the judgment of Lord Templeman in *ex p Wiley* to that effect. A court is unlikely to second guess a Minister who believes disclosure should be made which is the advice of Lord Woolf in *ex p Wiley*; one may add if the courts are reluctant to second guess a Minister's decision to release information *a fortiori* is this the case with the opinion of the Attorney-General. In other words, the Minister must exercise judgment before signing and must not be dictated to by another official. Appropriate advice must of course be sought and considered.

Following the Scott report, the Major Government announced that PII would only be claimed in future on a contents basis[8] This was confirmed by the incoming Labour Government.[9] The undertaking would only be binding on Crown bodies including the Crown Prosecution Service. It would not be binding on local government or the police and non Crown public bodies. Furthermore, the undertaking did not prevent class exemptions applying in a profligate manner in the FOIA 2000.

---

6   See Woolf and Jowell *Judicial Review of Administrative Action,* chapter 1 (5th ed 1995). The decision of Bingham LJ was *Makanjuola v Metropolitan Police Comr* [1992] 3 All ER 617, CA. In his report on Matrix Churchill Sir Richard Scott criticised the use by the government of public interest immunity certificates on a class basis in criminal trials. The government did not initially accept this criticism which drew forth further criticism from Sir Richard.

7   *Balfour v FCO* [1994] 2 All ER 588, CA and see Lord Scarman in *Burmah Oil* above. See *McQuillan's* case note 16 p 408 above and questioning of whether national security was at issue or a question of protection of informers. See generally: Simon Brown LJ 'Public Interest Immunity' (1994) Public Law 579.

8   HC Debs., Vol 287 col 949 and HL Debs., Vol 576 col 1507 18 December 1996.

9   HC Debs Vol 297 col 616 11 July 1997.

10 Conclusion—how nigh is the end?

What we know helps to make us what we are. The information we are able to use and build upon constitutes our past, our present and our future. It is small wonder that the protection and dissemination of information has attracted so much political and legal attention, for it is concerned with power and possession, wealth and influence, success and failure. It has as much relevance to the process of government as to our most intimate secrets. Very different kinds of information have been examined in this book. In some areas, for instance protection of private secrets by the law of confidentiality, the courts have generally adopted some sensible approaches in establishing where the protection of a private confidence ends and a public right to know begins. In *X v Y*[1] a newspaper was not justified in publishing confidential information about two doctors who had the Aids virus and which was leaked to the newspapers by employees in the authority. The public interest in this case was best served by maintaining confidentiality and thereby encouraging victims to identify themselves without fear.[2] The case of the murderers of James Bulger was also an occasion where confidentiality was extended to prevent death or injury (see chapter 7 p 333 et seq) On the other hand, the police were justified in giving information about the whereabouts of paedophiles to their temporary landlord which led to the termination of their residential licence (p 422 et seq).[3]

1   [1988] 2 All ER 648. See *Ashworth Hospital Authority v MGN Ltd* [2001] 1 All ER 991, CA.
2   *Re a Company's Application* [1989] Ch 477: blackmail by an ex-employee over confidential information which he threatened to send to FIMBRA; the court was not concerned with motives and it would be wrong to enjoin an employee who had relevant information. See *Mahon v Rahn (No 2)* [2000] 4 All ER 41 (CA). See also *W v Edgell* [1990] Ch 359.
3   *R v Chief Constable of C, ex p A* (2000) Times, 7 November.

The extension by the courts of confidentiality to protect without reservation 'public secrets' in the interlocutory proceedings of the *Spycatcher* case has a less happy aspect in its application, however much the courts declared that they were merely giving fuller articulation to the general principles of the law of confidentiality, and not confusing it with the law of copyright.[4] The progress of the law in this direction until Scott J's judgment in the case in December 1987, was reminiscent of erstwhile judicial attitudes which saw an extension of information about the operations of government as undesirable and unnecessary. The judicial extension protected the 'arcane mysteries' of government which we spoke of in general terms in chapter 1, the development of which we saw in chapter 3 and the contemporary practices of which we explored in chapter 4. The refusal of Scott J and higher courts to protect public secrets by the unmodified principles of equity as developed for private relationships was welcome and the adoption of a test of harm to the 'public interest' before publication will be restrained was doubly welcome. Of course the public interest is a fluid concept and different criteria will apply at interim and final hearings. But at least there is a legitimate expectation that the courts will engage in the balancing exercise. They have now had their position reinforced by HRA s 12 which concerns the grant of interim relief by the court where Art 10 ECHR rights may be affected. Relief should not be granted unless the court is satisfied that the applicant is likely to establish that publication should not be allowed at the full hearing. The wording is emphatic and does not seem to contain a discretion unless the court is so *satisfied*. Damages may be an appropriate remedy. If the court is not satisfied, relief should not be granted. The courts will, however, be sensitive to well-grounded claims of national security or personal danger. In s 12, there are safeguards against the non-representation or attendance of a respondent to prevent abuses of ex parte (one-sided) claims. In the case of material which is journalistic, literary or artistic, the court must have particular regard to the Convention right of freedom of expression and the public interest in publication.

Protection of an individual's confidentiality and privacy are often necessary to protect that individual's integrity and identity. Over-protection of governmental information can be destructive of integrity and identity. Taken to extremes, over-protection will not only prevent more participatory forms of democracy, it can undermine democracy itself. It will prevent the community contributing to meaningful and informed debate. It undermines freedom of speech. So much seems to have been present in the warnings of Lords Bridge and Oliver, Browne-Wilkinson VC and Scott J in the *Spycatcher* litigation. In chapters 1 and 9, it was

---

4   See *Ashdown v Telegraph Group Ltd* [2001] 2 All ER 370 for the limits of defences under the Copyright etc Act 1988 and Art 10 for a breach of copyright which was also a breach of confidence.

seen how courts have sought more recently to ensure that government claims are not abused.[5]

In chapter 5 we examined how government has to give information in order to observe certain democratic promises. Courts have sometimes assisted in a limited fashion in helping litigants to have these promises fulfilled. And it is true that the courts have insisted that private litigants be more open in all stages of litigation to save time and costs a process encouraged by the Civil Procedure Rules 1998. But where information cannot be conceptualised in proprietorial or quasi-proprietorial terms, the courts have traditionally lacked the wherewithal to foster 'communicative competence' between government and governed in the absence of constitutional principles of good and responsible government which they could invoke.[6] It was a matter of some regret that when confronted with leaflets describing the effects of the infamous poll tax which contained significant errors in information, the court refused to rule them unlawful because the errors were not so egregious as to fall foul of the *Wednesbury* test.[7] How far will the FOIA encourage constitutional principles of good and responsible government? As we saw in chapter 6, there are serious weaknesses in FOIA, but on the whole it should be viewed as a force for the good.

Intellectual property rights to genetic information are, it is widely claimed, seriously hindering medical treatment and scientific discovery. How far would the creation of a property right in information protect personal interests which at present are inadequately protected? Imagine that we accepted a legally protected definition of privacy as 'the claim of individuals, groups or institutions to determine for themselves when, how and to what extent information about them is communicated to others.'[8] Would we create more problems than we solved? We would be able to insist that whenever we gave information about ourselves it could only be used for the purposes for which we gave it. Otherwise, information about me cannot be used unless it has come into the public domain through my own choice or my actions. Even if we agreed that there are good grounds for invading privacy where a clear and identifiable public interest exists, eg the prevention of crime or disorder, much investigative journalism as we know it would cease if such a definition were accepted. Thirty years ago the Younger Committee expressed concern that the creation of a

5   See p 137 et seq and 418 and the cases of Tomlinson and Shayler.
6   See the interesting *R v Mid Glamorgan Family Health Services Authority, ex p Martin* [1995] 1 All ER 356 (p 332 above) where a public authority was not given complete discretion *vis à vis* its control of documents on an individual.
7   *R v Secretary of State for the Environment, ex p Greenwich LBC*, [1989] COD 530; see A McGougan (1990) Media Law and Practice 17.
8   AF Westin *Privacy and Freedom* (1967), p 7.

general right of privacy might seriously impede freedom of speech.[9]
Special provisions had to be inserted into the Data Protection Act 1998
to protect press and artistic freedom.[10] At present a non-statutory Press
Complaints Commission, with self-regulatory enforcement powers, hears
complaints from those who feel that journalists have overstepped the
bounds of responsible or acceptable reporting and it applies its code of
conduct. There have been two reports from a government-appointed
inquiry into freedom of the press, a report from the Commons Heritage
Committee and one[11] from the Lord Chancellor's Department on the press
and personal privacy. The general consensus has been for the creation of
a law of privacy—which our courts had not developed[12] although the
HRA 1998 may encourage the development of the law of confidentiality
to something approximating a law of privacy and the case law suggests
such a development[13]—the creation of a statutory ombudsman to
investigate complaints about intrusive journalism, prohibition of bugging
devices and other practices by criminal law,[14] a lay-dominated
Commission, a privacy tribunal and so on. In a public lecture before
demitting office as Master of the Rolls, Sir Thomas Bingham observed
that the judges may have to seize the initiative and develop a law of privacy
protection. This journey may have begun. The incorporation of the ECHR
and in particular Arts 8 and 10, will facilitate the development of a privacy
right and a free expression right as common law principles affecting
citizen state relations as well as relations between individuals. A
fundamental common law right of free expression has already been
recognised, although 'fundamental' must cede to doctrines of sovereignty.
By virtue of s 6 HRA, the courts are duty bound to act in accordance with
the Convention. Those who deny that the incorporation can affect private
relationships seem to be defying the principles of the Convention as part
of our law, there to assist in the development and interpretation of our
law, both statutory and common law. The Convention does not have to
be directly, horizontally effective to produce such an effect.[15] Article 8,

9   Cmnd 5012 (1972) para 42.
10   DPA 1998, ss 3 and 32.
11   Cm 2918 *Privacy and Media Intrusion* Press Complaints Commission 17 July
     1995.
12   *Kaye v Robertson* [1991] FSR 62 and *R v BCC, ex p Granada TV* [1995] 7 LS
     Gaz R 36; Gardiner (1995) NLJ, 17 February. See *Earl Spencer v UK* (1998) 25
     EHRR CD 105 where a claim by Earl Spencer for a breach of Art 8 was ruled
     inadmissible because domestic remedies had not been exhausted, viz those under
     the law of confidentiality.
13   See *Douglas and Zeta Jones v Hello! Ltd* [2001] 2 All ER 289, CA.
14   See Police Act 1997, Part III and Regulation of Investigatory Powers Act 2000,
     above chapter 1.
15   The leading protagonist against the incorporation of the Convention affecting
     private relationships is Sir R Buxton (2000) 116 LQR 48. In opposing him and
     arguing that it has such an effect, that it is horizontally effective, see Sir W Wade

it will be recalled, proclaims the right of *everyone* to respect for his private and family life, his home and his correspondence. Article 8(2) sets out the provisos for interference by the *state* (public authority) which is prescribed by law and necessary in a democratic society to protect a variety of legitimate interests.

The Press Complaints Commission is now lay dominated and it has strengthened its code. In 1994, a privacy commissioner to deal with complaints was appointed. This was Lord Wakeham a former minister in Mrs Thatcher's Government who has been widely regarded as very successful in the position. Unlike broadcasting, where there is a statutory watchdog and complaints body (see chapter 4 p 202 et seq), the press is self-regulatory and in July 1995 the Government accepted that self-regulation should continue with a 'toughened up' version of the code and a hot line between the chairman of the Commission and editors to try and avoid breaches. The latest version of the Code is that of 1 December 1999. The Code sets the bench-mark for the 'highest professional and ethical standards' which 'all members of the press have a duty to maintain.' It states that the public interest includes 'detecting or exposing crime or a serious misdemeanour; protecting public health and safety; preventing the public from being misled by some statement or action of an individual or organisation.' The Code covers: accuracy, opportunity to reply, privacy, harassment, intrusion into grief or shock, children, children in sex cases, listening devices, hospitals, reporting a crime, misrepresentation, victims of sexual assault, discrimination, financial journalism, confidential sources and payment for articles; the areas in other words which have caused repeated concern. The Commission should pay compensation from an industry fund to victims of intrusive reporting. There would be no new criminal offences and no law of privacy – although this last point is under the judicial agenda.[16]

Many who are forthright in their support of a free and independent press are equally critical of an irresponsible press. The English courts have not, for instance, accepted the approach to defamation of public figures that has been accepted in the USA and Australia – that a false statement made about an individual in public life is not actionable unless published knowing it was false or where the publisher was reckless as to its false nature.[17] The House of Lords has provided a series of tests to be satisfied

---

(2000) 116 LQR 217. My preferred position is that explained in M Hunt (1998) Public Law 423. See Lord Lester and D Pannick *Human Rights Law and Practice* (1999) pp 31-2: Section 6 [HRA] will apply 'because the state (acting through its courts) is obliged, under the Convention, to protect individuals against breaches of their rights...' including those perpetrated by individuals.

16 Press Complaints Commission *Privacy and Media Intrusion* Cm 2918 (1995). See, incidentally, *Bartnicki v Voepper* US Sup Ct 21 May 2001.

17 *New York Times v Sullivan* 376 US 254 (1964); *Lange v Australian Broadcasting Corp* (1997) 145 ALR 96.

before a defamation will be protected by qualified privilege – and these are demanding — and rejected the defence of 'political privilege'.[18] Where the publication is false but not actionable, should newspapers be compelled to publish a statement of inaccuracy? Where the Press Complaints Commission criticise a publication under one of the headings in the Code, the publisher must print its adjudication in 'full and with due prominence'. Making information about oneself a property right could create enormous restrictions on our freedom of speech. Abusive invasions of privacy are probably best settled by responsible self-regulation in the absence of a breach of private law, although the Government belief until fairly recently that no legislative support to protect privacy was necessary has been overtaken by the HRA.[19] Once again s 12 HRA will be available to protect freedom of publication unless the person seeking relief establishes to the court's satisfaction that publication should not be allowed and in addition to the matters referred to above, regard has to be had by the court to any relevant privacy code such as that of the press. Damages after publication may be adequate. They may not. Particular regard must also be had to Art 10 and freedom of expression and the journalistic, literary or artistic material involved and the court must regard the extent to which material has, or is about to become, publicly available or whether it would be in the public interest to publish it.

Even in those jurisdictions where privacy laws do apply, as in the USA, the courts have ruled, for instance that random employee urinalysis tests for drugs were not against the fourth amendment.[20] Employees are subject to increasing tests for drug or alcohol dependency and psychological and genetic testing to assess suitability for employment. In the ECHR Art 8 protecting privacy has been somewhat circumscribed in the area of national security.[1] A more general feature of modern government and society concerns the enormous powers of the state and its officials to demand information from individuals or companies in an ever-growing web of statutory compulsion which impinges on rights not to incriminate oneself

18 *Reynolds v Times Newspapers Ltd* [1999] 4 All ER 609, HL. In New Zealand, *Reynolds* has not been followed and qualified privilege could attach to political statements: *Lange v Atkinson* (2000) 8 BHRC 500 (CA NZ). See *Loutchansky v Times Newspapers Ltd* [2001] NLJ 643, CA.

19 In *Douglas and Zeta Jones* above an injunction was not awarded. See *Imutran v Uncaged Campaigns Ltd* [2001] 2 All ER 385 – HRA s 12 has only marginally shifted the balance in favour of publication. This seems to ignore the clear wording of s 12.

20 *Skinner v REA* 109 S Ct 1402 (1989); *NTEU v Von Raab* 109 S Ct 1384 (1989).

1   *Hewitt and Harman v UK* (1992) 14 EHRR 657 stated that holding files by MI5 on applicants was 'necessary in a democratic society' in spite of earlier ruling by the Court that such a holding was against the ECHR. In proceedings before the High Court Simon Brown LJ and Kennedy J refused to review the decision of the service though see note 16 p 381 above. See I Cameron *National Security and the European Convention of Human Rights* (2000).

or which sets ever-increasing limits to be 'let alone'. There have been significant differences between the domestic courts and EU courts and the Court of Human Rights in this field.[2] As we saw in chapter 7, the compulsory publication or notification of convictions and other matters has been permitted in order to vet those applying for jobs where there will be contact with children and vulnerable assets (see pp 335-336).[3]

Allowing others to determine exclusively the means by which they collect, use or disseminate information gives them the greatest of managerial prerogatives. As with all prerogatives, they are potentially inimical to shared responsibility, accountability and democratic values. Certain anaemic statutory provisions on disclosure cover national and multinational companies, but otherwise they are regarded as private commercial enterprises with a variety of somewhat exiguous duties[4] to actual or prospective creditors and shareholders[5] but few to the public at large other than on charitable or political donations. Information is published voluntarily on companies' environmental performance and 79 of the FTSE 100 companies produced an environmental report in 1996 although much of the information was not independently audited.[6] Where information supplied by companies to government bodies concerns commercial or industrial confidentiality or intellectual property rights, a House of Lords Committee has found that claims for confidentiality are routine.[7] Information supplied voluntarily by companies is subject to a mandatory exemption on access under the Environmental Information Regulations.

The Bill on a Right To Know—basically a FOIA—presented to the Commons by Mark Fisher in 1992 did have a section which would have made companies report on a series of items connected with wrongdoing, fatalities, court or other orders issued against them relating to safety,

---

2   See *Saunders v UK* (1997) 23 EHRR 313; see the decision of the ECJ *Mannesmannrohen-Werke v EU Commission* (2001) Financial Times: 21 January 2001: companies can be compelled to answer factual questions by the Commission; and note the growing number of statutes on compulsory disclosure of information and evidence.

3   Protection of Children Act 1999 and Care Standards Act 2000.

4   See eg Companies Act 1985, ss .366–383 on meetings and Financial Services Act 1986, Part I, chapter V and Part VII (see now Financial Services and Markets Act 2000), on conduct of business and insider dealing in the financial services sector, and Company Securities (Insider Dealing) Act 1985. Note the 'fair disclosure' regulation in the USA which seeks to ensure that ordinary shareholders gain access to information from companies on the same favourable terms as financial analysts working for major financial institutions: *Financial Times* 22 November 2000.

5   The duties relate to registers, accounts and reports.

6   See JE Parkinson chapter 17 in D Campbell and ND Lewis (eds), *Promoting Participation: Law or Politics?* (1999).

7   HL 9 (1996-97).

environmental and other concerns. These provisions did not make their way into the FOIA 2000. The benefits of 'efficient' and closed management of public institutions were seen when water authorities in the lead up to privatisation, were no longer caught by the Public Bodies (Access to Meetings) Act and their meetings were withdrawn from the public. This was justified by the responsible minister on the grounds that water authorities were no longer operating like public corporations, but more like private companies under the Companies Act, with executive and business responsibilities. This is the position *a fortiori* after privatisation. In the NHS, the boards of NHS Trusts only have to meet once a year and these provisions are generally treated in a somewhat desultory fashion.[8] Consumer committees in both the water and rail transport industries have to be open to the public, subject to various exemptions. The true democratic nature of much of our public affairs may be weak, but privatisation runs the risk of diminishing it further. Openness at all costs can lead to indecision and folly. Efficiency at all costs, without any balancing values such as openness, can lead to tyranny. Readers will recall that the extraordinary coverage of FOIA makes it particularly distinct in FOIA regimes because of the inclusion of many private bodies who are performing public tasks. It does not, however, provide an open meetings law like the laws in the USA (p 73 et seq).

Trade unions have often complained about the inadequate nature of information from managements employing their members concerning management proposals for future developments affecting the company and employees. The British tradition has seen a voluntarist, 'soft law' and non existent[9] approach, one which has meant that management most of the time is afforded enormous latitude. Since our entry into the EC, an increasing number of directives have sought to create the machinery for consultation and participation in commercial enterprises, as well as providing information in advance of decisions.[10] The Directive 94/45/EC on Works Councils attempted to achieve an effective and genuine flow of information from employers to employees, although 'sensitive information' as defined need not be disclosed. Confidential information should go no further than the employee representatives. There was nothing of significance to prevent the information being slanted in the employer's favour, and the provisions were watered down at the request of the European Parliament before the draft directive fell. The British provisions that did exist on employee involvement have been largely ineffectual.[11]

8   On NHS Trusts see Nolan Cm 2850 I, chapter 4.
9   Ie wide exhortatory provisions affording maximum opportunity for self-created standards: Employment Act 1982, s 1; Employment Protection Act 1975, s 99; Health and Safety at Work etc Act 1974, s 2(4) and (6); Transfer of Undertakings Regulations 1981, reg 10, etc. See now Employment Relations Act 1999.
10 See C Docksey (1986) MLR 281 for a full account.
11 Ibid.

The draft directive only applied to groups or undertakings employing 1,000 or more employees, and was only to exist in such groups where employee representatives were recognised for bargaining purposes and were certified as independent, ie a trade union. Participation based on employee share ownership is more popular, as a limited democracy based upon a property stake is acceptable whereas a democracy based on notions relating to human dignity and respect for individuals because they are individuals is a more difficult proposition. As is well known, the British Government elected to opt out of the Social Chapter of the Treaty of European Union at Maastricht but after the Labour Government electoral victory in 1997, the UK government signed up to the Social Chapter. The 1994 Directive was implemented in 1999.[12]

Closely related to managerial confidences are professional confidences. We have looked at these in the course of the book.[13] Through control of information, the professions can enhance their monopoly of domination, regulation and practice as well as their position *vis-à-vis* the communities they serve. The Law Society has, since October 1986, opened its meetings to its membership and has given limited press access to its meetings.[19] These seem likely to deal with the most routine and uncontentious items of business. The concession came at a time when solicitors through the Law Society reluctantly accepted a more 'independent' element in their client complaints procedures which have now seen the introduction of a Legal Services Ombudsman. In 1994, the Law Society opened its disciplinary hearings to the press and public. The Bar refuses to open up its disciplinary proceedings. As was noted in chapter 5, accountants have been pressurised by the Government to reveal information to the Bank of England, and now to the Financial Services Authority thereby breaking the confidentiality which they owe to their clients.[14] To seek a breach of similar confidence for lawyers would interfere with legal professional privilege. The compliance of the accountants' governing bodies ensured that the Government did not initially impose the duty by legislation, but by a voluntary self-regulatory code. This proved to be too weak and provisions are now contained in the Financial Services and Markets Act 2000.[15] Further spin-offs would see a far closer

12 SI 1999/3323.
13 Eg chapter 4 above, p 218 *et seq* and chapter 5, p 276 *et seq*. For the duty of confidentiality owed by a bank to its customers, see *Tournier v National Provincial Bank etc* [1924] 1 KB 461 and *Bank of Tokyo v Karoon* [1986] 3 All ER 468 and *Robertson v Canadian Imperial Bank of Commerce* [1995] 1 All ER 824, PC; *Christofi v Barclays Bank plc* [2000] 1 WLR 937, CA; see also *Barclays Bank plc v Taylor* [1989] 3 All ER 563 and Police and Criminal Evidence Act 1984, s 9(1) and Sch 1 and *Bank of Scotland v A* [2001] 1 WLR 751.
14 The Accounting Standards Committee is not open to the public, but follows 'notice and comment procedures'. See Financial Services and Markets Act 2000, Part XXII.
15 Ch 5 p 275 et seq above.

relationship between the profession and the state, as exists on the continent.[16]

The medical profession is probably under attack more than any other over its secretive administration. A complex web of arguments envelops this profession. Firstly, people do want greater access to those medical files that their doctor or health authority holds on them. Doctors' associations[17] claimed that if patients were allowed access to files, and if independent inquiries were conducted into medical practice, these developments would only encourage those who were hell-bent on litigation.[18] The Data Protection Act 1998 now covers such files with exemptions. Confidentiality helps to protect the professional status of doctors. This remains a major issue. The Access to Health Records Act 1990 was passed at a time when the medical profession and its relationship with government was at its lowest ebb for many years and in the changing managerial ethos of the health service where professional ethics were seen as an obstacle to efficiency drives the profession managed to extract from the Government few of the concessions which the legal profession, especially the Bar, did.[19] In health administration, the pressing issues feature the residue of largely unaccountable managerialism and professional power, as illustrated in repeated scandals, most recently in the case of the use of children's body parts without consent at Alder Hey hospital.[20]

Government and information

As a general premise, the law should only protect government information where a risk of a breach of national security is clearly established, where the safety of an individual would be compromised or where a clear and present danger would exist to an identifiable public interest by disclosure, such as economic or financial security, or where there would be an unjustifiable invasion of an individual's privacy or their legal rights.

16 The Companies Act 1989 made the Institute of Chartered Accountants the validating body for the profession. See Part III of that Act on investigation and information gathering powers of the authorities.

17 The British Medical Association. The Royal College of Nursing adopted a more relaxed attitude to change.

18 A grievance procedure for complaints of clinical judgment was agreed to, providing those cases which may go to litigation are weeded out: (DHSS) HC Circ (81) 5 and Hospital Complaints Act 1985 and Health Authorities Act 1995 and a new procedure was introduced in 1996. See S Kerrison and A Pollock (2001) Public Law 115.

19 Courts and Legal Services Act 1990 and Rozenberg *The Search for Justice,* chapter 3.

20 Report of Michael Redfern QC into Alder Hey Hospital, 30 January 2001.

'National security' requires clearer definition than we possess at present even, though no less a figure than Lord Lloyd has suggested that the phrase is not capable of definition but must always be shaped to differing contexts.[1] The ability of government to abuse information is limitless. The Matrix Churchill and the BSE sagas speak for themselves.

FOI or Right to Know Bill 1993

The interesting point about FOI bills presented by the Opposition to Parliament in John Major's premiership was that they had the support of today's political leadership and they were far more radical than FOIA 2000. Indexes were a legal requirement, for instance. This was not a feature of FOIA 2000. In fact, one benefit of a FOIA, believed Sir Douglas Wass, former Head of the Civil Service, was that it would force departments and agencies to attend to efficient record-keeping. This generally, he believed, was chaotic. The Public Records Office had attempted to produce some order in departments in respect to record-keeping. Greater efficiency in file-keeping had been one of the benefits of the open government policy adopted by some local authorities, eg Bradford city before the 1985 legislation affected local authorities. It was observed in chapter 6 that the introduction of FOIA 2000 is reportedly delayed until July 2002 because 'thousand of files' are missing.[2] Rights of individual access are unlikely to arise until 2004.

Under the 1993 Bill, the information commissioner was able to take up a complaint on his/her own initiation and may inspect exempt information regardless of a complaint. This could have been an effective way of ensuring efficient record keeping to facilitate public access. Unlike the position in Australia, New Zealand and under UK FOIA 2000, a minister was not given a power of veto but clearly right to appeal to the tribunal and judicial review would be open to ministers to attempt to withhold documents and information. It was expressly provided that the burden of proof before the Tribunal was upon the authority except where it relates to the competitive position of a third party who will then have to discharge the burden. Costs usually were to be borne by each party except where a party has behaved vexatiously or where a matter of important principle had been raised. In the latter case the authority pay the costs. In this earlier model, the Tribunal was modelled on the Data Protection Tribunal. 'It is likely that a large part of the Tribunal's work will involve *ex parte* representation, and hearings and deliberations *in camera*' it was stated in relation to an earlier prototype of the Tribunal. The length of time needed to process appeals would made it likely that

1   Norton Taylor in R Blackburn and R Plant *Constitutional Reform* (1999).
2   *The Guardian* 7 March 2001.

the Tribunal's emphasis was be on establishing precedents rather than resolving individual disputes. The commissioner was able to present cases before the Tribunal – a role expressly ruled out in FOIA 2000 – and it could see whatever documents it wished.

Several possible roles for the commissioner have been suggested over the last fifteen or so years: for instance that of overseer of public records and their administration; or auditor of a department's practice in providing access to information, especially where there are going to be highly variable workloads on departments and sections within departments and public authorities as under FOIA 2000. The Information Commissioner under the 2000 Act may advise departments but only where they invite her to do so. A final suggested role had been that of constitutional arbiter between ministers and civil servants in cases involving a serious difference of opinion or crisis of conscience, although this would be a role requiring a sensitive touch. It was not an outcome of deliberations between the Government and the Nolan Committee and its successor. The Public Interest Disclosure Act 1998 provides some safety valves for such matters but otherwise civil servants must be content with internal ventilation.

The 1993 Bill provided a replacement of the 1989 Official Secrets Act. This was singularly missing from the FOIA 2000. Many claim that the 1989 Act is now ready for pensioning off – like s 2 of the 1911 Act before it. This 1993 Bill sought to safeguard 'protected information' where unauthorised disclosure would do 'serious damage' to the interests of the UK. A public interest defence was provided to those who have disclosed protected information in contravention of the Act where they can prove that there was reasonable evidence that the material related to significant

(a) abuse of authority or neglect in official duty;

(b) injustice to an individual;

(c) individual or public danger to health and safety;

(d) unauthorised use of public funds; or

(e) other misconduct.

A civil servant would have to use internal procedures to ventilate a concern unless they proved useless or it was a matter of great urgency. There was also a defence that the information had become publicly available whether in the UK or elsewhere before the time of disclosure. Unlike earlier versions of the public interest defence civil servants did not appear to be entitled to go to select committees before exhausting internal procedures though clearly much is left to judgement. It is vital therefore that in any future bill reforming the OSA, these terms are left for the interpretation of juries, and not judges as the 1993 Bill sought to achieve, and certainly not the executive although offences are triable either way. The onus of establishing a defence will be on the defendant. The Public Interest Disclosure Act protects a civil servant from civil or administrative recriminations where they disclose information in accordance with that Act. It is well to remember that there are many employees who are not protected by that Act as was seen in chapter 4 (p 192). These will include security and intelligence officers as well as the police. The Act does not prevent a criminal prosecution where a disclosure is damaging and was unauthorised nor is such a disclosure (eg in breach of the OSA) protected under the Act. There are many who claim that the trial of former security officer David Shayler for offences under s 1 of the OSA will lead to the end of the 1989 Act as we know it and that the Act breaches the ECHR Art 10. The Law Lords have approved an absolute rule of secrecy for such officers albeit in the context of civil proceedings and where an account of profits was sought for wrongful publication.[3] The Act will remain because the respectable body of opinion going back to Franks in 1972 has expressed the view that there is a role for the criminal law to punish wrongful disclosure outside the area of espionage. That is not disputed. The role of the law should be to punish breaches causing serious damage where there is no public interest in disclosure.

The Public Interest Disclosure Act 1998 has improved the very unclear situation in which employees were placed where they disclosed wrongdoing. Although a disclosure might have been in the public interest, this would not prevent an employee being disciplined or dismissed. All studies showed that whistleblowers tended to end up badly disadvantaged as a consequence of their publicly spirited acts.[4] The nature of confidentiality flowing from an employment contract may well have justified a dismissal pre-empting any right to damages against an employer before the 1998 Act.[5]

> [T]his is a perfectly simple, straightforward case of a man bound by a contract to behave towards his employer with the same degree of confidence and trust as he is entitled to expect of them . . . the real gravamen of the employer's complaint which they found to be thoroughly reasonable and justifiable was that by sending the letter to *The Guardian* . . . he was in breach of trust to his employers.[6]

Civil servants do not, as of writing, have a contract of employment enforceable through the courts although the Government created a contractual status by legislation for limited purposes and rights akin to contractual ones have been acknowledged. Civil servants were under a contractual duty to provide information for the Scott inquiry. They do

3   *A-G v Blake* [2000] 4 All ER 385.
4   Y Cripps *Disclosure in the Public Interest* (2nd ed, 1994).
5   See HC 100 (1986–7).
6   *The Guardian* 24 April 1993. See now the revised Civil Service Code at p 186 et seq above.

have the protection of unfair dismissal legislation,[7] and certain public law rights.[8] They now have their position fortified by the Public Interest Disclosure Act. Nothing, however, will remove the taint of the 'beastly sneak' from such actions in the eyes of managers and employers. In reality, there will be no working relationship where those in the wrong are still in positions of power and trust over those who have disclosed in the public interest. Furthermore, where a whistleblower gives information to the press for reward, this will not be covered by the 1998 Act and the courts may not be sympathetic to the discloser in refusing to protect his identity under s 10 Contempt of Court Act 1981.[9]

An interesting provision was the clause in the 1993 Bill which requires an authority to grant access to documents containing exempt information where there was reasonable evidence of significant abuse of public office, misuse of public funds, danger to public health, individual safety or the environment, and where such public interest clearly outweighed any countervailing argument for secrecy or privacy. No such provision as this could be passed in the American FOIA. The UK FOIA has a public interest override but that does not apply to 'absolute exemptions' and nor does it apply to excluded information held by security and intelligence services.

Cost and utility of FOIA

How much will the Act cost to operate? In 1989, UK Government publicity services cost £200 million.[10] I have looked in chapters 1, 2 and 5 at the cost factor. The most commonly expressed apprehensions concern the enormous cost in financial terms of indexing, filing and systematising record holdings. Some estimates have said that FOIA will cover up to 70,000 bodies. There will then be the vast numbers of applications to be processed. The breadth of FOIA should not be forgotten. The debates on the Access to Personal Information Act rehearsed these arguments. The minister emphasised the numbers of manual files on individuals and expressed his concern over workload. We looked at cost figures for the American FOIA in chapter 2. In Australia, it is reported that there are about 30,000 requests for information pa – 90% of these cover personal

---

7   See Part V of Employment Protection (Consolidation) Act 1978, as amended.
8   *Council of Civil Servants Unions v Minister for Civil Service* [1984] 3 All ER 935, HL; *R v Secretary of State for the Home Department, ex p Benwell* [1985] QB 554; *R v Civil Service Appeal Board, ex p Bruce* [1988] ICR 649; *R v Chief Constable of Devon and Cornwall, ex p Hay* [1996] 2 All ER 711 at 724 d-g.
9   Above p 361 et seq.
10 The circular accompanying the Local Government (Access To Information) Act 1985 envisaged that the Act would involve no additional expenditure for local authorities.

records.[11] In Canada there are about 10,000 requests pa under the Access to Information Act.[12] Based on Canadian and Australian experience, the 1993 White Paper estimated the number of applications at 50,000-100,000 in the UK under the 1994 Code, a figure which dramatically over-estimated the actual use but these would not include DPA requests (see chapter 5).

What might we expect from FOIA? The operation of such laws was examined in chapter 2. However, the following provide interesting examples.

In the USA a tax analyst obtained previously undisclosed tax rulings issued by the Internal Revenue Service in response to letters from individuals and corporations. Congress changed the law to ensure that such rulings were published. A company used the Act to show that a competitor had used false information to secure a contract from a government department. It has been used by Honeywell Information Systems to obtain details of the Department of Defense's procurement regulations. New Mexico used the Act to obtain details of the federal government's compliance with environmental regulations applying to the disposal of nuclear waste in the state. A pharmaceutical industry trade body regularly uses FOIA to request copies of enforcement decisions of FDA inspectors. These are published by the industry in a newsletter as a guide to standards currently being required and as a check on arbitrary decisions—but it is only published internally *vis-à-vis* the industry. FOIA had shown that defence contractors were trying to claim entertainment expenses on procuring contracts from the federal government.[13] Under the US FOIA 1996, there is an emphasis on proactive disclosure of information which is likely to be widely sought or which has been the subject of two requests. This builds on earlier provisions.[14]

The whole point is that allowing government to be conducted in secrecy and darkness is destructive of effective accountability, of meaningful democracy and ultimately of effectiveness itself. We simply won't know how to test effectiveness. Our security and our national security are dependent upon us knowing what lies behind government actions and decisions. With this in mind, let us examine some problems with FOIA 2000.

---

11 Terrill in A McDonald and G Terrill (eds) *Open Government: Freedom of Information and Privacy* (1998).

12 Gillis ibid.

13 I am grateful to Maurice Frankel for this information. The FOIA was also used to obtain papers showing that Ronald Reagan narrowly escaped criminal indictment for his role in assisting the monopoly control of the US entertainment industry by the Musical Corporation of America: *The Guardian*, 13 January 1987.

14 See overseas examples in HC 398 I (1997-98) p xi.

Particular difficulties

Exemption of policy advice

The Act has many important and useful aspects. But it also has serious drawbacks. One of these concerns the exemption for the policy-making process and advice and disclosures which are prejudicial to the effective conduct of public affairs under FOIA s 35, which covers central government, and s 36 which covers public bodies generally. The policy advice exemption has a long history. The unacceptably wide remit of these sections was discussed in chapter 6 (above p 312 et seq).

Civil service organisations have generally welcomed the FOI proposals. But they have insisted on an exemption for policy advice: 'information in the nature of, or relating to, opinion or advice or recommendation tended [*sic*] by any person in the course of his official duties for the purpose of the formulation of policy within a department or authority to which this Act applies' said an earlier proposal. The First Division Association (FDA), representing leading civil servants, justified this exemption in the following terms:

> that while the Association wished to enhance the quality of public debate by better informing the public about government operations by timely provision of factual material, policy-making in a goldfish bowl was not to be welcomed.

The FDA has been adamant that identification of individuals will lower the quality of decision-making and could frequently have an adverse effect on the career prospects of the individuals concerned. Identification would cause civil servants to be more compliant with the wishes of ministers, rather than offering independent advice, since they would not wish to be publicly out of step with their ministers. They may be subject to retribution by an incoming government of a different political persuasion where their identity in giving advice can be established. But this is precisely the charge that is made against various senior civil servants today: that they are not sufficiently independent in their advice, they are the PM's people and the present conditions of anonymity help to conceal this. In Canada, policy advice, although it has wide protection, is not totally exempt, and the consequences so far have not undermined officials' neutrality or efficacy.[15] In other countries, a distinction has been drawn between the deliberative process of decision-making and the post-

15   See chapter 2 above, p 81 *et seq*. It does not exempt reasons for decisions affecting an individual's rights, or policy advice from outside consultants/advisers. See the evidence of the FDA to the Public Service Committee on *Ministerial Accountability and Responsibility* HC 313(i) 1995-6.

decision stage. In New Zealand, an exemption protects the confidentiality of advice tendered by ministers and officials and the 'free and frank expression of opinions' *unless* the public interest in knowing outweighs the confidentiality. It seeks to protect officials from improper pressure, it requires an objective test of harm and withholding information has to be *necessary*. The Campaign for FOI have also accepted that this is the world of *real politique* and no government would accept such access without at least a qualification such as in the New Zealand Act. UK governments are less liberal. Under the FOIA 2000, s 35 is subject to a public interest override.

But there is an inconsistency between this provision and statements in the White Paper *Modernising Government* where the Prime Minister spoke of widespread consultation with those outside government as early as possible in the policy-making process (see p 312 et seq above).

The Act states that statistical information is not exempt once a decision as to governmental policy is taken and in so far as the information was used to provide an informed background to the taking of the decision. Where information is not so used, it will be exempt unless it could be argued that in not being used it was not covered by s 35. It was not a part of the policy-making process. Furthermore, under the section, when making a decision on the public interest under s 2, 'regard shall be had to the particular interest in the disclosure of factual information which has been used, or which is intended to be used, to provide an informed background to decision-taking.' The statistics only come after the decision whereas factual information may come before or after the decision. In previous bills, this has included statistical data and test results; analysis, interpretation or evaluation of, or any projection based on, factual information, expert advice on a scientific technical, medical, financial, statistical, legal or other matter other than that protected by legal professional privilege. Overseas examples of information that cannot be withheld under such provisions include feasibility studies, plans and budgetary estimates, efficiency studies, environment impact studies, advice from consultants under contract.[16]

Advice would be caught by s 36 where in the reasonable opinion of a qualified person disclosure would or would be likely to inhibit the free and frank provision of advice, or the free and frank exchange of views for the purpose of deliberation or 'would otherwise prejudice, or would be likely to prejudice, the effective conduct of public affairs.' This latter formulation would cover infinitely more than control over timing of disclosures of information which is a matter of understandable protection. Early release could be damaging to legitimate interests of good government. But the blanket exemption of policy advice even after a

16 Campaign for FOI *FOI Bill Briefing No 3.*

decision is finished and operative, and even in anonymous form, is disappointing. In the reforms in local government it was seen how policy alternatives were to be disclosed. Such alternatives will be covered by these two sections. They are not absolute exemptions and are subject to the public interest test (although both Houses of Parliament are given an absolute exemption under s 36).

The First Division Association, the senior civil servants' trade union, have justified the exemption in terms which are redolent of Sir Robert Armstrong's memorandum upholding the confidentiality of the relationship between ministers and their servants. A FOIA's prime interest must surely be in facts and reliable information. Policy advice and alternatives to proposals must be open in order to inform and improve public debate, unless publicity would harm the proposal to such an extent that its purpose would be defeated *and* the public interest thereby injured. This is a question of the timing of release to avoid the defeat or frustration of legitimate plans. The question of identity of an internal adviser should not be fundamental,[17] unless an individual possesses the necessary information which will assist an inquiry into government practice. At that point the veil of confidentiality needs to be broken, and a select committee is the appropriate body to investigate. In the nature of government such matters are likely to involve an abuse of power, a breach of governmental trust, an untruth or high-handed exercise of public power. Only rarely are these matters of governmental right susceptible to legal examination before a court of law.[18]

The policy and advice exemptions under ss 35 and 36 go too far and constitute a weakness in spite of their own provisos. Once a decision is made, although it has been authoritatively stated that policy is a 'protean' concept,[19] then what should be missing is the name of the advice giver alone where s/he is a civil servant. As the exemption stands, it protects not only the identity, but also the content. It should be noted that the exemption applies to 'advice'. Presumably an advisory committee's report would be protected. What of an 'outside adviser' who is not a Crown servant? If formally commissioned, are they engaged in official duties? It would appear so.

These exemptions ultimately affect and belittle a right to freedom of expression – the basic right in democracy. If we lack the means effectively to criticise policy, then our criticism is of little or no consequence. Our position as citizens is to that serious extent undermined.

17 Both major parties claim that governments have made an issue of personalities by promoting 'like-minded' civil servants with whom they would not be able to work and whose identities they already know. There has been increased resort to special advisers who are not civil servants: HC 297 (2000-01).

18 See the former Civil Service Department's booklet, *Legal Entitlements and Administrative Practices* (HMSO 1979).

19 Nb *Bushell's* case, chapter 9 above, p 433 et seq per Lord Diplock.

Government contractors

We saw how the FOIA applies to a very wide range of bodies. To what extent will it apply to those carrying out public functions or public services under contract? Such bodies may well be designated by the minister for the purposes of the Act. They will then have to disclose information in accordance with the Act's provisions and its exemptions. The commercial interests and trade secrets exemption under s 43 are likely to feature widely here. These bodies may only be designated for certain purposes so that FOIA will only apply to such purposes. The public might be interested in the terms of the contract, payments and any special features. What unfavourable terms allocating risk have been saddled on the public authority? Under public private partnerships, for instance, it was envisaged that contracts should be awarded under the negotiated procedure (the most restrictive or least open) under the European Directives on Public Procurement as implemented. Any other award would be the strongest indication that this was not a PPP arrangement.

Designation could become a weapon of traditional secrecy in so far as it may be used as a threat by an authority to comply with its wishes. A very powerful contractor may insist that it is not designated and as many terms as possible remain confidential. Designation will be subject to judicial review.

Section 45 refers to the code of practice making provisions relating to the inclusion of terms in contracts entered into by public authorities covering access to information. Will duties exist on such contractors, ie companies, to provide information? Under the 1994 Code, as revised, they were under such a duty because they were within the terms of the 1967 Parliamentary Commissioner for Administration Act which governed the operation of the Code where contractors performed services for the public. The public service aspect might attract a complaint of maladministration. Arrangements will have to be made as between the department and contractor as to who should disclose the information and how. Section 75 and Sch 15 of the Deregulation and Contracting Act 1994 allow restricted or confidential information to be handed to contractors on terms that they give it the protection owed by ministers and civil servants. This will be implied by the contract as a matter of law. Nothing should require the disclosure of commercially confidential information except a greater public interest.

Where services are provided to government, there may well be considerations of intellectual property, commercial confidentiality or management and negotiating positions requiring confidentiality. The Guidance on the 1994 Code stated that disclosure under the Code will have to be decided on a case-by-case basis. This is a situation that ought to be covered clearly by contractual provisions relating to property rights in information or reports and confidentiality.

While the tendency in the law and practice has been to introduce greater openness and transparency into the tendering process, some of these tendencies have been driven by EC requirements implemented into our law, the general position relating to genuine commercial confidences of tenderers and contractors will be maintained. The *Guidance* on the Code on Access stated that the following should be disclosed:
- the identity of the successful tenderer;
- the nature of the job, service or goods to be supplied;
- the performance standards set (which should be output based);
- the criteria for award of contract; and
- the winning tender price or range of prices (maximum/minimum) paid.

The draft Code on FOIA 2000 Part V deals with contracts and states that confidentiality should not be guaranteed by a department where information is not confidential. Public authorities may be put under pressure to keep confidential the terms of a contract, its value and its performance. Wherever commercially viable, says the code on FOIA, public authorities should endeavour to obtain agreement that confidentiality should not protect such information. Under this lame provision, there is no guarantee that such information will be provided. Except where the contractor is designated, the duty of disclosure falls on the public authority. One should not overlook the public interest in disclosure where items of fraud, waste or mismanagement occur and the terms of the Public Interest Disclosure Act (above).

In Australia, contractors with public undertakings — who were supplying natural gas to public utilities — have been equiparated to public bodies, so a less demanding test of 'public confidentiality'[20] protected their 'commercially sensitive information' where it was requested outside an arbitration hearing for which the information was prepared:

> 'Why should the consumers and the public of Victoria be denied knowledge of what happens in these arbitrations, the outcome of which will affect, in all probability, the prices chargeable to consumers by the public utilities.'[1]

Third party challenges

Very frequently, parties who supply information to departments or agencies will want to be reassured that any confidential or commercially

---

20 See *Commonwealth of Australia v John Fairfax & Sons Ltd* (1980) 147 CLR 39 p 420 above.

1   *Esso Australia Resources Ltd v Plowman* (1995) 183 CLR 10 per Mason CJ at 32.

sensitive information will not be disclosed without that party being informed and having a right to challenge that department's decision if in favour of disclosure. The Government resisted calls to provide a third party procedure to facilitate challenge of decisions. Such a procedure was recommended by the Commons Select Committee on Public Administration. The Act simply provides in s 45 that a code of practice issued by the Secretary of State will advise on good practice to follow. This includes 'consultation with persons to whom the information requested relates or persons whose interests are likely to be affected by the disclosure of information.' The Code states that where legal rights of a third party are concerned, consultation should take place. Consultation is optional where rights are not involved. It may not be necessary where costs involved would be disproportionate. Consultation should take place to assist a decision on whether an exemption exists or on a discretionary public interest disclosure. A representative body may be an appropriate consultee. Non-response from a third party should not determine a decision on disclosure. Where the information is personal information on a data subject the terms of the DPA 1998 will have to be complied with.

When papers are sent in to public authorities it will be worthwhile indicating a belief that information should be exempted on grounds of commercial confidentiality. This will not be binding on the government/ holder in terms of the legal interpretation, but it will send a warning that it should not be disclosed without safeguards.

When information is peculiarly sensitive, companies may wish to warn departments that even disclosure of the existence of the documents containing the information could be damaging. Clearly, an element of 'wolf!' could be associated with this practice but genuine concerns should be communicated.

There is no doubt that the Act and guidance leave third parties in a poor position compared with procedures elsewhere. The US FOI did not originally provide for a third party notice whereby the provider of information, usually a business or company, which has supplied the department, etc with data on policies, operations or products, seeks to prevent the agency or department that collected the information from disclosing it to a third party in response to the latter's FOI request. This is now provided for by executive order as we saw in chapter 2. More recent access laws in other countries make statutory provision for a 'third party notice' to advise the provider of information that a request for information it provided has been made and Australian Federal law and state laws provide for similar legal procedures protecting the position of a third party.[2] The Code of Guidance accompanying the Code on Access gives much fuller detail on the kinds on information that would attract protection

2   See R Baxter (1997) JBL 199.

and previous FOI bills have given clearer guidance on what should and what should not be protected. The Commissioner is not given authority to deal with complaints from third parties, only from those who have made a request for information. Third parties will have to seek protection through actions for breach of confidence or judicial review where an authority is going to disclose information which concerns them or which they have provided. If they are not consulted, they will not know beforehand in order to prevent disclosure. This is not satisfactory.

In the USA the 'arbitrary, capricious and substantial evidence' standard is applied to review 'third party notice' decisions. This entitles the court to examine the whole record of the decision-making and provides discovery (disclosure) rights for a requester to help assess the process. This is distinguished from the *de novo* review where a requester challenges a refusal to hand over documents by the department. This amounts to a new decision on the merits by the court which can examine documents *in camera* if it wishes to assist in its decision.

There is also a practice in the USA which is of great practical importance. This is known as the 'Vaughn index' (see ch 2). By this process, agencies have to itemise and justify exemptions claimed for documents; their *ipse dixit* is not sufficient. Departments will have to provide compelling reasons and arguments why documents should be withheld and companies should be prepared to justify to departments, or the Commissioner or tribunal why they should be withheld. Something like the 'Vaughn index' might evolve from British practice.

Removing prohibitions on disclosure

Section 75 FOIA contains a provision allowing the Secretary of State to amend or repeal by order any enactment prohibiting disclosure of information. There are numerous such provisions in statutes.[3] The Public Administration Committee rightly considered this to be a very important provision – these provisions are also an exemption under FOIA by virtue of s 44. The Committee was concerned that a well-meaning intention might evaporate after initial enthusiasm and suggested that a Parliamentary committee rather like the Deregulation Committee established to examine deregulation orders under the Deregulation and Contracting Out Act 1994 should assume oversight for this task. It would provide the necessary encouragement and discipline. The suggestion was not taken up by Government.

---

3   An up-to-date list is in P Birkinshaw *Government and Information* (2nd ed, 2001) Annex B.

The practicalities

Access to information should include access to information in documentary form or in a computer or other memory store—the Act is pretty comprehensive in this regard. Computer print-outs, email attachments as well as papers should be available. An FOI office should be established with the necessary staff and facilities in each department and agency and larger public authority. Sir Douglas Wass has suggested[4] that each department would have one FOI office (rather like Companies House of the DTI at present), where general or policy papers could be requested. Personal papers would be kept separately at a local office level, if maintained in that form, or centrally on a file server or other device. Applications for information could be made personally by email request which is considered to be a request made in writing (s 8(2)(a)) or by post. Publication schemes containing information published voluntarily by public authorities are likely to be published on websites and, as discussed in chapter 6, these could be documents of vital significance. Factual and background information behind policy development could be published making them repositories of discussion and debate. They will contain, *inter alia*, details of information available for a fee. If the Government is serious about the virtues of joined-up government and citizen involvement, then these are the means through which dialogue may take place. The policy exemption cuts against the Government's pleas for 'joined-up policy making in *Modernising Government*.[5] This spoke enthusiastically about 'getting others involved' in policy 'early on' in the process.

The Government did not, as we saw above, include a duty on public authorities to provide indexes for the documents in their possession. If the European Council and Commission can provide such, then why not domestic public authorities? A request for documents on the Channel Tunnel, BSE, the foot and mouth disease etc would cover thousands of documents in the Department of Transport and in MAFF respectively. Two suggested alternatives are:

(1) an FOI officer to establish precisely the information being sought—favoured by Australia and Canada
(2) a sophisticated system of cataloguing papers and the unrestricted access to the catalogues so that each document could be identified by its file number or other identifier.

---

4   Former Head of the Home Civil Service and Secretary to the Cabinet. The following leans heavily on a paper given by Sir D Wass at a conference organised by the FOI Campaign on 1 July 1986. In spite of its age it contains prescient advice. The Government set up a group in 1999 to examine various aspects of FOIA introduction.

5   Cm 4310 para 6.

The problem with option 1 is that it is subject to possibly subjective interpretation and it might allow 'unofficial' exemptions of materials which the applicant will not know about. 'If [the requester]does not know, his right of appeal to some independent arbiter against the withholding of information becomes a cypher.'[6] It must be said that the FOIA places a duty on authorities (far more than Wass envisaged) to provide assistance, and the code identifies steps to assist requesters and training for officials.

The second option is more expensive and would take some years to implement fully. It would require comprehensive cataloguing by a department of all its papers and files, like catalogues of Company House, which would be available to the public in the FOI office. Writing some years ago, Sir Douglas Wass said: 'At present departments do not maintain satisfactory catalogues. Indeed the standard of cataloguing, indexing, registering and entitling of papers in government departments falls lamentably below the standards of even moderate librarianship.' Events reported in *The Guardian* in March 2001 concerning the delay in introducing the FOIA in Whitehall because of missing and badly catalogued files graphically support this criticism.[7] Sir Douglas goes so far as to say that current practices are a bar to efficient administration, and the suggested improvement would be a 'boon to departmental efficiency'. Option 2 would create a 'new discipline in relation to new documents' producing a decent filing system with cross-referencing.

If this were introduced, the questions would then be: how is the request met? How are requests for exempt information dealt with?

The FOI officer, Sir Douglas suggests, would inform the appropriate division of the request and it would examine the file to see whether exempt information is present. If it is not, the file would be released to the FOI officer, who would inform the applicant of the cost of reproduction. Help would be given to identify which portions he requires. If exempt, the file would have the exempt categories clearly identified and marked, and the applicant would only be allowed to examine the unexpurgated portion. Where possible, a decision on the public interest must be taken. Specific provision for redacting a document in this fashion is not contained in FOIA but if the practice were not observed it would be a ground of complaint to the IC. Sir Douglas thought the best way to deal with exemptions would be to categorise documents when they are requested, rather than created, unless presumably they are otherwise classified as 'Top Secret', 'Secret' etc.[8] Categorisation criteria can and have changed, and documents should not be marked exempt initially and perpetually.

Appeals will be made to a higher level officer within the authority against refusal – matters which are covered by the code of practice. The

6   Wass ibid.
7   *The Guardian* 7 March 2001.
8   But would still be subject to scrutiny in the court.

third stage would involve the Information Commissioner, who would have access to the whole file and whose decision would be binding, subject to appeal to the Tribunal. Exemption decisions would be made at an appropriate departmental level unless the information was politically sensitive, in which case it would be referred to higher authority.

Is FOIA 2000 enough?

The answer to this question depends upon what objectives one has in mind in promoting on to the statute book a Freedom of Information Act. In my estimation, open government is a more demanding objective than freedom of information. Freedom of information lobbyists inevitably, if not exclusively, operate on the basis that the more information that is made available, the better and/or the more democratic the process of government will become. Open government places its emphasis upon the opening up of the channels of government decision-making, and provision of information is one feature of open government. Other features, equally important, include the opportunity for wide debate before the government's proposals are finally confirmed or rejected. This has been attempted in central government and local government as we saw in chapter five. The Scottish Parliament has experimented with new arrangements for consultation and participation. A striking example at EU level involved the Charter of Fundamental Rights and the Convention formula adopted for the body mandated by the European Council for the preparation of the Charter. This comprised members from national governments, the EP, national parliaments and one from the Commission. Observers included members of the ECJ and Council of Europe. Members from various EU committees were invited to submit views along with the EU Ombudsman and 'other interested members from civil society.'[9] Shaw describes how public hearings were held and documents presented to the Convention were placed on the internet.

Not only the public, but inevitably MPs and Parliament, are left out of the process of policy-making until the decision is firmly concluded, and discussion of alternatives is really quite idle. While Blair's Government has under the initiative of *Better Government* programmes, Best Value and Joined up Government sought to engage in more consultation and feedback in developing policies for public services, the Government's pre-occupation with 'spin' in the presentation of policies caused a degree of scepticism. And, of course, information in the policy-making process and advice were given wide exemptions under FOIA. Many major inquiries of the last 20 years bear witness to this weakness of participatory

9   Jo Shaw (2001) European Public Law Issue 2 forthcoming.

democracy.[10] As was seen after the Hatfield rail disaster in October 2000, the Government refused to call an inquiry. So too does the refusal to discuss the policy behind a proposal of a government agency affecting national or regional interests. Central to openness is the giving of adequate reasons, full information about proposals and allowing for timely discussion of these. Timing, such an important feature of favourable presentation, is completely within Government control. Information under FOIA 2000, does not have to be disclosed where it is going to be published – how far away publication might be is not spelt out. With a subject matter that is inevitably complex, the provision of brute information is not adequate in itself. One needs to see 'outside' personnel with a sufficient degree of skill, expertise and independence assessing the information. As long ago as 1983, Sir Douglas Wass made a plea for such a body in his Reith Lectures.[10] The Outer Circle Policy Unit advocated a format for 'big public inquiries' in which a two-stage process would investigate the issues, obtain the necessary evidence, provide Parliament with the fruits if its research and then allow more locally specific inquiries to assess more particular points of objection.[11] This was never adopted. A former chief scientific adviser to the MoD has written that a permanent council of independent-minded scientists should be established to encourage ministers to challenge costly projects promoted by vested interests and to pierce the secrecy surrounding Britain's nuclear affairs.[12] These opinions inevitably come from 'former' senior or leading officials or politicians—rarely do they seem to occur when they are within the charmed circle of executive power. The council would advise the cabinet on projects put forward by departments. There remains a reluctance to open up decisions and decision-making across the spectrum of government to public scrutiny. It is as if the message that comes across is that such scrutiny is not a feature of strong government; it is a feature of weak government that has lost the plot. Ministerial responsibility has not gone in terms of its inward dimension. It remains a shell in terms of its outward dimension.

We are now moving inside the government machine. As we noted in chapter 4, the Westland, Matrix Churchill and BSE sagas supplied ammunition to those who advocate reform in our central government structure and culture.[13] A primary aim is for efficient and open internal administration at the higher levels of our government apparatus. We have

10   *Government and the Governed* (1984).
11   *The Big Public Inquiry* (Justice OCPU, 1979). At the Sizewell inquiry into pressurised water reactors, the CEGB bought essential equipment for a PWR reactor long before Sir Frank Layfield reported. In his report Sir Frank asked for 'full and accurate' records of the plutonium produced in civil reactors.
12   S Zuckerman *Star Wars In a Nuclear World* (1986).
13   Above pp 161 et seq.

spoken of the financial management initiatives and MINIS which were concerned with devolving responsibility and initiative down the management line. These have been taken over by other initiatives, most recently by public service agreements. Select committees have taken evidence which was in favour of establishing a French *cabinet* system in each ministry which would comprise senior civil servants and outside specialists to inform the minister more expertly on departmental and inter-departmental business.[14] Since the abolition of the Central Policy Review Staff (CPRS), there has been no co-ordinating body to appraise the overall impact of departmental or government policies from within while rising above the temptations of special pleading and inter-departmental bickering and bartering. Mrs Thatcher's Policy Unit provided an initiative on policy assessment and development for the Prime Minister—but not for the Government as a whole – and its role has expanded under Blair. Such a development, involving a detached overseer, it might be explained, is to make politics rational. John Major attempted more conventional Cabinet government and was sabotaged by his colleagues. Prime Minister Blair has resorted to task forces and special advisers from outside government, public service agreements and comprehensive spending reviews (see chapter 5 p 256 above) have established the framework of financial discipline. The impression is left that overall co-ordination is something from a bygone era. *Modernising Government*[15] emphasises joined-up government, putting service users if the driving seat. An IT strategy will be developed for information age government and greater coordination. Without that coordination no-one outside will have a chance at making any meaningful contribution the development of policy. FOIA as enacted may not assist that process.

The prize of success in British politics and administration is too great to give away. That prize is executive control of Parliamentary Sovereignty — even in post-devolution, post-HRA, post-FOIA Britain and Northern Ireland a unique prize for executive prerogative and outside a written constitution. Any attempts to foist a co-ordinated system of appraisal of departmental programmes, and to assess priorities in programmes such as those relating to the Public Expenditure Survey's activities in helping to formulate spending priorities for the budget report have until now failed. Programme analysis and review (PAR)[16] or CPRS[17] are clear examples. The comprehensive spending review (CSR) has provided more opportunity for transparency in spending decisions as we saw in chapter

---

14 HC 92 (1985–6), vol II; see HC 62 (1986–7); First Report for the TCSC on Ministers and Civil Servants and HC 293 (2000-01) on Special Advisers.
15 Above note 5.
16 See I Harden and N Lewis *The Noble Lie* (1986), pp 127–9.
17 See chapter 4 above, p 178.

5. In the past, the reasons for the failures embraced a complex variety of factors such as government scepticism, civil service jealousy, inadequate grasp of detail by the bodies concerned, and a less than thorough approach in their method of appraisal. CSR may be moving forward on a surer and more open basis. No one can demand that our government be omniscient; what is required is an improvement in the information flow between the higher ranks of government and the administration, between different tiers of government whether central, devolved or local and between the public and private sectors involved in service delivery or public performance, and the public. Improvement in information flow has a cost in relation to the investment of effort and the reduction of effective prerogative in government. An independent assessment of major proposals, or reviews of government priorities and programmes, would have to be published, and the government would have to account for its reasons for not complying with or accepting the recommendations.

Government is not big enough, it would seem, to do that. What is the best information about proposals and performance that is available?[18] How can the information be best understood and best utilised? What is there to stop the information being utilised in its best form and timeously? How do we increase our stock of knowledge and information? How do we assess the viability of different methods for interpreting information to appreciate it more fully? How do we collate information in the most complete form that is humanly possible? How do we ensure that our methods for selecting information and data are not partial, or not overly partial? That we have not, in other words, rejected good information because of subjective value preferences? I can see no compelling reasons why it would be contrary to the public interest to publish the vast bulk of such information. Indeed, it would be a positive asset. This would be equally true notwithstanding the reform of government departments into smaller policy units and the hiving-off of routine administrative tasks to governmental agencies or the Next Steps executive agencies and private contractors and devolution of power. With the revolutionary role of the

---

18 *Harden and Lewis*, pp 253–5, 282–3 and 305–6, place considerable faith in the example of the Social Security Advisory Committee established under the Social Security Act 1980. By s 9(4) it has the right 'to be provided with information reasonably necessary for the discharge of its functions' and the secretary of state must consult with it on proposals for a wide range of regulations. The Secretary of State must consider their report on the former's proposals and a copy of such report must be laid with the draft regulations. S/he must state how far s/he has given effect to the Committee's recommendations and reasons must be given for not following the recommendations. They have commissioned their own studies better to inform Parliament of social security regulations and policies. Ministers have not always paid due respect to the position and duties of the committee. The authors suggest a judicial rather than a parliamentary oversight of the operation of these provisions.

internet, there are vast opportunities for information sharing. We have to be aware of the fact that such a development may end the process of government as we know it. That process has probably begun anyway.

The increasing reliance upon private companies to carry out public business must be accompanied by legal assurances that government does not become 'all inside' and 'no outside' as was said before. The coming years will see growing demands that companies, and not just those performing tasks under contract for government or those designated by the Secretary of State under FOIA as a public authority, be made subject to greater openness and transparency if they are not to become, as Hobbes said 'like worms in the entrails of a natural man.'

We saw in chapter 5 how we rely upon Parliament to be informed and to impose accountability upon government, and how inadequately equipped Parliament is in its powers to extract information from a reluctant executive.[19] Recent events have brought this home rather dramatically. Before the inter-governmental conference to discuss the Treaty of Nice, the Government would not provide meaningful information to, and engage in meaningful discussion with, the Commons Select Committee on European Scrutiny.[20] However, the most prestigious of select committees, the Public Accounts Committee, has frequently complained of its inability, and government departments' inability, to obtain the necessary information. The community has to rely upon others to wield the tools of accountability. On some issues our society is structured in such a manner that we can only allow representative forms of government and accountability to act on our behalf. I have referred to instances and examples of how greater openness could help fuller accountability and a better-informed society. Nor should we forget the role of the US Sunshine Act and Federal Advisory Committee Act which I examined in chapter 2 and which opened up the meetings of federal agencies and advisory committees to the public. Open practices are developing but largely informally.

This brings us to FOIA 2000. It is a necessary safeguard—a boon to isolated individuals beset by all-powerful government. It does have the potential to address the private conduits and outposts of public business in a manner that other FOIAs do not. We should not be oblivious to the fact that the market might operate to ensure a supply of information brokers whose services will be used by those intent on exploiting a relatively new commodity. I have no doubt that the means to access is important. But unless the FOI movement is accompanied by a wide-ranging change in constitutional culture, institutions and practices, it must be questioned whether it will be of lasting utility to all but powerful organised interests

19 See R Dingwell (1986) MLR 489.
20 *Fourth Report* (1999-2000).

who have the resources to use it; to a few academics; to journalists; and to the occasional public-spirited individual. Enough has been said about the crucial role of the Commissioner, publication schemes and the Act's shortcomings. I hope these are remedied in the near future.

To provide safeguards against this happening, programmes of education should be provided to give guidance upon the existence of the legislation, how it works, what it does and how citizens can best use it. The Information Commissioner in Canada has argued for such programmes and she was been fully supported by the Standing Committee on Justice and Solicitor-General.[1] No one should expect that an FOIA will change the nature of government or the behaviour of the governed overnight. Much work, effort, goodwill and education will have to be provided. Progress and democratic development will take time. They are worth striving for. Unless, however, there is a change in attitude and ethos in our public administration and in the public/private interface, FOIA by itself will be something of a confidence trick. It is an inescapable development in democratic and responsible government. But an FOIA must be accompanied by more widespread changes in attitude and in major institutional reform if we are to be better informed and more open. Those are the necessary conditions to help reduce the abuse of power. The forces **and** the sources operating against such conditions should never be underestimated or overlooked.

---

1   *Open and Shut: Enhancing the Right to Know and the Right to Privacy*, Standing Committee on Justice and Solicitor-General (Ottawa, 1987). See p 87 above for the Government rejection of this report.

Epilogue – The EU Regulation on access: the final stages

The text of the draft Regulation agreed by the European Parliament early in May 2001 enhanced the recital on openness which strengthens democracy and respect for fundamental rights (see chapter 8). It states that wider access should be granted to documents in cases where the Institutions (EP, Council and Commission) are acting in their legislative capacity. The principles of the Regulation shall apply to 'all agencies established by the Institutions.' The reference to the 'without prejudice' nature of the Regulation vis a vis existing specific EC rules on access has gone as has the reference to 'loyalty' governing relations between the institutions and the Member States (MS) when the latter deal, basically, with requests for access to documents coming from the institutions. In its place comes 'loyal cooperation' and an exhortation that MSs 'should take care not to hamper the proper application of this Regulation' while respecting the security rules of the institutions. The Regulation is without prejudice to existing rights of access to documents of MSs.

A new article 1 seeks to ensure as wide access to documents as possible, to ensure the easiest possible exercise of this right and to promote good administrative practice on access.

The Regulation repeats that it will cover the Second and Third Pillars. Access to documents will be refused where it *would*, not could, undermine the public interest. The arguments for secrecy will have to be more specific. Refusal may be made on grounds of: public security; defence and military matters; international relations; financial, monetary or economic policy of the EC or a MS; and privacy and integrity of the individual. Access shall be refused where it would undermine the protection of commercial interests including intellectual property, court proceedings and legal advice and the purpose of inspections and audits but subject to a new public interest override in these cases. Deliberative documents for internal use and documents from outside the institution shall be refused if disclosure would seriously undermine the institution's decision-making process unless once again there is an overriding public interest in disclosure. Third parties shall be consulted and a MS may request the Institution not to disclose the document without its prior agreement. Except in clear cut cases, a MS shall consult an institution about disclosure of documents received from that institution.

Applications shall be decided upon within 15 days from their registration. This may be extended by an additional 15 days. Similar time limits to these apply to confirmatory applications (see chapter 8). Failure to comply allows the applicant to proceed to the ombudsman or court.

'Sensitive' documents which are classified and which deal basically with public security, defence and military matters are given special protection; this involves restricted access by officials dealing with requests who have necessary clearance and they may be registered (sic) and released only with the consent of the source.

The bar on commercial reproduction of documents has gone but copyright protection is maintained. The provision on registers has been extended. Direct access is provided for legislative documents and policy and strategy documents in electronic form. A new article 9b extends the range of documents to be published in the *Official Journal of the EC*. Article 9c provides that the institutions shall take requisite measures to inform the public of their right of access and MSs shall 'cooperate' with the institutions in providing information to citizens. Provision is made for the encouragement of good administrative practice in relation to access, the establishment of an inter institutional committee to examine best practice, conflicts or future development on access. An annual report of each institution will contain details of cases concerning refusals to grant access and the number of 'sensitive' documents not recorded in the register of documents. Agencies and similar bodies established by the legislator should possess rules on access conforming with those of the Regulation.

The general feeling was that the EP had done well to see through its major proposals although some parties were still disappointed by some of the concessions on 'sensitive' documents.

Index